Monetary Economics

Mervyn K. Lewis

University of South Australia, Adelaide

Paul D. Mizen

University of Nottingham

UNIVERSITY PRESS

OXFORD

UNIVERSITY PRESS

Great Clarendon Street, Oxford OX2 6DP

Oxford University Press is a department of the University of Oxford.
It furthers the University's objective of excellence in research, scholarship,
and education by publishing worldwide in

Oxford New York

Auckland Cape Town Dar es Salaam Hong Kong Karachi
Kuala Lumpur Madrid Melbourne Mexico City Nairobi
New Delhi Shanghai Taipei Toronto

With offices in

Argentina Austria Brazil Chile Czech Republic France Greece
Guatemala Hungary Italy Japan Poland Portugal Singapore
South Korea Switzerland Thailand Turkey Ukraine Vietnam

Oxford is a registered trade mark of Oxford University Press
in the UK and in certain other countries

Published in the United States
by Oxford University Press Inc., New York

British Library Cataloguing in Publication Data
Data available

Library of Congress Cataloging in Publication Data
ISBN-13: 978-0-19-829062-9
ISBN-10: 0-19-829062-4

9 10 8

Typeset by J&L Cosmoposition Ltd, Filey, North Yorkshire
Printed and bound in Great Britain by
Antony Rowe Ltd., Chippenham, Wiltshire

Monetary Economics

Preface

SOME people study the workings of computers because they have a thirst for knowledge and want to know how computers operate. For most of us, however, the need is more immediate and pressing; there is a problem—of communication—that needs to be solved (and it is true to say that without the miracle of e-mail, this book might never have been completed).

Monetary economics has also been problem-driven. Wicksell wrote *Interest and Prices* and Keynes the *Tract on Monetary Reform* because they were dissatisfied with the gold standard and wanted it replaced by a system of managed money. Cassel developed purchasing power parity to explain exchange rate and price movements after the First World War. Unemployment in the 1930s exposed the inappropriate assumptions of full employment and constancy of velocity upon which simple versions of the quantity theory were based, and ushered in Keynesian analysis. Inflation in the 1960s saw the analysis of inflation and inflation expectations, which led the quantity theory back into favour and provided the platform for the rational expectations revolution. The breakdown of the fixed exchange rate system ushered in floating exchange rates and, soon after, asset and monetary models of exchange rates to explain why rate movements were so volatile. Later, game theory approaches to optimal monetary policy were developed when credibility was being sought for exchange rate or inflationary policies.

We could have addressed these topics—that are still very much of current interest to researchers and policy-makers—in isolation, but we have sought instead to provide an historically informed, yet up-to-date, survey of the development of monetary theory and policy, accessible to fellow economists and students of monetary economics alike. The aim, simply, is to identify the principal building blocks which have shaped the literature—the key articles, the key theories, the key ideas and the key concepts. In doing so, we have tried to retain the flavour of the early contributions by adapting some of the original diagrams and using some of the original symbols, even though that has resulted in some differences in notation from chapter to chapter. Inevitably the content reflects our own perspective of what is of importance in monetary economics. Both of us have contributions to the literature on the demand for money and other topics in monetary economics. The volume draws on these ideas, along with others that have crystallized over a number of years, and we accordingly have obviously incurred numerous debts of gratitude to our co-authors, and to colleagues who have commented on the work. We would particularly like to thank Michael Artis, Nicoletta Batini, Alec Chrystal, Kevin Davis, Kevin Dowd, Leigh Drake, Andy Haldane, Norbert Janssen, James Juniper, Ben Martin, Stephen Millard, Katherine Neiss, Ed Nelson, Charles Nolan, Eric Pentecost, and Ryland Thomas.

With the scene of production moving between the University of Nottingham, the University of South Australia, and the Bank of England, we have incurred additional debts of gratitude. We thank Morna Tan for drawing many of the diagrams, and June Boot, Jill Brown, Judy Melbourne, and Donna Broadhurst for their patient work on the manuscript and, of course, their facility with e-mail. Each chapter has travelled many thousands of miles through the ether to receive improvements at the hands of co-authors now living some 11,000 miles and ten time zones apart. Theoretically this should have yielded substantial efficiency gains, as we could have virtually spent twenty continuous hours working on the manuscript in any working day. In practice we suspect that this was not the case, not on Sundays at least.

Finally, we thank our publishers Ruth Marshall, Tracy Mawson, Brendan George, and Miranda Vernon for their stoicism and forbearance.

Mervyn K. Lewis
Paul D. Mizen

Contents

Part One **Theory**

Part Two **Policy**

List of figures

List of tables

Part One

Theory

Chapter 1
The Nature of Monetary Economics

1.1 What is Monetary Economics?

A STUDY of monetary economics must first and foremost be concerned with analysing the role of money in the economy. In fact, money is a much older term than monetary economics, and was widely used as a title to cover the topic area (for example, Robertson, 1928; Harrod, 1969). The description 'monetary economics' came into popular usage when the topic of money generally came to be coextensive with macroeconomics. It continued to be used when the question of why money is a useful commodity began to be addressed in a rigorous theoretical way and the literature turned away from macroeconomics to examine the microeconomic foundations of the subject.

Monetary economics is now a very broad cathedral. How broad it is can be gathered from the two volume *Handbook of Monetary Economics*, edited by Benjamin Friedman and Frank Hahn, and published in 1990.[1] As might be expected there are chapters on inflation and growth, money supply, measuring money demand, the term structure of interest rates, nominal income targeting, rules and discretion, consumption and investment, money and output, credit rationing, inflation theory, costs of inflation, targets and instruments, and monetary rules and discretion. To these topics are added chapters on money in general equilibrium, money and trading, the optimum quantity of money, non-Walrasian equilibrium, liquidity, game theory approaches, overlapping generations models, the pricing of financial securities, and intertemporal asset pricing. The final chapter dealt with the open economy (there was an earlier companion eleven chapter volume on international macroeconomics).[2]

Clearly something has to be left out, and our approach to the content of monetary economics is more macro than micro, although that distinction is blurred in general equilibrium theory and new classical economics. Of our sixteen chapters, ten deal with theory and six with policy issues. Three of the chapters are devoted to open economy aspects, although the discussion of the exchange rate in particular is not confined to those three chapters. As explained in the preface, an overriding consideration has been to present topics roughly in their historical time perspective since the monetary economics literature has been largely fashioned in response to contemporary policy problems. As so much of monetary economics is British and American, the discussion of policy necessarily draws on that experience, although the implications of European monetary union are explored.

The sixteen chapters fall into eight groups. Two chapters consider the nature of money and alternative monetary systems. Two chapters examine the classical monetary system and the Walrasian heritage in terms of the work of Lange, Patinkin, and others. The next two chapters are on Keynesian monetary economics, based around Keynes, Hicks, and Tobin. Two chapters deal with monetarism, in the context of both a closed and open economy. Then, to complete the theory section, two chapters analyse rational expectations, credibility, and the design of optimal policy structures. In the policy and empirical section, two chapters are concerned with the econometrics of the demand for money, and two with transmission mechanisms and the control of interest rates and the money supply. Finally, there are two chapters on monetary policy more broadly, one dealing with exchange rates and the balance of payments, the other with constitutional issues and methods of inflation control.

In the remainder of this chapter we examine some of the characteristics of money. Monetary economics deals with the workings of a money economy, rather than a barter exchange economy. That is, it is concerned with an economy in which production and expenditures are made using money and incomes are received in monetary form. The first question to be asked is why money is used and what functions it performs. This is a very old question, but the answer keeps on changing, as the emphasis given to the medium of exchange, store of value, and unit of account function varies over time. In the classical quantity theory, as developed by David Hume, Adam Smith, and David Ricardo and refined by Irving Fisher, money was demanded and derived its importance from serving as a medium of exchange. By contrast, the Keynesian tradition has always emphasized money as a store of wealth, and this carried through to Friedman's 'temporary abode of purchasing power'. This focus did not change until the microfoundations literature swung the balance back towards the medium of exchange function, seeing money as a social device which simultaneously lowers uncertainty for market transactors, by reducing the costs of acquiring information, and allows a more efficient use of resources by reducing transactions costs and saving resources previously devoted to exchange operations. Only the 'new monetary economics' literature has made the unit of account function of money its focus, with the idea of separating this function from the others in order to bring about price stability.

A second question concerns the specialness of money: why is it important to study money? A related question if money is important is: important for what? Keynes was the first to argue that a monetary economy was quite different from a barter economy in terms of the role of money.[3] Adding money to a barter system means much more than introducing a contrivance of great convenience, linking (say) cloth and wheat, but otherwise transitory and neutral in its effects on real things and real assets. He argued that booms and depressions are peculiar to an economy in which money is not neutral.

Another question is how money comes into existence and what causes it to change over time. This book begins with the classical approach to monetary theory. Since that time the monetary system of the world has changed from bimetallism to the gold standard to the gold-exchange standard to Bretton Woods and to fiat money with floating exchange rates. Money has changed from metallic money to credit money. This process is tied up with financial innovation and deregulation which we will examine in later chapters. For the moment we stay with the three issues raised.

1.2 The Functions of Money

When a student is asked 'what is money' he has still no choice but to give the conventional answer. Money is defined by its functions: anything is money which is used as money: 'money is what money does.' And the functions of money are threefold: to act as a unit of account (or 'measure of value' as Wicksell puts it), as a means of payment, and as a store of value. (Hicks, 1967: ch. 1)

THIS pragmatic statement by Sir John Hicks gives no inkling of the debates which have taken place, at both a practical and theoretical level, about the role of money in the economy. At a practical level, most of the disputes arise because the three characteristics which are viewed as conferring moneyness upon an asset are to a large degree separable. Thus the 'something' used as a means of payment need not coincide with the 'something' that serves as a means of storing value (or purchasing power). We have already noted that the 'new monetary economics' school envisages separating the unit of account function from the others. At a theoretical level, economic theorists have notably failed to develop a generally accepted theoretical framework in which money has a distinctive role to play. In standard value theory, utility attaches to items which can be consumed or used in production. Money facilitates both consumption and production, but is not used directly for these ends, and it is thus difficult to slot into the conventional theoretical framework.

One way to approach the functions served by money is to consider the principal inconveniences that would be experienced in its absence. Suppose that there was an economic system that had no financial assets at all. There are at least three things that one could say about such an economy. First, there may be no commonly agreed unit with which to value things. Second, without money, the economy would be subject to all the inefficiencies of a barter system. Third, without money or other financial assets, the economy would probably have a relatively low level of investment and would tend to misallocate whatever investment it had; no unit could invest more than its saving because there would be no way to finance the excess, and no unit could invest less than its saving because there would be no financial assets in which to put the excess (we note that any durable good that served this purpose would become, by default, money).

If money were introduced into the economy, it would serve three functions: a unit of account and a unit of contract (or standard for deferred payment); a means of exchange or payment; and a liquid store of value. A means of payment will, of course, allow the economy to get rid of the inefficiencies due to barter. But money will do more that that; as a liquid store of wealth it will increase the efficiency of resource allocation by allowing private economic units to make investment expenditures in excess of their current saving by drawing down previously accumulated money balances.

Unit of account

The introduction of a unit of account in which to express and compare the values of different goods and services is also important for economic efficiency. The number of calculations required to achieve the valuation of goods in terms of goods increases sharply with the number of commodities involved.

Suppose that there is no money and there are only two commodities, X and Y; then there is only one calculation (the price of Y in terms of X or, as in all cases, its reciprocal, the price of X in terms of Y). Should we add a third commodity, say Z, we then have three calculations (the price of Y in terms of X, the price of Z in terms of X, and the price of Z in terms of Y). If we add a fourth commodity, say, W, we have six calculations, having to add the price of W in terms of each of the other commodities Y, X, and Z. With the addition of a fifth commodity, we have four more calculations, making ten in all. Each time we add a commodity, we add as many more calculations as there were previous commodities. If n is the initial number of commodities, the addition of another commodity increases the number of calculations by $n - 1$. The formula relating the number of calculations T to the number of commodities is then $T = {}^1/_2 n (n - 1)$. If we had 1,000 commodities, there would be $T = {}^1/_2 \times 1,000 \times (1,000 - 1) = 499,500$ calculations. With millions of commodities and hundreds of millions of people, the effort in these calculations would soon reach gigantic proportions.

A first function of money is to avoid such unnecessary calculations. Just as it is convenient to adopt common measures of length (inches, feet, yards), so it is to adopt a common language in which to express value. In no other way can values be arranged on a scale, and in no other way can an individual easily calculate the value of his or her possessions.

Consequently, a second function of money is to permit rational economic calculation to take place. A common unit of account, and prices expressed in such a unit, render comparable goods and services not otherwise comparable. Such comparability is necessary if the individual's choice is to be rational, in the sense of implying a transitive (i.e. non-contradictory) ordering of preferences. Valuing things in monetary terms is a way of formulating and ordering preferences.

Closely related to this, a third function of money as a unit of account is to transmit economic information. The market mechanism operates with consumers' money votes informing producers about market preferences, upon which production decisions are made. At the same time, prices inform households of the demand for their services. People need prices to decide in which activities they will engage and how best to perform this activity. A common unit of account, and prices expressed in its terms, thus serves to transmit economic information between people and so make possible specialization and a division of labour beyond the confines of the family unit.

Another function of money is to serve as a *unit of contract*. Whenever a purchase is made without paying cash, the purchaser is quoted a money price because money serves as a unit of account, but also agrees to pay later the money amount quoted. In this sense money is serving as a unit of contract as well as a measure in which values are expressed. Someone committed to pay a mortgage loan in some combination of cars, wheat, and clothes, for example, would have to form an estimate of the exchange value of each of these goods in the future. If the debts and assets are expressed in terms of money, one need only form an estimate of the value of one thing, money, in the future. There is the need only to form an estimate of general tendencies towards changes in the purchasing power of money.

However, as a unit of account money has a peculiarity. Although it is meant to be performing the same job as a yard or metre or kilogram in acting as a measuring rod, its value in terms of goods varies from year to year. Imagine the confusion if a metre was 39″ one year, 36″ the next, and 34″ the year after, yet this is regularly what happens with money and why inflation is so costly. As Sir Roy Harrod observes:

From its use as a measure of value flows the practical maxim that money ought to have a constant value, however constancy may be defined. One would think that this would be a most elementary objective of policy. It is a strange fact that after so many centuries of experience in so many countries man has not yet succeeded in providing for himself a money with a stable value. (1969: 4)

In many respects, then, money is a poor unit of account, and this begs the question of why it is used for this purpose. The common measure of value need not be dollars at all. We could calculate everything in terms of the number of bushels of wheat or fractions of bushels of wheat that have to be given up to buy commodities; or we could calculate everything in terms of gold, platinum, or anything else. Our measure need not even be something which actually exists; for example, the use of the guinea in Britain. For a certain period the guinea was a gold standard coin while the shilling was a silver standard coin, each of specified weight in gold and silver respectively, and it was also stated that 20s.—later 21s.—went to make up a guinea. Debts could be paid in golden guineas or silver shillings alternatively. But long after this ceased to be the case, the guinea was used as a unit of quotation in upmarket stores—a practice which lingered on in Britain (and the Commonwealth) for nearly 100 years to decimal currency conversion in 1971.

While there are examples of artificial contrivances used as units of account, for the most part (undoubtedly because the unit of account function is related to the other functions of money) there are seemingly benefits in concentrating all these functions with a single item. Only in times of serious monetary disorder is this not the case. For instance, in the period of great inflation in Germany after the First World War, paper Reichmarks continued to be handed around, and thus served as the medium of exchange, while in many transactions price quotations were made in terms of the dollar which thus served as a measure of value.[4] Much the same process has occurred in Latin American countries experiencing prolonged high inflation, although in them 'dollarization' has gone further and the US dollar has also replaced the local currency as exchange media and store of value.[5]

Medium of exchange

As a medium of exchange, the productive role of cash lies in avoiding the inconveniences and inefficiencies of barter. We use the term 'cash' advisedly, because despite predictions stretching back over fifty years that a cashless society is just around the corner, it would seem to be a long way off. Table 1.1 sets out estimates of transactions volumes in Britain in 1992. Although cash payments recorded are limited to those over £1 in value, cash accounted for 63 per cent of all transactions. Also, trial experiments in the town of Swindon with the new electronic purse, the Mondex card, indicate that people are most unwilling to give up the use of cash for plastic.

What exactly are the inefficiencies of barter vis-à-vis cash? Before examining them, it is perhaps sobering to note that throughout most of recorded history, barter has

Table 1.1 Transaction volumes in Great Britain in 1992

	Number (bn.)	%
Cheques	3.6	14
Paper credits	0.5	2
ATM cash withdrawls	1.1	4
Debit card purchases	0.5	2
Credit card purchases	0.8	3
Cash acquisition at counters, other than by cheque		
(e.g. passbook, withdrawal slip, plastic card)	0.3	1
Automated payments		
(i.e. Direct debit, standing order, direct debit)	2.0	8
Total non-cash transactions	8.8	34
PO order book cash payments		
(e.g. Child benefit, retirement pension)	0.9	3
Other cash payments over £1 in value	16.5	63
Grand total	26.2	100

Source: OECD.

been the norm. For example, in medieval times, rents were paid in labour or in kind; landlords obtained what they wanted by the direct service of their tenants and the tenants produced most of what they needed for themselves. In the form of counter-trade, barter remains alive in international trade. There has also been a revival of barter in domestic economies in terms of neighbourhood exchanges of babysitting and other household services; although hailed as a way of restoring community values and local cooperation, this bartering has attracted the interest of the taxation authorities.

There are also questions about the superiority of money exchanges at a theoretical level. People sell goods and perform services in order to obtain other goods and services in exchange. Money is not the ultimate commodity sought. Barter would seem to best symbolize the underlying realities of economic life. Why then is money used? There seem to be three reasons for this.

First, the use of money simplifies economic transactions; a barter transaction is much more complex than buying or selling with money. Its complexity stems from it being both a sale and a purchase and so involving *two* economic decisions: what, how much, and on what terms to sell; and what, how much, and on what terms to buy. Merging these two decisions into one complicates the decision process by doubling the number of variables that enter into it. Use of money as a medium of exchange, and the consequent breaking down of every barter transaction into separate sales and purchases, make possible a division of labour in the calculating process that yields returns in terms of increased rationality. One can deal more effectively with the problem of how best to sell services when free from the worry of how best to spend the proceeds.

Second, money replaces bilateral trading with multilateral trading, reducing the number of transactions needed to achieve a given degree of specialization. In order to engage in a mutually satisfactory barter transaction, one would need to undertake a whole chain of complementary barter transactions and so acquire the collection of goods and services most acceptable to the other party as means of payment. Such chains of complementary barter transactions would be long and complicated, costly in terms of time and effort, and risky unless conditional on the basic transaction being concluded. They can be short-circuited, their risk diminished, and the total number of transactions greatly reduced, by splitting every barter into the monetary transactions of a sale and a purchase. Money, above all, is a time-saver by enabling people to sell to one person and buy from another, or to sell in one place and buy in another, and the wider is the geographical area over which money is acceptable as a means of payment, the greater is the saving.

Third, the use of money increases the number of similar transactions, and the similarity of terms of contract enhances competition. If one thousand people want to buy bread in a money-using economy, they make similar transactions, constitute and belong to the same market, and by weight of sheer numbers create a competitive situation on the buying side of that market. In a barter economy, the same thousand people would form dozens of smaller, separate groups, according to whether they wished to pay for their bread with wine, shoes, haircuts, or some other commodity.

Clower (1967) shows how some of these advantages of using money could be

achieved under barter by a number of market innovations. As a first step from isolated barter, with bilateral exchanges, search and bargaining activities would be
greatly facilitated by the establishment of a 'community fairground', where individuals could meet other individuals desiring to engage in commodity trade. Transaction costs could then be reduced further by establishing within the fairground a
separate 'trading post' for each distinct pair of commodities traded. If provision were
made for *direct* trading of each good for every other good, a well-organized barter
economy would develop up to $n(n-1)/2$ markets in n commodities, and part of their
business would be arbitrage to ensure that price ratio between pairs of commodities
were consistent across pairs. However, such arbitrage is costly in terms of effort and
costs of taking speculative positions. A more convenient way to allow for *ultimate*
(indirect) pairwise trading of all commodities would be to establish trading posts for
all commodities *except* one, the exceptional commodity being distinguished from all
others by being tradable at all posts. This simplification of the complexities of the
barter economy would be tantamount to the introduction of money. (We consider
this case in more detail in Chapter 3.)[6]

The implications for trading costs of each of these market arrangements are illustrated by Clower in Figure 1.1. We notice, first, that the total trading cost curve associated with each successive innovation lies *everywhere* below its predecessor; that is
to say, there is an absolute (and possibly enormous) gap between trading costs in
highly organized as compared with moderately or unorganized markets. Because
market organization mainly affects transaction rather than waiting costs, however,

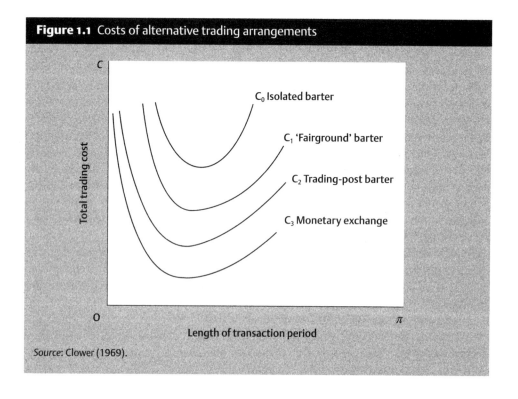

Figure 1.1 Costs of alternative trading arrangements

C_0 Isolated barter

C_1 'Fairground' barter

C_2 Trading-post barter

C_3 Monetary exchange

Total trading cost

Length of transaction period

Source: Clower (1969).

the minimum point of each successive cost curve lies ever closer to the 'work' axis. This corresponds to a second and socially very important consequence of organized trading arrangements: transaction periods become shorter and holdings of commodity stocks awaiting disposal through trade become smaller as the degree of sophistication of market organization increases.

An essential feature of a money economy is the existence of institutional arrangements whereby at least one commodity becomes universally acceptable in exchange for all other commodities. There are no specific trading rules in a world of barter; goods are simply traded for goods. In a money economy, however, goods buy money, and money buys goods—but goods do not buy goods in any organized market (Clower, 1969: 14).

Store of value

While money clearly 'matters' in its role as a medium of exchange, it does so only in a particular sense. The elimination of barter transforms economic life and permits specialization to occur, but once the social institution of money is established, variations in the form and quantity of the exchange medium itself may not have great significance, a point which Keynes made in 1937. Instead, he saw the importance of money stemming from its related function as a store of wealth.

In the Keynesian tradition, money has the characteristics of an asset with constant nominal purchasing power the capital value of which does not fluctuate with the rate of interest, so averting the uncertainties from market transactions by providing a reserve for emergencies. As a medium of exchange, money enables a person to buy elsewhere, other than where he or she sells, or from someone else, other than to whom the item is sold. Its store-of-value function enables the person to buy later than he/she sells. Most people want to delay consuming at least part of their earnings; and once consumption is postponed, there are many reasons for also postponing the buying of the goods to be consumed. The greater cost and inconvenience of storing goods instead of money, the deterioration and obsolescence of goods stored, the advantage in an uncertain world of storing general purchasing power instead of specific commodities, the desire to wait and be prepared for later opportunities of making a good buy, are some of these.

Relatively complex organizational units, such as families, firms, banks, governments, and countries, cannot easily coordinate plans for selling and buying, and this gives rise to the possibility of discrepancies between receipts and payments that can cause considerable fluctuations in cash holdings. The purpose of holding cash reserves is precisely so that cash reserves on hand can be used to make transactions in excess of income as the need arises, to take advantage of a good opportunity, or to tide over an emergency. The costs of a liquidity shortage can be high. If people have to balance receipts and payments too closely, they may have to pass up good bargains, borrow at expensive interest rates to pay emergency hospital bills or accident repairs, or fail to meet educational needs or pay taxes. Some irregularities in the stream of payments and receipts are inevitable, generating a demand to keep some excess cash on hand or in the bank to avoid the necessity for making costly sudden adjustments.

Money, however, is not the only store of value; most financial assets and some real assets serve the same function just as well. If nonetheless money is held, it must be for the sake of the advantages that the other assets lack. Collectively these are called *liquidity* (Lewis, 1990). Liquid assets are assets that are easily marketable or convertible into other assets, and cash is generally the most liquid of all assets by virtue of its medium of exchange function; it is readily and immediately accepted in payment by many people over a large geographic area. This *marketability* is the first aspect of liquidity. A second characteristic of liquidity is the *predictability* of the value of an asset at that future and usually unspecified moment of time when it will be used in payment. Shares, whose value fluctuates on the Stock Exchange, are not liquid in this sense; but predictability is not absolute, e.g. the market value of short-term bills and bonds varies within quite narrow limits. A third aspect of liquidity is *reversibility*: a value in payment that is little smaller than it was on receipt. Real assets lack reversibility. The extreme example is a car that loses value the moment it is driven out of the dealer's showroom: it is reversible only in a mechanical sense! Even financial assets, however, lack reversibility when their purchase and/or sale are subject to a commission or tax. Few people worry about the irreversibility of travellers' cheques, although they are subject to commission, but they are concerned about the flexibility of unit trusts (mutual funds) where administrative fees front-loaded into the acquisition price can result in a bid-ask spread which can be as much as 13 per cent (although market-makers normally operate 3–5 per cent). Finally, the size of the smallest unit in which dealings can take place in an asset is an important determinant of the flexibility of an asset in exchange, and is referred to as *divisibility*.

Nevertheless, liquidity is a matter of degree and to the extent that moneyness is associated with liquidity, then that is also. Liquidity summarizes a collection of characteristics which may be present to varying degrees in various assets. The concept is multidimensional and not measurable in any definite way. It is also subjective since marketability and predictability depend on evaluations by individuals of future conditions in the markets for particular assets. None of this makes for a clear differentiation of money from other assets.

Friedman (1961, 1969b) visualizes a distinction based on what came to be known later (e.g. Laidler, 1984) as money's 'buffer stock' role.[7] Friedman defines money as a 'temporary abode of purchasing power', a rather nebulous concept which seems to combine the store of value and means of exchange function. Indeed the two functions necessarily overlap, since the non-synchronization of transactions implies that economic agents will accumulate (or reduce) holdings of money balances as a result of transactions, with the recipients holding them as a store of value while time elapses until the next transaction. But a wide variety of assets could be used for the purpose of bridging the gap between the receiving and the making, of payments, and delineation of what is and what is not money is still arbitrary, as Friedman (1964) readily admits.

Thus, there would seem to be grounds for doubting the special importance of money in either the Keynesian or Friedman analysis. Once the medium of exchange function is downgraded, and the money stock treated as an asset yielding services much like other assets, then many other stores of value seem to stand on equal ground. Why should one or more of these asset stocks be singled out as having special significance? In the next two sections we look at two approaches to this question. Before doing so, however, we note a number of implications of money as a store of value.

Money as liquidity

As we have noted, 'moneyness' is often equated with liquidity. The relationship between the two envisaged is often bidirectional: money is the most liquid of all assets, and the most liquid assets come to be accepted as money. So long as the characteristics of liquidity, marketability, predictability, and so on are designated in terms of cash, money must definitionally be liquidity *par excellence*. But, as Okun (1981) wryly observes, the finding that money can be instantaneously and costlessly realised as money is no more remarkable than the expectation that the full peanut-value of peanuts can be realized immediately. Ultimately the purpose of wealth accumulation is to ensure command over future goods and services, i.e. the peanut value of money matters. The longer the time interval involved, the greater is the importance of predictability in real terms. When there is considerable doubt about the future purchasing power of money, and a wide divergence between capital certainty in real and monetary terms, liquidity preference is in effect inverted. 'The whole question of liquidity then takes on quite a different aspect, and money ceases to be the asset to which liquidity preference attaches' (Robinson, 1951: 249).

With his theory of liquidity preference, Keynes was not the first to analyse the store of value function of money. Eshag (1963) traces the development of the analysis of the demand for money from Marshall through the real-balance variant of the quantity equation of Pigou and Robertson through to Keynes. Nevertheless, Keynes was the first to draw attention to its significance for economic analysis and policy. This significance derives mainly in the fact that only this function creates a demand for holding money that can be analysed in terms similar to those used in analysing the demand for commodities—a point which Friedman (1956) later emphasized and made his own. As a store of value, money has close substitutes in other assets, and the proportions in which money is held with other assets depend on their differential advantages (such as yield) over money. The demand for holding money therefore is a continuous and elastic function of the yield of the competing assets. This feature both provides a demand curve for money and renders its supply a policy tool with which to influence the yield on other assets.

However, as we shall see later, the theories of the demand for money (liquidity) rarely encompass all of the relevant attributes which make money useful as a store of value, usually—and perhaps necessarily—focusing on one characteristic to the exclusion of the others. Marketability, reversibility, divisibility, and predictability all seem relevant attributes in the definition of what constitutes a liquid asset. A wealth-holder's portfolio selection is simple if all assets are fully predictable, marketable, reversible, and divisible: the portfolio offering the highest return will be chosen irrespective of whether wealth is being accumulated for the near or distant future, as the portfolio can be changed at any time. The Tobin–Markowitz models of mean-variance analysis, used in Chapter 6 for studying liquidity preference, single out imperfect predictability of asset returns as one reason to deviate from that simple strategy. But the assets under consideration in these models are assumed to be fully marketable, reversible, and divisible, and hence equally suitable in other respects to serve as temporary stores of purchasing power. Theories of the transactions demand for money change the concept of liquidity from the absence of risk to the absence of inconvenience. But in concentrating upon the impact of asset exchange costs on portfolio decisions they ignore not only unpredictability of yields on the assets but also other sources of market imperfections (low marketability, divisibility), including incomplete information about current and future earning prospects.

A final implication concerns the dividing line between money and those assets which are not quite money. The Radcliffe Committee (1959) saw no value in even attempting to draw a line between money and other assets in terms of moneyness, expressing the view that in 'a highly developed financial system' there are 'many highly liquid assets which are close substitutes for money', money being defined as 'immediately transferable purchasing power'. Without going quite to this extreme, there are grounds for thinking that the question of where money ends and other alternative assets begin may not be essential for economic analysis. For one thing, it is not needed for either the practice or for the comprehension of monetary policy. Also, money best performs its function as a store of value or temporary abode of purchasing power when it is held jointly with other financial and/or real assets. This complementarity is in sharp contrast with money's other functions. Because of the informational and other advantages of standardization and common acceptability, money cannot share with other items its unit of account or medium of exchange functions without some loss in the efficiency with which these functions are carried out. Another difference concerns the quantity of money. Money's role as a unit of account is, over a wide range, independent of its supply (although the efficiency of the function may be affected). Money's use as a medium of exchange is not independent of supply, but a shortage of money creates inconveniences somewhat different from those of ordinary market reactions to an excess of demand over supply. Money's store of value function links it more directly to other assets, although differences still remain in the character of market adjustments, which we now examine.

1.3 Money as a Special Asset

ONCE the medium of exchange function is downgraded, and money treated as an asset yielding services much like other assets, then many other stores of value seem to stand on equal ground. Why should one or more of these asset stocks be singled out as having special significance for economic activity? Friedman (1964) is particularly schizophrenic on this point. He says that 'no issue of principle is involved in the choice of definition.' More explicitly, he states that 'there is a priori no reason why a fairly narrowly defined subtotal of liquid assets should have any special importance' (Friedman and Schwartz, 1970: 127). In endeavouring to set out why a quantity theorist considers the demand for money to be more important than the demand for a commodity like pins, Friedman had to confess that 'it is not easy to state this point precisely' (Friedman, 1956). Yet, at the same time, he is the principal proponent of the view that 'money matters'.

The starting point has to be Friedman's view 'that there are important factors affecting the supply of money that do not affect the demand for money' (ibid. 16). The issue of the exogeneity/endogeneity of the money supply goes back to the Currency School–Banking School debates in the first half of the nineteenth century,[8] and revolves around the workings of a credit economy. In a credit economy, the statistically defined money supply consists mainly of the liabilities of financial intermediaries such as banks rather than central bank money. Should this fact alter our conception of how the money supply behaves? Ought the money supply be treated—as it typically is in textbooks—as a fixed amount, capable of being determined exogenously by a monetary agency like the central bank, or should it be regarded as an endogenous quantity, expanding and contracting in line with variations in the volume of credit provided by financial intermediaries?

In order to outline these issues, it may be helpful to think of the financial sector as consisting of three sectors. The primary sector is the monetary authorities—the central government and the central bank—which provide the primary liquidity or base money used as a reserve asset to honour deposit withdrawals by the banking system (or secondary sector). The tertiary sector consists of the non-bank financial intermediaries and the markets where debt instruments are traded, although the distinction between secondary and tertiary sectors is, in practice, blurred. Typically, the intermediaries in the tertiary sector use the liabilities of the secondary sector as reserve assets.

The tertiary sector was not of concern in the Currency School–Banking School debate, when the major issue was whether control of the primary sector gave control over the secondary sector, comprising the banking system. However, the Banking School view is readily extended to the tertiary sector, and indeed first was extended in the 1960s by the Yale School in the USA (Tobin, 1963; Tobin and Brainard, 1963) and more recently by the post-Keynesians (Moore, 1988; Chick, 1986; and Rogers, 1989). The argument is that no simple proportionality exists between the behaviour of the tertiary, secondary, and primary sectors. In particular, the inherent flexibility of the tertiary sector means that the supply of money (liquidity) adjusts to the demand for goods, rather than the reverse (Kaldor, 1970, 1986). Policies must be devised for the successful management of the tertiary sector, and these must be changing continuously both in form and intensity in line with financial developments and shifts in preferences for securities (Tobin, 1978). To this conception can be grafted ideas of 'financial fragility' inherent in financial intermediation and credit economy, which emanate especially from the writings of Minsky (1977, 1978, 1986).

Monetarists have also picked up on the significance of the tertiary sector in a credit economy, but come to very different conclusions. Thus they have argued that even in a developed credit economy the central bank can control the money supply via the so-called 'money multiplier' linking the monetary base to the statistically defined monetary aggregates. Moreover, they argue that the use of more general ways of controlling the secondary sector will automatically bring the tertiary sector into line with the secondary sector. Friedman and Schwartz (1963a) outline how an open market transaction in government securities might spread through the secondary and tertiary sectors to the level of spending via mechanisms involving the reserve base of both sectors and the structure of interest rates, so that the initial shock is transmitted—indeed, magnified. In this way, financial markets and the demand for goods dance to the behaviour of the supply of high-powered money.[9]

There is next the adjustment to equilibrium in the money market. If from a position of equilibrium there is a disturbance to money supply (say, an increase) then the adjustment process requires either an upward adjustment to the demand for money (via the arguments of the demand function) to absorb the added money, or a subsequent, negative, supply response—or some combination of both, depending on the extent of exogeneity/endogeneity in the money supply.

Notably, adjustments within the monetary sector itself are usually ignored or downplayed in the monetary economics literature. Own rates of interest on monetary assets are assumed to be either invariant (usually set at zero) or tied to market rates of interest (in the case of competitive money). Because money itself serves as the unit of account, then unlike other goods, money has no single definite price of its own which responds rapidly to economic forces in order that its market may be cleared. At a conference on monetarism held at Brown University in 1975, Milton Friedman posed the question 'What is the price of money?' and went on to answer his own question.

For the monetarist/non-monetarist dichotomy, I suspect that the simplest litmus test would be the conditioned reflex to the question, 'What is the price of money?' The monetarist will answer, 'The inverse of the price level'; the non-monetarist (Keynesian or central banker) will answer, 'the interest rate'. The key difference is whether the stress is on money viewed as an asset with special characteristics, or on credit and credit markets, which leads to the analysis of monetary policy and monetary change operating through organized 'money', i.e. 'credit', markets, rather than through actual and desired cash balances. Though not so obvious, the answer given also affects attitudes toward prices: whether their adjustment is regarded as an integral part of the economic process analyzed, or as an institutional datum to which the rest of the system will adjust. (Friedman, 1976: 316)

This elicited the following response from the chairman of the session, George Borts 'What am I, if I answer "one"?' which in fact was a better answer than Friedman's. The corollary of money having a fixed nominal price (but not a fixed real one) is that the adjustment to a monetary change must occur in the prices of *other* commodities or assets, so that many economists consider the market for money as the 'other side' of the market for goods or assets. Consequently, the 'price' of money is defined in terms of money substitutes rather than money itself. There is a fairly general agreement on this point, but rather less on what are the relevant money substitutes, as Friedman's quotation makes clear. The conditioning factor is the range of assets in the substitution chain. To monetarists, the price of money is the inverse of the general price level (of goods); to Keynesians the price of money is in terms of interest rates and yields (of other assets).

However, there are two provisos to the notion that the money market is the other side of the market for goods or assets. One proviso is that money remains the unit of account, so that whatever serves as the medium of exchange or means of payment acts as the unit of account for pricing. If the medium of exchange role of money were to be separated from the unit of account function, and something else used as a *numéraire* for pricing, then money would cease to have a fixed price (of unity) in terms of the unit of account. Money's price relative to that commodity or bundle of commodities chosen for the job could vary, and money would then be like any other commodity.[10]

The other, and at present more practical, proviso concerns the foreign exchange market. Our definition of the price of money in terms of the rate of interest or the price level is the case in a closed economy or what McKinnon (1984*b*) called 'an insular economy'. In a financially open economy there is also a foreign exchange market which allows the value of money to respond directly to monetary disequilibria. Market participants can react to a faster rate of domestic money creation by writing down the external value of the money supply. External purchasing power refers to the price of the monetary unit of one country in terms of the monetary unit of another country, with depreciation paralleling inflation. People can reduce the real value of money either by bidding up domestic prices or by lowering its external value. As before, the market for goods can be considered to be the 'other side' of the market for money, but a distinction needs to be drawn between money's value in terms of domestic goods and services and its value in terms of foreign goods and services.

If we accept the argument that the market for goods or assets is the other side of the market for money then much of the importance attached to money comes because decisions about money have effects which are both wide-ranging and speedy in operation (Cagan, 1958). Money is a component of most, if not all, balance sheets. In contrast with other assets and physical commodities which are much less widely distributed, changes in the quantity of money have broad effects on other markets. The breadth of the market for money makes it easy to spend or buy in large amounts quickly and without loss: it has perfect 'marketability' and 'predictability'. An individual's excess holdings of money (but not those of the community at large) can be speedily reduced by acquiring securities or goods, whereas stocks of other goods are likely to remain at a higher or lower level than is desired for a considerably longer time. Changes in the supply of money are likely to have more immediate effects upon economic activity than will changes in other assets.

If correct, such features may go some way towards explaining why monetary policy is seen by monetarists to be so pervasive. However, they cannot be the complete answer. Why don't disturbances in all of the $n - 1$ other markets in aggregate greatly outweigh those emanating from the money market? Decisions by the government to alter money are no different in principle from decisions of the public to alter their money balances (one affecting the supply of money, the other its velocity), yet a feature of monetarist literature is its emphasis upon government actions as a source of instability while the private demand for money is seen as highly stable. Certainly the government does have the ability to 'act on a scale that is extremely large relative to the actions of other independent economic groups' (Friedman, 1961). By virtue of its monopoly of note issue and controls over banks, the government has virtually unlimited power to inflate the currency. Restriction of the money supply is limited only by the amount of bonds it is prepared to sell and by the amount of taxes it is willing to levy. Also, political constraints may not operate in the short run, enabling a government to continue with an action, even if inappropriate, for a longer time than private groups. We shall return to this issue when examining monetary policy for it is of significance not only for the potency of monetary policy but also because of the potential for the monetary authorities to do great damage by reneging on low inflation promises.

1.4 Neutrality of Money

MONEY may be important, but important for what? A recurring theme in monetary economics—perhaps the key theme—is the neutrality of money and a major part of this book revolves around this issue. The 'neutrality of money' is a summary expression for the quantity theory of money proposition that a change in the quantity of money results in a proportionate change in the absolute price level, but leaves relative prices, the real rate of interest, real income, real wealth, and hence real output, unaffected. In the classical framework, for example, real economic outcomes are independent of nominal magnitudes, i.e. the nominal quantity of money and the level of nominal prices. The quantity of money determines the price level, but real magnitudes are determined by relative price ratios and all important features of the economic process can be understood as if there were a barter exchange of real goods and services. Money has no substantive role: in the traditional terminology, money serves as a 'veil' over the real sector. Monetarism added a significant new dimension to this, while otherwise maintaining faith with the classical quantity theory tradition. In the monetarist model, changes in the quantity of money can have a temporary or short-run impact on real variables, while the lasting impact of a monetary change falls on nominal values. Their version of neutrality—called *monetarist superneutrality*—is that real outcomes are independent of the rates of change, as well as the levels, of nominal prices. The monetarist combination of long-run neutrality and short-run non-neutrality enables an explanation of real-life episodes in which monetary disturbances apparently play a significant role, while providing a consistent interpretation of both inflation and deflation. In this important respect, monetarists follow in the footsteps of Irving Fisher and others in the quantity theory tradition who treated neutrality as a property of long-run static equilibrium, but not of the transition phases in which the business cycle is seen largely as the 'dance of the dollar' (Fisher, 1923).

Short-run non-neutrality of money is attributed by monetarists to nominal rigidities or mistaken expectations. In the long run, these rigidities wash out and errors in expectations are corrected, making real outcomes independent of monetary changes. Specifically, the model assumes the existence of 'natural rates' of both unemployment and interest rates, which are governed by real factors in the long-run equilibrium. Unemployment can either be above or below its natural rate in the short run, but in the long run will gravitate to the natural rate. The same is true of the rate of interest. Changes in either the demand for money or the supply of money can alter interest rates in the short run but eventually real forces outside the monetary system prevail, in the form of savings and investment or, what is equivalent, the demand for and supply of capital. Since money affects inflation, monetary forces can alter the nominal rate of interest, as the market rate incorporates an inflation premium. By implication, these inflation expectations become embedded in the term structure of interest rates. But the inflation-adjusted or real rate of interest is invariant to money and monetary policies, and so are the important real economic variables of the system.

Under Keynes's theory of liquidity preference, in contrast, the rate of interest itself is essentially a monetary phenomenon—governed by monetary policy—and the real economy adjusts to the rate of interest established by the monetary system, rather than the reverse. Holding wealth in monetary form gives people liquidity or, as Hicks (1974) described it, flexibility—flexibility to convert the money into consumption spending at any time, or flexibility to pour savings into money and become 'a bottomless sink for purchasing power' (Keynes, 1936: 231). Spending money or hoarding money can give rise to 'coordination failures', the consequence of which is that the demand for goods and services might diverge from supplies. Hence, to Keynes, an economy with money (and contracts and institutions based on money) behaves much differently from a barter world. Nor is money simply a 'veil': prices are not simply scaled up and down in response to a monetary change, as they might do under a change in the monetary unit. Expanding (or contracting) the money stock one hundredfold is not the same as an equivalent monetary reform in which the unit of account is adjusted (as in France in the 1950s when one new franc replaced 100 old francs). Thus, money is fundamentally non-neutral and so is monetary policy. Friedman's oft-repeated dictum 'inflation is always and everywhere a monetary phenomenon' has an antonym. In Keynes's words: 'fluctuations in effective demand can be properly described as a monetary phenomenon' (*Collected Works*, xxix: 85).

While the classical, Keynesian and monetarist positions do delineate the major dividing lines on the issue of whether or not monetary factors can permanently affect real variables, and whether monetary policy can have any lasting impact on the real growth of the economy, they are not the only competing views about the impact of changes in monetary variables on output and employment, real wages, inflation, the exchange rate, and the balance of payments. For example, the new Keynesian view provides a rationale for nominal price rigidities in terms of menu costs, custom pricing, wage contracts, and efficiency wage theory (e.g. Okun, 1981).

Another (and markedly different) view is provided by real business cycle theory—an offshoot of new classical macroeconomic theory. In real business cycle theory, economic fluctuations are equilibrium real phenomena, driven largely by productivity shocks, and independent of monetary events and policies (Prescott, 1986). Tobin (1992) argues that it is this theory which should rightly be seen as the modern descendant of classical economics. But in fact its true heritage should be traced to Yule (1927), Slutsky (1937), and Frisch (1933)—see Jacobs (1998). Yule showed that a shock to a harmonic process generates an irregular harmonic series. Slutsky demonstrated that a summation of random series can generate a cyclical pattern. Frisch provided an explicit framework for business cycles in terms of the propagation-impulse model which integrates random shocks into a model of business cycles. The economy is compared to a rocking-horse. To analyze cycles one needs to explain why the economy keeps fluctuating (the propagation mechanism) and how the economy starts fluctuating (the impulse mechanism). In real business cycle theory the source comes from unobserved 'technology shocks'. Because prices adjust promptly—there is market clearing in the short run and long run—monetary effects on the cycle are ruled out. Money is in fact assumed to be endogenous which accounts for any observed empirical correlation between money and output and prices and output.[11]

Real business cycle theory is thus not really part of monetary economics. But it does have firm roots in economic theory, being an outgrowth of rational expectations, and this revolution has been the single element which has most transformed and shaped modern monetary economics. Prior to its introduction, monetary economics had got bogged down into ultimately rather sterile debates about the significance of various elasticities and pricing rigidities. At one level, the rational expectations theory breathed new life into these disagreements and the debate about policy effectiveness (although in this case, ineffectiveness is a more apposite description). At another more fundamental level, rational expectations showed how theory could hurdle over these difficulties to present a clear view of the equilibrium macroeconomic relationships, much like that provided by perfect competition theory in microeconomics.

1.5 How Money is Established

So far we have put the cart before the horse, because we have failed to consider how the institution of money comes to be established. Jones (1976) argues that a medium of exchange will arise even in an economy which starts with barter. In his model, people note which commodity is the most frequently encountered (say onions). Some who are trading relatively rare commodities will reason that the probability of finding an exact match can be improved by an intermediate trade in onions and then another trade in the commodity of their choice—much as occurs in foreign exchange markets with the US dollar. Once these people begin to trade in onions, this raises the probability of finding someone to accept onions in trade and more traders will be induced to use onions. If this process continues then eventually the majority of trades will involve onions and onions will become the medium of exchange or vehicle currency.

This is, in fact, the story told by Menger (1892). In Menger's analysis, however, assets destined for acceptability as money are distinguished by their superior saleability (marketability). Traders discover that certain commodities are more marketable than others and are willing to hold more marketable ones for use in exchange. Others come to accept them in trades not because of their use in production but because of their marketability and value in exchange. The assets become more marketable and valuable as their demand as a medium of exchange increases relative to their non-monetary demand.

So as to qualify as candidates for this process, the assets should possess certain attributes such as stability of value, ease of transport and identification, durability, divisibility, and be easy to store and readily saleable: that is, the characteristics we have associated with liquidity. It is tempting to argue that assets which are highly marketable, reversible, divisible, and predictable evolve as money, so that liquidity confers moneyness. The difficulty with this line of reasoning is that an asset which lacks these attributes would soon acquire them should it become accepted as a medium of exchange. Moneyness would confer liquidity.

Nevertheless, it does seem apparent, as MacDonald and Milbourne (1990) argue, that if the chosen item, e.g. onions, is difficult to carry around (by other than Frenchmen!) there is an incentive for an individual to accept onions and issue paper claims against them which are easier to transport. There are historical parallels here. While gold (and more particularly silver) was accepted as a medium of exchange, such commodity money was difficult to carry in large amounts. Thus there existed an incentive for banks to accept gold and silver and issue banknotes against them, a role later taken over by central banks. Townsend (1980) and Lucas (1980) have shown that the portability of money is valuable when people have to move through geographically separated points in their trading, and because they cannot easily establish credit relationships, must carry money to indicate purchasing power. Portability is also emphasized by Kiyotaki and Wright (1989*a*) who extend the Jones model by making trading strategies endogenous. They show the existence of a fundamental equilibrium in which the good with the lowest storage cost is chosen as the medium of exchange. But fiat money will not be selected for this purpose unless people believe that it will be accepted by others.

Acceptability is indeed the nub of the issue. Each person accepts payment in money only because he expects others to accept it in payment from him or her. We value money only because we know that others do; and everybody is in the same position. The ultimate test of moneyness is acceptability by the public, although the social consensus which leads to acceptability as money is in common with many other social phenomena (legal norms, social conventions, clothing, language) far from fully understood. Indeed, Tobin (1980b) observed that money is like language. The speaking of English is useful only insofar as others do also: likewise, money is acceptable provided it is acceptable to others.

Money is in essence a pure illustration of consumer sovereignty: whatever is considered as good as money becomes money. The circularity involved means that to elevate something to the status of money, a social convention must be established; and it is not easy to establish this. Scitovsky (1969) suggests a number of ways by which this might be done.

One way would be for all members of a group formally to pledge amongst themselves to accept a certain object as a medium of exchange. This is how the European Union went about establishing a common currency. But the way in which it was done makes the euro very much a creature of the new millennium. It was a 'virtual' currency before it was a real one, and passed the market test of acceptability before entering circulation.

Another way of establishing such a social convention is for an authority to enforce acceptance of a money as payment. This is the basis of legal tender. The courts of every country enforce the acceptance of its national currency in discharge of legal obligations to pay. Note, however, that this is strictly limited. It means only that the government will accept its own pieces of paper in settlement of (certain) debts and that the courts will regard them as discharging debts. There is no obligation for private bodies to accept the money.

A third way is for an important member of the group unilaterally to accept in payment a certain form of money; if important enough, and the money convenient enough, other members of the group are likely to follow suit. The use of a currency reserve—one country's currency used as external reserve by other countries—is an example, payment of taxes in domestic currency is another.

A fourth way is for a commodity valuable in consumption and especially suitable as a medium of exchange gradually to acquire the status of money. Once the social convention is established, its use as money can persist quite independently of its value or continued use in consumption. The acceptance of gold, first as national money and later as international money, is the obvious example.

One more way of establishing the moneyness of something is to guarantee its convertibility into something else the status of which as money is already established. This is the historical explanation of the evolution of paper money, bank deposits, traveller's cheques, etc., as so many forms of money.

There is then the question of whether monetary economics itself needs to evolve as the environment changes, a view which comes through clearly in the later work of Hicks (1967, 1982, 1989). For example, Hicks in 1967 argued that monetary theory must evolve with the continuing evolution of the financial system. Making a distinction between 'metallic money' and 'credit money', his view at that time was that: 'In a world of banks and insurance companies, money markets and stock exchanges, money is quite a different thing from what it was before these institutions came into being' (1967: 158).

1.6 Conclusions

WE began by noting that monetary economics is a broad church. The range of questions posed in this chapter is sufficient to prove the point and even then we have not provided elaborate answers. Money has intrinsic attributes that make it special in terms of its functions, in terms of its properties as an asset and its interaction with the wider economic system in the short and the long term. It is unlike any other commodity since it has, by social convention, a usefulness and acceptability beyond that of other goods. Yet, in order to establish the social convention it does help for the money-to-be to have value for some other reason. A fall back value is a useful underpinning for money but where it does not exist, as in fiat systems, the basis of trust in money must be established by the stability of the monetary system. Both foundations are developed in relation to various types of monetary standard and are the subject of the next chapter.

Notes

1 An excellent review of this book is given by Sinclair (1991).

2 Jones and Kenen (1985).

3 Keynes (1933) and Dillard (1955).

4 Since the exchange rate generally anticipated the inflation rate this was good business. The German hyperinflation is examined in Ch. 7.

5 See Ch. 8 on currency substitution.

6 The inefficiencies of the double-coincidence of wants and thinly traded markets under barter are illustrated by an advertisement that appeared in a Protestant newspaper in the predominantly Catholic Republic of Ireland. It read 'Farmer, protestant (with tractor) seeks wife, protestant (with bailer). Please send photograph (of bailer).' Another advertisement illustrates further that while the double-coincidence of wants problem can be fully overcome in a monetary economy the

efficiencies of thinly traded markets cannot. The following entry appeared in the second hand column of a Dublin newspaper: 'Second-hand gravestone for sale. Would suit someone of the name O'Farrell'.

7 Buffer stock models are considered in Ch. 11. They are popular in British and Canadian work on the demand for money, but have made little headway in the USA.

8 The Currency school–Banking school controversy is considered further in Ch. 3. A general review is given by Anna Schwartz (1992). Cramp (1962) interprets the issues in terms of what we have called the tertiary sector.

9 The Friedman and Schwartz framework is outlined in Ch. 13. There is a body of literature, that we will not examine, which argues that bank intermediation has inherently 'special' characteristics. Bank credit creation may be more expansionary than that of other intermediaries (see Culbertson, 1958 and Guttentag and Lindsay, 1968). Or perhaps banks are creators of credit, while non-banks are merely middlemen (see Aschheim, 1961). Perhaps banks are capable of generating substantial amounts of money in excess of demand which cannot be extinguished (the 'hot potato' analogy), whereas non-bank's liabilities are predominantly demand-determined (Lewis, 1980). Or, the specialness may simply be a consequence of regulation, as argued by Tobin (1963) and taken up later under the 'legal restrictions' banner. To this extent, deregulation might be expected to have consequences for the role of banks in monetary policy, and we take up this particular point later.

10 That is the essence of the new monetary economics position (Fama, 1980; Cowen and Krosner, 1987; Harper and Coleman, 1992; Trautwein, 1993).

11 It is interesting that the real business cycle theorists and the post-Keynesians are agreed on this point.

Chapter 2
Monetary Standards

2.1 Monetary Systems

THE evolution of money and financial institutions from antiquity through to modern financial systems, based on a full complement of financial institutions and instruments, can be traced in Table 2.1, based on Goldsmith (1969) and Kindleberger (1984). It seems self evident that one type of analysis is needed for commodity systems, when money consists literally of units of physical commodities such as precious metals, another under fiat money involving inconvertible paper currency issued by the state, and a third in a credit money environment when the exchange media consist primarily of plastic cards and deposit liabilities of financial intermediaries. But in what way does the analysis change? The argument in this chapter is that the various monetary systems have a different monetary standard, and from this fact it follows that price determination and other monetary outcomes are going to change.

In the previous chapter we noted the view of Hicks that 'In a world of banks and insurance companies, money markets and stock exchanges, money is quite a different thing from what it was before these institutions came into being' (1967: 158). In his last work *A Market Theory of Money* (1989), he qualified his earlier statement in one important respect by arguing that all monetary economies, and not just those with developed financial institutions, have a basic credit element, so that the concepts of credit and the payment of debts are fundamental to understanding the role of money in market systems.

Any transaction involving the trading of either a commodity or a financial instrument can be seen to comprise three components:

- The contractual agreement specifying the terms of exchange, i.e. price, quantity and quality of the product, its physical characteristics, method of payment, liability provisions, location, and time for delivery.
- The delivery, i.e. the physical transfer of the ownership of the product.
- The payment.

In many auction markets there is no separation of these aspects. Thus in the wool auction market the type of wool, its quality, the amount, and the price is determined and almost immediately buyers are required to pay for and take delivery of the goods. The entire transaction takes place 'on the spot'.

Table 2.1 Forms of money and financial institutions	
Characteristic	Historical example
1. Only commodity money, no financial institutions, but occasional credit transactions	Early antiquity
2. Metallic money, bills of exchange and indigenous small-scale financial institutions (money lenders)	Classic antiquity: most parts of medieval Europe and large parts of Europe through the 18th century
3. Central bank the only, or predominant, financial institution	France, Russia (early 19th-century)
4. Deposit banks, and no central bank and no paper money	Medieval Italian cities (from 13th century on)
5. Multiplicity of note issuing and deposit banks, beginning of other financial institutions	Scotland in first half of 19th century: USA to 1913
6. Central bank, modern deposit banks; indigenous small-scale financial middlemen	Colonies in the period around independence
7. Central bank, deposit banks, beginnings of other financial institutions (particularly savings banks mortgage banks, development banks, and insurance companies)	Western Europe from mid-19th century to First World War
8. Full complement of financial institutions and instruments	USA from 1970s; Europe from 1980s

Sources: Adapted from Goldsmith (1969), Kindleberger (1984).

But this simultaneity is a rarity, and Hicks argues that the representative transaction is neither a simple 'spot' payment of goods for goods (under barter) nor of money for goods (under monetary exchange), but usually involves either deferred or advance payment in some way, so that the three components above are separated in time. When this occurs, the timing rule is that the contractual agreement comes first: in some cases the means of payment will be delivered before the goods and services (cash-in-advance or putting down a deposit), in others final payment comes after the delivery of goods and services (as in consumer or trade credit). However, the key element is that immediately after the initial contract is made two debts are automatically created, one in terms of 'money', the other in real goods and services.

Money's role is twofold in that it plays a part in fixing the terms of the original contract, and it is also the means by which the debt is settled. In the first it is performing a role which is an amalgam of the *unit of account* and *unit of contract* functions considered in Chapter 1. Hicks calls this the *standard of value*. In the second guise, money serves as a *means of payment*: a medium of exchange enables one to acquire the goods, and is needed to effect the final payment. Thus a credit card is a medium of exchange but not a means of payment, since the monthly bill must be settled finally with another medium. In many, if not most transactions, money will also act as a temporary *store of value* since it is necessary to store purchasing power if the purchase decision takes place later than the sale of goods and services. However, this function of money is not distinctive because there will always be other stores of value, possibly with better rates of return, which do not perform the primary monetary functions, e.g. government securities.

Consequently, Hicks says that we are left with only two distinguishing features of money: the standard of value and medium of payment functions. The essence of monetary exchange is the fixing of contracts in terms of 'money' and their ultimate settlement in money; the economic and financial system requires a basic monetary item—a standard—which both defines the measure of value and provides a basis for the ultimate repayment of debt. This monetary standard could take the form of 'hard money' such as gold or silver, or could be, as in contemporary systems, 'fiat money' such as base money or cash.

A monetary standard is not the same as money because even within a particular country there has rarely if ever been only one form of money used. In the past gold, silver, and banknotes and deposits have coexisted as exchange media or payment media. At present coinage, paper money, central bank money, and credit money of banks and other institutions are involved. Use of the word 'system' to describe this complex implies that there are definite relations of value between various moneys. A 'monetary system' refers to this whole and embraces a number of different types of money: that is, it refers to the set of policies and/or arrangements carried out by and through the monetary institutions which constitute the structure. An examination of different monetary systems compares the alternative arrangements for monetary management. By a 'monetary standard' we mean the criterion or reference point guiding these social arrangements and constituting the ultimate asset combining the twin functions of standard of value and means of payment. A study of the 'monetary mechanism' deals with the ways in which the various elements of the system interact and operate, and hence with the processes which enable achievement of the standard.

This chapter examines a number of different monetary regimes. In order to provide a framework for this discussion, Table 2.2 classifies monetary systems according to the reference point of the structure, i.e. the nature of the monetary standard. Most of the sixteen systems identified in the table can be classified under one of five heads: independent standards, single commodity-based standards, multi commodity-based standards, currency standards, and index standards. Two systems—the limping gold standard and the balance of payments standard—overlap these classifications.

A fiat money system can be defined as one based on claims such as paper money, coinage, and deposits at the central bank of a country which are not convertible by law or custom into anything other than themselves, and which have no fixed value in terms of any objective standard or monetary substance. This definition makes clear that fiat money is set apart from the other systems in not being linked with some external object, either directly or indirectly.

Table 2.2 Classification of alternative monetary standards

No external value	Some external value			
	One commodity	Two or more commodities	One or more currencies	Index standards
Fiat money Freely issued inconvertible token paper or credit money.	*Monometallism* A system based on one metal freely minted into coins which can be melted and exported. *Gold specie standard* Gold coins circulate along with banknotes which are convertible into gold coins on demand and for the smallest coin available. *Limping gold standard* Convertibility into metal rather than fiat money is at the authorities' discretion. *Gold bullion standard* Gold coins no longer circulate and banknotes can only be exchanged for gold bullion, often only by specified groups. *Gold exchange standard* Maintaining a country's currency convertible into the currency of a country on the gold standard, and so indirectly into gold.	*Bimetallism* Use of a monetary unit defined as a specific weight of silver or a specific weight of gold, both freely minted and standing in a fixed ratio to one another. *Symmetallism* The monetary unit is defined as a specific weight of silver *plus* gold. The two metals can be exchanged at a fixed price in terms of the monetary unit when combined in the legally fixed proportions, but their relative price is free to vary. *Composite commodity reserve standard* The monetary unit either consists of or is defined in terms of warehouse receipts of a fixed weighted bundle of commodities held in store or as a reserve asset.	*Exchange standard* The value of the domestic monetary unit is fixed in terms of the monetary unit of a foreign country. *Currency basket* The practice of fixing the value of the domestic money in terms of a composite unit comprising a number of foreign currencies, usually weighted according to trade. *Balance of payments standard* Use of monetary policy to maintain a defined equilibrium in the balance of payments.	*Tabular standard* The monetary unit would be defined as a specific combination of a selected group of commodities. The definition of the monetary unit would be adjusted periodically to offset movements in the prices of the selected group relative to all commodities. *Goods standard* The practice of maintaining stable by monetary management the value of money relative to an index of goods. *Earnings standard* Maintaining the value of money stable in terms of an index of wage earnings. *Labour standard* Expanding the money supply to accommodate full employment wage outcomes, as under an incomes policy.

For the other systems, the nature of the external linkage is the second criterion underlying the table, in particular whether the external object is one or more commodities, another currency or some index of items. Frequently, the external object is looked on as giving intrinsic value to money. Invariably, however, the monetary use gives value to the item chosen. What the external linkage really does is ensure confidence in money and sustain the social convention by protecting against the overissue of money and otherwise restricting the extent to which the authorities can debase the currency. Hence, within each category, the systems are ordered vertically from automatic to more managed systems, reflecting the method by which the linkage is brought about. Slight changes in the method of adjustment produce different classifications. A gold standard of any form carries implications for exchange rate relationships. An exchange standard is distinguished from a gold standard when stable exchange rates are the proximate goal of monetary policies and not the result of linking the monetary system to gold. A fiat money system converts into an index system, without any necessary change in institutional mechanisms, when there is a limitation of the amount of money so as to stabilize the prices of commodities (a goods standard) or of labour services (an earnings standard). Both standards imply the existence of a monetary constitution, which enables the required stabilization to be achieved (e.g. an independent central bank or a money supply role). When, instead, the quantity of money simply adjusts passively to accommodate wage outcomes at full employment, we have a labour standard of the Hicksian sort (Hicks, 1955).

Some of the systems have a long history; others such as symmetallism, tabular standards, and commodity reserve currency systems exist only in economic theory. They were proposed, and interest in them continues today, because none of the systems which have been in operation has so far provided a basis for measuring economic value which is comparable, in terms of uniformity and constancy, with the way that the adoption of the metre and kilogram has established them as the basis for measuring distance and weight — a fact which we noted earlier. Of the various systems, the commodity-based ones have been the most widely used and those involving the precious metals, gold and silver, have exhibited the greatest appeal in terms of stability of value.

2.2 Commodity Money

WHILE many commodities have served as money—cattle, salt, seashells, beads, and in more recent times, cigarettes—metallic money in the form of gold and silver (and before them, copper) have been the near-universal choice as local regional and international media of exchange. The history is a long one. Minting of gold and silver coins can be dated from the seventh century BC and although the precise beginnings of the use of the precious metals for storing value in bar form are lost in the mists of time, historians say that may have been a regular custom for 'thousands of years' (Toynbee, 1954). Many present-day moneys have metallic origins: the pound sterling dates back to the silver issue of William the Conqueror, with a penny then worth 1/240 of a pound (which was the case until 1971). The precious metals have desirable attributes: they are durable, meltable, and divisible into convenient denominations. They also have intrinsic worth in terms of value theory, for they have long been valued for non-monetary use and prized as ornaments and display.

Gold standard

Given the long history of commodity-based money, a gold standard of the universal form that we now associate with that description was in operation for remarkably short spans of time, 1879–1914 and 1925–31, and for many of those years its workings were the subject of fierce controversy. It would seem that the further we are from this period, the stronger is its emotional and historical appeal. Its advocates look upon the years before the First World War as an island of price stability and economic and personal freedom, brought about by a smoothly operating mechanism which automatically ensured balance of payments equilibria and stable exchange rates: 'commodity money is the only type of money that, at the present time, can be said to have passed the test of history in market economies' (Niehans, 1978: 140).

A *gold standard* can be said to exist when a country maintains equality between the value of the domestic monetary unit and a specified amount of gold. *Mint parity* provides an official valuation of the currency in terms of gold, and various provisions must exist to maintain the parity. Chief among these is *convertibility*. With free coinage and minting, it would pay an individual to have gold bars converted into coins should coins exhibit any tendency to rise in value relative to their gold content, and to reconvert the coins into bullion should coins fall in value. With freedom to export or import gold in unlimited quantities, the domestic currency is also kept equal in value to the stipulated weight of gold on world markets. Thus an *international gold standard* exists when a number of countries provide for convertibility between currency and gold and allow unrestricted export and import of gold. Such a system was not in place until 1879 and then only the USA, Britain, and Germany permitted full and automatic convertibility; France, Belgium, and Switzerland were effectively on 'limping standards' (Robertson, 1928; Bloomfield, 1959; Eichengreen, 1985) in which legal convertibility was at the option of the authorities, while many other countries (e.g. Japan, the Netherlands, Canada, Australia, Austria-Hungary) kept substantial external reserves in foreign exchange, and were on a form of 'gold exchange standard'.

Before 1879, Britain stood almost alone (with Portugal) in its attachment to gold. Gold suited Britain, in comparison with silver, because as the richest country a larger proportion of its monetary transactions could be conveniently carried out using gold, the higher-valued metal, but even so, the problem of ensuring adequate low-value coinage remained. In fact, convenience of the coinage has posed problems for the two monometallic standards. Under a silver standard, high-value coins would be excessively heavy. Under a gold standard, full-bodied low-value coins would be excessively tiny. The obvious solution is to have small-denomination silver coins circulate alongside gold coins, used primarily for high-valued transactions. This was the attraction of *bimetallism* which operated other than in Britain for the first three-quarters of the nineteenth century.

Bimetallism

Under a bimetallic system, a country's mint stood ready to convert either silver or gold into specified coins at a fixed gold/silver price ratio, set by law. Difficulties came about when countries maintained legal mint ratios between the two metals which were incompatible with each other and with market conditions. Undervaluation would see one of the metals disappear from circulation as Gresham's Law[1] came into operation, and the metallic money undervalued at the mint, the 'good money', would disappear, driven out of circulation by the 'bad money' overpriced at the mint (Dowd, 1996). Then bimetallism became *de facto* silver or gold monometallism unless the official mint ratio was readjusted in line with market equilibrium (or unless market conditions varied again). Indeed, one such readjustment in 1717 saw gold first emerge as the dominant currency in Britain, when Sir Isaac Newton, then Master of the Mint, set a mint ratio less favourable to silver than that ruling in France, pushing silver out of circulation and in effect putting England on a gold standard.

Price determination under gold

Gold provided Britain with a remarkable degree of long-term price stability. The price level of consumable goods on the eve of the suspension of the gold standard in 1931 was *in absolute terms* almost exactly the same as that in 1821. Sir John Hicks recalled as a child growing up in the early 1900s being aware that letter postage, from one part of Britain to another, was one penny and had been so for more than fifty years (Hicks, 1986). Nevertheless, prices in general were far from stable over shorter periods of time, as shown in Figure 2.1. During the nineteenth century, prices generally were on a declining path from 1816 to 1851, then had an upward path until 1873, and fell substantially until the end of the century. With the exception of the inflation of the Civil War years, the same trends are evident in the USA.

For any system in which the value of the currency is tied to a commodity standard (or any other external value), we can express the money price of goods as the product of the parity price of the standard commodity and the terms of trade between the standard commodity and other commodities, i.e.:

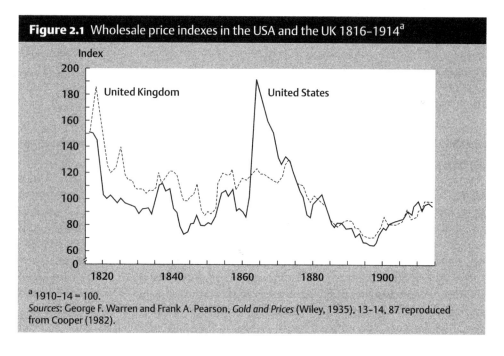

Figure 2.1 Wholesale price indexes in the USA and the UK 1816–1914[a]

[a] 1910–14 = 100.
Sources: George F. Warren and Frank A. Pearson, *Gold and Prices* (Wiley, 1935), 13–14, 87 reproduced from Cooper (1982).

$$\frac{\text{goods}}{\text{monetary unit}} = \frac{\text{goods}}{\text{standard commodity}} \times \frac{\text{standard commodity}}{\text{monetary unit}}$$

The essence of commodity-based money is to fix the relationship of the monetary unit (e.g. dollar or pound) to the standard, so leaving movements in the relative price of the standard commodity to goods in general as the sole source of fluctuations in commodity prices. It follows that if the aim is to achieve stability of prices, defined as some index of prices, the standard commodity should be one the prices of which move *pari passu* with those of the goods making up the chosen index.

On these grounds gold is far from ideal. Its value is likely to be upset by new mines or technical improvements in mining, by tastes in jewellery, and by hoarding. The 'automaticity' of the gold standard proved to be slow-working at best. In response to slow growth of gold production relative to trade and incomes, the idea was that commodity prices would fall, so raising the relative price of gold and making extra production profitable.[2] In fact, annual production of gold declined during the long period of falling prices from the 1870s to the 1890s and did not increase substantially before 1895, after which new discoveries in the Transvaal and the Klondike and new technology, saw gold production rise.

In the meantime, the process of deflation produced considerable hardship among debtors because nominal interest rates did not fall as rapidly as did commodity prices, so that real interest rates increased. (This behaviour has been the case in most periods of deflation, including the disinflation of the 1980s and 1990s.) The deflationary trend affected all nations with a gold standard, but was especially severe in the USA because it started with the inflated prices of the Civil War years, and from 1865 to 1879 when gold convertibility was resumed, price deflation averaged 6.5 per cent per annum.

Many at the time argued for a return to silver, and the issue was later fought out in the US presidential campaign of 1896.[3] Production of silver had expanded markedly, and with reduced demand from demonetization the price of silver halved between 1870 and 1895 (so giving the lie to the idea that the metal gives value to money—in reality, actual and potential monetary use gives the metal much of its value).

Symmetallism

Leading economists such as Edgeworth, Fisher, Marshall, Pierson, and Walras all came out against gold, most favouring bimetallism. Marshall's proposed alternative was *symmetallism* (Marshall, 1887), in which the monetary unit would be defined in terms of gold *and* silver rather than gold *or* silver, as under bimetallism. Under symmetallism, one can imagine, say, one ounce of gold and fifteen ounces of silver combined in one bar. Broadening the base to the two metals would lessen the impact of demand and supply variations affecting one metal alone, and thus lead to a less variable price level. In this respect, symmetallism is a forerunner of commodity reserve proposals in which a group of commodities would be chosen to be representative of prices in general.

Edgeworth (1895) considered that symmetallism had one major disadvantage. Unlike bimetallism, in which the money price of gold *and* silver is fixed, the relative price of gold and silver in terms of monetary units would fluctuate freely in world and domestic markets, as symmetallism might be introduced independently by countries without international agreement on a common bundle of gold and silver. If countries defined their currencies in terms of different bundles of gold and silver, the exchange rates between them would not be fixed and would need to vary. Fluctuating exchange rates were clearly out of temper with the times, which favoured the stable exchange rates provided by the use of one metal.

Tabular standards

Although he advocated symmetallism, Marshall actually much preferred a tabular standard—a constructed standard—for bringing about price stability, an idea later refined by Irving Fisher (1920) in his proposal for a 'compensated dollar' (see Patinkin, 1993; and Dowd, 1996, for recent expositions). Fisher recommended periodic discrete adjustments in the gold content of the dollar to keep a general price index nearly stable. A rise in the index would call for increasing the dollar's value by an increase in its gold content; a fall in the index would call for lightening the dollar. Consider the earlier relationship:

$$\text{dollar price of a basket of goods and services} = \text{gold price of basket} \times \text{dollar price of gold}$$

Any change in the gold price of the chosen basket of goods and services can be offset by an appropriate change by the minting authority in the dollar price of gold, leaving the dollar price of the basket unchanged.

Resource costs of commodity money

Enthusiasm for the alternatives to gold evaporated when gold production picked up and the declining path of prices in general gave way to an upward trend. Some of the deflationary consequences of falling gold production may in any case have been alleviated by the transition from predominantly commodity money to the increasing use of fiduciary money of one kind or another—banknotes and debt money such as bank deposits. There are strong economic incentives for this substitution to take place. A well-known deficiency of a commodity standard is the resource cost of tying up much of the commodity for monetary use. Growth of incomes and the demand for money over time require that labour and capital be used for digging gold from the ground in, say, South Africa and reburying it in central bank vaults in New York or London, as Sir Roy Harrod (1965) once remarked. These costs can be lowered by reducing the ratio of gold reserves to the domestic money supply.

A fractional reserve system is an arrangement in which at least two moneys circulate: a commodity such as gold in the form of currency, and credit money in the form of banknotes or deposits for which banks in turn hold gold as backing. If the banks can function effectively with gold reserves that are some fraction of their outstanding liabilities, so that the quantity of money is much larger than the stocks of gold, society gets its monetary services at a lower cost while individuals benefit from the explicit or implicit interest (services) which banks pay on deposits.

It was a feature of the gold standard that this economizing process occurred over time without design, undertaken by banks and other institutions engaging in financial intermediation which involves maturity transformation. Savers wish to 'go short' and keep part of their assets readily withdrawable at no risk of nominal capital loss to meet unexpected consumption shocks. Borrowers generally prefer to 'go long' in their financing requirements. These 'preferred habitats' leave room for banks to borrow funds at call, and lend longer. To successfully issue call obligations the bank must convince depositors that it can meet encashment demands. However, once the confidence exists, no one feels it actually necessary to make the conversion and the debt can serve successfully as 'money'. As we have said, consumer sovereignty dictates that whatever is regarded as being as good as money, becomes money. Banking depends on maintaining the trust and confidence of the depositors; so long as there is trust in the liabilities of the bank these can serve as money and augment gold for monetary use.

Gold exchange standard

Whether, in the circumstances of the nineteenth century, this process of financial innovation should be seen as a largely fortuitous development or induced by the combination of gold shortage, secular deflation, and high real interest rates remains a question which to our knowledge has not previously been asked. However, the innovations, in their turn, seem likely to have altered the character of the gold standard in ways which would become clearer under the later *gold exchange standard* of the interwar period, under which the pre-1914 practice of using gold-convertible currencies (especially sterling) to supplement gold as reserve assets became widespread. One effect of the growth of debt money was to weaken the influence of the automatic forces. While the whole superstructure of claims was still ultimately tied to gold—the monetary standard—by the redemption of bank liabilities and central banks' reserves of gold and gold-based assets, the indirect linkage meant that there could be no certainty that a country's money supply would always rise and fall automatically in line with gold movements as was expected under the 'rules of the game'. Further, the pyramiding of an increasing quantity of debt money on a limited quantity of gold held the potential for instability in times of crisis when the threat of gold conversions loomed (and indeed this is what happened in 1931 when many countries were forced off gold).

Exchange rates under gold

A gold standard requires that all paper and deposit money be interconvertible with gold at a fixed mint parity. This convertibility combined with the free trade in gold provided one mechanism by which foreign payments could take place. A person in England needing to make a payment in dollars could always take sterling notes to the Bank of England for conversion into gold bars at the official gold parity, ship the gold to New York, exchange the gold for dollars at the Federal Reserve Bank, and then arrange payment of the debt. Not surprisingly, most international transactions were not made in this way but were made instead, as now, through the foreign exchange markets. In order to buy dollar goods, Englishmen had to persuade someone to exchange sterling for dollars. Americans buying British goods had to persuade someone to change dollars for sterling. Either the total purchases of the two groups must balance, or members of one group had to be willing to accumulate the currency of the other, with the exchange rate adjusting to help bring this about—much the same as occurs at present. The difference from now was that exchange rates fluctuated only within strict limits, reflecting the existence of the indirect, roundabout payments mechanism described above.

Exchange rates were anchored to the mint par of exchange, i.e. the ratio of the gold content of one currency to that of another, simply because things related to the same thing must be related to each other. In 1816, the value of the pound was set equal to 113 fine grains of pure gold, while in 1834 the gold dollar contained 23.22 fine grains of pure gold, giving a mint par to exchange of $4.8665 = £1 prior to the First World War. Such was the permanency of all this that Hicks (1986) remembers as a schoolboy that it was simply taken for granted that one pound was equal to 4.86

US dollars, 25 French or Swiss francs, 20 German marks, a little less than 10 Japanese yen, and so on; moreover, these exchange rates were chanted from arithmetic books.

It was possible for exchange rates to vary from mint par, but they would usually do so only up to the limit implied by the cost of transporting gold in either direction between the two gold standard countries concerned. Suppose that in pre-1914 years, the cost of shipping gold across the Atlantic including freight, insurance, agency fees, and interest during the time of transit was about two cents per pound. Hence, in Figure 2.2, $4.846 constitutes the 'gold export point' for the UK, at which rate it would be advantageous to ship gold in payment rather than use the foreign exchange market. On the other hand, $4.886 is the 'gold import point' for the UK. These specie points constitute, respectively, the lower and upper limits to the movement of sterling in the market without producing gold shipments.

If, in response to a change in demand (e.g. D_2 in Figure 2.2), the exchange rate moved beyond the gold specie points, reserves of gold would flow to the country with relatively low prices from the country with relatively high prices, expanding the monetary base in the first and contracting it in the other. Under the automatic workings of the gold standard, this movement in the monetary base was expected to expand the total money supply in the low-price country and contract it in the country with high prices. Presumably, this would eventually bring their price levels into line with mint parities along the lines envisaged in Hume's price-specie-flow mechanism (Hume, 1752). The actual movements of gold would normally be carried out by arbitrageurs in the foreign exchange and bullion markets by exchanging currency for gold in the two countries.

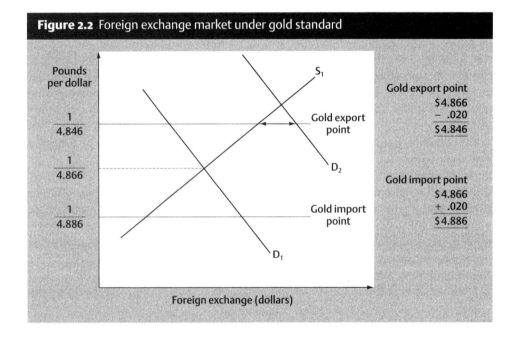

Figure 2.2 Foreign exchange market under gold standard

What is indisputable is that the gold standard did produce what is, especially by modern standards, a remarkable degree of exchange rate stability. Striking evidence of this stability comes from Giovannini (1992), and one of his calculations is reproduced in Figure 2.3. It reports logarithms of the spot exchange rates of the pound relative to the dollar, together with estimates of the gold points for the dollar from 1889 to 1908. Logarithms were used to highlight the size of the fluctuation bands, which were less than 2 per cent wide in the case of the dollar. Note also that the export (upper bound) and import (lower bound) points of gold fluctuate, as freight, insurance, and interest rates change. Giovannini's estimates of the gold points for the US dollar broadly match those of Officer (1986). What is notable from Figure 2.3 is that the spot exchange rate touches the gold export point only on one occasion, in August 1895, most likely in consequence of the collapse of the Morgan-Belmont syndicate (Garber and Grilli, 1986).

Adjustment mechanisms

Whether such stability came about via the specie flow mechanism of classical monetary theory is less clear, and—to judge from the extent of gold flows—probably unlikely. Other mechanisms which may have operated include adjustments in spending and employment, flows of capital (especially long-term lending emanating from London), trade and offsetting capital flows as predicted by the monetary theory of the balance of payments, and movements in the terms of trade between manufacturing and commodity exporting countries (see Eichengreen, 1985). It would also

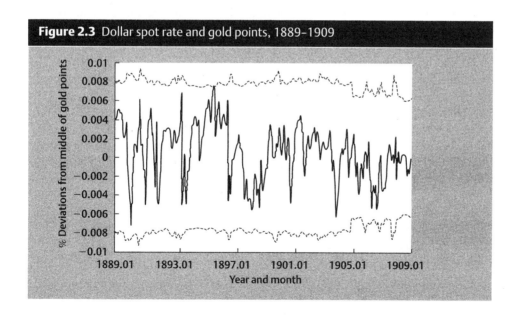

Figure 2.3 Dollar spot rate and gold points, 1889–1909

seem that the gold standard was, to a large degree, a managed system with central bank policy in some cases facilitating, and in other cases overriding, the 'automatic' adjustment process.

Central banks had a number of tools at their disposal such as intervention in the gold market, adjustments to the gold reserve, or changes in the regulations about convertibility (although intervention in the foreign exchange market was rare until the late 1930s when countries were no longer tied firmly to gold). For the Bank of England the main instrument was the Bank rate. Increases in interest rates had two principal consequences. One was to attract short-term capital flows which acted as a palliative for the situation by reducing or even reversing the gold flow. Walter Bagehot once remarked that '8 per cent will bring gold from the moon'. Such sensitivity of capital flows to interest rates owed much to the credible commitment to fixed exchange rates which the metallic standard offered: countries on gold were expected to be so forever, and moreover at the same parity. This continuity meant that it was possible at any time to give force to a statement that sterling or the dollar or any gold standard currency was relatively high or relatively low. As people became convinced of the fixity of rates, the process became self-reinforcing and capital more responsive. In this respect, to borrow Harrod's (1969) description, capital movements were 'helpful' to the authorities when protecting parity.

The other side of an increase in interest rates was to tighten credit, discourage spending, and to deflate home demand, so reinforcing the restriction of the money supply due to the contraction in gold stocks and the monetary base. As debt money assumed a larger part of the money supply, and more money came to be created as a byproduct of the lending activities of banks, interest rates and conditions in the credit market came to be seen as the cornerstone of monetary policy. As capital flows induced by the Bank rate increasingly offset the initial gold flows, eliminating the need for the monetary base actually to force a reduction in money, reliance was placed upon credit and not money supply policy to bring out the adjustments to incomes and prices needed for longer-term stabilization of the trade and exchange rate position. It is easy to see from these institutional practices, the origins of the Keynesian way of thinking about money in terms of interest rate and credit conditions, so contrary to Friedman and his 'litmus test' (see Section 1.3).

Consequently, for most gold standard countries, stable exchange rates, instead of being the result of linking monetary units to gold, became in Irving Fisher's description 'the criterion of monetary stability' (1934: 1). Monetary policy was thought of primarily in terms of maintaining a constant exchange value in terms of other currencies, with foreign rather than domestic convertibility the governing objective. With this tendency to elevate the exchange rate to the status of the monetary standard in place of gold, it was a short step from the gold standard to Bretton Woods and the era of fixed exchange rates.

2.3 Fixed Rates

MORE familiar in recent decades than tying money to one or more commodities is tying the home currency to some foreign currency at a fixed rate of exchange. There is a large variety of ways in which this is still done, ranging from exchange rate targeting to currency board systems (and even monetary union), and these techniques are examined in Chapter 15. Although normally thought of in terms of the Bretton Woods era, the practice began under the gold exchange standard when smaller countries fixed their exchange rate to a larger currency which was itself convertible in gold. Indeed, in these terms it might be said that the Bretton Woods system *was* a gold exchange standard. The system gets its name, incidentally, because it was established by a meeting of forty-four countries in Bretton Woods, a village in New Hampshire in July 1944 (and the system got under way in 1945 after the end of the war).

In order to provide some structure to our discussion, Table 2.3 compares various monetary regimes in terms of exchange rate arrangements, international reserves, inflation control, and monetary independence. Under the rules of the Bretton Woods system, which established international institutions such as the IMF and the World Bank, member countries of the IMF were required to define the parity of their currencies in terms of gold and to maintain what amounted to indirect convertibility into gold via the stabilization of exchange values and gold prices. A parity in terms of gold implied, as under the gold standard, an official exchange rate between the currency concerned and other currencies, in particular the US dollar.[4] The key currency of the system was the dollar as only the USA allowed its currency to be convertible (for external purposes) into gold—moreover at the 1934 parity of \$35 per ounce. Exchange rates were to be maintained within ± 1 per cent of parity, creating, albeit artificially, analogues of the old gold points (but wider); and there was indirect convertibility into gold much as under a gold exchange standard. In addition, intervention took place in the London gold market to ensure that the private market price of gold did not differ from \$35 per ounce by much more than the cost of shipping gold from New York to London. Both defining features of a commodity currency standard—parity and convertibility—were thus present. To all appearances a gold standard of sorts was still in operation (Harrod, 1969, called it a 'modified gold standard').

However, in other respects the role of gold was downplayed. No country redeemed money domestically into gold, and in many countries private hoarding of gold was prohibited. While IMF member countries maintained convertibility through the foreign exchange market, that conversion was no longer at a parity meant to be immutable. Par values could be altered for any (non-dollar) currency adjudged to be in fundamental disequilibrium (although it was implicit that the gold parity of the dollar would not change, the dollar being in effect 'as good as gold').

This fixed-but-adjustable exchange rate mechanism grew out of the interwar experiences and the idea was to combine the best features of gold and fiat money. The

Table 2.3 Comparison of different monetary regimes

	Gold standard 1879–1914	Gold Exchange Standard 1925–31	Bretton Woods 1945–68	Dollar Standard 1968–71	The 'Non-System' 1972–	ERM 1979–98	EMU 1999–
Exchange rate regime	Fixed gold parities	Fixed gold parities	Fixed gold parities	Fixed parities	Floating	Fixed parities	Fixed parities single currency
Exchange rate variability	Within gold export and import points	Gold bullion shipping points	±1%	±1%	Complete	Bands of ±2.25% ±6% ±15%	None
Exchange rate realignments	Parities irrevocable		One-sided at discretion of individual country	Possible for non-US currencies	Complete	Required a common decision of all members	None: common currency or irrevocably fixed parities
Nature of reserves	Gold institutionalized	Gold and gold-backed currencies	US dollar institutionalized	US dollar	National fiat currencies	Mixed: ECU official reserves balances; DM and US dollar used for interventions.	Fiat currencies
Key currency	Sterling	Dollars and sterling	US dollar institutionalized as intervention and vehicle currency	US dollar	US dollar as vehicle currency	None institutionalized: evolved to country with strongest currency e.g. DM.	Euro
Balance of payments adjustments	Symmetric rules of game	Asymmetric due to sterilization policies	Burden fell on deficit countries	Burdens fell on deficit countries	No rules of game	Symmetric intervention obligations of all members; but asymmetric sterilization	As in region of country
Inflation control	Depended on gold price	Link to gold weakened	Relied on USA maintaining gold convertibility	Relied on USA	Depends on individual country	Relied on Germany	Depends on European Central Bank
Monetary independence	Restricted	Limited	Limited	Limited, except for USA, without controls	Possible	Limited, except for Germany	None: centralized monetary policy

Source: Based on Lewis (1993).

gold standard provided exchange rate stability along with a set of rules and cooperation in promoting free trade and capital movements, but was regarded as contributing to depression when countries deflated to defined fixed parities. Fiat money,
it seemed, led to inflation and unstable exchanges, but did enable countries to
recover from unemployment by not having to deflate prices to bring them into line
with gold parities. What emerged was the system of rigid, but adjustable parities.
Exchange rates would normally be kept fixed, with the widened 'gold points' allowing some margin for market clearing of imbalances.

A number of writers have spoken of the four so-called 'desirables' of international
monetary arrangements, namely fixed exchange rates, free trade, monetary autonomy, and free capital movements (see Artis and Lewis, 1993). While the four are
meritorious, they also constitute an 'inconsistent quartet'. Policy-makers who simultaneously seek to attain these four objectives will be unsuccessful, for at best only
three of the four can be achieved, and something has to give. Under the gold standard, monetary autonomy was sacrificed. In the interwar years, fixed exchange rates
were sacrificed, and there was some compromise to free trade and capital movements. Architects of the Bretton Woods system envisaged that official controls over
capital flows would reconcile the inconsistency, and were consequently prepared to
compromise on freedom of capital flows. Countries agreed to a 'code of conduct'
dealing with cooperation, trade convertibility and orderly exchange arrangements,
yet continued restrictions on capital markets were envisaged and tolerated. The IMF,
for its part, undertook to promote stability of exchange rates by lending out
resources ('drawings') to help countries ride out minor fluctuations in the demand
and supply of foreign exchange, while permitting orderly changes in parity to
correct a 'fundamental disequilibrium'. Exchange rates would thus be brought into
conformity with misaligned price levels—not the other way around as under the
gold standard.

On this depiction, the Bretton Woods system could not accurately be described as
a gold standard. Nor could it be termed an exchange standard, for stabilization of the
exchange rate was compromised by the trade-off of external for internal stability. To
the extent that the authorities sought a stable growth of employment it might be
said that the countries were on an *employment standard*.[5] If the commitments to the
IMF were adhered to, it might be more accurate to call Bretton Woods a *balance of payments standard* (Mason, 1963). Action to correct a balance of payments disequilibrium
by either deflationary or inflationary policies or an adjustment to par values implied
making the balance of payments the criterion of policy.

If so, the Bretton Woods system was soon transformed into a fixed exchange rate
standard, with maintenance of the existing parity central to policy formulation. This
was not due to any unwillingness of the IMF to approve exchange rate changes for it
was never difficult for member countries to alter parity, and sometimes these were
at the urging of the IMF itself. Rather, countries became increasingly reluctant to
change parities for an amalgam of reasons. Revaluations were domestically unpopular because they jeopardized the competitiveness of export- and import-competing
industries. Devaluation called into question the competence of economic policy-
makers, and its avoidance was a sort of international 'virility test'. Countries with

large external borrowings in their own currency felt obliged to make every possible effort to maintain the value of their currencies at the level which prevailed when the debts were incurred. Finally, there was the problem of speculation and of 'unhelpful' capital movements.

Under the gold standard, capital movements were 'helpful' because exchange rate parities were credibly fixed by the gold specie points. The ±1 per cent ranges in the Bretton Woods system provided no similar assurance, mainly because many governments were not prepared to follow through with the policies to maintain them. Moreover, countries liberalized the controls over capital movements that the founding fathers of Bretton Woods appear to have taken for granted. Speculators were able to bet against the willingness of the authorities to sustain the parity. To make matters worse, the method of changing rates in large discrete jumps—the adjustable peg—made obvious the direction of change, allowing speculators the luxury of a one-way bet. A government contemplating an adjustment to parity had to figure that a change might merely encourage speculators to expect an alteration in response to future payments difficulties, so making things more difficult 'next time round'. Future policy credibility and the avoidance of increasingly large and destabilizing speculation pointed to the desirability of using the adjustable peg provisions of the IMF system as seldom as possible (Houthakker, 1977).

This transition to a fixed exchange rate regime highlighted the system's internal contradictions. With the exchange rate instrument unused, this left the 'adjustment' problem—the policy problem of how external balance was to be attained in an environment in which countries were unwilling to sacrifice internal balance to defend existing exchange rate parities. Mundell (1962,1963b) argued that by an appropriate use of the two instruments of fiscal and monetary policy it might be possible to attain internal and external balance under fixed exchange rates without recourse to commercial policies which would be undesirable for trade. This 'appropriate use' involved assigning fiscal policy to internal balance and monetary policy to external balance, the latter requiring that interest rates be varied inversely to the strength of the balance. Deficit countries could thus raise interest rates to correct the balance of payments, and at the same time cut taxes or increase spending to offset the contractionary effects of tight monetary policy upon employment.

For most countries Mundell's solution offered only a short-run palliative. The price of a Mundell 'solution' to a lack of competitiveness is a capital account surplus matching the current account deficit which, if capital markets are rather imperfect (as they were then) may not be sustainable. There was also the question of economic growth. Continued reliance upon high interest rates in deficit-prone countries was seen as inimical to high investment and growth. Countries were thus left reliant upon direct controls. Surplus countries tried to sterilize the money supply from the consequences of the accretion of international reserves, while applying, among a number of instruments, ceilings and taxes on the interest rates paid to foreigners and special reserve requirements on foreign deposits, which served to ameliorate the effects but did not correct the underlying payments position. Deficit countries applied import quotas and export subsidies, two-tiered exchange rates (a rate less favourable than parity for overseas investment by residents) and exchange controls. As the market found ways around these restrictions, policy-makers were faced with the choice of tightening existing controls and introducing ever more draconian measures—which to them were increasingly tedious to operate—or find some way of escaping from the straitjacket of fixed parities. Floating exchange rates emerged as the only escape route, and the major countries went down this path after 1971.

2.4 Fiat Money

THE present international monetary system is one in which national monetary authorities monopolize the supply and the management of inconvertible paper moneys. A fiat money standard is one based on claims such as paper money, coinage, and deposits at the central bank of a country which are not convertible by law or custom into anything other than themselves, and which have no fixed value in terms of any objective standard or monetary substance. In the past, the value of the internal currency was intrinsic or was maintained in a fixed or nearly fixed relationship to a monetary substance or some other external standard of value. For example, in 1816 and again in 1925, the value of the pound sterling was laid down as a specific weight of fine gold (113 grains) to which the value of sterling was to be kept equal. After the Second World War, national currencies were maintained at a fixed rate of exchange relative to the US dollar, itself backed by a gold commitment. That all changed in 1971.

The significance of that change has been characterized by Milton Friedman:

The world's current monetary system is, I believe, unprecedented. No major currency has any link to a commodity. What economists call outside money consists entirely of government fiat in the form of paper currency, minor coin, and book keeping entries such as deposits at US Federal Reserve Banks. The major earlier episodes in which governments departed from a specie standard and issued irredeemable paper money were expected to be temporary, and most of them were. The others ended in disaster, as in the hyperinflations after World Wars I and II. They were followed by monetary reforms that restored some relation between the currency and a commodity. Only since President Nixon ended Bretton Woods by closing the gold window on August 15, 1971, have the United States and all other major countries explicitly adopted monetary systems in which there is no link to a commodity and no commitment to restoring such a link. (1986: 643)

The period since 1971 is not the first time that the link between major national currencies and a commodity base has been severed. And not all such periods have been inflationary. During the 1930s much of the world employed paper money, yet in many cases its value was maintained as successfully as it had been when based on a commodity. Moreover, it can be argued that the closing of the US 'gold window' in 1971 was simply part of the same evolution that was already giving rise to the gathering inflationary momentum of the late 1960s and early 1970s, and that the departure from gold was symptomatic of these inflationary tendencies rather than the reverse. But there can be little doubt of the symbolic significance of the break as the culmination of a long evolutionary process.

It is a matter of record that, worldwide, the years since 1971 have generally been ones of high inflation. Figure 2.4 shows that consumer prices since 1970 have more than doubled in Germany, and increased threefold in Japan and more in France and the USA. In Britain, prices have increased ninefold over these years. These price movements have been accompanied by other signs of economic instability. Smith, Smithson, and Wilford (1990) provide striking graphical evidence of the greater volatility of exchange rates post-1971. McKinnon (1996) calculates the volatility of long-term interest rates in Britain and the USA. Since 1973 the volatility has been two to four times higher than under Bretton Woods and eight to ten times higher than under the pre-1914 classical gold standard.

Milton Friedman's statement 'inflation is always and everywhere a monetary phenomenon' is so familiar that it is easy to overlook that inflation need not be a monetary phenomenon and has the potential to be so only in a fiat money system. When money either is a commodity or has a value tied to a commodity, inflation is ultimately a story of fluctuations in the prices of goods in general relative to that other commodity. In that sense, inflation under a commodity standard might be said to be a *real* matter, not a monetary one. With the universal adoption of independent paper money since 1971, the value of fiat money cannot be explained by such factors.

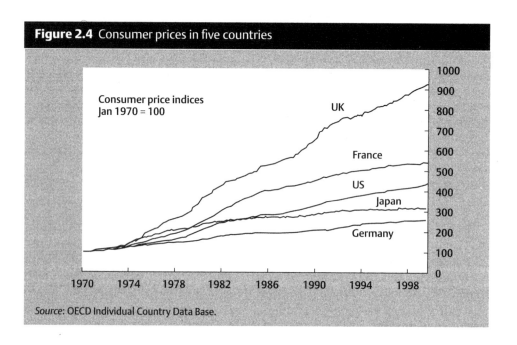

Figure 2.4 Consumer prices in five countries

Source: OECD Individual Country Data Base.

The non-system

What is the nature of the present system? What determines the value of money? What implications follow for economic policy-making? What is the monetary standard that guides policy? Many leading experts, notably Williamson (1976), have seized upon the absence of constraints to characterize present arrangements as a 'non-system', by which they mean the absence of an explicit set of rules. This follows a long tradition in monetary economics of defining a fiat money system in negative terms — for example as a 'monetary system in which the value or purchasing power of a monetary unit is *not* kept equal to the value of a specific quantity of a particular commodity or of a group of commodities' (Kent, quoted in Mason, 1963: 183). Viewed in these terms, the present system has no agreed rules upon international behaviour. Issuers of money do not promise to exchange it for gold or any other commodity. Many countries do not make their money convertible at a fixed rate into another currency. No limits are placed upon money creation. Countries can choose inflation, deflation, any fiscal-monetary policy mix, fast or slow growth. They can lend or borrow as much as they choose.

However, absence of a 'system' in the sense meant by Williamson need not imply disorder. Order in monetary arrangements can be induced spontaneously[6] as well as by design; coordination can arise voluntarily without coercion; actions can be constrained without there being any central direction. The consensus has been established in the present 'non-system' through gentlemen's agreements between members of the G7 such as the Louvre and Plaza Accords, which agreed acceptable ranges for exchange rate fluctuations. These are the distinctions which underlie Corden's (1983) insightful observation that present monetary arrangements have similarities with one of the oldest of systems, namely *laissez-faire*—in Corden's words, the present system is one of 'international financial *laissez-faire*'.

Old-fashioned (and nowadays politically incorrect) textbooks on economic principles used to begin with parables about housewives going off to market each day for shopping. Their actions are not managed or centrally directed, but neither are they uncoordinated or unconstrained. Coordination comes through the market place. Household purchase plans are drawn up on the basis of preferences and expected prices. When confronted by posted selling prices, these plans are revised along with market-clearing prices. So it is internationally. Economic entities formulate plans about exports and imports, consumption and savings, holdings of money and assets. These decisions are integrated, revised, constrained, and coordinated through the international market places for goods, services, and assets, by exchange rates and interest rates and overall demands and supplies.

A special twist comes from the different currencies employed. Continuing the householder analogy, it is as if a songwriter, artist, or author must sell his or her work before every purchase. The intrinsic value of the music sheet, canvas, or manuscript is very small, but if the works of art are valued they exchange for goods in the market for amounts well in excess of this value. Our author, say, at one time might well live in the lap of luxury but if preferences change and his writings fall from favour, then he must work harder to pay his way. So it would seem is the case with countries; 'fiat money has no intrinsic value other than what the issuing government (central bank) manages to establish' (McKinnon, 1984b: 20).

The value of fiat money

This is not to say that fiat money has no value. While having no intrinsic value, and thus no non-monetary demand, it is valued by individuals because of its ability to purchase other goods: the value of the monetary unit is the claim on goods and services which holders acquire when it is transferred to others. This was recognized by J. S. Mill (1871).

After experience had shown that pieces of paper, of no intrinsic value, by merely bearing upon them the written profession of being equivalent to a certain number of francs, dollars or pounds, could be made to circulate as such, and to produce all the benefit to the issuers which could have been produced by the coins which they purported to represent; governments began to think that it would be a happy device if they could appropriate to themselves this benefit, free from the condition to which individuals issuing such paper substitutes for money were subject, of giving, when required, for the sign the thing signified. They determined to try whether they could emancipate themselves from this unpleasant obligation, and make a piece of paper issued by them pass for a pound, by merely calling it a pound, and consenting to receive it in payment of taxes. And such is the influence of almost all established governments, that they have generally succeeded in attaining this object: I believe I might say they have always succeeded for a time, and the power has only been lost to them after they had compromised it by the most flagrant abuse.

In the case supposed, the functions of money are performed by a thing which derives its power for performing them solely from convention; but convention is quite sufficient to confer the power; since nothing more is needful to make a person accept anything as money, and even at any arbitrary value, than the persuasion that it will be taken from him on the same terms by others. (1871: 542)

Hence, despite being intrinsically useless and produced at little or no cost, money usually has an exchange value well in excess of its resource cost. The factors influencing the value of money, like that of any economic substance, can be proximately classified in terms of 'demand' and 'supply'. Demand here refers to monetary demand. This creates somewhat of a dilemma since the existence of a monetary demand presupposes that the money has value, yet there is no non-monetary demand at all for the money. Here is the essence of Kareken and Wallace's (1981) and Wallace's (1990) contention that nominal values in the present system are 'indeterminate'. On the other side of the equation, the influence of supply in determining value is readily apparent. If each monetary unit exchanged in terms of its marginal cost of production then there would be a literal paper standard — a commodity system based on paper. It follows that if each dollar or pound can be exchanged for goods of greater value than the cost of printing the unit, then it is due to some scarcity or artificial restriction upon supply. This puts the emphasis upon the conditions governing the issue of money. Hence, the successful operation of a paper money system relies on restraint by the issuing authority and/or budget agency.

The benefits and costs of fiat money

Fears that this needed restraint would not be exercised have led to much of the hostility to a fiat money system. For example, Yeager, speaks of

the preposterousness of a fiat unit, which has whatever value supply and demand fleetingly accord to something supplied and demanded *entirely* for monetary purposes—the dollar of government base money, the scruffy dollar bill. (1992: 731)

As another example, Leijonhufvud (1987) dubbed fiat money regulated not in accordance with any clear rules or criteria but rather in accordance with the changeable and largely unfettered discretion of a monetary authority as a 'Random Walk Monetary Standard'.

Opposition to fiat money has not been confined to theorists. The limited experience in the 1930s with paper moneys and floating exchange rates led men of affairs at the time to contemplate with considerable trepidation a continuing system of free paper currencies. Consider, for example, the view of Sir Theodore Gregory.

The dangers which the universal adoption of independent standards involves are that such a step would encourage the already strong tendencies toward economic nationalism; that it would bring about perpetually fluctuating rates of exchange; and that it would at any moment of difficulty facilitate the abuse of the printing press by governments . . . the existence of universal paper standards threatens an indefinite continuance of chaos in the monetary affairs of the world unless agreement is reached as to general price policy. But such an agreement would make an international adopting of paper unnecessary, for the same ends could then be reached under an international gold standard.' (Gregory, 1933:612)

Despite such warnings, it is easy to understand why those such as Keynes (1923), seeking 'a scientific treatment of currency questions', have found paper currencies seductive. The attractiveness of commodity-based money lies in the track record of price and exchange rate stability. A well-managed paper money system can in principle do at least as well, and perhaps better, in realizing these goals by overcoming the short-run price variability which results from lags in the response of commodity-based money supply to variations in demand. Indeed, many central banks were originally established in order to bring about a more 'elastic' supply of money and water down the rigidities of a commodity monetary standard. But, importantly, a paper standard can achieve these ends at very much lower resource cost since the inefficiency inherent in tying up stocks of a valuable commodity for monetary use is eliminated. If supplied correctly, paper money can be created at near-zero social cost — due to its trivial intrinsic value. In this respect, as Yeager notes, 'ideally managed government money is a beguiling idea' (Yeager, 1992: 732).

The worldwide adoption of fiduciary paper money undoubtedly is an acknowledgement, even if unstated, that the advantages of an inconvertible monetary standard are substantial. However, as Milton Friedman (1986) has noted, the true cost to society is much higher when there is monetary mismanagement. The costs then include the effects upon economic decision-making of the unstable exchanges and higher and more variable inflation which we noted has occurred. Resources will then be diverted into hedging against price-level uncertainty via markets for swaps, futures, options, and other derivatives.

The essential issue is how the undoubted benefits of fiat money can be obtained without incurring these costs. In opting for a worldwide system of paper moneys, modern central bankers have entered uncharted waters (Lewis, 1994). Nevertheless, however limited is our experience of fiat money in terms of the broad sweep of monetary history, the properties and workings of a fiat money system have been analysed extensively in monetary theory. David Hume's (1752) fancy that 'by miracle, every man in Great Britain should have five pounds slipped into his pocket on one night', Milton Friedman's (1969) unique 'helicopter money' events, whereby an extra $1,000 in bills is dropped from the skies, and Patinkin's (1965) 'market experiments' are ones in which the monetary injections are of fiat money. There is a real sense in which it can be said that economic reality has caught up with, and to this degree made practically relevant, mainstream monetary economics based around the quantity theory of money—the topic of the chapters which now follow.

Notes

1 For an explanation of Gresham's Law see Harrod (1969) and Burstein (1963). The law is so frequently mentioned in monetary economics that it is worth reproducing Harrod's wonderful account at some length.

The law states that 'bad money drives out good'. If the authorities issue new coins into a circulation that has become somewhat worn, the new coins will at once disappear, whether into hoarding or for foreign payment, so that matters will not have been mended. Thus the coins in actual circulation would continue to get worse and worse. The only device that the authorities could think of was to reduce the standard amount of metal in a coin of given name, say the penny, so that the new coins were of lighter weight than the old worn coins. Either could be used to discharge debt. Thus it was the new coins that were the 'bad' money relatively to the old, and the new coins thus drove the old out of circulation . . . But this result was only achieved by reducing the standard value of the coin, otherwise known as debasement. This reduction of value was not, it may be believed, usually effected from perversity or mischievousness, but was the only known device for countering Gresham's Law and keeping the coinage in reasonably good shape.

In England this process was terminated by the personal intervention of Queen Elizabeth I. . . . By the time that Queen Elizabeth I came to the throne, the coinage in circulation was already in disorder owing to the processes above described. Queen Elizabeth desired a new issue. Her adviser, Sir Thomas Gresham, pointed out **that in** the event of a new issue there would have to be a reduction in the standard content of the coins owing to the operation of the well-known law which, owing, presumably, to the lucid way in which Sir Thomas Gresham described it to Queen Elizabeth, has since been known as 'Gresham's Law'. But Queen Elizabeth was not willing to follow in her father's footsteps and authorise a further debasement of the standard content of the coins, and told Sir Thomas Gresham that there must be no such debasement. Doubtless he again stressed Gresham's Law. Queen Elizabeth said that in that case all the old coins must be collected and brought in to the mint so that they could no longer drive out the new coins. We may well believe that Sir Thomas Gresham expostulated that this was 'administratively impossible'. But Queen Elizabeth insisted that it should be done. And it was done. Edicts were issued ordering that those not complying with the Queen's orders should be 'hanged, drawn and quartered'.

This recoinage constituted a new chapter in current history. There was no further debasement of the pound, apart from a small adjustment in 1601 (about 2%), until 1931. Who will arise to check our modern-type debasement? The penalties would not need to be so severe! (1969: 7–8).

2 The alleged automaticity is examined by Harrod (1965).

3 William Jennings Bryan campaigned for silver and is renowned for his Cross of Gold Speech ('ye shall not crucify mankind on a cross of gold'). His campaign was doomed by the rash of gold discoveries in that year which put prices on an upward path.

4 Consider, e.g. the position of the following European currencies in early 1970, prior to the breakdown of the Bretton Woods system, using figures drawn from Mundell (1973).

	Gold 'Content' (grams)	U.S. Cents equivalent	Units per US dollar
Pound	2.13281	240.0	0.416667
Deutschmark	0.242806	27.3224	3.66
French franc	0.16000	18.004	5.55419
Lire	0.001421	0.160	625.000
Guilder	0.245489	27.624	3.620
Belgian franc	0.017773	2.28167	43.726
US dollar	0.888671	100.0	1.000

The par values of the currencies were defined in terms of gold, but were usually quoted vis-à-vis the 1949 gold dollar. The dollar exchange rates are calculated by dividing the gold content of the national currencies by the gold content of the dollar; the national currency prices of the dollar are the reciprocals of the dollar prices of the national currencies ($2.40 in the case of sterling). To keep the exchange rates fixed, central banks bought and sold dollars at upper and lower support points. Thus the Bank of England intervened in the exchange market to sell dollars (and buy pounds) when the market price of the pound went down towards $2.38; and to buy dollars (and sell pounds) when the market price went up towards $2.42. The other central banks also intervened at support points three-quarters of 1% above and below the dollar parity.

5 Buchanan (1962: 165, n. 2) He doubts whether an employment standard should be called a monetary standard at all.

6 Spontaneous monetary systems are examined in Gallarotti (1989).

Chapter 3
The Classical Theory of Money

3.1 The Classical Heritage

FEATURES of the classical model are central to monetary theory. The most obvious reason is that it is where monetary economics began. The classical approach to monetary theory covers the time period from 1790 to 1936. In terms of subject matter it ranges over most of the major topics of monetary economics and provides a consensus view from which many economists now, and certainly few economists at the time, would seek to depart. These classical views were codified by J. S. Mill in his *Principles of Economics* (1848) and from 1870 to 1914 constituted what Laidler (1993b) describes as a 'golden age'. It was only after this period that detractors emerged to challenge its pre-eminence. This challenge provides a second reason for regarding classical monetary theory as central; every subsequent attempt to understand monetary theory has resulted either from a rejection of, or the re-espousal of, its core elements. For example, the seemingly hostile Keynesian analysis was shaped as much by the classical model as were the contributions of Patinkin, and the two types of monetarism associated with Friedman and Lucas. It is probably fair to say that the classical model occupies a vital place in monetary theory similar to the place of perfect competition in microeconomics. Even if one does not fully accept it, one still has to be aware of it for the purposes of comparison and the evaluation of the alternatives. It is a benchmark against which every other theory can be compared and contrasted.

This chapter elaborates on the classical model. Reactions and reaffirmations of it are examined in later chapters. Conventionally, but perhaps unrealistically we analyse the classical model in a Walrasian context, presupposing the existence of a coordinated market for the exchange of goods between buyers and sellers at mutually agreed prices. Since much of the classical model is about the real side of the economy (production and exchange), we show that markets can operate under conditions of barter without the existence of money. The workings of a monetary economy are then contrasted with a barter economy to demonstrate that money is a desirable and efficient social institution. Once we accept the role of money in society, we can then examine how money overlaps with the real economy and explore the transmission mechanism of monetary policy in terms of its direct and indirect consequences on the real activity. We emphasize that these are short-run effects, however, and that in the long run money is neutral.

3.2 The Walrasian System

THE Walrasian system was a system of general equilibrium. It was devised in a formal manner by Leon Walras in his *Elements of Pure Economics* (1954), but was anticipated to a large extent by Cournot, who had realized that a complete understanding of the economic system required a consideration of all markets, not partial models of individual markets and exchanges. Blaug explains that

Cournot thought that the problem of general equilibrium was beyond the resources of mathematical analysis. Walras' genius lay not only in seizing upon the problem that Cournot had recognized, but in showing that it is capable of being solved, at least in principle. Oddly enough, Walras lacked the mathematical finesse of Cournot, or for that matter of Marshall or Wicksell, and his demonstration is not only mathematically clumsy but ambiguous and unfinished. Yet there is an architectonic quality to the whole performance that has led some commentators to credit Walras with the supreme achievement of theoretical economics. According to Schumpeter, Walras' *Elements* is nothing less than the 'Magna Carta of exact economics'. (Blaug, 1968: 575–6)

Walras provided a system of pure exchange for a general system of many markets, all of which clear simultaneously. The Walrasian market involves the supply and demand for all goods at once and is therefore a *general equilibrium* system. In this chapter general equilibrium analysis is retained because it allows a direct link with subsequent critiques of the classical system. Many leading classical economists, however, such as Alfred Marshall preferred to use *partial equilibrium* systems to analyse economic questions. These deal with one set of supply and demand equations at a time.

The central feature of the general equilibrium world is the Walrasian market place.[1] Walras envisaged a formal market structure, operating by certain rules, which would ensure that trade could take place in commodities even if there was no money to facilitate trade. This became known as a *Walrasian market* coordinated by a Walrasian auctioneer acting under a specified set of rules. Specifically, the following rules would enable trade between buyers and sellers to take place in a way that was organized and not sporadic.

1. Trade takes place on particular days (market days). All trading would take place within the market day and accounts would be settled at the end of the day between traders.
2. Traders enter the market with a bundle of goods to be sold, which they had either received as an endowment or produced in the period since the previous market day. These goods constitute the supplies of goods to be traded. Traders then enter

the market with the intention to trade their own bundle of goods for other goods which other traders had brought to market.

3. The auctioneer acts as the coordinator of the market place, and would seek relative prices of one good in terms of another, at which traders would be willing to exchange goods. This process known as *tâtonnement* or 'groping' would take place until a satisfactory set of relative prices could be found to ensure the markets for all goods cleared. This is similar, or perhaps encompasses, the idea of Edgeworth that buyers and sellers establish provisional contracts which are renegotiated or 'recontracted' until a satisfactory solution is agreed upon. The end of recontracting results in acceptable prices for exchange, and in Walras's market the end of 'groping' signals an acceptable solution to the general equilibrium problem for all market participants.

4. When satisfactory prices are found the exchange takes place between suppliers and demanders. The relative prices so established ensure that demand is equal to supply in all goods and no one is disappointed. Thus all buyers and all sellers are assured of the fact that they can exchange their goods and attain a satisfactory equilibrium at the prevailing relative prices determined by the outsider. The market then closes.

By this process equilibrium could be obtained, without requiring the use of money, through the activity of an auctioneer who would bring together the suppliers and demanders of goods and agree on relative prices to clear the markets. In the pure exchange economics of Leon Walras and Jean Baptiste Say, the system could work without money at all as the next section will show, but the exchanges are conducted more efficiently with money than without. For the present we consider how the economy could work if money did not exist.

A barter economy

In order to develop the properties of the classical system we need to focus on the nature of the supplies of and demands for goods in the Walrasian market.

We assume that there are many goods and that these are labelled goods $1,2,3 \ldots n-1$ and are denoted as quantities x_i, where $i = 1,2,3, \ldots, n-1$. At this stage the quantities refer to real tangible products; the nth good (money) appears in the next section. These $n-1$ goods are supplied by traders from their initial endowments or are goods produced in the period before the market day, and we write the total supply of good x_i as S_i, which refers to the supply in the ith market. Since the supply is provided out of an endowment received at the beginning of the period or out of production that took place before the trading day begins, this total supply is best regarded as a fixed stock which cannot vary in response to relative prices or income. It is generally agreed that the supply side was underdeveloped in Walras's model, so we do little to restrict his model by taking it as given.

The demand for goods $i=1,2,3 \ldots, n-1$ are written as D_i and these are functions of relative prices and income, which is given by the total value of the endowments received. Consequently, the demand function can be written as

$$D_i = f(p_2/p_1, p_3/p_1, p_4/p_1 \ldots, p_{n-1}/p_1, \sum_{i=1}^{n-1} (p_i/p_1)S_i). \tag{3.1}$$

It is important to remember that prices are not specified in monetary terms because money does not exist. Rather, prices are expressed in relative terms in one of two ways. In the first, the relative price of the goods is given in terms of one special good chosen to be the reference or *numéraire* against which everything else takes its value, e.g. goods may be priced in terms of gold. Alternatively, the average price of goods is determined and price of any one good is given in comparison to the average. As a result of either method, the demand for goods can be described as a function of $n-2$ relative prices of all the $n-1$ goods. For example, the absolute price level could be a weighted average of the prices of the goods calculated using weights w_i:

$$p = \sum_{i=1}^{n-1} w_i \, p_i. \tag{3.2}$$

The process of *tâtonnement*, conducted by the auctioneer, establishes an equilibrium between the fixed supplies of the goods brought to market and the demands, which do vary with the relative prices for which he/she searches. The auctioneer's existence is critical to the operation of the market, since without this service there is no one to coordinate the market and ensure that participants play by the rules. Yet there is no obvious incentive for anyone to take on this role since they receive no reward for their effort and do not directly participate in trade themselves. Thus it is rather like the old joke about the economist on a desert island who assumes the existence of a tin opener to open the can washed ashore with him. The auctioneer, like the tin opener, has a vital function to perform for the analysis to proceed in an environment in which every trader is a price taker but has to be assumed into existence. Price-making is left to the auctioneer.

A convenient way to consider the process by which the auctioneer determines equilibrium in each individual goods market is by the calculation of the excess of demand for each good over the available supply. Excess demand indicates to the auctioneer that the relative price of the good must rise in order to clear that market and establish equilibrium, whilst excess supply indicates that the price must fall. In terms of the demand and supply relationships above the excess demand can be written as

$$ED_i = D_i - S_i \tag{3.3}$$

with the excess supply merely the negative of excess demand. Since D_i is a function of relative prices and income, and supply is predetermined for any particular market day, excess demand is also a function of relative prices and income.

$$ED_i = f(p_2/p_1, p_3/p_1, p_4/p_1 \ldots, p_{n-1}/p_1, \sum_{i=1}^{n-1} (p_i/p_1)S_i) - S_i. \tag{3.4}$$

This excess demand function can be calculated for any of the goods markets $i = 1, 2, \ldots, n-1$ individually and gives information to the auctioneer about whether the particular market is in equilibrium. In addition, the auctioneer has the task of overall coordination and must set relative prices that will achieve equilibrium in all markets simultaneously. An obvious question is whether this is in fact possible. It was Walras's contribution to economic theory to prove that it *is* possible to find a set of relative prices that equilibriates all markets simultaneously. The proof, which was named *Walras's Law* by Oscar Lange in his book *Studies in Mathematical Economics and Econometrics* (1942), was a direct application of Say's Law of markets to the market structure which Walras described. So we begin by describing Say's Law.

Jean Baptiste Say (1821) put forward the proposition that 'supply creates its own demand'. The simplicity of the statement belies its profound implications, which amounts to much more than 'what is sold is bought'! These implications are most clearly expounded by Schumpeter:

> More clearly than did others, Say perceived . . . that . . . [u]nder division of labour, the only means normally available to everyone for acquiring the commodities and services he wishes to have is to produce—or take part in the production of—some equivalent for them. It follows that production increases not only the supply of goods in the markets but normally also the demand for them. *In this sense*, it is production itself ('supply') which creates the 'fund' from which flows the demand for its products: products are 'ultimately' paid for by products in domestic as well as in foreign trade In consequence, a (balanced) expansion in all lines of production is a very different thing from a one-sided increase in the output of an individual industry or group of industries. To have seen the theoretical implications of this is one of Say's chief performances. (Schumpeter, 1954: 616)

The Law shows that the total value of the supplies (either from endowments or production) must equal the total value of the demands for them. In the terminology that we have used so far this can be written as the sum of the value of demand equals the sum of the value of supply:

$$\sum_{i=1}^{n-1} p_i D_i = \sum_{i=1}^{n-1} p_i S_i \tag{3.5}$$

or by rearrangement

$$\sum_{i=1}^{n-1} p_i ED_i = 0 \tag{3.6}$$

This is no more than to say that if there are excess demands in some of the $n-1$ markets, then there must be offsetting (i.e. negative) excess demands in the others. Application of this conclusion to the Walrasian market was the means of proving the useful result that if we observe equilibrium in all but one market, then we know that the final market must be in equilibrium, even if we do not observe it. Expressed alternatively, since the supplies represent the endowments of goods provided at the beginning of each period (or those produced before the market day), the Law states that demands in aggregate cannot exceed the supplies in aggregate. This is in essence a budget constraint which ensures that the total value of goods obtained through trading cannot exceed the amount available for sale.

The conclusion drawn from Say's Law of Markets by Walras in his application of it to a barter economy was not just that the auctioneer *can* find a set of relative prices to clear all the markets simultaneously, but that the market does not clear until he does so. Thus, under the rules of the Walrasian market, all markets must always clear and the proposition that supply creates its own demand is always true. For this reason Say's Law is identically true and is written in the strong form of an identity as

$$\sum_{i=1}^{n-1} p_i\, ED_i \equiv 0 \tag{3.7}$$

The results of this proposition are significant. All the demands in all the markets must equal the supplies or, where there is an excess of demand over supply in one market, there must be a compensating excess supply in at least one other market, so that in aggregate the excess demands sum to zero.

Hence we find that

While it is possible for a particular good to be produced in excess relative to other goods, it is impossible for all goods to be produced in relative excess

and:

One must not say 'general overproduction' or 'general underproduction' for that is a logical impossibility. But, of course, it is only a logical impossibility in a barter economy. Overproduction must be relative to something, and by talking of goods in an economy without mentioning money, we have excluded anything relative to which goods can be produced in excess. An oversupply of one particular product means an underdemand for it in terms of all other products, for the supply of other products given in exchange for it represents the demand for this product; excess supply of one good necessarily means excess demand for at least one other good. Hence, in a barter economy there can be no such thing as an excess of supply over demand for all goods. But in a *monetary* economy a general excess supply of *commodities* is a logical possibility, for it simply implies that there is an excess demand for money. (Blaug, 1968: 145–6)

We now consider this point.

A monetary economy

We must address the question of how the conditions and functioning of the market alter when we replace a barter economy with a monetary one in which there exists an *n*th good which is readily accepted as a unit of account, means of exchange, and crucially a store of value. In the first place, the relative prices are specified in monetary units rather than in terms of other goods. This means that prices are money prices and the monetary unit is regarded as the *numéraire*, which accords with what most people think of as prices, but could still amount to a relative value to a commodity such as gold. Secondly, goods can be exchanged for money and third, if it is storable, then purchasing power can be held over from one market day to the next. This allows individuals to defer purchase, or if there is a loans market, make purchases in advance.

By introducing money as the nth good then we can still apply Walras's Law, but we must now add up the demands and supplies over n goods rather than $n-1$ goods. Thus,

$$\sum_{i=1}^{n} p_i D_i = \sum_{i=1}^{n} p_i S_i \qquad (3.8)$$

or, alternatively

$$\sum_{i=1}^{n-1} p_i D_i + p_n D_n = p_n S_n + \sum_{i=1}^{n-1} p_i S_i. \qquad (3.9)$$

where D_n and S_n are respectively the demand for and supply of money and p_n is the relative price of money. What this tells us is that by rearrangement of the above expression the value of the excess demand for money $p_n(D_n - S_n)$ is equal to the value of the excess supply of goods on the real side of the economy. This has important implications for Walras's Law and Say's Law since the excess supply of goods on the real side of the economy was what the previous section considered under barter conditions. In that discussion it was shown that the excess supply (equal to minus the excess demand) was identically equal to zero. Now that we have money in the equation it is clear that for excess supply to be equal to zero the excess demand for money must be zero too. Hence, it is only when the monetary side of the economy is in equilibrium that the real side of the economy is in equilibrium. Of course, this can be true if the demand and supply of money are equal, but it can also be the case that it is not true if money demand exceeds supply or vice versa. It is the possibility that the real side of the economy may not necessarily be equilibriated which gives rise to the conclusion that Say's Law does not automatically hold in a monetary economy. It is possible to say that it may hold, but it is not possible to say that it must hold. Say's Law holds as an equality, but not an identity, in a monetary economy and it no longer follows as an inevitable consequence of the process of finding relative prices at which the market can trade.

Thus, some suppliers may find that demand is not sufficient to relieve them of their stocks available for sale, and others may find that there is more demand for a good than supply available to meet it if the demand for money and the supply of money are not equalized. For example, there is the possibility that some traders may demand money to be held as a store of value until the next market day and as a result of this use of money as a commodity to be held as a store of purchasing power some traders could find that there is insufficient demand for their products. This possibility concerned many classical economists, since the hoarding of money appeared to imply that oversupply would result in some goods markets.

The issue of oversupply was a phenomenon which many classicals inferred from Walras's analysis using Say's equality, but John Stuart Mill was quick to point out that the same Law which indicated that oversupply could result in the case of one or a few commodities also inferred that a general oversupply of all industries could not result from the hoarding of money by buyers. He argued that the notion of a general depression of all industries from this cause is impossible due to the working of Say's Law. What he was prepared to argue was the notion that, since money is not held for its own intrinsic qualities but for the purchase of goods, and that since money may be convenient as a means to defer the purchase of goods to another period in time (enabling the separation of earning and spending):

[I]t may very well occur, that there may be, at some given time, a very general inclination to sell with as little delay as possible, accompanied with a general inclination to defer all payments as long as possible [an excess demand for money]. This is always actually the case in those periods which are described as periods of general excess. And no one, after sufficient explanation, will contest the possibility of general excess, in this sense of the world. (Blaug, 1968: 153)

The important point about his equilibria in a world described by Say's equality is that such conditions would be temporary.

In equilibrium conditions in a monetary economy, however, it is simultaneously true that the value of the money demanded would be sufficient to cover the purchases of goods

$$p_n D_n = \sum_{i=1}^{n-1} p_i S_i. \tag{3.10}$$

and the supply of money would be enough to cover the value of the demand for goods and would hence meet the 'needs of trade', that is

$$p_n S_n = \sum_{i=1}^{n-1} p_i D_i. \tag{3.11}$$

This follows from Say's equality, which brings the demand and supply for goods and money to balance.

Hence, quoting from Mill's *Principles*:

As the whole of the goods in the market compose the demand for money, so the whole of the money constitutes the demand for goods. The money and the goods are seeking each other for the purposes of being exchanged. They are reciprocally supply and demand to one another. It is indifferent whether, in characterising the phenomena, we speak of the demand and supply of goods or the supply and demand for money. These are equivalent expressions. (Mill, 1848: 298)

Of course, all this is doing is to confirm the role of money as a medium of exchange, but before going on to deal with further details of a monetary economy we should note that Walras's general equilibrium system consists of n excess demand equations which are functions of relative (money) prices only, i.e.

$$ED_1 = f(p_1/p_n, p_2/p_n, p_3/p_n, p_4/p_n \ldots, p_{n-1}/p_n, \sum_{i=1}^{n} (p_i/p_n)S_i) - S_1.$$

$$ED_2 = f(p_1/p_n, p_2/p_n, p_3/p_n, p_4/p_n \ldots, p_{n-1}/p_n, \sum_{i=1}^{n} (p_i/p_n)S_i) - S_2.$$

$$\ldots \qquad \ldots$$

$$ED_n = f(p_1/p_n, p_2/p_n, p_3/p_n, p_4/p_n \ldots, p_{n-1}/p_n, \sum_{i=1}^{n} (p_i/p_n)S_i) - S_n. \tag{3.12}$$

Thus although the price of money p_n, (referred to as the absolute price level) enters the excess demand functions it does so as the denominator of all the relative price terms. As a result the excess demand functions do not change when the absolute price level changes because it affects all the relative prices equally through the denominator. This characteristic, which is a vital feature of the classical monetary economy, is known as the *homogeneity postulate*. The choice of the name reflects the fact that the absolute price level enters the excess demand functions in such a way that it leaves the function unchanged, that is, the same as before or 'homogeneous' with the previous definition.

In mathematics, a function is homogeneous if the variables in the function can be multiplied by a constant and still remain equal to the function itself multiplied by that same constant raised to some power. The function with this property is said to be homogeneous of degree z where z is the power to which the constant is raised. In general terms if we have a function such as $y = f(x)$ and multiply the variable in the function by a constant a then the function is homogeneous if the constant a can be taken out of the function and raised to the power z without changing the meaning of the relationship, i.e. $f(ax) = a^z f(x)$ then the function is said to be homogeneous of degree z with respect to a. So, if $a = 3$ then we can say that the function is homogeneous of degree zero if $f(3x) = 3^0 f(x) = f(x)$; or homogenous of degree one if $f(3x) = 3^1 f(x) = 3f(x)$; or degree two if $f(3x) = 3^2 f(x) = 9f(x)$ and so on.

In the case of the classical monetary economy, the function $f(x)$ can be thought of as an excess demand function, x can be thought of as the prices of goods and a as one over the absolute price level. We know that changing absolute prices leaves the excess demand function unchanged, and the only way that this can be done is by taking a outside the function in such a manner that the function does not change its value. If a is taken outside the function and raised to the power zero, i.e. $z = 0$, the excess demand function is homogeneous of degree zero. Although this result seems innocuous it proves to be a strong assumption, as the next chapter will explain, but before going any further it is important to show how the classicals dealt with the absolute price level which remains indeterminate in the Walrasian general equilibrium system as a result of the homogeneity postulate.

3.3 The Quantity Theory

THE classical economist's method of dealing with the absolute price level was through the quantity theory. In its starkest form, it is a strict statement that the value of money is determined by the quantity of money alone, as proposed by Locke for example, and can be viewed as a restatement of Say's identity.[2] In less extreme versions it is regarded as a tendency which represents an equilibrium relationship between the circulation of a given money stock and the value of transactions which it is used to purchase. A commonly accepted representation of the theory is given by

Mill (1848: 300) as: 'The money laid out is equal in value to the goods it purchases', which can be written as

$$MV = PT, \tag{3.13}$$

where M is the money supply in circulation, V is the velocity of money, P is the general price level, and T the volume of transactions in the economy. It is easy to understand the meaning of money supply, price, and transactions levels, but velocity is a more difficult concept. Consider the following from Robertson's *Money* (1922):

On Derby-day two men, Bob and Joe, invested in a barrel of beer, and set off to Epsom with the intention of selling it retail on the race-course at 6d a pint, the proceeds to be shared equally between them. On the way Bob, who had one threepenny-bit left in the world, began to feel a great thirst, and drank a pint of the beer, paying Joe 3d as his share of the market price. A little later Joe yielded to the same desire, and drank a pint of beer, returning the 3d to Bob. The day was hot, and before long Bob was thirsty again, and so, a little later, was Joe. When they arrived at Epsom, the 3d was back in Bob's pocket, and each had discharged in full his debts to the other: but the beer was all gone. One single threepenny-bit had performed a volume of transactions which would have required many shillings if the beer had been sold to the public in accordance with the original intention! (Robertson, 1922: 36)

As Robertson amusingly demonstrates, the concept of velocity of circulation indicates the work rate that money achieves—that is, the volume of transactions covered per period of time. Since the value of all the transactions *must* be met by the money used to pay for them, for the current supply to be able to be exchanged for the goods sold the currency must circulate at a sufficient rate. In Marshall we find this relationship simply expressed as

The total value of a country's currency, multiplied into the average number of times of its changing hands for business purposes in a year, is of course equal to the total amount of business transacted in that country by direct payments of currency in that year. (A. Marshall, 1923: 47)

or returning again to Mill it is described in more detail:

If we assume the quantity of goods on sale, and the number of times these goods are resold, to be fixed quantities, the value of money will depend upon its quantity, together with the average number of times the piece changes hands in the process. The whole of the goods sold have been exchanged for the whole of the money, multiplied by the number of purchases made on average by each piece. Consequently, the amount of goods, and the transactions being the same, the value of money is inversely as its quantity multiplied by what is called the rapidity of circulation. And the quantity of money in circulation, is equal to the money value of all the goods sold, divided by the number which expresses the rapidity of circulation. (Mill, 1848: 300)

As a simple statement it is hardly possible to disagree, as the quantity theory takes on the nature of a truism in its plainest form, but complications arise from two sources. First, there are different opinions about the definition of terms such as money, velocity, volume of transactions, and the general price level. Second, there are different interpretations about the relationship between the variables in the quantity theory especially with regard to those that are active and those that are passive in causing price changes.

The definition of money, M, took on a significance in the literature since classical economists in Europe tended to consider metallic money alone whilst classicals in America considered both metallic money and sight deposits. Fisher (Yale) in particular referred to the velocity of money and checkable deposits as separable, whilst Marshall (Cambridge) did not. Likewise the concept of velocity was treated differently by the many economists who used the term. In the first place there arose a confusion through the meaning of the term which some took to be the total money stock circulated over a period of time, whereas it should properly be defined as the rate of circulation of those money balances that are used over time to conduct transactions. Second, there were further difficulties introduced because velocity was misleadingly implied to be constant by definition. To an extent this error was encouraged by the institutional stability of velocity over long periods of time, and the notion of velocity degenerated to one of a constant in theory from the observation of constancy in practice. In fact, these errors were introduced as simplifications by those other than the leading writers. Nowhere in the writings of Marshall or Fisher can the notion of a constant velocity be found, except an illustration quickly modified to show that velocity was a variable dependent on confidence (i.e expectations) and credit market conditions.

For example, the Cambridge cash balance approach, used by Marshall in his evidence to the Gold and Silver Commission 1888–9 and later to the India Currency Committee in 1899 defined the quantity theory as a form of demand for money function. In its crudest form, it was assumed that velocity was approximately constant and that the demand and supply for money were equal so that the stock of money holding could be represented as a proportion of the value of transactions in the following way:

$$M=kPY. \tag{3.14}$$

Implicitly, if $k=1/5$ then velocity has a fixed value of 5.

Eshag (1963) traces the evolution of the Cambridge approach through oral evidence, lectures, and other obscure sources through to the publicly available writings, which emerged much later in the form of Pigou's article on 'The value of money' (1917) and Marshall's *Money, Credit and Commerce* (1923). There is much evidence that the theory had been developed by Marshall as early as 1871, well before he applied it to contemporary problems, in the form of advice and memoranda to various committees. Certainly by the time Wicksell wrote *Interest and Prices* in 1898 he was aware of Marshall's views and made extensive references to the transcript of the Gold and Silver Commission 1888–9.

The situation in America was quite the opposite. Irving Fisher's *Purchasing Power of Money* (1911b), far from being hidden in private evidence to Royal Commissions, received considerable public attention. Part of the success of Fisher's book was that it was the result of twenty years of monetary thinking, clearly explained and neatly tied into existing works by Ricardo and Mill. This approach was quite a contrast, as it transpired, to Marshall's attempt to express his views in *Money, Credit and Commerce*. Regrettably, in an attempt to ensure clarity, Fisher reduced the quantity theory to a simplified form, which allowed others to misinterpret crucial features—although he could hardly be accused of failing in this respect himself. In particular, his treatment of velocity as 'to all intents and purposes' stable, introduced the misunderstanding that it could be, or should be, thought of as necessarily stable.

In the U.S. version of the quantity theory the causality ran from money to prices such that

$$P = f(M, V, 1/T), \tag{3.15}$$

and the quantity of money was considered to be the most active variable in the function. It should be noted with care, however, that Fisher did not infer that MV equals PT, in the general form of the equation stated above, but that values of V, M, and T infer values of P which arise from an equilibrium relationship. Generally speaking, movements in money would be translated proportionally into movements in prices although velocity and volume of trade were by no means considered constant. Fisher listed several determinants of trade and velocity that can be interpreted as 'deep' parameters of individual tastes and institutional technology. Hence, trade would depend variously on (i) conditions affecting producers, (ii) conditions affecting consumers, and conditions connecting producers and consumers by which he meant transportation, freedom of trade, monetary conditions, and business confidence. Velocity, on the other hand, would vary with (i) individual habits in arrangement of accounts, (ii) the payments system and its efficiency, and (iii) other general causes amounting to social conditions and proximity. Thus the model was far less crude than Locke's model or the popularized versions of Fisher.

Resulting from the two approaches, there emerged in the literature a distinction between the quantity theory of the Cambridge School based on the stock of money balances held and the Fisherian version later adopted in Chicago, referring to the turnover of money. Robertson summarized the Cambridge cash balance approach as a definition of 'money sitting', i.e. a stock concept of the quantity theory based on a particular value of money at a *point* in time and the other version as 'money on the wing', implying a flow approach, which defined the amount of money over an *interval* of, say, a year. Pigou illustrates the stock–flow distinction very well in the following statement: 'One aspect of this reality can be displayed by way of an instantaneous photograph. In such a photograph no indication will appear of any process of movement. The picture will comprise, not flows at all, only stocks' (A. C. Pigou, 1923: 20). In line with Robertson's analogy, the quantity theory of the Cambridge school involves a still picture of the stock of money required for a given level of transactions, whilst the Fisher view offers a moving picture of the flows of money and transactions.

Although the two theories were different they were not necessarily inconsistent, although the differences were highlighted in the neoclassical period to a large extent as an attempt to explain the transmission mechanism between money and prices in the light of the institutional characteristics of the day. Many of the features were the subject of subsequent criticism but as a truism and a general equilibrium tendency, the theory remains immune to its critics.

Nevertheless, the quantity theory of money was a *theory* and not just a truism. Indeed, it was not just a theory but *the* theory during the classical and neoclassical period. David Laidler explains in the overview of his book *The Golden Age of the Quantity Theory,* that

[t]o the monetary economist, the period 1870–1914 was a golden age, in more than one sense. Most obviously and literally, in those years the Gold Standard developed from something close to an exclusively British institution into an international monetary system which even today is held up as a model of stability. But this was also the period in which the quantity theory of money, conceived of as a theory of the general price level, reached the peak of its development. In the years before World War I, both well-known formulations of that theory—the transactions approach mainly associated with Irving Fisher, and the stock supply and demand for money approach of Alfred Marshall and his pupils—were brought to full fruition by their exponents. This fact, and the then ruling idea that it was the principal business of monetary economics to explain the behaviour of the general price level, combined to give the quantity theory a more central position in monetary economics than it has enjoyed at any other time, whether before or since. (Laidler, 1993*b*: 1)

The quantity theory had a remarkable position in classical theory, a position that had grown from simple origins in the work of Locke, Cantillon, and Hume, some two or three centuries earlier. Laidler notes that one of the notable features of the quantity theory was its continuity even when institutions and economic conditions were subject to alteration. It is an exaggeration to say that it has remained a crucial and central feature of classical theory because of its fundamental position in monetary economics. The theory was the classical's explanation of the behaviour of prices and the relation that they had to money balances. The relationship indicated a direct and proportional effect that gave money a central place in determining the absolute and general price level. Money was neutral in the system, leaving real variables unaffected, but it influenced prices in a one-for-one fashion. The concept of neutrality and the theory of variations to the money supply, the main cause of price movements, i.e. nominal variables, led to a view that money was in fact a veil.[3]

3.4 The Classical Dichotomy and Money as a Veil

USING the Walrasian excess demand equations to explain the real side of the economy in terms of relative prices, and the quantity theory to explain the monetary side, by tying down the absolute price level, gave the classicals a workable system of price determination for the whole economy. By *dichotomizing* their model, and splitting it into two distinct and separate halves, they were able to define both the set of relative prices and the absolute price level required for equilibrium in the real economy. In principle, the real sector could work with any level of absolute prices which was determined in the separate quantity theory equation. For this reason, money was referred to as a *veil*, because the real sector could operate perfectly well on the basis of relative prices with absolute prices as a superficial covering to the whole process. Schumpeter summarizes the position as follows:

Then, as Walras himself observed, the equation of monetary circulation would indeed be 'external to the system of equations that determine economic equilibrium' and then there would be some warrant for saying that Walras' system is essentially a 'real' or numeraire system, complete as such, on which he threw, as a separate piece of apparel, the 'veil of money'. (Schumpeter, 1954: 1025)

One of the best accounts is to be found in Pigou's book *The Veil of Money* (1941). Here, Pigou describes the resources which are provided by nature in the form of land, capital, and labour which together contribute to the production of real income. Since production tends to be specialized, a large number of exchanges are needed for individuals to reach their desired consumption bundle. In these Walrasian-like transactions, goods are not necessarily exchanged for goods, as money can act as an intermediary to facilitate exchange. The notion of money as a veil, however, implies that whilst it can act as an intermediary, it is not *necessary* for exchange that it should do so. Thus he writes:

In general, a man receives as real income only a small extent of those things which his own particular work has contributed in producing. By far the predominant part of his real income he obtains by exchanging, and exchanging against money, so that money income, which is the obverse of money expenditure by final buyers—not, of course, intermediaries—is the purchase price, or value, of the communities real income. It is in connection with this exchanging that monetary facts and happenings come into being. They differ from 'real' facts and happenings in that, unlike these they have no *direct* significance for economic welfare. Take the real facts and happenings away and the monetary facts and happenings necessarily vanish with them, but take money away and, whatever else may follow, economic life would *not* become meaningless—there is nothing absurd about the conception of a self-sufficing family, or village group, without any money at all. In this sense money *is* a veil. It does not comprise any of the essentials of life! (1941: 24)

Pigou quickly goes on to add that while money is not essential it remains important and useful as a social contrivance. But once the institution takes root and is established the amount of money, in nominal units, is irrelevant to its function. In principle, at least, the world's trade and production could be financed by a single dollar (and a calculator—or cleaver—to divide it up into sufficiently small units). In terms of the Walrasian model this means that whatever the stock of money determining the nominal value of the absolute price level, p_n, relative prices at which real goods exchange will be unaffected, due to the homogeneity postulate. In this way the classical dichotomy and the idea of money as a veil follow automatically from the acceptance of the homogeneity postulate.

3.5 The Transmission Mechanism

The direct effect

IT is now time to consider the nature of the transmission mechanism between money and prices in the classical model. The quantity theory is an equilibrium condition which states that money and prices will tend to move together, although Fisher in particular noted that there could be temporary departures from this strict equality. Fisher was not the first to do so. Wicksell in Interest and Prices dealt with the mechanisms by which prices were affected by changes to the money stock and provided one of the clearest restatements of the direct and indirect transmission mechanisms since Henry Thornton and John Stuart Mill respectively 100 and 50 years earlier.

The direct mechanism refers to the straightforward effects on demand and hence prices of an increase in the money stock. This mechanism has been known since the writings of Cantillon (1734) and Hume (1752). If the stock of money rises but the volume of goods for which money is exchanged remains the same, then, since more money will be chasing the same quantity of goods, the price of goods will necessarily rise and will continue to rise until they have risen in proportion to the increase in the stock of money. Hume illustrates the proposition in the following way:

> Suppose four-fifths of all the money in Great Britain to be annihilated in one night, and the nation reduced to the same condition, with regard to specie [gold or commodity money], as in the reigns of the Harrys and Edwards, what would be the consequence? Must not the price of all labour and commodities sink in proportion, and everything be sold as cheap as they were in those ages? (Hume, 1752)

The principle can be illustrated by drawing the demand and supply for money on a diagram with the quantity of money on the horizontal axis and the price of money in terms of what it will buy on the vertical axis. The supply of money is assumed to be exogenous and so it is a vertical line. The demand for money is given by the quantity theory equation, which we represent in the Cambridge cash balance form as $M=kPY$.

The demand curve represents the real value of money in terms of goods, or to put it another way, the value of goods in real terms that must be forgone to obtain a unit of money. Using Figure 3.1, taking an initial point of intersection between demand curve, D, and supply curve, S, at point E, we consider the effects of doubling the money supply. The doubling of the money supply is shown by an outward shift of the supply curve to S'; the immediate effect on demand is to shift the curve outwards as prices fall establishing a new equilibrium at E'. The mechanism operates as the doubling of the money supply creates an excess supply of money and prices begin to rise as there is an excess demand for goods (corresponding to the excess supply of money). Prices rise until the excess demand for goods and the excess supply of money are eliminated, and it is the point where prices have doubled. By increasing the money supply again to $3M$ prices increase proportionately to $\frac{1}{3P}$, leaving real balances unchanged at E''.

Joining the points E, E', and E'' describes a curve, XX, which is a rectangular hyperbola. The area described by the rectangle under the curve is the quantity of money times the price of money in terms of goods which is $M \times (1/P)$, the real balance. Since the curve is a rectangular hyperbola the real balance at any point on the curve, including points E, E', and E'', stays the same and the increase in the money supply has no final effect on the real sector. Money is neutral.

The indirect effect

The indirect mechanism, first proposed by Thornton (1802) in *An Enquiry into the Nature and Effects of the Paper Credit of Great Britain*, adopted by Ricardo and rediscovered by Wicksell, is less straightforward, but essentially begins with a change to the money supply and its subsequent impact through the interest rate. It comes into play because Thornton introduced into the analysis a banking system, that takes deposits and makes loans. When the money supply is increased as before, some of the extra cash will be deposited in a bank. The bank would then have an excess of funds from which to increase the supply of loans to others. From a simple demand and supply analysis of the loan market, it can then be shown that the price of loans (the interest rate which Wicksell called the 'market rate') would fall. Following the injection

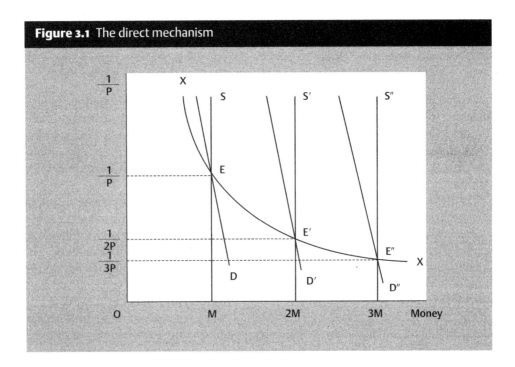

Figure 3.1 The direct mechanism

of extra money the market rate would fall below the rate of return required to clear the loans market, which Wicksell called the 'natural rate' (approximately equal to the rate of return on newly created capital). As a result there would be the opportunity for entrepreneurs to borrow at the market rate to invest in newly formed capital and earn a return at the natural rate of interest. In these circumstances the demand for loans would rise as entrepreneurs seek to make profits from investment in capital goods and the demand would continue to rise until the rates were again equal. In the process of stimulating the loans market by lowering the rate of interest the monetary expansion would also boost the demand for goods, raising prices indirectly. Wicksell went on to show, in a mechanism known as the cumulative process, that so long as the market rate was below the natural rate the effect would create continuously changing prices, i.e. inflation.[4]

To illustrate the working of this process consider Figure 3.2 which depicts the demand and supply for money and loans. When the money supply increases from M to M' the equilibrium in the money market changes from E_m to E'_m in response to the change in the interest rate determined in the loans market. As a result of the increase in the money supply the banks are able to increase the supply of loans available and the interest rate falls from the natural rate r_n to the rate r_m which is a market-determined rate. The interest rate remains at that level until the demand for loans, which increases following the fall in interest rates, pushes it up again to r_n. The expansionary effect of the excess demand for capital goods will raise prices which will push the demand for money up to D'_m. Note that the rate of interest r_n is compatible with both equilibria in the money market E_m and E''_m.

The notion of the indirect mechanism was accepted and used by both Ricardo and Mill. Ricardo argued that in the circumstances of the late eighteenth century and

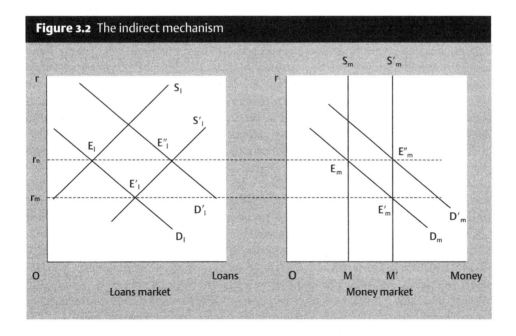

Figure 3.2 The indirect mechanism

early nineteenth century, when Britain was at war with France and suffering from severe balance of payments difficulties, that the Bank of England was depreciating the currency at a rapid rate by keeping the interest rate charged on its tenders to the private sector (the discount rate) too low. Under normal times the exchange rate would be regulated by the flow of gold (specie) into and out of the country; however, during the Napoleonic wars the Bank of England ceased to make the pound convertible and this broke the link to automatic stabilization of the currency versus other currencies. The Bank was, therefore, unchecked in its actions involving the minting of the currency—it could produce whatever it wished and the resulting inflation would *not* cause an outflow of gold. Ricardo raised these points in his tract *The High Price of Bullion: A Proof of the Depreciation of Bank Notes*, accusing the Bank of keeping the market rate artificially low and thus generating inflation in a manner that Wicksell would rediscover a century later. The Bank defended itself stoutly by arguing that it issued its notes only on discount of short-term commercial paper which was sound. This was known as the real bills doctrine. Ricardo argued that the Bank was conducting an unwelcome monetary policy (through the indirect effect) while the Bank kept its line that it was facilitating trade in a passive way, but responsibly. The Bullionist Controversy raged on with the indirect mechanism at its heart, until 1844 when the Charter Act separated the operations of the Issue and Banking Departments within the structure of the Bank of England.

These arguments led to the development of two rival camps: the Currency School and the Banking School. The former, in line with Ricardo, stated that a mixed paper–gold currency should vary with the outflow of gold, just as a pure gold currency would. Their point was that the foreign exchanges should determine the value of the currency (and not, as they saw it, the behaviour of the Bank of England Issue Department). The latter suggested that the real bills doctrine, known since the time of Adam Smith, and the 'needs of trade' acted as a natural regulator to currency issue. If this were so, they argued, currency and credit would be stable. The Currency School could not hope to tie down credit with their mechanism, since credit could grow beyond the limits set to the currency by gold, but the real bills doctrine would ensure that both currency and credit would be stable. Although the arguments were regularly rehearsed and each side had its period of supremacy, the doctrine of real bills continued even into the twentieth century and was written into the Federal Reserve Act of 1913. We noted in Chapter 1 that the issues were revived in the context of the growth of non-bank financial intermediaries and markets in the post-Second World War era.

Both the direct mechanism and the indirect mechanism also have their counterparts in the works of later writers in the classical tradition, most notably in Robertson and Pigou.[5] The direct effect is to be found in both Robertson and Pigou as a form of the real balance effect in which the wealth of the nation is increased temporarily until the ensuing demand for goods and rise in prices restores real balances to their initial level. This effect is examined in more detail in the next chapter when we consider Patinkin's analysis. The indirect mechanism was reiterated by Ohlin and Robertson in the loanable funds theory which again revolved around the market rate, determined by the supply and demand for loans, and the natural rate.

Thus, the direct and indirect effects formed the building blocks of the classical transmission process, in which the indirect mechanism could become more varied as the financial system became more complex. Nevertheless, the essential elements did not change. Money is neutral in the sense that a change to the stock of money results eventually in an equivalent rise in the price level. The interest rate is determined in the real sector by the natural rate of interest on newly formed capital and is compatible with any nominal level of money supply in that the loan market clears at the natural rate irrespective of whether the money supply is at its original level or twice its original level. In this sense the interest rate is a real variable, determined by the real sector, rather than a monetary one. Loanable funds was the preferred mode of analysis.

3.6 Loanable Funds

IN the classical world the rate of interest is regarded as a real variable, determined by real forces of saving and investment. Money does not alter the rate of interest in the long run, and changes to money supply result in equiproportional changes to prices. Interest rates can be affected in the short term, but they are soon brought back to their long-run value, which is dependent on the rate of return on new capital. The key word is neutrality. Interest rates are invariant to money supply changes in the long term since they will be determined by productivity (governing investment) and thrift (savings). The leading exponents of the loanable funds theory of interest rates are Ohlin (1937) from the Swedish School, who derived his ideas from Wicksell (1898), and in England, Robertson (1937). Whilst the ideas were developed considerably by these authors the basic mechanism can be found in Thornton (1802).

If we consider the total stock of funds available for supply and the total demand for funds, then we can say that according to the classical theory of interest the 'price' of funds is given by the equilibrium between supply and demand. The supply of funds comes from savings while funds are demanded for investment in physical capital. Thus the factors that govern saving and investment behaviour such as the return on capital (productivity) and the desire to save (thrift) determine the price of loanable funds, the interest rate. This point can be illustrated by drawing a demand schedule for funds (investment) and a supply schedule for funds (saving) on a graph indicating quantity of funds and the price of funds—the interest rate. Clearly, the equilibrium illustrated by point E, determines the price, r, and the quantity, L.

In a more financially developed economy we could represent savers as demanders of bonds and investors as suppliers (or issuers) of bonds. Then we would find that the total stock of savings would be equal to the total supply of funds which would equal the total demand for bonds. Likewise, the total stock of investment would equal the demand for funds and this would equal the total stock of bonds issued by investors. Thus schedules, I and S, could be thought of as schedules for the total supply of

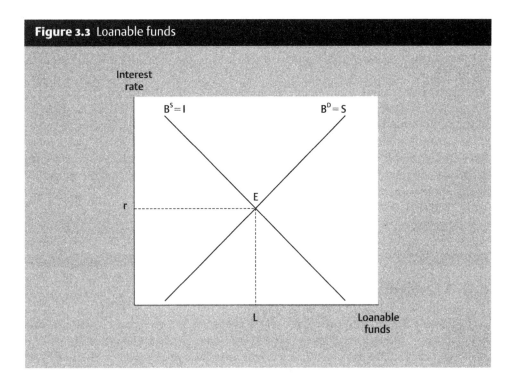

Figure 3.3 Loanable funds

bonds and the total demand for bonds respectively—the bond market is now acting as the place where stocks of funds are exchanged between savers and investors.

Hence

$$B^D = S \quad \text{and} \quad B^S = I. \tag{3.16}$$

Implying that if $B^D = B^S$, then $I = S$ and this occurs at equilibrium E, where the interest rate is r and the total stock of funds available is L (Fig. 3.3).

If we consider a model which deals not in stocks but flows, we can show that altering the amount of money has no influence on the rate of interest. To consider flows we determine the demand for new bonds and the supply of new bonds. The supply of new bonds may arise from two sources—first, companies may issue new bonds and, second, individuals may relinquish bonds in order to build up money balances. Note that before we were considering total stocks of bonds and therefore changes could only occur due to new investment (issuance of bonds) not from individuals wishing to rearrange their portfolios. If we represent the flow supply of bonds (the supply of new bonds) as $\tilde{B}^S$ and new investment as $\tilde{I}$, then

$$\tilde{B}^S = \tilde{I} + \triangle M^D, \tag{3.17}$$

where $\triangle M^D$ is the change in the demand for money balances in the period.

Likewise the demand for new bonds arises from new saving and changes to the money supply arranged by the authorities through open market operations. Hence the demand for new bonds, $\tilde{B}^D$, and the new saving, $\tilde{S}$ are related:

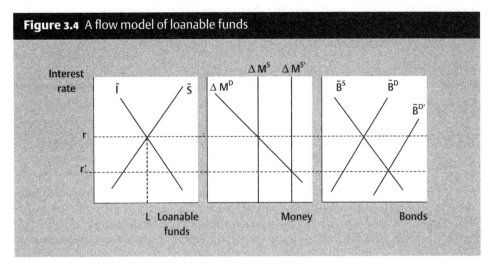

Figure 3.4 A flow model of loanable funds

$$\tilde{B}^D = \tilde{S} + \triangle M^S. \tag{3.18}$$

Now, plotting $\tilde{B}^D$, $\tilde{B}^S$, $\tilde{I}$, $\tilde{S}$, $\triangle M^S$, and $\triangle M^D$ on a diagram relating to the price of funds and the quantity of funds we find that there is a level of the interest rate that ensures that there is an equilibrium between new supply and new demand for bonds. Thus:

$$\tilde{B}^S = \tilde{B}^D \quad \text{implies} \quad \tilde{I} + \triangle M^D = \tilde{S} + \triangle M^S \tag{3.19}$$

and since investment, saving, and the demand for money can be thought of as functions of the interest rate this represents an equation that can be solved for an optimal level of the interest rate, r. This interest rate clears the bond market, the money market, and the saving–investment equation. This is illustrated in Figure 3.4.

The important point to note is that Robertson, Ohlin, Wicksell, and others considered the rate of interest that clears the money, bond, and investment–saving relationship to be determined in the long-run by the real forces that determine investment and saving decisions. It can be shown on Figure 3.4 that a monetary expansion, shifting $\triangle M^S$ and $\tilde{B}^D$ to the right, would result in a temporary fall in the interest rate but through the indirect mechanism this process would ultimately be reversed and the rate of interest would return to r.

3.7 Conclusions

IN this chapter we have explored the nature of a classical economy, progressing from a simple barter-exchange model in a Walrasian market context to a model in which money overlaps the real workings of the economy. Whilst money has been shown to be an efficient and desirable social institution it has no long-run real effects in the classical view. The implications of the direct and indirect mechanisms of monetary policy operate only over the short term; ultimately money is a veil and has neutral effects on the real aspects of the model such as supply and demand of goods, the relative prices of goods exchanged, and the interest rate.

Notes

1 Much of modern pure theory of money is couched in terms of Walrasian markets, although we will concentrate on the classical system here. We turn to modern Arrow–Debreu general equilibrium frameworks in Ch. 4.

2 Locke suggested that there was a strongly proportional relation between real money balances (purchasing power), the ratio of the volume of trade, and velocity of circulation. This is a stricter relation than those versions of the quantity theory discussed in this section because nominal money and prices are not independent.

3 The concept of neutrality is a familiar one due to its revival in monetarist and new classical thinking due to Friedman and Lucas. We will return to this issue in Chapters 7 and 9.

4 Note that through this process there is a connection between the money supply and the real economy, which operates through the loan market and the market rate of interest.

5 Both Pigou and Robertson were known for their defence of the classical writers and particularly Marshall.

Chapter 4
Patinkin and the Walrasian Heritage

4.1 Patinkin's Critiques

THIS chapter deals with the legacy of the classical system. We begin with Don Patinkin's analysis of the classical model and the role of the real-balance effect, analysing its implications and evaluating Patinkin's contribution to monetary thought. We then turn to monetary theory based on the general equilibrium framework of Kenneth Arrow and Gerard Debreu. Overlapping generations models with money in the utility function and Clower's cash-in-advance constraint are considered in turn. While these models bring us right up to date, disrupting the strict chronological order of monetary theory, they are closest in spirit and character to the theoretical models outlined in this chapter. We therefore deal with them here.

Patinkin came to the view that the classical model was flawed, since the real side, based on the Walrasian market, and the quantity theory, both of which were described in the last chapter, give incompatible descriptions of the workings of the whole economy. Central to the point at issue is the 'invalidity' charge which Patinkin levelled at the classical dichotomy. The accusation is that there exists a mathematical inconsistency in the classical system so long as it is maintained that relative prices can be determined in the real sector independently of the aggregate price level, determined in the monetary sector. Patinkin's reasoning is based on the fact that in a Walrasian system the monetary and real sectors cannot be kept apart, since money-holding decisions result from the decision to sell or buy goods. Since monetary and the real decisions are made simultaneously, any excess demand for goods must have implications for the excess demand for money, and any attempt to partition the sectors is invalid. Patinkin's contribution to monetary theory was to suggest a simple correction to the classical system—including real money balances in the excess demand function for goods—to ensure that the real and monetary sides of the model are compatible.

Patinkin approached the classical model in the light of initial criticisms made by Lange (1942), on the grounds that the classical system was internally inconsistent. Patinkin (1965) followed Lange in taking a representation of the classical world similar to the general equilibrium system outlined in the previous chapter and proceeded in stages, first examining a Walrasian system excluding money, and then the monetary version of Walras's model. He then attempted to reconcile the Walrasian excess demand for money with the counterpart derived from the quantity theory. He quickly realized that this could not be done and this analysis formed the basis of his attack. Patinkin argued that the two excess demand equations demonstrate that the classical model is indeterminate in the absolute price level, overidentified in the number of equations and unknowns, and is inconsistent in its treatment of the excess demand for money. These points are taken up in the following sections.

4.2 Determination of Prices

THE first issue we will investigate is Patinkin's assertion that the classical model is not fully identified, since it has an incompatible number of variables and equations. Consider the $n - 1$ excess demand equations of a Walrasian system without money. Patinkin showed that these could determine the $n - 1$ relative prices provided there was an arbitrary method of weighting them to sum to unity, which we have written as a weighted average of relative prices (equation n). To demonstrate this he arranged the $n - 1$ excess demand equations with the nth equation giving a value to absolute prices, and then showed that to determine $n - 1$ relative prices, $n - 1$ linearly independent equations are required. We reproduce the n equations and $n - 1$ unknowns in such a system in Table 4.1.

At first sight there is an apparent mismatch between equations and unknowns, since there are $n - 1$ excess demand equations plus the absolute price equation but only $n - 1$ relative prices to be determined. This can be reconciled by the

Table 4.1 The Walrasian system

No.	Equations	Unknowns
1	$ED_1 = f(p_1/p_n, p_2/p_n, p_3/p_n, p_4/p_n \ldots, p_{n-1}/p_n, \sum_{i=1}^{n}(p_i/p_n)S_i) - S_1$	p_1/p_n
2	$ED_2 = f(p_1/p_n, p_2/p_n, p_3/p_n, p_4/p_n \ldots, p_{n-1}/p_n, \sum_{i=1}^{n}(p_i/p_n)S_i) - S_2$	p_2/p_n
...	...	...
$n-1$	$ED_{n-1} = f(p_1/p_n, p_2/p_n, p_3/p_n, p_4/p_n \ldots, p_{n-1}/p_n, \sum_{i=1}^{n}(p_i/p_n)S_i) - S_{n-1}$	p_{n-1}/p_n
n	$p_n = \sum_{i=1}^{n-1} w_i p_i$	

application of Walras's Law. When $n - 2$ equations are in equilibrium the $n - 1th$ equation will also be in equilibrium and the system will have only $n - 1$ *independent* equations, since one of the excess demand equations can be inferred from the others.

Since the original demand and supply equations are homogeneous of degree zero in the prices $p_1, p_2, \ldots, p_{n-1}$, they depend only upon the $n - 2$ relative prices p_1/p_{n-1}, $p_2/p_{n-1}, \ldots, p_{n-2}/p_{n-1}$. Likewise the excess demand functions depend only upon the $n - 2$ relative prices $p_1/p_{n-1}, p_2/p_{n-1}, \ldots, p_{n-2}/p_{n-1}$. Through Walras's Law the excess demand functions depend only upon these relative prices and not on the absolute price level. That is, the functions are homogeneous of degree zero in prices and homogeneous of degree one in relative prices. We can determine relative prices in this system but not money prices and hence the absolute price level is indeterminate.

To establish this point Patinkin considered the consequences of altering relative prices of some goods from their equilibrium values. He showed that the discrepancy between actual and equilibrium prices would serve to alter the excess demand for these goods in such a way that the relative prices would be pushed back towards equilibrium. The discrepancy would create a positive excess demand if prices were lower than equilibrium prices or an excess supply if the prices were higher than the equilibrium values which would force prices back in the direction of equilibrium, stopping only when prices were equal to their equilibrium values. With absolute prices, on the other hand, Patinkin showed that a change in absolute prices would leave excess demand functions unaltered as a result of the homogeneity postulate. Absolute prices would not affect excess demand functions because they are homogeneous of degree zero. Hence, any level of absolute prices would be compatible with the equilibrium set of relative prices, any absolute price level chosen arbitrarily would be an equilibrium price level, and any multiple of the absolute price level would also be an equilibrium price level.

The real sector would be able to operate on the basis of the relative prices which are perfectly defined without reference to a specific level of absolute prices. Even the equation which supposedly calculates the absolute price does not properly define it, since it is the product of an arbitrary weighting of the individual goods prices. Hence, we can say that on the real side of the model the absolute price level is not defined and this is a direct consequence of the homogeneity postulate, which turns out to be a strong assumption. As a result, Patinkin concluded that the classical barter model could determine relative prices but not the absolute price level.

4.3 Invalidity of the Classical Dichotomy

THE introduction of a monetary side to the classical model may be regarded as a way to overcome the objection of identification and indeterminacy in the previous section. After all, the absence of an equation defining the price level on the real side of the economy could be satisfied by the addition of an equation to describe it on the monetary side of the model. The classical model certainly had an additional equation on the monetary side in the form of the quantity theory, which specified the absolute price level in terms of income, money, and velocity. It was claimed that the problem could be resolved simply by dichotomizing the pricing process in such a way that the relative prices were determined by the real sector and the absolute price level by the quantity theory. Having shown that the real side of the Walrasian system in itself could not identify the absolute price level, Patinkin considered the introduction of money (by the addition of the quantity theory equation to the Walrasian system) to evaluate this claim. His conclusion, however, was that the dichotomy between the real and the monetary sides of the model is invalid and inconsistent.[1]

His analysis centred again on the excess demand functions. The system which comprised the $n - 1$ excess demand functions for goods, the equation defining the weighted average of relative prices, and the quantity theory could now identify all the relative prices and the absolute price level. Accounting for Walras's Law, which reduces the independent equations to n, the number of equations and unknowns to be determined is equal, thus the Walrasian model (augmented by the quantity theory) is identified and determinate in the absolute price level. This can be shown by considering the number of equations and unknowns in Table 4.2.

Although the model is determinate and identified it can be shown to be inconsistent and invalid on further examination. By considering the excess demand equations again, Patinkin showed that the excess demand for money on the real side and the monetary side of the model were treated inconsistently.

Patinkin's invalidity hypothesis was expanded by considering the monetary side of the classical model where the money supply, M^S, is constant and the demand for money, M^D, described by the quantity theory equation, in the following way:

$$M^S = M = constant \qquad (4.1)$$

$$M^D = kp_nY, \qquad (4.2)$$

where k is an institutional constant, p_n is the absolute price level, and Y is the aggregate output of the system. The excess demand function for money from this side of the model is

$$M^D - M^S = kp_nY - M. \qquad (4.3)$$

This depends on the absolute price level through the quantity theory equation but does not depend on relative prices at all.

Table 4.2 The Walrasian system and the quantity theory

No.	Equations	Unknowns
1	$ED_1 = f(p_1/p_n, p_2/p_n, p_3/p_n, p_4/p_n \ldots, p_{n-1}/p_n, \sum_{i=1}^{n}(p_i/p_n)S_i) - S_1$	p_1/p_n
2	$ED_2 = f(p_1/p_n, p_2/p_n, p_3/p_n, p_4/p_n \ldots, p_{n-1}/p_n, \sum_{i=1}^{n}(p_i/p_n)S_i) - S_2$	p_2/p_n
. . .	. . .	. . .
$n-1$	$ED_{n-1} = f(p_1/p_n, p_2/p_n, p_3/p_n, p_4/p_n \ldots, p_{n-1}/p_n, \sum_{i=1}^{n}(p_i/p_n)S_i) - S_{n-1}$	p_{n-1}/p_n
n	$p_n = \sum_{i=1}^{n-1} w_i p_i$	
$n+1$	$M = kp_n Y$	p_n

The excess demand for money from the real side, however, is given as the sum of the excess demand for goods as a result of Walras's Law. This can be written as a function of relative prices in the following way:

$$ED_n = \sum_{i=1}^{n-1} ED_i = \sum_{i=1}^{n-1} f(p_1/p_n, p_2/p_n, p_3/p_n, p_4/p_n \ldots, p_{n-1}/p_n, \sum_{i=1}^{n-1}(p_i/p_n)S_i) - S_i. \quad (4.4)$$

Clearly, as has already been demonstrated in the previous section, this depends solely on relative prices and not on the absolute price level. Thus there is, at the very basic level, an inconsistency in the variables in the excess demand for money represented by the monetary and the real sides of the same model. As an illustration of this point consider the effect on the excess demand for money function following a change in the absolute price level. The excess demand for money derived from the monetary side of the model registers a change through the absolute price level that has an effect on the term $kp_n Y$: in the same expression derived from the real side of the model the absolute price level has no effect because of the homogeneity postulate.

As a consequence of this inconsistency in the model the excess demand for money function in the real sector was shown to be homogeneous in prices of degree one (such that the absolute price level leaves the equilibrium unchanged) whilst the excess demand function derived from the quantity theory could be shown to be non-homogeneous in prices. Non-homogeneity means that it is impossible for the variable, in this case the absolute price level, to be taken outside the function and raised to some power leaving the original function unchanged in value. This result arises because the demand for money on the monetary side of the model is determined by the quantity theory, and depends on the absolute price level in such a way that the absolute price level has a proportional effect, whilst the supply of money does not depend on the absolute price level at all. Hence the subtraction of one from the other to generate the excess demand function yields a non-homogeneous function in the absolute price level.

Clearly, the excess demand functions differ, and it was Patinkin who showed that there was an inconsistency between the real and the monetary sectors as a result of the different definitions of the same term from different parts of the model. In the real sector, absolute prices are indeterminate and do not affect the excess demand functions whilst in the monetary sector the absolute price level is determinate and excess demand for money is dependent upon it. But through Walras's Law the excess demand for money is equal to the value of the excess demands in the real sector and if the latter depend on relative prices alone then the former must depend on relative prices alone. This inconsistency suggests that the two parts of the model are irreconcilable as they stand.

As a result of this inconsistency the two sides of the model were regarded by Patinkin as incompatible: the absolute price level could not be irrelevant in one derivation of excess demand and singularly important in another derivation of the same equation. Put another way, it is impossible for the real sector to depend solely on relative prices whilst in the monetary sector the excess demand for money is dependent only upon the aggregate price level. Patinkin drew from this feature the conclusion that the system was fundamentally inconsistent and could not be reconciled by dichotomizing the operation of commodity markets and the monetary market effectively separating the Walrasian system from the quantity theory. The attempt by some economists to lash the two together whilst keeping the determination of relative and absolute prices apart was the heart of the classical dichotomy. Patinkin's analysis undermined this approach and showed that the sectors could not be held apart in a general equilibrium system. Since money-holding decisions result from the decision to sell goods, the demand for money and the supply of goods are simultaneous, and hence the excess demand for money and the excess supply of goods must be compatible. Any attempt to partition the sectors produces an inconsistency as Patinkin clearly proved.

4.4 The Real-Balance Effect

PATINKIN not only showed that the classical model, built on the foundations of the quantity theory, Say's identity and Walras's Law, was invalid and inconsistent, but he provided a solution.[2] This came in the form of the real-balance effect, which is defined as the effect of real (money) balances on the excess demand functions for goods. Patinkin defines this effect as 'an increase in the quantity of money, other things being held constant, [that] influences the demand for a commodity just like any other increase in wealth' (Patinkin, 1965: 20).

This simple amendment has profound implications for the nature of the classical system, since it resolves all of the inconsistencies, invalidities, and indeterminacies identified in the previous sections, although, as might be expected, it raises some problems of it own. Patinkin himself makes the claim that

The real balance effect in the commodity markets plays a central role ... It is therefore worth emphasizing at the outset that the fulfilment of this analytical role depends not on the *strength* of this effect but only on its *existence*. ... It must also be emphasized that, for the simple exchange economy with which we are now dealing, the assumption that there exists a real balance effect in the commodity markets is the *sine qua non* of monetary theory [italics in original]. (Patinkin, 1965: 21)

In order to assess these claims we can allow for the existence of the real-balance effects by simply introducing the nth commodity (S_n) to our excess demand functions:

$$ED_1 = f(p_1/p_n, p_2/p_n, p_3/p_n, p_4/p_n \ldots, p_{n-1}/p_n, \sum_{i=1}^{n} (p_i/p_n)S_i + S_n/p_n) - S_1$$

$$ED_2 = f(p_1/p_n, p_2/p_n, p_3/p_n, p_4/p_n \ldots, p_{n-1}/p_n, \sum_{i=1}^{n} (p_i/p_n)S_i + S_n/p_n) - S_2$$

. . .

$$ED_{n-1} = f(p_1/p_n, p_2/p_n, p_3/p_n, p_4/p_n \ldots, p_{n-1}/p_n, \sum_{i=1}^{n} (p_i/p_n)S_i + S_n/p_n) - S_{n-1}, \quad (4.5)$$

where S_n/p_n equals the real money supply. Adding real money balances is equivalent to introducing an additional wealth effect as we have already seen. Yet the change is important because it allows an additional factor, besides the endowment of goods, to shift the excess demand function akin to a wealth change. This can take place through a change in S_n or a change in p_n, since both variables enter the term for real balances. An increase in the money supply from S_n to S'_n is equivalent to a positive wealth effect, raising the excess demands for all commodities together as real balances increase. Alternatively, a fall in p_n would bring about the same result

This simple modification has considerable implications. Most obviously, the absolute price level now enters the real side of the model, and the excess demand functions are no longer dependent solely on relative prices. A change in the absolute price level, p_n, has a wealth effect that increases (or decreases) all the excess demand functions together. The previous dichotomy of price determination is no longer valid: commodity market equilibria depend on both relative and absolute prices, and the excess demand functions are no longer homogeneous of degree zero in absolute prices. However large or small it may be in practice, the existence of the real-balance effect disposes of the classical dichotomy and money is no longer a veil.

We can now understand what brings about homogeneity. In the case above, the absolute price level enters the excess demand functions in an additive way, as an additional influence on endowed income, rendering the excess demand functions non-homogeneous. Homogeneous functions are those that contain additive terms under special conditions such that only relative prices matter (absolute prices are homogeneous of degree zero). With real balances included additively, the special conditions are not satisfied and the function becomes non-homogeneous: the homogeneity postulate is discarded. Note that the non-homogeneity of excess demand functions on the real side of the model is consistent with the conclusion that excess demand for money on the monetary side of the model is also non-homogeneous. The excess demand function for money derived from the Walrasian model using Walras's Law is now

$$ED_n = \sum_{i=1}^{n-1} ED_i = \sum_{i=1}^{n-1} f(p_1/p_n, p_2/p_n, \ldots, p_{n-1}/p_n, \sum_{i=1}^{n} (p_i/p_n)S_i + S_n/p_n) - S_i. \tag{4.6}$$

The existence of the additive term, S_n/p_n, makes the function as a whole non-homogeneous. The consequence of this is that the excess demand function is consistent with that derived from the quantity theory, which is also non-homogeneous.

$$ED_n = M^D - M^S = kp_nY - M. \tag{4.7}$$

Hence the conclusion that the model is inconsistent with itself is not true in Patinkin's modified classical model once it includes a real-balance effect; the excess demand for money results in a non-homogeneous function whether it is calculated on the real or the monetary side of the model.

Other implications follow. Excess demand functions are all affected uniformly, in the sense that any increase in real balances leads to an increase in excess demands across the board, and vice versa. Say's Law no longer holds *as an identity*. Say's identity implies that excess demands for goods should identically sum to zero but this can no longer hold if *all* excess demand functions rise with a positive change to real balances. An assumed increase in real money balances cannot simultaneously boost excess demands in all commodities whilst also maintaining the condition that excess demands for goods sum identically to zero.

The excess supply of money should result in an excess demand for goods if Walras's Law (which has not been discarded) is true. In Patinkin's modified version of the classical model the excess demand for goods increases with an excess supply of money, which takes the form of an increase in nominal and real money balances. These excesses in supply in the monetary market are matched by excesses in demand in the goods markets, ensuring that Walras's Law holds for the system as a whole ($\sum_{i=1}^{n} ED_i = 0$). Thus Say's Law holds as an equality, even though Say's identity can be shown to be untenable, since

$$\sum_{i=1}^{n-1} ED_i = 0 \text{ if } ED_n = 0. \tag{4.8}$$

Having considered the impact of the real-balance effect we must now turn to the dynamic effects of an assumed increase in nominal and real balances by looking at the goods market and money market equilibria in subsequent time periods. The excess demand for goods arising from the excess supply of money might reasonably be expected to cause a rise in prices of commodities and hence of the general price level in subsequent periods. This is indeed the case and forms the basis of the stability and neutrality of the model. It ensures stability because it describes the mechanism by which prices will alter to move the system back towards equilibrium to remove the disequilibria described by excess demands for goods and excess supplies of money. It ensures neutrality because the new equilibrium will occur at the point where the excess demands are zero and this will take place when the prices have risen proportionately with the increase in the money supply. Thus the real-balance effect, which took place initially because of a disturbance to equilibrium arising from an exogenous increase in nominal and real money balances (at the original price level), will be restored to equilibrium once prices rise sufficiently to restore the real balances to their original level.

Operation of the real-balance effect can be illustrated using the standard indifference curves and budget constraints of microeconomic analysis and this requires in turn that we develop a utility function with real balances in the function. The first assumption is that money yields utility (we will deal with this in more detail later in the chapter). Patinkin's justification is that money represents potential consumption or future purchasing power and on this basis provides satisfaction to individuals just as present consumption provides satisfaction, except that the actual satisfaction of consumption is deferred to a future date.[3]

$$U = U(x_1, x_2, x_3, \ldots, x_{n-1}, M/p_n). \tag{4.9}$$

The budget constraint is derived from Walras's Law, since this describes the relationship between the demand and supply of commodities and the demand and supply for money, i.e. the goods and the resources to pay for them. Hence

$$\sum_{i=1}^{n} p_i D_i = \sum_{i=1}^{n} p_i S_i \tag{4.10}$$

giving

$$\sum_{i=1}^{n-1} (p_i/p_n) D_i + S_n/p_n = \sum_{i=1}^{n-1} (p_i/p_n) S_i + D_n/p_n, \tag{4.11}$$

where S_n is the money supply (M^s) and D_n is the money demand (M^d), thus

$$\sum_{i=1}^{n-1} (p_i/p_n) D_i + M^S/p_n = \sum_{i=1}^{n-1} (p_i/p_n) S_i + M^D/p_n. \tag{4.12}$$

Notably, this is just an aggregation of the excess demand functions and it is through the budget constraint therefore that the real-balance effect enters the analysis. That is, the demand for commodities depends on relative prices and real balances. This will become more apparent when, having solved the model using constrained optimization in the usual way, to maximize utility subject to the budget constraint, the comparative statics of the equilibrium level of money balances and goods consumed are compared.

Diagramatically this can be shown by drawing the budget constraint and the indifference curves in such a way that the highest attainable indifference curve is reached subject to the budget line, with equilibrium described by the tangency position between the two. But, since there are $n - 1$ goods plus money in the analysis, we would have to draw an n-dimensional diagram to illustrate equilibrium. If we make a simplification as the classicals did, splitting the economy into a monetary and a real part, we can illustrate the effects on a normal two-dimensional diagram. Thus we take the individual goods and form a measure of aggregate goods consumption, G, on the horizontal axis representing the real side, and represent real balances, M/p_n, on the vertical axis. To draw the budget constraint on the diagram we need to know the slope of the line, but since goods and real-money balances exchange for each other in the ratio one to one, the slope must be minus one (i.e. 45 degrees). We can then superimpose the indifference curves on top of the budget constraint to illustrate the equilibrium position by a tangency point.

In Figure 4.1 the initial endowment of goods and money is given by the combination $[(M/p)_0, G_0]$ at point $(M/p)_0 G_0$, which can be transformed into any other combination on or inside the budget line by the process of exchange. The equilibrium point, other things remaining constant, is illustrated by point E_1 which gives a utility-maximizing combination of money and goods of $[(M/p)_0, G_0]$. The endowment point need not correspond with the initial equilibrium point as it does here but it greatly simplifies matters later on if we make this assumption.

Patinkin considered an initial endowment at $(M/p)_0, G_0$ which was subsequently disturbed by the injection of money to a point $(M/p)_1, G_0$. The additional supply of nominal money balances causes a real-balance effect, which shifts the budget constraint outwards, since at the original prices the new level of real balances has a greater command over real goods than before. The shifting budget constraint shows the effect of the real-balance effect on goods in total. The point $(M/p)_1, G_0$ which corresponds to the new endowment point of money and goods does not represent the

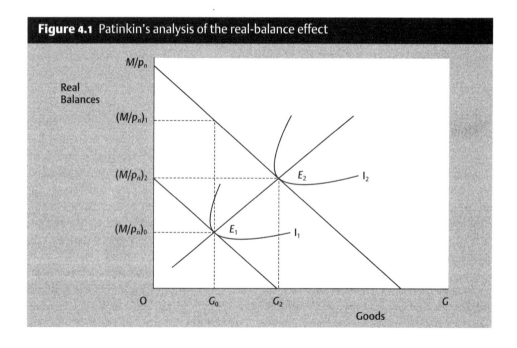

Figure 4.1 Patinkin's analysis of the real-balance effect

equilibrium position, however, since a higher indifference curve, I_2, can be attained by transforming some money balances into goods, moving along the budget constraint to a point such as E_2. Hence, it can be seen that the real-balance effect acts as a wealth effect shifting the budget constraint outwards from the origin, which allows the individual to attain a new equilibrium at E_2 where the new combination of real balances and goods is $[(M/p)_2, G_2]$ and utility is higher than before.

In Patinkin's calculations the impact of the real-balance effect was a permanent wealth effect which had properties that resulted in stability and neutrality in the long run. In Figure 4.1, we have a real-balance effect which is not neutral or stabilizing. This is the case because real balances at E_2 are greater than those at E_1. Prices at E_2 are the same prices that existed at E_1 before the real-balance effect took place, making real balances larger over all.

Archibald and Lipsey

The introduction of the stability property and restoration of the neutrality result was the work of Archibald and Lipsey (1958).[4] Their contribution was to point out that the equilibrium E_2 is not a *permanent equilibrium* position if the model is to be consistent with the stability and neutrality properties. Instead E_2 must be considered a *temporary equilibrium* which pertains to one trading day only. The reason for calling it a temporary equilibrium is that the position cannot be maintained, even if no other exogenous changes take place, as a result of the impact of the upward pressure on prices. The pressure comes from the fact that individuals have excess real money balances to offload, or to put it another way, they have excess demand for goods which drive the prices of goods up. Archibald and Lipsey showed that once the equilibrium E_2 is regarded as a temporary equilibrium, then we can consider a sequence of these equilibria before we reach one that is permanent. A temporary equilibrium pertains only to one trading day and we must analyse a sequence of trading days up to the point that neutrality and stability are assured before we reach a permanent equilibrium position. Only when we have attained the permanent equilibrium can we truly say that we have worked out the full implications of the real-balance effect. The implication of this finding is that the real-balance effect requires a sequential analysis, which is dynamic in nature, rather than the static approach developed by Patinkin.

Fortunately, it is possible to illustrate a sequence of days using the same diagrammatic method as Patinkin. Archibald and Lipsey took the equilibrium E_2 in Figure 4.1 as the first step in the dynamic process, which results from the real-balance effect. They then considered what would happen on the next trading day, which we illustrate in Figure 4.2. From the position E_2, individuals would be left with real balances corresponding to $(M/p_n)_2$. The goods received in that trading day would be consumed by the beginning of the next one so that at the beginning of the next trading day individuals would hold their new endowment of goods received every period G_0 and the remaining money balances. This would give a combination of $[(M/p_n)_2, G_0]$ through which the budget constraint would have to pass since only combinations which are exchangeable for $[(M/p_n)_2, G_0]$ would be available to the individual in this period. The resulting equilibrium position would be a new temporary equilibrium point such as E_3, giving $[(M/p_n)_3, G_3]$, which maximizes utility subject to the new constraint at period-two prices. From this point and the money balances held at the end of the period, the next budget constraint and equilibrium could be calculated. In each successive period the budget constraint would move closer to the origin as the remaining real balances at the end of each period fell.

The reason that real balances fall in the first place is because the excess supply of money is being dissipated by individuals as they purchase goods, inevitably leading to a rise in the price level for goods. This is another way of saying that the excess demand for goods pushed up prices as the additional real money balances injected into the system 'chase' the endowment of goods available for consumption, given by the endowment G_0 in each period. Since this happens every period, the budget constraint shifts inwards every time period as real balances fall and there are a succession of temporary equilibria until prices have risen proportionately with the money supply and a permanent equilibrium is re-established.

This derives the neutrality result that insists that the real balances should be the same as they were before the real-balance effect took place. Since the endowment of goods received every period has not changed during successive periods the permanent equilibrium is E_0—the position from which we started. The impact of Archibald and Lipsey's work was therefore to show that there is no permanent real-balance effect. There is a temporary expansion of demand, which pushes prices up in proportion to the increase in the money supply, but there is no lasting effect on the

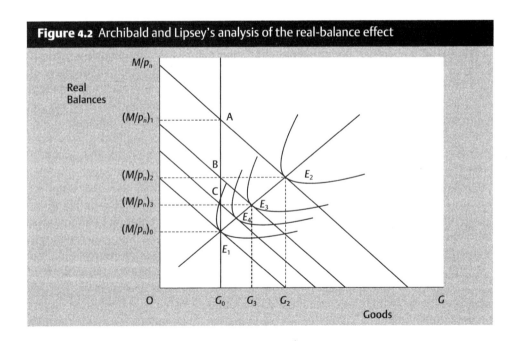

Figure 4.2 Archibald and Lipsey's analysis of the real-balance effect

goods market or real money balances. Neutrality is the rule and the departure from the permanent position is only temporary.

Liviatin

The assumption that a permanent equilibrium exists that is unique and stable is taken for granted, by both Patinkin and Archibald and Lipsey, but the analysis of Liviatin (1965) to which we now turn, shows that the existence of a permanent equilibrium is by no means a foregone conclusion. Liviatin introduces interest-bearing securities into the modified classical model of Patinkin and Archibald and Lipsey, which formerly included only money balances—a safe non-interest-bearing asset—and real perishable goods which had no store of value function. With interest-bearing assets added, the nature of the endowment received every period alters since the endowment contains not only real perishable goods but also a rate of return, which represents the yield on a durable asset. Circumstances may then arise in which there is no permanent equilibrium or, if a permanent equilibrium exists, no assurance that departures from it will be followed by stabilizing adjustments to return to it after a number of periods. In order to explain these cases we will illustrate the Archibald and Lipsey model using Liviatin's apparatus and then consider the three cases in turn.

The Liviatin apparatus is a skeletal form of the budget lines and indifference curves in which there are two loci which represent temporary and permanent equilibrium positions. Figure 4.3 shows the Archibald and Lipsey model with the points of temporary equilibrium on the SS' locus and points of permanent equilibrium on the LL' locus. Thus E_1, E_2, and E_3 lie on the temporary equilibrium locus whilst points A and B lie on the permanent equilibrium locus. This juxtaposition reveals that it is the act of redistribution from points such as A and B to points which are utility-maximizing tangencies that is the cause of rising prices. Without this redistribution there would be no pressure on prices and these points would be permanent equilibria (although Pareto-inefficient ones inconsistent with utility maximization). Note also that only E_1 lies on both the temporary and the permanent equilibrium loci by virtue of the fact that this is the initial equilibrium consistent with the regular endowment.

Consider now the Liviatin extension in which there is an interest-bearing asset, B/p_n, yielding a rate of return r each period which must be added to the endowment every period. As a consequence, the endowment received is no longer constant but is variable and it will depend on the real perishable goods component, G_0, and a return to a durable good of $r.B/p_n$. We represent the yield on the durable good in terms of the amount of perishable goods that the individual can purchase. Thus the initial endowment is G_0, the endowment in period one is $G_0 + G_1$, the endowment in period two is $G_0 + G_2$ and so on. Now the LL' locus is upward-sloping as a consequence of the yield on the asset and three possibilities arise. The first is illustrated in Figure 4.4 and corresponds most closely to the Archibald and Lipsey model, except that the LL' locus is upward-sloping not vertical. The equilibrium in this case exists

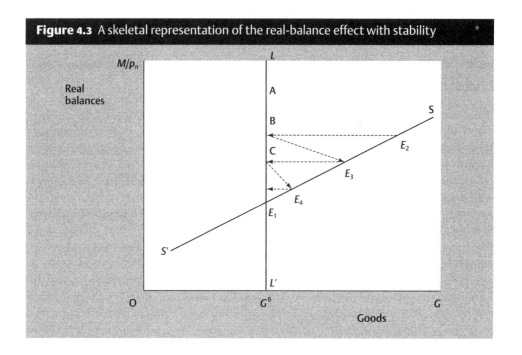

Figure 4.3 A skeletal representation of the real-balance effect with stability

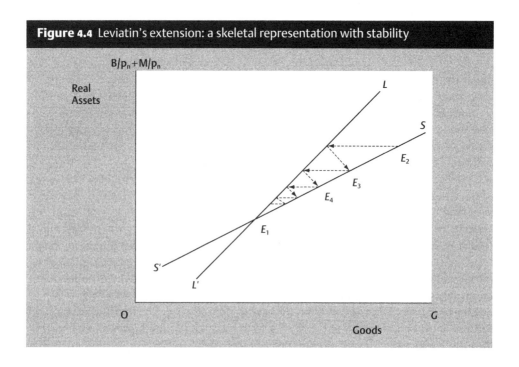

Figure 4.4 Leviatin's extension: a skeletal representation with stability

and is unique and it is stable since a real-balance effect moving the temporary equilibrium to E_2 causes a series of price rises as described before. These in turn reduce real balances until they equal the original equilibrium level E_1. The only difference between this model and Archibald and Lipsey's model is that the endowment each period is not constant.

We now consider in Figure 4.5 a situation in which the permanent equilibrium exists and is unique but not stable. In this case the SS' locus is steeper than the LL' locus which means that following a real-balance effect shifting the temporary equilibrium to E_2 the system is unstable. The path following a move to E_2 implies ever-increasing goods and real money balances. From the position E_2 rather than receiving a goods endowment, which shifts the budget constraint inwards, the opposite is true resulting in an outward shift of the budget constraint. From this new endowment position the redistribution of the goods, money balances combination yields a higher level of money balances than at the endowment point pushing prices down (not up). This process continues in ever-greater steps in an explosive fashion. The result in this case is that even a small departure from the equilibrium point E_1 can result in a highly explosive unstable path for prices and real money balances.

The final case relaxes the assumption that an equilibrium exists in the first place. In this case, illustrated in Figure 4.6, the SS' and LL' loci do not intersect at all. As drawn, the LL' locus is steeper than the SS' locus but the intersection does not occur in the positive quadrant of the diagram. Since negative quantities of goods and real balances do not exist, the permanent equilibrium does not exist. For the case drawn, the real-balance effect results in a movement to E_2 but the resulting fall in prices does not bring the system back to the full equilibrium. Prices continue to rise

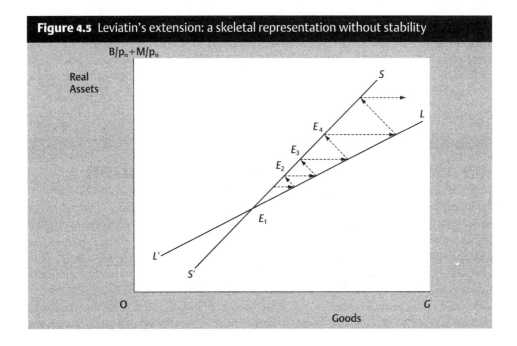

Figure 4.5 Leviatin's extension: a skeletal representation without stability

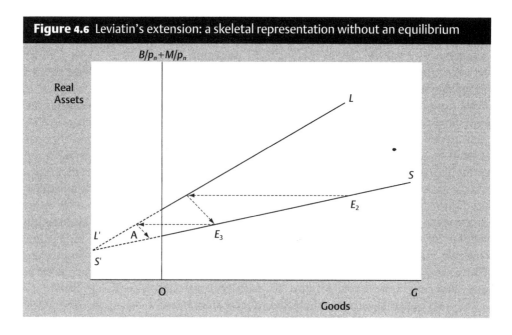

Figure 4.6 Leviatin's extension: a skeletal representation without an equilibrium

until the point A is reached where the goods, real balances combination indicates a zero holding of goods. Had we drawn the LL' locus less steep than the SS' locus and non-intersecting, the result would have been ever-falling prices until prices were zero and real balances were infinite. In either case no permanent equilibrium results.

In practice, whilst all three of these cases are possibilities, by the observation of stability of the monetary system and the existence of levels of money balances and goods that do not drive real balances to infinity or goods consumption to zero, we have to conclude that the first case is the best description of the world. Under any other scenario we could infer an inconsistency in the model since individuals are assumed to be rational yet their rational actions lead to irrational outcomes.

4.5 Evaluating Patinkin's Contribution

THE conclusion to which Patinkin was inevitably drawn by his analysis was that the Walrasian system, relying as it does on Walras's Law and Say's identity, is indeterminate in the absolute price level. Introduction of the quantity theory defines the absolute price level but leaves the dichotomized determination of relative and absolute prices and excess demands inconsistent and invalid. Patinkin's solution was to introduce the concept of the real-balance effect. This section evaluates Patinkin's work and requires us to consider the long-term implications of his findings. In doing this we assess the novelty of the real-balance effect as a concept and the implications of the effect over the long run. If we compare Patinkin's original published papers with the first and second editions of his book *Money, Interest and Prices*, then it is apparent that Patinkin made considerable modifications to his model to account for minor points and objections raised by other economists. There are two major issues to be considered (i) whether the classical model was in need of the real-balance effect at all and (ii) whether the model incorporating a real-balance effect achieves the stable and consistent model it set out to create.

In the first place, it is worthwhile pointing out that the classical system was not without its defenders. Patinkin's contribution was based on a mathematical form of the classical model due to Lange (1942), his research supervisor at Chicago. There were however, many others who used quite different (i.e. non-mathematical) apparatus to explain the classical model. Their point of view was championed by Robertson, who, in private correspondence with Patinkin, raised the issue of whether the classical and neoclassical economists such as Mill, Marshall, Walras, Wicksell, and others were really guilty of the accusations levelled by 'the counsel for the prosecution, Patinkin' concerning the dichotomy between relative and absolute prices in classical monetary theory. Robertson argued that the classicals *did* recognize the real-balance effect, even before Patinkin introduced it as the solution to the 'inconsistencies' in the Walrasian model based on Walras's Law, Say's identity, and the quantity theory. Robertson argued that the classical model was never really inconsistent and that Patinkin drew his conclusions from a mathematical form of the model which did not convey the subtleties of classical writings. On this issue there was to be little eventual disagreement between Robertson and Patinkin, since both accepted that the neoclassical economists, and Robertson himself in his own work, had recognized the real-balance effect. There was a related issue, however which was more contentious. Patinkin alleged that the neoclassical economists had not employed the real balance as a means of stabilizing the monetary sector, nor had Robertson in his writings. Robertson contended otherwise and on this point they agreed to disagree.

On the second point, a number of arguments can be rehearsed to question the long-term influence of the real-balance effect. Archibald and Lipsey and also Liviatin concluded that the real-balance effect is important but only as a transitory phenomenon the effect of which dies away with a rise in prices. Money is still neutral and there is no money illusion. Even the argument that the real-balance effect ties down the price level and makes the absolute price level determinate was in a sense invalidated by Harry Johnson's (1962) observation that the presence of an interest rate can serve the same purpose. His point was that once an interest-bearing asset exists, the classical model can be shown to be determinate and consistent since the interest rate alters the demand for consumption and investment goods as well as the demand for money and bonds. Therefore, even without the real-balance effect, the real and monetary sectors are interrelated, the dichotomization breaks down and the absolute price level is determinate. The clear implication is that there was no real need in the first place for the real-balance effect.

Patinkin's reworking of the classical model dominated monetary theory for over a decade. Whatever one concludes now about the novelty and influence of the real-balance effect, it is clear that Patinkin's analysis remained within the classical framework and that his lasting contribution was in conceptualizing a mathematically consistent system building on the earlier work of Lange (1942). A far more serious challenge to the classical model had come from Keynes's *General Theory*. Before we turn to that model we outline later developments in the Walrasian heritage adopted by theorists working with the Arrow–Debreu model.

4.6 The Walrasian Heritage

Arrow–Debreu model

THE Arrow–Debreu model of general competitive analysis (Arrow and Debreu, 1954) is founded on two basic principles: optimizing behaviour on the part of individual entities in the presence of prices taken as given by them and the setting of prices so that, given this individual behaviour, supply equals demand on each market. Consider the case of an economy with $n-1$ goods (i), h households (H), and f firms (F), with costless exchange and information about exchange. We must evaluate the behaviour of firms and households, and then the outcome of the competitive process.

Firms are assumed to maximize profits, and for a single firm the optimizing behaviour is

$$\max \pi^f = f(p_1, p_2, p_3, \ldots, p_{n-1}), \tag{4.13}$$

where π^f is the profits of the individual firm and $(p_1, p_2, p_3, \ldots, p_{n-1})$ are prices facing the firm, subject to the technical production relationship characterized by its transformation surface, defined by

$$T(y_1, y_2, y_3, \ldots, y_{n-1}) = 0, \tag{4.14}$$

where y_i is taken to be an output if positive and an input if negative. As a solution to this process we obtain a firm's demand and supply function for goods (demand for inputs, supply of output),

$$D_i^f(p_1, p_2, p_3, \ldots, p_{n-1}) : S_i^f(p_1, p_2, p_3, \ldots, p_{n-1}). \tag{4.15}$$

Consumers maximize utility gained from consuming goods $(x_1, x_2, x_3, \ldots, x_{n-1})$

$$\max u(x_1, x_2, x_3, \ldots, x_{n-1}) \tag{4.16}$$

subject to a budget constraint for an individual

$$\sum_{i=1}^{n-1} p_i x_i = \sum_{i=1}^{n-1} p_i \bar{x}_i + \pi^h, \tag{4.17}$$

where $\sum_{i=1}^{n-1} p_i x_i$ is the total value of consumed goods, $\sum_{i=1}^{n-1} p_i \bar{x}_i$ is the value of the consumer's initial endowment (including labour services), and π^h are the profits received during the period, where

$$\sum \pi^f = \sum \pi^h \tag{4.18}$$

and all profits earned by firms are distributed as dividends. From these, we derive

$$D_i^h (p_1, p_2, p_3, \ldots, p_{n-1}) = S_i^h (p_1, p_2, p_3, \ldots, p_{n-1}), \tag{4.19}$$

the analogues of consumer supply and demand functions.

For any commodity i, there will be total demands and supplies at any given set of prices, viz.

$$S_i = f (p_1, p_2, p_3, \ldots, p_{n-1}) \tag{4.20}$$

and

$$D_i = f (p_1, p_2, p_3, \ldots, p_{n-1}) \tag{4.21}$$

We require for equilibrium

$$D_i = S_i \text{ for each } i = 1, 2, 3, \ldots, n-1, \tag{4.22}$$

i.e. multi-market clearance.[5] Alternatively, following the Hicksian tradition (Hicks, 1939), we can define the excess demand for any commodity i, x_i, as the sum over all individuals and firms of demands and supplies. The general equilibrium of the economy is then the set of prices which equate all excess demands to zero,

$$ED_i (p_1, p_2, p_3, \ldots, p_{n-1}) = 0 \; i = 1, 2, 3, \ldots n-1. \tag{4.23}$$

Three features of equilibrium should be noted. First, although there appear overall to be n equations in $n - 1$ unknowns (see Table 4.1), the equations are homogeneous, and no solution can be unique, since any positive multiple of all prices is also a solution to the set of equations. Thus if nominal prices are halved or doubled, e.g. ($2p_1, 2p_2, 2p_3, \ldots, 2p_{n-1}$), there will be no difference to behaviour and real demands and supplies will be unchanged. The system is consistent with a large number of nominal outcomes.

Second, Walras's Law defines the linear dependence among the n equations. In effect, the equations really only determine $n - 2$ price ratios, but the equations are not independent. If $n - 1$ equations are satisfied, then the $n - 1$th must be by Walras's Law, which equates the total values of demand and supply in the economy. Note that Walras's Law holds for all values of prices (Patinkin, 1987).

Third, a distinction exists between full and temporary equilibrium. Full (or Arrow–Debreu) equilibrium is when all goods—current and future—can be exchanged now, via a complete set of futures markets. Temporary equilibrium exists when only present commodities are exchanged. Under conditions of full equilibrium a decision to save, and refrain from present consumption, means that one can buy now the future goods needed and therefore provide information for producers to undertake production decisions next period. Simultaneously a decision to invest can be undertaken by buying inputs now and selling future production on the futures market to those currently saving. In this way, there is no imbalance between future demand and supply due to savings decisions. The contrast with Keynes is sharp, and the following quotation indicates that he was not unaware of the implications.

An act of individual saving means—so to speak—a decision not to have dinner today. But it does *not* necessitate a decision to have dinner or to buy a pair of boots a week hence or a year hence or to consume any specified thing at any specified date. Thus it depresses the business of preparing today's dinner without stimulating the business of making ready for some future act of consumption. It is not a substitution of future consumption-demand for present consumption-demand—it is a net diminution of such demand. Moreover, the expectation of future consumption is so largely based on current experience of present consumption that a reduction in the latter is likely to depress the former, with the result that the act of saving will not merely depress the price of consumption-goods and leave the marginal efficiency of existing capital unaffected, but may actually tend to depress the latter also. In this event it may reduce present investment-demand as well as present consumption-demand.

If saving consisted not merely in abstaining from present consumption but in placing simultaneously a specific order for future consumption, the effect might indeed be different, for in that case the expectation of some future yield from investment would be improved, and the resources released from preparing for present consumption could be turned over to preparing for future consumption. Not that they necessarily would be, even in this case, on a scale *equal* to the amount of resources released; since the desired interval of delay might require a method of production so inconveniently 'roundabout' as to have an efficiency well below the current rate of interest, with the result that the favourable effect on employment of the forward order for consumption would eventuate not at once but at some subsequent date, so that the *immediate* effect of the saving would still be adverse to employment. In any case, however, an individual decision to save does not, in actual fact, involve the placing of any specific forward order for consumption, but merely the cancellation of a present order. Thus, since the expectation of consumption is the only *raison d'être* of employment, there should be nothing paradoxical in the conclusion that a diminished propensity to consume has *cet. par.* a depressing effect on employment. (Keynes, 1936: 210–11)

The role of money

Insofar as monetary economics is concerned, a major stumbling block is that there is no role for money in the Arrow–Debreu system, either as a medium of exchange or as a unit of account. All prices are expressed in terms of a *numéraire*, but this need not be money; it could be a historical unit like the guinea or a fictional measure such as the 'bancor' (as indeed, in Arrow and Hahn, 1971). The budget constraint of consumers evidences no need for a medium exchange. Considering (4.17), the transformation of the initial endowment into a final consumption bundle could occur through a direct exchange of, say, apples ($\bar{x}_1$) for oranges (x_2), as noted by Clower (1967).

Standard economic theory offers two reasons why entities should hold money. One, underlying the transactions demand for money, is the time and trouble needed to obtain money when needed for a transaction (e.g. by selling securities). The other, in line with the 'diversification' or 'speculative' demand for money, is the desire for risk aversion obtained by holding some part of wealth in unprofitable but safe form. Neither, however, applies in this case. Once entities know market prices they are able to take it for granted that they can transact on these terms, and the process of exchange—by assumption—is costless and entirely anonymous. Moreover, if money were held it would be held for later transactions, since money separates the act of sale of goods and services from the subsequent purchase. But this role is not needed if there were in existence a full range of futures markets. For example, should there be imperfect knowledge about the terms for the future supply of grain, a miller could make future contracts for labour services contingent upon that supply.

How, then, are we to get money into the system? There are a number of approaches to this issue.[6]

Overlapping generations

Under this approach, introduced by Samuelson (1958), money is a device for accomplishing an intertemporal reallocation of consumption. At any time, the economy consists of the young and the old, and the exposition is simplified by assuming that each transactor lives for two periods and receives income as an exogenous endowment of one unit of a single good while young and nothing while old. This immediately generates a motive for saving. With people saving when young, we require another group of people to be dissaving; with no investment, aggregate saving must be zero in equilibrium. This can be accomplished by having generations overlap. At each point in time there will be an old and a young generation alive, who are identical except for the phase of their life.

One method of generating a need for financial assets is to assume that goods are not storable. Then there will be a demand for financial assets as a means of transferring purchasing power from one period to the next. Without money (or some other asset), there would be no way that such a transfer could take place: the young could lend to the old but the old would not be around to repay the debt when the current young became old. Samuelson suggested that money in the form of paper currency would solve the problem. When the model commences, the old have all the money there is. Realizing their imminent demise, they will want to convert it into consumption. They can do this only by inducing the young to accept money in exchange for goods. The young would then sell some of their output for currency. The creation of money allows the old to trade with the young and allows the old to consume more than they could under barter. In turn, the young accept the money and thereby allow the old to increase consumption because they know for certain that the next generation of young will do the same for them.

In such a model, money has a role only as a store of value, a function that could equally well have been performed by other assets. In fact, an asset like land or physical capital which possesses positive marginal products will dominate money as a means of transferring consumption from one period to the next, so that the economy would quickly evolve to a non-monetary one. In itself, the overlapping-generations model does not exploit the medium-of-exchange advantage that money possesses. Tobin (1980b, 1992), in particular, has criticized Wallace (1980) and others for suggesting that these models explain the existence of money on the grounds that the model 'unrealistically assigns to money the function of being the sole or the principal store of value that links one generation to the next' (Tobin, 1992: 774).

Further problems arise if we model such an economy as being of finite duration. If there is a terminal date, then clearly at that time no person will wish to hold paper money—it cannot be consumed and it must be worthless. But this fact, under full and perfect information is known to entities at the moment preceding the final date. If they hold money to transfer to the final date, they will be forgoing current consumption for no future benefit. No one will wish to hold paper money at the moment immediately preceding the final date, and it will also be worthless at that time. Continuing in this manner, we can deduce that money must therefore be worthless at every date. Since money is worthless one minute before midnight, it must be worthless today and the economy unravels. Thus, as Hahn (1982) argues, a theory of a monetary economy cannot be established by this route.

How can we get around this logical conundrum? One possibility is to simply ignore it. As Tobin notes:

[W]e do not all and will not all expect with certainty the end of the world at any definite time. We always do, always will, assign some probability to its continuation. Since there are many other paradoxes involved in thinking about human behaviour in a world with no chance of a future beyond a definite time, it is best not to take that prospect seriously in economic modelling. (1992: 774)

Another escape route is to introduce a new and largely *ad hoc* element into the analysis. This might take the form of postulating that there is an inescapable law requiring people to pay fixed money sums, e.g. taxation, to the government at the final date using the paper money. Alternatively, there might be some other form of legal restriction to enforce the holding of money.

Money in the utility function

The simplest way that money can be reintroduced into the overlapping-generations framework in the presence of other assets is to focus directly on the ease with which transactions can be made with whatever we are defining as money, relative to other assets. Money thus buys goods more cheaply than do other assets, in Hahn's (1982) terminology. Some authors thus assume that real balances (denoted $\frac{M}{p_n}$, where

$$p_n = \sum_{i=1}^{n-1} w_i p_i)$$

bring utility, and modify the utility function (4.16) each period to be

$$u \left(x_{it}, \left[\frac{p}{p_n} \right]_t \right) \text{ for } i = 1, 2, 3, \ldots, n-1. \tag{4.24}$$

The technique has been utilized by Samuelson (1947), Patinkin (1965), Friedman (1969), and many later authors, including Brock (1974), Fischer (1979), Weiss (1980*b*), and Obstfeld (1984).

Not surprisingly, inserting money in the utility function produces a demand for money even though it is dominated in its rate of return by other assets. Brock (1974) has provided two illustrations designed to justify this practice: in one example, real balances are an argument of 'liquidity costs' which appear in the individual's budget constraint; and in the second, real balances influence the 'shopping time' involved in making trips to the bank. Feenstra (1986) has fully developed the first of these examples, and has established a functional equivalence between using liquidity costs in the budget constraint and money in the utility function. Consequently, there would seem to be little difference between using liquidity costs and money in the utility function, although one qualification is in order since any variables which affect liquidity costs also enter the derived utility function. Fischer (1974) has explicitly considered the role of such variables (particularly the interest rate) in his analysis of money in the production function. This is another way of assigning utility to money, in this instance by giving it marginal productivity: in effect, treating it as a factor of production to a productive enterprise.

The idea of putting real money balances as an argument in an individual's utility function has generated a lot of controversy. This technique has been criticized by Clower (1967), Hahn (1982), Kareken and Wallace (1980), and Tobin (1980). Tobin contends that 'the practice of putting money stocks in the utility function is reprehensible.' Hahn considers it to be 'harmless if properly done and interpreted,' but 'can also and has also held back the development of a proper monetary theory'. One criticism of this type of model concerns whether money is yielding utility *directly* or *indirectly* through transactions costs, and we note the alternative approaches above. In this respect, Clower (1967) has argued that money in the utility function does not yield a theory where money plays a special role in transactions. Finally, Kareken and Wallace (1980) take exception to what they regard as the implicit theorizing of this approach since it does not allow the underlying model consistency to be checked.

In the alternative approaches considered below, the focus of attention is upon the constraint function rather than the utility function, as a way of giving money a role in the system. We look first at Clower's rule.

Cash-in-advance models

An alternative way to introduce money is to assume that money must be acquired before any transactions, and thus consumption, can be undertaken. This is known as the Clower (1967) or *cash-in-advance* requirement. We will develop the analysis using Clower's logic but it is worth noting that the cash-in-advance constraint has received a great deal of prominence in macroeconomic theory since Clower's day principally due to work by Robert Lucas and co-authors, e.g. Lucas and Stokey (1987).

Consider again the budget constraint (4.12) employed by Patinkin. The maximizing behaviour of the consumer when money plays a role is

$$\max u \left(x_1 \dots x_{n-1}, \frac{M}{p_n} \right) \tag{4.25}$$

subject to

$$\sum_{i=1}^{n-1} p_i x_i + M = \sum_{i=1}^{n-1} p_i \bar{x}_i + \bar{M}, \tag{4.26}$$

where the left-hand side of (4.26) indicates the values which the individual ends up with and the right-hand side indicates the values of the initial endowments of commodities and money. Does the budget constraint define a monetary economy? Clower answers no, on the grounds that a direct exchange of $\bar{x}_i$ for x_i is not ruled out.

Clower then asks: (i) what is the distinguishing characteristic of money?—to which the answer is a medium of exchange—and (ii) what is a monetary economy? His answer to the second question is the catch phrase: *money buys goods and goods buy money, but goods do not buy goods.* Thus money does not simply economize on transactions balances it is a prerequisite for exchange and therefore, he argues, the restriction ought to be the central theme of a money economy.

In order to implement this restriction, Clower proposes that the Patinkin-style utility function be replaced by

$$\max u \left(x_1 \dots x_{n-1}, \frac{M}{p_n}, \frac{m}{p_n} \right) \tag{4.27}$$

subject to the constraints

$$\sum_{i=1}^{n-1} p_i x_i + M = \sum_{i=1}^{n-1} p_i \bar{x}_i + \bar{M} \text{ for } i \text{ such that } x_i \geq \bar{x}_i \tag{4.28}$$

and

$$m = \sum_{i=1}^{n-1} p_i(\bar{x}_i - x_i) \text{ for } i \text{ such that } x_i \leq \bar{x}_i, \tag{4.29}$$

where m denotes monetary receipts. In (4.27), the condition $x_i \geq \bar{x}_i$ means that net purchases must be backed by a readiness to supply money in exchange (from $\bar{M}$). In (4.28) the condition $x_i \leq \bar{x}_i$ means that all net sales involve the receipt of money. Thus the combined effect is that for every commodity sold, the individual acquires money, while every one bought must be from money holdings.

However, there is still a problem. In the previous situation, individuals were subject to only one constraint. In Clower's model, they are subject to two constraints, and to this extent are presumably worse off. If Clower's framework really is that of a monetary economy, then people are worse off than under barter. In any case, it can be argued that the cash-in-advance requirement postulates what should be explained; there is nothing in the model to explain why the economy uses a medium of exchange. Barter must be ruled out for money to exist and in this sense money does not dominate it.

What, then, are we to do? Basically, there are two approaches to the Clower dilemma. One is to introduce transactions costs and/or risk to explain why money is valued and used, and this is the basis of most existing work on the demand for money, examined in later chapters. Transactions costs presumably explain why we prefer our employer to pay us in money rather than in vouchers to attend lectures in, say, astrophysics, because of the extra costs of converting these vouchers into the goods which we would prefer to consume. Imperfect information enters this story, too, for the monetary exchange is likely to be conducted on more predictable terms than the planned exchange of the non-monetary commodity. How can the quality or value of a commodity be assured?

The other approach is arbitrarily to impose the cash-in-advance restriction (or alternatively insert money in the utility function),[7] and appeal to either legal restrictions or social and institutional arrangements to justify why this has been done.

Legal restrictions

The earlier requirement in the overlapping-generations approach to the effect that debts must be settled in legal tender is one example of a legal restriction designed to enforce the use of currency or paper money issued by the monetary authority. Such a requirement has been employed by 'legal restrictions' theorists as a way of getting money into the system, invoking legal arrangements such as the condition that taxes be paid in money or certain other institutional features. Among the latter might be that certain other financial assets (for instance, Treasury bills) are not finely divisible in terms of the minimum amounts that one can buy (e.g. multiples of $100,000). These minimum parcel sizes presumably act to inhibit use of the securities for monetary use.

For example, in order to account for why economic entities hold intrinsically worthless paper money, Wallace (1983) offers a legal restrictions theory of the demand for money. He suggests three relevant restrictions: (i) that central banks artificially create a demand for money (fiat currency) by forcing commercial banks to hold reserves at the central bank in the form of currency; (ii) the failure to allow private money creation; and (iii) the issuing of bonds in large denominations. If interest-bearing government bonds were issued in any denomination and there was no requirement to hold reserves in currency, then no one would hold fiat currency. Consequently, a reserves requirement and the non-divisibility of bonds are jointly required to generate a demand for money.

As counter-examples, Makinen and Woodward (1986) and White (1987) provide historical illustrations where Wallace's assertion does not appear to hold; in one case (France during the First World War) currency was preferred to a small denomination interest-bearing bond, and in the other case (Scotland under the free banking era from 1716 to 1844) there were neither required reserves nor a prohibition upon private money, yet zero-interest banknotes circulated as money. There are, of course, practical problems of calculating and paying accrued interest if small denomination bonds are used as a medium of exchange, and the same difficulties apply to the idea of private interest-bearing currency, as advocated by free bankers such as Hayek (1976*a*), King (1983), and Dowd (1988).

4.7 Conclusions

THIS chapter and the previous one have ranged over a number of areas of pure economic theory developed over two centuries. We first covered the classical model and Patinkin's critique along with the elaborations by Archibald and Lipsey and Leviatin. The last section of this chapter has brought us right up to date with Arrow–Debreu models, money in the utility function, cash in advance models, and legal restrictions theories. The unifying feature of all of these models is the Walrasian general equilibrium framework.

The major criticism of this methodology was to come from Frank Hahn (1982) who made the claim that despite the theoretical advances of the Arrow–Debreu model 'the foundations of monetary theory have not yet been laid.' His reasoning was based on the fact that the best developed model of the economy could find no room for money: 'The best developed model is, of course, the Arrow–Debreu version of a Walrasian general equilibrium. A world in which all conceivable contingent future contracts are possible neither needs nor wants intrinsically worthless money' (Hahn, 1982: 1).

The result of this critique was an attempt by Hahn and others to build a non-Walrasian model of money where money had intrinsic features that made it indispensable. The foundation for such models is a Keynesian view of money in which frictions exist and money has a distinctive and special character. In the next chapter we consider the Keynesian model in detail. It did not seek to modify or adjust the classical structure as Patinkin and Arrow and Debreu had done, but aimed to construct a completely new framework for macroeconomic analysis based on new foundations. In the process it was necessary to undermine and demolish the classical model.

Notes

1 Patinkin levelled his charge in a series of papers in the late 1940s and early 1950s. The Nobel laureates William Baumol, Gary Becker, and James Tobin were involved in the debate and Sir Dennis Robertson cast himself in the role as the defender of the faith. The debate is summarized in Mizen and Presley (1996).

2 This solution was elaborated in great detail in his book *Money, Interest and Prices*. The first edition appeared in 1956 but a revised second edition appeared in 1965 and this

is usually the version cited. Patinkin explained the workings of the real-balance effect in a microeconomic and a macroeconomic context. In this chapter we consider the microeconomic analysis for two reasons, first the microfoundations of macroeconomics has become more fashionable in recent years and, second, Patinkin's analysis is set up in a macroeconomic framework that maps most closely to a Keynesian approach, presumably because the 1950s and 1960s were the heyday of Keynesian macroeconomics, and this makes it slightly less accessible to modern readers.

3 Patinkin argues that in a system without futures markets, it is plausible that individuals would want to transfer purchasing power to the future, and where there is uncertainty about the future income streams, money would be a vehicle for doing so because of its convenience yield. There is thus a retreat from full (Arrow–Debreu) equilibrium (discussed in the next section) in two respects. One is an absence of markets in which all goods, including future goods, can be exchanged now, i.e. temporary rather than full equilibrium. The other is that there is no longer perfect information about future prices or future exchanges. The conditions for full equilibrium are examined in Arrow and Hahn (1971) and Arrow (1974).

4 Archibald and Lipsey were the first authors to consider the real-balance effect in a dynamic context. They were able to show that real-balance effects that overturned the neutrality of money were temporary. This means that money is a veil in the longer term but wealth effects arising from impulses to real balances can have temporary effects on the real sector. These results are replicated in modern classical models by impulse response functions that show wealth effects to die away over the medium term.

5 This requirement is not needed for freely available goods, such as air. Here supply exceeds demand, but the economy is not out of equilibrium because of it. Thus for equilibrium we require

$$D_i(p_1 \ldots p_{n-1}) \leq S_i(p_1 \ldots p_{n-1}) \, i = 1 \ldots n-1. \tag{4.22a}$$

for each commodity, and there is strict inequality only if $p_1 = 0$. See Arrow (1974: 260).

6 Surveys of the issues are provided by Hahn (1982), Brock (1990), and MacDonald and Milbourne (1990).

7 Feenstra (1986) shows that the method of entering money directly into the utility function can be explicitly derived from an optimizing model with transactions costs or uncertainty, and that the cash-in-advance model is a special case of the money in the utility function approach.

Chapter 5
Keynes's *General Theory*

5.1 Keynesian Monetary Economics

KEYNES provided the first significant challenge to classical theory. The new approach, largely contained in the *General Theory*, represented a break from the conventional classical wisdom, based around Say's law and the quantity theory, and the later neo-orthodox reinterpretation of Patinkin, because money was not neutral and of considerable importance for real things. In terms of monetary theory, the most fundamental issue raised by Keynes lay in his attack on the traditional separation of monetary and value theory, according to which relative prices are determined by the 'real' forces of demand and supply and the absolute price level is determined by the quantity of money and its velocity of circulation. It is he, rather than Patinkin, who first questioned this 'classical dichotomy', as it has become known, and in this, as in many other respects, the *General Theory* revolutionized economists' thinking. Most of the literature in following decades can be seen either as an application of Keynesian ideas or as a counter-attack on them.

His monetary economics delved into the psychology of the demand for money and individuals' expectations of the future. Much of this analysis centred on the motives for money, as a liquid asset, entering financial portfolios including liquid interest bearing assets—an individual's 'liquidity preference'. In this framework the interest rate takes on a new meaning as the determinant of an individual's preference between more liquid and less liquid assets, rather than as the determinant of the choice between present and future consumption (as the classicals had conventionally interpreted it).

The rate of interest is not the 'price' which brings into equilibrium the demand for resources to invest with the readiness to abstain from present consumption. It is the 'price' which equilibrates the desire to hold wealth in the form of cash with the available quantity of cash. (Keynes, 1936: 167)

The idea that an individual might have preferences over the liquidity of a portfolio based on the yield and the expectations of future yields of its constituent elements introduced a new dimension to monetary analysis and interest rate determination. It also implied limitations upon monetary policy, by placing restrictions on the efficacy of the direct and indirect mechanisms that the classicals had always relied upon. A confrontation with the classical view was inevitable because of the radically different interpretations of as the rate of interest and the ability of the economy to automatically right itself. The subsequent disagreements over policy prescriptions polarized the economics profession for more than a generation. These issues are elaborated below.

5.2 The Importance of Money

KEYNES had no doubt about the importance of money. In a little-known paper written in 1933, he outlined the task which lay before him 'to work out in some detail a monetary theory of production to supplement the real exchange theories', for 'booms and depressions are phenomena peculiar to an economy in which money is not neutral' (1933: 411). Keynes returned to this issue in chapter 17 of the *General Theory*, a chapter ignored by many, if not most, interpreters of Keynes (e.g. Patinkin, 1976). Its concerns are the differences between real exchange economics and monetary economics, and the important characteristics of money. These are matters which were taken up by general equilibrium theorists forty years later—see Ostroy (1973), Ostroy and Starr (1974), Ulph and Ulph (1975) and Hahn (1977).

Keynes commenced chapter 17 of the *General Theory* by posing the question 'wherein the peculiarity of money lies as distinct from other assets'. His answer turned on three characteristics of money: (i) its high liquidity premium and low carrying costs; (ii) its negligible or zero elasticity of production; and (iii) its negligible elasticity of substitution.

In comparing money with other assets, allowances must be made for the presence of non-pecuniary services. The total net return from an asset can be sub-divided into three elements: the pecuniary returns r_{mt}; the non-pecuniary service flow, r_{pt}; and the convenience costs (the cost of holding the asset and acquiring the pecuniary and non-pecuniary yields), r_{at}. The pecuniary return is the interest or dividend income received in the case of bonds, debentures and shares, while for capital assets and consumer durables the return is in the form of services supplied in lieu of rentals, or services which assist in production. Most assets suffer wastage over time and there are transactions costs involved in acquiring or disposing of them. Keynes called these the 'carrying costs'. Finally, there are the non-pecuniary services, summarized by the word 'liquidity', and covering attributes such as ease and speed of disposal (marketability), certainty of value at future dates (predictability), divisibility, and protection from theft. The return implicit in these services can be measured by the explicit return which must be sacrificed to acquire the asset. The net return can be written as

$$r_{nt} = r_{mt} + r_{pt} - r_{at}. \tag{5.1}$$

These own rates, as Keynes called them, may be expressed in terms of the asset itself or in terms of any other asset such as wheat or land. Normally the own rates are expressed in terms of money, so that the net return is in terms of holding a dollar of the asset per year.

Characteristically, the pecuniary yield on capital assets exceeds the convenience costs, and the non-pecuniary service flow is negligible. Stocks of finished goods usually have high holding costs relative to the expected yield and liquidity services. Money is peculiar in having a non-pecuniary service flow that exceeds its convenience costs, while its pecuniary return is either zero (in the case of cash) or often established by government regulation (in the case of demand deposits, for example).

It is an essential difference between money and all (or most) other assets that in the case of money its liquidity premium much exceeds its carrying cost, whereas in the case of other assets their carrying cost much exceeds their liquidity premium. (Keynes, 1936: 227)

Consequently, money is the asset whose own rate is the most reluctant to fall. Unlike other goods, money has no single definite price of its own which responds rapidly to economic forces in order that its market may be cleared by variations in its yield. The adjustment occurs in the prices of *other* commodities or assets, as an excess demand or an excess supply of money spills over into other markets. The 'price' of money is either 'the' rate of interest (to Keynesians), the inverse of the general price level (to monetarists) or (as noted earlier) its external purchasing power, i.e. the exchange rate that gives the price of domestic money in terms of foreign money.

To deviate somewhat at this juncture, there is the obvious question of how financial deregulation may alter this characteristic since it rests on the key institutional fact that the nominal interest return on money is fixed, usually at zero. To the extent that deregulation allows banks to pay a market-governed interest rate on bank deposits, then this part of the money supply bears a rate of return which can respond to market forces. Nevertheless, paper money and coinage still has zero interest, and to this extent an important component of the money supply retains the attribute of having a fixed return. This issue is examined later in chapter 14.

Reinforcing this attribute is money's *negligible elasticity of production*. An increase in the demand for an ordinary product is met in part by an increase in price (a lowering of the own rate) and in part by higher production, which reduces the impact upon other markets. This is not so in the case of money, because it is not produced like ordinary commodities. Under a gold standard, additions to the demand for gold will not add significantly to employment, except in the case of gold-producing countries. With fiat currency, it is normal for the government to monopolize the issue of cash.

These two features of money provide the essence of Keynes' explanation of depressions and his invalidation of the Say's Law-type proposition that the supply of labour is the demand for goods produced by labour, so that real supply and real demand are necessarily equal. Without money, an individual could save only by accumulating real goods and dissave only by disgorging accumulated goods, in both cases with little or no effect on aggregate production. But in a monetary economy, an increase in the hoarding of money means a reduction in labour effort required, and real supply can (at least temporarily) exceed real demand.

Similarly, an increase in the *supply* of money assumes special significance. Imagine that the government conducted an open market purchase of a commodity by selling some other commodity that it was storing. The price of the commodity being purchased would rise and that of the commodity being sold would fall. More production would be demanded of the commodity purchased and less of the commodity sold and, depending on the relative supply elasticities, the changes in the two outputs will tend to cancel each other out. When money is used in the open market purchase the offsetting responses do not arise and the effects run in one direction.

A third feature was seen by Keynes to reinforce the importance of shifts in the demand for money and make it the source of persistent unemployment; namely that 'it (money) has an elasticity of substitution equal, or nearly equal, to zero'. By contrast, most capital assets have a non-zero elasticity of substitution. If their price rises under the influence of expanding demand, substitutes flow in and check the rise in the value of the asset in question. In the case of money, such substitution is thought to be less likely.

Thus, not only is it impossible to turn more labour on to producing money when its labour-price rises, but money is a bottomless sink for purchasing power, when the demand for it increases, since there is no value for it at which demand is diverted, as in the case of other rent factors, to substitute some other factor for it. (Keynes, 1936: 231)

To Keynes, these three characteristics make money central to the problem of unemployment. Its liquidity premium is a 'measure of our disquietude', while the low carrying costs make it relatively costless (except for foregone earnings) to hold wealth in monetary form. A preference for the hoarding of money is not easily satisfied by other assets, and its low elasticity of production means that an increase in supply does not rise to meet an increased demand. There is a 'flaw in the price mechanism' because money is unlike other goods.

Unemployment develops, that is to say, because people want the moon;—men cannot be employed when the object of desire (i.e. money) is something which cannot be produced and the demand for which cannot be readily choked off. (Keynes 1936: 235).

These views of Keynes about the importance of money are disputed by Frank Hahn (1977). He repeats Keynes' observation that the existence of money is not necessary to repudiate Say's Law. 'Any non-reproducible asset will do, . . . land would have the same consequence and so would old masters.' According to Hahn, 'Keynes was fully aware of this and this is why he devoted so much space to the theory of choice amongst alternative stores of value'. Money is 'one of a number of non-reproducible assets. All such assets must compete with each other as well as with reproducible ones. . . . The equilibrium outcome in the labour market is of course not independent of the number of different assets there are and so the existence of money contributes to the outcome. But that . . . is all'. He concludes: 'there is nothing to suggest that in a world of costless mediation without money with say a fixed land wage, the story would be different . . . . The special properties he [Keynes] claimed to find in the demand for money turn out to make no difference in kind to any theoretical proposition'.

Keynes anticipated this criticism in part by his third characteristic of money—its low elasticity of substitution—which he introduced to 'distinguish money from other rent elements' (ibid. 231). Land shares with money the attribute of having a zero or negligible elasticity of production, but when prices rise other factors can be substituted for it. With money, there are some substitutes which involve real resources, such as the hiring of accountants and the development of cash-flow systems, but these substitutions are generally thought to be minor for small variations in the exchange value of money or over short periods of time.

Yet substitutability is a matter of degree, and the question of whether money has close substitutes or whether it is different from other assets, particularly as a store of value, is empirical. Money may have a lower elasticity of substitution than land, but more than the other non-reproducible item cited by Hahn of old masters (that is, unless new paintings or undetected counterfeits are a close substitute for old works). Also money's elasticity of substitution is not unchanging and a sophisticated financial system may be capable of throwing up substitutes for money in many forms.

Substitutability in demand is only part of the answer, for Hahn's views are far removed from the world of monetary policy. Consider Hahn's old masters, and suppose that the Bank of England were to conduct an open market purchase of securities (bonds) by selling off some of its portraits. At a formal level the effects which ensue can be described in terms much like those which would ensue from the 'sale' of money. In order to effect the transaction the price of bonds will be bid up, while the bargain prices going on art works would attract dealers in the bond market to temporarily become holders of art. But they will not wish paintings (previously money) to become a permanent component of their portfolio, and the secondary effects will commence as they sell the paintings (previously money) and reacquire securities of various types, with effects fanning out through the various credit markets. Many of the securities acquired by dealers will presumably be newly issued by investors encouraged by the lower interest rates to produce durable assets.

Nevertheless, there are important qualitative differences between the two cases. The undesirably large holdings of money are more easily disposed of than are the stocks of old masters, so that the secondary and subsequent effects of the open market operation get under way fairly quickly, and with little transaction costs. Because there are many more takers for money than there are for paintings, the effects are wide-ranging and not confined to any narrow segment of the capital market (Cagan, 1958; Yeager, 1968). In short, the 'market' for money is much better than the market for other assets. With old masters only the first-round effect and the disposal of the paintings by the bond dealers is likely to be of use to policy. With money the first round effects are minor relative to the (so-called) 'secondary' effects which reverberate through the capital market. In the USA, the income velocity of narrow money, M1, is six times a year, while transactions velocity (calculated as the ratio of bank debits to current deposits) is, phenomenally, over 100 times that figure. The first-round effects last less than a month!

5.3 The Motives for Holding Money

BUT first money has to be held, and Keynes's starting point was to ask: 'Why should anyone prefer to hold his wealth in a form which yields little or no interest to holding it in a form which yields interest [?]' (Keynes, 1936: 168).[1]

His answer was implied in the way he posed the question. He specified the decision as a choice about

what form he will hold the command over future consumption which he has reserved, whether out of current income or from previous savings. Does he want to hold it in the form of immediate, liquid command (i.e. in money or its equivalent)? Or is he prepared to part with immediate command for a specified or indefinite period, leaving it to future market conditions to determine on what terms he can, if necessary, convert deferred command over specific goods into immediate command over goods in general? In other words, what is the degree of liquidity preference? (Keynes, 1936: 166).

For the answer he turned to the motives for holding money stating:

The three divisions of liquidity-preference which we have distinguished above may be defined as depending on (i) the transactions-motive i.e. the need of cash for the current transaction of personal and business exchanges; (ii) the precautionary-motive i.e. the desire for security as to the future cash equivalent of a certain proportion of total resources; and (iii) the speculative-motive, i.e. the object of securing profit from knowing better than the market what the future will bring forth. (Keynes, 1936: 170).

The transactions motive

As a means of exchange, money does have a valuable function to perform and the first motive was the use of money for the purposes of conducting transactions in the economy.

One reason for holding cash is to bridge the interval between the receipt of income and its disbursement. The strength of this motive in inducing a decision to hold a given aggregate of cash will chiefly depend upon the amount of income and the normal length of the interval between its receipt and its disbursement. (Keynes, 1936: 195)

The relationship between money held and nominal income was regarded as essentially the same as a quantity theory equation written in the Cambridge cash balance form, $M = kp_nY$. This implied that a constant proportion of nominal income held at the beginning of the period would be run down as expenditure took place until the balances fall to zero by the time of the next payment. If expenditures were reasonably steady across the period and income was received at regular intervals then the pattern of receipt and expenditure could be shown as a saw-tooth pattern in actual money balances.

Following the receipt of an income, M, at the point of payment, balances are run down steadily as expenditure is incurred until the balance reaches zero just before the next payment of M is due. The average balance in these circumstances is given by M/2. The saw-tooth pattern and the average balance are illustrated in Figure 5.1.

In Figure 5.1 we can consider how the transactions demand for money alters with the interval between payments. If we extend the interval between payments from weekly to monthly payments, which implies an interval four times as long as before, the fourfold increase in the payment interval results in a fourfold increase in the income payment per period (to keep income constant) which entails an initial and average money balance which is four times higher than before—2M (= 4 × M/2) will be held on average over the period rather than M/2. This result follows from the assumption that the expenditure over the period occurs at the same steady rate and reduces the initial balance at the same pace as before; that is, the slope of the saw-tooth has not altered at all.

In this example, transactions balances are determined as much by institutional arrangements as by the income of the individual. Since the level of money balances must be sufficient to provide for the transactions that are expected to take place in the interval before the next pay day, the length of the payment period has an influence on the holdings of money. If the interval is a long period of time, such as a year, then average money balances will be commensurately higher.

Rarely, however, will the choice of payment intervals be in the hands of the individuals. Usually employers adopt the same interval for all their employees, following the norm for a particular employment category within their own industry, and ultimately these standards are given by custom and practice in the economy as a whole. These institutional factors can be taken as largely given at any moment of time. There is some room for individual choice in the model, but to a considerable extent the regular pattern is determined by receipts and expenditures in the form of income from salary or wage payments and outgoings from mortgage payments, standing orders and the like. Thus Keynes suggested that the transactions motive

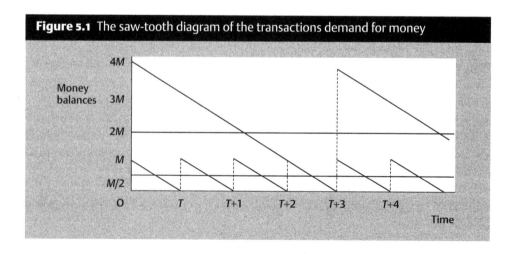

Figure 5.1 The saw-tooth diagram of the transactions demand for money

would depend on the mechanics of obtaining and delivering cash in the process of spending what has been earned. This could also involve 'the cheapness and reliability of methods of obtaining cash, when it is required, by some form of temporary borrowing, in particular by overdraft or its equivalent' (Keynes, 1936: 196).

If these same institutional features were sufficiently regular, transactions balances could be regarded as a constant proportion k of nominal income. Over the short interval which Keynes had in mind this may not be a strong assumption, but if we were to consider several decades changes to institutional arrangements would certainly become important. A relatively recent example would be the effect of the introduction of credit cards and debit cards. The proportion of money income held in cash has likely fallen as a result; payments can be placed on a credit card before paying the sum off at a later date.[2]

The precautionary motive

The second motive is clearly identified in the *General Theory* but less developed than the others. It is akin to the transactions motive but distinct from it by virtue of the fact that it is governed not by predictable and regular expenditures but by uncertain and irregular ones. For this reason it is treated as a separate motive from the transactions motive, which is entirely based on planned and expected income and expenditure. Since the motive relies on the lack of knowledge attached to the timing and magnitude of expenditures relative to the income stream it is called 'precautionary', indicating that additional balances are held for the unexpected, over and above what Keynes regards as the *normal* requirements for planned expenditures. Balances are held 'To provide for contingencies requiring sudden expenditure and for unforeseen opportunities of advantageous purchases' (Keynes, 1936: 196).

In practice, Keynes and many others have lumped the transactions and precautionary motives together on the grounds that they meet expected and unexpected transactions. Keynes put these two motives together because he wished to distinguish them from the third speculative motive, his primary innovation to the demand for money.

The speculative motive

The speculative motive is concerned with money holdings in a financial portfolio composed of only two assets, money and bonds. Bonds are risky assets which have a positive rate of return whilst money is safe but has a zero rate of return. Funds put in money represent 'immediate, liquid command', whereas in the case of bonds, as Keynes put it, future market conditions determine the terms on which deferred command over goods can be converted into immediate command over goods (see earlier quotation). Thus each holder of bonds faces a risk that the price of the bond may vary, which could be favourable (a capital gain) or unfavourable (a capital loss), and it is the response to the likelihood of a capital gain or loss relative to the interest earned on the bond that determines the demand for them. In a two-asset portfolio, money provides the alternative. Individual investors will try to avoid capital losses on bonds by holding money and will attempt to profit from capital gains by reducing money holdings, so that the demand for money will be influenced by 'the object of securing profit from knowing better than the market what the future will bring forth' (Keynes, 1936: 170).

The actual capital gain or loss is determined by the workings of the bond market where the future price of the bond is inversely related to the future interest rate. But the important thing is what is expected to happen. Investors in the bond market do not know in advance what the future interest rate or the future price will be, but they form expectations about it. If the interest rate is expected to fall relative to the present then the future price of the bonds will be higher than the current price. If interest rates are expected to rise then the future price of bonds will be lower than the current price. In a bond market where the prevailing view is that the future interest rate will rise relative to the present there will be an expectation of falling bond prices which creates an excess supply of bonds and an excess demand for money. The opposite would be true in a bond market where the majority expect the future interest rate to fall—here expected prices in the future would be above current bond prices and there would be an excess demand for bonds. Thus the demand for money, which is the important factor in the analysis, depends on the market's expectations of the future rate of interest.

In Keynes's conception, market expectations were formed on the basis of the current level of interest rates relative to what was regarded as 'normal'. If interest rates were above their normal level, then the expectation would be that they would fall in the future to bring them back in line with the norm. Conversely, if interest rates were below normal, then the expectation would be of a rise in interest rates in the future. Thus bond prices (i.e. the interest rate) are 'sticky'.[3] An interest rate above the normal rate would create expectations of rising bond prices and would raise the demand for bonds and reduce the demand for money. A rate lower than normal would entail a rise in the demand for money as the demand for bonds began to decline. The decisions would be taken by many individuals with different opinions, however, and as Keynes notes:

different people will estimate the prospects differently and any one who differs from the predominant opinion as expressed in market quotations may have a good reason for keeping liquid resources in order to profit, if he is right, from its turning out in due course that the [present discounted value of investments on the basis of the term structure of interest rates] were in a mistaken relationship to one another. (Keynes, 1936: 169).

In his 1958 paper 'Liquidity Preference as Behaviour towards Risk', James Tobin outlines a theory of liquidity preference which he considers (although some disciples of Keynes may not agree) 'essentially the original Keynesian explanation'. Drawing on Tobin's analysis, we suppose there to be a fixed level of financial wealth (W_t) which is held in either money (M_t) or bonds (B_t):

$$W_t = M_t + B_t. \tag{5.2}$$

The expectation of an investor as to the return on the portfolio, $E(RP_t)$, can be calculated as the return to money and the return to bonds in the proportion that they are held in the portfolio. Since money is non-interest bearing and safe the return to money is zero and hence the return to the portfolio will be composed of the return from bond holdings alone, made up of the interest rate and the capital gain or loss.

$$E(RP_t) = (r_t + g_t)B_t + (0)M_t = (r_t + g_t)B_t. \qquad (5.3)$$

The capital gain is the percentage change in the price of the bond between the current period and the next which can be calculated as

$$g_t = \frac{p_{t+1}^e - p_t}{p_t} \qquad (5.4)$$

and since the price of a bond is the present discounted value of future returns represented (in the case of a consol or perpetuity) as

$$p_t \cong \frac{1}{r_t}, \qquad (5.5)$$

we can substitute for p_t in the equation for g_t and obtain an expression for the expected return to the portfolio in terms of the interest rate. Thus

$$E(RP_t) = r_t + ((r_t/r_t^e) - 1) \qquad (5.6)$$

From this expression we can identify whether it is optimal to hold bonds or money and this is based on the rate of interest known as the *critical rate*. The critical rate is the rate of interest which makes the rate of return on bonds and the capital gain equal; at this rate the total return on bonds equals zero and the speculator is indifferent between bonds and money viz.

$$r_{ct} = \frac{r_t^e}{r_t^e + 1}. \qquad (5.7)$$

Once we know the critical rate we can determine the speculator's behaviour because if the current rate of interest is above the *critical rate* the expected return on bonds exceeds that on money and hence all wealth will be held in bonds. If the current rate is below the critical rate then the capital loss will eliminate any positive return from the interest on bonds and hence the speculator will hold money balances and no bonds. We may note that, in terms of the Tobin style analysis, this behaviour is determined by an individual's *definite expectations* about future interest rates, or, in other words, definite expectations about changes in the prices of capital assets (in this instance, bonds).

For the individual the result is that liquidity preference will react to the interest rate in the form of a step function, with a discrete switch between money and bonds at the critical rate. This is represented on Figure 5.2 by the switch from zero money balances to unity when measured as a proportion of total financial wealth (OW') as the interest rate falls below r_{ct} as indicated by the heavy vertical lines $LMNW'$, in terms of Tobin's analysis. Tobin goes on to note that the situation is different if there are pre-existing holdings of bonds, the value of which increases as the rate of

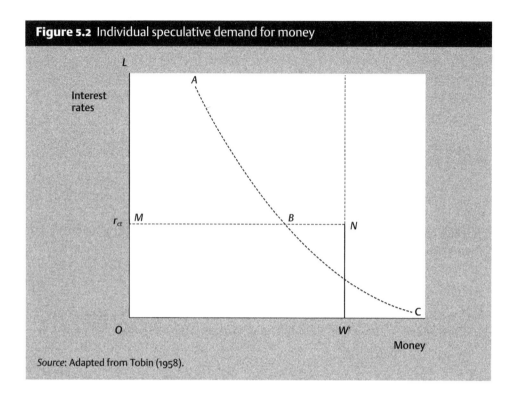

Figure 5.2 Individual speculative demand for money

Source: Adapted from Tobin (1958).

interest falls. Then the investment balances of an individual would not be constant at W' but would depend on r_t in a manner illustrated by the curve ABC. Accordingly, the step function would become $LMBC$ with the switch from zero money balances to total wealth at r_{ct}. In either form, the individual step function is quite different from the familiar smooth, continuous inverse relationship between money and interest rates.

In aggregate, individual opinions on the expected future value of the rate of interest will likely to differ and this means that there will be a spread of critical rates which will determine for each individual investor when to switch between money and bonds. The result will be something that approximates a smooth curve: 'the schedule of liquidity preference relating the quantity of money to the rate of interest is given by a smooth curve which shows the rate of interest falling as the quantity of money is increased' (Keynes, 1936: 171).

Such an aggregate relationship is shown in Figure 5.3. At actual rates above the maximum of individual critical rates the aggregate demand for money is zero, while at rates below the minimum critical rate it is equal to the total investable funds for the whole economy. Between these two extremes the demand for money varies inversely with the rate of interest r_t. This is shown as the curve $LMNW$. Strictly speaking, the curve is a step function, but if the number of investors with a range of critical rates is large it can be approximated by a curve.

When there are pre-existing holdings of bonds, the investment balances for the whole economy would follow a curve like ABC in Figure 5.3, instead of being constant

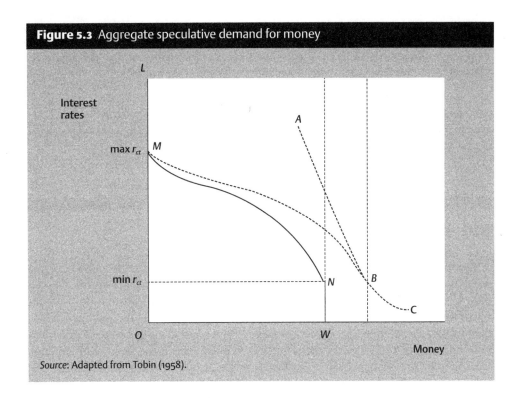

Figure 5.3 Aggregate speculative demand for money

Source: Adapted from Tobin (1958).

at *W*. The demand for money would then be described by *LMBC* in both figures. Correspondingly the demand for bonds at any interest rate is the horizontal distance between *LMBC* and *ABC*.

It is the variety of opinion which ensures that speculative activity is not destabilizing in the aggregate. If all individuals had the same critical rate of interest based on the same expectations, the rate of interest would cause no alteration in money balances up to the point that the critical rate was reached at which point there would be a wholesale switch out of one asset and into another.

[O]pinion about the future of the rate of interest may be so unanimous that a small change in present rates may cause a mass movement into cash. It is interesting that the stability of the system and its sensitiveness to changes in the quantity of money should be so dependent on the existence of a variety of opinion about what is uncertain. (Keynes, 1936: 172)

Putting all of Keynes's motives together, the demand for money depends on a transactions-precautionary motive determined mainly by the level of income and on the speculative motive based mainly on the rate of interest and expectations.

Let the amount of cash held to satisfy the transactions- and precautionary-motives be M_1, and the amount held to satisfy the speculative-motive be M_2. Corresponding to these two compartments of cash, we then have two liquidity functions L_1 and L_2. . . .

$$M = M_1 + M_2 = L_1(Y) + L_2(r),$$

where L_1 is the liquidity function corresponding to an income Y, which determines M_1, and L_2 is the liquidity function of the rate of interest r, which determines M_2. It follows that there are three matters to investigate: (i) the relation of changes in M to Y and r, (ii) what determines the shape of L_1, (iii) what determines the shape of L_2?' (Keynes, 1936: 199–200)

The demand for speculative balances was believed by Keynes to be the most significant feature of the monetary side of the *General Theory*. This was because they had a crucial impact on the transmission of monetary policy, operating through expectations via the liquidity function L_2 to the rate of interest.

5.4 Liquidity Preference Theory

LIQUIDITY preference implied a different role for the rate of interest. In the classical economic system, the rate of interest was seen as a rate of return required to equilibrate the market for capital resources. Interest encouraged the abstention from current consumption on one side (to provide the supply of funds) and encouraged the demand for investment funds on the other (by creating a favourable comparison with the rate of return on investment goods) which made the borrowing of funds worthwhile. The problem was to establish a rate of interest that would ensure that the demand for funds and their supply were equal and this occurred on the real side of the model where the return on newly acquired capital tied down the 'natural' rate of interest.

For Keynes the question was very different. He did not ask what rate of interest would be necessary to encourage individuals to forgo current consumption for consumption tomorrow. Rather, he asked how individuals would prefer to store their forgone current consumption: should it be held in money or bonds? When there are two assets this question becomes one of a preference about liquidity and is resolved by the individual who has a preference ordering that requires greater or lesser liquidity. In these circumstances the rate of interest becomes the reward for parting with liquidity, not consumption, as reflected in the liquidity preference schedule.

Many of the debates about the *General Theory* revolve around the theory of interest rate determination. Liquidity preference theory would seem to provide a very different interpretation of events from the loanable funds theory of Ohlin and Robertson. First, liquidity preference theory considers the money market, and the interest rate equates the demand for money (involving the liquidity preference schedule arising from a speculative motive) and the supply of money. Loanable funds theory concentrates on the bond market, or more strictly on the market for loanable funds, and the interest rate equilibrates the supply and demand for loans. Second, liquidity preference is a stock theory since it utilizes demand and supply functions which are specified in terms of stocks of money balances, whereas loanable funds is based on flows of funds, measuring the increase in the demand and supply of loan resources over a period of time.

Nevertheless, there is a close connection between them. In equilibrium it can be shown that whether the rate of interest is determined in the money market under stock conditions or in the bond market under flow conditions is largely semantic. Given the wealth constraint, equilibrium in one market implies equilibrium in the other.

Hicks in *Value and Capital* (1939) was the first to show the formal equivalence of the two in a full Walrasian-type system of general equilibrium. Since Walras's law permits the elimination of one of the equations in equilibrium, one can omit either the excess-demand-for-money equation, leaving a loanable-funds theory of interest, or the excess-demand-for-securities equation, leaving a liquidity preference theory of interest. This result prompted a mischievous observation by Abba Lerner. Suppose that the excess demand equation for a commodity (e.g. peanuts) is eliminated. The system then incorporates both a loanable funds and a money equation, one of which must be used to determine the price of the excluded good. What does one have then—a liquidity preference theory of peanuts?

Lerner also illustrated the equivalence of the two approaches, and we reproduce his diagrammatical analysis below renumbering his figure in line with ours (Lerner, 1939).

Keynes says that the rate of interest is the price that equates the supply and demand for cash. Professor Ohlin says that it is the price that equates the supply and demand for credit. The identity of meaning of these two propositions is shown in Figure [5.4].

At each rate of interest—and the corresponding value of the assets—people will wish to distribute their wealth in a certain proportion between cash and other assets. At a higher rate of interest, people will wish to hold less cash, partly because of the higher award for holding other assets, partly because the value of other assets shrinks relatively to the value of a given

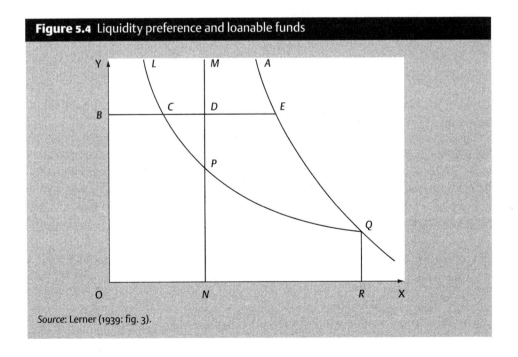

Figure 5.4 Liquidity preference and loanable funds

Source: Lerner (1939: fig. 3).

amount of money, and partly because at the higher rate of interest investment and income will be less.

Keynes calls the L curve the demand for money and the M curve the supply of money, measuring both of these in the familiar way from the Y axis towards the right. The rate of interest is determined by the equilibrium shown at P, where the demand for BC is equal to the supply BD. Professor Ohlin looks at the picture from the other side, measures his quantities from the A curve towards the left. The M curve then measures the supply of assets which is the demand for credit, and the L curve measures the demand for assets which is the supply of credit. The equilibrium giving us the rate of interest is shown at P, where the supply of credit, ED, is equal to the demand for credit, EC, and it is thus that the rate of interest is determined. Our figure shows very simply that the equation of BC to BD is the same thing as the equation of EC to ED (647–649).

Finally, Lerner comments on Hicks' treatment:

Dr Hicks emphasizes the arbitrary nature of the choice between speaking in terms of loans or of cash, declaring that, if we equate the supply and demand for money, the equation of the supply and demand for loans follows automatically, and, if we equate the latter, the former equation is otiose. This is shown very clearly in our Figure. (650)

Both 'proofs' are carried out as though the theories were built on stock concepts. Yet the loanable funds analysis is normally couched in terms of flows. What of the stock-flow distinction? Fellner and Somers (1949) showed that stock analysis and flow analysis of monetary equilibrium were in fact equivalent—stock equilibrium results in flow equilibrium, and vice versa.

Consider the loanable funds theory specified in flows. The accumulation of bond supplies can take place in two ways: through alterations to the flow demand for money or through investment; likewise the flow demand for bonds can be a result of changes to the money supply (open market operations) or saving. Thus

$$\tilde{B}_t^D \Delta M_t^S + S(r_t) \tag{5.8}$$

$$\tilde{B}_t^S = \Delta M_t^D + I(r_t). \tag{5.9}$$

This is a flow explanation of the rate of interest, which enters through the saving and investment functions, based on the loanable funds market.

Equally, a stock view can be obtained if we introduce two additional equations which explain how flows are used to adjust stocks. Investors are assumed to have a desired stock of bonds which they demand and suppliers to have a desired stock to offer to market. Adjustment equations then relate stocks to flows. If the adjustment takes place over one period, the change is actually equal to the flow demand for or supply of bonds, hence

$$\tilde{B}_t^S = ([B_t^D]^* - B_t) \tag{5.10}$$

$$\tilde{B}_t^D = ([B_t^S]^* - B_t) \tag{5.11}$$

If $\overset{N}{B_t^D} = \overset{N}{B_t^S}$, i.e. there is flow equilibrium, this implies that $[B_t^D]^* = [B_t^S]^*$ (which is a stock equilibrium condition) meaning that the stock–flow distinction is unimportant in equilibrium situations. Flow equilibrium ensures stock equilibrium and vice versa.

In disequilibrium, the situation may be very different as Johnson (1962) noted. Just as the debate between Patinkin and the classicals was sterile in equilibrium but meaningful in disequilibrium so the liquidity preference–loanable funds difference is really only an issue in disequilibrium. In disequilibrium, liquidity preference theory states that interest rates will be determined primarily in the money market with activity in the bond market mirroring events occurring elsewhere. Under loanable funds the reverse is true. Fellner and Somers argued that, as the rate of interest is the price of securities, it is more sensible to regard it as determined by the demand for and supply of securities than by the demand for and supply of money. By contrast, Klein (1950) maintained that the rate of interest would change in response to an excess demand for or supply of money, not an excess supply of or demand for securities.[4]

Does it matter? The answer must be in the affirmative, precisely because the *General Theory* was written to address disequilibrium situations such as the great Depression of the 1930s. The conclusions it draws are most applicable to these and similar circumstances, and many of the points have re-emerged in the context of the Japanese economy in the late 1990s (IMF, 1998; Krugman, 1998). An important feature of the determination of the rate of interest in the money market by liquidity preference schedule is the possibility of constraints to monetary policy. One such constraint—the liquidity trap—prevents the interest rate from falling below some minimum level.

In nominal terms, interest rates cannot fall far below zero because of the existence of cash. No-one would invest $100 today to receive only $99 in a year's time, say, given the alternative of holding $100 in riskless cash. But if holding currency is seen to be risky and costly because of possible theft or loss, people may prefer to hold bank deposits or bills, even if these assets have a negative rate of interest. In terms of Equation 5.1, a non-pecuniary service flow may offset the lack of a pecuniary return.

However, a liquidity trap is not about what is technically feasible but is governed by expectations of future rates of interest. Once the rate of interest falls to some low level there may no longer be anyone who believes that it is likely to fall in the future, rather the opposite situation is more likely, as everyone will be expecting a rise in interest rates in the future. In effect, all individuals are considered to have passed their critical rate of interest and to have shifted their portfolios into money balances. Since an interest rate rise is expected, the market is anticipating a fall in bond prices relative to the currently high price, and a capital loss for bond-holders. No one can then be persuaded to hold bonds and increases in the supply of money will be willingly held at the prevailing (low) rates of interest. A money supply increase will be 'absorbed' by an increase in the income velocity of circulation of money (in the language of the quantity theory of money). In practical terms, this represents a scenario in which a unanimity of expectations has been created by the extremely low level of the interest rate relative to the normal rate anticipated.

How realistic a possibility is the liquidity trap? Keynes (1936, p. 207) refers to 'the possibility ... that ... liquidity preference may become virtually absolute' but went on to add: 'whilst this limiting case might become practically important in future, I know of no example of it hitherto.' (1936: 207).

Empirical studies got bogged down on the question of whether 'absolute liquidity preference' refers to the slope or the elasticity of the liquidity preference function, but on either score 'the evidence lends little or no support to the 'trap' (Meltzer, 1963: 549). Nevertheless, the existence of a liquidity trap in Japan in 1998 seemed real enough to the IMF:

> The very low level of nominal short-term interest rates in Japan places an important constraint on the extent to which monetary policy can be used to stimulate economic activity. In general, no amount of monetary easing can drive interest rates on risk-free assets significantly below zero, given that the (zero) return on holding cash would dominate that on assets yielding a negative nominal return. As nominal interest rates reach zero, then, investors would choose to hold all of their financial wealth in cash rather than in interest-bearing assets, implying that the supply of loanable funds would also fall to zero. Keynes termed this constraint on monetary policy the 'liquidity trap' ... Given that interest rates in Japanese money markets are already below $\frac{1}{2}$ of 1 per cent, there is little scope for the monetary authorities to further reduce short-term interest rates (1998: 70).[5]

5.5 Keynes and the Classics

LIQUIDITY preference and the liquidity trap were central to Keynes's attack on classical orthodoxy. He had plenty of practical objections to the classical economic policy prescription of cutting real wages to remove involuntary unemployment. For one thing, there was the observation that wage bargains are made in terms of money wages, not in terms of the real wages to which traditional analysis of the labour market relates. Workers will usually resist reductions in money wages. But more important was his position that real wages are not determined by the nominal wage derived from the labour market alone, but in conjunction with the general price level in the whole economy. An individual worker can reduce his real wage by lowering money wages, but generalized wage cuts may be another matter. Cuts to money wages may merely see prices change in almost the same proportion, leaving the real wage and the level of unemployment practically the same as before. Alvin Hansen likened this to a baseball crowd: 'if *everyone* stands up in the bleachers, no one will be able to see any better than before' (1949: 119).

These were important practical considerations outlined in chapter 2 of the *General Theory*, but they were not in themselves enough. Keynes realised that to kill an idea he needed a new idea—a new theory. He had first to show what was wrong with the logic of the classical position, and then erect a new framework in its place. This was the burden of the rest of the *General Theory*, and his new theory of money was essential to both goals.

The first step was to establish that the classical view of there being no obstacle to full employment depended crucially on acceptance of the classical theory of the rate of interest. His starting point was the Say's Law doctrine that 'supply creates its own demand' and its corollary 'the axiom of parallels' that an individual act of saving (abstaining from consumption) inevitably leads to a matching act of investment (supplying consumption to be invested in the production of capital wealth). Keynes argued that there is no necessary nexus between the two decisions. Under classical theory, employment depends on Say's Law, but achievement of Say's Law relies on the rate of interest being determined entirely in the market for loans and being the variable which brings savings and investment into equality. If this theory of interest breaks down, then so too does the classical theory of employment.

I consider that the difference between myself and the classicals lies in the fact that they regard the rate of interest as a non-monetary phenomenon, so that an increase in the inducement to invest would raise the rate of interest irrespective of monetary policy—though they might concede that monetary policy was capable of producing a temporary evaporating effect. (1973, xiv: 80)

Keynes's own sequence is quite different, and effectively reverses the 'axiom of parallels' (as he called it) by which an increase in saving leads to a matching increase in investment. Rather than supply creating its own demand, demand creates its own supply; investment rather than savings becomes the driving force. As Meade put it: 'Keynes's intellectual revolution was to shift economists from thinking normally in terms of a model of reality in which a dog called *savings* wagged his tail labelled *investment* to thinking in terms of a model in which a dog called *investment* wagged his tail labelled *savings*' (1975: 82).

If we start (as Keynes did) with the propensity to consume, employment depends on the quantity of investment. Given the marginal efficiency of capital, investment depends on the rate of interest which, given the quantity of money, depends on liquidity preference. Since the rate of interest is determined in the market for money, and interest is the reward for parting with liquidity, the greater is the preference for holding savings in the form of money, the greater is the rate of interest required for giving up liquidity. Liquidity preference may keep the interest rate too high for the full employment level of investment to be generated. The interest rate problem prevents supply from creating its own demand.[6]

Nowadays our views on all of this are conditioned by the synthesis and diagrammatic representation of the Keynesian and classical position in the form of the IS-LM model by Hicks (1937) and Hansen (1949, 1953). The attraction of the IS-LM model was its versatility and simplicity which opened the debate to the wider economics profession and made it the workhorse of applied macroeconomics. The 'astonishing performance'[7] of Hick's article 'Mr Keynes and the Classics', coming so soon after the *General Theory* was published,[8] was to clarify and to bring to a broad (and sustained) measure of agreement, what the classical and the Keynesian theories really were saying. It also indicated some of the essential differences between the two approaches using a common apparatus—the IS-LM diagram. It had initially been unclear whether the *General Theory* was really more general than the 'true' classical model or the 'representative' classical model based on Pigou's theory of employment. Certainly Keynes's was not a general equilibrium model, and this was where Hicks's IS-LM came in, as the most dominant and long-lasting of several attempts to put the *General Theory* into equations and diagrams.

Rather than provide the reader with a potted account of Hicks's argument, we reproduce at length below some key passages from his original article (page numbers come from the American Economic Association re-publication and again we have taken the liberty of altering the figure number):

Now let us assume the 'Cambridge Quantity equation'—that there is some definite relation between Income and the demand for money. Then, approximately, and apart from the fact that the demand for money may depend not only upon total Income, but also upon its distribution between people with relatively large and relatively small demands for balances, we can write

$$M = kI.$$

As soon as k is given, total Income is therefore determined.

In order to determine I_x, we need two equations. One tells us that the amount of investment (looked at as demand for capital) depends upon the rate of interest:

$$I_x = C(i).$$

This is what becomes the marginal-efficiency-of-capital schedule in Mr Keynes's work.

Further, Investment = Saving. And saving depends upon the rate of interest and, if you like, Income. $\therefore I_x = S(i,I)$. (Since, however, Income is already determined, we do not need to bother about inserting Income here unless we choose.)

Taking them as a system, however, we have three fundamental equations,

$$M = kI, I_x = C(i), I_x = S(i,I),$$

to determine three unknowns, $I, I_x, i \ldots$

As against the three equations of the classical theory,

$$M = kI, I_x = C(i), I_x = S(i,I),$$

Mr Keynes begins with three equations,

$$M = L(i), I_x = C(i), I_x = S(I).$$

These differ from the classical equations in two ways. On the one hand, the demand for money is conceived as depending upon the rate of interest (Liquidity Preference). On the other hand, any possible influence of the rate of interest on the amount saved out of a given income is neglected. Although it means that the third equation becomes the multiplier equation, which performs such queer tricks, nevertheless this second amendment is a mere simplification, and ultimately insignificant. It is the liquidity preference doctrine which is vital.

For it is now the rate of interest, not income, which is determined by the quantity of money. The rate of interest set against the schedule of the marginal efficiency of capital determines the value of investment; that determines income by the multiplier. Then the volume of employment (at given wage-rates) is determined by the value of investment and of income which is not saved but spent upon consumption goods.

It is this system of equations which yields the startling conclusion, that an increase in the inducement to invest, or in the propensity to consume, will not tend to raise the rate of interest, but only to increase employment. In spite of this, however, and in spite of the fact that quite a large part of the argument runs in terms of this system and this system alone, *it is not the General Theory*. We may call it, if we like, Mr Keynes's *special theory*. The General Theory is something appreciably more orthodox . . .

In order to elucidate the relation between Mr Keynes and the 'Classics,' we have invented a little apparatus . . .

With that apparatus at our disposal, we are no longer obliged to make certain simplifications which Mr Keynes makes in his exposition. We can reinsert the missing i in the third equation, and allow for any possible effect of the rate of interest upon saving; and, what is much more important, we can call in question the sole dependence of investment upon the rate of interest, which looks rather suspicious in the second equation. Mathematical elegance would suggest that we ought to have I and i in all three equations, if the theory is to be really General. Why not have them there like this:

$$M = L(I,i), \ I_x = C(I,i), \ I_x = S(I,i)?$$

The Generalized General Theory can then be set out in this way. Assume first of all a given total money Income. Draw a curve CC showing the marginal efficiency of capital (in money terms) at that given Income; a curve SS showing the supply curve of saving at that *given* Income (Figure [5.5]). Their intersection will determine the rate of interest which makes savings equal to investment at that level of income. This we may call the 'investment rate.'

If Income rises, the curve SS will move to the right; probably CC will move to the right too. If SS moves more than CC, the investment rate of interest will fall; if CC more than SS, it will rise. (How much it rises and falls, however, depends upon the elasticities of the CC and SS curves.)

The IS curve (drawn on a separate diagram) now shows the relation between Income and the corresponding investment rate of interest. It has to be confronted (as in our earlier constructions) with an LL curve showing the relation between Income and the 'money' rate of interest; only we can now generalise our LL curve a little. Instead of assuming, as before, that the supply of money is given, we can assume that there is a given monetary system—that up to a point, but only up to a point, monetary authorities will prefer to create new money rather than allow interest rates to rise. Such a generalised LL curve will then slope upwards only gradually—the elasticity of the curve depending on the elasticity of the monetary system (in the ordinary monetary sense).

As before, Income and interest are determined where the IS and LL curves intersect—where the investment rate of interest equals the money rate. Any change in the inducement to invest or the propensity to consume will shift the IS curve; any change in liquidity preference or monetary policy will shift the LL curve. If, as the result of such a change, the investment rate is raised above the money rate, Income will tend to rise; in the opposite case, Income will tend to fall; the extent to which Income rises or falls depends on the elasticities of the curves.

When generalised in this way, Mr Keynes's theory begins to look very like Wicksell's; this is of course hardly surprising. There is indeed one special case where it fits Wicksell's construction absolutely. If there is 'full employment' in the sense that any rise in Income immediately calls forth a rise in money wage rates; then it is possible that the CC and SS curves may be moved to the right to exactly the same extent, so that IS is horizontal. (I say possible, because it is not unlikely, in fact, that the rise in the wage level may create a presumption that wages will rise again later on; if so, CC will probably be shifted more than SS, so that IS will be upward sloping.) However that may be, if IS is horizontal, we do have a perfectly Wicksellian construction; the investment rate becomes Wicksell's natural rate, for in this case it may be thought of as determined by real causes; if there is a perfectly elastic monetary system, and the

Figure 5.5 The generalized *General Theory*

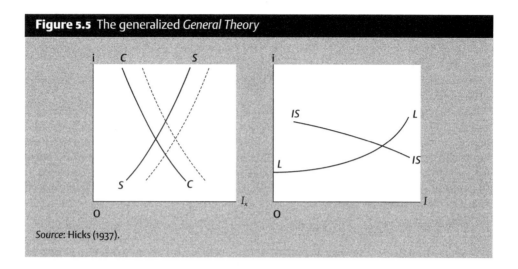

Source: Hicks (1937).

money rate is fixed below the natural rate, there is cumulative inflation; cumulative deflation if it is fixed above.

This, however, is now seen to be only one special case; we can use our construction to harbour much wider possibilities. If there is a great deal of unemployment, it is very likely that $\partial C/\partial I$ will be quite small; in that case IS can be relied upon to slope downwards. This is the sort of Slump Economics with which Mr Keynes is largely concerned. But one cannot escape the impression that there may be other conditions when expectations are tinder, when a slight inflationary tendency lights them up very easily. Then $\partial C/\partial I$ may be large and an increase in Income tends to raise the investment rate of interest. In these circumstances, the situation is unstable at any given money rate; it is only an imperfectly elastic monetary system—a rising LL curve—that can prevent the situation getting out of hand altogether. (Hicks, 1937: 463–475)

What comes through in these extracts is the remarkable freshness of the analysis. Nowadays we would use Y rather than I for income, I rather than I_x for investment and LM instead of LL (LM stands for liquidity preference = money supply). In other respects, however, little else has changed and this is an indication of the extent to which Hicks shaped the subsequent literature. Moreover, Hicks's treatment was very much better than what one typically learns today. He allows for elasticity in the money supply function (and correctly, too, only up to a point) due to interest rate policies followed by the central bank. In addition, Keynes's theory is linked with that of Wicksell as well as with the Cambridge quantity theorists (Hicks cited Marshall, Lavington and Pigou).

The issue which has come through most strongly is that Hicks's 'generalized' system has room both for Keynes's 'special theory'—in which saving is determined by income, investment is relatively interest-inelastic, and liquidity preference rules interest rates—and also for at least some versions of the 'Treasury View' which Keynes wrote the *General Theory* to refute. In the IS-LM system, everything depends on the slopes of the curves. Keynes's theory and the classical analysis emerge as 'special cases' of the true 'general theory', with Keynes's special case considered to be the most useful for policy.

Perhaps this is why Keynes, upon reading 'Mr Keynes and the Classics', wrote to Hicks 'I have found it interesting and really have next to nothing to say by way of criticism' (*Collected Writings*, xiv: 80), despite publishing soon afterwards a restatement of the *General Theory* which emphasized uncertainty, the indefinite character of actual expectations, and the effect on market decisions of all sorts of vague doubts and fluctuating states of confidence and courage (Keynes, 1937)—all of these factors would seem to be at some variance with the static nature of Hicks's article.

Interestingly, Robertson (1937) seemed to make many of the same points, although he blamed Keynes as well as Hicks. Robertson liked the simplicity of IS-LM (and had earlier been successful in persuading Hicks to change some aspects which had misrepresented the classical position). However, the real issue was the appropriateness of the IS-LM model as a mechanism for examining the disagreements between Keynes and the classics. Since IS and LM curves defined equilibrium conditions they could not be used to resolve the liquidity preference–loanable funds debate, as the two theories were indistinguishable in equilibrium. Another question to be resolved was whether a liquidity trap existed, but this was secondary to whether the determination of the interest rate took place in the market for money or for loans. Keynes (and Hicks as well) simplified matters down to a money–bonds choice, but for the classicals there was a fundamental connection between the rate of interest and the holding of real assets. In the classical framework, the interest rate was determined in the productive sector and to isolate money and bonds from real capital was entirely inappropriate.

Pigou's reaction was more concerned with the possibility that Keynes's work could imply that unemployment equilibrium could persist. He noted:

The architects of [classical political economy] never had any doubt that, provided only thorough-going competition exists among wage-earners, there must be a tendency towards full employment, and, apart from changes and frictions, there must actually be full employment. (Pigou, 1945: 20)

Despite this strong statement, Pigou admitted that he was not in favour of 'attacking the problem of unemployment by manipulating wages rather than by manipulating demand' (1945: v). Rather his concern was with diagnosis, not policy, and his argument rested on the basis that if consumption was determined by real wealth rather than current income then wealth effects ('Pigou effects') could raise the income-interest rate combination (IS curve) and achieve a full employment equilibrium even with the liquidity trap blocking interest rate falls. An increase in real wealth would lead to a rise in consumption which, as one of the determinants of the IS curve, would cause the IS curve to shift to the right. Wealth effects would come from the impact of falling prices in raising the real value of existing money value claims against the government (and overseas) sector (if prices fell enough anyone holding a dollar bill could be effectively a millionaire) producing a version of the real balance effect upon goods markets which we have already seen in the work of Patinkin.[9]

5.6 Hicks and the Term Structure

THE discussion so far has been presented in terms of a single interest rate. Obviously, however, there is a whole array of interest rates in the market. Suppose that we continue with the assumption that the only forms of wealth are paper assets and money. Paper assets can nevertheless be of two kinds: short-term and long-term. Correspondingly we have a short and a long interest rate. What governs the relationship between short-term and long-term interest rates, or in other words, the term structure of interest rates?[10]

Keynes (*General Theory*: 167) defined the rate of interest as 'the reward for parting with liquidity for a specified period' and went on to note that 'it is convenient to mean by the rate of interest the complex of the various rates of interest current for different periods of time, ie. for debts of different maturities' (ibid. 167 n. 2). It would seem to follow that just as Keynes said that liquidity preference would give an advantage to cash over bonds, so liquidity preference would provide an advantage to short-term over long-term securities, as a result of which holders would demand a smaller reward for holding shorts.

Consequently, in the same way that the 'interest rate' equilibrates the net return to holding money and 'securities', the term structure of interest rate equilibrates the net return to holding securities of varying terms to maturity and money. Keynes used liquidity preference to describe a preference of the market, abstracting from differences in yield, for assets that are immune to capital losses produced by interest rate changes. Since the risk of capital losses attributable to holding securities is directly related to the term to maturity, security yields ought also to vary directly with terms to maturity. The shorter the term to maturity of a security, the smaller is its vulnerability to capital loss, and hence the greater its liquidity and the smaller the yield differential between that security and money. Therefore, by implication, liquidity preference constitutes a theory of the term structure of interest rates.

This extension of liquidity preference theory in this way to the term structure was supported by both Lusher (1942) and Lerner (1944) and, combined with risk aversion, it implies a positively sloped yield curve i.e. long rates higher than short rates. The argument is that liquidity preference treats the interest rate as the price for sacrificing liquidity, and the longest securities, where more liquidity is sacrificed, should always bear the greatest return.

In fact, this was the yield curve pattern which ruled in the USA continuously from 1931 to the end of the 1950s, but downward sloping segments re-emerged in the 1960s and have become commonplace in recent decades. Durand's (1942) analysis of high-grade corporate bonds from 1900 to 1942 showed that yield curves sloped strongly upward in thirteen years, were close to horizontal in twelve years, and clearly declined in seventeen years. Such evidence runs counter to the view that the yield curve must always be positively sloped.

The main alternative, and by far the most widely accepted explanation of the term structure, is based on the expectations hypothesis or the modified version of it, both set out by Hicks in *Value and Capital* (1939). Simply stated, the unmodified version of this theory runs essentially as follows. If one-year rates are now 1 per cent and if one-year rates are expected to be 3 per cent next year, then two-year rates today will have to be in the neighbourhood of their average, 2 per cent. Only such a relationship can equalise returns for a two-year investment by the two avenues available: the purchase of a two-year security, or investment in a one-year obligation followed by reinvestment in another. Though individuals may not all be able to invest for the full two-year period, speculators will force the approximate equality.

This example may be generalized by stating that long rates will tend to be an 'average' of expected short-term rates over the intervening period. Because of compounding this is a complex kind of weighted average. It should be noted from the generalization that it implies expected yields over any given holding period, including capital gains or losses, must be equal on all securities, long or short. If expectations are uniform and held with perfect confidence, securities of different term become perfect substitutes for one another. One important implication of this theory is that from the yield curve at a given time it is possible to derive or 'dig out' the future short-term rates expected by the market up to the maturity of the longest security on the yield curve. The corollary is that there is nothing to prevent the yield curve from sloping either positively or negatively, since long rates are modified averages of shorts.[11]

The formula relating longs and shorts derives from Hicks (although the expectations theory itself dates back to Irving Fisher, 1930). His procedure is to equate the receipts that might be obtained by two investment procedures—one in a single long (option 1) and the other in a sequence of shorts (option 2)—assuming that all funds are retained in the investment until ultimate maturity of the long-term security. That is, interest is compound, and coupons are reinvested as they are received (and at the same rate). The first strategy available to an investor with P to spend, and an intended holding period of n years, is the option to buy an n-year bond. The maturity value of option 1 is $P_1 (1 + R)^n$, and the maturity value of option 2 is P_2 (which equals P_1 by hypothesis) multiplied by $(1+ r_1) (1+ r_2) \ldots (1+ r_n)$. Setting these two values equal to one another and cancelling out the P_1 we obtain Hicks's equation:

$$(1 + R)^n = (1 + r_1)(1 + r_2) \ldots (1 + r_n). \tag{5.12}$$

Solving this for R we obtain:

$$R = [(1 + r_1)(1 + r_2) \ldots (1 + r_n)]^{\frac{1}{n}} - 1. \tag{5.13}$$

where P represents principal, $r_1, r_2 \ldots \ldots r_n$ represent the series of assumed short rates, and R represents the long rate which is equivalent for the investor to a sequence of short-term investments.

Viewing the term structure of interest rates at any point in time as containing an implicit set of forward interest rates and calculating the long rate as this average of them is, strictly speaking, a matter of arithmetic only. The expectations hypothesis provides economic content to the tautology by treating the forward rates as *unbiased* estimates of expected future rates (Meiselman, 1962). If, in fact, forward and future rates are identical, then any given structure accurately predicts all future and for-ward interest rates. An upward-sloping yield curve means that future interest rates would tend to be higher than current, and conversely for a declining yield curve.

But Hicks argued that forward rates are *biased* estimates of the relevant expected future rate, due to the presence of liquidity preference. Each forward rate is com-posed of two conceptually separate elements: (*i*) the expected rate, where expected is defined as the mathematical expectation, and (*ii*) some positive risk or liquidity premium. The effect of the latter is to make each forward rate a biased estimator of the relevant expected future rate and to be higher than the expected rate by the amount of the risk premium. This is the result of risk aversion, causing some bor-rowers to prefer to borrow for a long rather than a short period of time. Because of this 'constitutional weakness', short-term and long-term securities are imperfect substitutes.

The forward market for loans (like the forward market for commodities) may be expected to have a constitutional weakness on one side, a weakness which offers an opportunity for spec-ulation. If no extra return is offered for long lending, most people (and institutions) would prefer to lend short, at least in the sense that they would prefer to hold their money on deposit in some way or other. But this situation would leave a large excess of demands to borrow long which would not be met. Borrowers would thus tend to offer better terms in order to persuade lenders to switch over into the long market (that is to say, enter the forward market). A lender who did this would be in a position exactly analogous to that of a speculator in a commodity market. He would only come into the long market because he expected to gain by so doing, and to gain sufficiently to offset the risk incurred.

The forward rate of interest for any particular future week . . . is thus determined . . . at that level which just tempts a sufficient number of 'speculators' to undertake the forward contract. It will have to be higher than the short rate expected by those speculators to rule in that week, since otherwise, they would get no compensation for the risk they are incurring; it will, indeed, have to exceed it by a sufficient amount to induce the marginal speculator to undertake the risk. The forward rate will thus exceed the expected rate by a risk premium which corresponds exactly to 'normal backwardation' of the commodity markets. If short rates are not expected to change in the future, the forward rate will exceed the current short rate by the extent of the premium; if short rates are expected to rise, the excess will be greater than this normal level; it is only if short rates are expected to fall that the forward rates can lie below the current rate.

The same rules must apply to the long rates themselves, which . . . are effectively an average of the forward rates. (Hicks, 1946: 146–7)

In effect, Hicks looks to an amalgam of expectations and liquidity preference theory because the term market for loans is dominated by the lender's side of the market, where lenders are viewed as essentially speculators who have risk-aversion, and who regard long loans as riskier than short loans. They therefore require compensation for providing borrowers with 'insurance', or a 'hedge', against the consequences of interest rate changes which takes the form of a risk or illiquidity premium needed as an inducement to hold a longer-term security. Viewed alternatively, liquidity pref-erence provides an advantage to short-term securities, over long, as a result of which holders demand a smaller pecuniary reward for holding shorts.

Under this modified version, the actual yield curve is composed of expected future short-term rates and liquidity premiums for longer-term commitments. Algebraically, the liquidity premiums are expressed by adding the term L to expected short-term yields in the basic equation, i.e.

$$(1 + R)^n = (1 + r_1)(1 + r_2 + L_2)\ldots(1 + r_n + L_n) \tag{5.14}$$

There is then the question of the nature of the liquidity premia. Are they relatively constant or do they vary with the level of interest rates? Are the premia relatively stable over time?

Figure 5.6 based on Kessel (1965), indicates two possibilities. In both panels, the liquidity premium (L) curve is shown rising with term to maturity. This component of observed interest rates could, conceptually, slope either positively or negatively, and may change from one period to another. The r_1 and r_2 curves represent the yield curve as it would be under an unmodified expectation hypothesis, the first when current short-term rates are low and the other when they are high. Observed yields at any point in time would be the sum of the appropriate L and r curves. The result of the configuration in panel A is that yield curves could take shapes between R_1 and R_2, a majority being positively sloped because of the positively sloped L curve assumed. But in times when rates are very high relative to historical standards the dominance of the expectations component may produce negatively sloped curves like R_2 even if L does exhibit positive slope. Panel B presents an alternative possibility. If the L curve is much more sharply curved at short maturities and then flattens

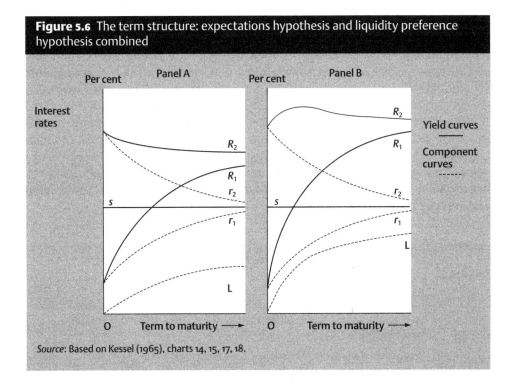

Figure 5.6 The term structure: expectations hypothesis and liquidity preference hypothesis combined

Source: Based on Kessel (1965), charts 14, 15, 17, 18.

rapidly, and if the r curve resembles r_2, the combination may well produce a 'hump' in the intermediate to short-term range. Such humped curves have been observed quite often at times of high rates in recent decades.

A composite analysis of expectations and liquidity preference along these lines has considerable intuitive appeal on at least two counts. First, it represents a marriage (not unlike Hicks's IS–LM) of Keynesian and neoclassical theory in which both elements retain some explanatory power. Second, the modification provides a ready rationale for the four main yield-curve shapes encountered in practice: upward-sloping, downward-sloping, horizontal, and humped. Moreover, one can allow for the liquidity preference component to vary in both intensity and form from one time period to another. Generally speaking, empirical testing of the term structure supports this modified framework. While expectations remain the dominant influence, the pure form is usually rejected. There is an upward bias, but liquidity premia do not increase uniformly over the whole span of forward rates, and appear to vary over time. Nevertheless, liquidity premia do seem to exist in some form, along with a variety of other factors such as taxation and institutional preferences (preferred habitats).[12]

5.7 Conclusions

KEYNES provided a psychological underpinning to the decision to hold money when interest-bearing alternatives were available. The simple delineation of the motives was to uncover a completely new theory of the rate of interest and consequently of the role and scope of monetary policy transmission to real economic activity. This created a breach with the dominant classical theory and provoked a defensive reaction from its supporters such as Robertson and Pigou. Hicks forged the bridge between the two approaches in terms of both the level and structure of interest rates. In the immediate post-war period these ideas became the common currency of macroeconomists. In monetary theory this consensus developed into a search for microfoundations for the Keynesian motives and it is to this work, principally by the three Nobel laureates, William Baumol, Hicks (again) and James Tobin that we now turn.

Notes

1   This echoes the question of Hicks: 'What has to be explained is the decision to hold assets in the form of barren money, rather than in interest—or profit-yielding securities.' Hicks (1935:18).

2   Even so, we should note the argument of Tobin (1958):

The traditional theory of the velocity of money has, however, probably exaggerated the invariance of the institutions determining the extent of lack of synchronisation between individual receipts and expenditures. It is no doubt true that such institutions as the degree of vertical integration of production and the periodicity of wage salary, dividend, and tax payments are slow to change. But other relevant arrangements can be adjusted in response to money rates. For example, there is a good deal of flexibility in the promptness and regularity with which bills are rendered and settled.

Hence the demand for narrow money balances continues to be a subject for econometric research notwithstanding the extent of financial innovation since Keynes's time.

3   As Kaldor (1939) noted: 'It is . . . not so much the uncertainty concerning future interest rates as the inelasticity of interest expectations which is responsible for Mr Keynes' "liquidity preference function"'(1939: 15).

4   In a dynamic context, an excess demand for money does not necessarily imply an excess supply of securities, since it may be accompanied by an excess supply of goods. (Johnson, 1962).

5   What constitutes a very low level? Obviously that depends on people's expectations. Historically, we may observe that the lowest level to which the Federal Reserve Bank of New York's discount rate was reduced during the 1930s was 1%, while yields on prime commercial paper of 4–6 months fell to a low of 0.56% in 1939. During Britain's period of 'cheap money' from June 1932 to November 1951, Bank rate remained at 2% (except for a brief time at the outbreak of the Second World War). By comparison, at the end of September 1998, overnight interest rates in Japanese money markets had fallen to 0.20% p.a. In November 1998 nominal rates actually fell below zero so that bondholders were paying banks to hold their Japanese investments!

6   While this reasoning was enshrined in the *General Theory*, Keynes's ideas had been evolving for some years. In the three Harris Foundation Lectures given at the University of Chicago in June 1931, Keynes provided 'An Economic Analysis of Unemployment'. The gist of the argument was that the interest rate was too high. Falling marginal productivity of capital required falling interest rates, but the Federal Reserve imposed tight money in 1929 just when cheaper money was needed, sparking off a worldwide credit contraction (1973, xiii: 343–67, esp. 351).

7   The description is that of Robert Skidelsky (1996).

8   The *General Theory* was published in February 1936, and Hicks's paper was read to the Econometric Society in September 1936.

9   In fact, Patinkin originally called his real balance effect a 'Pigou effect'. See Patinkin (1965: 19, n. 13). Patinkin called it a 'bad terminological choice'. Pigou effects come from 'outside' assets, i.e. outside money and government bonds, not just from real money balances. The distinction between 'outside' (i.e. base) money and 'inside' (i.e. credit) money owes to Gurley and Shaw (1960).

10   Some definitions may be useful.

  Yield curve—a yield curve is a graphical representation of the pattern of redemption yields ruling on securities of varying terms to maturity.

Redemption Yield—by redemption yield we refer to that uniform rate of discount which, when applied to the expected stream of receipts to be obtained from holding a security until its redemption, just suffices to equate the value of this expected stream of receipts to the current market price of the security.

Holding Period—the term 'holding period' is applied to the period over which an investor intends to hold securities.

'Short' and 'Long' Rates—the term 'short' rate of interest is the rate of return on a bond with a short-term to maturity, a 'long' rate is the rate on long bonds. The difference is arbitrary (provided short bonds are shorter than long bonds).

11 The following appear to be the basic assumptions of the expectations theory:

(1) All the securities to be examined are identical in every respect except their term to maturity, and possibly their redemption yield and coupon rate. They are all riskless, look and smell the same, and so on. This assumption guarantees that there should be no other reason, outside the scope of the theory, for preferring shorter to longer bonds or vice-versa.

(2) Investors are 'rational' i.e. they aim to maximise the net expected yield from investing in securities, over any specified holding period.

(3) Investors unanimously hold with confidence a set of expectations about future short rates.

(4) There is perfect arbitrage between securities of different terms. There are no obstacles to switching from long to short bonds or vice versa. We neglect transactions costs and assume away all other legal, financial, etc. deterrents to perfect arbitrage.

12 A brief summary of the theories and evidence is given in Malkiel (1992).

Chapter 6
Portfolio Theory

6.1 The Nature of Portfolio Analysis

PORTFOLIO theory is a central feature of modern monetary and financial economics. From its origins as a way of thinking about how investors cope with risky assets, it has developed into a complete branch of economics in its own right. The purpose of this chapter is to introduce the use of portfolio approaches from the initial work of Hicks and others through to the Baumol–Tobin results and beyond.[1] The approach will give new insights into the three motives for holding money identified by Keynes and in this respect it is an extension of the Keynesian view of monetary economics.

Before considering the first developments by Hicks, it is worth summarizing the common features of almost all modern portfolio analysis.

1. Since portfolio theory involves choice between assets there are a minimum of two assets in the choice set and often three or more. The theory involves the determination of choice between one asset and the other(s); assets can be real or financial, and are regarded as substitutes.
2. It is implicit in (1) that the assets differ in their characteristics as to risk and return. The characteristics of the assets are summarized by the expected yield and a measure of 'risk', usually described following Markowitz by the variance or the standard deviation of the returns. This approach is referred to as the 'mean-variance approach' to portfolio allocation. The construction of the portfolio depends on the 'return' and the 'risk' to each asset and these individual characteristics will apply to the portfolio as a whole in proportion to the size of the holding of the assets in the portfolio. Thus, the expected return to the portfolio will be:

$$E(R) = p_1 E(R_1) + p_2 E(R_2) + \ldots + p_n E(R_n), \tag{6.1}$$

where p_i = proportion of portfolio made up of asset i; and $E(R_i)$ is the return to asset i, and evidently $\sum_{i=1}^{n} p_i = 1$. Likewise, the variance of the return to the portfolio is

$$V(R) = p_1^2 V(R_1) + p_2^2 V(R_2) + \ldots + p_n^2 V(R_n) \tag{6.2}$$

3. Economic investors will tend to hold mixed portfolios. Different characteristics as to risk and return make combinations of assets in the portfolio desirable unless investors have a strong preference for one particular attribute such as liquidity or high risk. Diversification allows an investor to choose the mixture of asset types,

such as money and bonds, so as to produce risk and return characteristics for the portfolio as a whole that would maximize utility for a given level of wealth. Diversification also has the advantage of reducing the overall risk of the portfolio, since the investors do not have 'all their eggs in one basket'.[2] The more negatively correlated the returns to the assets in the portfolio, the greater the benefit from diversification in terms of risk reduction.

4. The portfolio approach is a general equilibrium approach analysing several real and financial asset markets together, hence total financial wealth acts as a constraint on choice, determined otherwise by the utility from the chosen risk–return combination of all the assets concerned. Changes to wealth, rates of return, and risk introduce income and substitution effects between types of assets.

5. Transactions costs in the sale and purchase of assets can introduce frictions into the model which restrict the extent to which investors are prepared to substitute into and out of these assets. These transactions costs need to be set against the expected return of the portfolio in order for an individual to decide whether an asset substitution is worthwhile.

6. The treatment of expectations concerning future returns and the degree of certainty/uncertainty[3] with which they are held has a very great influence on the way investors behave. Generally expectations are considered to be rational but not held with perfect foresight.

These features have emerged over a considerable period through the work most notably of Hicks (1935) , Baumol (1952), Markowitz (1952), and Tobin (1956, 1958). The following sections explain in greater detail how these common features emerged and demonstrate the implications for monetary economics.

6.2 Hicks and the LSE Tradition

MANY observers trace the beginnings of portfolio analysis to the pioneering article of Henry Markowitz (1952), but we begin on the other side of the Atlantic. In 1929, Lionel Robbins (later Lord Robbins) became Professor and Head of the Economics Department at the London School of Economics and under his leadership the LSE adopted an influential new research programme on money. Hicks, who was appointed as a junior lecturer in 1929 after studying mathematics and economics at Oxford, was very influential in its development and elaboration. One shrewd observer remarked that Hicks demonstrated how Robbins's programme could be realized in theory. At much the same time as Hicks's appointment, Paul Chambers took up graduate studies in the Department of Economics at the LSE whilst working as an Inspector of Taxes. His thesis on the pure theory of credit was supervised by Hayek and Robbins, but he evidently also learnt from Hicks.

The starting point of Chambers' analysis was an article by Hicks, 'Equilibrium and the Trade Cycle', republished in Hicks (1973), which conjectured that monetary theory falls outside of equilibrium theory. Chambers published his conclusions in an article in 1934, and it is on this evidence that the early development of portfolio theory is based. The article falls into three main parts, which represent the general setting of the problem, predictable fluctuations and unpredictable fluctuations. The prescience of the work is immediately apparent by the similarity that the section on predictable fluctuations shows to the later analysis of the transactions motive by Baumol (1952) and Tobin (1956). In the section on unpredictable fluctuations, Chambers introduced risk into the determination of portfolio allocation. He again acknowledged his debt to Hicks who had pointed out to him the usefulness of using a frequency curve to determine the features of a portfolio using the mean value and the standard deviation of returns. This subsequently became known as the mean-variance approach.

Using a two-dimensional diagram to illustrate the new portfolio method along with indifference curve analysis to describe risk and return combinations, Chambers explained that:

Retaining the two-dimensional diagram . . . we now measure on [the vertical axis] and on [the horizontal axis] the mean values and the standard deviations respectively for the different ways in which the whole capital can be invested. These are not simply the measurements of a single investment of the whole capital in one lump. Each point on an indifference curve now represents not a single investment at that point but the separate investment of all the units of capital, possibly all at different mean values and standard deviations, the resultant of which gives the mean value and standard deviation at that point. The number of different possible combinations depends on the number of units into which the capital can be divided, and, although this number is likely to be very large, the effective range of combinations depends upon the market conditions and is much more limited. (Chambers, 1934: 46)

Continuing, he showed that diversification would be a sensible strategy to minimize the risk associated with a portfolio:

The investment of a number of units at the same mean value and standard deviation does not involve the investment of all of them in the same enterprise, since, from a fairly elementary principle of probability, it is clear that the standard deviation is smaller if the chances are in-dependent, and, therefore a combination of independent investments will always have in total a lower standard deviation than a single investment which has the same mean value and standard deviation as the separate investments individually. Put more popularly, the risk is less if the eggs are in a number of independent baskets instead of being all in one, when the chance of falling is the same for each basket. (ibid. 46)

Given that the paper examines reasons for holding safe assets and risky assets, this represented a considerable step towards a theory of portfolio choice. The analysis, albeit in a non-mathematical form, is at least as detailed as that of Hicks (1935) and Tobin (1958) in terms of the richness of ideas.

Hicks's 1935 paper 'A Suggestion for Simplifying the Theory of Money' was also a precursor of modern portfolio theory. Hicks had turned to monetary theory in 1932 after a request from Robbins to translate Hayek's *Prices and Production* model into mathematics (Hicks, 1982: 6). This led to a new research strategy: to elaborate monetary theory in line with the theory of risk. For this purpose, Hicks turned to his reformulation of the theory of ordinal utility with R. G. D. Allen in 'A Reconsideration of the Theory of Value' (Hicks and Allen, 1934). With tools such as the marginal rate of substitution, the indifference curve, the elasticity of substitution, and the expenditure curve, Hicks was able to consider new approaches to portfolio theory. His first thoughts were presented in the paper 'The Application of Mathematical Methods to the Theory of Risk', presented at the meeting of the Econometric Society in Leyden, 1933. In this paper, according to a report by Marshak (1934), Hicks applied probability theory to the capital account of the community. He suggested the representation of the prospect of an investment by a frequency curve, representing the probabilities of yields as they appear to the investor, and discussed in detail one particular case in which the mean value and the standard deviation were employed. In a risky situation the investor must choose between assets with high risk-return characteristics and safer assets with lower risk but lower return. His knowledge of the law of large numbers led him to conclude that opting for one asset with particular characteristics as to risk and return could be dominated by a hedging strategy based on diversification over a number of assets. In dealing with the problem in this way, Hicks was the first to consider mean-variance analysis in the choice of a range of assets, which Tobin readily acknowledged when he used this method twenty years later.

Hicks's simplifying theory of money was much broader than Keynes's liquidity preference theory, in recognizing that the individuals' asset choice was wider than money and bonds. Moreover, it argued that marginal utility analysis should be applicable to money:

We now realise that the marginal utility analysis is nothing else than a general theory of choice ... People do choose to have money rather than other things, and therefore, in the relevant sense, money must have a marginal utility. (Hicks, 1935: 63)

As early as 1933 Hicks had noted that

In advanced communities, a representative individual may be considered to hold his assets in innumerable different forms which may, however, be broadly classified: Cash, Call loans, Short-term loans, Long-term loans, Material property (incl. shares). Broadly speaking, there is an increasing risk-element as we go from left to right; and again, broadly speaking, there is a higher promise of return in the same direction to compensate for increased risk. The distribution of assets among these forms is governed by relative prospects of return and by relative risk factors. (1933: 529)

Thus the decision to hold money is part of a decision concerning a portfolio, with a generalized balance-sheet, incorporating all the assets and liabilities. General equilibrium analysis was applicable. The two questions to be addressed were: how will people allocate their wealth and what are the determinants of this allocation? One factor was transactions costs or 'frictions'; there are costs of transferring assets from one form to another comprising both objective elements, i.e. brokerage charges, as well as more subjective elements. When calculating the net advantage from an investment, these costs should be subtracted from the yield of the investments.

Thus, so far as we can see at present, the amount of money a person will desire to hold depends upon three factors: the dates at which he expects to make payments in the future, the cost of investment, and the expected rate of return on investment. The further ahead the future payments, the lower the cost of investment, and the higher the expected rate of return on invested capital—the lower will be the demand for money. (Hicks, 1935: 68)

Another factor was the possibility of capital appreciation or depreciation with respect to the asset portfolio, ie. risk. The risk factor influences two variables, the expected period of investment and the expected net yield of the investment. An increase in one of these risks will make people less willing to undertake the investment. Hicks represented the expected yield by the mean return, and the risk factor by a measure of dispersion of a probability distribution:

Where risk is present, the *particular* expectation of a riskless situation is replaced by a band of possibilities, each of which is considered more or less probable. It is convenient to represent these probabilities to oneself in a statistical fashion, by a mean value, and some appropriate measure of dispersion. (No single measure will be wholly satisfactory, but here this difficulty may be overlooked.) Roughly speaking, we may assume that a change in the mean value with constant dispersion has much the same sort of effect as a change in the particular expectations we have been discussing before. The peculiar problem of risk therefore reduces to an examination of the consequences of a change in dispersion. Increased dispersion means increased uncertainty. (ibid. 69)

But the law of large numbers creates a difference between the risk of one particular investment and the risk incurred by undertaking a number of separate risky investments.

These persons who have command of large quantities of capital, and are able to spread their risks, are not only able to reduce the risk of their own capital to a fairly low level—they are also able to offer very good security for the investment of an extra unit along with the rest. (ibid. 72)

When many assets are held the risk is lowered because not all the returns on the assets in the portfolio will fall and rise together, and in practice a well-diversified portfolio will include assets which tend to have offsetting behaviour. This strategy mixes assets the returns of which have a negative covariance, reducing the total risk on the diversified portfolio in comparison to investing in one risky asset, without altering the return.

Risk and transaction costs, as elements in the determination of the allocation of wealth, were regarded as similar to price in value theory. Hicks's further 'Suggestion' that one should investigate how the demand for money changes under the influence of a change in total wealth, laid out the skeleton of portfolio theory.

Why did twenty years elapse before the next significant contribution? It would seem that the publication of the *General Theory* turned the main debate in monetary economics to the efficacy of monetary policy and the liquidity trap. In the context of the Depression years and post-war reconstruction, monetary theory in general took a back seat. The focus of attention was on the role of government in stimulating aggregate demand through fiscal intervention and few Keynesians at least were thinking about monetary issues. Portfolio theory had to await the revival of monetary policy after the Treasury-Federal Reserve Accord[4] of 1951 and the resurgence of interest following the work of Baumol (1952) and Tobin (1956, 1958) in the United States.

6.3 Portfolio Approach to Transactions Demand

THE rationale for transactions demand in the Keynesian model suggested that individuals would hold money balances to meet the immediate needs of transacting in goods markets. But in a world in which transactions are known with certainty, it does not really explain why purchasing power should be held in a non-interest-bearing form. If the transactions patterns were well known, it would be more profitable to hold purchasing power in interest-bearing assets (i.e. bonds) and disinvest into money at the point that liquidity is needed to settle transactions. Hicks dealt with this point by introducing 'frictions' which made switching between assets costly. Once there is a cost of adjustment the individual will consider making arrangements to avoid excessive conversions and this may account for the existence of transaction balances, even when an interest-bearing asset exists and transactions patterns are known.

Baumol (1952) and Tobin (1956) took up this suggestion and developed a theory of the transactions demand for money of an individual based around the existence of a brokerage fee incurred every time wealth is switched between assets. There are only two assets, money (M) and bonds (B), and financial wealth is:

$$W_t = M_t + B_t. \tag{6.3}$$

Drawing on inventory theory, the transactions demand for money emerges from a cost-benefit analysis of investing in interest-bearing assets as opposed to holding non-interest-bearing money. The expected return on bonds is calculated using the rate of return which is the interest rate, r_t, times the average bond holding over the period, $\bar{B}_t$, thus:

$$R_t = r_t \bar{B}_t. \tag{6.4}$$

The cost of holding bonds is the payment in brokerage fees incurred every time wealth is switched between money and bonds, this is made up of the brokerage fee, c_t, times the number of switches between money and bonds in either direction, N:

$$C_t = c_t N. \tag{6.5}$$

The aim of the individual is to determine that level of bond holdings which will jointly maximize the returns from interest income and minimize brokerage costs or, what amounts to the same thing, the optimal amount of money to be held for transactions balances and the number of switches from bonds to money. The individual could choose to hold all wealth in money for the whole period but for any given rate

of interest and brokerage fee it may be possible to do better by investing a proportion of wealth in bonds and disinvesting a certain amount of wealth from bonds into
money at given intervals. The Baumol–Tobin analysis determines the optimal
number of switches between money and bonds, in set proportions, Q_t, each period in
time, and thus indicates how high the average money balance should be. By assumption at the end of the analysis all wealth will have been switched into money so that

$$W_t = Q_t N. \tag{6.6}$$

Taking the relationship between wealth and money and bond holdings we can write
this in terms of averages

$$\bar{W}_t = \bar{B}_t + \bar{M}_t \tag{6.7}$$

and using the fact that we know from the saw-tooth pattern of transactions balances
that average money balances are equal to half the money balances received each
period, which in this case is equal to half the amount of wealth disinvested from
bonds each period,

$$M_t = Q_t/2, \tag{6.8}$$

we can now rearrange some terms to define Q and N in terms of $\bar{M}$ and $\bar{W}$ as follows

$$Q_t = 2\,\bar{M}_t \tag{6.9}$$

$$N = 2\bar{W}_t/Q_t = \bar{W}_t/\bar{M}_t. \tag{6.10}$$

We are now in a position to maximize the return, R_t, from interest subject to the
brokerage costs, C_t. We write the costs and benefits in terms of $\bar{W}_t$ and $\bar{M}_t$ as follows:

$$\pi_t = R_t - C_t = r_t(\bar{W}_t - \bar{M}_t) - c_t\,(\bar{W}_t/\,\bar{M}_t). \tag{6.11}$$

If we maximize subject to $\bar{M}$ and set the result equal to zero, we then get

$$r_t - c_t(\bar{W}_t/\bar{M}_t^{\,2}) = 0. \tag{6.12}$$

The first term is the marginal benefit of holding bonds, namely, the interest rate, and
the second term is the marginal cost based on the brokerage fee. Rearrangement
gives the optimal average money balances as:

$$\bar{M}_t = \sqrt{\frac{(c_t(\bar{W}_t)}{r_t}} \tag{6.13}$$

This is Baumol's square-root rule and it pins down not only the average money
balance but also the optimal proportion of wealth to be disinvested each period and
the number of switches be made.

   Intuitively it is easier to understand this result by drawing the marginal cost and
benefit curves on a diagram, but instead of thinking about the marginal cost and benefit in terms of bonds we will do so in terms of average money balances. We know that
the marginal benefit of holding a higher average level of bonds is the interest rate,
so when we consider the marginal benefit from the point of view of average money
balances we can see that the marginal benefit of holding more money on average
will be the lost interest (i.e. minus the interest rate). Likewise when we consider that

the marginal cost increases with average bond holding we will be able to understand that as average money balances rise the marginal cost incurred through brokerage fees will fall. The cost and benefits are drawn relative to average money holdings in Figure 6.1, labelled MR and MC respectively, and we find a point of intersection between the two curves which gives the optimal level of average money holdings, $(\bar{M}\bar{W})^*$

If we plot the net return (π) against the proportion of wealth held in money balances on average in Figure 6.1 we find that the choice of $\bar{M}^*$ at the point of intersection maximizes the net return at E, $(\bar{M}/\bar{W})^*$. The point of maximization depends on the marginal revenue and marginal cost curves and hence on the given levels of the interest rate and the brokerage fee; if either of these were to change, then the optimal average money balance would change too. A decrease in the interest rate is illustrated in Figure 6.2, here the marginal benefit of holding higher average bond levels falls and hence the marginal benefit of holding higher money balances rises. The marginal benefit curve shifts towards zero, to a smaller negative number, from MR_1 to MR_2 and the marginal cost curve remains unchanged, hence the optimal average money balance rises on Figure 6.2 from $(\bar{M}_1/\bar{W})^*$ to $(\bar{M}_2/\bar{W})^*$. The net return falls on Figure 6.2 in response to the fall in the interest rate and the optimal point moves to the right from E_1 to E_2 where average money balances are a higher proportion of average wealth since $(\bar{M}_2/\bar{W})^*$ is greater than $(\bar{M}_1/\bar{W})^*$.

The transactions model is conducted in a world of certainty in which there is no risk attached to bonds. Since in the discussion of the portfolio approach to precautionary and speculative demand there is risk, and later we will want to combine

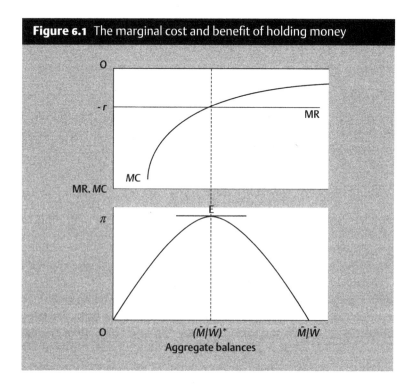

Figure 6.1 The marginal cost and benefit of holding money

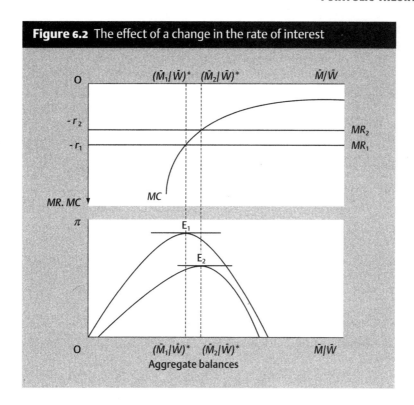

Figure 6.2 The effect of a change in the rate of interest

transactions, precautionary and speculative approaches, we redraw the net return diagram to include both risk and return characteristics of the interest-bearing asset. On the top panel of Figure 6.3 is the trade-off between risk and return for the interest-bearing asset, which in this case is simple since there is no risk. The opportunity locus, describing the choices of risk-return combinations available to the investor, is a horizontal line along the axis given by $0A$, and the investor who has a preference for more return and less risk chooses a point consistent with utility maximization at A. This is a corner solution which gives the maximum return available with no trade-off for risk compared with other points on $0A$. The lower panel shows Figure 6.2 rotated through 90 degrees and shows that the maximization point A is consistent with the maximum net return at E_1. The proportion of average money balances to average wealth is given on the vertical axis as $(\bar{M}_1/\bar{W})^*$ as before.

Considering a fall in the interest rate in Fig. 6.3 yields the same result as before but in a slightly different way. The reduction in the rate of interest shortens the opportunity locus to $0B$ since the maximum return available is now B rather than A and the choice is to hold bonds at a level consistent with a corner solution to maximize utility. The new equilibrium is still consistent with the maximum net return on the lower panel as before, and is given by E_2, but average money balances rise as a proportion of average wealth to $(\bar{M}_2/\bar{W})^*$ with the fall in interest rates. In each case the optimal level of money balances, even with a positive rate of return on

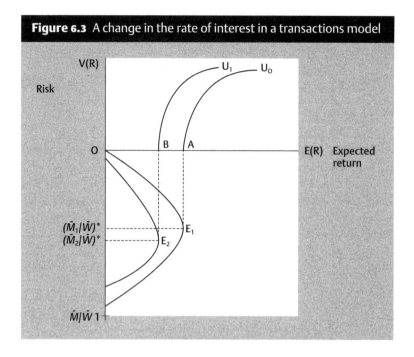

Figure 6.3 A change in the rate of interest in a transactions model

the alternative asset is not zero. This result means that the transaction cost makes holding money for transactions purposes worthwhile—since this avoids incurring excessive costs by substitution between bonds and money. Stated alternatively, there is an optimal number of times to make the substitution between bonds and money, and this results in a positive average money balance.

6.4 Portfolio Approach to Precautionary Demand

THE principal objection to the Baumol–Tobin transactions model is that it is conducted in a certain world in which bond holding is not risky. This section overcomes the objection by introducing risky bonds which gives an opportunity locus which trades off risk and return. The precautionary model under the portfolio balance approach is the one which is most familiar since it is often used to justify the existence of a diversified portfolio. Diversified portfolios as we have already seen are less risky because risky investments can be offsetting if their returns are negatively correlated. It is unsurprising to find that many investors who aim to avoid the economic costs of uncertainty will tend to manage their portfolios in a precautionary fashion and hence diversify their assets. Organizations such as pension funds which put a large weight on achieving a stable and dependable income stream from their investments will diversify extensively.

The basic premiss of the precautionary model, that a higher rate of return is a compensation for taking on a greater level of risk, goes back a long way, certainly to Hicks (1935) and probably earlier if we consider insurance principles. Tobin (1958) used this observation to explain diversification on the grounds that the investor gains utility from a higher rate of return but loses utility from taking on risk and that a trade-off between risk and return can be achieved by diversification between the two assets, bonds and money. By investing in a greater proportion of bonds the investor gains more return and more risk; by holding more money the investor loses interest income but gains by reducing risk. Implicitly we consider the typical investor to be risk-averse, but we do not require this to be so, and can relax the assumption later.

Tobin (1958) considered the expected return to the portfolio, as under the transactions approach but with the possibility of riskiness associated with capital gains or losses. Financial wealth is held in either money or bonds as before and both the risk and the return on money are equal to zero. Any expected return from the portfolio comes from bond holdings. The expected return is equal to the average interest rate plus the average gain or loss times the average bond holding over the period, but since the average gain or loss is equal to zero (by assumption) the expected return is solely a function of interest income:

$$E(R_t) = [E(r_t) + E(g_t)] \, \bar{B}_t, \tag{6.14}$$

where $E(r_t) = \mu$ and $E(g_t) = 0$. The variance of the return is determined by the variance of the gain/loss. Since the gain/loss is $V(g_t)$ the variance of the return to the portfolio can be calculated as

$$V(R_t) = V(g_t) \, \bar{B}_t. \tag{6.15}$$

From this we can see that there is a positive relationship between the risk and return to the portfolio, since we can rearrange the equation above and substitute it into the equation for the expected return to the portfolio to give

$$E(R_t) = r_t V(R_t)/V(g_t). \tag{6.16}$$

Both the rate of return and the variance of the gain/loss are positive, hence there is a positive relationship between the rate of return and the risk of the portfolio, which gives an upward-sloping opportunity locus, drawn in Figure 6.4 and labelled *OA*.

We can now use Figure 6.4 in conjunction with indifference curves (indicating preferences of investors) to determine the preferred portfolio mix. If the investor is to maximize the return to the portfolio, then the portfolio must consist of all bonds and the maximum risk at point *A*. If no bonds are held so as to avoid risk altogether, then there will be a zero return to the portfolio on average represented by point *O*. If the investor is risk-averse and gains utility from a higher return and lower risk, then the preference will be to trade off risk and return in a diversified portfolio (point E_1) and we can trace the proportion of average money balances to average wealth, lying between zero and one, in the lower half of the diagram.

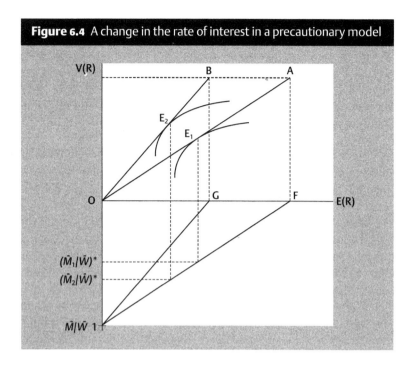

Figure 6.4 A change in the rate of interest in a precautionary model

When the interest rate falls, the opportunity locus rotates inwards, reflecting the fact that the interest income available from the portfolio is reduced from a level vertically above F to a level vertically above G while risk is unchanged. The maximum available return is given by G on the horizontal axis, hence the line representing the relationship between proportion of average money balances in average wealth and the return also rotates inwards. Depending on the shape of the indifference curves the proportion of average money balances to average wealth may rise or fall. We have drawn the diagram to show a rise in money balances at E_2, which results in the average level of money balances to wealth increasing to $(\bar{M}_2/\bar{W})^*$. It is consistent with the transactions model to assume that the proportion of money balances will rise as the interest rate falls since the opportunity cost of holding money has fallen, although there is nothing to say that the shape of the indifference curves should imply a fall in bond holding if the investor seeks to maintain a target level of interest income, for example. In the case where the portfolio composition does not shift, this will be because there is a strong income effect which dominates the usual substitution effect arising from changing interest rates.

If we consider a change to the riskiness of bonds in Figure 6.5 we can see that the maximum return would be maintained above point F, since the return is unchanged, but the maximum risk will increase from σ_1 to σ_2, rotating the opportunity locus from OA to OB. With a family of indifference curves as before, the proportion of average money balances to average wealth is likely to increase, reflecting the fact that the same return is associated with a higher level of risk than before.

Throughout the analysis here we have assumed that the indifference curves are

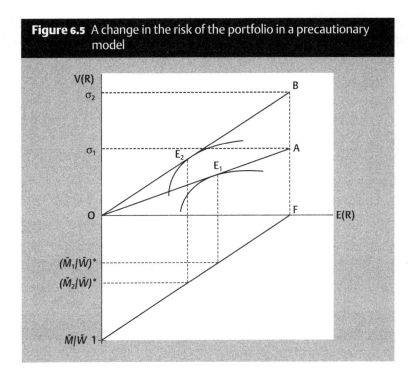

Figure 6.5 A change in the risk of the portfolio in a precautionary model

positively sloped reflecting risk-averse behaviour and concave to the horizontal axis reflecting a tendency to diversify the portfolio. Given that many if not the vast majority of investors demonstrate a preference for less risk for a given return, often by adopting diversified portfolios, this is not unreasonable. There are nevertheless two other possibilities: individuals may be risk-loving 'gamblers' or risk-averse 'plungers'. In the first case their indifference curves will be negatively sloped demonstrating a willingness to accept lower returns in order to indulge in the possibility of unusually high capital gains associated with high risk. The risk lover will choose a corner solution at the highest level of risk on the opportunity locus as shown in Figure 6.6(a), and will thus hold all bonds.[5] Gamblers do not diversify their portfolios since this will reduce the risk and lower the utility derived from the portfolio. Changes to the rate of interest or the riskiness of bonds will not alter the gambler's preference to be holding all bonds, although it will change the level of utility gained from holding a portfolio composed entirely of bonds.

For the risk-averse plunger the indifference curves are positively sloped but are convex to the origin leading the investor to 'plunge' for a portfolio which is completely bonds or completely money rather than adopt a diversified portfolio of both assets. As the diagram is drawn, the plunger opts for all bonds at point A, which dominates a diversified portfolio at point E. Changes to interest rates cause abrupt changes to portfolio composition since the plunger will opt for either all money or all bonds, changing between the two in response to changes in interest rates and risk.

The model we have considered has some precautionary and some speculative features. We can see that if the majority of investors are risk-averse diversifiers then

Figure 6.6(a) Preferences of a risk lover

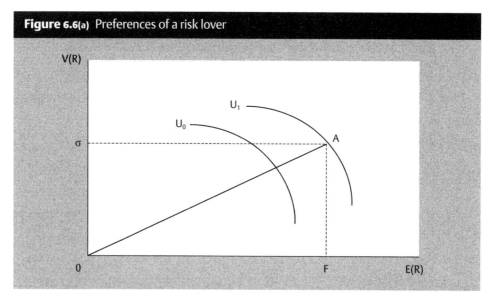

Figure 6.6(b) Preferences of a risk-averse plunger

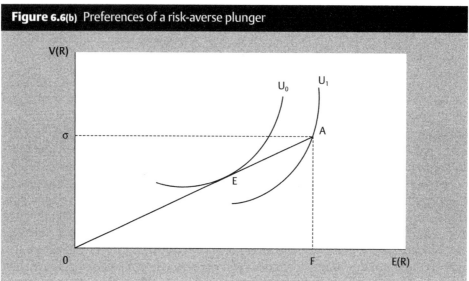

the model is precautionary in character. If on the other hand the investors are primarily risk-averse plungers or risk-loving gamblers, then the model has the instability associated with the speculative motive. We prefer to describe the model above as a precautionary one which can account for the types of investors, such as pension funds, that seek to maintain a balance between risk and return. In the next section we look at a model which deliberately deals with the instability associated with speculative behaviour.

6.5 Portfolio Approach to Speculative Behaviour

THE important insight from Keynes's notion of the speculative motive was the instability that it generates in money and bond holdings. Once the interest rate alters in such a way that the critical threshold is crossed, investors no longer believe that capital gains will be realized from changes in the price of bonds derived from the expected direction of future interest rate movements. Individually, the behaviour of investors is of the (0,1) variety. In aggregate, this response is smoothed when there is diversity of opinion amongst the investors, but when there is herding behaviour that causes investors to 'follow the leader' in the market the sensitivity remains.

Considering the analysis when the rate of interest is below the critical rate, we know from Chapter 5 that the capital loss will outweigh the interest income on the bond, so that the more bonds that are held in the portfolio on average the greater will be the loss on the portfolio as a whole. The investor's utility-maximizing strategy is to disinvest from bonds and hold money, since a zero return is better than a negative return. Diagramatically, we can draw the opportunity locus as line OA in the negative quadrant of the portfolio balance diagram in Figure 6.7. In this model the expectations about future interest rates and thus the capital gain are held with certainty, so the risk of holding bonds is zero. This explains why the opportunity locus is a horizontal line. As the proportion of average money balances to average wealth increases the capital loss from holding bonds decreases, reaching zero where the portfolio is completely composed of money at C, where $\bar{M}/\bar{W} = 1$. Thus on the lower left-hand quadrant the relationship between the composition of average money balances in the portfolio and the rate of return is given by AC.

We can now examine the opposite case, where the interest rate exceeds the critical rate. The investor can be sure that there will be a capital gain from holding bonds and the return on the portfolio will rise in proportion with the average bond-holding. If the individual holds all bonds the return will be maximized, as the line BC indicates on the lower right-hand quadrant of the diagram. Again the opportunity locus is flat because the individual has certainty about the future interest rate so there is no risk to trade off the high return from holding all financial wealth in bonds.

If the interest rate is below the critical rate, then the individual will choose the corner solution O which is consistent with utility maximization, holding all money and no bonds. If the interest rate is above the critical rate, then the investor will hold all bonds and no money, since any wealth not held in bonds is forgoing certain income on the portfolio. The choice when interest rates are above the critical rate is again a corner solution and thus the individual will act somewhat like the risk-averse plunger in the precautionary model (although the model here has no risk), jumping from all money to all bonds and vice versa with changes to the interest rate.

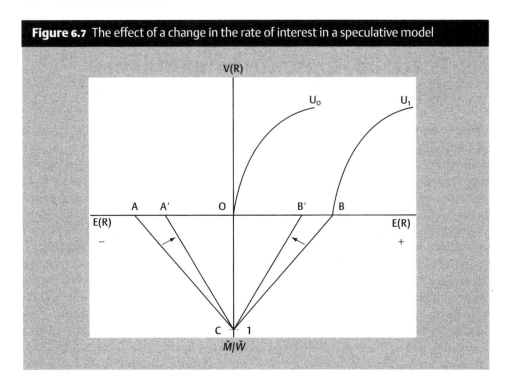

Figure 6.7 The effect of a change in the rate of interest in a speculative model

Consider the effect of interest rate policy under these conditions. We can think of four scenarios which depict all the possible reactions to changing interest rates. The first two involve a rise or a fall in the interest rate which does not cross the critical rate; in these cases the calculation as to the benefit of holding money or bonds is unaltered in sign. If the interest rate is below the critical rate initially and remains so after the change, then no alteration will take place in the composition of the port-folio, which will remain composed entirely of money. Likewise if the interest rate is above the critical rate and remains above that rate after the change, then the com-position will be unchanged from before. The only effect on the diagram will be to shorten the opportunity cost locus due to the lower interest rate (and hence lower maximum available return), and the chosen point will still remain at the same corner solution at O. This would also be true in the case where an interest rate rise had been considered when the interest rate was initially above the critical rate. In both of these cases interest rate policy would be ineffective, since it would not alter the composition of investor's portfolios, merely altering the expected return from the portfolio and leaving the optimal corner solution unchanged.

The other two cases represent situations where the change in the rate of interest crosses the critical rate. If the rate of interest was formerly below the critical rate and was changed in such a way that it was subsequently above it, then all financial wealth would be switched from money to bonds. If the reverse were true, then all wealth would be switched from bonds to money. The result of this kind of change to the rate of interest would be a transfer of all financial wealth from one asset to another, creating substantial instability in the demand for money and for bonds. The corner solutions chosen are shown for a fall in rates (opportunity loci OA' and OB'). With a fall in the interest rate initially above the critical rate such that the opportunity locus shortens from OB to OB' the investor shifts from point B to point B' there is no portfolio reallocation. Alternatively, with a fall in the interest rate to below the critical rate from a position originally above it, the investor swaps from B to O, divesting from all bonds.

6.6 **Integrating the Approaches**

THE main criticism of the speculative model is that, while it explains the instability of an investor's demand for money and bonds in isolation, it does not explain diversification. With this, and other criticisms, in mind we have dealt with all the motives in a consistent manner so that they can be integrated together so as to allow for different motives at the same time. If we wanted a model that could explain both the instability and diversification, then we could integrate the speculative and precautionary models together. The effect of including a precautionary model (with risk) with the speculative model (without risk) is to combine opportunity loci which are upward-sloping with the V-shaped lower quadrants of the speculative model. Drawing these in Figure 6.8 we find that the behaviour is dichotomized according to whether the interest rate is below or above the critical rate. When the interest rate is below the critical rate the model gives the same result as the speculative model since all assets are held in money and the corner solution O is the chosen point. When the interest rate is above the critical rate the investor behaves with the precautionary motives, since although there is an expectation of a capital gain this is accompanied by non-zero risk. Hence the investor diversifies the portfolio, choosing equilibrium point E when there is an expectation of a capital gain on bonds, and average money holding as a proportion of wealth is given by $(\bar{M}_1/\bar{W})^*$.

If we wanted to account for transactions behaviour as well, allowing for risk, capital gains, and transactions costs, then the diagram can be altered to allow for the influence of net return analysis due to Baumol and Tobin. This is illustrated in Figure 6.9 which shows that the lower right-hand quadrant has a somewhat curved-V shape which results from combining this quadrant from Figures 6.3 and 6.8. The opportunity locus would look similar and would result in choices between a corner solution at O when the interest rate was below the critical rate and a diversified portfolio at equilibrium E when interest rates were above the critical rate. All the points on the opportunity locus between point O and point D dominate the range DB since they give the same return for a lower level of risk. Thus the investor will never choose points on the negatively sloped parts of the lines in the upper and lower right-hand quadrants so long as they are risk-averse diversifiers. If investors were risk lovers, they would choose either point D or point B depending on the exact slope of the indifference curves.

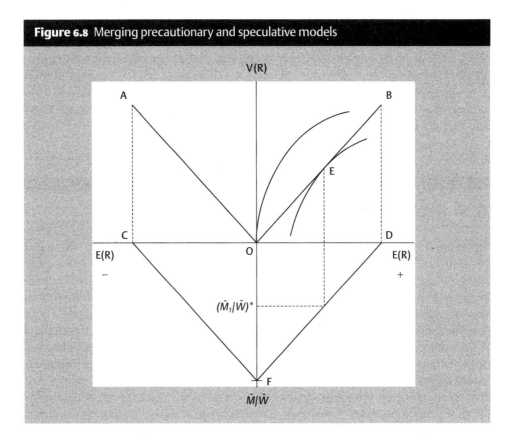

Figure 6.8 Merging precautionary and speculative models

Clearly even allowing for the other motives by including the impact of risk and transactions costs, the effect of an expected capital loss on bonds when interest rates are below the critical rate is a dominant feature of the models. In this sense the models are truly Keynesian in character because liquidity preference is central to the analysis. The conclusions regarding the liquidity trap would follow through in these models if there were a rate of interest that was sufficiently low or unanimity of opinion that bond holding would result in a capital loss.

6.7 Extension to Other Assets

HOWEVER, the conclusions about the liquidity trap depend on the nature of the portfolio menu available, and the assumptions made. Tobin (1966) provides two alternative frameworks which demonstrate this point in terms of pure diversification behaviour.

In the first, the two assets considered are not money and bonds, but 'currency' and 'capital' (claims on real assets). This change makes a considerable difference. Both

Figure 6.9 Merging transactions: precautionary and speculative models

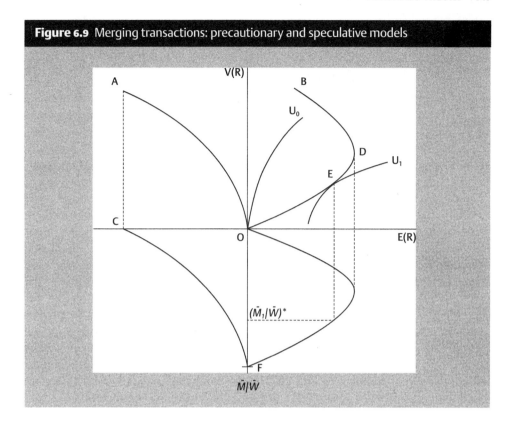

money and bonds are denominated in money terms. The same is not true of capital, for both the yield on capital and the value of capital relative to consumer goods involve risk. When we allow for price changes, the expectation and risk of return on currency reflect possible changes in the price level of consumer goods. Let x_1, E_1 and σ_1 stand for the portfolio share, expected return, and risk of currency, and x_2, E_2 and σ_2 for capital. Then the portfolio characteristics are:

$$E(R_t) = x_1 E_{1t} + x_2 E_{2t} \tag{6.17}$$

and

$$V(R_t) = x_1^2 \sigma_1^2 + x_2^2 \sigma_2^2 + 2 x_1 x_1 \rho_{12} \sigma_1 \sigma_2 \tag{6.18}$$

where $\rho_{12} = \dfrac{\sigma_{12}}{\sigma_1 \sigma_2}$, the coefficient of correlation of the two returns.

Minimizing $V(R)$ with respect to x_1 and x_2, subject to $x_1 + x_2 = 1$, gives

$$x_1 = \frac{\sigma_2^2 - \rho_{12} \sigma_1 \sigma_2}{\sigma_1^2 + \sigma_2^2 - 2\rho_{12} \sigma_1 \sigma_2} \tag{6.19}$$

and

$$x_2 = \frac{\sigma_1^2 - \rho_{12}\sigma_1\sigma_2}{\sigma_1^2 + \sigma_2^2 - 2\rho_{12}\sigma_1\sigma_2}. \tag{6.20}$$

That is, in general, the minimum-risk portfolio includes both assets. In the case of $\rho_{12} = 0$ (risks on capital and currency are independent), the minimum-risk portfolio includes both currency and capital in inverse proportion to their variances. This result holds even though capital is more risky than currency.[6] All available portfolios entail some risk, and the minimum-risk position is no longer 100 per cent currency. In these circumstances, the liquidity trap cannot be generated by aversion to risk.

Tobin also extends the risk diversification model to consider portfolios of more than two assets. The case examined is selection amongst assets A_1, A_2, and A_3, which could be money, bonds, and equities. In this situation, the opportunity set is not represented by a single line or curve, but by a region, the shape of which will obviously be governed given Equation (6.18) by the correlations between the three assets. However, in general, the risk-averter's portfolio will be diversified among the three assets. The flavour of the analysis can be appreciated by supposing, for example, that A_1 and A_2 have a correlation of $+1$ but A_3 which is introduced into the portfolio is independent of them. The opportunity set is shown in Figure 6.10. The locus for A_1, A_2 combinations is a straight line. The locus when A_3 is introduced is produced by combining A_3 with combinations of A_1 and A_2. Starting at the bottom left hand, we first combine A_1 and A_3.Then the combination X of A_1 and A_2 is combined with A_3, and the opportunities lie along the hyperbola connecting A_3 with X. And so on for Y, Z, etc.

The envelope, or frontier, of all of these hyperbolas, which is given by the solid curve MNA, constitutes the efficient locus for a risk-averter, and the portfolio will be diversified as between the three assets. The minimum-risk portfolio is M, which because of the special assumption about A_1 and A_2 contains only two assets, A_1 and A_3. In the general case, it too will combine the three assets.[7] But it is not normally confined to the lowest-risk asset.

Many extensions of this type of analysis are possible. As well as increasing the number of assets in the portfolio, the selection over a number of periods can be considered involving either sequential reinvestment decisions or in continuous time (Samuelson, 1970; Merton, 1971). In such multiperiod analysis, additional matters which must be addressed are the investor's lifespan, the probabilities attached to that, and the nature of the (stochastic) process generating the returns. A wide range of outcomes are possible and the results are less tractable than the simpler models considered here.

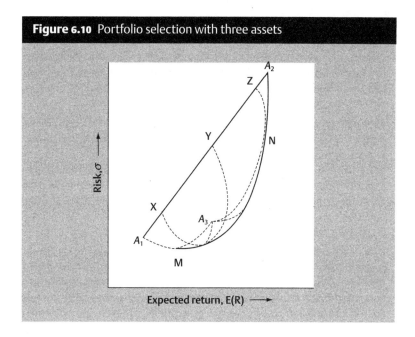

Figure 6.10 Portfolio selection with three assets

6.8 Conclusions

THIS chapter has developed the theme of portfolio analysis insofar as it deals with monetary economics and originates from the work of monetary economists. Portfolio theory itself is clearly a foundation for the management of financial assets in a much broader sphere than monetary economics. The approach has been developed much further by academics in the fields of finance, investment and risk management, actuarial science, and so forth. Indeed much of what might be perceived as monetary economics in practice is the application of portfolio analysis techniques.

In the next chapter we consider the analysis of the demand for money based on the work of Friedman and the monetarists, which involves many assets including non-financial as well as financial assets. It is quite different in character and conclusions from the work of Hicks, Baumol, and Tobin but, as Patinkin (1972) has pointed out, in terms of the nature of the analysis, it is much closer to Keynes than to the portfolio balance approaches considered above.

Notes

1 The modern mathematical theory of financial investment and portfolio selection can really be said to have begun with the work of Markowitz (1952, 1959) who developed the mean-variance model. However, the general approach itself can be traced back to

Hicks (1935) and others, at least insofar as monetary analysis is concerned, as we explain below.

2 Clearly, however, the baskets must have independent fates if diversification is to reduce risk. Should the risk be that the basket carrier goes 'bottom up', putting eggs into two baskets, one on the left hand and one on the right, will not do the trick. See the later discussion in Sect. 6.2.

3 Although risk and uncertainty are often used interchangeably, Knight (1921) drew a distinction between them. A situation involves risk if the randomness facing individuals can be expressed in terms of specific numerical probabilities (either objectively or subjectively). Where they cannot assign actual probabilities to the alternative possibilities, the situation is said to involve uncertainty. The main approach to modelling choices under uncertainty (as opposed to risk) is the state preference approach involving states of the world or states of nature (Arrow, 1964; Hirschleifer, 1966; Yaari, 1969).

4 In the Accord of 4 March 1951, the Federal Reserve was relieved of responsibility for supporting the government securities market at pegged prices. During the war years, the Federal Reserve agreed to maintain fixed interest rates on long-term government bonds and limit fluctuations in short-term interest rates. The Accord allowed greater fluctuations in the prices of government securities, and by rendering bonds a less close substitute for money, made portfolio selection analysis more relevant.

5 Bleaney (1993: 10–11) reconsiders the view of Tobin (1958) that risk-loving implies increasing marginal utility with a mean preserving increase in the variance of the return to the portfolio. Bleaney observes that this implies risk lovers should have portfolios entirely committed to bonds or money, depending on their preferences, when expected returns are negative, yet the psychology literature suggests that investors take small gambles with negative returns. His suggestion is that risk lovers seek uncertainty which gambling as a commodity provides, not maximum risk. When the risk lovers are treated in this way their preferences are represented by indifference curves that are convex to the origin.

6 The opposite circumstance is of interest too. Suppose that currency has both a lower expectation of return *and* more risk than capital. Currency would still feature in a risk-averter's portfolio.

7 The exceptions in this case are if there were high positive correlations among the asset returns or if there were an asset which is riskless.

Chapter 7
Friedman, Monetarism, and the Quantity Theory

7.1 Monetarism and the Quantity Theory

IN a survey 'The Keynesian Revolution and the Monetarist Counter-Revolution' delivered to the American Economic Association, the Canadian economist Harry Johnson (himself a leading monetarist) predicted that monetarism would peter out as a challenge to the then prevailing Keynesian orthodoxy (Johnson, 1971). In one respect, Johnson was wrong, because monetarism went on to usurp Keynesianism as the conventional wisdom and came to influence policy-making throughout the world. But, in another respect, Johnson proved to be correct, for monetarism (like many 'isms') did eventually peter out, although not in the way that he anticipated. As it was to turn out 1968 was a vital year for monetary theory.

Ironically, both the rise of monetarism and its later fall can be traced to the one source, for Johnson failed to foresee the impact that Milton Friedman's Presidential Address to the American Economic Association, published in 1968, would have upon macroeconomics (Friedman, 1968*a*). In the lecture, Friedman shifted the primary focus of monetarism from the money market, and the stability of relationships there, to the labour market, and the characteristics of economic relationships in that market. In reaffirming and emphasizing those monetarist postulates about labour market behaviour, which had previously been implicit, Friedman introduced the notion of 'the natural rate of unemployment' in conjunction with a crucial role for expectations (soon to become 'rational')—concepts that proved to be the sparks which sustained monetarism into the 1980s.

Initially, the 'natural rate hypothesis', the 'rational expectations revolution', and 'new classical economics' were seen as part of the monetarist agenda, marking the transition from Mark I Monetarism to Mark II Monetarism (Hoover, 1984). Eventually, however, those ideas proved to be its downfall. The core of monetarism has always been that 'money does matter' (Friedman, 1956). Moreover, 'money matters' at two distinct levels; for inflation in the long run, and economic activity and the upswings and downswings of the business cycle in the short run. In 1956, it was the short-run effects alone which were subsumed under the heading 'money matters':

Money does matter—any interpretation of short-term movements in economic activity is likely to be seriously at fault if it neglects monetary changes and repercussions and if it leaves unexplained why people hold the particular nominal quantity of money in existence. (Friedman, 1956: 3)

This particular emphasis proved to be monetarism's undoing. The simplicity of monetarism was lost when under the influence of the rational expectations revolution 'monetary changes' needed to distinguish 'unanticipated' from 'anticipated' ones. Later, the monetary explanation of economic fluctuations came to be supplanted by non-monetary factors under the 'real business cycles' banner.

1968 was also the year when the word 'monetarism' was first used (not by Friedman but by Karl Brunner, 1968). Previously Friedman and his followers had gone under the label of 'the Chicago School' or 'quantity theorists', because of their adherence to the quantity theory of money. 'Monetarism' as a label caught on, although the earlier descriptions confirm an intellectual tradition dating back to at least 1752 when David Hume perceived that an increase in the amount of currency in the economy provided a stimulus to demand and to price inflation in economies without the industrial capacity to provide more goods, thus sketching out the essence of the quantity theory of money. Hume also noted the tendency for currency growth to cause balance of payments deficits, thus providing the fundamentals of the monetary theory of the balance of payments which forms the theoretical core of international monetarism.

Many who called themselves monetarists displayed little evident interest in these issues. This is because monetarism came to be associated with a particular view about markets—what Charles Goodhart (1978) dubbed as a 'market optimist' view. There has always been a cleavage in economics between those who believe that markets work more-or-less in a textbook fashion and those who do not, the latter often advocating government intervention to correct perceived market failures. Keynesians, by and large, have tended to be 'market pessimists', especially with respect to the workings of the labour market. Monetarists are 'market optimists' partly because of Friedman and the Chicago School but also because monetarism, even if defined narrowly as a set of theoretical and empirical propositions relating the money stock to other important economic variables, rests on a particular view about how a system of markets works. While the economics profession has focused upon debating the propositions about money and has seen them as defining the monetarist–Keynesian divide, the general public's use of those labels is more usually based on the free market versus interventionist distinction.

Interestingly, this division of views about markets also has historical roots in an eighteenth-century debate, the focus of which was whether or not the economic system should be centrally controlled through a feudal hierarchy or left to the operations of decentralized and uncontrolled markets. Hume and Adam Smith challenged the prevailing orthodoxy, which held that without an authoritarian system the economy would degenerate into Hobbesian chaos. They argued that rational, self-interested individuals would engage in trade within a framework of laws and ethics if given the opportunity to do so. Smith relied on the 'invisible hand' to ensure beneficial results, while Hume and other British philosophers laid the foundations of a scientific methodology based on empiricism rather than theology. It is not stretching a point to see Hume's position as a forerunner to Friedman's 'positive' economics, i.e. evaluating theories in terms of their predictive content to make economics more 'scientific'. Nor is it fanciful to say that many market optimists see interventionist governments as the modern-day equivalent of feudalism in terms of the theories of James Buchanan, Gordon Tullock, and others of rent-seeking lobbyists, excessive regulation and the squandering of resources in the public sector (see, for example, McKenzie and Tullock, 1978).

Under Smith and Hume's influence, classical political economy, which concentrated on income distribution between groups such as capitalists, workers, and rentiers gave way to neoclassical economics with its attention on rational individuals interacting through competitive markets. By the early twentieth century, neoclassical economics had evolved to a central orthodoxy which saw a system of microeconomic markets yielding full employment of resources through the operation of the relative price system. Macroeconomics was summarized in terms of the quantity theory which had been inherited as part of the tradition and refined on one side of the Atlantic by Irving Fisher (1911b) and on the other side by A. C. Pigou (1917), Alfred Marshall (1923) and, perhaps confusingly, J. M. Keynes (1923), in his early writings. It was the intention of Friedman, in particular, not only to build on this simple framework of the quantity theory of money but to argue that monetarism was a natural continuation of that ancient line—hence the use of the word 'restatement'.[1]

7.2 Friedman's Restatement

FRIEDMAN commences by arguing: 'The quantity theory is in the first instance a theory of the *demand* for money. It is not a theory of output, or, of money income, or of the price level' (1956: 4).

What does this mean? Consider the Cambridge version of the quantity theory

$$M_t = kP_t y_t = \frac{P_t y_t}{V}. \tag{7.1}$$

This expression can be interpreted as a demand for money function, with $k \left(= \dfrac{1}{V} \right)$ behaviourally determined. It is not a theory about nominal income, $Y_t = P_t y_t$, because a supply of money function and a redefinition of equilibrium is needed to get from (7.1) to the determination of income. Similarly, it cannot be a theory about P_t or y_t separately unless we know what determines the other. For example, if real income is constant and the money supply is exogenously determined, then the time path of prices is given by the demand for money function. With velocity or its inverse k constant, the quantity equation becomes a theory of price determination.

The mechanism of price inflation runs in terms of the demand and supply of money. Velocity, V, reflects the desire of people to have money rather than the goods included in Y_t. The quantity is related to a period of time so that V is the frequency during the period with which each dollar, on average, is spent on money income, $P_t y_t$. This frequency is low if people wish to hold relatively large amounts of money relative to income, high if they spend it quickly after receipt. Thus the demand for money can be visualized as

$$M_t' = \frac{P_t y_t}{V} \text{ or } \frac{M_t'}{P_t y_t} = \frac{1}{V'} , \qquad (7.2)$$

where V is the desired velocity of money. There is equilibrium when the demand for money is equal to the supply of money, i.e. $M_t' = M_t$. If the supply of money is then increased, people will have excess money balances to spend. If the flow of goods and services is given, and the desired velocity of money is unchanged, commodity prices P_t rise until M_t' is once more equated with M_t.

Irving Fisher and the quantity theorists tended to treat the ratio $(M_t / P_t y_t)$ as a constant $(1/V)$ for reasons outlined in Chapter 3. Keynes made that ratio depend upon the interest rate and the state of expectations. Friedman recast Keynesian liquidity preference into a theory in which wealth-holders choose amongst various assets with known or anticipated returns, so downplaying the role of imperfect information. Like others, however, he made no attempt to examine the nature of the services provided by money. Money is defined as a 'temporary abode of purchasing power'—a cross between the transactions and store of value roles—but thereafter the demand for money is treated much like the demand for any commodity, and analysed in terms of the budget constraint, relative prices, and tastes and preferences.

Capital assets

Friedman's contribution to pure monetary theory has been to treat money as a durable capital asset rather than, as in standard value theory, a consumption service. This characteristic means that relative prices are in terms of intertemporal rates of return, while the budget constraint must be cast in terms of wealth rather than income. A distinction is drawn between the demand for money by ultimate wealth-holders, to whom money is one form in which to hold wealth, and firms, to which money is a capital asset providing productive services which are combined with other forms of capital. Some attempts were made later to model money as a factor of production (Prais, 1975), but not much resulted from this line of thought, and certainly Friedman made little of it in his analysis of the demand for money which, in the main, revolved around the wealth-holders' preferences, for the analysis relates to an individual wealth-owning unit (1956: 14, para 13), and aggregation issues are ignored.

Wealth

Each individual is envisaged to have a balance sheet encompassing the desired composition of assets and the preferred distribution of liabilities, so that overall the individual obtains a desired wealth position including the desired holding of money. If one were analysing the demand for pins or peanuts, the budget constraint would be cast in terms of income, e.g. personal disposable income. In the case of money, the analogue of the budget constraint should be couched in terms of wealth—either in terms of the overall scale of the balance sheet or a measure of net worth. Friedman is not clear on this point, and suggests the use of real income or permanent income as an index or surrogate for wealth. However, he does recognize that wealth which is held in the form of human capital cannot readily be converted into monetary form. Thus the larger is w (the fraction of wealth held in non-human form), the larger is likely to be the holding of money.

Friedman then considers four different forms in which wealth can be held: money, bonds, equities, and physical capital.

Money

The nominal return on money depends on how money is defined. It may be (i) zero, as it generally is on currency or base money; or (ii) negative, when demand deposits are subject to net service charges; or (iii) positive, as it sometimes is on demand deposits on which interest is paid and generally is on time deposits. Friedman does not make clear whether the return on the deposit component of money is market-determined or subject to regulation. Money also has an implicit yield in terms of safety, liquidity, convenience, etc.

Bonds

Friedman's standard bond is a claim to a perpetual income stream in nominal units, and the return to the acquirer consists of the coupon payments along with the capital gains or losses. Consider the stream of income purchased by $1.00 invested in bonds at time $t = 0$, viz.

$$[r_b]_0 + [r_b]_0 \cdot \frac{d}{dt}\left[\frac{1}{[r_b]_t}\right] \tag{7.3}$$

where:

$\dfrac{1}{[r_b]_t}$ = price at time t of a bond yielding $1.00 per annum,

$$\frac{d}{dt}\left[\frac{1}{[r_b]_t}\right] = \text{rate of change of bond prices per unit of time,}$$

$$\frac{\dfrac{d}{dt}\left[\dfrac{1}{[r_b]_t}\right]}{\dfrac{1}{[r_b]_0}} = \text{rate of change of bond prices per unit of time } per\ dollar\ invested.$$

Differentiating (7.3) with respect to time gives

$$[r_b]_0 - \frac{[r_b]_0}{[r_b]_t^2} \cdot \frac{d[r_b]_t}{dt} \tag{7.4}$$

which can be approximated by

$$[r_b]_0 - \frac{1}{[r_b]_t} \frac{d[r_b]_t}{dt} \tag{7.5}$$

at time zero. This expression defines the nominal return from holding $1.00 of wealth in bonds.

Equities

An equity is treated by Friedman as being equivalent to the standard bond with a purchasing power escalator (indexation) clause. Thus the nominal return to the holder

=   the constant nominal amount (ie. dividend) received each year

±   increases or decreases in this nominal amount due to price level changes

±   any change in the nominal price of equity due to changes in interest rates and/or price levels.

These assumptions mean that the preceding formula for bonds can be used with appropriate amendments. In (7.3)

$$[r_b]_0 \text{ is replaced with } [r_e]_0 \frac{P_t}{P_0},$$

where $[r_e]_0$ is the market interest rate of equities defined analogously to $[r_b]_0$ (in effect the dividend yield) and P_t is the general level of prices. Also, in (7.3) we replace

$$[r_b]_0 \frac{d}{dt}\left[\frac{1}{[r_b]_t}\right] \qquad \text{with} \qquad \frac{[r_e]_0}{P_0} \cdot \frac{d}{dt}\left[\frac{P_t}{[r_e]_t}\right],$$

where $1/[r_e]_t$ is the price at time t of an equity yielding $1.00 per annum.

Here we may note that $\dfrac{d}{dt}\left[\dfrac{1}{[r_e]_t}\cdot\dfrac{P_t}{P_0}\right]$ is the rate of change of equity prices per unit of time. When this magnitude is divided by $1/[r_e]_t$, what results is the rate of change of equity prices per unit of time per dollar invested, which is the expression given above.

Combining the two new components, the rate of return per dollar invested in equities is:

$$[r_e]_0 \frac{P_t}{P_0} + \frac{[r_e]_0}{P_0}\cdot\left[\frac{P_t}{[r_e]_t}\right]. \tag{7.6}$$

Differentiating we obtain:

$$[r_e]_0 \frac{P_t}{P_0} + \frac{[r_e]_0}{[r_e]_t}\cdot\frac{1}{P_0}\frac{dP_t}{dt} - \frac{P_t}{P_0}\cdot\frac{[r_e]_0}{[r_e]_t^2}\frac{d[r_e]_t}{dt} \tag{7.7}$$

which can be approximated by

$$[r_e]_0 + \frac{1}{P}\frac{dP}{dt} - \frac{1}{[r_e]_t}\frac{d[r_e]_t}{dt} \tag{7.8}$$

at time zero. The return on equity is governed by the dividend flow and changes in equity prices due to variations in the general price level or because of interest rate changes.

Goods

Wealth may also be held in the form of physical goods such as consumer durables or tins of food on the shelf. These differ from bonds or equities in that the income stream is 'in kind' rather than in monetary terms. In addition, to the extent that the items stored or held as a capital asset appreciate or depreciate in money value along with the general level of prices, these assets may be regarded as yielding a nominal return comprising two elements: stream of services provided ± appreciation or depreciation in price.

At time zero, the expected price appreciation or depreciation can be approximated by

$$\frac{1}{P_t}\frac{dP_t}{dt}, \tag{7.9}$$

where P_t is, as before, the general level of prices. An increase in the expected rate of changes of prices (i.e. in inflation) raises the cost of holding wealth in the form of money.

Tastes

Finally, the demand for money will depend on the tastes and preferences of individuals for the peculiar income and service streams provided by the various assets, in particular (although not solely) the preference for the non-pecuniary services of money—safety, liquidity, convenience, etc. One variable which Friedman saw as likely to be important in governing the taste for liquidity was the degree of economic stability expected to prevail in the future (Friedman, 1961). The argument implies that wealth-holders are likely to attach more value to liquidity when they expect economic conditions to be unstable than when they see a more certain future. Events such as wars and the onset of major economic declines seem likely to be associated with expectations of greater instability and with larger holdings in money balances. However, this idea was difficult to model and express in quantitative terms, and proved to be something of a dead end.[2]

The demand function

Putting these elements together gives us the following demand function for money

$$M_t = f(P_t, [r_M]_t, [r_b]_t - \frac{1}{[r_b]_t} \frac{d[r_b]_t}{dt}, [r_e]_t - \frac{1}{[r_e]_t} \frac{d[r_e]_t}{dt} + \frac{1}{P_t} \frac{dP_t}{dt}, \frac{1}{P_t} \frac{dP_t}{dt}, W_t, w_t, u_t)$$

(7.10)

where M_t = nominal money balances demanded
  P_t = price level
  W_t = total wealth, measured as the capitalized value of the flow of income, i.e. Y_t/r_t where Y_t is income and r_t is the rate of discount.
  w_t = fraction of wealth held in non-human form
  u_t = variables influencing the 'taste' for money (or liquidity preferences).

Equation (7.10) can be simplified in several ways, viz.:

(i) if we suppose that bond and equity yields are expected to be stable over time, in which case

$$\frac{d[r_b]_t}{dt} = \frac{d[r_e]_t}{dt} = 0$$

(ii) if $\frac{1}{P_t} \frac{dP_t}{dt}$ in the equities term can be represented by that for commodities;

(iii) and if $[r_b]_t$ and $[r_e]_t$ together are an adequate measure of r_t,

then we obtain the demand function

$$M_t = f(P_t, [r_M]_t, [r_b]_t, [r_e]_t, \frac{1}{P_t} \frac{dP_t}{dt}, Y_t, w_t, u_t).$$

(7.11)

Finally, with the homogeneity postulate, the demand function can be assumed to be independent of nominal units, and to depend on 'real' magnitudes. Consider, first, prices. Equation (7.11) can then be written as

$$\frac{M_t}{P_t} = f([r_M]_t, [r_b]_t, [r_e]_t, \frac{1}{P_t}\frac{dP_t}{dt}, w_t, u_t), \tag{7.12}$$

i.e. as a demand for real money balances. In terms of nominal income, the function can be expressed as

$$\frac{M_t}{Y_t} = f([r_M]_t, [r_b]_t, [r_e]_t, \frac{1}{P_t}\frac{dP_t}{dt}, \frac{P_t}{Y_t}, w_t, u_t) \tag{7.13}$$

$$= \frac{1}{V([r_M]_t, [r_b]_t, [r_e]_t, \frac{1}{P_t}\frac{dP_t}{dt}, w_t, \frac{Y_t}{P_t}, u_t)} \tag{7.14}$$

Rearranging, we obtain

$$M_t V = P_t y_t \tag{7.15}$$

where $P_t y_t = Y_t$. Here is the usual quantity theory of money where V is income velocity.

Thus Friedman reformulated the quantity theory with velocity hypothesized to be a constant function but not a constant number. If the function is stable, velocity will vary systematically and predictably in response to the variables contained within the function, but that is the extent of the variation. Variations in M_t will then have predictable consequences for $P_t y_t$.

7.3 The Quantity Theory Position

IN a recent assessment of Friedman's work, his longstanding co-author Anna Schwartz attributes much of Friedman's success in the 1970s to 'his empirical emphasis', i.e. to the fact that 'he framed his arguments in the form of testable hypotheses' (Schwartz, 1998). This characteristic was less to the fore when making his restatement of the quantity theory. Then Friedman did not elucidate a set of testable propositions but instead laid inheritance to the quantity theory as an 'approach' or point of view—something that cannot be written down precisely—which runs back to via the Chicago School to earlier writers such as Irving Fisher. 'To the best of my knowledge, no systematic statement of this theory as developed at Chicago exists. And this is as it should be, for the Chicago tradition was not a rigid system, an unchangeable orthodoxy, but a way of looking at things' (Friedman, 1956: 3).

Moreover, at one of the crucial points in his argument, Friedman makes claims not about the quantity theory, but about what 'the quantity theorist' 'accepts', 'regards', and 'holds' (Backhouse, 1991):

The quantity theorist accepts the empirical hypothesis that the demand for money is highly stable . . .

The quantity theorist . . . also regards it [the demand function for money] as playing a vital role in determining variables that he considers of great importance for the analysis of the economy as a whole . . .

The quantity theorist also holds that there are important factors affecting the supply of money that do not affect the demand for money. (Friedman, 1956: 16)

By 1970, however, Friedman had embraced the term 'monetarism' and the empirical approach was evident in the ten 'key propositions of monetarism', set out in Table 7.1. By way of comparison, Tables 7.2–7.5 provide some alternative definitions of monetarism by James Tobin, Doug Purvis, Thomas Mayer, and Anna Schwartz. Tobin (1972) outlines six aspects based on Friedman's *Theoretical Framework* (Friedman, 1971).[3] Purvis (1976) and Mayer (1978) introduce some of the Keynesian–monetarist debates about the transmission mechanism and the stability of the multiplier, none of which would seem to be central to Friedman. Anna Schwartz (1998) is the only one to move beyond the confines of a closed economy, despite the fact that advocacy of floating exchange rates has been a consistent theme of Friedman (see Friedman, 1953*b*), and that floating exchange rates are the building blocks of open economy monetarism (see next chapter).

Table 7.1 Friedman: the key propositions of monetarism

1. There is a consistent though not precise relationship between the rate of growth of the quantity of money and the rate of growth of nominal income. If the quantity of money grows rapidly, so will nominal income and conversely.

2. This relation is not obvious to the naked eye over short periods, because it takes time for changes in monetary growth to affect income and how long it takes is itself variable. The rate of monetary growth today is not very closely related to the rate of income growth today. Today's growth depends rather on what has been happening to money over a past period.

3. On the average, a change in the rate of monetary growth produces a change in the rate of growth of nominal income about 6 to 9 months later. This is an average. Sometimes the delay is longer, sometimes shorter.

4. The changed rate of growth of nominal income typically shows up first in output and hardly at all in prices . . . If the rate of monetary growth is reduced, for example, then about six to nine months later, the rate of growth of nominal income and also of physical output will decline. However, the rate of price rise will be affected very little. There will be downward pressure on the rate of price rise only as a gap emerges between actual and potential output.

5. On the average, the effect on prices comes some 9 to 15 months after the effect on income and output, so the total delay between a change in monetary growth and a change in the rate of inflation, averages something like 15 to 24 months. That works both ways.

6. Even after allowance for the delay in the effect of monetary growth, the relation is far from perfect. There is many a slip 'twixt the monetary change and the income change.

7. In the short run, which may be as much as 5 or 10 years, monetary changes affect primarily output. Over decades, on the other hand, the rate of monetary growth affects primarily prices.

8. It follows from the propositions I have so far stated that *inflation is always and everywhere a monetary phenomenon* in the sense that it is and can be produced only by a more rapid increase in the quantity of money than in output.

9. Government spending may or may not be inflationary. It clearly will be inflationary if it is financed by creating money, that is, by printing currency or creating bank deposits. If it is financed by taxes or by borrowing from the public, the main effect is that the government spends the funds instead of the taxpayer or instead of the person who would otherwise have borrowed the funds. By itself, fiscal policy is not important for inflation. What is important is how the spending is financed.

10. A change in monetary growth affects interest rates in one direction at first but in the opposite direction later on. More rapid monetary growth at first tends to lower interest rates. But later on, as it raises spending and stimulates price inflation, it also produces a rise in the demand for loans which will tend to raise interest rates. In addition, rising prices introduce a discrepancy between real and nominal interest rates.

Source: Extracted from Friedman (1970, pp. 22–26).

Table 7.2 Tobin on Friedman's 'quantity theory'

1. Emphasis on the distinction between the real and the nominal quantity of money and on the fact that what matters to rational individuals is the real quantity.

2. Use of the quantity identity, or some variant, as an organizing framework for macroeconomic analysis.

3. Belief that the central equation of macroeconomics is that of the demand for money to largely exogenous supply.

4. Interest in the determinants of the demand for money, and the size and direction of their effects.

5. Assertion that in the short run, nominal income is proportional to the supply of money, although changes in nominal income may affect output as well as prices.

6. Assertion that real magnitudes are in long-run equilibrium independent of the nominal quantity of money, so that nominal magnitudes—prices, money incomes—are simply proportional to the nominal quantity of money.

Source: Tobin (1972).

Rather than seeking to examine all of the dimensions of monetarism, we select four aspects along with supporting quotations from Friedman's work.

1. The absence of a 'fundamental flaw in the price mechanism' and a tendency to 'a long-run equilibrium position characterized by full employment of resources' (Friedman, 1971: 15–16).
2. 'The quantity theory in all its versions rests on a distinction between the *nominal* quantity of money and *real* quantity of money' (Friedman, 1973: 37).
3. Monetary changes exert only a transitory effect upon the (real) rate of interest. 'The interest rate is not the price of money. The interest rate is the price of credit.' 'There is a liquidity effect which operates but it is a short-term effect.' 'A higher

Table 7.3 Purvis's historical 'Characteristic Propositions' of monetarism

1. 'The Quantity Theory of Money'.
2. The demand for money is interest inelastic.
3. The demand for money is more stable than the Keynesian consumption function.
4. The lags in the effects of monetary policy are long and uncertain.
5. The transmission process entails a broad set of substitution relationships involving more than just money and bonds, and working through channels other than simply through 'the interest rate'.
6. Prices (including nominal wages) are sufficiently flexible that output is (approximately) maintained at its full employment level.
7. The real interest rate is (approximately) a constant.
8. Fiscal policy doesn't matter.
9. The (private sector) of the economy is more stable in the absence of discretionary stabilization policy than in its presence; further, the path of real output is independent of any systematic behaviour of the nominal stock of money.

Source: Purvis (1980).

Table 7.4 Mayer's 'structure of monetarism'

1. The quantity theory of money, in the sense of the predominance of the impact of monetary factors on nominal income.
2. The monetarist model of the transmission process.
3. Belief in the inherent stability of the private sector.
4. Irrelevance of allocative detail for the explanation of short-run changes in money income, and belief in a fluid capital market.
5. Focus on the price level as a whole rather than on individual prices.
6. Reliance on small rather than large econometric models.
7. Use of the reserve base or similar measure as the indicator of monetary policy.
8. Use of the money stock as the proper target of monetary policy.
9. Acceptance of a monetary growth rule.
10. Rejection of an unemployment–inflation trade-off in favour of a real *Phillips* curve.
11. A relatively greater concern about inflation than about unemployment compared to other economists.
12. Dislike of government intervention.

Source: Mayer (1978).

Table 7.5 Schwartz on Friedman

1. Inflation is always and everywhere a monetary phenomenon—central banks cause inflation.

2. Monetary authorities should follow a rule rather than exercise discretion—activist monetary policy is a source of instability.

3. Fixed exchange rates are a source of instability.

4. Monetary collapse causes depression.

5. Misperceptions about the price level can lend to deviations of output from what it would otherwise be.

6. In the long run there is no relation between the rate of inflation and the rate of unemployment, that unemployment returns to its normal rate, regardless of the rate of inflation.

Source: Schwartz (1998).

---

rate of increase in the quantity of money, leaving out the Fisher effect, will end up with interest rates back where they started.' 'No permanent effect on the real rate remains.' (Friedman, 1968*b*: 12, 44–47).

4. 'Substantial changes in prices in nominal income are almost invariably the result of changes in the nominal supply of money.' 'The stock of money is a key variable in policies directed at the control of the level of prices.' 'Government deficits are expansionary primarily if they serve as a means of increasing the stock of money' (Friedman, 1973: 39, 62, 64).

All of these propositions can be questioned. For example, the first might be better treated as an assumption ('real income is determined outside of the system') than as a conclusion of Friedman's analysis, which relies either upon 'Pigou effects' of falling prices upon consumption or upon rather loose appeals to the notion of Walrasian general equilibrium. The second, according to Tobin (1972), is not in serious dispute amongst theorists of all schools, although it is probably the case that Friedman made this idea his own and made more of it than most. Third, the constancy of real interest rates for the purposes of monetary analysis rests on some very special assumptions about the invariance of the marginal productivity of capital—what Burstein (1963) described as the 'Chicago Special case' in Knightian analysis. The fourth reflects Friedman's distinction between two versions of the quantity theory, operating at two levels, which he calls the 'analytical' and the 'empirical':

On an analytical level it is an analysis of the factors determining the quantity of money the community wishes to hold; on an empirical level, it is the generalization that changes in desired real balances (in the demand of money) tend to proceed slowly and gradually or to be the results of events set in train by prior changes in supply, whereas in contrast, substantial changes in the supply of nominal balances can and frequently do occur independently of any changes in demand. The conclusion is that substantial changes in prices or nominal income are almost invariably the result of changes in the nominal supply of money. (Friedman, 1971: 3)

Nevertheless, much of the flavour of Friedman's position can be conveyed using the 'simple common model' of his 1971 theoretical framework, which corresponds to the standard textbook IS–LM model, viz.:

$$S(y_t, r_t) = I(r_t) \tag{7.16}$$

$$L(y_t, r_t) = \frac{M_t}{P_t}, \tag{7.17}$$

where the variables have the same meanings as in earlier chapters. This system has two equations but three unknowns—Friedman's 'missing equation'. Closing out the system can be achieved in a number of ways: fixing y_t, fixing P_t, tying P_t, y_t together by means of a Phillips curve, or by combining $P_t y_t = Y_t$ to give a theory of nominal income.

Adopting the first, viz.:

$$y_t = y_0 \tag{7.18}$$

enables us to obtain the simple quantity theory propositions outlined earlier. Equation (7.17) then determines the equilibrium rate of interest, say r_0, along the lines of loanable funds theory. Substituting y_0 and r_0 into (7.17) means that M_t and P_t vary proportionately.

The result is shown in Figure 7.1, where from A we suppose there to be an increase in the money supply from M_0 to M_1. With prices initially unchanged at P_0, the LM curve moves from LM_0 to LM_1, lowering interest rates to r_1 and stimulating consumption and investment spending. As prices respond, the LM curve shifts back to

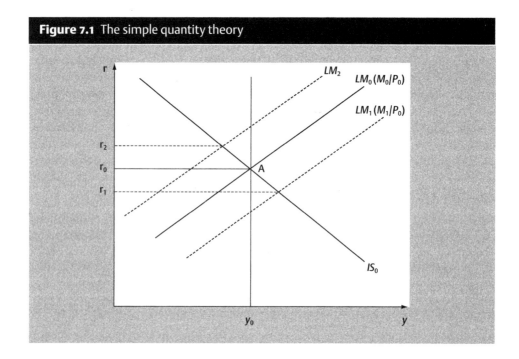

Figure 7.1 The simple quantity theory

LM_0. Prices continue to rise until the price expansion exactly matches the monetary expansion.

A number of features are noteworthy:

1. The monetary expansion initially increases real money balances, but the resulting price rise restores real balances to the starting level. Real balances increase, in these terms, only if larger real balances are demanded by money-holders in aggregate. This is the basis of proposition (2) above.

2. A monetary expansion produces an initial reduction in the rate of interest (the 'liquidity' effect) but when prices rise interest rates end up where they started. Conversely, from A an increase in liquidity preferences (shift in the demand for money) will immediately raise rates to r_2 (an upward movement in the LM curve to LM_2), but the fall in prices needed to generate the larger real balances desired will see interest rates return to r_0. Thus a change in either money supply or money demand produces only a transitory change in interest rates, in line with proposition (3) above.

3. If monetary forces result in no permanent change in interest rates, what governs the level of real interest rates? They are anchored at the intersection of the IS curve with the y_0 line at that level which equates investment with full employment savings. An increase in planned investment (demand for loanable funds) will raise equilibrium real interest rates; an increase in savings (supply of loanable funds) will lower real interest rates. Real rates will thus respond to changes in productivity and thrift—that is real variables not nominal ones.

4. Consider now the behaviour of velocity. For simplicity, suppose that the elasticity of the demand for money with respect to real income is unity. We can then rewrite (7.17) as:

$$L(r) = \frac{M_t}{Y_t} \qquad (7.19)$$

where $1/L(r)$ is the income velocity of money. In response to a monetary expansion, velocity falls transitorily as the lower interest rates induce adjustments in desired money holdings and bring desired velocity into equality with actual velocity.[4] When prices rise, so too do interest rates and velocity. The proportionate change in prices restores interest rates and velocity to their 'normal' levels. Expenditure flows are on a mirror image path to interest rates and velocity, rising temporarily and then returning to their normal level.

This sequence, but with interest rates left out of the story, is virtually identical to that of Irving Fisher (1911b):

'The chief purpose is to set forth the causes determining the purchasing power of money. This purchasing power has been studied as the effect of five and only five, groups of causes. The five groups are money, deposits, their velocities of circulation, and the volume of trade. These and their effects, prices, we saw to be connected by an equation called the equation of exchange $MV + M'V' = \Sigma pQ \ldots$

To set forth all the facts and possibilities as to causation we need to study the effects of varying, one at a time, the various magnitudes in the equation of exchange. We shall in each case distinguish between the effects during transition periods and the ultimate or normal effects after the transition periods are finished . . .

Velocity of circulation is the average rate of 'turnover', and depends on countless individual rates of turnover. In the long run and for a large number of people, the average rate of turnover, or what amounts to the same thing, the average time money remains in the same hands, will be very closely determined. It will depend on density of population, commercial customs, rapidity of transport, and other technical conditions but not on the quantity of money and deposits nor on the price level. If the quantities of money and deposits are doubled, there is nothing, so far as velocity of circulation is concerned, to prevent the price level from doubling. On the contrary, doubling money, deposits, and prices would necessarily leave velocity quite unchanged. The velocity of circulation either of money or deposits is independent of the quantity of money or of deposits . . .

It may be claimed—in fact it has been claimed—that such an increase results in an increased volume of trade. We now proceed to show that (except during transition periods) the volume of trade, like the velocity of circulation of money, is independent of the quantity of money. An inflation of the currency cannot increase the product of farms and factories, nor the speed of freight trains or ships. The stream of business depends on natural resources and technical conditions, not on the quantity of money. Since then, a doubling in the quantity of money (1) will normally double deposits subject to check in the same ratio and (2) will not appreciably affect either the velocity of circulation of money or of deposits or the volume of trade, it follows necessarily and mathematically that the level of prices must double . . .

One of the objectors to the quantity theory attempts to dispose of the equation of exchange as stated by Newcomb, by calling it a mere truism. While the equation of exchange is, if we choose, a mere 'truism' . . . 'Truisms' should never be neglected. The greatest generalisations of physical science, such as that forces are proportional to mass and acceleration, are truisms, but, when duly supplemented by specific data, these truisms are the most fruitful sources of useful mechanical knowledge. (Fisher, 1911*b*: 149–58)

Responding to Fisher's call for 'specific data' to supplement the 'truism' of the equation of exchange, we conclude this section by reproducing in Figure 7.2 a recent analysis from 1960–1990 of the monetary growth–inflation relationship using a cross-section study of 110 countries (McCandless and Weber, 1995: 10). They conclude that 'growth rates of the money supply and the general price level are highly correlated, with a correlation coefficient close to one.'

7.4 Nominal and Real Interest Rates

DOUBLING (or halving) the quantity of money is a useful one-off illustrative exercise, but continued monetary changes (and accompanying price changes) would bring about a change to expected inflation, driving a wedge between nominal and real interest rates. As a first approximation, we might suppose the real sector of Friedman's 'simple common model' to be unaffected by expected inflation. That is, following Bailey (1971), the assumption is that real consumption, real investment, and real

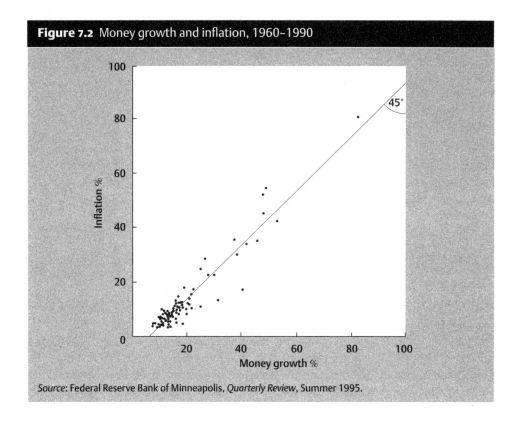

Figure 7.2 Money growth and inflation, 1960–1990

Source: Federal Reserve Bank of Minneapolis, *Quarterly Review*, Summer 1995.

income (along with employment and real wages) can all be analysed without reference to prices or expectations of continuing price changes (inflation). As Bailey asks,

Won't firms invest more, and hire more labor, if they expect the price level to rise, and won't households consume more and save less? Not necessarily. Firms will invest more if they expect the price level to rise and they do not have to pay a correspondingly higher rate of interest, or its equivalent, for the capital to invest. They will hire more labor if the price level rises more than the wage level. But whether they have to pay a higher rate of interest depends on expectations in the money market; if they do have to pay a rate of interest that rises by just the same amount as the expected rise in the price level, they have no incentive to invest more than they would otherwise. (1971: 72)

This brings us to the money market. Consider, for example, Friedman's demand for money function and the money, bonds, and equities choice (along with the special assumptions made about the behaviour of equities). As Friedman noted:

If there were no differences of opinion about price movements and interest-rate movements, and bonds and equities were equivalent except that the former are expressed in nominal units, arbitrage would of course make

$$r_b - \frac{1}{r_b}\frac{dr_b}{dt} = r_e + \frac{1}{P_t}\frac{dP_t}{dt} - \frac{1}{t_e}\frac{dr_e}{dt},$$

or, if we suppose rates of interest either stable or changing at the same percentage rate,

$$r_b = r_e + \frac{1}{P} \frac{dP}{dt}$$

that is, the 'money' interest rate equal to the 'real' rate plus the percentage rate of change of prices. In application the rate of change of prices must be interpreted as an 'expected' rate of change . . . (1956: 9)

Where there was previously no expectation of inflation, such arbitrage takes care of the bonds–equities relationship. The cost of holding money vis-à-vis equitites (or real assets) is then given by the real rate plus the expected rate of inflation $(r_t + \dot{p}^e_t)$ or vis-à-vis bonds by the nominal (or money) rate of interest (i_t), so that (7.17) becomes

$$\frac{M_t}{P_t} = L(y_t, i_t) = L(y_t, r_t + \dot{p}^e_t),\tag{7.20}$$

where $i_t = r_t + \dot{p}^e_t$[5].

As a consequence of the assumed behaviour, expenditure sector relationships summarized by the IS curve depend on the real rate, while the LM curve is governed by the nominal rate. Figure 7.3 illustrates the position. Before the onset of expected inflation, IS_0 and LM_0 depict the real and monetary sector equilibrium. Since the graph is in terms of the nominal rate, anticipated inflation itself does not alter the LM curve. But expected inflation shifts the IS curve to IS_1. For each value of r the level

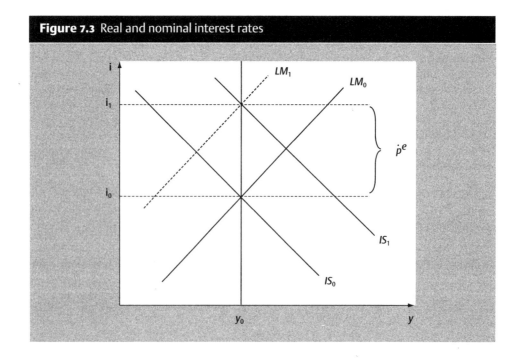

Figure 7.3 Real and nominal interest rates

of real income that is consistent with real sector equilibrium is the same as before, but each value of r now corresponds to a value of i higher by $\dot{p}^e$. The price level must rise to maintain equilibrium at y_0, shifting the LM curve to LM_1

Thus the overall effect is to raise the nominal rate of interest by the expectation of inflation—the Fisher effect[6]—leaving the real rate of interest and real income unchanged in equilibrium. However, the expectation of inflation does not generate continuous price rises, i.e. inflation. Rather the expectation itself results in a once-for-all increase in the price level above the level prices would have been if no inflation were expected. This single limited rise in the price level is needed to produce the smaller real money balances now demanded. There is not a continuous flight from money; because of the higher cost of holding money balances, fewer are required. In terms of the equation of exchange, there is an increase in the velocity of money and an associated increase in prices.

7.5 Inflationary Equilibria

BOTH of the previous sections have examined one-off changes in prices. In order to analyse continuous price changes we need to begin with a sustained monetary expansion. Again assume a full employment equilibrium with the money stock and prices constant, and interest rates (real and nominal) of 5 per cent per annum. That is (letting $\dot{M}$ represent the growth rate of the money supply and $\dot{P}_t$ the growth rate of prices), $\dot{M}_t = 0$, $\dot{P}_t = 0$, $i_t = r_t = 5$ per cent p. a.

Let that equilibrium be disturbed by a sustainable (and initially unanticipated) increase in the money stock of 10 per cent p. a. The 'static' quantity theory would predict that prices will increase at the same rate, i.e. $\dot{P}_t = \dot{M}_t = 10$ per cent p. a., with velocity constant. But that implies that the rate of interest in real terms becomes, and stays, negative. The missing element is expectations. People will come to expect a 10 per cent inflation and require that an inflation premium of that magnitude be built into interest rates. If so, the nominal rate of interest (i) rises to 15 per cent, leaving the real rate (r_t) unchanged at 5 per cent p. a. (i.e. 15 per cent per annum minus the 10 per cent per annum expectation). But at the higher nominal rate of interest, less money *is* demanded. A once-for-all increase in the price level is needed (additional to the 10 per cent per annum increase) to reduce money balances in real terms (i.e. to increase the velocity of money). In the transition to the new equilibrium, prices for a time increase more rapidly than the increase in the quantity of money. The new equilibrium path has $\dot{M}_t = 10$ per cent p. a., $\dot{P}_t = 10$ per cent p. a., $i = 15$ per cent p. a., $r_t = 5$ per cent p. a. This can be sustained so long as the money supply continues to expand at 10 per cent per annum, and expectations are geared to that growth.

In order to examine the possible impacts on interest rates, we effectively combine Figures 7.1 and 7.3. This combination is shown in Figure 7.4. Beginning, as before with IS_0, LM_0, and the interest rate i_0, the immediate effect of the monetary expansion is to

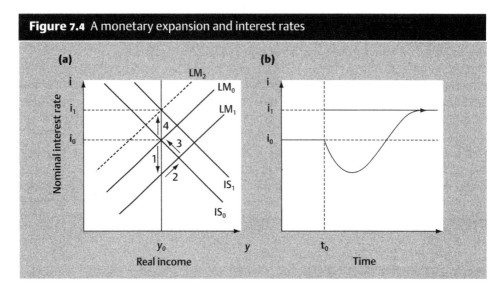

Figure 7.4 A monetary expansion and interest rates

cause interest rates to fall (sequence (1) in 7.4*a*). Friedman (1968*a*) called this the 'liquidity effect'. As spending is stimulated, interest rates rise (sequence (2)). When price rises, interest rates return to i_0 (sequence (3)). The two were referred to by Friedman as the 'income effect' upon interest rates. Nominal interest rates eventually rise to i_1, when inflation expectations respond to the monetary expansion. Friedman described this as the 'price expectations effect' (sequence (4)).

If the monetary expansion had been fully anticipated, interest rates would in theory rise directly to i_1. But on the scenario outlined above (Friedman's account) interest rates initially fall and later rise—eventually, of course, to a level above the starting position, as shown in Figure 7.4*b*. In Friedman's words: 'A change in monetary growth affects interest rates in one direction at first but in the opposite direction later on' (see Table 7.1, #10). At the time he went on to note:

That is why throughout the world interest rates are highest in those countries that have had the most rapid rise in the quantity of money and also in prices—countries like Brazil, Chile, Korea and Israel.

In the opposite direction, a slower rate of monetary growth at first raises interest rates but later on, as it reduces spending and price inflation, it lowers interest rates. That is why interest rates are lowest in those countries that have had the slowest rate of growth in the quantity of money—countries like Germany and Switzerland. (Friedman, 1973: 29)

How long does it take for interest rates to adjust to money? Friedman suggested that the liquidity effect may last six months, and the income effect about twelve months, so that interest rates took 'something like 18 months' to return to their initial level. However, he estimated the price expectations effect to be much slower, so slow in fact that it may take ten to twenty *years* for interest rates to get to the final equilibrium level! These estimates are broadly consistent with the lags calculated by Irving Fisher (1930). Fisher argued that it takes twenty to thirty years for price expectations to adjust fully to inflation and thus twenty to thirty years for interest rates to adjust fully as well. Later, however, Friedman and Schwartz (1982) reported that the long lags had disappeared in the post-war years.

Some lag in the adjustment of interest rates to inflation is consistent with the tendency for measured real rates of interest to vary inversely with sharp changes in the inflation rates. There would seem to be only a partial adjustment of nominal rates to inflation. For example, real rates fell when inflation accelerated in the 1970s and rose when inflation decelerated in later decades. There are, however, other explanations. One is the difficulty of measuring expected inflation and thus *ex ante* real rates of interest. The other is the presence of wealth effects. Metzler (1951) showed that unanticipated inflation due to money creation from open market operations would lower the real rate of interest. Using much the same model, Robert Mundell (1963*a*) argued that *anticipated* inflation would also lower the real rate of interest. In his analysis, interest rates fully adjust for inflation expectations, but nominal rates rise by less than expected inflation, stimulating economic growth. This comes about because real cash balances decline, and the reduced wealth stimulates savings, lowering the real rate of interest and increasing investment.

However, monetarist superneutrality has always been an empirical, as well as a theoretical, idea. Neutrality refers to the notion that one can conceive of a static, non-inflationary equilibrium which is invariant to monetary changes. Monetarist superneutrality is the idea that an inflationary equilibrium can be considered in much the same way, so that variations in monetary growth find reflection predominantly in inflation, once the transition effects upon interest rates, output, and unemployment are over. The study referred to earlier which examined the monetary growth—inflation relationship in 110 countries also found there to be no consistent relationship one way or the other between inflation and real output growth. This is shown in Figure 7.5.

Of course, what we have outlined here (under highly special assumptions) is the transition from a non-inflationary equilibrium to an inflationary one. Inflation

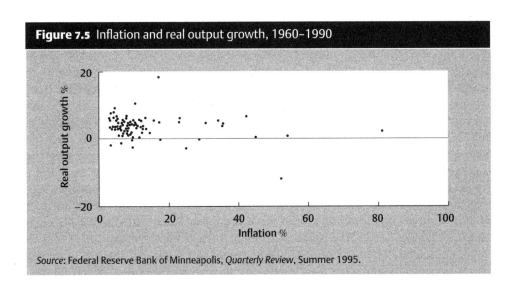

Figure 7.5 Inflation and real output growth, 1960–1990

Source: Federal Reserve Bank of Minneapolis, *Quarterly Review*, Summer 1995.

begins at zero and is disturbed by an unanticipated monetary expansion of 10 per cent per annum. For a time, inflation rises above 10 per cent per annum as the monetary effect upon prices is supplemented by a one-off increase in velocity. However, once things settle down, and inflation expectations and nominal interest rates are geared to the underlying inflation rate, inflation should proceed at a steady 10 per cent per annum—so long as the growth rate of monetary expansion does not accelerate.

Some inflations clearly *do* accelerate. During the German inflation from August 1922 to November 1923, inflation averaged 322 per cent per *month* but at the end accelerated to such an extent that prices were rising at the rate of 32,400 per cent a month. The world record increase occurred in Hungary from August 1945 to July 1946 when inflation averaged 19,800 per cent per month and accelerated to a peak of 4.2×10^{16} per cent per month in the final month. What causes inflation to accelerate to these levels? Can the view that 'inflation is always and everywhere a monetary phenomenon' be sustained for such episodes of hyperinflation?

7.6 Hyperinflation

HYPERINFLATION is generally (and arbitrarily) defined, following Cagan (1956), as periods when the rise in prices exceeds 50 per cent per month. Inflation of this magnitude took place in Austria, Germany, Hungary, Poland, and Russia after the First World War, in Greece, Hungary, China, and Taiwan at the end of the Second World War and in Bolivia, Peru, Argentina, Brazil, Poland, Nicaragua, and Yugoslavia in the 1980s. The German hyperinflation remains the best known, and the most extensively researched, and provides an instructive example of the processes involved. It also illustrates the varied explanations offered to explain the phenomenon of hyperinflation.

Runaway inflation can derive from three sources. First, it may be set in train by the depreciation of the foreign currency value of the currency, which raises the cost of imports and the cost of living. Second, it may be due to upward adjustments to wages, for example, under trade union pressures. Third, the inflation may stem from a budget deficit and money creation. Of course, all three are likely to interact, but they have been put forward as competing (if not mutually exclusive) hypotheses of the German inflationary experience. Contemporary German writers favoured the first. They blamed reparations payments imposed on the German nation after the war as the primary source of the trouble which led to the collapse of the mark, reinforced by speculative capital—both foreign and German—fleeing the country. Their explanation was challenged by Professor Bresciani-Turroni (1931), an Italian member of the Reparations Committee, who (in a book translated into English in 1938) blamed a budget deficit which was financed by increasing the amount of money in circulation. Joan Robinson (1938) in her review of this book saw the rise in money wages as critical because—in what would now be seen as a structural view (Feldman,

1993)—German workers were bearing an undue share of the burden being placed on society and were 'faced with starvation. Wage rises had to be granted.' In her view ... the quantity of money was important, not because it caused inflation, but because it allowed it to continue' (Robinson, 1938: 74–5).[7]

Three puzzles

This then was the background against which Phillip Cagan provided the first systematic analysis of the relationship between the quantity of money and the price level during hyperinflation. Not only was his the first econometric treatment of the subject, it was the first application of the adaptive expectations–distributed lag technique to monetary data. It was also the first to explore the dynamics of hyperinflation and supply a framework for addressing three puzzles of monetary behaviour during such episodes. One is the behaviour of velocity and the apparent 'flight from money'. The simple quantity theory predicts proportionality between money and price movements. During periods of very rapid inflation, prices increase much more rapidly than money balances, so much so in fact that real money balances (M/P) shrink to a fraction of their initial value. In the German case, real money balances fell to only 3 per cent of their starting level.

A second puzzle is the shortage of money. As W. Arthur Lewis observed of Germany:

The printing presses were working full-time, but were unable to print all the money that people needed to buy goods at the inflated prices. If the inflation was due to 'too much money chasing too few goods', how could there be a shortage of money? (1949: 27)

The third puzzle is: why the money creation? If the inflation originated through the balance of payments or from workers' wage demands, these factors at least explain why the government changed the money supply (to prevent unemployment). But if the money supply creation is the cause of inflation, then the question becomes: 'why did the quantity of money increase and by so large an amount?' (Cagan, 1956: 77).

Cagan's starting point is a Friedman-type demand for money function (Eq. 7.12) in which real money balances demanded vary with the cost of holding money, income or wealth, and tastes. Real money balances, we have seen, change dramatically during hyperinflation. The quantity theorist has to explain the movements and, in so doing, show that the behaviour of real money balances results from movements along, rather than shifts of, the demand function. In addition, the explanatory factors within the demand function must be intimately linked with money supply variations. This is the import of Friedman's contention that [t]he quantity theory is ... the generalization that changes in desired real balances (in the demand for money) tend to proceed slowly or gradually or *to be the result of events set in train by prior changes in supply*' (Friedman, 1968b: 434—our emphasis).

Considering the arguments of the demand function, real income is not invariant during hyperinflation but is relatively constant in comparison with the vast change in real balances. Likewise, the return on bonds (interest) and equities (dividends) exhibit greater stability than the return from holding non-perishable consumer goods, given by the rate of depreciation in the value of money, i.e. the rate of change of prices. This variable is the one chosen by Cagan to measure the cost of holding money under rapid inflation.

The specific form of the demand function is

$$\ln \left(\frac{M}{P} \right)_t^* = -\alpha E_t - \gamma \qquad (7.22)$$

in which $E_t = \left(\frac{1}{P} \frac{dP}{dt} \right)^e$ i.e. the expected rate of change of prices and t = months.

The elasticity of real money balances desired, $(M/P)^*$, is proportional to the expected rate of change in prices.

The next step is the market-clearing condition, which is simply

$$\ln \left(\frac{M}{P} \right)_t = \ln \left(\frac{M}{P} \right)_t^* . \qquad (7.23)$$

That is, the price level is bid up (or down) as people spend money balances, to bring equality within the month between actual and desired real balances.

What is then required is a specification of the expectations-forming mechanism. This takes the general form

$$\left(\frac{dE}{dt} \right)_t = \beta (C_t - E_t) \qquad (7.24)$$

Where C_t is the *actual* rate of changes in prices at month t. One particular specification is the distributed lag relationship:

$$E_t - E_{t-1} = \beta (C_{t-1} - E_{t-1}),$$

which we rearrange as

$$E_t = \beta C_{t-1} + (1 - \beta) E_{t-1}.$$

Since

$$E_{t-1} = \beta C_{t-2} + (1 - \beta) E_{t-2}$$

By successive substitution we obtain:

$$E_t = \beta C_{t-1} + \beta (1 - \beta) C_{t-2} + \beta (1 - \beta)^2 C_{t-3} + \ldots$$

$$= \beta \sum_{\tau = 0}^{\infty} (1 - \beta)^\tau C_{t-1-\tau}. \qquad (7.25)$$

Here the coefficients or weights $\beta (1 - \beta)^\tau$ decline in geometric progression in successive periods, with the implication being that people form their expectations adaptively on the basis of the inflation they have been experiencing, giving more weight to the recent past than to the distant past.[8]

Measurement

Cagan's actual specification was a little more complicated than this, but the idea was the same. His was

$$E_t = \frac{(1 - exp^{-\beta}) \sum\limits_{x=-T}^{t} C_x exp^{\beta x}}{exp^{\beta t}}, \qquad (7.26)$$

where $-T$ is an arbitrary lower limit before which prices are assumed to be constant. Feeding this into the demand function, he obtained

$$\ln\left(\frac{M}{P}\right)_t = -\alpha \left[\frac{1 - exp^{-\beta}}{exp^{\beta t}} \sum\limits_{x=-T}^{t} C_x exp^{\beta x} \right] - \gamma + \varepsilon_t. \qquad (7.27)$$

The index of cash balances at the end of, say, month 5 would be found by setting $t = 5$

$$\ln\left(\frac{M}{P}\right)_5 = -\alpha \, \frac{1 - exp^{-\beta}}{exp^{5\beta}} \sum\limits_{x=-T}^{5} C_x exp^{\beta x} - \gamma,$$

and if $-T$ were fixed at -5, there would be eleven terms making up weights for E (i.e. the actual rate of change of prices for the current and preceding ten months).

Estimation took place by the method of trying out different βs, constructing the associated E series which were then fed into the demand function, choosing that β which gave the best fit. While the procedure is laborious, Griliches (1967) in his survey of distributed lags argued that if the model is correct and the search procedure finds the β which maximizes goodness of fit then the estimates are maximum likelihood ones. Cagan applied the technique to seven hyperinflations. Figure 7.6 shows the scatter picture for Germany with monthly observations from September 1920 to November 1923. By and large, the results suggest a systematic response of real balances to the cost of holding money, with the off-the-line observations attributed to money balances being larger than predicted towards the end of hyperinflation because of anticipated monetary reform.

Implications

This demand for money function provides the quantity theorists' answer to the first of the three puzzles outlined at the beginning of this section. The basic postulate of the monetarist position on inflation is the existence of a stable demand function for money into which the expected rate of inflation enters as the cost of holding money. As inflation accelerates, there is a predictable movement along this function, not a shift of the function, with transactors wanting to hold less real balances.

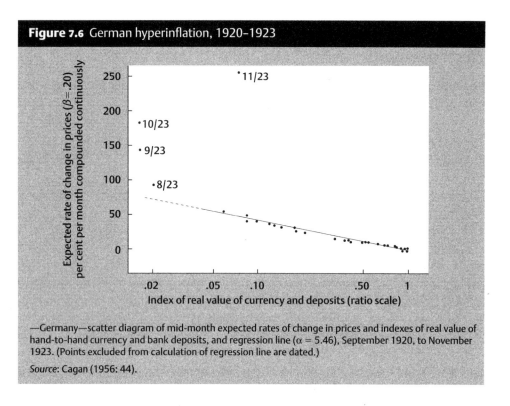

Figure 7.6 German hyperinflation, 1920–1923

—Germany—scatter diagram of mid-month expected rates of change in prices and indexes of real value of hand-to-hand currency and bank deposits, and regression line ($\alpha = 5.46$), September 1920, to November 1923. (Points excluded from calculation of regression line are dated.)

Source: Cagan (1956: 44).

This expectation of inflation is not an exogenous force upon velocity but is determined by past inflation and thus by past injections of money.

The quantity theorists' answer to the second puzzle also revolves around the demand for money function. There are two forces operating upon real balances from prices. The first is that given this demand function, as prices rise the public eventually comes to expect the rate of inflation and adjust the stock of real balances desired (or the ratio of real balances to real income—the Cambridge 'K') to the inflationary trend. The second aspect is that with any given expectation of inflation, people want to hold a certain amount of real money balances. In order to maintain real balances constant in the face of inflation, the public has to accumulate *nominal* money balances at a rate equal to the rate of inflation. The faster prices rise, the faster money must be acquired, producing a shortage if the printing presses cannot keep pace.

The third puzzle is the question posed by Cagan 'Why did the quantity of money increase and by so large an amount?' (1996: 77). His answer was twofold: (i) printing money was a convenient way to provide the government with real resources, and (ii) the effectiveness of this method declined over time and so required even larger issues. Here we come to a major monetarist theme—inflation as a tax.

7.7 The Inflation Tax

To the quantity theorist, inflation is viewed as imposing a tax on holdings of real balances. People add to money balances at the same rate as inflation in order to keep real balances constant. This sacrifice of real income constitutes the equivalent of a tax on the holders of real balances, while from the viewpoint of the issuer of money it constitutes revenue available for government expenditure.

Suppose that the government wishes to increase spending: how might this increased expenditure be financed? If the government does not want to borrow, there are two choices: (i) taxation or (ii) money issues.

Consider first taxation. One possibility would be to tax money balances[9]. Taxpayers might be required to go to the tax office (i.e. the Inland Revenue, Nottingham not Bethlehem), turn out their pockets, and have their money balances counted. With a tax rate of 50 per cent, the tax collector would confiscate half of the money holdings. This payment would provide the government with the money needed to undertake spending. If the reduction in spending by those taxed is matched by increased spending by the government, zero inflation could be the result.

An alternative is for the government to undertake the same expenditure and pay for it by printing money. Suppose that the money supply is increased by 50 per cent, producing an increase in prices of 50 per cent. Real money balances are unchanged, but in the meantime the government has acquired command over real resources. It gains real resources when the public hands over goods and services (e.g. the provision of teaching services) in exchange for the pieces of paper issued by the government. In this case, the real resources gained are

$$50\% \text{ (i.e. } \dot{M} = \dot{P}) \times \text{real money balances} \left(\text{i.e. } \frac{M}{P} \right),$$

which is exactly the same as the *explicit* tax on money balances, when the revenue (like any form of taxation) equalled

$$\text{tax rate (i.e. 50\%)} \times \text{tax base} \left(\text{i.e. } \frac{M}{P} \right).$$

Accordingly, inflation is regarded as simply another form of taxation, in effect an *implicit* tax on real balances, providing the revenue for government expenditure.[10] In Cagan's words:

Issuing money was a method of raising revenue by a special kind of tax—a tax on cash balances. This tax is often appealing because it does not require detailed legislation and can be administered very simply. All that is required is to spend newly printed notes. The resulting inflation automatically imposes a tax on cash balances by depreciating the value of money.

The base of the tax is the level of real cash balances; the rate of the tax is the rate of depreciation in the real value of money, which is equal to the rate of rise in prices. Revenue (in real terms) from the tax is the product of the base and the rate. (1956: 78)

But why does the inflation accelerate? A simple extension to a figure used by Harry Johnson (1963) can be used to illustrate Cagan's argument. In Figure 7.7, the rate of inflation (actual and expected) is measured on the vertical axis, real balances are measured on the horizontal axis, and the demand for real balances is represented by the demand for money function, D. With price stability, real balances demanded are OM. From this position suppose that inflationary finance occurs and an inflation rate of OP results. If zero inflation is still expected, tax revenue is given by the area OPQM. Once the inflation is established and expected to continue at OP, the demand for real balances declines to OM^1 due to the cost of holding money under inflationary conditions. As a result the tax base is eroded, and the revenue from the inflation tax declines to $OPRM^1$. If revenue and expenditure are to be maintained, the 'tax rate' needs to be increased to OP^1. But once that rate comes to be expected, the 'tax rate' needs to be raised again, setting in train a sequence of successively higher inflation rates. This is what appeared to happen.

Because of the lag in expectations, many months passed before real cash balances declined very much. When the balances finally began to decline by substantial amounts, the revenue decreased from the high level of the beginning months. The revenue could be enlarged, as for a short time it was, only by inflating at successively higher rates. Rates were quickly reached, however, that completely disrupted the economy, and they could not be long continued. The attempt to enlarge the revenue in the closing months thus produced the characteristic pattern of hyperinflations: price increases did not peter out; they exploded. (Cagan, 1956: 80)

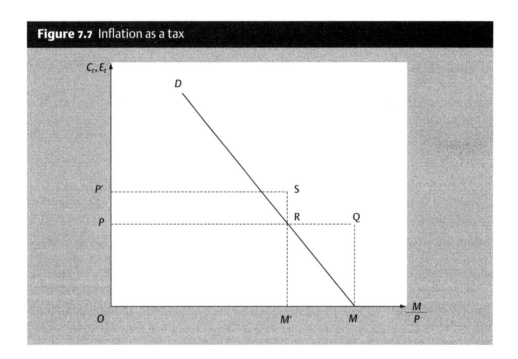

Figure 7.7 Inflation as a tax

7.8 Conclusions

MONETARISM grew out of Friedman's restatement of the quantity theory and the empirical regularities surrounding money supply changes, but it did not take hold until inflation emerged as a major problem after the mid-1960s. Quantity theorists had a ready-made framework for analysing nominal and real interest rates and the dynamics of inflation. The latter was most clearly reflected in Cagan's model of periods of very rapid inflation—hyperinflation—but this informed the general notion of inflation as a form of taxation and a particular view of the processes of inflation as dominated by money creation, and its impact upon inflation expectations, rather than institutional features of the wages–prices nexus.

If the quantity theory approach to inflation was to be useful in studying the less virulent forms of inflation which typified the experiences of most economies, then many of the factors suppressed in the hyperinflation model would need to be reintroduced. In particular, interest rates would have to be added back into the demand-for-money function, the interaction between wages, prices, and unemployment would need to be examined, and a more complex treatment would have to be given to the formation of expectations, particularly in light of the rational expectations revolution.

Most of the criticisms, in fact, of Cagan's analysis of hyperinflation have revolved around the formation of expectations. Sargent and Wallace (1973), Frenkel (1977), and Sargent (1977) have all reinvestigated Cagan's model in this light. If money creation is the driving force behind price changes, transactors would presumably become aware of the government's resort to the printing press rather than other means of revenue-raising. Expectations of inflation would focus in on the government's budgetary position and the money-issuing implications of it, rather than respond adaptively to past inflation. Should it be possible to estimate the rate of money creation in this way, this estimate could be translated into a path for prices directly, short-circuiting the processes previously operating through aggregate spending.[11]

Quite clearly, the introduction of such rational-expectations ideas has important ramifications for the operation of monetary models. These are explored in Chapter 9. First, however, we translate the quantity theory results into the open economy.

Notes

1 In his restatement of the quantity theory of money Friedman (1956) spoke of an oral tradition sustained in Chicago during the 1930s and 1940s. Patinkin (1969) could find scant evidence of this intellectual inheritance (an oral tradition is not worth the paper it is written on?), while Covick (1974) brilliantly satirizes the notion in his article 'The quantity theory of drink—a restatement'.

2 Friedman's emphasis on the expectations of economic stability variable was part of his more general attempt to downplay the importance of interest rates in the demand for money and explain velocity in terms of permanent income. However, the postwar rise in velocity proved difficult to account for in these terms, and the greater economic stability was one potential candidate (Friedman, 1966).

3 Tobin in fact rejects all except the sixth—neutrality of money—as representative of the quantity theory.

4 The implication, in terms of time lags, is that velocity leads fluctuations in interest rates in this sequence. This differs from the lags in the usual specification of the demand for money function (see Lewis, 1978). In Ch. 11, the velocity preceding interest rates sequence forms part of the exogenous money-buffer stock idea.

5 This is the relationship in continuous time. In discrete time, the condition becomes

$$(1 + i_t) = (1 + r_t)(1 + \dot{p}^e_t)$$

giving

$$i_t = r_t + \dot{p}^e_t + r_t \dot{p}^e_t$$

or

$$r_t = \frac{1 + i_t}{1 + \dot{p}^e_t} - 1$$

which allows for the expected erosion of the periodic interest payments as well as the capital value of a bond denominated in money terms.

6 The so-called 'Fisher tax effect' allows for bond-holders to be compensated both for expected inflation and for income taxation on the periodic interest payments, viz.:

$$1 + i_t(1 - tx_t) = (1 + r_t)(1 + \dot{p}^e_t)$$

giving

$$i_t = \frac{(1 + r_t)(1 + \dot{p}^e_t)}{1 - tx_t} - 1$$

and

$$r_t = \frac{1 + i_t(1 - tx_t)}{1 + \dot{p}^e_t} - 1$$

where tx_t is the (marginal) tax rate on income received as interest.

7 There is then the question of whether such monetary accommodation to prior wage increases should be seen as consistent with a quantity theorist explanation of inflation. Morton first raised this issue:

To be successful then in their assumed policy, labor unions must also control banking policy . . . Labor leaders may act foolishly and at times impetuously, but they will not continually beat their heads against a stone wall. (1950: 109).

8 The idea of the weighting coefficients declining systematically as we go further back in time was originally suggested by Irving Fisher in 1925 and was revived and extended later by Koyck (1954) and Nerlove (1958). Cagan's was only the second study to employ the technique in econometric work.

9 The taxing of money balances was, in fact, an in-built feature of the monetary system which operated in late Anglo-Saxon Britain. Silver coins were issued with a restricted period of legal tender, two to three years, after which they had to be returned to the local 'moneyer' (mint) and exchanged for new issue. Due to the practice of paying out only 8 or 9 new coins for every 10 returned, the coin-making process netted a valuable surplus to the King. Lacey and Danziger (1999) provide a fascinating account to life in England just prior to the Danish and Norman invasions of the eleventh century.

10 Earlier we indicated a number of ways in which government expenditures could be financed: borrowing, taxation, and money creation. The corollary of the quantity theorist view is that there are only two. If money creation does not add to inflation, then it is borrowing at zero interest. If money creation generates inflation, then it is taxation. Either way, it is not an alternative to borrowing or taxation.

11 There are also important implications for the model's estimation. If money creation is geared to achieving a certain revenue base in real terms, monetary growth will itself depend on the inflation rate, rendering the quantity of money statistically endogenous to inflation. Real money balances depend on inflation, but inflation feeds back to the nominal money supply introducing estimation biases. One alternative, used in the German hyperinflation case, is to employ the forward premium on foreign exchange as a measure of the cost of holding money, since the market marked down the exchange value of the Mark in line with their expectations of inflation. Such anticipatory behaviour may account for the German view, noted earlier, that the foreign exchanges 'caused' the inflation.

Chapter 8
Money and Exchange Rates

8.1 The Quantity Theory in an Open Economy

MONETARY theory has been developed mainly in the context of a closed economy. Irving Fisher's quantity theory of money, Keynes's *General Theory* and Patinkin's monetary experiments are all examples of closed-economy reasoning. Closed-economy analysis could be appropriate in either one of two quite different circumstances. One would be if we were dealing with what in effect is a unified world economy, employing a uniform currency. The other situation would be for a national currency to be linked to other currencies by completely flexible exchange rates.

This section extends the quantity theory results of the previous chapter to these two situations. In the first, the quantity of money is entirely endogenous, and the analysis runs in terms of the monetary theory of the balance of payments under fixed exchange rates. In the other circumstance, the quantity of money becomes a policy variable, and the floating exchange rate is linked to other monetary variables by means of the 'four-way equivalence theorem'. But, as we will argue, this theorem is an equilibrium relationship, and subsequent sections examine models of exchange rate behaviour based on the experience of freely floating rates.

Fixed rates

A unified world currency has never existed, except perhaps before 1914 when most of the major countries in effect used gold as currency. Even then, as we saw in Chapter 2, the gold standard was not uniform in its operation and there were a variety of 'limping' standards. It would seem that Keynes may have been beginning to think along the lines of a unified world system in the *General Theory*, where his attention had moved beyond Britain specifically to an Atlantic Community of wealthy economies and the policy actions needed to be taken by them to lift the world economy out of the slump. Amongst this group, remedies involving devaluation, protectionism, and other 'beggar-thy-neighbour' policies would be unhelpful in compari-son with those which would help to generate new investment.

Later, of course, Keynes went explicitly down the unified world economy path dur-ing the Bretton Woods conference in 1944 with his proposal for a unified world cur-rency—the Bancor—issued by the International Clearing Union, his version of the IMF. In such a world, the quantity theory would be applicable at a global level, but for any country or part of the unified currency system, the quantity of money is entirely endogenous, determined by the demand for money.

Something approaching this result applies to a worldwide system of fixed exchange rates such as that which operated from 1945 to 1971 under the aegis of the IMF. In such a system, individual countries retain money-creating powers but so long as they adhere to the fixed-rate peg lose the ability to have an independent monetary policy. Instead, excess money spills over into the balance of payments (in ways orig-inally outlined by David Hume) as domestic money creation is offset by a loss of international reserves. This loss reduces the quantity of money to a level consistent with the demand for money. Here we have the essence of the *monetary approach to the balance of payments*, developed by Harry Johnson (1958, 1972).

A starting point for the monetary approach is the now standard (but novel back in 1958) accounting identity which shows the way the balance of payments in a small country is linked with the domestic monetary system.

$$(X - Z) + K = \triangle R = \triangle M - DCE. \tag{8.1}$$

The left-hand side of (8.1) divides transactions with the rest of the world into those on current account $(X - Z)$ and capital account K, and the net balance implies an accommodating change in the foreign reserves $(\triangle R)$ of the central bank. As additions to domestic money balances come from external money flows and expansions of domestic credit, the right-hand side of (8.1) expresses reserve flows as the difference between new money $\triangle M$ and domestic credit creation (DCE). In this way 'it is evident that a balance-of-payments problem is monetary in nature and that it is fundamen-tally related to the fact that the banking system can create credit' (Johnson, 1958: 18).

As with all monetarist analysis, the basis is a demand for money function which is a stable function of a small number of variables, viz.:

$$M' = P.L(y, i), \tag{8.2}$$

where the symbols take on their normal meaning. Instead of (Eq. 8.1) we need to focus on stocks,

$$M = R + D, \tag{8.3}$$

where D is the domestic assets of the banking system contributing to the money sup-ply. If monetary equilibrium prevails, we obtain

$$R + D = P.L(y, i). \tag{8.4}$$

For the analysis to be operational, the arguments of the demand function need to be predictable or independent of the money supply. Johnson achieved the latter by some very special assumptions about economic and financial integration involving *purchasing power parity* and *interest rate parity* which serve to fix domestic prices and interest rates. If national output is of internationally traded goods and no restrictions on trade such as tariffs and quotas exist, perfect international commodity arbitrage (the 'law of one price') requires that

$$P = eP^* \tag{8.5}$$

or in growth rates

$$\dot{P} = \dot{e} + \dot{P}^*, \tag{8.5a}$$

where P^* is world prices in terms of world money (for example, US dollars) and e is the exchange rate (price of world money in terms of domestic money). If domestic and foreign securities are substitutes, perfect capital mobility ensures the equalization of expected net yields including the expected rate of increase of the domestic currency price of foreign exchange ('uncovered interest rate parity'), that is

$$i = i^* + \pi \tag{8.6}$$

in which i^* is the interest rate on foreign securities and π is the expected rate of depreciation of the domestic currency. With exchange rates fixed e is constant (assumed $e = 1$) and $\pi = 0$. By making the further assumption that $y = y_0$ (full employment), (8.4) can be rewritten

$$R + D = P^* . L(y_0, i^*). \tag{8.7}$$

Once the adjustment to world levels is complete and all the right-hand side variables are fixed, it follows that if $L(y_0, i^*)$ is stable, credit creation involving domestic assets (D) is *offset* by an equal and opposite decrease in reserves (R) until equilibrium is restored. In the words of Harry Johnson

a balance-of-payments deficit can occur only if the domestic monetary authority allows domestic credit to expand faster than the public wants to expand its money holdings, with the result that the public gets rid of the otherwise excessive balances though a balance-of-payments deficit and a reduction in the international reserves backing the domestic money supply—in other words, domestic credit substitutes for international reserves in the backing of the money supply. (Johnson, 1976: 16)

It may be noted that the offsetting reserve flows could originate from responses in the current account, via spending, or in the capital account, via asset adjustment (Hume's 100 canals).[1] Kouri and Porter (1974) examined the role of offsetting capital flows. Casual support for this mechanism is provided by the necessity for some countries (e.g. Britain, USA) in the late 1960s and early 1970s to operate capital controls to keep capital from flowing out, while others (Germany, Switzerland) had to erect barriers to keep capital from flowing in and loosening anti-inflationary policies.

Floating Rates

The other circumstance in which closed-economy reasoning might be considered appropriate is for an individual country, which determines the quantity of national currency internally, but allows the price of that currency in terms of other countries to be determined without any intervention in the foreign exchange market. With no intervention, the change in international reserves in (8.1) is fixed by the authorities (in terms of various strategic objectives). The simplest assumption is $\Delta R = 0$ so that $\Delta M = DCE$. In that case, the money supply remains under the control of the domestic monetary authorities, and there is the potential for quantity theory-type results to ensue from money supply disturbances. What are these results in an open economy context?

The closed economy inflationary equilibrium—'monetarist superneutrality'—involved

(a) prices rising in proportionality to the rate of monetary change,
(b) expectations of inflation adapting fully to the underlying rate of inflation,
(c) the Fisher effect with nominal interest rates rising by the expectation of inflation, and
(d) real rates of interest unchanged.

For an open economy, the analogues are summarized by the so-called 'four-way equivalence theorem', embracing

(a) purchasing power parity,
(b) the international Fisher effect,
(c) interest rate parity,
(d) expectations theory of exchange rates and
(e) the Fisher open hypothesis.

These are summarized in Figure 8.1, and discussed in turn below.

Purchasing power parity

The concept of purchasing power parity (PPP) was developed by Gustav Cassell (1925) who used it as a way of explaining the depreciation of the mark and other European currencies in the hyperinflations after the First World War.[2] It was subsequently criticized by Keynes (1930) and fell into disuse until revived by Harry Johnson and others as part of the monetary theory of the balance of payments, either in the strong (or absolute) version (8.5) or in the weak (or relative) version (8.5a).

There are a number of different views of the economic forces underlying PPP. One relies on goods arbitrage in an integrated, competitive world market free of all frictions in which case the price of any good i will be the same in all locations when converted into a common currency (e.g. US dollars), i.e. $P_i = eP_i^*$. If arbitrage enforces parity across a sufficiently wide range of individual goods, so that the price of each

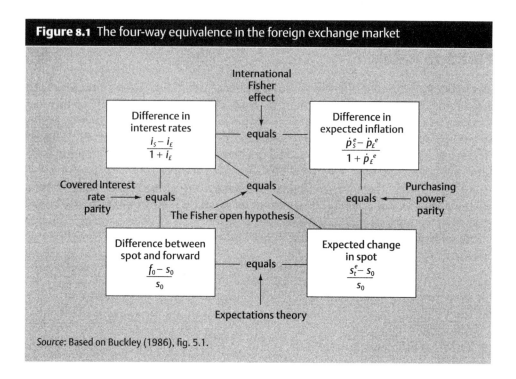

Figure 8.1 The four-way equivalence in the foreign exchange market

International Fisher effect

Difference in interest rates
$$\frac{i_s - i_\pounds}{1 + i_\pounds}$$

equals

Difference in expected inflation
$$\frac{\dot{p}_s^e - \dot{p}_\pounds^e}{1 + \dot{p}_\pounds^e}$$

Covered Interest rate parity → equals

equals

equals ← Purchasing power parity

The Fisher open hypothesis

Difference between spot and forward
$$\frac{f_0 - s_0}{s_0}$$

equals

Expected change in spot
$$\frac{s_t^e - s_0}{s_0}$$

Expectations theory

Source: Based on Buckley (1986), fig. 5.1.

good, expressed in terms of dollars, is equalized across countries, PPP may extend to aggregate price levels. In that case, PPP is 'the disarmingly simple empirical proposition that, once converted to a common currency, national price levels should be equal' (Rogoff, 1996: 647).

As an empirical proposition the goods arbitrage approach faces several hurdles: not all goods are traded, barriers to trade exist, and not all commodities exhibit the high degree of substitutability needed to ensure costless, instantaneous arbitrage. These factors do not necessarily prevent the usefulness of PPP in explaining exchange rate movements, but they do mean that there are impediments to arbitrage in the form of trade and information costs which preclude the strict equalization of prices across countries, as a variety of empirical studies have shown—even in the case of the Big Mac index (Pakko and Pollard, 1996).

Another difficulty with the arbitrage approach, building up from individual price equalization, is that it does not explain why *e* rather than *P* adjusts to equalize (8.5). For this we need a theory of aggregate price determination, and monetarist analysis employs PPP under fixed rates to predict what domestic money prices will be and under floating rates to predict what the exchange rate will be. The monetary theory of the balance of payments is adapted into a monetary theory of exchange rates by presuming PPP to be a monetary phenomenon. With fixed rates, international reserves adjust the quantity of money to an equilibrium governed by PPP. Under flexible rates, reserves are fixed and in this case it is the exchange rate which adjusts to the long-run requirements of PPP. In this second view of PPP, a monetary approach to exchange rate determination emerges as an outgrowth of purchasing power parity theory and the quantity theory of money. Combining (8.5), viz.:

$$P = eP^*$$

with the quantity equation in each country gives

$$M = kPy \tag{8.8}$$
$$M^* = k^* P^* y^* \tag{8.9}$$

and therefore

$$e = \frac{P}{P^*} = \frac{M/ky}{M^*/ky^*} \ . \tag{8.10}$$

The idea here is that the price level in each country is related to the respective national money supply and money demand, with PPP via the exchange rate in equilibrium tying the price levels together.

In the third view, PPP emerges as underpinning equilibrium in the balance of payments. When Friedman (1953b) and Johnson (1969) presented the case for flexible exchange rates they envisaged that the rate would adjust to the point where the demand for foreign exchange to buy imports (Z) and make other current payments would equal the supply resulting from exports (X) and other current receipts. Suppose that exports and imports both depend on relative prices (Swan's cost ratio)[3] and real income (Alexander's absorption effect).[4] Equilibrium requires

$$X\left(y, \frac{eP^*}{P}\right) = Z\left(y, \frac{eP^*}{P}\right) \tag{8.11}$$

and for a given $y = y_0$, this is defined by

$$\frac{eP^*}{P} = \alpha. \tag{8.12}$$

If $\alpha = 1$ we have absolute PPP and when $\alpha \neq 1$ we have relative PPP when (8.12) is expressed in terms of rates of change.

In all three cases discussed above, the presumption is that the spot rate of exchange at any date is underpinned by relative price levels in the two countries (assumed to be USA and UK). The precise formulation in Figure 8.1 comes from relating the price to the spot exchange rate at time $t = 0$, s_0, and to that expected at time t, s_t^e, viz.:

$$s_0 = \frac{P^\$}{P^£} \tag{8.13}$$

$$s_t^e = \frac{P^\$(1 + \dot{p}_\$^e)}{P^£(1 + \dot{p}_£^e)}. \tag{8.14}$$

After substituting we obtain

$$\frac{s_t^e - s_0}{s_0} = \frac{\dot{p}_\$^e - \dot{p}_£^e}{1 + \dot{p}_£^e} \tag{8.15}$$

in which it is predicted, on the basis of PPP, that the exchange rate changes in line with the difference in inflation between the two countries.

The international Fisher effect

In a closed economy, the Fisher effect required nominal interest rates to reflect both the real rate of interest and the expected rate of inflation. A stronger version expects that, in equilibrium, the adjustment to inflation will be fully in nominal rates, leaving real rates unchanged. The international Fisher effect envisages that this adjustment occurs in each country, with the addition that real rates are equal across countries. The argument is that in a world where capital is mobile, expected real rates of return should tend to equality as investors switch between assets in search of the highest yields, especially in the Eurocurrency and other financial markets. Nominal rates will differ for these assets, but by virtue of different inflation expectations. Thus

$$(1 + i_\$) = (1 + r)(1 + \dot{p}_\$^e) \tag{8.16}$$

and

$$(1 + i_£) = (1 + r)(1 + \dot{p}_£^e) \tag{8.17}$$

Deducting one from the other and dividing through by $(1 + r)$ gives

$$\frac{i_\$ - i_£}{(1 + i_£)} = \frac{\dot{p}_\$^e - \dot{p}_£^e}{(1 + \dot{p}_£^e)} \tag{8.18}$$

so that the difference in nominal interest rates reflects the difference in expected inflation.

Interest rate parity

The next leg of Figure 8.1 relates interest rate differentials to the spot-forward exchange rate differential in terms of covered interest arbitrage. The term 'covered' refers to the fact that the transaction involved, e.g. an investment that exploits interest rate differentials, is covered in terms of exchange rate risk by means of a forward transaction. One way to approach matters is to consider, say, a US exporter receiving £X in one year. This could be covered at time $t = 0$ by means of a forward foreign exchange transaction, guaranteeing proceeds at time $t = 1$ in terms of US dollars of

$$f_0 \cdot X,$$

where f_0 is the current forward $/£ exchange rate (New York quotation). An alternative hedge would involve using the money market. At time $t = 0$, the exporter could borrow £$X/1 + i_£$. At $t = 1$, £X will be due on the loan and this can be discharged using the export receivables. In the meantime, the amount borrowed (£$X/1 + i_£$) could be converted to dollars at the current spot exchange rate s_0 (giving $\$ \dfrac{X}{1 + i_£} \cdot s_0$), and invested in the US money market, giving proceeds of

$$\frac{X}{1 + i_£} \cdot s_0 (1 + i_\$)$$

in terms of US dollars at time $t = 1$.

If arbitrage ensures that each method of covering yields the same amount, then

$$f_0 . X = \frac{X}{1 + i_£} \cdot s_0 (1 + i_\$), \tag{8.19}$$

which when simplified and rearranged gives

$$\frac{f_0 - s_0}{s_0} = \frac{i_\$ - i_£}{1 + i_£}, \tag{8.20}$$

the interest parity relationship.

Expectations

So far we have established that in equilibrium:

(i)   the spot-forward differential equals the interest rate differential,
(ii) the interest rate differential equals the difference in expected inflation, and
(iii) the difference in expected inflation equals the expected change in the spot rate.

Logically, it ought to follow from this sequence that the spot-forward differential equals the expected change in spot and in fact this link is the final leg of Figure 8.1. This interrelationship constitutes the basis of the expectations theory.

The question addressed by the expectations theory is how the actual spot rate turns out, say in six or twelve months, in relation to the six-month forward rate or the twelve-month forward rate that could be contracted now. Expectations theory contends that the expected spot rate is equal to the forward *unbiased* predictor of the future spot rate. A twelve-month forward rate of $1.66 to the pound would exist only because traders expected the spot rate to be $1.66 to the pound. With an anticipated rate higher than this, nobody would use the forward rate to sell sterling (and vice versa for those wanting to buy sterling).

This is the conclusion in the absence of risk. What the future rate actually will be is uncertain. Should transactors care about this risk, they might be willing to pay something different from the expected spot rate to avoid foreign exchange risk. Then the unbiased forward rate condition may not hold.

Similar doubts surround the diagonal in Figure 8.1—the Fisher open hypothesis— which reflects the idea that differences in the interest rates should be underpinned by the movement in the spot rate of exchange. Known also as the uncovered interest parity,[5] encountered earlier, the hypothesis states that expected returns on interest-bearing securities will be equal, regardless of the currency of denomination. This hypothesis holds only if securities that are similar except for currency are perfect substitutes. If not, a risk premium will apply to the higher-yielding assets.

It needs to be remembered that, with the exception of covered interest rate parity which does hold all of the time (so much so that in Eurocurrency markets it is used for quoting interest rates in different currencies),[6] the four-way equivalence illustrated in Figure 8.1 refers to equilibrium conditions, and must be viewed in the same light as the neutrality propositions considered earlier. This is particularly so of PPP which forms the starting point for the remainder of this chapter.

8.2 Asset Models of Exchange Rates

WHEN the era of floating exchange rates was ushered in after 1971, economists had two main tools of analysis. One was the flow theory of exchange rates which visualized that the exchange rate was governed by the demand for foreign exchange to buy imports (demand for traded goods) and the supply of foreign exchange from the sale of exports (supply of traded goods). The other tool of analysis was purchasing power parity.

Neither, it was soon shown, provided a good basis for explaining exchange rate movements. Viewed as the result of goods arbitrage, PPP provided at best a long-run approximation, and much the same was true also of the current account balance story. As part of the quantity theory applied to open economies, PPP seemed much like an appendage, tacked on at the end of the story (rather like the classical dichotomy) to reconcile nominal magnitudes (in this case, price levels) determined separately from the exchange rate.

The problem with the flow theory is that only a small, and rapidly shrinking, fraction of foreign exchange transactions seem to involve, either directly or indirectly, trade transactions. Most transactions in foreign exchange are asset-holding decisions which result in capital inflows or outflows of one sort or another. While capital inflows or outflows can be added to the flow model to augment the demand and/or supply of foreign exchange, the model itself cannot explain how large these flows are or how long they last.

Asset models were developed with the aim of providing a better framework for analysing the determination of exchange rates in a freely floating system operating worldwide. As a class of model, the asset models are in the 'portfolio balance' tradition pioneered by Tobin (1969) and Tobin and Brainard (1968).[7] The Hicks–Keynesian IS–LM model dealt with two assets (money and bonds) and one rate ('the' rate of interest). Tobin (1969) considered portfolio balance amongst three assets (money, bonds, and capital) to determine two rates: the bond rate and the required return on capital. But his was a closed-economy analysis.

When a portfolio-balance approach is extended to an open economy system of generalized floating rates, there is an immediate problem of how the analysis is to be made tractable. With N countries, we would have N moneys, $NJ + N$ assets, NJ rates of return and $N-1$ exchange rates. At the very minimum, there would seem the need to model two countries. Branson (1977) and Black (1977) manage with one.

Four assets are contained in the Branson model: domestic money, foreign money, domestic securities, and foreign securities. Neither money is assumed to bear interest and the terms on which one money exchanges for the other is, at least formally, the exchange rate. Thus the exchange rate in the first instance is the relative price of national moneys because money serves as the medium of exchange and unit of account. A full analysis would allow all assets to be internationally traded, but this is watered down in a number of ways. No currency substitution is generally allowed, so that residents of neither country hold the other currency. However, net claims on foreigners are held by the domestic private sector in the form of interest-bearing assets. Foreigners are assumed only to hold foreign money and the foreign asset, which means that there are no valuation effects on foreign wealth from changes in the exchange rate, allowing foreign demand for foreign bonds to be ignored.

Consequently domestic money and bonds are held only in the home country, and there is just one internationally traded asset, the foreign asset (F). With these assumptions, asset market equilibrium results when the following conditions hold:

$$W = M + B + eF \tag{8.21}$$

$$M = m(i, i^*, \pi)W \tag{8.22}$$

$$B = b(i, i^*, \pi)W \tag{8.23}$$

$$eF = f(i, i^*, \pi)W$$
$$= (1 - m - b)W \, , \tag{8.24}$$

where W is domestic net wealth, M is domestic currency, B is domestic securities and e, the home price of foreign exchange, translates the foreign currency value of F into home currency. As arguments of the demand functions, expressed as proportions of W, i and i^* are the domestic and foreign interest rate respectively, and $\pi = E(e_t - e_{t-1}/e_{t-1})$ is the expected depreciation of the domestic currency.

Stocks of M, B and F are given to domestic holders at each point of time. These stocks interact with the demand functions to generate market (i.e. asset) equilibrium. Because of the wealth constraint, only two equations of (8.22), (8.23) and (8.24) are independent. Given i^*, π, M, B, and F then two equations determine e, i. The pairs of domestic interest and exchange rates (i . e.) satisfying the three market-clearing conditions are plotted in Figure 8.2 to give a money market equilibrium curve (MM), a domestic bond market equilibrium curve (BB) and a domestically held foreign asset equilibrium curve (FF). The slope of each curve follows from the equations.[8] The FF curve is flatter than the BB curve because domestic demand for domestic bonds is more responsive than domestic demand for foreign assets to changes in the domestic interest rate.

The exchange rate e_0 in Figure 8.2 satisfies asset market requirements. But the exchange rate must also give equilibrium in the balance of payments. There is a

Figure 8.2 Asset market equilibrium in an open economy

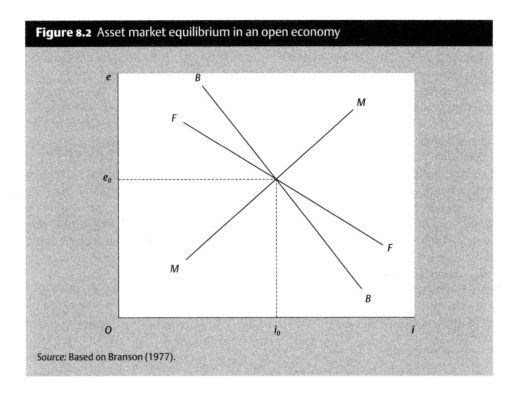

Source: Based on Branson (1977).

direct parallel here with closed-economy Keynesian modelling. In the standard IS–LM model, the interest rate initially (and on an hour-to-hour and day-to-day basis) is dominated by asset market stock conditions in the form of the demand and supply of money (the LM curve). However, this rate will have implications for expenditures and the *flow* of savings and investment (the IS curve). Eventually, the rate of interest must establish stock–flow equilibrium. So it is in the case of the exchange rate.

What happens if the exchange rate as determined in asset markets is not consistent with the balance of trade, and export and import flows? Since we are dealing with freely floating rates (no change to official reserves), a current account imbalance implies a non-zero capital account and changing stocks of foreign assets (foreigners are precluded from holding domestic assets). If the trade account is in surplus, the country will be accumulating foreign assets (i.e. foreign money and/or securities). If the trade position is in deficit, residents will be losing foreign assets. These trade-induced asset changes will, in turn, alter asset market conditions.

Figure 8.3 depicts what happens to asset markets if the stock of foreign assets increases, perhaps in response to a trade surplus. There is an increase in wealth, which in this case has taken the form entirely of foreign assets. However, people will not wish for the greater wealth to be held only in foreign assets, and will want to re-balance their portfolios by adding to money holdings and bonds. Thus, *BB* and *MM* will shift down. As transactors sell *F* to add to *M* and *B*, the exchange rate will appreciate. This relationship between *F* and *e* is shown in the bottom panel, depicting asset market equilibrium.

Figure 8.3 Asset market responses to a trade surplus

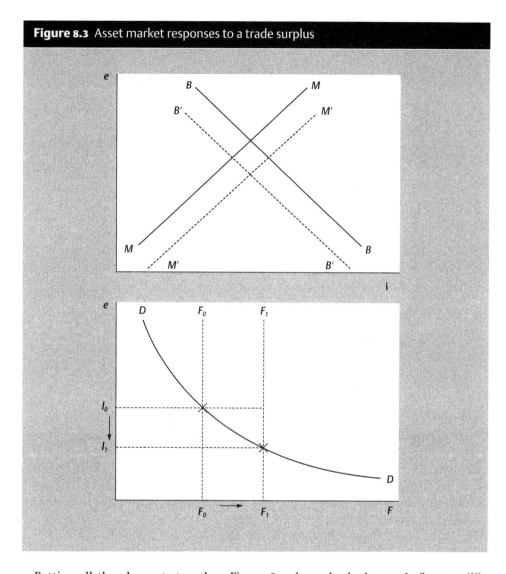

Putting all the elements together, Figure 8.4 shows both the stock–flow equilibrium, and the process of adjustment from short-run to long-run equilibrium. The right-hand side illustrates stock equilibrium in respect of the demand (D) and supply (S) of foreign assets. With a given stock of foreign assets, F_0, stock equilibrium or asset market conditions generate the exchange rate e_0. This value of the exchange rate permits the existing stocks of assets to be willingly held. But the left-hand side shows what happens to the flow balance of trade if the short-run or asset equilibrium fails to correspond to long-run flow equilibrium, in terms of dd, the demand for traded goods (import demand) and ss, the supply of traded goods (exports). The left-hand side thus gives the traditional flow story of exchange rate determination.

Starting at the asset market position and exchange rate e_0, it is apparent from the flow market that this exchange rate results in a trade surplus of bc shown in the left-

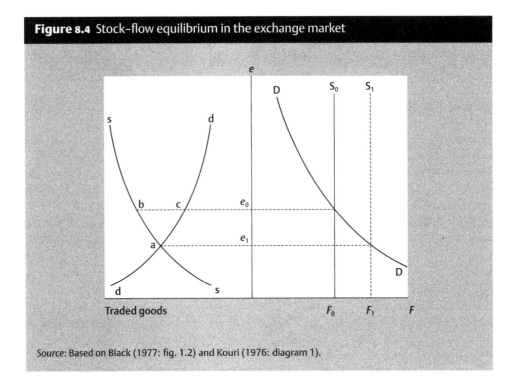

Figure 8.4 Stock–flow equilibrium in the exchange market

Source: Based on Black (1977: fig. 1.2) and Kouri (1976: diagram 1).

hand panel, which enables domestic residents to increase their net foreign assets. These accumulations modify the short-run stock equilibrium and produce a new exchange rate which gives a different current account position, and so on. Eventually the process converges to a long-run equilibrium at the exchange rate e_1, where stock equilibrium prevails and the current account is balanced (that is, $(X - Z) = K = 0$). In this way, the exchange rate is both the relative price of national moneys and the relative price of national outputs.

The broad conclusions of this analysis are as follows:

1. The exchange rate adjusts to a long-run equilibrium determined by purchasing power parity, as predicted by the flow theory of exchange rates which formed the basis of traditional analysis.

2. In the short-run, however, the exchange rate is governed by asset market conditions, and is determined along with the rate of interest by the interaction of asset demands and asset stocks.

3. Asset stocks (money, bonds) are altered by monetary policy and budgetary decisions. Because the exchange rate results from what happens in asset markets, it (like the interest rate) is an important channel whereby monetary policy (and fiscal policy) is transmitted to the domestic economy.

4. Expectations about the variables which determine asset behaviour seem likely to play an important role. Indeed, the implication of the theory is that exchange rates may respond much like asset prices in other markets, such as the equity

market, and be subject to speculative pressures, bandwagon effects, and other features of asset markets.

From what we know about exchange rate behaviour in the two decades since the asset theory was developed the last three points seem indisputable. Asset-holding decisions dominate the exchange market on a day-to-day basis. Policy changes do alter exchange rates (and interest rates). Expectations (about policy and many other matters) generate asset market disturbances upon the exchange rate.

It is the first conclusion—that the location of the equilibrium rate is driven by PPP—which is perhaps the most controversial. How long should the convergence to PPP take and how large should the short-run deviations be? There can be no hard-and-fast rule here, but it is interesting to note the observations of Haberler:

It seems that as a matter of fact under normal circumstances (i.e. when trade is not drastically controlled and regimented, and when the comparison is confined to periods that are not separated by great structural upheavals, e.g. prewar with postwar periods) the PPP theory holds in an approximate fashion in the sense that it would hardly be possible to find under such circumstances a case where an equilibrium rate is say, 15–20 per cent off purchasing power par. (1961: 51)

Figure 8.5 shows much larger deviations than that. Rogoff (1996: fig. 2) reports equally large disparities.

If we recall that PPP was formulated by Cassel in the light of the monetary disturbances after World War I, then we could appeal to the argument of Bruce and Purvis: 'PPP should be interpreted as a *comparative-statics* result arising from a monetary disturbance, embodying the essential feature of *monetary neutrality*' (1985: 839).

Such a view is entirely consistent with the idea of PPP being the open economy and exchange rate equivalent of domestic monetarism. It follows that the source of the non-neutrality may lie outside of the monetary sector, and this is the basis of the Dornbusch monetary model of exchange rates.

8.3 Monetary Models

DORNBUSCH (1976) provided the first, and most famous, monetary model of exchange rates. His model differs substantially from the portfolio-balance models. However, the speed of adjustment, specialization, and size-of-country assumptions necessary for deriving this model are quite similar to those used in deriving the portfolio balance models of Kouri (1976), Branson, Black, and others. Like them, Dornbusch assumes that home and foreign goods are imperfect substitutes and that goods markets adjust slowly relative to asset markets so that domestic prices and real output are fixed in the short-run. He assumes, as they do, that domestic money is held only in the home country. He also assumes that the domestic country is small relative to world asset and goods markets, so that it faces a fixed foreign interest rate and price level.

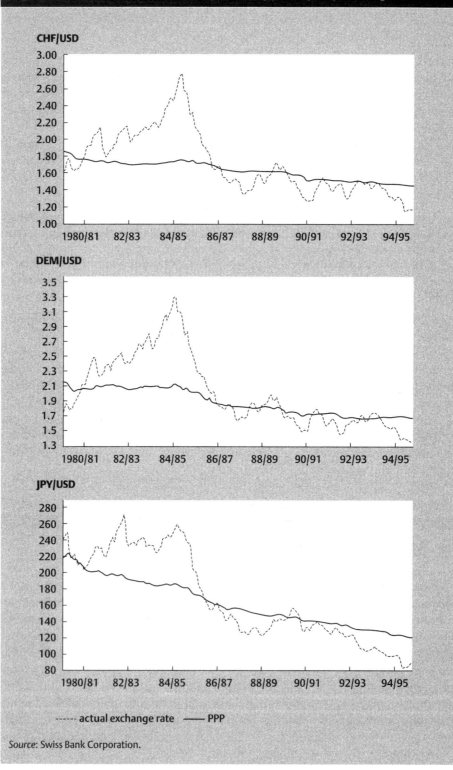

Figure 8.5 Actual and calculations of purchasing power parity exchange rates

----- actual exchange rate ——— PPP

Source: Swiss Bank Corporation.

Dornbusch's key assumption—one that separates the monetary approach from the portfolio-balance approach—concerns substitutability of the assets. Monetary models differ from portfolio-balance models by assuming domestic and foreign interest-earning assets to be perfect substitutes, so that asset holders in each country are indifferent between the two. Additionally wealth effects are assumed to have no role in determining the exchange rate. It is possible, therefore, to focus on money market equilibrium for short-run exchange rate determination.

Consider again (8.22) above, viz.:

$$M = m(i, i^*, \pi)W.$$

The assumption about asset substitutability reintroduces uncovered interest rate parity (8.6), i.e.

$$i = i^* + \pi$$

in that domestic and foreign bonds are perfect substitutes other than the expectation of exchange rate change. Therefore, we do not need equations for B and F because their earlier role was one of determining i and i^* separately.

The next step is to deal with π. This is achieved by assuming 'semi-rational' or 'consistent' expectations of the form

$$\pi = \theta(\bar{e} - e). \tag{8.25}$$

The exchange rate is expected to adjust partially toward an equilibrium value $\bar{e}$, governed by PPP.

Replacing wealth with an income formulation of the demand for money function yields a function of the specific form used by Dornbusch

$$\frac{M}{P} = Y^\phi \, exp^{-\lambda i} \tag{8.26}$$

or in logarithms

$$m - p = \phi y - \lambda i, \tag{8.26a}$$

where m, p, and y are the logarithms of money, prices, and real income.

Rearranging and substituting (8.25) into (8.26a) we obtain

$$e = \bar{e} - \frac{1}{\lambda\theta} [p - m + \phi y - \lambda i^*]. \tag{8.27}$$

This is the key equation of the model and, for given values of m, y, i^*, and $\bar{e}$, relates the current (spot) exchange rate to the level of prices.

The workings of the Dornbusch model are set out in Figure 8.6. Asset market equilibrium is given by the AA line which shows the combinations of price levels and exchange rates that clear the money market.[9] For any given price level, the exchange rate adjusts instantaneously to clear the asset market. Thus the system is always on an AA line. But long-run equilibrium requires also that we be on the 45° line, which has the exchange rate moving proportionately with the price level (given a constant P^*) to maintain eP^*/P unchanged in line with PPP.[10] As with the asset model in the pre-

Figure 8.6 Exchange rate overshooting

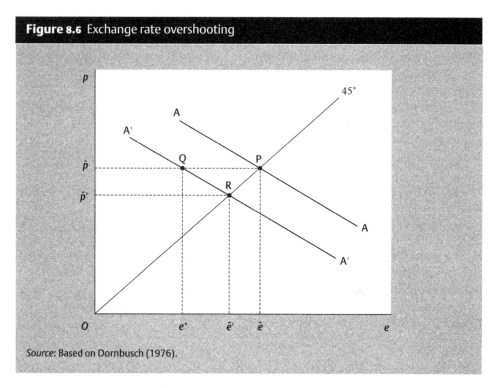

Source: Based on Dornbusch (1976).

vious section, we have a short-run asset market equilibrium and a long-run goods equilibrium involving PPP.

Consider, now, a reduction in the quantity of money (due say to monetary policy) which shifts the *AA* line to *AA'*. The new long-run equilibrium involves a movement from P to R with a lower price level $\bar{p}'$ and an appreciation of the exchange from $\bar{e}$ to $\bar{e}'$. But how do we get to this position and how quickly? Dornbusch was the first to show that the answers depended crucially on what is assumed about the speed of adjustment in the different markets. Some monetary models—the so-called 'flexible price' models—supposed that all prices in the economy, whether they be wages, prices, or exchange rates, are perfectly flexible both upwards and downwards in both the short-term and the long-run (e.g. Frenkel, 1976; Mussa, 1976; and Bilson, 1978). These models incorporated a role for inflation expectations and assumed that purchasing power parity holds continuously. A particularly interesting (indeed remarkable) statement of this monetarist line of thinking is provided by Kreinin and Officer:

> While the adjustment of a balance of payments deficit or surplus takes place via money market equilibrium under both the fixed and floating systems, there is a difference in how this equilibrium is attained. Under fixed exchange rates, quantities of money adjust *gradually* through reserve flows to bring equality between actual and desired money stock. Under floating rates, money market equilibrium occurs *quickly*, if not instantaneously, through domestic price changes that alter the valuation of the money stock. (1978: 20)

By contrast, Dornbusch pioneered the 'sticky price' monetary models in which wages and prices are largely inflexible in the short-run, leaving only exchange rates to change in response to monetary policy.[11] Let us suppose, then, that wages and prices are sticky. If, immediately, prices are unchanged, the system must move from P to Q for the asset market to clear. That is, at the price level $\bar{p}$, the exchange rate must move to e'' to induce people to hold a smaller stock of money. Only as prices fall will the exchange rate converge to the new long-run equilibrium level $\bar{e}'$. In the meantime, the exchange rate overshoots its long-run position.

The commonsense of this result can be understood readily if we assume at the original equilibrium that domestic and foreign interest rates are both 10 per cent per annum. Suppose that the home economy now introduces a tightened monetary policy stance which reduces the quantity of money and raises the domestic rate of interest, to say, 12 per cent per annum. With foreign and domestic securities perfect substitutes, interest parity requires that the now higher domestic interest rate be combined with the expectation that the home currency *depreciates* by 2 per cent per annum vis-à-vis the other currency. But how can this be if the home currency *appreciates*? The answer is for the domestic currency to appreciate so much that everyone expects it to depreciate from its current, abnormally high level. That is, the home currency must *over-appreciate* as compared with the long-run equilibrium position.

Another way to view this result is in terms of the balance of payments. Consider again equation (8.1). Under a floating exchange rate regime,

$$(X - Z) + K = \triangle R = 0.$$

In the very short-run, the trade account $(X - Z)$ can be regarded as predetermined. This means that the adjustment must take place *within* the capital account. As a consequence of the increase in domestic interest rates relative to foreign interest rates, the covered interest differential may encourage a capital inflow based on interest arbitrage. However, there cannot be a *net* capital inflow if the current account remains unchanged. Either the forward premium must rise sufficiently so that a covered interest differential does not open in favour of the home country or a speculative capital outflow must match the inflow from interest arbitrage. This latter result can be achieved if the exchange rate rises sufficiently above its long-term value to a point that an expectation of depreciation results.

In broad terms, the model seemed to make some sense of the surge in the US dollar from 1980 to 1984, which features so prominently in Figure 8.5. After the Federal Reserve tightened monetary policy unexpectedly in 1979–80, the US dollar rose well above its expected PPP value. The US dollar started to fall in 1985. Then, following a period of looser monetary policy, the dollar seemed to be 'under-shooting'.

However, there are misgivings as to whether this can be the entire story. If rigidities in nominal wages and prices are to blame, then it is not clear that deviations as long as those shown in the figure could persist. Friedman, we recall, argued that prices adjust to monetary shocks with a 'long and variable' lag of between twelve and twenty-four months. One would consequently expect to observe a substantial degree of convergence to PPP over one to two years. Evidence suggests that this is not the case (Rogoff, 1996).

Another potential source of exchange rate stability comes from the persistence with national monetary targeting policies in the face of extensive currency substitution. We now look to models of currency substitution.

8.4 Models of Currency Substitution

THE term 'currency substitution' was first used by Calvo and Rodriguez (1977) when extending the paper on exchange rate determination by Kouri (1976). While an asset market approach, Kouri's model restricted the assets to home currency and foreign currency, and this choice of menu provided a basis to explore currency substitution. The phrase 'currency substitution' refers to the demand for domestic money by foreign residents and the demand by domestic residents for foreign currency. Currencies may be substituted for many reasons but it is always related to the underlying advantages that accrue from the holding of one currency relative to the holding of another. These advantages may be in terms of rates of return or in the 'services' that one currency offers relative to another. Models of currency substitution explain the demand for each currency in relation to the relative rewards that they offer.

Thus by currency substitution we mean demand-side currency substitution. This stands in distinction from the supply-side substitution which occurs under fixed exchange rate regimes when central banks stand ready to exchange currencies at rates of exchange which are fixed and known in advance. When exchange rates are flexible, individual transactors have an incentive to hold foreign currencies which is not present with perfect supply-side currency substitution, as is the case in a monetary union, and may not be present in the case of a 'usually-fixed-sometimes-adjustable' exchange rate regime. Instead of governments or central banks holding such reserves of foreign exchange as they require in order to finance their exchange guarantee, there will be some compensating increase in private sector demand.

In this respect, Krueger (1983) first categorized models of currency substitution into two types: monetary models and global models. These correspond respectively to a model based on the monetary approach to the balance of payments and to an approach based on open economy money demand functions. The *monetary currency substitution models* interpret current balance surpluses (deficits) as an excess demand (supply) for foreign currency by domestic residents. These models can be considered to be models of the monetary approach to the balance of payments in which the capital account and capital markets are ignored since interest-bearing assets do not exist in these models. The *global currency substitution models* view the relevant money supply as the world money supply, within the context of a highly developed and interdependent world capital market. The issue for this class of currency substitution models is the liquidity services which different types of money provide to the holder, based on the motives for diversifying money holdings.

The motivations suggested for diversifying money holdings across currencies of

Table 8.1 Classification of currency substitution models

1. Monetary currency substitution models
   No distinction between foreign money and foreign bonds
   Kouri (1976), Niehans (1977), Calvo and Rodriguez (1977), Barro (1978)

2. Global currency substitution models
   (a) Money services models
       (i) *Two-stage portfolio allocation*
           No bonds in model portfolio choice
           Miles (1978), Joines (1985), Bergstand and Bundt (1990)
       (ii) *Single-stage portfolio allocation*
           Includes both bonds and money in the equilibrium
           Ratti and Jeong (1994), Milner, Mizen and Pentecost (1996)
   (b) Portfolio balance models
       Bonds and money choices made simultaneously
       Girton and Roper (1981), McKinnon (1982), Cuddington (1983), Branson and Henderson (1985)

denomination are transactions-based and speculative. A transactor who buys goods invoiced in a range of currencies will have a corresponding need at the point of purchase for currency of the right denomination. Costs of exchange suggest, as do costs of liquidating an alternative asset in the standard theory of money demand, that a mixed portfolio of moneys may be desirable in this case. Not all these needs can necessarily be programmed in advance, though a perception that they may arise gives substance to a precautionary demand for foreign-currency-denominated money. The second motive is speculative: holding money in foreign denomination hedges the risk of an exchange rate change if expenditures on foreign goods are planned in any case; it also affords a means of speculating on exchange rage changes which may dominate alternative investment vehicles when costs and ease of acquisition and liquidation are taken into account.

Global currency substitution models can be further subdivided by the way they represent domestic residents' portfolios of assets. *A two-stage portfolio allocation model* assumes that there is a restricted portfolio choice. In the first stage the portfolio is divided between money and bonds. When these proportions have been determined, transactors then divide up these independent portfolios between domestic bonds and foreign bonds and between domestic money and foreign money in the second stage. McKinnon (1984a) called the division of liquid assets between domestic and foreign moneys direct currency substitution.[12] Since the portfolios are independent, by construction, we need only consider the allocation of the money portfolio between domestic and foreign cash balances. *A single-stage portfolio allocation model* uses a portfolio balance model in which all assets are available to portfolio holders and a combination of assets is chosen that maximizes the return of the portfolio subject to a minimal level of risk in a single-decision process. Finally, the *portfolio balance model* allows simultaneous and unrestricted choice between domestic and foreign money and bonds. The allocation of wealth is determined by the rates of return to the available assets, and is subject to no constraint except that the total asset stocks should equal total wealth.

We now give further consideration to each type in turn.

Monetary currency substitution models

The monetary substitution models emphasize that the accumulation of foreign currency balances can only come about through the current account surplus or deficit: this is a flow approach to the currency substitution question. The key idea is that domestic residents hold their real financial wealth, W, in domestic money, M, and foreign money, M^*, that is:

$$w = M/e + M^*, \tag{8.28}$$

where e is the nominal exchange rate defined as the domestic price of foreign currency, so that M/e is the value of the domestic money supply measured in units of foreign currency, and W is therefore also measured in foreign currency. The asset demands depend upon the level of wealth and the rate of inflation, π (asterisks denote foreign variables), so that:

$$L = L(W, \pi) \quad L_1 > 0, L_2 < 0$$

$$L^* = L^*(W, \pi) \quad L^*_1 > 0, L^*_2 < 0. \tag{8.29}$$

With the money markets in equilibrium, the ratio of home money to foreign money is given as:

$$\left[\frac{M}{eM^*}\right] = \frac{L}{L^*} = l(W, \varepsilon), \tag{8.30}$$

where ε is the expected depreciation of the home currency, equal to the domestic inflation rate when foreign prices are stable. In a stationary state the relative demands for money depend only upon domestic wealth.

Currency substitution in this model depends upon the monetary policy pursued by the domestic authorities. An unanticipated rise in domestic monetary growth will lead to a depreciation in the domestic currency. This depreciation will stimulate the demand for domestic tradables abroad leading to a current balance surplus. This surplus will be financed by domestic residents accumulating foreign currency balances until the surplus is eliminated by the appreciation of the real exchange rate. Thus the attempt to expand the rate of monetary growth results in a process of currency substitution, in that the proportion of domestic real financial wealth held in foreign currency is higher at the end of the period than at the beginning. Foreign currency balances have therefore been partly substituted for domestic currency balances.

A weakness of these models is that they assume that the capital inflow is solely in the form of money: no bonds are permitted in the analysis. This feature makes the models most applicable to economies where there are not well-developed financial and capital markets but does not make them very useful for identifying currency substitution in countries where bond and other financial markets are well developed.

Global currency substitution models

The two-stage portfolio allocation model has also been labelled the money services model, since allocation is based on the provision of liquidity services which different moneys provide. It offers a restrictive set of portfolio choices. The process of currency substitution takes place as individuals switch between different currencies in the liquid asset portfolio. The decision to alter the liquid asset composition of portfolios is independent of the non-liquid asset position.

The model due to Joines (1985) and Bergstrand and Bundt (1990), looks at domestic residents' and foreign residents' demand for domestic and foreign currencies. In this model the supply of domestic currency, M, is held by both domestic, M^D, and foreign residents, M^F, and the foreign supply of money, M^*, is also held by both domestic, M^{*D} and foreign residents, M^{*F}. Therefore we have the following identities:

$$M = M^D + M^F \quad \text{and} \quad M^* = M^{*D} + M^{*F}. \tag{8.31}$$

The demand for each money, K, depends on the price level, P, relevant to the currency, the level of real income relevant to the 'home' resident, and both domestic and foreign rates of interest, r and r^*. Thus money market equilibrium conditions are given as:

$$M^D + M^F = PK^D(r, r^*)Y + PK^F(r, r^*)Y^* \tag{8.32}$$

$$M^{*D} + M^{*F} = P^* K^{*D}(r, r^*)Y + P^* K^{*F}(r, r^*)Y^*. \tag{8.33}$$

A well-known model by Miles (1978) implicitly assumes that $M^F = M^{*F} = 0$, focusing attention solely on the domestic demand for each currency, so we have:

$$\frac{M^D}{M^{*D}} = \frac{PK^D(r, r^*)Y}{P^* K^{*D}(r, r^*)Y}. \tag{8.34}$$

Assuming purchasing power parity and noting that the real income terms cancel, we have:

$$\frac{M^D}{eM^{*D}} = \frac{K^D(r, r^*)}{K^{*D}(r, r^*)}, \tag{8.35}$$

which in logarithms is approximately equal to[13]

$$\log\left(\frac{M^D}{e\,M^{*D}}\right) = \sigma \log\left(\frac{\theta_1}{\theta_2}\right) + \sigma \log\left(\frac{1 + r^*}{1 + r}\right), \tag{8.36}$$

where the degree of currency substitution is given by σ which according to this approach should be positive, and so the ratio of domestic to foreign currency balances held by domestic residents depends directly upon the foreign rate of interest and inversely on the domestic rate.

An alternative to Miles's assumption, that $M^F = M^{*F} = 0$, is the restriction that $M^{*D} = 0$. This has been applied by Bergstrand and Bundt (1990) to consider another asymmetric case, where domestic residents do not hold foreign money, but foreign residents hold domestic money. Any currency substitution must accordingly be undertaken by foreign residents, and represented by the coefficient on the foreign rate of interest in non-residents' demand for home currency:

$$\frac{M^F}{P} = K^D(r, r^*)Y^* \tag{8.37}$$

or in logarithms

$$\log \frac{M^F}{P} = \alpha_0 + \alpha_1 r + \alpha_2 r_t^* + \alpha_3 \log Y^*. \tag{8.38}$$

One advantage of this specification is that it includes foreign real income, Y^*, which represents a portfolio size of growth variable missing from Miles's analysis. The dependent variable is simply the level of real domestic money balances held by non-residents which has the advantage of not requiring the assumption of purchasing power parity in its construction. The term r^* represents the opportunity cost of holding domestic money and so, as it falls, foreigners will switch out of foreign money into domestic money, because although they cannot make an acquisition of bonds to reduce the total holdings of money (decided upon in the first stage), they can reallocate their holdings between domestic and foreign currencies. Conversely, if r^* falls (and r remains unchanged) then there is a lower opportunity cost of holding foreign currency and a tendency to switch from domestic to foreign money. In common with Miles's model, the use of the interest rate to capture currency substitution means that the hypothesis cannot be distinguished from capital mobility in practice.

The single-stage portfolio allocation model is also reliant on money services provided by alternative currencies, but it is based on dynamic optimization, emphasizing rather more clearly the demand for money as a medium of exchange, and different from the restricted money services models by explicitly recognizing bonds. In this framework introduced by Ratti and Jeong (1994), the fraction of real resources necessary for transactions is given by a function, V, which is inversely related to the level of money services, S, such that $V = V(S)$.

As before, the level of money services is provided by both domestic and foreign currency, M and M^* respectively, so that

$$S = S\left(\frac{M}{P}, \frac{M^*}{P^*}\right) \quad S_1 > 0, S_2 > 0. \tag{8.39}$$

The consumer seeks to maximize utility from consumption over all future periods subject to a wealth constraint and a savings, or asset accumulation, constraint. As such, the wealth constraint includes both domestic and foreign money and bonds and additions to wealth can be in the form of any of the assets. Ultimately the marginal utilities of domestic and foreign cash balances depend directly upon the real exchange rate and the uncovered interest rate parity condition:

$$\frac{S_1\left(\dfrac{M}{P},\dfrac{M^*}{P^*}\right)}{S_2\left(\dfrac{M}{P},\dfrac{M^*}{P^*}\right)} = \left(\frac{P}{eP^*}\right)\left(\frac{r}{r^*(1+\varepsilon)}\right). \tag{8.40}$$

Assuming that the money services function has a constant elasticity of substitution (CES), rearranging and taking logs this can be written as:

$$\log\left(\frac{M}{e.M^*}\right) = \log\left(\frac{\theta_1}{\theta_2}\right) - \sigma\log\left(\frac{P}{e\,P^*}\right) - \sigma\log\left(\frac{r}{r^*(1+\varepsilon)}\right), \tag{8.41}$$

where as before σ is in the elasticity of currency substitution and M/eM^* gives the relative shares of domestic and foreign money balances in the portfolio in equivalent units. Although this specification of the money services model is the most general, it suffers from a number of inconsistencies and limitations, not least that it omits to include a scale variable in real income or wealth. Second, in the derivation PPP is assumed to hold so that P/P^* can be replaced by e on the left-hand side of the equation. This implies that the real exchange rate is constant, but the real exchange rate appears as an explanatory variable on the right-hand side of (8.41). Clearly there is an inconsistency here since if PPP holds continuously, then the constant real exchange rate should be part of the constant term and Miles's model results. If it is not constant, then the substitution of e for P/P^* is invalid. Third, the measure of currency substitution in (8.40) is a multiplicative term consisting of PPP and uncovered interest rate parity (UIP) which has no obvious economic interpretation.

The *portfolio-balance approach* was initially developed for an open economy by McKinnon and Oates (1966) as an extension of Tobin (1958) for asset demands in a closed economy. More recently, Girton and Roper (1981), Cuddington (1983), Branson and Henderson (1985), and Zervoyianni (1988, 1992) have extended the model to include the possibility of currency substitution. As in Tobin (1958), these models all assume that transactors maximize the returns to their wealth subject to a given level of risk. This is the most general model since people can hold four different assets and switch between them simultaneously. Domestic money is viewed as a riskless asset, since there is assumed to be no domestic inflation, while domestic bonds are risky in that their prices may vary. The rate of return on foreign bonds is simply the rate of interest plus the expected depreciation of the domestic currency, since for domestic residents it is the home currency value of bond returns which is important. The rate of return on foreign money, in the absence of inflation, is again zero. The relative return on the cash part of the portfolio is given by the expected depreciation of the exchange rate. If domestic inflation is expected to be higher than foreign inflation, the domestic currency is expected to depreciate and the demand for domestic currency will fall relative to foreign currency.

These models view the demands for all assets as directly related to their own yields and inversely related to the yields on all other assets. Consequently, the demand for domestic money balances by domestic residents is given as:

$$\frac{M^D}{P} = m(r, r^* + \varepsilon, \varepsilon, Y), \tag{8.42}$$

and the demand for foreign money balances by domestic residents as:

$$\frac{eM^{*D}}{P} = m^*(r, r^* + \varepsilon, \varepsilon, Y), \tag{8.43}$$

So that the relative demands are given as:

$$\frac{M^D}{eM^{*D}} = \eta(r, r^* + \varepsilon, \varepsilon, Y). \tag{8.44}$$

The main advantage of this approach, compared to the money services approach, is the fact that it allows the impact of currency substitution and capital mobility to be measured independently. Note that in the context of the portfolio-balance model currency substitution is seen as a precautionary phenomenon, and hence the expected depreciation of the domestic currency is frequently viewed as the expected difference between home and foreign inflation rates. The principal difficulties with the portfolio-balance approach derive from the empirical application of the model. The potential correlation between r, $r^*+ \varepsilon$, and ε (see Cuddington, 1983) probably goes some way to explaining why this model seems to perform the best for countries where the risk premium is time-varying, driving a wedge between these variables. Secondly, there are problems with the measurement of the expected depreciation of the exchange rate. The forward premium and the inflation differential both under-predict the actual change in the exchange rate, while using the actual rate itself puts strains on the degree of rationality with which expectations can reasonably be assumed to follow (see Froot and Frankel, 1989).

8.5 Some Implications

THIS chapter examined the basic building blocks of open economy modelling and then outlined the characteristics of three different classes of models of exchange rate behaviour—the asset model approach, monetary models, and currency substitution models. The broad conclusions—brought out most clearly in the asset models—that asset-holding decisions dominate the exchange market in the short- to medium-run, and that there can be marked shifts in preference as between currencies, driven by expectations, seem to accord with actual behaviour.

The monetary model of Dornbusch was extremely influential. It generally highlighted the role that expectations play in determining exchange rates and at the same time demonstrated that volatile exchange rates cannot necessarily be seen as evidence of inefficiencies and instabilities in asset markets. Rather, the failure of the exchange rate to move in line with purchasing power parity can be attributed to stickiness in wages and prices which pushes all of the short-run adjustment onto the asset markets. Yet, there are reasons to question the model both in terms of the formation of 'consistent' exchange rate expectations and the hypothesis that inflation responds sluggishly to the pressure of excess demand in goods markets. Neither may be consistent with optimizing behaviour, and this is the topic of the next two chapters.

That a high degree of currency substitution has potentially significant effects upon exchange rates cannot be doubted. Without currency substitution, only one money would be relevant—as is in fact the standard assumption of open economy monetary analysis. With two moneys it is clear that, if the two are highly substitutable in people's portfolios, quantitative control of either one, or or both independently, is meaningless and can result only in a volatile exchange rate between the two when people attempt to change the composition of their holdings. An analogy would be attempting to hold constant the stock of pears and of apples separately when the relevant variable is the sum of apples and pears. Seemingly capricious switches from apples to pears occasioned by the appearance (say) of minor blemishes in the appearance of one or the other will—because the two are by hypothesis highly substitutable—occasion wild swings in the relative price of pears to apples.

Moreover, in the absence of an understanding of currency substitution, authorities may easily follow inappropriate monetary policies. What appears to be an expansionary stance of policy in the light of a rapid expansion of the domestic money supply may turn out to be an unchanged stance of policy because of strong international demands to hold the local currency. Reacting to the false signal by domestic policies to restrain what seems to be the 'excessive' monetary growth could lead to excessive exchange rate instability.

In these circumstances, McKinnon (1984*b*, 1988) suggested that exchange rates should be held constant and that the leading countries (USA, Japan, and Germany) should coordinate their domestic credit expansion so as to stabilize world money supply growth. His argument provided intellectual support for policy coordination of the type in the *Plaza Agreement* and *Louvre Accord* in that excessive exchange rate variability appears costly and strong negative externalities attach to monetary policies working actively through the exchange rate simply because one currency's appreciation is another's depreciation. As in other cases, the optimal response to externalities is to internalize them. In this context, internalization requires world (or at least North American, European, and Japanese) monetary cooperation.

Empirical evidence in favour of currency substitution is, however, mixed. There is plenty of evidence of asymmetrical currency substitution, notably in some developing countries, where residents use the US dollar widely, but for currency substitution among the industrial countries which might in principle be more symmetrical, the evidence is sometimes more elusive. This is examined when we consider the empirical work on the demand for money.

Notes

1 Hume wrote that international trade brings 'money to a common level in all countries, just as "all water, wherever it communicates, remains always at a level"' (*Essays*, 335-6).

2 Versions of the PPP have been traced back to the Salamanca School in sixteenth-century Spain, to the bullionists in the eighteenth century, and to classical economists such as Ricardo, Mill, and Marshall. This history is outlined in Viner (1937), Schumpeter (1954), and Officer (1984).

3 Swan (1955, 1960). While the cost ratio on Swan's internal–external balance model is generally interpreted in US textbooks as eP^*/P (and in some cases as the exchange rate alone), in fact Swan defined the cost ratio as 'the ratio of an index of international prices (prices of imports and exports) to an index of local wages' (386). He was dealing with a small open economy (Australia) for which both export and import prices are set internationally. International prices would need to be converted to domestic prices via the exchange rate (which was fixed when Swan wrote). Also, by defining the cost ratio in terms of wages, Swan was allowing for centralized wages policy, which operated in Australia (and in parts of Europe) at that time. That has never been the case in the USA—hence the different treatment.

4 Alexander (1952). As real income increases, more of domestic production is 'absorbed' by domestic expenditure, stimulating imports and leaving less available for export.

5 To distinguish it from covered interest parity considered earlier. Similarly, the Fisher open hypothesis is to be distinguished from the Fisher closed hypothesis, i.e. the international Fisher effect examined before.

6 Thus a euro-sterling rate, say, will be quoted by a bank as the euro-dollar rate and the relevant forward discount or premium. See Lewis and Davis (1987: Ch 9).

7 The asset or portfolio-balance models for an open economy are surveyed in Jones and Kenen (1985), in particular in chapters by Branson and Henderson, Frankel and Mussa, and Bruce and Purvis.

8 The *MM* curve is upward-sloping because a rise in the domestic interest rate i reduces demand for money requiring a rise in the exchange rate e (depreciation), which increases wealth by the valuation effect on holdings of foreign assets, thereby increasing demand. The *BB* curve is downward-sloping because a rise in i increases demand for domestic bonds requiring an appreciation, which decreases wealth by the valuation effect, thereby decreasing demand for bonds. The *FF* curve is downward-sloping because as i rises, demand for foreign bonds decreases, depressing the exchange rate e (appreciation) to bring the domestic currency value of foreign bonds supplied into line with lower demand.

9 An increase in the price level reduces real money balances, raising interest rates and the attempted shift from foreign assets to domestic money gives rise to an incipient capital inflow that appreciates the spot rate.

10 The 45° line passes through the origin on the assumption that by an appropriate choice of units, domestic and foreign prices are initially equal.

11 Later Frankel (1979) integrated the two approaches into a general one which has the 'flexible price' and 'sticky price' monetary models as special cases.

12 McKinnon (1996: 44), explains that 'direct currency substitution means two (or more) currencies compete as a means of payment within the same commodity domain' whilst 'indirect currency substitution refers to investors switching between non-monetary financial assets, say "bonds", denominated in different currencies in a way that indirectly influences the domestic demand for transactions balances.'

13 The model is based on a money services production function (CES) such that

$$S = \left[\theta_1\left(\frac{M}{p}\right)^{-\rho} + \theta_2\left(\frac{M^{*D}}{p^*}\right)^{-\rho}\right]^{-\frac{1}{\rho}}$$

where ρ is the elasticity of substitution.

Chapter 9
Rational Expectations

9.1 New Classical Economics

THE two previous chapters have examined open economy and closed economy monetarism, the latter in particular championed by Milton Friedman as a revival of the Chicago quantity theory. In this chapter we turn to another kind of monetarism, also from Chicago and also closed economy but in this case supported and advocated by Robert Lucas. The foundations of Lucas's version, which has become known as new classical economics (or, as Hoover (1988) put it, monetarism mark II),[1] lie in the notion of 'rational' expectations. Our first task will be to introduce and define that concept. The chapter will then explore the implications of the rational expectations hypothesis and consider the role of monetary policy in such a world.

Before doing so, we consider the main differences between monetarism mark I and monetarism mark II, which by virtue of the prominence of the leading advocates of these schools can be viewed as a contrast between Friedman and Lucas. Taking Friedman and the original monetarist analysis first, we find that theoretically it is a partial equilibrium approach in the Marshallian style. The principal feature is the interaction between the supply of and the demand for money and the consequences for monetary policy, considered largely in isolation from the other supply and demand functions in the wider economy. Money is treated analogously to a durable good and the theory builds on the quantity theory relationship, in the form of Friedman's restatement. Throughout Friedman's work, the emphasis is on the effects of monetary policy, while his training as a statistician is reflected in the importance placed upon the forecasting ability of the final empirical specification. For this purpose, the demand for money function is quickly reduced from a theoretical model with many variables to a small parsimonious one to which statistical tools can be successfully applied—success being the predictive performance of the model over long runs of data.

The move from mark I to mark II came when the priority shifted from the demand for money, and the constancy of velocity, to the labour market and the issue of full employment output. Friedman provided the link between the two with the introduction in his 1968 paper of the concept of the 'natural' level of unemployment. Prior to the 1968 paper, Friedman had contented himself with the established view that full employment was a theoretical possibility. But that was quite different from establishing that the full employment equilibrium would actually be attained in a world of apparent rigidities and sluggish adjustment, and without Keynesian demand management policies.

Friedman in 1968 argued that any expansion of output and employment from demand management was a transitory phenomenon, lasting only until expectations of inflation caught up with the ongoing inflation rate. Then the stimulus to demand from lower real interest rates and from prices outstripping wages would be lost. Once expectations of inflation caught up, whatever was expected would have to be added to any inflation generated by excess demand. Furthermore, if there was a one-for-one relationship between expected inflation and wage inflation it was easy to demonstrate that inflation would accelerate so long as excess demand persisted. Friedman argued that there was a natural rate of unemployment which was consistent with zero wage inflation.

Friedman's analysis of inflation and unemployment was a persuasive one, but he had no analysis of fluctuations around the natural rate other than those induced by government policy—in line with his monetary interpretation of the Great Depression.[2] Monetarists needed a theory of how the private sector by itself gets into, and more particularly gets out of, recessions, i.e. a theory of self-correcting business fluctuations. Friedman was also vague about the character of full employment or its apparent inverse, the natural rate of unemployment. The new brand of monetarism filled in those gaps by adding rational expectations and the assumption of continuous market-clearing.

However, in doing so, Lucas's model differed crucially in that it relied on a general equilibrium method, and was rooted more firmly in a Walrasian tradition than was Friedman's monetarism. In these models the emphasis is upon consistency between different parts of the model because, from the general equilibrium nature of the system, a correctly specified monetary model relies on the other components of the model being correctly identified and modelled. Misspecifications in one part of the model affects all of the other parts and so the Lucas model relies heavily on a consistent and accurate theoretical model with an abstract but consistent treatment of the mathematics. In contrast to Friedman's approach, Lucas was far less concerned about practical issues and predictive performance, although he and other 'new classicals' have drawn some very strong policy conclusions from the theory including the likely signs and magnitudes of the parameters of the model. The cohesiveness and consistency of the model to acceptable microfoundations is all important. It is because of its similarity, in terms of its method and its policy results, to the classical economic system discussed in Chapters 3 and 4 that Lucas's approach has been called new classical economics.[3]

9.2 The Formation of Expectations

THE formation of expectations is central to monetary economics since all but the most elementary aspects are dynamic. Dynamics introduces a time dimension by focusing on change from one period to another. Inevitably, some of the changes will be concerned with the likely future value of some economic variable, such as prices or the money supply, in relation to the present. The question that immediately arises is whether the present can inform us about the future and in particular whether a forecast can be made about a series from information available to us today. This leads us to the process of expectation formation.

There are many ways that expectations can be formed and we will not seek to deal with all of them.[4] Our interest is in explaining how expectations formation can alter the properties of a monetary model, and we illustrate this point with a few simple examples beginning with the simplest, *static expectations*, where the expected value of some variable p_t, given information up to time $t - 1$, is denoted $E_{t-1} p_t$ and is constant i.e.

$$E_{t-1} p_t = p. \tag{9.1}$$

It can also be said that future expectations will all be equal to p, and so long as the variable does not deviate from p in practice, the expectation will be correct, and there will be no expectational error:

$$p_t - E_{t-1} p_t = 0 \tag{9.2}$$

This is obviously a special case, and most economic series would likely vary from a fixed value. Any variation in p_t when expectations are static will result in expectational errors that are non-zero.[5]

It would be reasonable to consider the possibility of learning in such a context and one way to allow for this is to permit *adaptive expectations*. The adaptation occurs when expectational errors are observed and the expected value of the variable in the previous period $E_{t-2} p_{t-1}$, is updated by the expectational error $(p_{t-1} - E_{t-2} p_{t-1})$. By adjusting the prior expectation by the previous mistake a new expectation is formed based on the formula

$$E_{t-1} p_t = E_{t-2} p_{t-1} + \varphi \; (p_{t-1} - E_{t-2} p_{t-1}) \tag{9.3}$$

where the term on the left–hand side is the new expectation, the first term on the right–hand side is the expectation from the prior period and the second term is the previous expectational error or 'mistake', while φ is a weight between zero and one. From this formula we can see that

$$E_{t-2} p_{t-1} = E_{t-3} p_{t-2} + \varphi \, (p_{t-2} - E_{t-3} p_{t-2}) \tag{9.4}$$

and by substitution of 9.4 into 9.3 we can show, by repeated substitution that

$$E_{t-1}\,p_t = \varphi\,p_{t-1} + \varphi\,(1-\varphi)\,p_{t-2} + \varphi\,(1-\varphi)^2 p_{t-3} + \ldots +$$
$$(1-\varphi)^{n+1}\;E_{t-n-2}\,p_{t-n-1} \quad (9.5)$$

If n is large, then $(1-\varphi)^{n+1} \to 0$ and the expectation is simply a function of the past history of the variable p_t. Each value of p_t in the past has a weight and the weight declines geometrically to ensure that the recent past has more influence than the distant past. By this means, an expectation can be formed about the future based on past history of the variable itself.[6]

There are three main objections to this schema: (i) the expectation is entirely backward-looking so it cannot anticipate future events; (ii) the weighting of the past based on φ is arbitrary; and (iii) the procedure is prone to systematic errors. Consider a surprise event in the evolution of the variable p_t that was not previously anticipated. Given that there has been a surprise, there will be an expectational error, $(p_{t-1} - E_{t-2}\,p_{t-1})$, and this will be used to adjust future expectations according to the weight φ. The unfortunate property of this expectational scheme is that, unless $\varphi = 1$, the adjustment will be partial and not complete. In fact, even if no other shocks or surprises ever occur, the expectation will always differ from the true value because the shock is never fully adjusted for in present expectations.

This result indicates that there will always be a systematic error in expectations following an unexpected shock. The extent of the systematic error will depend on φ; the smaller it is the greater the systematic error since less of the expectational error will be incorporated into the current expectation in each period. The sole exception to this rule is the case where $\varphi = 1$, and this is a situation where

$$E_{t-1}\,p_t = p_{t-1} \qquad\qquad (9.6)$$

which says that the expectation equals the previous value of the variable, and the expectational error is completely eliminated in the fully revised expectation $E_{t-1}\,p_t$. This is the case of *rational expectations*.

The notion of rational expectations was originally defined by John Muth (1960, 1961) in the context of microeconomics and it remained in obscurity until used by Lucas (1972) to establish the beginnings of new classical macroeconomics.[7] The research that led Muth to the conclusion that expectations should be formed rationally was developed at Carnegie-Mellon University in the late 1950s and early 1960s. While Muth was considering the interaction between the real world and expectations formation, his colleague and co-author, Herbert Simon was also considering the issue. The two came to very different conclusions from their deliberations. Simon considered that optimizing problems were too complex for most economic decision-makers to process fully. He developed a limited optimization scheme based on the principle of 'satisficing', which seeks acceptable but not necessarily fully optimizing solutions to complex problems. Simon considered that individuals who were 'boundedly rational' would reach satisfactory solutions on the basis of the satisficing principle rather than attempt to solve a complex optimization problem. Muth, on the other hand, found it unacceptable that expectations were separable from a theoretical model which accurately represented reality. His view was that expectations that did not consider all relevant information and discarded pertinent data were 'irrationally formed'. In his eyes, individuals *were* capable of handling real world complexity in expectations formation—their forecasts within the model would be no worse than those made by the economist who has the model.

The question we must address is how an individual behaving rationally would form an expectation in order to remove systematic errors. This is a complex problem since many economic series are randomly distributed, and they follow a path in which the next period's value is equal to the previous value plus a random term, ε_{t+1}:

$$p_{t+1} = p_t + \varepsilon_t + 1 \tag{9.7}$$

The basic philosophy behind rational expectations, derived directly from Muth, is that *all* available and relevant information is used to make the best possible guess of the future value of a particular economic variable—that is $\varphi = 1$ in our previous example. Errors can still be made but these will be essentially random, with a mean of zero, and display no discernible pattern. The concept of rational expectations does not allow *systematic* mistakes to be made in expectations formation; moreover, these will be less than those associated with any other forecasting model.

At a practical level, the expectation of the future value of the variable can be found by computing the mathematical expectation of the variable based on all information available up to the time that the expectation is formed. The mathematical representation of the above is

$$E_t(p_{t+1}) = E_t(p_t) + E_t(\varepsilon_{t+1}) \tag{9.8}$$

The expectation of the previous price is easy to calculate since it can be observed in the information set. The expectation of the random term can be determined from knowledge of its probability distribution, and although the exact value of ε_{t+1} cannot be known, its mean and variance can be inferred from its distribution. The expectation of the random term can be determined using this information (since $E_t \varepsilon_{t+1}$ is equal to the mean of the random term) to give our expectation of its future value. From the fact that it is a random, unpredictable shock term we know that the mean will be zero (if it had a non-zero mean we could use that information to help predict its value) but it is defined as the unpredictable part and therefore must have a zero mean. From these pieces of information we can say that $E_t p_{t+1} = p_t$. That is, our best guess of the future value of the economic variable is its past value since the only thing we know about the difference between the current and the future value is that it is unpredictable, but will be zero on average.

The important characteristic of rational expectations is that they do not include systematic errors. Strictly speaking, this means that the expectational errors, $(p_{t+1} - E_t p_{t+1})$ should be uncorrelated with any information, I, that is available at the time of forming expectations. This principle is known as the *orthogonality principle* and ensures that

$$E_t \left((p_{t+1} - E_t \, p_{t+1}) . I_t | I_t \right) = 0. \tag{9.9}$$

If there is information in I_t that can help to remove expectational errors, then it would have been included in the original expectation and thus, without it, the expectation is not fully rational (some information has remained unused).

Two versions of rational expectations can be distinguished. In the strong form, the individual is assumed to know the correct underlying model which generates the values of this economic series. The definition of information in this case includes all information including economic theory and econometric information which bears on the true data generation process. In weaker forms of rational expectations models, it is acknowledged that information collection is not costless and that orthoganality should hold up to the point that the marginal benefit exceeds the marginal cost of collection. Even under the weak form, if there are sufficient numbers of participants, such errors that do exist should reasonably be offset in aggregate by the Law of Large Numbers.[8]

The application of the idea of rational expectations is a central feature of the new classical models and it is the basis for many important and interesting results, but it is only in conjunction with the additional assumption that markets clear continuously that it yields the radical classical results that the following sections will elucidate.

9.3 The Phillips Curve and Lucas's 'Islands Model'

ONE of the first areas to receive attention from Lucas was the relationship between wage–price inflation and the level of economic activity—the Phillips curve. It was in the theory of the labour market that the Phillips curve was most vulnerable, for it was never more than an empirical regularity in search of a theory. The New Zealand economist A. W. Phillips (1958) had shown that a logarithmic relationship between the unemployment rate and wage inflation in Great Britain from 1861 to 1913 was able to be fitted satisfactorily to data for 1948–57. The relationship was such that high unemployment was associated with low wages growth, while low unemployment was combined with a rapid growth of wages. That was generally interpreted as one between excess demand and those variables. A stimulus to demand (say from government spending) would increase output and reduce unemployment, but the cost of that achievement was higher inflation. Conversely, a reduction in demand would reduce inflation, but at the cost of increased unemployment. Those trade-offs were an accepted part of policy formulation in the 1960s, for Phillips curves had been found to exist in most major countries.

During the late 1960s and early 1970s the relationship had received renewed attention from economists because the apparently stable negative relationship between inflation and unemployment identified by Phillips and others had come into question as new data appeared to indicate both rising inflation and lower economic activity. Friedman suggested that the reason for the success of the Phillips curve in its original 'misspecified' form over the late 1950s and 1960s was the low level of inflation in that period which meant that nominal changes and real changes to wages did not diverge much over the period. His prediction was soon afterwards shown to be true as the inflation rate accelerated in the early 1970s, widening the gap between nominal and real changes to wages, and the empirical regularity which provided the main justification for the Phillips curve broke down.

Friedman (1968a) and Phelps (1970) put forward the hypothesis that this was because the process by which wages were negotiated, which determined the rate of inflation, involved expectations of future conditions. Their contention was that the Phillips curve was failing to account for the impact of expectations on the wage inflation process and as a result of the misspecification was failing to explain the true nature of the relationship between inflation and unemployment. The misspecification of the Phillips curve was revealed by two inconsistencies with neoclassical economics which Friedman corrected by specifying the relationship in real rather than nominal terms and as a relationship between the *level,* not the change, of the wage and the rate of unemployment. To deal with the first of these issues Friedman expressed the Phillips curve in real terms, and 'augmented' it with price expectations, enabling the model to predict accurately the change to prices over the period for which wages were being negotiated. Without this adjustment money illusion would never be corrected, workers would continue to mistake nominal for real changes to their wages and would never learn from their mistakes. To deal with the second issue, he noted that should the relationship be written in terms of the change to wages and the rate of unemployment then there should be a 'natural rate of unemployment' to which the economy would converge in the absence of disturbances. The natural rate represents the long-run level of unemployment consistent with any level of nominal wage inflation, given that there is no money illusion and that price expectations correct for nominal changes in wages.

The statistical evidence for a negative relationship, Friedman suggested, was due to temporary money illusion and the possibility that in the short-run there could be an exploitable trade-off between inflation and unemployment. In the long term the true change to the real wage would become apparent as nominal prices and wages were observed; this would mean that expectations would change and the short-run deviation from the natural rate of unemployment would be corrected. In the expectations augmented version of the Phillips curve, there can be no money illusion in the long-run and the Phillips curve must be vertical at the natural rate of unemployment.

In diagrammatic terms the rational expectations augmented Phillips curve can be illustrated in Figure 9.1. Drawing the graph with the change in money wages on the vertical axis and unemployment on the horizontal axis, the original Phillips curve is labelled *AA* and shows a negative relationship between wage inflation (π) and unemployment. Friedman's model concurs with this curve in the short run when there is money illusion to overturn the neutrality result, so *AA* is a short-run expectations augmented Phillips curve, but *BB* represents the long-run Phillips curve which is vertical above the natural rate of unemployment, U^*. To consider the dynamics of

Figure 9.1 Expectations augmented short-run and long-run Phillips curves

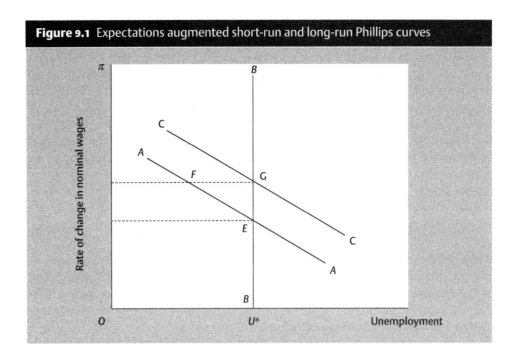

price expectations in this context, suppose that the labour market clears at a real wage consistent with expectations that prices will be equal to some value p_0. Suppose that after the settlement of the contracts in the labour market the price level is increased to p_1 so that the real wage falls from w/p_0 to w/p_1. So long as money illusion prevails in the short run the economy will move from point E to point F where the level of unemployment has fallen and the inflation rate is higher. This is only a temporary position which holds until it is perceived that the price level has risen and real wages have fallen. Once this is the case, expectations of prices are revised and the economy returns to the natural rate but at a higher level of inflation than before, on the short-run Phillips curve CC. This serves to illustrate that there are many short-run Phillips curves, each consistent with an expected level of inflation—there is not a unique negative relationship between inflation and unemployment. It was because of the successive shift of short-run Phillips curves outwards as price expectations rose that the apparent strong negative relationship broke down in the early 1970s.

We turn now to Lucas, who was quick to appreciate the wider significance of the informational errors. His contribution was to pick up on the notion that expectations entered the process of inflation generation and, by accurately specifying theoretical microfoundations, to explain how expectations formation could affect the inflation process. This was a first indication that Friedman's concern for predictive accuracy was not enough for Lucas who wanted to develop a coherent and consistent underlying theory. Friedman had used neoclassical principles to come to his conclusions but had no formal model behind them; it was the development of a formal model which Lucas provided in the form of the 'islands model', in Lucas and Rapping

(1969) and Lucas (1972, 1973), that gave the new classical results academic legitimacy and theoretical respectability.

Lucas's approach was to imagine a theoretical model in which inhabitants lived on a number of islands. Inhabitants were able accurately and continuously to determine the prices on their own island $p_t(z)$ but could only infer from these the likely contemporaneous prices on other islands and hence the general price level p_t, which they could observe accurately only with a lag. These assumptions replicated the idea that people are often better informed about their own enterprise and the local economy than they are about the economy at large. The restriction on information about prices implied that the inhabitants would need to form expectations about the contemporaneous general price level using the information on the behaviour of prices on their own island

$$E_z(p_t) = E(p_t | p_t(z), \Omega_{t-1}),$$
(9.10)

where $E_z(p_t)$ is the expectation of sellers in market z of the general price level p_t, given information on prices in market z at time t ($p_t(z)$) and last period's information on the general price level and other factors Ω_{t-1}. Suppose the information from the past period expectation of prices in time t is weighted with the information from market z to allow expectations to be formed as

$$E_z(p_t) = \theta \, p_t(z) + (1 - \theta) \, E_{t-1} \, p_t.$$
(9.11)

Then the seller in market z faces a signal extraction problem: there is a signal in the data but it is contaminated by market-specific noise. The solution to such a problem results in:

$$E_z(p_t) = \left(\frac{\theta^2 \, \text{var}(p_t(z)) + (1 - \theta)^2 \, \text{var}(E_{t-1} \, p_t)}{\theta^2 \, \text{var}(p_t(z))} \right) . p_t(z).$$
(9.12)

It was assumed that the inhabitants would need to know the general price level in order to be able to conduct negotiations over wages in the labour market. The inhabitants were assumed to be fully rational using all available information to calculate their expectation of the general price level. The labour supply is assumed to be elastic and the market is assumed to clear continuously without the hindrance of nominal wage rigidities. Firms with which inhabitants negotiated are profit-maximizing.

In such a model Lucas considered the intertemporal substitution problem faced by the inhabitants who have a choice of taking leisure today or leisure tomorrow—a rise in wages entails both an income effect and a substitution effect as greater wages create incentives to reduce working hours, in response to the level of income earned, and to increase hours, in response to the marginal return to the extra hours worked. Lucas suggested that the dominance of the substitution effect over the income effect was responsible for the observed negative correlation between prices and output levels. Through the use of the model it was possible to show that expectations about changes in real wages could alter the labour supply by encouraging or discouraging intertemporal substitution between leisure today and leisure tomorrow. The correspondence between decisions to work (or not work and hence be unemployed) and the behaviour of real wages period to period, which depend heavily on expectations of the general price level, create a Phillips curve trade-off. From this foundation, the Phillips curve could be regarded as a solution to the labour market problem when the price level is imperfectly observed. Labour supply simply responds to the expected real wage from one period to the next on the basis of expectations of the general level of prices. The solution is micro-consistent in that it has a firm foundation in utility maximization and yields predictions about the way that expectations influence the macroeconomy.

The formulation of the Lucas–Rapping labour supply model gave a new micro-foundation for the Phillips curve relationship, backing up some of Friedman's claims that expectations augmented models in real terms were the correct way to think about the relationship. But in certain respects the model went beyond Friedman and was more strict in its interpretation of the role of expectations. In Friedman's model the natural rate was a result of unspecified frictions in the labour market which led to a rate of unemployment to which the economy would tend to converge. In the Lucas–Rapping model the inhabitants of the islands are unemployed because they are unable to negotiate a real wage sufficient to compensate them for forgoing current leisure and thus are *voluntarily* unemployed. In the event that the minimum acceptable wage could not be reached the inhabitants would prefer to opt for leisure rather than work in the current period. Thus, in the Lucas model there are no *involuntarily* unemployed: all inhabitants maximize their utility without restriction due to the 'frictions' which Friedman had mentioned in his model and their choices are equilibrium ones consistent with their preferences.

The Lucas–Rapping model asserts that it is only the random and unpredictable contemporaneous events for which expectations cannot account that lead to departures from the natural rate of unemployment. Their notion of expectations is a fully rational one in which all information is used to update expectations such that there are no systematic errors. Consequently departures from the vertical long-run Phillips curve, *BB* in Figure 9.1, occur only for one period after which the error is incorporated into the information set, and future expectations take account of it. In other words movements along the short-run Phillips curve occur only as one-period departures from equilibrium, whilst in Friedman's case they can persist so long as money illusion exists, which may be for several periods.

The implications of this last point become apparent once the Phillips curve is rearranged into a form resembling an aggregate supply curve. Consider the expectations augmented Phillips curve which can be written as

$$p_t = (y_t - y^*) + E_{t-1} p_t + \varepsilon_t. \tag{9.13}$$

In this form the equation is a relationship between the price level and the departures from the natural rate of output (which can be thought of as a scale variable which proxies for unemployment) and the expectations of prices based on the information available in the previous period. Here there is an error term, indicating that random events can affect prices.

By rearrangement, it is possible to write equation (9.13) in such a way that output deviates from the natural rate when unexpected events cause changes to prices which expectations cannot account for in the current period:

$$y_t = y^* + (p_t - E_{t-1} p_t) - \varepsilon_t. \tag{9.14}$$

This has become known as the Lucas supply function or 'surprise' function since only unexpected surprises cause output to deviate from the natural rate. Note that the surprise effect is only influential for one period, after which it becomes part of the information set and is incorporated into the process of expectations formation. In the next section we consider the major implications of specifying the aggregate supply function in this way in terms of the limitations that it places upon economic policy-making. In particular, we can show that systematic policy becomes ineffective and that the result is a strong neutrality proposition which creates the similarities between Lucas rational expectations models and traditional classical economics.

9.4 The Policy Ineffectiveness Theorem

THE basic policy ineffectiveness proposition draws on the assumption that expectations are rational, making the best use of all available information. Given that departures from the natural rate of output (unemployment) can only occur as a result of surprises to the price generation process, because of unforeseeable and unpredictable events, it is only unanticipated policy that can affect the level of output in the economy through this mechanism. Any systematic policy can be fully anticipated and neutralized through the prices response. Output cannot be altered by systematic (Keynesian demand management) methods, only by surprising or fooling the general public into making expectational errors.

This strong conclusion was first proposed by Sargent and Wallace (1975) in a simple model made up of aggregate supply and aggregate demand equations, a money demand function, and a monetary policy rule. The aggregate supply function is the Lucas 'surprise' function. Aggregate demand depends on the expected real interest rate, that is, the nominal interest rate, R_t, and the expected change in the general price level (inflation) given by $(E_{t-1} p_{t+1} - E_{t-1} p_t)$:

$$y_t^D = (R_t - (E_{t-1} p_{t+1} - E_{t-1} p_t)). \tag{9.15}$$

The demand for money depends on income, y_t, prices, p_t, and nominal interest rates, R_t, that affects nominal money balances, m_t^D, according to a fixed parameter, χ, and is written as

$$m_t^D = p_t + y_t - \chi R_t. \tag{9.16}$$

Finally there is a monetary policy rule under which the government adjusts the money supply to the condition of the economy measured by the difference between output last period and its natural rate.

$$m_t^S = \eta(y_{t-1} - y^*) + \varepsilon_t. \tag{9.17}$$

The crucial factor here is the role of the feedback term in the monetary policy rule, η, which is the systematic part of monetary policy.

Solving the system, Sargent and Wallace assume that markets clear, and by equating the money demand and supply, $m_t^D = m_t^S$, the interest rate can be determined as a function of prices and output, since

$$p_t + y_t - \chi R_t = \eta(y_t - y^*) + \varepsilon_t, \tag{9.18}$$

hence

$$R_t = \{\eta(y_t - y^*) + \varepsilon_t - p_t - y_t\} \frac{1}{\chi}, \tag{9.19}$$

Equating the aggregate demand and aggregate supply, $y_t^S = y_t^D$, gives

$$y^* + \alpha(p_t - E_{t-1} p_t) = R_t - (E_{t-1} p_{t+1} - E_{t-1} p_t) \tag{9.20}$$

and substituting for the interest rate they are able to derive an expression entirely in terms of prices, the natural rate of output, expectations of prices, and coefficients of the model η, α, and χ given as

$$(\chi + 1)y^* + \alpha(\chi + 1)[p_t - E_{t-1}p_t] = \varepsilon_t - p_t - \chi[E_{t-1}p_{t+1} - E_{t-1}p_t] + \alpha\eta[p_{t-1} - E_{t-2}p_{t-2}]. \tag{9.21}$$

From this equilibrium expression, the system can be closed by assuming that expectations are formed rationally. Using Muth's method where prices are split into an equilibrium value, $\bar{p}$, and the part due to shocks $\{\varepsilon_t, \varepsilon_{t-1}, \varepsilon_{t-2} \dots\}$ such that

$$p_t = \bar{p} + \phi_0\varepsilon_t + \phi_1\varepsilon_{t-1} + \phi_2\varepsilon_{t-2} + \dots \tag{9.22}$$

they show that

$$E_{t-1} p_t = \bar{p} + \phi_1\varepsilon_{t-1} + \phi_2\varepsilon_{t-2} + \dots \tag{9.23}$$

and hence that

$$(p_t - E_{t-1} p_t) = \phi_0\varepsilon_t \tag{9.24}$$

By substituting these terms back into (9.20), it can be shown that output is unaffected by the operation of systematic monetary policy, since η does not enter the final solution for y_t.

This result can be demonstrated by using Muth's method of undetermined coefficients to define prices and expectations in the equilibrium expression, in which case ϕ_0 is not a function of η. Substituting the terms for prices and expectations into the equation and collecting terms in ε_t, ε_{t-1}, ε_{t-2}, we can define the coefficients ϕ_0, ϕ_1 and ϕ_2 in equilibrium. Prices must be equal to $\bar{p}$ in equilibrium, implying that ε_t, ε_{t-1}, and ε_{t-2} must drop out and hence their coefficients at that point must take values to ensure that they are eliminated. These can be found by collecting coefficients on those terms, for example, with ε_t:

$$\varepsilon_t : \phi_0 + \alpha(\chi + 1)\phi_0 = 1 \tag{9.25}$$

so if $\phi_0 = 1/(1 + \alpha(\chi + 1))$ the ε_t term drops out. Repeating for all coefficient values for ϕ_0, ϕ_1, ϕ_2, etc. ensures that all shocks, $\varepsilon_t, \varepsilon_{t-1}, \varepsilon_{t-2} \ldots$ drop out.

In terms of Lucas's aggregate supply function we know that only ε_t and ϕ_0 appear in the equation for output:

$$y_t = y^* + \alpha(\phi_0 \varepsilon_t) = y^* + [\alpha/(1 + \alpha(\chi + 1))]\varepsilon_t. \tag{9.26}$$

Notably η does not appear. Therefore systematic monetary policy, operating through η, cannot affect the level of output. Policy, as described by the monetary feedback rule, gets built into the evolution of the price level and its systematic effect is neutralized by the responses of the general public. The only option left to the government in this case is to adopt a non-systematic or 'surprise' policy, which by its very nature is unable to achieve anything but a temporary deviation from the natural rate and is completely offset in the following period when expectations are revised. Even if the government were to choose this option, it becomes apparent that its effect in comparison to doing nothing is not beneficial. Consider the variability of output when the government acts randomly to affect the money supply. The variance of output, $\text{Var}(y_t)$, is now positively increased by the impact of the variation in the money supply, $\text{Var}(\varepsilon_t)$ in the following way:

$$\text{Var}(y_t) = \left[\frac{\alpha}{1 + \alpha(1 + \chi)} \right] \cdot \text{Var}(\varepsilon_t). \tag{9.27}$$

Raising the variability of output might be considered to reduce welfare rather than improve it. The conclusion is that it is pointless for a government to attempt *systematically* to engage in stabilization policy by means of monetary (or fiscal) feedback rules and detrimental for them to do so in an unsystematic way.

The ineffectiveness proposition can be illustrated by means of a diagram in the same way that the expectations augmented Phillips curve was illustrated in the previous section. In fact there are many similarities between the two since the surprise supply function is a rearrangement of the expectations augmented Phillips curve as we noted above. In Figure 9.2 the aggregate supply and aggregate demand functions are illustrated, and these are graphical representations of the equations discussed above. In the initial state there is an equilibrium at point E at the natural rate, y^*. The use of systematic monetary policy will be ineffective and will not result in any movement in the aggregate demand or aggregate supply curves since the effect is fully anticipated in the expectations term. Only surprises affect aggregate supply and aggregate demand and the figure shows the case of a positive unanticipated monetary shock. The aggregate supply function does not shift initially because the monetary policy was unexpected and the increase in prices was not anticipated in the expectations term. Aggregate demand does shift out as the effect of the positive monetary shock is to increase the level of demand in the economy. This leads to a new equilibrium at F, where output is higher than the natural rate at y_1, but this is only temporary and lasts only one period before the information about the shock is incorporated into the information set upon which expectations are based, and the

Figure 9.2 The effect of expectations on prices and output through aggregate supply

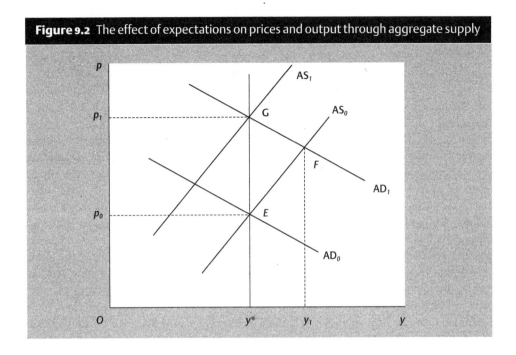

aggregate supply curve shifts inwards as this happens. The economy returns to the natural rate again at y^*, but at a higher price level at point G, as a result of the positive monetary shock. The effect of the unsystematic policy in the form of a monetary surprise is a temporary boost to output, reversed in the subsequent period and resulting only in a higher price level thereafter, much like the sequence of events illustrated in Figure 9.1, where the effect of unexpected price increases was a temporary deviation from the natural rate of unemployment.

The argument has not always gone the way that new classicals would have expected, however. Two criticisms emerged from within their own camp, suggesting that the models are *ad hoc,* since they are not derived from the optimization behaviour of individuals, and that they are too simple in their treatment of the monetary policy process. In an attempt to address one of these points, Sargent and Wallace (1981) introduced bonds into the analysis to allow for bond-financed government spending. Having done so, monetary policy was tied to the behaviour of the government deficit and the stock of bonds. When stocks of money and bonds are related to the deficit, which is a flow, the problem of government finance becomes a dynamic problem of the choice over the financing strategy. Since deficits must be financed by money creation or issues of additional government bonds, monetary policy may be constrained by fiscal policy through the level of outstanding debt. Past decisions over bond issue can have enduring implications for future monetary policy—in this sense the problem is dynamic—and choices made in the present or the past can be a constraint on the possible paths for policy in the future. It is unsurprising that having discovered these features of their models Sargent and Wallace called their paper

'Some Unpleasant Monetarist Arithmetic' because the monetarist foundations did not produce the expected monetarist policy conclusions they had hoped to find.

There have been two reactions to the policy ineffectiveness theorem. New classicals have embraced the results and advocated the abandonment of demand management employment policy and its replacement by 'supply-side policies' to influence factors in the economy which govern the natural rate itself.[9] One important aspect of that agenda was the development of real business cycle theory—'real' to signal that the business cycle is caused by factors unrelated to changes in the money supply (in contradistinction to Friedman and Schwartz, 1963a) or to countercyclical monetary and fiscal policies. Instead, business cycles are seen to be the result of changes in total factor productivity, due to new technology, new products, and alterations to workers' skills. An above-average rate of growth of productivity in one period, for example, acts as a spur to new investment opportunities, so that the impulse persists for some time. Recessions are the result of several quarters of below-average productivity growth. As noted in Chapter 1, the whole approach bears similarities to the Yule–Slutsky–Frisch idea of business cycles being generated by exogenous shocks within a propagation-impulse model, without any obvious role for countercyclical policies.[9]

Others have argued against the policy ineffectiveness theorem by emphasizing conditions in which the ineffectiveness proposition might not hold. It is to these exceptions that we now turn.

9.5 Exceptions to the Policy Ineffectiveness Rule

FOUR sets of conditions may result in the policy ineffectiveness rule not applying in practice, allowing governments a measure of influence over the level of output through monetary and fiscal policy. The first two cases deal with the nature of the information set available to the general public.

Different public and private information sets

Commenting on the strong policy ineffectiveness result of Sargent and Wallace, Robert Barro observed that 'The efficacy of public activism then requires an appeal to an information or computational advantage for the government' (1981: 58). Around the same time, Turnovsky (1980), Weiss (1980), and King (1982), showed that the Sargent and Wallace result derives from the assumption that both the public and the private sectors have access to the same information set. This assumption was challenged by Minford (1992) on the basis that the government collects most of the key information on the price level, money supply, output, and so on, and only a certain amount of it is revealed to the public. The government also has access to information before it is put in the public domain.

Because of this informational and time advantage, it is suggested that the authorities can respond to economic situations before the public becomes aware of them through published data, and can systematically affect output through monetary or fiscal policy without expectations offsetting or reversing the policy action. The public cannot anticipate and counteract actions which are effectively surprises based on the private information.

Turnovsky, Weiss, and King show that it is possible that the information asymmetry may in fact work in the other direction but nevertheless still leave a role for systematic monetary policy. If the private sector has both the global connections and the resources to access information independently of the public sector, it may have an advantage over the government.

In many areas the private sector is in constant touch with market conditions and can observe first-hand the behaviour of prices. Turnovsky, Weiss, and King start from the premiss that present and future behaviour by the private sector will be influenced by their expectations of future conditions and prices. Even though the government has no information advantage, and no means of directly affecting the variance of output by a systematic policy rule, it can nonetheless alter future output through the impact of present policy on the private sector's expectation of future prices. While the government may be at an informational disadvantage it does have the opportunity to influence output by playing on the expectations and the behaviour of the private sector. As one possible manifestation of this, we shall see in the next chapter on policy design that policy announcements and their likely effects on private sector actions are a central feature of modern-day monetary policy.

Partial information sets

A similar and related condition comes from the observation by Marini (1985, 1986) and Minford (1986) that information is not necessarily complete and that partial information may open up the possibility of systematic monetary policy which cannot be anticipated by the public. In this case the public and private sector have the same information set, but it is incomplete for both and as a consequence the ability of the public to counteract the policy of the government is limited.

Marini defines the information set available in some market, z, as $\Omega_t(z)$. This is less than the full information set at time t, Ω_t, and consists of the full information available at time $t - 1$ plus market specific information $p(z)$ so that $\Omega_t(z) = \Omega_{t-1} + \{p(z)\}$. Not only are there expectational surprises due to $[p_t - E(p_t \mid \Omega_t)] = \varepsilon_t$ but there are further surprises, v_t, due to the gap between full information, Ω_t, and the partial information set, $\Omega_t(z)$.

The situation seems a realistic one as current information is not revealed all at once: some information such as on interest rates and exchange rates is available on a more or less continuous basis but data on prices, output, and the money supply are available only once a month or once a quarter, leading to a degree of uncertainty about this. Based on the information from the continuously available series, a 'signal extraction' procedure can be used to guess the likely behaviour of other economic series in much the same way as the inhabitants of Lucas's islands inferred the general price level from their observation of the local price data. Inevitably this is more crude than knowing the true data, and the errors that are introduced can create room for systematic policy to operate.

Automatic stabilizers

A third case deals with the systematic component of policy, which is not under the direct control of the government but is a result of policy rules, derived from the state of the economy. The most obvious example in this category is the payment of social security and the receipt of taxes which vary with the business cycle in an automatic fashion and are only influenced directly by the government when they change the legislative arrangements of the automatic rule. It has been shown by McCallum and Whittaker (1979) that the introduction of an automatic stabilizer of this type into the aggregate demand function is sufficient to establish that systematic policy, operating through a legislative rule, is able to influence fluctuations in output around its natural rate.

If we take a tax stabilizer and augment the original output demand function to include a tax term comprising a tax elasticity, τ, and a term σ reflecting the elasticity of expenditure to temporary changes in taxation then

$$y_t^D = (R_t - (E_{t-1} p_{t+1} - E_{t-1} p_t)) - \sigma \tau y_t. \tag{9.28}$$

The final solution depends on the same parameters as before (in the Sargent–Wallace case) but the tax stabilizer has a systematic effect on the variance of output.

9.6 Contracts and New Keynesian Economics

A FURTHER case is by far the most important because it marked the beginnings of a new school of thought which has emerged to counter the strong classical propositions. The school has developed into the New Keynesian school and began by considering the microfoundations of the price- and wage-setting process in the Sargent and Wallace model. It is perhaps instructive to note that the challenge to the rational expectations literature is not concerned so much with the concept of rational expectations itself but the accompanying assumption of rapid adjustments in competitive instantaneously-clearing markets.[10]

Models with overlapping contracts were first put forward by Fischer (1977), Taylor (1979, 1980), and Phelps and Taylor (1977). The most important feature was the notion that a relevant economic variable such as wages may be set contractually, with some given proportion of the contracts coming due at different times. These contracts would typically be set for the current time period and would stretch for more than one period into the future. In Taylor's model the contractual variable is the price changed by one seller in relation to other sellers' prices—half of the sellers change their prices in one period and half in the next. Each contract lasts for two periods and is therefore overlapping with a previous contract in the first period and with a subsequent contract in the second period.

To illustrate the idea further, we take Fischer's model of wage-setting that has a wage-setting framework with a workforce split into two groups: the first group negotiates a wage contract for the next two periods at time t whilst the second group negotiates a similar two-period contract at time $t + 1$. The negotiations of each group will be contingent on all information available to them, which in practice means information up to time $t - 1$ for the first group and information up to time t for the second group. Any events which occur in time t can be acted upon by the second group, who negotiate their contract on the basis of information up to period t, but for the first group who negotiated a two-period contract in time t on the basis of information up to time $t - 1$, the events cannot be responded to until renegotiation of their contract at time $t + 2$.

The nominal wage in period $t + 1$ is given by

$$W_{t+1} = \frac{1}{2} \left({}_{t-1}W_t + {}_tW_{t+1} \right), \tag{9.29}$$

where ${}_tW_{t+1}$ indicates a wage negotiated in time $t + 1$ on the basis of information available up to time t. Wages are based on the achievement of the level of real wages and are therefore dependent on price expectations, hence

$$ {}_{t-1}W_t = E_{t-1}\,p_{t+1} \tag{9.30}$$

$$ {}_tW_{t+1} = E_t\,p_{t+1} \tag{9.31}$$

and therefore by substitution

$$W_{t+1} = \frac{1}{2} \left(E_{t-1}\,p_{t+1} + E_t p_{t+1} \right). \tag{9.32}$$

If we define the aggregate supply function as dependent on the real wage rate

$$y_{t+1} = -\alpha(W_{t+1} - p_{t+1}) + y^*, \tag{9.33}$$

then substituting for the nominal wage rate gives

$$y_{t+1} = \frac{\alpha}{2}\,(p_{t+1} - E_{t-1}\,p_{t+1}) + \frac{\alpha}{2}\,(p_{t+1} - E_t\,p_{t+1}) + y^*. \tag{9.34}$$

It will be noticed that the supply function differs from the Lucas supply function in that half the workforce is subject to a contract which is based on information from two periods ago. The fact that expectations about p_{t+1} are made using information up to $t - 1$ means that the events of time t do not impinge on these workers' behaviour. It is the exploitation of the fixed multiperiod contract that introduces the possibility of stabilization policy using systematic monetary policy. The existence of a fixed contract ties the hands of half the workforce at any one time removing their ability to respond to systematic monetary policy, even though it may be perfectly observed and anticipated. Thus it is argued that so long as fixed contracts exist there will be the potential for stabilization policy to work for a time.

The New Keynesian justification for fixed contracts is to be found in the 'menu costs' argument, which states that there are fixed costs of changing prices of goods at a microeconomic level including that of labour. Writing contracts for a number of periods minimizes these costs. The new classical response to this approach has been to accept that contracts are a reality of everyday life but to question the nature of the pricing and contracts implied by the New Keynesians. The 'menu costs' literature often simply *assumes* that the costs relate to changes in nominal prices (which then means that changes in monetary policy leave nominal prices unaffected and alter real variables). But this assumption merely brings in money illusion by the back door. Why are buyers and sellers not concerned with relative prices, and maintaining prices in real terms? That is, why are menus not printed in real terms rather than nominal prices (McCallum, 1993)?

Also, most importantly, new classicals object to the non-contingent character of nominal wage contracts in New Keynesian models, which they argue does not tally with real world experience. In reality, wage contracts are full of contingency clauses allowing for bonuses, overtime arrangements, lay-off conditions, and other factors which might alter during the life of the contract. Once one accepts that contracts can be written in a conditional manner, then it become less likely that 'fixed' contracts can be exploited by governments for systematic monetary policy purposes. This is especially so if the workforce believes that the government is likely to try to take advantage of the fixed nature of the contractual arrangements. Subclauses allowing changes to the conditions of employment on the basis of changing external circumstances introduce a contingent element to contracts which will prevent governments from using systematic monetary policy.

9.7 The Lucas Critique

A **KEY** macroeconomic question in the late 1970s was whether the aggregate supply curve was best thought of as a new classical formulation or an alternative type. Sargent and Wallace (1973) used tests of the direction of causality between economic variables to try to validate Lucas's new classical model on econometric grounds, concluding that the new classical approach was not inconsistent with the data. Barro (1977, 1978) attempted to confirm these results by modelling directly the aggregate supply relationship. In order to do this he specified the money supply process and from it derived estimates of the unexpected changes to monetary policy. He then introduced both variables into a model to explain output and found that whilst anticipated monetary policy did not have a statistically significant effect on output the unexpected component did—seeming to confirm the new classical approach. Shortly after the publication of these results, however, Sargent (1979) established from theoretical first principles that these econometric approaches could be misleading. His reasoning was to become known as the *observational equivalence* argument by which it is possible to show that a model which seems to show that *systematic* monetary policy can affect output can be rearranged with some reasonable additional assumptions to show the contrary, i.e. that only *unanticipated* policy can affect output. The problem for the econometric work is that while these models have different assumptions which set them apart in theory, they are observationally equivalent in practice because it is not possible to specify them in such a way that they can be separated on econometric grounds when estimated in reduced form.

Consider the following example. Suppose the aggregate supply function is defined as

$$y_t = \alpha m_t + \beta m_{t-1} + \chi y_{t-1} + \varepsilon_t, \tag{9.35}$$

where m_t is the money supply, y_t is output, and ε_t is an error term. By lagging this relationship and repeatedly substituting it back into the equation to eliminate lagged output terms, output can be shown to be a function of past money supply

$$y_t = \alpha m_t + (\beta + \alpha\chi)m_{t-1} + \ldots + \varepsilon_t. \tag{9.36}$$

A systematic money supply rule based on the previous level of the money supply, m_{t-1}, and a random component u_t, such as

$$m_t = \delta m_{t-1} + u_t \tag{9.37}$$

would be influential on output.

Consider now the equation above relating output to lagged money supply. We know that

$$E_{t-1} m_t = \delta m_{t-1} \tag{9.38}$$

and by adding and subtracting terms for $E_{t-1} m_t, E_{t-2} m_{t-1}$ from this equation we can rewrite the relationship between output and lagged money supply as a relationship between output and unanticipated money supply shocks:

$$y_t = \phi(m_t - E_{t-1} m_t) + \gamma(m_{t-1} - E_{t-2} m_{t-1}) + \ldots + \chi y_{t-1} + \varepsilon_t. \tag{9.39}$$

This model shows that unsystematic 'surprises' in the money stock affect output, but this has been derived from exactly the same equations as the model which purported to show that *systematic* monetary policy can affect output. With the additional assumption that the public make rational expectations about monetary policy, the two models can be said to be observationally equivalent. The general implication is that any estimated reduced-form equation which an econometrician discovers in the data is compatible with many different structural models with different theoretical priorities and policy implications.

Lucas introduced a rider to this debate which became a turning point in relation to the econometric estimation of economic models involving expectations, known as the *Lucas critique*. His observation was that many reduced-form models treat the expectational terms in the same way as they treat the structural parameters of the model, that is, as if they are given and unchanging. The obvious objection to this practice is that, unlike structural parameters, expectations are liable to change with the policy process. Models which do not treat them in such a way that this change can be accommodated will generally give misleading results. In the context of the new classical rational expectations debate, the main issue is how expectations of government policy influence the nature of the model and how the modellers should build into their models behavioural equations relating expectations to government policy regimes. Models which replace behavioural relationships with mechanical devices will collapse as the regime on which they were based changes, and thus adaptive methods of dealing with expectations which are backward-looking will in general prove inadequate. Lucas's point is that expectations should not be treated as exogenous, but should be regarded as *endogenous* to the models that they influence.

Lucas concludes his article in the following way.

This essay has been devoted to an exposition and elaboration of a single syllogism: given that the structure of an econometric model consists of optimal decision rules of economic agents, and that optimal decision rules vary systematically with changes in the structure of series relevant to the decision maker, it follows that any change in policy will systematically alter the structure of econometric models.

For the question of the short-term forecasting, or tracking ability of econometric models, we have seen that this conclusion is of only occasional significance. For issues involving policy evaluation , in contrast, it is fundamental; for it implies that comparisons of the effects of alternative policy rules using current macroeconometric models are invalid regardless of the performance of these models over the sample period in *ex ante* or short-term forecasting. (Lucas 1980: 126)

Many small-scale econometric models of the type built by Treasury or central bank economists use recent history to estimate a set of equations purporting to describe the present structure of the economy. The equations are then used to study (simulate) the effect of various policy changes, e.g. a reduction in interest rates or increase in government spending. Simulations of alternative policies, so goes the Lucas critique, are generally invalid because the estimated parameters of the model reflect the policies which were in vogue in the past. Employ different policies and the parameters would be different, thereby rendering as misleading the simulations based on unchanging parameters. Since the models are mostly used to evaluate the effects of alternative policies, the critique is particularly apposite. Even if similar policies were adopted, responses would be different next time round as the private sector acquires information about the nature of government policy. Because the estimated equations have expectations effects built into them, the equations are likely to be unstable (and thus unreliable) over time. The response of many policy institutions has been to build a large structural model with expectations modelled explicitly to attempt to avoid this trap.

9.8 Conclusions

IN terms of its impact upon the economics profession, the rational expectations revolution in macroeconomics and monetary analysis has often been likened to the Keynesian revolution nearly half a century before. But whereas classical economists objected to the rigid pricing, exogenous expectations, and 'animal spirits' of the Keynesian analysis, which underpinned the case for interventionist policies, many object today to the leap of faith in new classical economics.

Stripped to its essentials, the concept of rationality in expectations involves nothing more than the assumption that economic man (or woman) forms and acts upon expectations of future events in a rational, rather than an arbitrary or *ad hoc*, manner. Since actions based upon incorrect premisses of what the future has in store result in unwanted costs, it pays to use available information to improve the accuracy of such forecasts. In most cases that matter, professionals are employed to gather and process information on behalf of the public—obvious examples include unions, pension funds, and life assurance companies, which act on behalf of the public in specialist roles.

This relatively unobjectionable principle is pushed to extremes which often strain the bounds of belief. For example, all individuals are assumed to possess sufficient (indeed omniscient) information about the structure and workings of the economy in order to be able to correctly predict the most likely outcome following any currently observable development. But the structure of the economy is always changing, as technology, tastes, and government interventions change. If these changes occur frequently enough, it may never be appropriate to assume that people's forecasts are optimal forecasts.

Moreover, in most of the models, the behaviour of the economic variables that individuals must forecast is itself affected by the way the individuals form expectations. A rational-expectations equilibrium can be achieved only when people have adopted a way of forecasting that is consistent with the implications for the economy of their own way of forecasting. Given the time that this is likely to take in view of the complexity of the economy, it would seem that transactors would only learn slowly about how to forecast.

In justification, rational expectations theorists borrow from the 'as if' methodology of Friedman's positive economics (Friedman, 1953a). The great (Brazilian) soccer player Pele, we presume, did not study the laws of aerodynamics. But he behaved *as if* he understood the complex mathematical formulae involved when he shot for goal. By parallel reasoning, the rational-expectations models assume that economic entities behave *as if* they know the structure of the economy so that they can calculate the optimal forecasts that constitute their expectations. Better results are obtained by assuming complete rationality than by assuming the reverse.

Nevertheless, it is probably fair to say that when the propositions of rational expectations and continuous market-clearing were first advanced, many economists thought of them as over-statements designed to provoke controversy and attract attention to a more moderate position to follow. However, the 'overstatements' have triumphed without a moderate back-up ever being revealed. Why has this occurred?

One reason, we suggest, is the parallel with microeconomics. The basic building blocks of microeconomics—demand and supply analysis, welfare economics, and resource allocation—all rest on the assumptions of perfect competition, i.e. complete homogeneity, atomistic markets, full mobility, and perfect knowledge. In a course on micro theory, time will be given to imperfect competition[11]—monopoly, oligopoly, and monopolistic competition—but perfect competition is the core. A study will be made of asymmetric information—adverse selection (hidden knowledge) and moral hazard (hidden actions)—but perfect knowledge remains the essential starting point. In much the same way, the rational expectations equilibrium provides the formal, theoretically tidy solution in macroeconomics.[12]

The second reason, quite simply, is the failure to agree on an alternative. There has been some work on differently informed individuals, on sticky-price RE models, and on the likelihood of 'bubble' or 'sunspot' solutions in rational expectations models, but the alternative expectations mechanisms e.g. adaptive expectations, have little support.[13] Fully flexible, instantaneous market-clearing price behaviour may be a characterization but the attempts to combine some form of monopolistic competition with 'menu costs' have failed to win widespread support.

Thus it is the rational expectations-based agenda which has laid the foundation for new approaches to the analysis of monetary policy based on economic behaviour and feedback rules. Having recognized the Lucas critique and that the regime matters, and that economic behaviour will vary as the regime varies, economists began to consider the effect of government announcements of impending changes to regimes and the degree of belief associated with those announcements. This introduced considerations of the role of game theory and suggested that individuals might make strategic responses to government announcements. It is to the development of strategic behaviour, announcements, and credibility in monetary economics that we now turn.

Notes

1 Because macroeconomics has in many ways returned to a position similar to that propounded by neoclassical economics and the Austrian school of Hayek, mark II monetarism is alternatively described as 'new classical' or 'neo-Austrian'.

2 In the book *A Monetary History of the United States*, Friedman and his co-author Anna Schwartz argued that the contraction was not caused by a collapse of investment plans and a decline in velocity, but by monetary mismanagement. The quantity of money had fallen, and banks had been allowed to collapse, and those events dragged velocity, investment spending, and output down with them. Friedman and Schwartz also swamped the economics profession with business cycle studies to show that other recessions had also been due to faulty monetary policies.

3 Other leading contributors are Robert Barro (1976) and Thomas Sargent and Neil Wallace (1975).

4 Some of the alternatives are surveyed in Shiller (1978).

5 It then depends whether expectations change in the light of events and are endogenous as the model evolves, or whether they are in some respect exogenous. An example of the latter is Keynes's 'animal spirits'.

6 Alternatives to adaptive expectations are *regressive expectations*, in which variables are expected to return gradually to a fixed level independent of their recent past behaviour, and *extrapolative expectations* in which the recent direction of change in the variables is expected to continue.

7 Some of Muth's ideas were picked up by Whittle (1963), Nerlove (1967), and Lucas and Prescott (1971).

8 The most basic criticism of many rational-expectations models is that they make implausible claims for individual transactors' ability and willingness to compute, as compared with other expectations mechanisms such as adaptive expectations. Schiller (1992) provides an interesting example. Suppose people were asked on a monthly basis to forecast the rate of increase of the price of a seasonal commodity, say, fresh tomatoes. Many would be aware that fresh tomatoes are more expensive in the winter, when they must be grown in hothouses or brought in from greater distances. Not all people would know this, and many who did know about the seasonality in price would not know its magnitude. But certainly a distributed lag with smoothly declining coefficients on actual tomato price changes, i.e. *adaptive expectations*, is not what one would immediately think of to model their expectations.

   If simple expectations proxies can be queried for modelling the expectations of consumers, there is no doubt that it would be inappropriate to use such proxies to model the behaviour of tomato producers. Some of them specialize in producing hot-house tomatoes and time their production for the winter months. They must know in which month prices are higher, and by how much they tend to be higher. Since tomatoes must be planted months ahead of the anticipated demand for them, the supply must depend on expectations formed in advance by producers, as well as on seasonal factors affecting the cost of production. We might then model the supply function of tomatoes by finding a way to predict the price of tomatoes (using, say, seasonal dummies and other information) and substitute the prediction in place of the expectation in the supply function. The result would be a *rational-expectations model*.

9 Kydland and Prescott (1991) calculated that real business cycle theory can account for about 70% of post-war business-cycle fluctuations in US ouput. However, as Chatterjee (1999) notes, many of the factors that characterized pre-war business cycles (e.g. bank crashes and money supply contractions) have been removed from the post-war sample due to policy changes, perhaps leaving fluctuations in productivity as the dominant source (in much the same way that modern medicine and hygiene have removed many old diseases, leaving cancer and heart ailments as the major causes of death). Lucas (1994) foreshadowed this possibility in his retrospective review of Friedman and Schwartz (1963b).

10 Even New Keynesians use rational expectations in their models, but they do not assume fully clearing markets in the short run.

11 But not in Friedman's Price Theory.

12 Notably, however, the approach is quite different. In microeconomic analysis, one begins with perfect competition and moves on to the imperfections. In macroeconomics, one typically begins with the 'imperfections' (eg. Keynesian multipliers etc.) and moves on to rational expectations.

13 One interesting development, however, is the idea of an 'adaptively rational equilibrium' in which economic decision-makers base decisions upon predictions of future values of endogenous variables, in which each predictor is a function of past observations. People adapt their beliefs over time by choosing from a set of different predictors (or expectations functions) with a rational choice based on the predictors' past performance. See Brock and Holmes (1997).

Chapter 10
Optimal Policy Design

10.1 Issues in Policy Design

ONE of the main characteristics of monetary policy analysis in the 1980s and 1990s has been the use of game theory to explain the strategic interaction between the government and the public. This approach is a natural extension of the rational expectations literature, and grows out of the policy ineffectiveness theorem by allowing the likely future strategic behaviour of the government to alter the expectations of the public and vice versa. If the government can be fully trusted and the future announcements of policy are fully credible, then the public will rationally expect the announced policies to be carried out. In contrast to the Sargent–Wallace finding, however, policy impotence does not necessarily result. The government can act strategically to use systematic policy announcements to influence the expectations of the public and thereby systematically alter the future evolution of the economy. In this way announcements can be used to the government's advantage to steer expectations and the behaviour of the public conditioned upon them, provided that they are believed.

Credibility is the crucial issue here, and the first contributions to the literature by Kydland and Prescott (1977) and Barro and Gordon (1983b) showed that, despite the obvious benefits from making policy announcements that are credible, there are short-term temptations to deviate from the announced line.[1] With less than full credibility, governments may make announcements that they do not keep; this introduces a central role for a game to take place between the government and the public. A large part of the literature on optimal policy design is about creating conditions under which the government has an incentive to aim for a socially desirable policy objective and keep its commitment to announced monetary policy. In the more recent literature, the strategy involves the delegation of responsibility to a third player, the central bank, and the game then involves designing agreements between the government, the central bank, and the public that yield optimal policy outcomes. The establishment of the need for regulation or the design of an institutional arrangement between the government and the central bank can help to overcome time-inconsistency problems. Delegation to a conservative central banker, the design of a penalizing contract, or a target for inflation can add marginal costs to deviating from the socially optimal inflation rate and thus deter cheating.

Much of the recent literature on policy design acknowledges these points and the use of contracts and targets for central banks and policy-makers has passed from active current research to institutional orthodoxy. Now the issue is how the central bankers should conduct policy in order to hit their target or fulfil their contract.

Many authors have proposed so-called optimal rules for policy-makers, by which they mean guides for policy instruments given a well-defined objective and a known economic model. The suggestions vary from inflation targets to money targets, nominal income targets, and even open-economy combinations of monetary conditions indicators. Few policy-makers would claim that the models are known, even if the target for policy is clear. The response to risk and uncertainty in economic models has been the theme of very recent research in order to establish *how* a policy-maker should go about setting instruments of monetary policy. The following sections explore these theoretical issues that have had a profound influence upon central bank practice in recent years.

10.2 Time Inconsistency

THE first paper to bring the issue of time inconsistency into the public domain was the paper by Kydland and Prescott (1977). *Time inconsistency* refers to the notion that the optimal policy that a government chooses to follow may not remain consistent from one time period to the next. In particular, if the government makes an announcement today and the public believes it and acts upon it, the very act of commitment by the public can alter the conditions that the government faces when tomorrow arrives, making an alternative policy optimal. It is the changing nature of the optimal policy that creates time inconsistency between one period and another. A time-consistent policy on the other hand would be one where the authorities have no incentive to change their behaviour in subsequent periods from that which was announced at the beginning. It is difficult to think of an example of a time-consistent policy in economics because the commitments of the public, on the basis of the initial announcements, almost always ensure that the nature of the problem is different when re-optimized in subsequent periods. The policy that is genuinely the best policy, as viewed from knowledge of conditions today, is unlikely to remain the best policy when tomorrow comes. There is a compelling case for the re-optimized policy to be followed by the authorities even if it means departing from announcements since there are Pareto improvements for society as a result. Kydland and Prescott used these arguments in a formal way to establish that optimal policy is not invariant and that the expectations of the public (in this case over the consistency of the government) can influence the nature of the optimization from one period to the next. In this section we introduce a formal example used by Kydland and Prescott before developing some intuition using the example of the flood plain.

Theory

The theory covers two periods, 1 and 2, in which there are two states of the world given by x_1 and x_2 and two instruments that are under the government's control, Π_1 and Π_2.

The state variables are dependent on the settings of the instruments in the following way:

$$x_1 = X_1(\Pi_1, \Pi_2) \qquad\qquad (10.1)$$

$$x_2 = X_2(x_1, \Pi_1, \Pi_2). \qquad\qquad (10.2)$$

This indicates that the state in the first period depends on the (expected) settings of the policy instruments in periods 1 and 2, whilst the state variable in the second period depends on the state in period 1 and the (expected) settings of policy instruments in periods 1 and 2. The sequencing is important for this model: the government is supposed to make announcements, then the public form expectations about state variables, finally the government sets the policy instruments in the full knowledge of expectations that have been set. Clearly, the government can influence the state in both periods by its announcements over the choice of instrument settings in periods 1 and 2 through expectations. In period 2, the state in period 1 is history and so is the setting of the instrument in period 1, but the choice over the instrument in period 2 is still variable.

Kydland and Prescott show that a government that maximizes an objective function such as

$$S(x_1, x_2, \Pi_1, \Pi_2) \qquad\qquad \text{(10.3)}$$

will find it optimal to set different (time-inconsistent) values for the instrument in period 2. Both of the policy choices will be optimal but the choice in the second period is conditional on the precommitted actions of the public in period 1.

To illustrate this point we can show that the optimal value for Π_2 in period 1 is:

$$\frac{\partial s}{\partial x_2} \cdot \frac{\partial X_2}{\partial \pi_1} + \frac{\partial s}{\partial \pi_1} + \frac{\partial X_1}{\partial \pi_1}\left(\frac{\partial s}{\partial x_1} + \frac{\partial s}{\partial x_2} \cdot \frac{\partial X_2}{\partial x_1}\right) = 0 \qquad\qquad (10.4)$$

whilst in period 2, reoptimizing, conditional on the precommitted actions of the public gives:

$$\frac{\partial s}{\partial x_2} \cdot \frac{\partial X_2}{\partial \pi_2} + \frac{\partial s}{\partial \pi_2} = 0. \qquad\qquad (10.5)$$

Since these two results are different, there is a time inconsistency between optimal policy settings in periods 1 and 2. Unless $\dfrac{\partial X_1}{\partial \pi_1}$ is zero (indicating that policy has no impact on state 1) or the bracketed term is zero (suggesting that the net effect of state 1 on the loss function is nil), both of which are unlikely, the optimal policies are not the same. They are time-inconsistent. It will make it easier to follow the logic of the theoretical argument if we illustrate the point using Kydland and Prescott's flood plain example.

The flood plain example

The public chooses whether to build or not to build houses on a flood plain, and these choices correspond to the state variables in the theory above. The instruments are the government's decisions whether or not to build dams to prevent floods from occurring. The government has an incentive to declare that it will not build dams to deter the public from building on the flood plain and the combination of no building and no dams is the government's optimal outcome. Yet if the government is believed to care about the welfare of its citizens, the public may build on the flood plain in the knowledge that, once the houses are built, the government will provide the dams to protect them. This is the public's ideal outcome and is to be preferred over no houses and no dams (i.e. the government's first choice). The preference ordering, where H = houses, D = dams, NH = no houses, and ND = no dams, and > indicates strictly preferred to is:

Government:

NH+ND > H + D > H + ND

Public:

H+D > NH + ND > H + ND

Hence the decision whether to build houses depends on the public's perception of the credibility of the government's resolve not to build dams. If the resolve of the government is perceived to be weak, then the public will build houses in the knowledge that the government will most likely build dams to protect them (despite the fact that the public and the government are agreed that the outcome that houses but no dams is the worst possible outcome). If the resolve of the government is perceived to be strong, then the public will be deterred from building houses and save the government budget the expense of building dams. The final outcome depends on the credibility of the announcements not to build dams if houses are built, or to put it another way, the extent to which the government really cares for the public. When credibility is low and the government is perceived to care then, despite the initial optimization that results in no dams, after a reoptimization in the second period, in the knowledge that houses have been built, dams will be built by the government.

Time inconsistency undermines public belief in the government's announcements. The challenge has been to create conditions or devices to ensure that a government has every incentive to stick to its announcements even after reoptimizing. If the government can show that such a mechanism eliminates the incentive to alter optimal behaviour, its announcements become credible once again. Thus a mechanism for ensuring credibility exists that does not rely on tightly framed rules that unduly constrain the authorities, ability to respond to shocks that may hit the economy. The next three sections develop this theme.

10.3 Credibility and Reputation

A MAJOR advance to the concept of time inconsistency and optimal policy was made by Barro and Gordon (1983b). Their model has been the workhorse of most subsequent analysis of optimal policy design. Like Kydland and Prescott, they assume that the government controls the policy instruments that affect the state of the economy through the expectations of the public. The government has an objective function, which it maximizes, and this objective function is the same as that for society in general. It is written as

$$L = \left(\frac{a}{2}\right)(\pi_t)^2 - b(\pi_t - \pi_t^e)\ a,b > 0, \tag{10.6}$$

where L is a loss function, π_t is current inflation, and π_t^e is expected inflation. The loss function is quadratic in inflation in order to capture the fact that inflation is costly. The term $b(\pi_t - \pi_t^e)$ can be thought of as impact of an output term based on the Lucas supply function, $y_t = b(\pi_t - \pi_t^e)$, so that the government cares about inflation and output with weights determined by the values of a and b. It captures the benefits to the policy-maker associated with unanticipated inflation. In this simple model the state is given by inflation and, since we assume that the authorities can control inflation directly, the instrument is inflation as well. These simplifications are not required but we make them in order to explain the model more straightforwardly.

The timing in this model is crucial. The first event to occur is an announcement by the government of its future intended course of action, i.e. a monetary policy stance is declared, which in this case refers to a profile for inflation. Second, the public form expectations about the future value of inflation and act upon those expectations in such a way that they are committed to follow through even if events turn out differently from the way that they expected. Last of all, the government implements monetary policy in the full knowledge of the expectations of the public so that the actual outcome is a function of the expectations of the public, $\pi_t = \phi(\pi_t^e)$. This is the government's reaction function.

We plot these relationships in Figure 10.1. Taking the axes as π_t and π_t^e we can plot the relationship between the government's action and expected inflation, which is upward-sloping line, $\pi_t = \phi(\pi_t^e)$. The intercept and the slope of the line will be determined by the loss function that the government faces, i.e. the trade-off between inflation and output. This line has a slope less than one since the increase in expected inflation causes the actual rate to rise, but since actual inflation is disliked by the government and incurs a cost through the loss function the government increases the actual inflation rate less than proportionally. The rational expectation

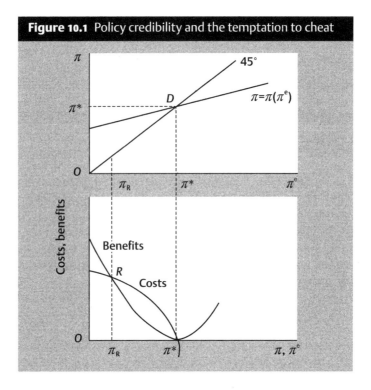

Figure 10.1 Policy credibility and the temptation to cheat

of inflation, π_t^e, should be equal to the actual inflation rate, π_t, by definition so this can be represented as the 45° line. The equilibrium outcome will be at π^*_t where the two lines intersect, and therefore satisfies rationality (it is on the 45° line) and the reaction function of the authorities.

Barro and Gordon consider three possible policy scenarios for monetary policy, which they label as discretionary equilibrium, a rule-based equilibrium, and reputational equilibrium. We consider these in turn.

Discretionary equilibrium

Under this scenario the policy-maker optimizes the objective function on the assumption that the expectations of the public do not change in response to the actions of the government. The government announce an intention to achieve a zero inflation rate to the public and the government believes that the public expectation of inflation π_t^e is zero. Hence, taking the first derivative of the objective function with respect to the inflation term

$$\frac{dL}{d\pi_t} = a\pi_t - b = 0 \tag{10.7}$$

implying that the optimal inflation rate, given the assumption that the announcement of $\pi_t = 0$ is

$$\pi_t^d = \frac{b}{a} > 0 \tag{10.8}$$

where superscript d indicates discretion.

The presumption of the authorities that the inflation expectations of the public is zero is false, however, and when the public realize that a discretionary policy is being followed they expect inflation to be b/a. In other words they realize that policy is time-inconsistent and can see that the government has an incentive to deviate from $\pi_t = 0$. As a result of the public response to government action, the loss function takes a value of

$$L^d = \frac{1}{2} \frac{b^2}{a} \tag{10.9}$$

which can be confirmed by substitution $\pi = b/a$ and $\pi^e = b/a$ into the loss function L above (10.6). Clearly this does not take the value of zero that the authorities were aiming for because the public expectation deviates from the government's announcement. The government lacks credibility and has no way of convincing the public that it will deliver on its announced policy because the public knows that when the government reoptimizes conditional on $\pi_t^e = 0$ the optimal setting for inflation will be b/a. In the case where the policy is set for only one period and there are no subsequent periods (the so-called one-shot game) the government will always cheat. Only if the game is a multiperiod game will the public have the option to 'punish' the government if they cheat. The real world is better characterized as a multiperiod setting in which the government might try to build up reputation. One way it can do this is to follow a rule for monetary policy.

Rule-based equilibrium

One way for the government to gain some credibility for its announcements is to bind itself to a policy rule. The government now announces an intention to follow a rule, which is binding, such as $\pi_{t+i} = 0$ for all future periods $i = 0, 1, 2, \ldots, n$. If expectations equal the announcement so that $\pi_t^e = 0$ then the loss function will be $L^r = 0$.

But as before, once the public forms an expectation of a zero value for inflation, the government has an incentive to cheat. This arises because the loss function can take a lower value, i.e. less than zero, if the government creates some 'surprise' inflation. The gains to the government are (for an inflation rate equal to b/a, which is optimizing conditional on $\pi_t^e = 0$):

$$L_t^r = \frac{1}{2} \frac{b^2}{a} . \tag{10.10}$$

This appears to be the same as the discretionary case but since the rule applies to many periods we must consider what would happen in periods $t + 1$, $t + 2$, etc. What we find is that the public is not to be fooled in the second period ($t + 1$) by the announcements of the government. Far from believing $\pi_{t+1} = 0$ they expect $\pi_{t+1}^e = b/a$.

The government is *punished* in period $t+1$ for *cheating* in period t and the punishment is given by the value of the loss function which is $L_{t+1} = b^2/a$ when $\pi_{t+1} = 0$. Overall, the government loses since the gain from the previous period was only half of this value. However, since the government sets the inflation rate after expectations are formed by the public it is likely to set $\pi_t = b/a$ and the resulting loss function will then be

$$L^r_{t+1} = \frac{1}{2}\frac{b^2}{a}. \tag{10.11}$$

If there is any discounting at all, then future losses will count for less than present gains and the authorities will still have an incentive to cheat on the rule. Returning to Figure 10.1, we can draw the benefits versus the costs of cheating. Any temptation to cheat is related to the absolute distance between the reaction function $\pi = \phi(\pi^e)$ and the 45° line. The benefit from cheating is greatest when the reaction function is far from D and falls to zero at D. The cost of cheating—calculated by the discounted sum of the loss function when society punishes the authorities for cheating—is dependent on the departure of the actual inflation from the rate that the public believe will occur. As we approach D the cost falls and becomes zero at D, after D the loss is negative. Any outcome that creates benefits in excess of costs will not prevent the authorities from cheating. In general, many rules correspond to this type and are unenforceable. Barro and Gordon define these as *unfeasible policy options*. Some rules will fail to deter cheating, but others will be sufficient to prevent reneging. The rules that will be enforceable lie between R and R', where the cost exceeds the benefit of cheating. In these cases the punishment period is long and the sum of all the present discounted losses exceeds the present gain sufficient to deter cheating. This subset of enforceable rules called 'reputational equilibria' by Barro and Gordon is considered in the next section.

Reputational equilibria

The set of feasible rules are based on those that are enforceable, in the sense that there are no incentives for the government to cheat. Effectively the loss function cannot be reoptimized to find an inflation rate that deviates from the announcement and hence the public believes that the announcement is credible. Should the authorities deviate from their announced inflation rate it can be shown that the subsequent punishment over a given interval will result in an inferior value for the loss function sufficient to deter the authorities from attempting to do so in the first place. In this sense the rule or policy is enforced by the threat of punishment.

With the exception of the last case there is a tendency for inflation to take a value equal to b/a. This is known as the inflation bias inherent in the economy and is dependent on the relative weights on inflation (squared) and output in the loss function for society. The source of the bias is to be found in the fact that the government can and does inflate after expectations are set by the public because it has an incentive to do so. This is the time-inconsistency issue at work. The fact that the government has no means of precommitting to a zero inflation rate (except under a special set of reputational equilibria) is the nub of the problem. Barro and Gordon show that discretion is potentially more damaging to society (inferred from the loss function and the effect on output through the Lucas supply function) than a rule even though a rule restricts policy flexibility. Amongst the rules that are feasible (the reputational equilibria) the government has a means of credibly committing to an inflation rate that can tie down public expectations to the advantage of society. The feasible rules work because they raise the marginal cost of inflating to the government through the punishment—they only work because the game between the public and government is repeated many times and the behaviour in one period influences credibility in subsequent periods.

Some advances on the reputational solutions to the credibility problem were made by Backus and Driffill (1985), Canzoneri (1985), Vickers (1986), and Cukierman and Leviatin (1991). In these models governments are perceived to belong to certain types: either 'dry' governments (inflation fighters) or 'wet' governments (discretionary).[2] Due to asymmetric information about the true type, the public must infer the type by observing the behaviour. This leads to a signal extraction problem of the type we considered in the previous chapter on rational expectations. The problem for the public is that even a wet government may attempt to build reputation as a dry type and the wets and drys may be difficult to distinguish since both have an advantage to appear to be dry whether they are or not.

As a result of this mimicry any government that announces a zero inflation policy will not be fully credible. Despite the fact that the government may be genuinely dry, the public has an incentive to attach at least a small probability that it is really wet. The dry government has then an incentive to announce a small positive inflation rate since the public expect the rate will be positive not zero and the loss function can be best minimized by reducing the gap between π_t and π_t^e. Thus even with reputational solutions an inflation bias may remain if there is imperfect information about government type; even dependable policy-makers may find it optimal partially to accommodate inflationary expectations.

10.4 Conservative Preferences

An ingenious solution to this problem was suggested by Rogoff (1985). His idea was to introduce a third player into the game, the central bank, and to allow the government to delegate responsibility to the central bank. If the preferences of the central bank are known (overcoming the problems of asymmetric information) and the preferences are more conservative than the government (towards lower inflation), then the inflation bias could be diminished.

Suppose the preferences of the central bank can be described as the following loss function

$$L_t^{cb} = \frac{a}{2} (\pi_t^e) - c(\pi_t - \pi_t^e).$$

(10.12)

We recall that the term $c(\pi_t - \pi_t^e)$ comes from the Lucas output supply function and thus that the relative weights a and c represent the preferences towards or away from inflation. When c is lower than b in the loss function for government and society, then output gets a lower relative weight to inflation in the loss function of the central bank.

By delegating to a central bank with these preferences the government can reduce the inflation bias. The solution to the loss function for the central bank is, on the basis of an announcement of a zero inflation rate, equal to:

$$\frac{\partial L_t^{cb}}{\partial \pi_t} = a\pi_t - c = 0$$

(10.13)

implying

$$\pi_t = \frac{c}{a} > 0.$$

(10.14)

The inflation rate is lower than the equivalent case under the government and hence the inflation bias $c/a < b/a$. It is always optimal, as judged by the value of the loss function, to appoint a central banker with more conservative preferences than society and the government whatever the equilibrium strategy adopted.

An alternative way of considering the issue was considered by Cukierman (1992) who took a loss function as

$$L = \frac{a}{2} (\pi_t^2) - d(\pi - \pi_t^e),$$

(10.15)

but the parameter d reflects the preferences of both the government (b) and the central bank (c):

$$d = \phi c + (1 - \phi)b$$

(10.16)

and ϕ is the degree of independence of the central bank. Were $\phi = 1$, then the model would be identical to Rogoff's model, but if $\phi = 0$ the model would be Barro and Gordon's original model. The solution implies $\pi_t \to b/a$ as $\phi \to 0$ and $\pi_t \to c/a$ as $\phi \to 1$.

Lohmann (1992) has shown that the approach of Rogoff and Cukierman could be improved still further if the central bank is conservative, independent, *and* subject to the threat of government override if policy deviates from its optimal value. The central bank is independent and more conservative but any inherent tendency to cheat is checked by the knowledge that the government can override the central bank effectively setting $\phi = 0$ if it violates some preconditions on behaviour. This acts as an additional disincentive to the central bank to prevent cheating since it will be further punished by being overridden by the government if it does violate its announced policy.

Rogoff's approach has been the main theoretical underpinning for central bank independence but it is subject to a number of obvious criticisms. First, unless we rule out imperfect information, how does the government know the central bank has more conservative preferences than society? Here we again come across the problems, mentioned in the previous section, of discerning the commitment type since the less conservative types have an incentive to behave as if they too are conservative. Second, how does a central bank commit to announcements in a more credible way than the government? The bank has preferences against inflation (and perhaps more so than society) but there may still be incentives to cheat (governors require reappointment and like to be popular).[3] The government in Lohmann's model can monitor the bank but, as McCallum (1993) points out, the government was the untrustworthy policy-maker in the first place and may have little incentive to monitor conscientiously. Third, if delegation is a solution to the problem of precommitment at what point does this process end? Should the central bank delegate further to a more conservative body? Finally, we have the argument of Walsh (1995a, 1998) and Svensson (1997) that it is not the preferences of the central bank that matter but the design of an appropriate institutional structure. An authority deviating from its announcement must weigh up the costs versus the benefits of cheating. While loss of reputation is one punishment which creates a disincentive to cheat, Walsh and Svensson argue that explicit, contractual arrangements, which penalize the central bank directly would operate more effectively and transparently.

10.5 Contracts and Targets

THE issue of incentives and disincentives leads us into the literature on contracts and targets by Walsh (1995) and Svensson (1997). The notion that there is a design process for institutional structure and policy objectives draws on the principal-agent theory found in industrial economics to explain shareholder–manager interactions. Since incentives differ, or to put it another way, utility functions do not contain the same arguments, contracts and objectives must be set to introduce additional considerations in order that behaviour is tilted towards the best outcome.

In Carl Walsh's model, the central bank governor is offered a state-contingent wage contract which adds the inflation outcome to his own personal loss function. This is a specific example of a transfer function from government to central bank (in this case positive but it could be a penalty instead). The new loss function facing the governor of the central bank is now:

$$L_t^{cb} = L - t, \tag{10.17}$$

where L is the social loss function and t is the transfer payment contingent on the state of inflation. It can be shown from this that if we take the first derivative with respect to inflation, setting this equal to zero:

$$\frac{\partial L_t^{cb}}{\partial \pi_t} = \frac{\partial L}{\partial \pi_t} - \frac{\partial t}{\partial \pi_t} = 0. \tag{10.18}$$

The solution implies that

$$\frac{\partial t}{\partial \pi} = \frac{b}{a} \tag{10.19}$$

the change in the transfer function with the state variable (inflation) should equal the inflation bias b/a. Walsh demonstrates that this can most easily be achieved by setting a linear transfer function such as

$$t = t_0 + \frac{b}{a} \pi_t, \tag{10.20}$$

where t_0 is an intercept and $(b/a)\pi_t$ is the part that makes t state-contingent. Intuitively the transfer function raises the marginal cost of deviating from an optimal policy of $\pi_t = 0$ sufficiently to deter cheating. The solution relocates the commitment problem that gave rise to the inflation bias in the Barro and Gordon framework in the first place. The simplicity of the arrangement is to be found in the fact that the government does not need to observe the state to determine the transfer payment because the bias itself is not state-contingent. All that needs to be done is to set the transfer equal to the bias and make the final level of the transfer equal to the bias times the level of inflation, which can be observed. This overcomes the asymmetric information problem identified by Canzoneri (1985), Backus and Driffill (1985), Vickers (1986), and Cukierman and Leviatin (1991). In addition it leaves the central bank free to use monetary policy in response to shocks that may hit the economy.

Contracting has been explored further by Persson and Tabellini (1993) and Walsh (1995a) to show that dismissal rules can achieve similar results to wage contract incentives, but without the politically unpopular implications of wage contracts (wage increases are invoked during periods of tight monetary policy). Contracts are set by governments so the structure is subject to the same features and criticisms as the Rogoff model but the transparent way in which contracts are drawn up and enforced overcomes some of the problems identified by McCallum (1993). The public way in which contracts are written and monitored produces the openness and accountability that has become a major feature of central bank independence in practice.

Targets for independent central banks, introduced by Svensson (1997), operate in a similar way to contracts and can be shown to be equivalent incentive-enhancing devices. Instead of introducing a (linear) cost penalty to the loss function of the central bank, targets add an extra term as follows:

$$L_t^{cb} = \frac{a}{2} (\pi_t)^2 - b(\pi_t - \pi_t^e) + \frac{f}{2} (\pi_t - \pi_t^T)^2, \tag{10.21}$$

where $(\pi_t - \pi_t^T)^2$ represents the squared deviation of actual from target inflation with a weight $f/2$ attached to it. This is a flexible targeting rule for inflation, in that it does not require that the target should be hit every period but allows the central bank to trade off the target against other objections in the loss function. The marginal cost of deviating from the target is represented by an increase in the loss function of the central bank by $f/2$ for a unit deviation from target.

We can now compare the result of inflation targeting with that of the Rogoff conservative central banker. In Rogoff's case the inflation bias is reduced from b/a to c/a, and in the target case inflation is reduced to $\dfrac{b}{(a+f)} - \dfrac{f}{(a+f)}\pi^T$. If π^T equals the socially desired rate, equal to zero in this model, then the inflation bias is $\dfrac{b}{(a+f)}$. This can be shown to be similar to the Rogoff result since by re-writing the loss function as

$$L_t^{cb} = \frac{(a+f)}{2}(\pi_t)^2 - b(\pi_t - \pi_t^e) \tag{10.22}$$

$$\pi_t = \frac{b}{(a+f)}. \tag{10.23}$$

A greater relative weight is attached to inflation, i.e. $\left(\dfrac{a+f}{2}\right)$ instead of $a/2$ and this is equivalent to assigning a lower relative weight to $(\pi_t - \pi_t^e)$. In other words $\dfrac{(a+f)}{b}$ may achieve the same relative effect as $\dfrac{a}{c}$.

Svensson (1997) has shown that a similar relationship exists between a linear inflation-contracting approach and inflation targeting. Setting an inflation target equal to the social optimum minus the inflation bias is equivalent to implementing an inflation contract, i.e.

$$\pi^T = \pi^* - b/a =- b/a, \tag{10.24}$$

where π^* $(=0)$ is society's preference for inflation. To show this we can write

$$L_t^{cb} = \frac{a}{2}(\pi_t)^2 - b(\pi - \pi_t^e) + \frac{f}{2}(\pi_t - \pi_t^T)^2$$

$$= L + \frac{f}{2}(\pi_t - \pi_t^T)^2$$

$$= L + \frac{f}{2}(\pi_t - \pi_t^* + \pi_t^* - \pi_t^T)^2.$$

$$L_t^{cb} = \frac{g}{2}(\pi_t - \pi_t^*)^2 + h(\pi_t - \pi_t^*) + \frac{g}{2}(\pi^* - \pi^T)^2. \tag{10.25}$$

It can be shown that $L_t^{cb} \equiv L - t$ if $g = 1$ and $h = g(\pi_t^* - \pi_t^T) =- b/a$. The result then follows. The requirement that $g = 1$ is equivalent to setting the preferences of the central bank equal to the preferences of society, whilst the choice of $h =- b/a$ makes the loss functions equal under the contract solution and the target. By rearrangement, the value of the target can be obtained from $g(\pi^* - \pi^T) =- b/a$ for $g = 1$.

10.6 Types of Policy Rules for Central Banks

UP to this point, we have assumed that the instrument and the target for monetary policy is inflation. In this section we allow for a wider choice of instruments
and targets that have been suggested in the economic literature; inevitably we will
need to consider the relation between them and this introduces policy rules. The
main purpose of a policy rule is to provide a guide to monetary policy formulation
that is clear and transparent. The type of policy rule will differ depending on the
instruments of monetary policy, i.e. short-term nominal interest rates or a narrow
measure of money. It will also differ according to the target for monetary policy and
the subset of variables considered relevant to the relationship between policy instrument and target. In general, policy rules should satisfy the following criteria. They
should be

1. clear and simple so that it is easy to discern which component of the rule is driving the monetary policy instrument;
2. dependent on variables that can be measured accurately in a timely fashion;
3. readily estimated by econometric methods; and
4. able to explain the past history of the monetary policy instrument. If they fail to
   do so the reason should be apparent, and the rule should still explain monetary
   policy in times that policy performance was 'good'.

The most famous policy rule is the Taylor rule (popularized and introduced independently by John Taylor and Dale Henderson) and we will consider that first. Other
alternatives include the McCallum rule, the nominal income rule (Bean, 1983), and
the monetary conditions index, all of which have been suggested and implemented
by central banks. There have been attempts to create forward-looking policy rules;
these are discussed last.

Taylor rules

The instrument of a Taylor rule applies to the setting of the short-term nominal
interest rate (i_t). The rule is written as

$$ i_t = \pi_{t-1} + \theta_1(\pi - \pi^*)_{t-1} + \theta_2\left(\frac{(y - y^*)}{y^*}\right)^{t-1} + (i_t - \pi_t)^*. \tag{10.26} $$

where π_{t-1} is the inflation rate, $(\pi - \pi^*)_{t-1}$ is the deviation of inflation from its tar-
get/desired rate, $(y - y^*)/y^*$ is the deviation of output from its natural rate relative to
the natural rate, and $(i_t - \pi_t)^*$ is the equilibrium real rate of interest. t is a time subscript and θ_1 and θ_2 are set equal to 0.5 so that the rule is aggressive with respect to
past inflation (π_{t-1}), i.e. that coefficient is greater than 1 so the short-term nominal
rate rises by more than inflation, but less so with respect to output. Broadbent (1997),

Ball (1997), and Svensson (1997) have argued that the 'optimal' weights, chosen to minimize the variance of inflation and output, might be higher than this. A Taylor rule satisfies the criteria outlined at the beginning since it is simple, measurable, easily estimated, and timely, and has performed well on historical US data.[4] The rule has been used by policy-makers to assess whether the central bank has followed an appropriate policy trajectory in the USA and the UK (Barker, 1996; Yellen, 1996; Greenspan, 1997).

The rule has had to address a number of criticisms. First, the measurement of target/desired levels of output, inflation, and real interest rates is problematic. The determination of the NAIRU, and its near relation the natural rate of output, for the Taylor rule is fraught with difficulties. Many central banks have resorted to a Hodrick–Prescott filter to obtain a best-guess of y^*_t but this has its own drawbacks. Target inflation, likewise, has been difficult to estimate. Although the target has been quantified in the UK, NZ, Australia, and Canada in recent years by policy-makers, the target level in periods when supply shocks, e.g. oil price rises, hit inflation rates has been harder to determine. Estimates of the equilibrium real rate of interest can be extracted from financial instruments such as indexed government bonds, but the errors that creep in due to errors in expectations, or worse still using *ex post* real rates rather than *ex ante* ones, can lead to an inflation bias in either direction. Since central bank policy affects the *ex ante* rate, the rule may not be a suitable guide to policy-makers if constructed on *ex post* data.

Second, for open economies the rule ignores the effect of the exchange rate. The poorer performance in the UK relative to the USA, which is far more closed, may be a reflection of this omission. The impact of exchange rate appreciations or depreciations on inflation may introduce the effect indirectly but attempts to model the open-economy Taylor rule must make assumptions about the speed with which exchange rate effects 'pass-through' to domestic prices (Ball, 1998).

Recently, Batini and Haldane (1998) have extended the Taylor rule to include a forward-looking dimension that would be required if lags in monetary transmission were taken into account. Their rule is written as

$$i_t = \gamma i_{t-1} + (1 - \gamma)i^*_t + \theta(E_t \pi_{t+j} - \pi^*), \tag{10.27}$$

where i_t is the short-term real interest rate, i^*_t is the equilibrium real interest rate, $E_t \pi_{t+j}$ is expected inflation j periods ahead, and π^* is the inflation target. By searching over possible values of γ, θ, and the forward-looking horizon j they conclude that the optimal response (given by the smallest output variability–inflation variability combination) is for a forward-looking horizon of six to eight quarters ahead. This horizon corresponds to Friedman's long-standing position on the length of the lag in the effect of monetary policy. Referring to Table 7.1, we can see that he argues monetary policy changes feed through to output six to nine months later and to prices after fifteen to twenty-four months.[5] It also matches the forecast horizon adopted by the Bank of England and other central banks (based on rather similar estimates of the policy lags).

Svensson (1998) has considered inflation targeting as a policy strategy for central banks and draws some useful parallels with the literature on policy rules. Monetary policy implementation must allow for lags in the transmission mechanism, and inevitably this creates the need to look forward. Inflation targets are not targets for today but targets for tomorrow since today's interest rate policy will not affect inflation today.[6] Svensson has argued that using the forecast of inflation as an intermediate variable is the solution to the problem and the inflation target becomes an inflation forecast target equivalent to a Taylor rule. Inflation targeting can be considered as a particular example of a *targeting rule*. Unlike *instrument rules*, which give guides to the setting of policy variables such as the short-term interest rate, the money supply, and so on, targeting rules specify an actual loss function to be minimized as a function at a small number of intermediate or final target variables.

If we take our loss function which is linear in output, we will get a more restrictive result than Svensson so at this point we assume a Svensson loss function, which is different from the one used in the previous section, i.e.

$$L_2^{sven} = \frac{1}{2} \left((\pi_t - \pi_t^T)^2 + k(y_t)^2 \right). \tag{10.28}$$

We minimize an expected loss function over many periods

$$\tilde{L}_t^{sven} = E_t \sum_{i=1}^{n} \delta^i \left(L_{t+i}^{sven} \right) \tag{10.29}$$

subject to

$$y_t = b(\pi_t - \pi_t^e) \tag{10.30}$$

and

$$\pi_{t+1} = \pi_t + \alpha y_t + \varepsilon_t, \tag{10.31}$$

where ε_t is an error term and k, α, and δ are parameters.

The solution indicates that the two year ahead conditional inflation forecast is

$$E_t(\pi_{t+2}) = \pi_t^T + \gamma(E_t \pi_{t+1} - \pi_t^T) \quad \text{or} \quad E_t(\pi_{t+2}) - \pi_t^T = \gamma(E_t \pi_{t+1} - \pi_t^T) \tag{10.32}$$

that is, a partial adjustment towards the target π_t^T that makes some allowance for the previous period's discrepancy between the forecast and the target weighted by γ.[7] The inflation forecast is a function of the short-term interest rate and therefore changes to the instrument will drive the intermediate variable, $E_t(\pi_{t+2})$, and ultimately the goal variable, (π_{t+2}), towards the target π_t^T.

By substitution of the forecast values into the partial-adjustment expression, Svensson shows that the inflation-targeting strategy can be written in the form of a Taylor rule

$$i_t = \pi_t + \theta_1(\pi_1 - \pi_t^T) + \theta_2 y_t, \tag{10.33}$$

where θ_1 and θ_2 are parameters given by the structure of the model. It is possible to show that this expression can be written as a rule in terms of the inflation forecast. Hence inflation targeting can be thought of as a targeting rule, and since variables other than the inflation rate enter the rule, it is regarded as a *flexible* rather than a *strict* inflation-targeting rule.

McCallum rule

The McCallum rule defines the instrument of monetary policy as the narrow money base, (M0). The rule is written as

$$M0_t = k_{t-1} - v_{t-1} + \theta_3(z^* - z)_{t-1} \tag{10.34}$$

where $M0_t$ is the growth rate of nominal narrow money supply, k_{t-1} is a target level of money growth, v_{t-1} is a lagged sixteen-month moving average of velocity growth and $(z^* - z)_{t-1}$ is the deviation of a nominal income growth from the target rate, z^*. θ_3 is a parameter weight and t is a time subscript; all variables are in natural logarithms.

If the economy is at target growth rate for output and money demand equals its desired level (i.e. $v_{t-1} = 0$ and $(z^* - z)_{t-1} = 0$), then $M0_t = k_{t-1}$. Thus, in a dynamic sense, McCallum's rule approximates to a Friedman money growth rule where k_{t-1} is the growth rate. This interpretation has led many economists to consider the McCallum rule as a dynamic monitoring range for narrow money, which is endogenously supplied by the central bank.

The rule has many of the advantages and disadvantages of the Taylor rule. It is used as a check on medium-term policy in many central banks, but after a disastrous experiment with targeting of broader monetary aggregates in the early 1980s many central banks have relinquished monitoring ranges for monetary aggregates, including M0, altogether. Yet the Bundesbank, the most celebrated money targeter, used a reference growth rate value for money of 5 per cent for many years and the ECB has been given M3 a reference growth of 4.5 per cent per annum. One explanation for this is that the quantity of money was seen to be the nominal anchor in the German system. Over- and under-shooting of the ranges, that might have been taken to suggest that monetary references were failing, was merely an attempt to deal with perceived permanent shifts in velocity that the McCallum rule suggests should have been accommodated. Nevertheless, money is not an instrument as such (nor is it a target that many central banks use) and the role of the McCallum rule is to guide to the setting of the actual policy instrument in a consistent fashion with the M0 path that would have been prescribed had they followed the rule.

The McCallum rule is a strict version of a nominal income rule. Some prominent authors such as James Meade (1978), James Tobin (1980a)—both Nobel Laureates—Samuel Brittan (1981), and Charles Bean (1983) have argued that policy should be guided by a nominal income target. Whilst income data are less timely than either price or monetary measures, money GDP can be thought of as a velocity-corrected money supply target and as ranking alongside prices as an ultimate target of policy.

Bean shows from a simple labour market-clearing model with a wage outcome, that the sensible objective for policy-makers in the face of uncertainty about future demand and productivity, would be to minimize the variance of output, y_t, from the full information level y^*_t. The optimal policy rule requires the authorities to target nominal income to its expected value in order to achieve this since the real output deviation from target depends on nominal income and price surprises:

$$(y_t - y_t^*) = \beta[\alpha\phi(x_t - E_{t-1}x_t) + (1 - \phi)(p_t - E_{t-1}p_t)], \tag{10.35}$$

where $(x_t - E_{t-1}x_t)$ is the surprise to nominal income, $(p_t - E_{t-1}p_t)$ is the surprise to prices, and β, α, and ϕ are parameters from the underlying model of labour supply and demand.

If $\phi = 1$, then nominal income-targeting is optimal, and this occurs if the labour supply is perfectly inelastic. Even if the labour supply is elastic to some degree, then nominal income targets will produce better responses to productivity shocks if the aggregate demand function for the economy responds less than one for one in proportional terms to prices.

Major objections to nominal income targets have been raised by Poole (1980). Nominal income can be regarded as a velocity-adjusted money supply strategy, but if the reality is that the income velocity of money is volatile and unpredictable, forecasting may be difficult when we allow for transmission lags. Alternatively, there may be considerable uncertainty surrounding the relationship between money, prices, and income. In the face of parameter uncertainty, a gradualist policy may be needed. We examine this in Section 10.7 below.

Monetary conditions indices

Some central banks, such as the Reserve Bank of New Zealand and the Bank of Canada, have given attention to a monetary conditions index (*MCI*). An *MCI* gives an indicator of the tightness of monetary policy by forming a weighted average of percentage changes in the logarithm of the exchange rate and the percentage point changes in the interest rate. Hence in nominal terms an *MCI* might be

$$MCI_t = a_1(e_t - e_{t-1}) + a_2(i_t - i_{t-1}) \tag{10.36}$$

or in real terms

$$\text{Real } MCI_t = b_1(s_t - s_{t-1}) + b_2(r_t - r_{t-1}). \tag{10.37}$$

where e_t is the nominal exchange rate, and i_t is the nominal interest rate, s_t is the real exchange rate, and r_t is the real interest rate and a_1, a_2, b_1, and b_2 are chosen (or estimated) parameters. In both cases the nominal (or real) exchange rates and nominal (or real) interest rates are related to their previous period's value, but the comparison could be made over a time horizon of a month, quarter, year, or relative to some (equilibrium) base year.

MCIs can be used both for informational purposes and as intermediate targets and are regarded as useful for countries that are small and open, where the exchange rate consequences of monetary policy matter. Ball (1998) generalizes an optimal rule to include the open economy, deriving an *MCI* equivalent as the policy rule. In a model based on an IS curve, and an open economy Phillips curve, given by

$$y_t = -\alpha_1 r_{t-1} - \alpha_2 s_{t-1} + \alpha_3 y_{t-1} \tag{10.38}$$

$$\pi_t = \pi_{t-1} + \beta_2 y_{t-1} + \beta_3 (\triangle s_{t-1}) \tag{10.39}$$

a positive relation between the exchange rate and the interest rate and $s_t = \theta r_t$ would translate a domestic Taylor rule into a rule for the exchange rate or a rule for a combination of the interest rate and the exchange rate where $\theta = a_2/a_1$ in our nominal MCI.

Yet the models have a number of fairly obvious theoretical and empirical weaknesses. The first is that the equation $s_t = \theta r_t$ simply expresses the exchange rate as a linear function of interest rates (equivalent to a change of units). A more forward-looking relationship would bring in the real interest rate and inflation expectations, or alternatively a genuinely open economy model might use the uncovered interest parity equation in order to close the model, which would allow foreign as well as domestic interest rates to affect the exchange rate.

Second, the MCI involves the addition of an endogenous policy instrument, the exchange rate, to an exogenous policy instrument, the interest rate. If the equation relating the exchange rate to the interest rate is correct, then the exchange rate is a function of the interest rate and hence the MCI is just collapsible into two summable forms in the interest rate (King, 1987).

Third, the MCI does not tell us from where the monetary policy tightness (looseness) is coming, nor can it disentangle the sources of shocks. The policy response of the central bank might be quite different if the index changed due to the effects on the exchange rate of monetary policy developments abroad instead of domestic influences. The Bank of Canada, one of the most ardent supporter of MCIs, does precisely this to disentangle the sources of shocks so that it can determine its optimal response.

Fourth, the empirical estimation of MCI models is prone to difficulties associated with the statistical treatment of non-stationary variables like the exchange rate and the interest rate, the non-constancy of the weights estimated as the model parameters in this context, the possibility of omitted variables, the role of dynamic relationships, and so on.

In practice, it seems that a Taylor rule consistent with an inflation target is likely to be the best strategy to follow. It does not prevent the policy-makers from considering other data such as money, nominal income, the exchange rate, unemployment, or whatever. Indeed, many central banks target one particular variable but monitor many other things that might be regarded as useful and timely indicators of economic conditions under a 'looking-at-everything' approach. Having made the choice of the nature of the rule, the next section considers *how* a central bank should operate a monetary policy rule and that introduces the issue of uncertainty.

10.7 Policy Rules in an Uncertain World

HAVING considered the various policy rules that a central bank may wish to use to guide policy, we must now consider how uncertainty alters the policy setting. Theil (1958) showed that, although the world *is* uncertain, the policy-maker should act as if the world were certain (the theory of 'certainty equivalence'). One of the earliest studies to consider a world of uncertainty was William Brainard (1967) and it is still the seminal work. Brainard's paper allows for different types of uncertainty to affect the parameters of the model. He contrasts additive errors with multiplicative errors, which involve positive covariances between targets and the settings of monetary instruments themselves.

Brainard argues that these two sources of uncertainty need to be carefully distinguished. The first is, as it were, 'in the system' and invariant to policy behaviour. The authorities should proceed with the optimal strategy as if their best guess of the behaviour of the economy is certain knowledge. If the nature of the uncertainty is not additive but multiplicative, then the policy should not follow 'certainty equivalence' but instead adopt a gradualist or conservative policy response. Because the second type of uncertainty is directly contingent upon the strength of policy, in order to avert risk, policy-makers should lower their sights and accept a lower expected value of goal achievement, not seeking to fully restore the goal variables to their desired levels.

We will consider each case in turn, but first we must introduce a static framework relating instruments and targets of monetary policy. Suppose that the relationship between each instrument and target is given (deterministically at first) as

$$x_j = \Phi_{jk} u_k, \tag{10.40}$$

where x_j are a series of j targets and u_k are a set of k instruments, whilst each Φ_{jk} relates the two. We could think of these equations as the inverse of the policy rules considered in the previous section. From the work of Tinbergen (1952) we know that the number of independent instruments (j) must be at least equal to the number of targets (k) for all targets to be met. In the event that the targets exceed the instruments ($j > k$), Theil (1958, 1964) suggested that the policy-maker should aim to minimize a loss function weighted according to the importance of each target to the policy-maker by the coefficient, Ψ_j.

$$L = \sum_{j=1}^{n} \Psi_j (x_j - x^*_j)^2 \tag{10.41}$$

given $x_j = \Phi_j u_k$, the optimal policy setting is found by partially differentiating and setting equal to zero to give

$$\frac{\partial L}{\partial x_j} = 2\Psi_j(x_j - x^*_j) = 0 \tag{10.42}$$

for each j and by substitution of $x_j = \Phi_j u_k$, gives

$$u_k^* = \Phi_j^{-1} x_j^*. \tag{10.43}$$

With $k < j$ instruments only k targets can be hit.

This is a deterministic case; we now consider additive and multiplicative errors.

Additive errors

We consider a special case with one instrument and one target, related as follows

$$x_1 = au_1 + \varepsilon, \tag{10.44}$$

where ε is an error distributed $N(0, \sigma_\varepsilon^2)$. Since $E(\varepsilon) = 0$ we can show $E(x_1) = aE(u_1)$ and we return to the deterministic case in expectation—the 'certainty equivalence' case.

The variance term σ_ε^2 is not dependent on the policy-setting, i.e. is not a function of u_1 or x_1, and arises because future non-policy forces may be incorrectly predicted. We can split the loss function into the expected deviation from target and the variance of the error by using the expected loss

$$
\begin{aligned}
E(L) &= E(x_1 - x_1^*)^2 \\
&= E(x_1 - E(x_1) + E(x_1) - x_1^*)^2 \\
&= (E(x_1) - x_1^*)^2 + Var(x_1) \\
&= (au_1 - x_1^*)^2 + \sigma_\varepsilon^2. \tag{10.45}
\end{aligned}
$$

Again the solution implies

$$u_1^* = \frac{x_1^*}{a}, \tag{10.46}$$

the same solution as before (where $a = \Phi_j$), for $k = j = 1$.

Multiplicative uncertainty

Suppose that the uncertainty was not additive to x_1 but rather multiplicative, in that the uncertainty was in parameters and their relation to errors. For example, the strength and timing of policy forces may be misjudged. If $a \sim N(\mu, \sigma_a^2)$ and was related to ε through a covariance term $\eta_{a\varepsilon}$, then the loss function would be (in expectation)

$$E(L) = (\mu_1 . u_1 - x_1^*)^2 + \sigma_a^2 u_1^2 + \sigma_\varepsilon^2 + 2\eta_{a\varepsilon} . u_1, \tag{10.47}$$

the optimal policy would give

$$u^* = \frac{(\mu_1 x^* - \eta_{a\varepsilon})}{(\mu_1^2 + \sigma_a^2)}. \tag{10.48}$$

Certainty equivalence no longer holds (i.e. $x_1^* \neq au_1^*$); now the mean, variance and covariance of the parameter with the error appear in the optimal solution for the monetary policy instrument. Since a larger value of μ and σ_a^2 implies greater variation in the instrument to x_1^*, then $(E(x_1) - x_1^*)$ will grow with σ_a^2. This means that too much variation in the instrument increases the risk of missing the target, hence policy-makers should be more cautious if uncertainty is multiplicative.[8]

Lessons for policy-makers

Blinder (1997) suggested that this second result should make policy-makers more cautious—they should adopt Brainard's 'conservatism principle'. This is supportive of Friedman's concern that central banks should adopt a predictable and simple rule for policy given the long and variable lags in the transmission mechanism. Phelps (1988) puts the point well:

William Brainard in a well-known paper (1967) also makes a contribution to the Monetarist stance. The Monetarist premise is that to put all your eggs in the activist basket—going for the highest average performance—is to adopt a risky portfolio; on the other hand, nothing ventured, nothing gained. Brainard spells out a model in which the optimum policy action is to take a 'small step' because big steps cause too much variance per unit of return. The message differs little in spirit from that of Friedman, though the latter was interested in demonstrating the theoretical possibility that no action would be better than any quivering move in the probably right direction.[9] (Cited in Hall *et al.* 1998)

Fischer and Cooper (1973) found that Friedman's predictability was greatly to be preferred, suggesting that central banks should heed the comment attributed to Robert Solow that, 'if you don't know what you are doing, don't do much of it.' Brainard uncertainty encourages caution, and if policy is to be adopted it should be done in small doses. Hence the assignment of one instrument to one target is discouraged in favour of small adjustments in the use of several instruments. This undermines the Tinbergen counting rule between instruments and targets; the more instruments the better with multiplicative uncertainty, since many small changes in many instruments is greatly to be preferred to a few large changes in a limited number of instruments.[10] It also encourages many small steps in policy instruments rather than one large adjustment, so that policy-makers take successive autocorrelated steps in setting interest rates, for example, rather than one large cut. Goodhart (1996), Lowe and Ellis (1997), Estrella and Mishkin (1998), Sack (1998), Sheutrim and Thompson (1998), and Yates and Bhundia (1998), have all shown that short-term policy instruments are autocorrelated due to the phenomenon of 'interest rate smoothing' in the UK, the USA, and Australia. Sack's study is representative. He concludes

the Fed appears reluctant to make aggressive changes in the Funds rate, choosing instead to adjust rates gradually so that many months pass before the peak of the Funds rate response is reached. (1988: 12)

He deduces this from the fact that the response to various shocks is less than the optimal response derived from a small empirical model of the economy. Brainard (multiplicative) uncertainty accounts for a considerable portion of the observed gradualist response.

In the 1998 Keynes Lecture to the Fellows of the British Academy, Charles Goodhart argued that central banks *do* act in this way. Large step changes and frequent reversals give the market the jitters. If policy reactions are dramatic, the market assumes that the central bank knows something (perhaps untoward) that they do not and an adverse reaction can occur even if it is not warranted. Based on recent evidence, the BIS concludes:

> There is some evidence that a dislike of reversals of this sort is not uncommon in the industrial countries. Central banks generally move interest rates several times in the same direction before reversing policy. Moreover, the interval between policy adjustments is typically considerably longer when the direction is changed. . . As the size of the steps at turning-points is not systematically larger than at other times, this pattern of adjustments risks being interpreted as a tendency to move 'too little, too late'. One possible rationalisation for such behaviour is un-certainty about the policy impulses. Such uncertainty is likely to be greatest at the turning-points of the interest rate cycle. A further reason for wishing to avoid frequent interest rate reversals is the desire to provide clear guidance to markets, both to strengthen the pass-through along the yield curve and to avoid destabilising markets. BIS Annual Report (1998: 68–9)

In effect, the argument is that in a world in which central bankers are accountable changes must be justified, not in terms of parameter uncertainty, long lags, or predictions from optimal rules, but in general terms through the media to the public at large. The need to explain the reasoning behind policy changes creates a cautious response to events, especially when rates are moved upwards. Reversals in particular are seen as a 'change of mind' and are equated with inconsistency and unreliability, so changes to rates are usually only adopted if there is enough evidence to suggest that the next change will be in the same direction—albeit by small increments. By making changes in such a manner that is regarded as 'consistent' (many changes in the same direction) which can be validated *ex post* as 'the right policy' (few reversals), central bankers create the credibility that they desire. What is more, when rate changes or reversals do occur, the response to the stimulus will be sharp, since the change is liable to indicate the genuine requirement for a series of steps in the same direction. Central banks can then avoid the well-known problem of crying wolf once too often, so that when they do act the policy response is immediate (Woodford, 1998).[11]

Dynamic models

The results of Brainard were all devised in static models but the results carry over to a dynamic context. Using multiperiod models with uncertainty makes the model more complicated, and in some cases intractable (Aoki, 1977), but Chow (1977) has shown that 'certainty equivalence' in the additive case and the smoothing result in the multiplicative case hold true for certain tractable dynamic settings. A recent example by Wieland (1998) has a dynamic loss function

$$L = E_t \sum_{i=1}^{n} \delta^i \left[(\pi_{t+i} - \pi_{t+i}^*)^2 + \omega(u_{t+i}^* - u_{t+i})^2 \right] \tag{10.49}$$

where π_t is inflation, u_t is unemployment and a star denotes the target.

Inflation is driven by a Phillips curve and unemployment is a random walk; policy-makers control the short-term interest rate, which reduces inflation but increases unemployment with rising rates. Hence policy-makers may follow an optimal rule such as

$$i_t = i_{t-1} + \beta_1(\pi_{t-i} - \pi^*_{t-i}) + \beta_2(u^*_{t-i} - u_{t-i}). \tag{10.50}$$

Multiplicative uncertainty is introduced through the Phillips curve as

$$\pi_t = \pi_{t-i} + \beta_3 u_t + \varepsilon_t, \tag{10.51}$$

where $\beta_3 \sim N(\mu, \sigma^2_\beta)$ and $\text{Corr}(\beta_3, \varepsilon_t) = \eta_t$. The results follow through as for the static case.

Weiland considers that policy-makers may be passive learners as in Sack's (1998) model, in which they take the nature of the model (particularly the variance/covariance matrix) as given, or they may be active, taking into account the response of the model to their policies. With an active learning rule the policy-maker will be more interventionist than under the passive rule but more gradualist than the 'certainty equivalence' case. Applying his model to the Bundesbank policy pre- and post-unification, Weiland shows a passive rule explains actual money and inflation outcomes quite well, but an active rule would have returned inflation (money) to target more quickly at the expense of more volatile short-term interest rates.

Notably, the notion of uncertainty has made a welcome return to economic models, and the contribution of Knight (1921) in distinguishing between risk and uncertainty has been revived. Brainard's model refers strictly to 'risk'—imperfect information that can be quantified and described by probability distributions—but new models by Sargent (1998) and Stock (1998) deal with 'robust rules' under Knightian uncertainty (when actual probabilities cannot be assigned).[12] The 'robust rules' are devised as the best response under the worst-case scenario chosen by a minimax strategy in a game between the policy-maker and nature. A minimax strategy involves the policy-maker identifying the worst case scenario and then choosing a policy rule that minimizes the loss function in that case. So taking M as the estimated model, and $\triangle$ as deviations from the model, the policy-maker selects the worst $\triangle$ from the possible distribution of shocks and computes the loss function L under that scenario (this is the max part of the problem, i.e. $\text{Max}_\triangle L(M + \triangle, r)$). Given the worst-case scenario the policy-maker then chooses a value for the policy instrument, r, to minimize the loss function (this is the min part, i.e. $\text{Min}_r \text{Max}_\triangle L(M + \triangle, r)$). Onatskio and Stock (1999) show that rather ironically these models suggest a more *active* response may be more desirable under uncertainty, in contradiction of Brainard.

Evidently, these models are at the very forefront of monetary policy design and it is difficult to judge how important they will be for practical purposes. Stock and Sargent view the potential for these models to be as revolutionary as rational expectations was to conventional macroeconomics in the 1970s and 1980s. There are a number of drawbacks to robust rules that follow from the fact that a policy-maker following a robust rule would be inclined to be overpessimistic about the state of the world. This would make the policy-maker overly aggressive under 'normal' conditions, so that the policy-maker would be likely to get the 'sack' for overeagerness long before a bad state of the world actually occurred. Worse still, if a minimax strategy were actually followed by a policy-maker, it might be concluded that the possible dangers under a worst-case scenario of travelling to work were so severe that the optimal response to minimize them would be simply to stay at home! The solution, if this strategy is to be useful for practical purposes, is to identify a sensible range of severe shocks to the model that can be realistically taken as worst cases to limit aggressiveness or excessive personal caution. Clearly, there is much more to learn on this topic.

10.8 Conclusions

A MAJOR contribution in recent years to monetary economics has been the design of institutions and policy rules that lead to 'optimal policy'. Very often these involve games between governments and central bankers, the general public and even nature itself. Under certain conditions policy-makers may be motivated to re-optimize or 'cheat', but incentives can be devised so that they choose to follow an optimal path. Even when policy-makers have a desire to aim for the optimal path, rules and strategies must be established to deal with the nature of the environment in which they are to be conducted. This is a complex task and is still very much a matter for ongoing research.

Notes

1 Even if one finds the credibility story hard to swallow it must be acknowledged that the literature is still seminal since it introduces for the first time the idea that policy-makers face incentives and the design of the incentives can alter policy outcomes.

2 This particular terminology was first introduced into the public domain by Mrs Thatcher during the recession of the early 1980s. Those in the Conservative Party who supported the government's anti-inflationary policies were dubbed 'drys' while those who did not were called 'wet'.

3 Paul Samuelson once remarked that the Fed was 'captured' by its independence and desire to retain it.

4 This is somewhat of an illusion, however, since the weights were chosen by Taylor from historical relations in US data. The weights may be less satisfactory and the rule less effective for the UK, a more open economy, although recent work by Ed Nelson (Nelson, 2000) suggests the weights are close to Taylor's for the period 1992–97.

5 Following Friedman (1948) it has been customary to distinguish three lags: '(1) the lag between the need for action and the recognition of this need; (2) the lag between the recognition of the need for action and the taking of action; and (3) the

lag between the action and its effects.' The first two categories have subsequently been called the 'inside' lag, and the third the 'outside' lag. The estimates reported here are Friedman's for the outside lag.

6 One is tempted to add unless fully and unanimously anticipated by transactors able to act upon the information costlessly in completely flexible, instantaneously clearing markets!

7 Where

$$\gamma = \frac{k}{k + \delta\alpha^2} \quad f(k) \quad \text{and} \quad f(k) = \frac{1}{2}\left(1 - \frac{k(1 - \delta)}{\delta\alpha^2} + \sqrt{\left(1 - \frac{k(1 - \delta)}{\delta\alpha^2}\right)^2 + \frac{4k}{\alpha^2}}\right).$$

8 The exceptions are when $\eta_{a\varepsilon}$ is large and negative or when covariances overturn this result

9 Cited in Batini *et al.* (1998).

10 This is because uncertainty also exists about the relative effectiveness of the various instruments. Brainard shows that this risk is reduced by 'diversifying' policy amongst the range of instruments and using several of them in combination. Actions involving small changes in a wide number of instruments are preferred to actions involving large changes in some. However, the force of this particular aspect is reduced if one is confident that the monetary policy instrument is the most effective for controlling inflation.

11 This is the theory, but practice can and will differ. It was only in 1989 that interest rates in the UK were nearly doubled in a short space of time to institute the most severe contraction in British monetary history. And in 1997, Asian central banks did not have the luxury of making small, discrete policy adjustments. When it comes to practice, 'The golden rule is that there are no golden rules' (George Bernard Shaw).

12 Probabilities cannot be assigned for two reasons. First, the number of possible states of the world is vast, making the task too great for practical purposes, but second, not all the states are known and it is an unfeasible task to assign probabilities to states of the world that are unknowable at the present.

Part Two

Policy

Chapter 11
Modelling the Demand for Money

11.1 Introduction

MODELLING the demand for money concerns the estimation and quantification of the demand for money function, utilizing data and econometric methodology. While basically empirical it must be informed by the theory. This chapter provides an overview of recent work, beginning with the most basic issue of how to define the variables such as money, income, rate of return, and prices. This serves to illustrate the variety of choices that need to be made before any attempt at estimation can start. Once the variables have been isolated, there are a number of important econometric considerations to ensure that the estimated function actually is a demand for the money function.

The historical development cannot be ignored either, as illustrated by the initial success and subsequent collapse of the Goldfeld equation in the mid-1970s. This heralded a new era in empirical work. Various attempts to rescue the demand for money function from its ignominious fall from grace (and revive monetary targets) have been a catalyst for most of the research agenda over the last twenty-five years.

11.2 Practical Issues

Measurement of variables

THEORY suggests a relationship between an endogenous variable m, and the exogenous or explanatory variables, p, y, and i. But we need to define what we mean by these, and make choices between competing measures.

The first edition of Mrs Beeton's *Cookbook* was said to have begun with the advice (no doubt apocryphal) 'first kill the ox'. The appropriate starting point with the demand for money function is to define money, but unlike the aforementioned animal money is not so clearly identifiable. Rather there is a whole spectrum of

Figure 11.1 Relationships among monetary aggregates and their components

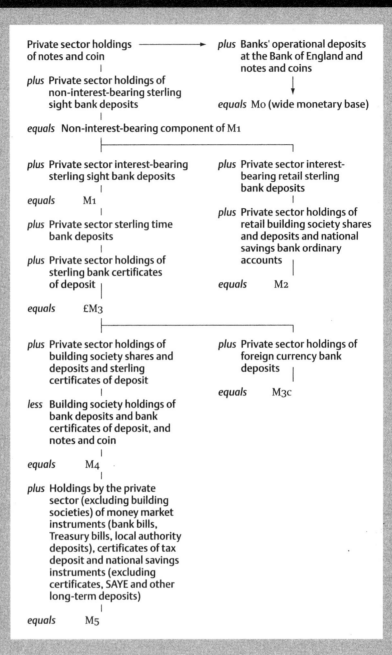

Source: Adapted from Bank of England Quarterly Bulletin, May 1987.

assets of varying liquidity and acceptability. Using Figure 11.1 we can illustrate this point using the conventional monetary aggregates M0, M1, M4 for the UK. The monetary base M0, the narrowest definition of money, constitutes the notes and coin held by the general public plus the deposits which the banking system keeps at the Bank of England. If we add interest-bearing and non-interest-bearing sight deposits (current accounts) to notes and coins, then we obtain the definition M1, which is also regarded as useful for measuring those balances liable to be used for transactions. Adding further components produces progressively broader monetary aggregates that incorporate monetary assets with successively declining liquidity. The addition of non-marketable interest-bearing deposits to M1 gives M2 in the UK (although in the USA M2 corresponds to M4 for the UK, by including savings instruments). Sterling M3 (£M3) then adds the non-interest and interest-bearing holdings of assets by the non-bank private sector. M4 and M5, now the more widely used broad measures of money, include building society deposits and certain short-term money market instruments such as Treasury Bills, local authority deposits, and national savings instruments. All of these aggregates are in sterling and ignore the foreign currency deposits of domestic residents even when they are held in the UK banks.

The first choice, then, is between narrow or broad money, depending on whether we are interested in the medium of exchange or payment function of money, associated with transactions behaviour, or its store of value function, linked with saving. Another consideration, particularly if the function is to be estimated over a considerable period of time, say thirty years or more, is that some components may have altered with respect to liquidity due to innovation and deregulation. A simple aggregation of the components may be unwise. Such changes have led some economists such as William Barnett to question the validity of simply adding up the components with equal weights. His alternative is that the weights should vary according to the 'moneyness' of each. The Divisia aggregation scheme (the formal definition of which is left to the next chapter) adopts this approach.

Once chosen, the monetary aggregate can be included in nominal or real terms. Usually a real definition of money balances is employed, imposing a coefficient of unity on the price variable in the money demand function by appeal to the theoretical property of homogeneity.[1] Nominal balances must then be deflated by a measure of the price level. One option is to use a basket measure of the price level such as the consumer price index (CPI) measuring prices of a range of goods at retail outlets (in the UK it is referred to as the retail price index (RPI)) whilst the wholesale price index (WPI) measures prices in a similar way at the 'factory gate', excluding some services and the impact of indirect taxes. Another option is to use price deflators for gross domestic product (GDP) or total final expenditure (TFE) obtained by dividing the current price measures by the constant price measure to give an index of prices relative to the base period. The vast majority of studies use one of the price deflators.

The monetary aggregate selected affects the choice of the scale or income variable. A narrow definition of money, based on the medium of exchange function, where the demand for money represents purchasing power for transactions, would normally be matched with GDP or TFE to measure total transactions in the economy. Nevertheless on theoretical grounds there is a question mark over the validity of linking the *stock* of money at a point in time to a measure of transactions over a period of a year or a quarter, which is a *flow* variable. Desirably, stocks should be explained by stocks and flows by flows.[2] However, in practice, the waters have been muddied because current income has been used as a proxy for permanent income, which in turn can be thought of as analogous to wealth, which is a stock term (Friedman, 1956).[3] In principle, Keynesians suggest current income to reflect transactions and precautionary behaviour, while monetarists prefer permanent income because current income includes temporary as well as permanent income and may over- or under-state the levels of sustainable purchasing power.[4]

Recently the suitability of income measures in general has been questioned. Since income excludes many intermediate transactions to avoid double counting it also excludes many intermediate exchanges. Some authors have argued for expenditure rather than income as the scale variable because it avoids these problems (see Goldfeld and Sichel, 1990; Mankiw and Summers, 1986; Hall, Henry, and Wilcox, 1990). Another change is that wealth terms have been added explicitly. Evidence of Grice and Bennett (1984), Hall, Henry, and Wilcox (1989), and Adam (1991) in the UK point to better performance from models of the demand for broad money when wealth is included than when it is left out. Wealth in most cases refers to financial wealth, although non-financial measures, such as valuation of the housing stock, appear to have become more important. The main practical problem is the lack of reliable wealth measures.

The next decision is the choice of the opportunity cost variable. The main question to address here is how many assets are genuine alternatives to money, for this will determine what interest rate (or rates) to include. A yield on a government bond is likely to be preferred by Keynesians as a proxy to 'the' rate of interest, while monetarists would be more inclined to include a number of rates as the returns on equities, bonds, capital goods, and other assets. But this still leaves a considerable choice. For many applications, the issue is not so much to do with the particular rates but how to capture the information in long and short interest rates accurately. This is a matter of choosing a representative rate for the long rate, such as the twenty-year government bond yield or the consol rate, and a short-term interest rate on an asset with a maturity of say three months, such as a three-month Treasury Bill or the three-month interbank rate. The three-month rates move closely together as Figure 11.2 shows, so choosing any one of them is likely to give a good indication of the opportunity cost to money of assets with a short term to maturity. The long term rate is likely to give a better indication of the opportunity cost of money incorporating expectations of the future inflation rates. Including both rates in the same demand function can create estimation problems since these rates are likely to move together. This problem can be overcome by calculating the long–short differential.

Cagan (1956) pioneered the role of the expected rate of change of prices in the demand for money function, but his was a study of hyperinflations. Inflation has not been at particularly high levels in most industrialized countries, although at certain points such as during the oil price shocks, it jumped to high levels. Hendry and Mizon (1978), Hendry (1979, 1985), and Hendry and Ericsson (1991) include inflation as a separate explanatory variable. They and others (see Budd and Holly, 1986; Hall,

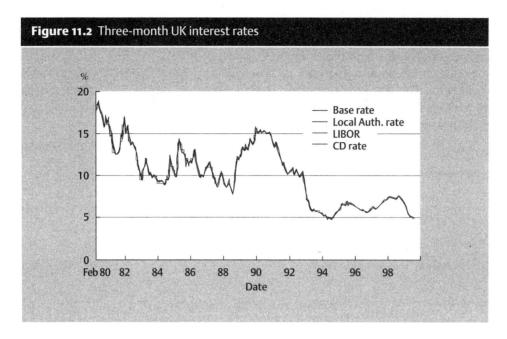

Figure 11.2 Three-month UK interest rates

Henry, and Wilcox, 1989) found that inflation does have an independent effect, per-haps because until the mid-1980s sight deposit accounts in the UK and the USA were non-interest bearing and inflation imposed a significant loss in purchasing power on idle balances.

As a result of deregulation and financial innovation, money has begun to pay inter-est. Barro and Santomero (1972) and Klein (1974) were the first to compute the implied rate of return on money in demand for money functions but the significance of this term has become much greater since the advent of explicit rates on current accounts in the 1980s. Most subsequent studies include an own rate of return on money, such as the seven day deposit rate (that is most relevant to the personal sec-tor) or the rate on certificates of deposit (which represents the rate available to com-panies), often as a differential against the alternative three-month rate (see Taylor, 1987; Grice and Bennet, 1984; Kent, 1985; Adam, 1991; Hendry and Ericsson, 1991).

Specification and functional form

The next step in our monetary 'Cookbook' is to examine the econometric issues and the functional form. Collecting and organizing the data involve choices about the fre-quency of observations, the sample length, and the reliability of the data. For some countries the financial data are available at annual, semi-annual through to quarterly or monthly observations, but the national accounts data are collected less frequently (usually quarterly). In many developing countries, few quarterly data are available and empirical work relies on annual series and longer runs (Ghatak, 1983). Nevertheless, using longer sample lengths has some merits because the random component has less influence due to the smoothing effect of temporal aggregation. Some go further. Friedman and Schwartz (1963a, 1982) deliberately used smoothing methods to average out behaviour over business cycles.[5]

Whatever sample and frequency is chosen, data are usually converted into natural logarithms. This has several benefits. First, it smoothes out the data in comparison to un-logged data. Second, the parameter estimates resulting from an estimated equation are elasticities and are easier to interpret. Consider the regression

$$\ln y_t = \beta \ln x_t + \alpha + \varepsilon_t. \tag{11.1}$$

The parameter, β, is

$$\beta = \frac{d\ln y_t}{d\ln x_t} \simeq \frac{\%\triangle y_t}{\%\triangle x_t} \simeq \frac{\triangle y_t / y_{t-1}}{\triangle x_t / x_{t-1}} = \frac{\triangle y_t}{\triangle x_t} \cdot \frac{x_{t-1}}{y_{t-1}}. \tag{11.2}$$

When the regression is run in levels:

$$y_t = \beta_1 x_t + \alpha_1 + \varepsilon_t, \tag{11.3}$$

then $\beta_1 = \dfrac{dy_t}{dx_t} \equiv \dfrac{\triangle y_t}{\triangle x_t}$ and needs to be converted to an elasticity by multiplication by $\dfrac{x_{t-1}}{y_{t-1}}$. This is cumbersome and needs to be done for every variable—it is simply easier to take logarithms of the data at the beginning.

Third, equations in logarithmic form allow non-linear specifications to be estimated in such a way that the powers are elasticities. A non-linear function form, which is difficult to estimate such as

$$y_t = AX_t^B exp^{Cz_t} \tag{11.4}$$

can be easily estimated in a log-linear format as

$$\ln y_t = \ln A + B \ln x_t + Cz_t + \varepsilon_t. \tag{11.5}$$

Since most empirical researchers use logarithmically transformed data, we refer to lower-case variables as natural logs throughout.

The sole exception to this rule is the treatment of interest rates. Since these are measured in percentages in the first place, the variable does not have to be logged in order to produce an elasticity. In (11.5) the parameter, C, is referred to as a semi-elasticity since

$$C = \frac{d\log y_t}{dz_t} \simeq \frac{\triangle y_t / y_{t-1}}{\triangle z_t} = \frac{\triangle y_t}{\triangle z} \cdot \frac{1}{y_{t-1}}. \tag{11.6}$$

This is not identical to an elasticity but is very similar and can be interpreted in much the same way.

Once we have adopted a log-linear format we can cover a vast range of functional forms represented by powers on explanatory variables (these are the elasticities estimated in the model). The models can be treated as if they were linear in estimation since the variables are entered linearly into the regression. Non-linearities can still exist, through products of explanatory variables e.g.:

$$y_t = \alpha + \beta\, x_t.z_t + \varepsilon_t \tag{11.7}$$

or through non-linearities in parameters e.g.:

$$y_t = \alpha + \beta\,(1-\alpha)\,x_t + \varepsilon_t. \tag{11.8}$$

But most models are specified as linear-in-variables, linear in parameters.

The identification problem

The possibility that the demand for money function may represent more than one economic relationship cannot be assured even when the variables are confirmed as exogenous. The identification of the estimated relationship with a demand for money function makes certain assumptions about the exogeneity of the money supply process. If the nominal money supply is truly exogenous and varies independently of the demand for it, then the estimated demand for money relationship will be correctly identified (in real terms). If, on the other hand, the money supply is endogenous, responding to the demand for money in a passive sense, then the estimated relationship will not be a true reflection of the demand for money function. Instead the relationship will represent a line of best-fit between points of monetary equilibrium. In this case the explanatory variables affect both the supply and the demand for money, and the demand for money function cannot therefore be identified from econometric estimates.

To demonstrate this point consider the Figure 11.3. In the first panel, money supply is considered exogenous, as a result it is possible to identify a variable or set of variables which shift the supply function but leave the demand function unchanged. As the identifying variable changes the supply function shifts from S_0 to S_1 to S_2 but the demand for money function does not shift. The econometric estimation of the demand for money function yields a line of best-fit for the points of equilibrium between supply and demand, labelled A, B, C, and correctly identifies the demand for money function.

In the second panel the supply of money is endogenous. The demand and the supply of money both shift in response to the same set of variables and there is no variable which can uniquely identify the demand or the supply function. When the demand for money function is estimated the econometric model fits a line of best-fit to the equilibrium positions A, D, E, which do not identify a unique demand for money function. In this particular case, the econometric estimates of the demand for money suggest that the demand function is not as steep as it is in reality.

The lesson to be learned from this is that the estimation of the demand for money function must be conducted with caution, since there are many econometric pitfalls which can befall the unwary. A clear understanding of the nature of the relationships between the independent variables as well as the demand and supply of money are necessary preconditions before attempting to isolate a seemingly simple demand for money relationship.

Figure 11.3 The identification problem

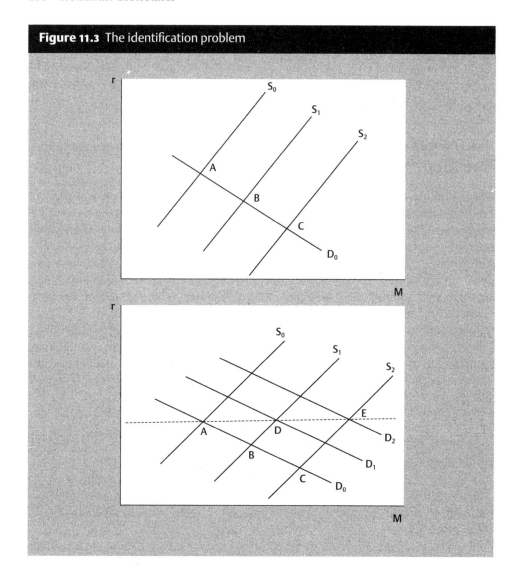

Lags and dynamics

The correct identification of the function as demand rather than supply is a necessary step before we can examine with any confidence the long-run relationship between money income, prices, and interest rates. Equally important for the specification of the short-run model is an appreciation of the dynamics of adjustment from a current balance to a desired (long-run) balance.

The long-run desired level of money balances can be thought of as the level of real balances consistent with theoretical requirements given the values of the exogenous explanatory variables. If we assume that these balances are known at any point in time as the result of an optimization process, then the short-run demand for money can be thought of as a temporary balance (completely consistent with optimizing behaviour) conditional on the desired long-run objective and the speed of adjustment towards it. Writing the long-run equation as

$$m_t^* = \alpha p_t + \beta y_t + \gamma R_t + \varepsilon_t \tag{11.9}$$

we can write the short-run adjustment problem as the aim to minimize the cost of deviating from the target, m_t^*, and the cost of making an adjustment to money balances. Following Chow (1966), we assume that the cost function is quadratic:

$$C = [a_1(m_t^* - m_{t-1})^2 + a_2 (m_t - m_{t-1})^2]. \tag{11.10}$$

Taking the derivative and setting equal to zero gives:

$$\frac{dC_t}{dm_t} = 2a_1(m_t^* - m_{t-1}) + 2a_2 (m_t - m_{t-1}) = 0. \tag{11.11}$$

Hence

$$(m_t - m_{t-1}) = -\frac{a_1}{a_2} (m_t^* - m_{t-1}) \tag{11.12}$$

or

$$(m_t - m_{t-1}) = \triangle m_t = -\frac{a_1}{a_2} (m_t^* - m_{t-1}) = \theta(m_t^* - m_{t-1}). \tag{11.13}$$

In which the adjustment to equilibrium (m_t^*) takes place at a given rate based on the cost of adjustment a_2 relative to the cost of deviating from the target a_1. Clearly this equation gives information about the adjustment process; and dynamics and the lag structure of the short-run equation are shown to be related. A proportion of the deviation from target is eliminated every period by a dynamic change to money balances. According to the cost function the result is consistent with an optimization of the adjustment process, hence the choice of the sequence of balances $m_{t-2}, m_{t-1}, m_t, m_{t+1}, \ldots$ is optimal even though they are not necessarily equal to the long-run desired money balance, m_t^*.

More general forms of adjustment involving more complex lag structures will be considered below with error correction models and autoregressive distributed lag structures. For the moment we restrict ourselves to a consideration of the implications of a single lagged dependent variable in the functional form. To do so we substitute the long-run equation into the short-run adjustment process to give:

$$m_t = \theta (\alpha p_t + \beta y_t + \gamma R_t) + (1 - \theta)m_{t-1} + \theta\varepsilon_t. \tag{11.14}$$

There is an immediate question about this. The parameter θ represents the speed of adjustment to disequilibrium in the money demand equation and unless this is unity, in which case the lagged dependent variable drops out and adjustment is instantaneous, the adjustment is sluggish. A smaller value of θ implies a slower adjustment process, this can be confirmed from the relationship $\triangle m_t = \theta(m_t^* - m_{t-1})$. The parameter α represents the responsiveness of nominal money balances, m_t, to prices, p_t. If $\alpha = 1$, as is often the case by construction of the model in terms of *real* money balances, then there is an instantaneous response of nominal balances to prices but a sluggish response of nominal balances to deviations from equilibrium. Laidler (1993) has argued that this leads to an inconsistency in the treatment of adjustment.

The inclusion of a lagged dependent variable can be also questioned on econometric grounds. When a lagged dependent variable is included in a regression equation (i.e. nominal money balances in our model) the parameter estimates can be biased. The result emerges if the error term for the long-run equation is positively correlated; then the parameter on the lagged dependent variable will be biased upwards. The problem can be overcome but if it remains undetected it may leave the researcher to draw inference about the speed of adjustment, θ, that is unwarranted, since an upwardly biased estimate on the lagged dependent variable implies a slower adjustment speed than it should.

11.3 Historical Overview of Empirical Work

HAVING considered the empirical issues, we can now review some of the work that has been done.

Long-run estimates of the demand for money

Long-run studies have assumed an equilibrium relationship between real money balances, income, and interest rates of the form

$$m_t^* = \alpha p_t + \beta y_t + \gamma R_t + \varepsilon_t, \tag{11.15}$$

where α, β, and γ are parameters to be estimated, m_t^* denotes the desired level of money balances, p_t is the price level, y_t is the level of output, and R_t is the interest rate. All variables in lower case are in logarithms and ε_t is an error term.

The first statistical studies of the demand for money were in fact of Keynes's liquidity preference function, based on a distinction between active and idle balances, and were undertaken, first, by Arthur Brown (1939) for the UK and then for the USA by James Tobin (1947). These were followed in the UK by Paish (1958, 1959) and Dow (1958) based on graphical analyses (see Figure 11.4). In the USA, the first econometric study of the overall demand for money function was by Henry Latané (1954), followed by Meltzer (1963), who found a negative relationship with interest rates using annual US data from 1900 to 1958, and Laidler (1966a, b) who came to the same conclusion and showed stability for the subperiods 1892–1916, 1919–40, 1946–65. Work on the UK by Kavanagh and Walters (1966) and Laidler (1971) gave similar results creating the belief that the long-run demand for money function was stable and predictable with a significant negative relationship between money balances and interest rates. Subsequent studies reported in Tables 11.1 and 11.2 have not

Table 11.1 Long-run studies of the demand for money in the UK

Authors	Sample period	Money variable	Income variable	Interest rate	Elasticity with respect to		Comments
					Income	Interest rate	
Kavanagh and Walters (1966)	1880–1961	M1	National income	Consol rate	1.15	−0.31	
		M2	National income	Consol rate	1.27	−0.46	
	1926–60	M1	National income	Consol rate	0.96	−0.50	
Laidler (1971)	1900–65 excl. war years	M2	Permanent income	Consol rate	0.80	−0.57	
				Treasury bill rate	0.67	−0.15	
Graves (1980)	1911–66	M1	National income	Commercial bill rate	0.30	−0.10	Instability in standard equations; includes variable for urbanization and age of distribution populations
Friedman and Schwarz (1982)	1874–1975	M2/M3	Net national product	Commercial bill rate less own rate	0.88	−0.19	Dummy variables for inter-war and post-war shifts
Batts and Dowling (1984)	1880–1975	M1	Net national product	Commercial bill rate	0.57	−0.07	Instability evident around war years and possibly 1970s
		M2	Net national product	Commercial bill rate	0.47	−0.08	
Artis and Lewis (1984)	1920–81 excl. 1973–6	M2	GDP	Consol rate	1.00	−0.59	Possible shift during war years
Longbottom and Holly (1985)	1878–1975	M2/M3	NNP	Commercial bill rate less own rate	1.08	−0.09	Dummy variables for shift in war years. Possible instability in 1930s. Inclusion of CDs gives instability in 1970s
Hendry and Ericsson (1991)	1875–1970	M2/M3	NNP	Long rate	1.00	−0.40	National debt/real income ratio significant

Table 11.2 Long-run studies of the demand for money in the USA

Study	Data	Money variable	Income variable	Interest rate	Elasticity with respect to Income	Elasticity with respect to Interest rate	Comments
Latané (1954)	1919–52	M1	GNP	Long-term Corporate bond yield	1.00	−0.70	Velocity measure used Income elasticity constrained to unity
Meltzer (1963)	1900–58	M1 M2	NNP Wealth	Corporate bond yield Corporate bond yield	1.05 1.32	−0.79 −0.50	Compares income, wealth and and permanent income
Laidler (1966a)	1919–60 1892–1960	M2 M2	Permanent income Permanent income	Corporate bond yield Corporate bond yield	1.15 1.51	−0.72 −0.25	Also uses first differences
Chow (1966)	1897–1958 excl. war years	M1	Permanent income	Corporate bond yield	1.06	−0.74	Using lagged money stock
Laidler (1971)	1900–65 excl. war years	M2	Permanent income	Long-term Corporate bond yield CP rate	0.93 1.31 1.26	−0.79 −0.39 −0.19	
Khan (1974)	1901–65	M1	Permanent income	Corporate bond yield Commercial paper rate	0.65 1.09	−0.30 −0.12	Evidence of some instability when short-term rate used
Gandolfi and Lothian (1976)	1929–68	M2	Permanent income	Bond rate less own rate on deposits	1.20	−0.46	Instability reflected in changes in intercepts
Laumas and Mehra (1977)	1900–74	M1 M2	Permanent income Permanent income	Long-term bond rate Long-term bond rate	0.90 1.07	−0.46 −0.28	No evidence of change in parameters
Friedman and Schwartz (1982)	1873–1975 cycle average data	M2	NNP	Difference of commercial paper rate over own rate	1.15	−0.19	Dummy variable to allow functions to shift during inter-war and at end of war
Lucas (1987)	1900–85	M1	Permanent NNP	CP rate	0.97	−0.07	Instability unless income elasticity is constrained to unity
Wenninger (1988)	1915–87 quarterly	M1 M2	GNP GNP	CP rate CP rate	0.86 1.04	−0.36 −0.14	Persistent pattern of instability for M1, less so for M2

Figure 11.4 Interest rates and the demand for money, 1921–1958

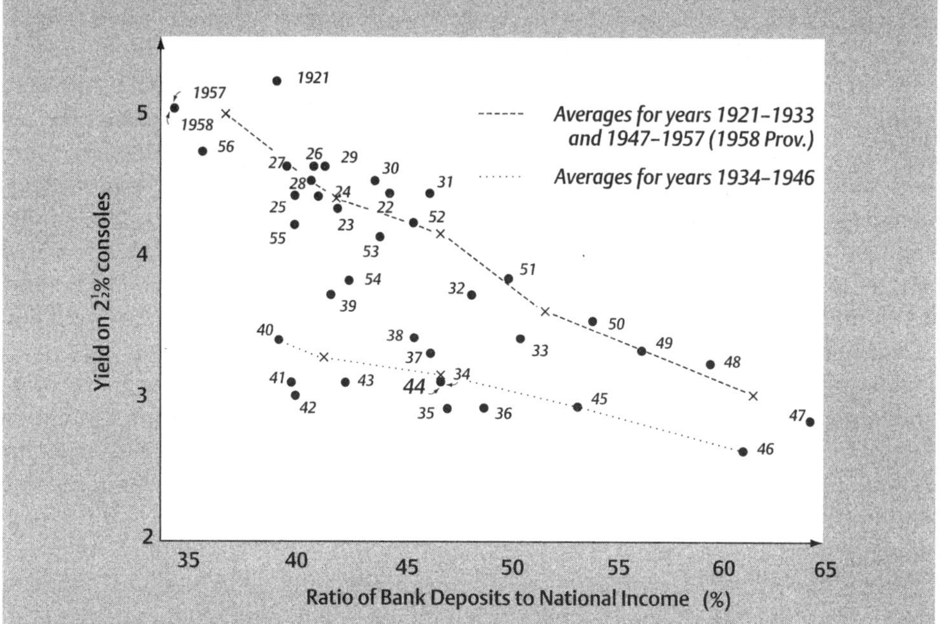

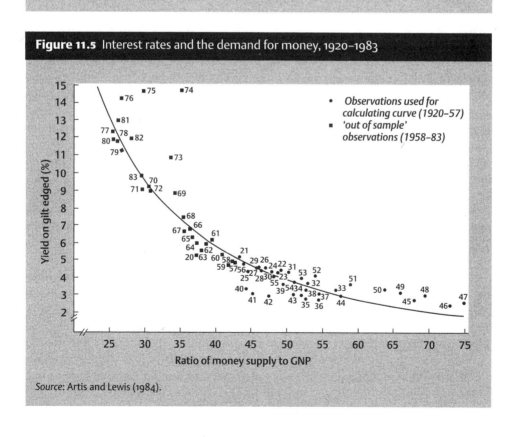

Source: Paish (1959).

Figure 11.5 Interest rates and the demand for money, 1920–1983

Source: Artis and Lewis (1984).

undermined the conclusions that the coefficients on income and prices imply income elasticities of around unity and the homogeneity of nominal money demand in prices. These results appear to be remarkably robust to the choice of scale variable and to the breadth of monetary aggregate.

In more recent examinations a similar range of results seems to apply. Artis and Lewis (1984) redrew and re-estimated Paish and Dow's graphical analysis for an extended data set confirming the original relationship (see Figure 11.5). Patterson (1987) suggested more rigorous techniques but effectively corroborated the main findings including the critical price and income elasticities. In effect, the Artis–Lewis equation can be thought of as the long-run relationship underlying a short-run dynamic model of the type employed by Patterson, as Cuthbertson (1991) has pointed out. This is a useful insight because it enables us to write the equation as a function of two variables, the ratio of money supply to nominal income, (M/PY) and the interest rate (r).

Plotting the data for Artis–Lewis and Patterson shows clearly the inverse relationship between (M/PY) and r predicted by theory: in fact the regression line (calculated using the data used by Paish and Dow) is very like the demand for money schedule printed in most macroeconomic textbooks. There are some departures from the line during the war years and the high inflation episodes in the mid-1970s but the relationship is otherwise remarkably constant.

Other authors such as Friedman and Schwartz (1982) reported a similar stability in their estimates of the long-run money demand function in both the UK and the USA. Friedman and Schwartz used a cycle-averaging technique to convert data into averages over business cycle phases, to eliminate the short-run cyclical component. Hendry and Ericsson (1983, 1991) argued that the method loses vital information and arbitrarily determines temporary departures from the equilibrium relationship effectively imposing regularities on the long-run money demand function. Despite the severe criticism of their methodology, the results of Friedman and Schwartz have stood the test of time, and appear to have become the accepted norm. Ironically, Longbottom and Holly (1985) found evidence confirming Friedman and Schwartz's model for the UK using Hendry's own methodology, and Hendry and Ericsson themselves confirm the existence of a stable demand for money function over the period 1875–1970. These long-run results point to a more substantial and reliable relationship in the demand for money function than is evident in the short run.

Estimates of the demand for money short run

Up to the mid-1970s there was a consensus that the demand for money could be accurately represented by a long-run equation denoting equilibrium and a process of partial adjustment to describe the dynamics. As we have seen, the partial adjustment hypothesis introduced short-run dynamics to explain how money balances would be adjusted in the event that current balances, m_t, did not correspond to the desired long-run level, m_t^*. The rationale in terms of error-learning was that individuals would observe the difference between the actual and desired levels of money balances in the previous period and would make adjustments to their actual balances in such a way as to reduce the gap. The adjustment process could be described using Chow's method (11.12), giving (11.14) as the empirical specification. This model was estimated using both annual and quarterly data for both the UK and the USA from the beginning of the 1970s and it performed well, fitting the data within the sample and predicting accurately out of sample.

Laidler and Parkin (1970) and Goodhart and Crockett (1970) were the first to use the partial adjustment model in the UK, followed by Goldfeld (1973) in the USA, and initially these models appeared to perform well. Other studies are reported in Table 11.3 for both the USA and the UK and the negatively signed interest rate coefficient is again confirmed although there is much more disagreement over its magnitude. The short-run model provided the necessary information required for monetary policy and so stable was the relationship that the 'Goldfeld equation' became the standard framework.

On reflection, two features should have pointed to its later difficulties in the mid-1970s when the model appeared to falter and ultimately broke down. In the first place there was an inconsistency between the quarterly and the annual demand for money results. The annual studies assumed that there was full adjustment within a single year (one observation), and when quarterly data were introduced it became possible to put this assumption to the test by examining the speed of adjustment parameter, θ which quantifies the amount of adjustment taking place in each of the four quarters. The results suggested that the actual speed of adjustment was less than 50 per cent, and occasionally as low as 15 per cent, of the difference between the actual and the desired level of money balances in one year. The adjustment to equilibrium took much more than one year. Lags of this length surprised many economists since the findings implied that the money market was more sluggish than initially had been thought.

The second inconsistency appeared in the estimated interest rate elasticities. Theory suggested that it was reasonable to expect close money substitutes to have high interest elasticities since only a slight change in interest rates ought to provoke a redistribution of portfolios. Evidence from the short-run money demand studies indicated that the reverse was the case. Longer-term securities appeared to have higher interest rate elasticities with money despite the fact that they might be considered to be poorer substitutes. The statistical reason for this result was the lower amplitude of the cyclical fluctuations in interest rates on longer-term assets compared with short rates. Expectations of future short-term rates are generally considered to be the dominant influence on the yield curve but the authorities tend to conduct transactions at the shorter end of the market which may have an effect. If so, the functional form which implies that interest rates exogenously determine money balances with a long lag will be called into question. We return to this point when we consider the responses to the instability of the short-run demand for money function, but before we do so we consider in more detail how the short-run demand for money function foundered.

Table 11.3 Short-run studies of the demand for money in the UK and USA

Study	Data	Money variable	Income variable	Interest rates	Elasticity with respect to Income	Elasticity with respect to Interest rate	Comments
USA							
Heller (1965)	1954–9	M1 M2	GNP GNP	Commercial paper rate Commercial paper rate	1.08 1.41	−0.10 −0.18	No adjustment lags
Goldfeld (1973)	1955–72	M1	GNP	Commercial paper rate Time deposit rate	0.53	−0.05 −0.12	Nominal adjustment
Garcia-Pak (1979)	1952–76	M1	GNP	Commercial paper rate	1.26	−0.96	Implausibly long lags
Boughton (1979)	1960–77	M1	GNP	Commercial paper rate Time deposit rate Commercial paper rate	* 1.20	* −0.11	Lagged coefficient exceeds unity; instability after 1973
Gordon (1984)	1956–72	M1	GNP	Savings deposit rate	0.43	−0.03	Instability offer 1972; need to add supply shocks
Anderson (1985)	1960–83	M1	GNP	90-day bankers' acceptances	(1) 0.83 (2) 0.86	−0.24 −0.64	(1) Standard equation. Long lags found (4-year average lag) (2) Interest rate adjustment Average lag 3 quarters
Baba, Hendry and Starr (1992)	1960(3)– 88(3)	MI	GNP	Treasury bill rate long bond—Treasury bill spread	0.51	−3.96	Overcomes the instability of the Goldfield equation but questionable elasticities

UK

Study	Period	Money	Scale variable	Interest rate variable	Scale coeff.	Interest coeff.	Notes
Laidler and Parkin (1970)	1955–67	M2	GDP	Treasury bill	0.59	−0.02	
Goodhart and Crockett (1970)	1955(3)–69(3)	M1	GDP	3mo LA	1.25	−1.05	
				Consol	1.09	−0.00	
	1963(2)–9(3)	M3	GDP	3mo LA	1.41	−0.21	
				Consol	1.54	−0.51	
Price (1972)	1964(1)–70(4)	M3	GDP	Consol	(1) 2.29	−0.37	(1) Personal sector
				3 mo LA	(2) 2.77	−0.36	(2) Corporate sector
Hacche (1974)	1963(40–72(4)	M1	TFE	3mo LA	0.70	−0.06	
				Consol		−0.21	
	1963(4)–72(4)	M3	TFE	3mo LA	*	*	(2) Inserting interest rate variable for shift after 1971
					1.00	−0.25	
Artis and Lewis (1976)	1963(2)–73(1)	M1	GDP	Consol	1.24	−0.66	Instability in 1971
	1963(2)–73(1)	M3	GDP	Consol	(1) 3.89	−0.46	(1) Standard equation
					(2) 1.21	−0.34	(2) Interest rate adjustment equation
Hamburger (1977)	1963(1)–70(4)	M1	GDP	3mo Eurodollar	0.67	−1.07	No adjustment lags in model; Instability in 1972
Coghlan (1978)	1964(1)–76(4)	M1	TFE	3mo LA	1.01	−0.30	Complex adjustment lags; No instability
Boughton (1979)	1963(2)–77(3)	M1	GDP	3mo LA	1.32	−0.51	Instability in 1971
	1963(2)–77(3)	M£	GDP	Consol	•	•	Instability evident
Grice and Bennett (1984)	1963–78	M3	TFE	Return on gilts	0.32	0	Dynamic instability present; dummy variable added
Goodhart (1984a)	1963(4)–73(4)	M3	TFE	Local authority rate CD rate	0.66	−0.19	Picks up evidence of round tripping

Study	Data	Money variable	Income variable	Interest rates	Elasticity with respect to		Comments
					Income	Interest rate	
Anderson (1985)	1960–83	M1	GDP	(1) Treasury bill rate (2) Treasury bill rate	0.68 0.70	−0.45 −0.49	(1) Standard equation (2) Interest rate adjustment
Taylor (1987)	1964(2)–85(4)	£M3	TFE	Long bond yield 3 month Treasury Bill/ deposit rate spread	1.00	−0.26	First use of cointegration for broad money in UK
Hall, Hendry and Wilcox (1990)		M1 M4	TFE GDP	Consol rate	1.0 1.0	−0.03	First attempt to use multivariate cointegration methods
Hendry and Ericsson (1991)	1878–1970	M2	NNP	Long term rate own yield on money	1.0	−7.0	A critique of the Friedman and Schwartz model of Monetary Trends in the US and the UK. Friedman and Schwartz regarded it as an alternative not a contradiction
Fisher and Vega (1993)	1977(1)–92(4)	Sectoral M4	Personal sector real disposable income. Corporate sector Real financial wealth	3 month Treasury bill/ deposit rate spread Long bond yield/ LIBOR spread	0.5 1.0	−1.92 −8.82	Among the first published sectoral estimates of M4. Includes wealth variable explicitly

11.4 Instability in the Money Demand Function

IN Britain, it was the work of Hacche (1974) that showed conclusively that the partial adjustment model was unable to predict accurately outside of sample for the period after 1971, recording significant negative forecasting errors for broad, narrow, and sectoral aggregates. In the USA, Goldfeld (1976) came to the same conclusion showing that his model broke down from 1974, overpredicting money balances and implying that there was some 'missing money' the existence of which had yet to be explained. Despite considerable effort on both sides of the Atlantic the model was not easily corrected to account for the inexplicable events of the period.

Initial attempts to understand the episode focused on the unusual monetary conditions which had led to greater financial innovation. Hacche experimented with the yield on certificates of deposit as an additional explanatory variable in an otherwise unchanged partial adjustment model, restoring some of the predictive performance of the money demand function. Investigation by Artis and Lewis (1974, 1976), however, concluded that in experiments with different aggregates in real, nominal, and per capita terms, even excluding CDs altogether, it was not possible to reverse the conclusion that the partial adjustment model suffered from serious prediction errors. Goldfeld, in the USA, added the interest on NOW and thrift accounts to the otherwise standard money demand function, and, whilst he did remove the over-predictions to some degree, he remained unconvinced that this was the root cause of the problem. These unexplained patterns of behaviour in the 1970s introduced a new agenda for empirical studies of the demand for money, which had ceased to be much more than routine applications of the accepted Goldfeld model. Both Goldfeld (1976) and Artis and Lewis (1976) concluded that the theory behind money demand estimation needed overhauling and in many respects the research agenda of the next twenty-five years was set by the breakdown of the partial adjustment theory.

Three possibilities were to form the basis of new research:

1. One conclusion was that the basic money demand function was misspecified all the time and its acceptable performance was coincidental. If this were the case, then the annual extensions to the data set and the increase in the number of studies were eventually bound to reveal the misspecification. The way to rectify the money demand equation would be to respecify the model for the whole period.

2. A related possibility was that the long-run equation, which had remained much more stable than the short-run equation, was correctly specified but that the short-run dynamics were incorrectly understood. In this case the dynamic specification for the model would need to be overhauled although the long-run relationship could remain intact.

3. Alternatively, while the demand function was correctly specified for the 1960s,

a structural break may have occurred in the mid-1970s, which would have changed the nature of the relationship from that point on. In that case, the model would need respecifying only for the period after the break.

We consider the first under the heading *buffer stock models* and the second and third points under the heading *econometric advances*.

11.5 Buffer Stock Models

IN a far-sighted comment on Goldfeld's paper which exposed the breakdown in the USA, William Brainard made two observations. In the first place he noted that in the case of the missing money 'Inspectors Perry and Gordon of the Price Squad must take a certain pleasure in finding that their colleagues working on the money side of the street are encountering difficulties just like those that plagued them in the case of the vagrant Phillips curve' (1976: 732). In this Brainard was making the point that it was surely not a coincidence that two of the most important equations for economic policy-making—the Phillips curve and the demand for money function—had failed in similar economic circumstances. Common causes should have been suspected and investigated.

His second observation concerned the treatment of the dynamics of the demand for money and the effect of factors such as transitory income and money supply shocks. If the partial adjustment model was to be believed, the LM curve shifted in a very spectacular fashion in response to transitory income receipts and money supply shocks during the period under investigation by Goldfeld, which seemed contrary to a transactions model. More plausible, Brainard suggested, would be an explanation which is consistent with the transactions model where 'money balances serve as a buffer stock, or a temporary abode of purchasing power, and one would expect the transitory income to be absorbed passively in money holdings in the short run' (1976: 735).

Buffer stock models pick up this last point and recognize that there can be departures from equilibrium in the money market based on commonly accepted micro-economic principles. The idea that all individuals hold their long-run desired money balances at all times and are continuously on the LM curve is replaced by the more realistic view that temporary departures can be rational and optimal. There are four groups of models to be considered. First, *flow disequilibrium models* question the direction of causality between money and other variables reversing the money demand relationship to make money balances exogenous and some other variables, e.g. prices, income, or interest rates endogenous. Second, *shock-absorber models*, introduce expectations into the analysis and allow unexpected and anticipated events to affect the money demand function in different ways. The third group of models extend the shock-absorber principle to an infinite horizon of future events and are known as *forward-looking buffer stock models*. Lastly, there are a separate group of models based on

Table 11.4 Buffer stock models of the demand for money

Authors	Sample	Money variable	Countries	Main findings
Flow disequilibrium models				
Artis and Lewis (1976)	1953(1)–73(4)	M1 M2	UK	Slow interest rate adjustment found to be responsible for instability in money demand function
Laidler (1980)	1953(1)–78(1)	M1	USA	Tests of interest rate model, sticky price model, and expenditure models with money as an explanatory variable
Shock absorber models				
Carr and Darby (1981)	1957(1)–76(4)	M1	UK, USA, Canada, France, Germany, Japan, Netherlands, Italy	Unexpected money supply shocks augment the partial adjustment model
MacKinnon and Milbourne (1984)	1953(1)–78(4)	M1	USA	Overturns the Carr–Darby result
Carr, Darby, and Thornton (1985)	1957(1)–76(4)	M1	USA	Re-establish the original shock absorber model
Cuthbertson and Taylor (1987b)	1964(2)–81(4)	M1	UK	Confirm Carr and Darby results generating shocks from ARIMA and Kalman Filter models
Boughton and Tavlas (1989)	1964(1)–85(4)	M1/M2	UK, USA, Japan (1973(1)–85(4)), France, Germany	Establishes international credentials of the buffer stock model
Forward-looking models				
Kanniainen and Tarkka (1986)	1960(2)–82(4)	M1	USA, Australia, Germany, Finland, Sweden	Some support for a forward-looking model
Cuthbertson and Taylor (1987b)	1963(1)–83(3)	M1	UK	Strong support for a forward-looking model
Muscatelli (1988)	1963(1)–84(4)	M1	UK	Test against a general error correction model (ECM), favours the ECM
Hendry (1989)	1964(3)–79(4)	M1	UK	Tests forward versus feedback model. Favours general-to-specific model on the basis of econometric evidence
Mizen (1992)	1966(1)–89(2)	M1 M4	UK	Tests the validity of broad versus narrow money model of forward-looking model
Mizen (1994)	1966(1)–89(2)	Personal sector M1/M4 Corporate sector M1/M4	UK UK	Tests the Cuthbertson and Taylor forward-looking model on sectoral data

the *inventory management approach* that have a quite different microeconomic foundation to the previous types of buffer stock models.

Flow disequilibrium models

After the initial failure of the demand for money function a number of authors questioned the direction of causality implicit in money demand functions. In the standard interpretation at the time the money stock was supposed to be caused by the independent variables such as price, income, and interest rates. Artis and Lewis (1976) and Laidler (1982) asked whether causality might in fact run the other way (especially in a period of floating exchange rates) with the nominal money supply exogenous and the other variables endogenous—Artis and Lewis (1976) and Lewis (1978) selecting interest rates, Walters (1965), Laidler (1982), and Wren-Lewis (1984) choosing the price level, and Jonson (1976) using expenditures. The general procedure was to invert the money demand function by isolating the dependent variable and taking the remaining variables to the other side of the equation, as follows:

$$z_t^* = m_t^S - f(\mathbf{X_t}), \tag{11.16}$$

where $f(\mathbf{X_t})$ is a function of a vector of independent variables, z_t is the chosen dependent variable, and m_t^S is the money supply. The chosen variable z_t is supposed to adjust slowly according to a partial adjustment approach as follows:

$$z_t - z_{t-1} = \theta(z_t^* - z_{t-1}) \tag{11.17}$$

and the equation for z_t^* is substituted into it and rearranged to give a correctly specified money demand function.

Considering the Artis and Lewis (1976) model in which the dependent variable is the interest rate, a money demand function can be written in the form:

$$(m - p)_t = \phi + \beta y_t^p + \gamma R_t, \tag{11.18}$$

where p_t, is prices, y_t^p is permanent income, and R_t is the interest rate. Interest rates follow a partial adjustment process to adjust to the equilibrium rate R_t^*

$$R_t - R_{t-1} = \theta (R_t^* - R_{t-1}) \text{ for } 0 \le \theta \le 1. \tag{11.19}$$

By substituting the long-run equation for R_t^* into this adjustment model gives:

$$R_t = \frac{\theta}{\gamma} ((m - p)_t - \phi - \beta y_t^p) + (1 - \theta) R_{t-1}. \tag{11.20}$$

This equation was estimated for the UK using M1 and M2 over the period 1953(1) to 1973(4), and was tested by Laidler (1980) for the USA using M1. In each of these cases autocorrelation was found to be quite severe and Laidler showed that there was also simultaneous equation bias.

Laidler (1982) suggested a similar alternative based on the idea that the money demand equation 'might be interpreted as a price level adjustment equation in an economy where nominal balances are exogenous'. Therefore inverting a money demand equation gives the equilibrium price level

$$p_t^* = m_t^S - f(\mathbf{X_t}) \tag{11.21}$$

and with a 'sticky' price level which adjusts slowly according to a partial adjustment mechanism as follows

$$p_t - p_{t-1} = \theta\,(p_t^* - p_{t-1}) \text{ for } 0 \le \theta \le 1 \tag{11.22}$$

the equation could be written

$$p_t = (1 - \theta)\,p_{t-1} + \theta\,m_t^S - \theta\,f(\mathbf{X_t}). \tag{11.23}$$

Laider then showed that by adding money balances to both sides, a version of the standard money demand equation could be derived, but with a crucial change in the final term. Here $(m_t - p_{t-1})$ has replaced $(m_{t-1} - p_{t-1})$ in the original equation—a minor and probably insignificant change in periods of low inflation, but vital and important during periods when quarter-on-quarter changes to money and prices are large, as they were in the 1970s. The new equation is:

$$(m - p)_t = \theta\,f(\mathbf{X_t}) + (1 - \theta)(m_t - p_{t-1}). \tag{11.24}$$

The model is one of a price equation which does not overshoot, but rather allows buffer stocks in money balances to be held in the short-run while over the longer-run the price level adjusts partially to the equilibrium price level. Wren-Lewis (1984) tested this model, empirically assessing the relevant variables and lag lengths required in the $\mathbf{X_t}$ vector. This process suffers again from simultaneous equation bias—a criticism which Laidler himself noted. At a theoretical level the model omits a number of variables which could be considered important in determining prices. In this sense, it is derived from the money demand function alone, and does not allow other areas of the economy besides the monetary sector to impinge on prices. The likelihood that the other variables would later evolve in response to the money supply shock, in addition to the evolution of the chosen dependent variable, to bring the money market to equilibrium meant that they could not be treated as exogenous variables except in the very short-run. Attempts to incorporate these insights into larger models with many endogenous variables can be found in Jonson and Trevor (1979) for Australia, Spinelli (1979) for Italy, Laidler and O'Shea (1980) for the UK, and Laidler and Bentley (1983) for Canada.

When 'reverse-causation' was initially broached, there was the belief that it implied overshooting of the arguments of the demand function in response to an exogenous money supply shock, along the lines of Tucker (1966). Using the interest rate as an example in the standard partial adjustment money demand function the short-run interest elasticity is greater than the long-run elasticity and therefore over-shooting occurs. The problem with this interpretation was that there was no ob-servable evidence to suggest that the short-run interest rate, or for that matter the price level or the output variable, exhibited overshooting of the long-run value in practice. Nor is it clear that there should be. Starleaf (1970) argued that the standard partial adjustment model cannot be applied to situations where the money stock is exogenous, and overshooting in any case relies on the money market always clearing.

The buffer stock concept was therefore introduced to explain how the market coped with a money supply shock by absorbing the impact of the shock in a buffer stock rather than by causing the short-run value of the dependent variable to over-shoot its long-run value. This meant that the response of an individual who experienced a shock to the money supply was to increase or decrease money balances held to offset the shock and in the long-term to return to desired money holdings as the interest rate, price level, or expenditure level changes.

Shock-absorber models

An alternative approach was taken by the models which introduced expectations, and built on the work by Lucas (1973), Sargent and Wallace (1975), and Barro (1977, 1978) examined in Chapter 9. Under rational expectations, an expected change to the nominal money supply is neutral, since the impact is taken up in the price level and other nominal variables. It was noted by Carr and Darby (1981) that the partial adjustment mechanism proposed by Chow (1966) fitted this case. However, it did not deal well with an *unexpected* shock to the money stock.

Carr and Darby (1981) added a 'surprise term' to allow money supply shocks and temporary income to push real money balances 'off' the demand for money for some time. An unexpected money supply shock would not be neutral, and would differ in its effect on money demand from anticipated supply shocks. Empirical research seemed to confirm that an unexpected shock to the money stock had very little impact on prices. Accordingly, a quantity effect, operating through real money balances, must take up the shock. If this were so, then, under the partial adjustment model, the desired level of money balances would have to increase markedly in order to keep real money balances on the short-run money demand function. But for this to be possible the impact on real variables, income, and interest rates, would be very great and Carr and Darby showed by means of an example that the requirements were totally implausible. Having demonstrated Starleaf's objection to the Chow partial adjustment mechanism in the face of (in this case unexpected) nominal money supply shocks, they went on to incorporate a 'surprise term' into the original partial adjustment mechanism.

The 'surprise term' was introduced in two ways. Firstly, the term $(m_t - m_t^a)$ was added to the partial adjustment model to reflect unexpected, 'off' the demand curve nominal money supply shocks, where m_t^a is the anticipated money supply, and m_t is the actual money supply; and, secondly, transitory income, y_t^T was included since money was suggested to be the temporary abode of any unexpected variations to income. The result was an equation which allowed for positive and negative variations to money balances in response to unexpected events in the short run and is very similar to the original partial adjustment equation since

$$m_t = (1 - \lambda)m_{t-1} + \lambda m_t^* + p_t + by_t^T + f(m_t - m_t^a) + u_t, \tag{11.25}$$

where transitory income, y_t^T is defined as current minus permanent income and long-run 'desired' money holdings, m_t^*, are described as a function of permanent income, and interest rates; λ, b, and f are coefficients from the modified partial adjustment model.

If the coefficients f and b are significantly different from zero the partial adjustment specification omits crucial buffer stock variables. During periods of relative calm the former model would be expected to perform reasonably well, but when the expectational errors become more important they will be the cause of serious forecast errors as observed in the mid-1970s.[6] Carr and Darby (1981) and Carr, Darby, and Thornton (1985), tested the model, using a two-stage least squares simultaneous equation method of estimation, taking the sample period 1957(1) to 1976(4) for the UK, USA, Canada, France, West Germany, and the Netherlands. The results supported the hypothesis that unexpected money supply shocks have an impact on the demand for money, suggesting that the real money stock is a shock absorber but rejected the hypothesis that transitory income is held in money balances. Cuthbertson and Taylor (1987b) retested the Carr and Darby method for narrow definition of money in the UK. The anticipated money supply series, m_t^a, was generated using the one-step-ahead predictions from a Kalman filter process, which improved on the ARIMA process used by previous authors.[7] The unanticipated money supply shocks, m_t^u, were extracted as the difference between this series and the actual money stock. In general, the results supported the Carr and Darby model as an acceptable model.

Forward-looking models

In many respects the forward-looking models are very similar to the shock-absorber models but instead of allowing the individual to be surprised by current monetary policy alone they allow expectations of future monetary policy to influence current money balances. Departures from current period equilibrium result not just from unexpected events but from anticipated events ahead of the present time period. If adjustments to money balances take place now, in anticipation of future events, or if money balances are held as a result of unforeseen shocks, money serves as an inventory function. The important microeconomic point is that, for the individual, money balances are more than a response to current conditions alone, and transition from one equilibrium to another in anticipation of future events can take place over a number of periods.

Inherent in this kind of framework is the notion that it may be in the individual's interest not to make instantaneous adjustments to money balances because of the time required for search (Kanniainen and Tarkha, 1986), or because of high costs of adjustment in the short run (Cuthbertson and Taylor, 1987a). Costs of asset adjustment were the basis of the original partial adjustment model used by Goldfeld (1976), but have been generalized in the buffer stock model to include the future as well as the present.[8]

The model of Cuthbertson and Taylor (1987a) is a representative example. It is derived from the same type of cost function as the partial adjustment model but generalized to allow for the cost of being out of equilibrium, and the cost of actually adjusting balances in the future as well as the present, and it can be seen that by setting $i = 1$ the model reverts to the original partial adjustment model. The cost function is

$$C = E_{t+i-1} \sum_{i=1}^{\infty} D^i [a_1(m_{t+i} - m *_{t+i})^2 + a_2(m_{t+i} - m_{t+i-1})^2] \qquad (11.26)$$

which states that adjustment is based on the squared deviation from desired money balances, m_t^* (the cost of being out of equilibrium) and the squared deviation from last periods' money balances (the cost of actually adjusting balances). Money holdings, m_t, are made up of planned components m_t^p, based on the minimisation of an intertemporal cost function, and unplanned parts m_t^u due to unanticipated shocks

$$m_t = m_t^p + m_t^u \qquad (11.27)$$

and the 'desired' level of money holdings is given as before by

$$m_t^* = ay_t + bp_t + cR_t. \qquad (11.28)$$

Taking the first derivation of the cost function and setting this equal to zero yields, after some manipulation, the demand for money equation

$$m_t = \lambda m_{t-1} + (1 - \lambda)(1 - \lambda D) \sum_{i=1}^{\infty} (\lambda D)^i E_{t-1} m *_{t+i} + m_t^u, \qquad (11.29)$$

where λ is equal to (a_1/a_2), D is a discount factor set 0.97 for empirical work and unexpected shocks to money balances, m_t^u are explicitly modelled as part of the equation. The second term reflects anticipated future changes to the desired level of the demand for money which will affect current money balances in such a way that the adjustment takes place slowly, minimizing the cost function, in advance of the expected change. The shock terms affect money balances immediately with the effect decaying over time as the individual moves back to long-run equilibrium by a slow real-balance effect.

The empirical results of Cuthbertson and Taylor (1987a) are estimated for M1 in the UK using quarterly data 1963(1) to 1983(3) using three-stage least squares. The coefficients were found to be significant and correctly signed. The coefficient λ gives an estimate of a_1/a_2, which is an indication of the ratio of the relative weights placed on the deviation from 'desired' money balances and on adjustment in the multiperiod cost function. They show that the adjustment costs are 'something like thirty times more important than deviations of the actual from desired holdings in the loss function' (1987a: 73). In terms of the model, the presumption is that because the cost of adjustment is large in relation to the cost of maintaining a disequilibrium, the individual would rather avoid adjustment costs than move faster towards the desired level of money balances.

Inventory management models

The third type of buffer stock model is based on the inventory principle. The microstructure of these models draws on Miller and Orr (1966), Akerlof (1973, 1979), Akerlof and Milbourne (1980), and Milbourne (1987). These models are more useful for explaining the cash management practices of the company sector and were not developed specifically to address the instability of the money demand function in the 1970s, but they go a long way to explain why disequilibrium may be observed.

The basic idea is that a holder's money balances are managed within a target zone defined by a target level, z_i corresponding to an equilibrium level of money balances with thresholds above and below z_i beyond which balances cannot move. Balances fluctuate up and down with receipts and payments and the entity accepts any level of money balances with the range even if it deviates from the target level. Balances are adjusted to the target level only when the upper or lower threshold is reached: they are brought to the target when they hit the lower bound and likewise are adjusted downwards only when they hit the upper bound. Otherwise, they are allowed to wander within the zone without adjustment in what may appear to be a completely random fashion. In this way, the model minimizes the number of adjustments, making large but discrete changes when necessary. Departures from equilibrium money balances can exist and persist for some time whilst still remaining fully consistent with optimizing behaviour.

The behaviour of the money balances can be described in the following way. Consider a level of money balances, m_i. There are three possible ways that an individual firm can find itself holding this level of balances at time t. First, if the money balances last period were m_i and if there is no change in period t then the balances this period will be m_i. Alternatively, if the money balances last period were just above m_i at $m_i + 1$ and if there is a change of -1 to the money balances in period t, then the balances this period will be m_i. Likewise, if the money balances last period were just below m_i, at $m_i - 1$ and if there is a change of $+1$ to the money balances in period t, then the balances of this period will again be m_i. Therefore, to indicate by the notation $f_i(m_i,t)$, the probability of holding m_i balances at time t, the short-run probability of money holdings being m_i at time t, can be calculated as

$$f_i(m_i,t) = p(.)f_i(m_i + 1, t - 1) + s(.)f_i(m_i, t - 1) + q(.)f_i(m_i - 1, t - 1) \qquad (11.30)$$
$$1 \leqslant m_i \ h_i - 1 \ and \ m_i \neq z_I.$$

This shows that the probability of holding m_i at time t is given by the sum of the probabilities of m_i, $m_i + 1$, and $m_i - 1$ coinciding with the probabilities of a zero, negative or positive adjustment $s(.)$, $p(.)$, and $q(.)$ respectively, which would result in m_i balances at that point in time. The conditions also ensure that money balances lie on or between the two thresholds and do not equal the target.

The probability that the individual holds money balances corresponding to the target level balances is correspondingly

$$f_i(z_i, t) = p(.)f_i(z_i + 1, t - 1) + s(.)f_i(z_i, t - 1) + q(.)f_i(z_i - 1, t - 1) \qquad (11.31)$$
$$+ p(.)f_i(h_i + 1, t - 1) + q(.)f_i(h_i - 1, t - 1).$$

This equation indicates that the probability of being at the target level is equal to the probability that a current change to the money balances the individual on a threshold (which immediately returns the individual to the target level of money) and the probability that the change adjusts money balances onto the target. It is equivalent to saying that the probabilities that m_i, $m_i + 1$ or $z_i + 1$, and $m_i - 1$ or $z_i - 1$, coincide with the probabilities of zero, negative or positive adjustments $s(.)$, $p(.)$, and $q(.)$ respectively which would result in a movement on to the target level (or to the threshold and hence realignment to the target level).

The short-run equilibrium is found by calculating the mathematical expression for the expected value of m as the sum of all possible values of m_i times their corresponding probabilities, denoted by $f_i(m_i, t)$, viz.:

$$f_i(0) = 0. \qquad (11.32)$$

$$f_i(h_i) = 0. \qquad (11.33)$$

$$\sum_{m=1}^{h_i-1} f_i(m_i) = 1. \qquad (11.34)$$

The probability of being on either the lower or the upper threshold is zero (because it causes the individual to immediately realign to the target), and the probability of being between them is therefore certain. The Miller and Orr result thus explains the behaviour of money balances between the thresholds, showing that the use of money as an inventory to cover departures from equilibrium in the short-run can be optimal. Although relatively new to monetary economics, buffer stock schemes of this form are well known and widely used in industrial production and agricultural problems and have been developed more generally for use in wider macroeconomic applications.[9]

A final assessment

If we accept the buffer stock notion (Laidler, 1984), then it follows that the original demand for money functions broke down because they misspecified the nature of the relationship between the observed money holdings and the equilibrium money stock. Buffer stock models, based on microfoundational principles, are better able to explain the behaviour of the demand for money in a more turbulent period, and moreover do so with a theory which encompasses the original partial adjustment model. Introducing expectations about the future and allowing for the impact of unexpected and 'surprise' events replicated for the demand for money Friedman's additions to the Phillips curve.

The reasons for this seem obvious now. The partial adjustment model suffered from much the same limitations in an inflationary environment as did the original Phillips curve. It was specified as a function of current variables which adjusted to events only by examining the deviation from the intended equilibrium in the previous period; as such it was adaptive and backward-looking without reference to future events. While this did not matter in stable conditions where inflation was low and last period's conditions were a reasonable guide to the conditions of the present and future periods this was not the case in the double-digit inflationary environment of the 1970s. The model needed to be augmented with expectational terms which allowed for future monetary needs as well as the needs dictated by the present. The buffer stock model based on an *intertemporal* cost function (as opposed to a current period cost function) recognizes that money demand in the present is affected by expectations of future economic conditions and the likely monetary needs in subsequent time periods. The buffer stock model is able to deal with unexpected events and temporary shocks to the money supply and income, whilst the partial adjustment model ignored these possibilities.

11.6 Econometric Advances

$\mathbf{E}$CONOMETRIC advances offered the additional explanations for the poor performance of the Goldfeld equation, by suggesting that misspecified dynamics in the short run or misspecified econometrics altogether were responsible. There have been many contributions to econometric methodology that have improved our statistical understanding of the breakdown of the money demand function—and this section explores some of the steps along the way.

Spurious regressions and stationarity

During the early 1970s, it was discovered that some econometric results were the result of certain statistical properties common to the variables included in the regression rather than due to any genuine underlying relationship between the variables themselves. These regressions were dubbed *spurious regressions* by Granger and Newbold (1974). The common feature in the variables was the dominant effect of the statistical behaviour of the individual variables (the stochastic trend) resulting from the fact that most economic variables included in their regressions were generated by random walks. These types of variables are called *non-stationary* because they do not have a constant mean (i.e. they do not revert to any fixed value) and have an infinite variance. They evolve in an unpredictable fashion described by a random walk. When these variables are regressed against each other the common dominant feature of a stochastic trend can and does lead to the incorrect conclusion that the variables are related in an economic sense. The point about spurious regressions is that they need not be *economically* related and the relationship can be an entirely artificial feature arising from the underlying data-generation process for each series.

The first step in an estimation is now a test for the time-series characteristics of each individual variable used in the study. These tests are known as stationarity tests or unit root tests; they determine whether the variables are derived from a non-stationary data-generating process such as a random walk òr some stationary alternative. If the variables are stationary, they have a constant mean to which they revert periodically, and a finite variance. When variables are specified in a form that they are stationary, classical regression theory is valid. Spurious regression problems should be avoided by ensuring that all the variables in the regression are stationary since this removes the stochastic trend responsible for the 'spurious' result.

Non-stationary variables can be transformed to stationarity by differencing, but simply differencing all the variables is not the solution to uncovering the underlying relationship between them. Instead we must turn to the important step forward made by a number of econometricians who were students and colleagues of Dennis Sargan of the London School of Economics in the 1970s.

The general-to-specific methodology

The solution he proposed, which has been followed up by Davidson, Hendry, Srba and Yeo (1978) and Hendry (1979), was to elaborate upon the dynamic lag structure of the models in an attempt to capture the data-generation process. This has become known as the general-to-specific methodology. Instead of defining a long-run demand for money equation with a partial adjustment model to explain the dynamics, the approach began with a much more general model which included the lagged levels of price, income, and interest rate variables to measure the equilibrium relationship and many lagged terms representing changes to these variables. This 'Hendryfication' is based on the notion that the econometrician or applied economist is concerned to discover the true data-generation process for an economic relationship. The procedure involves four main steps.

1. The first is to discover the subset of all possible variables of interest that can be used to model the economic relationship. This is a matter of variable choice, identification, and economic theory considered earlier.

2. From these variables one must specify the variables to be explained and those that are to do the explaining—the exogenous or conditioning on the right-hand side and the endogenous, left-hand side variable. In most demand for money equations, real money balances are the endogenous variable and the remaining are exogenous. In buffer stock models, real money balances are often exogenous and one of the other variables is taken as the endogenous variable, e.g. price (Laidler 1982), interest rates (Artis and Lewis 1976).

3. In this stage, a choice of functional form, very general in the first instance, is reduced to a specific structure by empirical testing and elimination. The initial structure might take a form something like

$$y_t = \alpha + \sum_{i=1}^{n} \beta_i y_{t-i} + \sum_{i=0}^{n} \delta_i x_{t-i} + \varepsilon_t, \tag{11.35}$$

where n is the lag length chosen for the model. This structure is known as an auto-regressive distributed lag model (ADL) and has the advantage of being very flexible. Sufficient restrictions imposed on the ADL would give the Goldfeld equation, as illustrated below, but in the spirit of general-to-specific modelling we would model the ADL and attempt to find a specific model consistent with the underlying data-generation process. We could test whether a restricted functional form, based on a partial adjustment model, with a more restricted dynamic structure is acceptable by setting parameters in the ADL model to zero. If $\beta_i = 0$ for $i > 1$ and $\delta_i = 0$ for $i > 0$ then the ADL becomes

$$y_t = \alpha + \beta_1 y_{t-1} + \delta_0 x_t + \varepsilon_t. \tag{11.36}$$

But in the spirit of general-to-specific modelling we would model the ADL and attempt to find a specific model consistent with the underlying data-generation process. We could then test whether the restricted functional form, based on a partial adjustment model, is more acceptable.

4. The final stage is to estimate the model and determine the simplest structure consistent with the data.

Thus the general-to-specific modelling strategy provides a versatile dynamic structure, which can be tested down to the parsimonious model by eliminating statistically insignificant variables. The model is theory-based but its structure is data-determined and validated by statistical tests of restrictions to the dynamic form. Its more flexible approach to the short-run dynamics enabled improvements on the econometric performance of the partial adjustment model.

Cointegration and error correction models

The most important step to econometric theory and practice in the last two decades is undoubtedly the innovation by Engle and Granger (1987), who found that it was possible in some cases to take certain combinations of individually non-stationary variables and combine them in some linear way to form a series that is stationary. In this way integrated variables could be combined to remove non-stationarity when they form a cointegrating relationship. The concept of *cointegration* has since revolutionized the empirical literature in every area of economics and this transformation is very evident in empirical work in monetary economics.

If we define two series x_t and y_t as integrated of order d, then d is the number of times the variable must be differenced to achieve stationarity. A series that is stationary is $I(0)$, and a series that needs to be differenced once to be stationary is $I(1)$. Most economic data are $I(1)$ or $I(0)$. Suppose x_t and y_t are $I(d)$, we can find a cointegrating relationship between x_t and y_t if we can combine terms in some linear way by the parameter vector, (1α), to reduce the order of integration from d to a lower level, b

$$(y_t - \alpha x_t) \sim I(b). \tag{11.37}$$

In monetary applications y_t might be the real money stock and x_t might be a set of explanatory variables and the estimated parameters, α. So long as the residuals from a demand for money equation are stationary, even if the original variables are individually non-stationary, then the function is not a spurious regression. Since the relationship is reliable and not a statistical artefact, a cointegrating relationship is often referred to as a long-run equilibrium equation.

Once a cointegrating relationship has been found between a group of economic variables there exists a dynamic adjustment process explaining how departures or errors from the long-run equilibrium are corrected. This mechanism is known as the *equilibrium correction mechanism* (ECM). The ECM defines the dynamic adjustment or lag structure of the model and can be thought of as a short-run counterpart to the long-run equilibrium relationship.

In the light of Engle and Granger's contribution, the reason for the superior performance of the general-to-specific model on econometric grounds can be readily understood, and it relates back to the spurious regression problem. The equilibrium correction model has a form very similar to the parsimonious model derived by Davidson *et al.* (1978) using their general-to-specific methodology. Cointegration implies that an equilibrium correction model exists, and this explains why the general-to-specific modelling strategy is able to perform well in explaining the short-run dynamics of the money demand function. In effect, it is a good approximation to the equilibrium correction model associated with the long-run money demand function. For example, we can rewrite the ADL model (11.35) as

$$\triangle y_t = (\beta_1 - 1)(y_{t-1} - x_{t-1}) + \sum_{i=1}^{n} \xi_i \triangle y_{t-i} + \sum_{i=0}^{n} \zeta_i \triangle x_{t-i} + \nu_t, \tag{11.38}$$

where ξ_i and ζ_i are functions of α, β_i, and ν_t is an error term. The term $(\beta_1 - 1)(y_{t-1} - x_{t-1})$ is the cointegrating relationship, whilst the remainder is a dynamic lag structure. The only difference between this equation and the Engle–Granger model is that the latter explicitly embeds a cointegrating relationship that explicitly corresponds to the long-run equilibrium equation.

Current practice in econometric analysis of demand for money functions utilizes the cointegration method. Some refinements have allowed the estimation of the long-run and the dynamics simultaneously using the Johansen procedure (Johansen and Juselius, 1990). With this technique, the demand for money can be modelled in a system with other interrelated demand functions and can be estimated while allowing for other 'endogenous' relationships between the variables normally included on the right-hand side of the money demand equation as explanatory variables.

11.7 Conclusions

IN this chapter we have surveyed a vast range of empirical literature on the modelling of the demand for money. The material covers early models of the long-run function, simple dynamic specifications, and subsequent reformulations, based on econometric theory, in the light of misspecifications evidenced by the predictive performance. Econometric advances have helped to release the demand for money function from the partial adjustment straightjacket and, by freeing up the dynamics to allow for alternative short-run relationships, it has been possible to account for some of the instability in the estimated equations. From a practical point of view the econometric developments have restored a lot of the forecasting performance and predictive power of the demand for money function (see Hendry and Ericsson, 1991, for the UK and Baba, Hendry, and Starr, 1992, for the USA), although the simplicity and ease of interpretation of the old approach has had to give way.

While we have been able to cover one major new branch of theoretical modelling based on the buffer-stock approach we have not yet touched on two other advances: the development of Divisia aggregates in response to growing financial innovation, and the reclassification and extension of models based on supplements or extensions to simple sum aggregates. These tie in much more closely with the financial innovations that took place in the 1980s and it makes sense to explain those innovations before discussing the attempts to model them. This forms the basis of the next chapter.

Notes

1 Some studies by Coghlan (1978), Courakis (1978), and Boughton (1991) suggest that the price coefficient should be freely estimated and only restricted to unity if warranted by the data. When the parameter on the price variable is freely estimated, however, it is often not possible to reject the homogeneity restriction (see Spencer, 1985; Goldfeld and Sichel 1987; MacKinnon and Milbourne, 1988; and Hall, Henry, and Wilcox, 1989).

2 Patinkin (1972) helpfully elaborates on the distinction between stocks and flows using wealth and income as examples in ch. 1 of his *Studies in Monetary Economics* (NB reference Harper international edn., Harper & Row, Singapore).

3 Friedman put the distinction in the following terms:

> From the broadest and most general point of view, total wealth includes all sources of 'income' or consumable services. One such source is the productive capacity of human beings, and accordingly this is one form in which wealth can be held. From this point of view, 'the' rate of interest expresses the relation between the stock which is wealth and the flow which is income, so if Y be the total flow of income, and r, 'the' interest rate, total wealth is $W = Y/r$.
>
> Income in this broadest sense should not be identified with income as it is ordinarily measured. The latter is generally a 'gross' stream with respect to human beings, since no deduction is made for the expense of maintaining human productive capacity intact; in addition, it is affected by transitory elements that make it depart more or less widely from the theoretical concept of the stable level of consumption of services that could be maintained indefinitely. (1956: 4–5)

4 Early studies by Feige (1967) and Laidler and Parkin (1970) for the USA and UK respectively, sought to determine whether income or wealth was the most appropriate scale variable. Both concluded in favour of permanent income although the evidence was weaker for the UK.

5 There are, of course, important issues beneath the surface. Suppose that we have ten years of data, covering two complete business cycles. How many 'true' observations do we have? Two (business cycles), four (Friedman and Schwartz half-reference cycles), or ten (annual data). Does using quarterly data really give us four times as many 'true' observations as the use of annual data? Frequency domain methods, e.g. spectral analysis of monetary series, brings out some of these questions. In the time domain, where the distinction between 'legal' and 'true' degrees of freedom may be less apparent, it becomes important to correctly extract the information from the series by allowing for autocorrelation and cointegration in the underlying data.

6 Why were the mid-1970s so turbulent? One reason was the transition from fixed to floating exchange rates, against the backdrop of a large expansion in international liquidity and an international commodity boom. The other was the large change to absolute and relative prices caused by the fivefold increase in oil prices during the Yom Kippur War in 1973.

7 Cuthbertson and Taylor introduced a Kalman filter as a way of dealing with the expectations learning scheme embedded in the forward-looking model. The model suggests that a typical economic variable x_t is explained by three components—a permanent component, π_t, a seasonal component, μ_t, and a transitory component, ε_t. These are modelled as

$$x_t = \pi_t + \mu_t + \varepsilon_t$$
$$\pi_t = \pi_{t-1} + \beta_t + \theta_t$$
$$\beta_t = \beta_{t-1} + \zeta_t$$

Previous attempts to model expectational learning had used auotregressive integrated moving average (ARIMA) models to do so. These imply that a series, x_t, can be modelled as

$$\Phi(L)\triangle^d x_t = \Theta(L)\varepsilon_t,$$

where $\Phi(L)$ and $\Theta(L)$ are polynomials in the lag operator of length p and q respectively and ε_t is an error variable. The variable to be forecast is differenced d times.

8 This approach has been developed largely by Kanniainen and Tarkha (1986), Cuthbertson (1986, 1988), and Cuthbertson and Taylor (1986, 1987a, 1989, 1992) as a generalization of the minimization of costs of adjustment, which underlies the Carr and Darby model, into a multiperiod framework.

9 These schemes are designed for a number of purposes, including production smoothing and income or price stabilization. See Newberry and Stiglitz (1981) and Blinder and Maccini (1991).

Chapter 12
Demand for Money and Financial Innovation

12.1 The Process of Financial Innovation

CHANGE in the financial sector is not a new phenomenon. The second half of the nineteenth century saw the decline in bimetallism and the rise of the gold standard, a fall in the usage of notes and growth of cheque deposits, the formation of limited liability banking which saw banks transformed from small regional country partnerships to national and international organizations, and the globalization of markets in trade and finance. Structural change then lasted for nearly fifty years.

Judging from the evidence of the past two decades it would seem that structural change in banking and financial markets is once again a major force. Evolution in financial markets is the normal way by which the financial sector adapts to changes in technology, demand, and government regulation. This process of adjustment is exemplified in new products, new processes, and new markets and market arrangements. But it is not sufficient for an event to be new or novel in order to be innovative. For a financial change to be an innovation it must truly alter or displace some existing activity or practice in a significant way. The distinction between evolution and innovation is thus at root arbitrary.

Financial innovation can be in the form of a new product, or a new process for supplying or delivering an existing product, or be in terms of market arrangements. Table 12.1 gives some examples under these three headings, further subdivided into those primarily affecting retail or personal financial activities and those operating at a wholesale or corporate level. These distinctions, however, are not hard and fast ones. For example, process innovation, first evident in the 'back office', has moved increasingly 'out front' with the emergence of automatic teller machines (ATMs), point-of-sale terminals (SWITCH or EFTPOS), and 24–hour telephone and Internet banking. These process changes have so altered the nature and characteristics of the service provided that the distinction between process and product innovation has become less relevant. In a similar way, the introduction of the secondary mortgage market has altered the liquidity characteristics and pricing of the traditional home mortgage instrument, and changed the delivery system by spurring the growth of independent mortgage providers (mortgage banks and brokers). Money market

Table 12.1 Major financial innovations

A. Products	B. Processes	C. Market arrangements
Retail	*Retail*	*Retail*
Money market mutual funds	Automated teller machines	Secondary mortgage markets
Money market accounts	Point of sale terminals	Joint ventures
Cash management accounts	Electronic funds transfer	Financial service centres
Sweep accounts	Electronic trading	Financial conglomerates
Index-linked securities	Automated clearing systems	Bancassurance
Personal equity plans		
Housing equity loans		
Wholesale	*Wholesale*	*Wholesale*
Rollover credits	Automated clearing houses	Eurocurrency markets
Medium term notes	CHIPS, CHAPS	International banking facilities
Leveraged buyouts	Automated securities trading	Financial futures markets
Interest rate and currency swaps	Euroclear	Repurchase markets
Options, swaptions	Electronic delivery of securities	Over-the-counter markets
Caps, floor and collars		
Hedge funds		

mutual funds have been classified as a retail innovation, but their real significance was in eroding the distinction between retail and wholesale products, processes and markets (Lewis, 1986*b*).

Theories of innovation

There are a large number of studies of financial innovation, but no readily agreed distinction like that in R & D research between demand pull and science push (see Voss, 1984). Demand pull refers to situations where the market, i.e. the customers, ask for a new product or modifications of an old one. Ideas come through close contacts with customers. When there is science push the ideas come from scientific developments that enable firms to make products that the consumers do not demand because they cannot imagine them or evaluate their usefulness. A good example of this process is the development and marketing of the Xerox machine.

Most analyses of financial innovation have, in one form or another, used a microeconomic framework, based around the profit-maximizing financial firm operating under regulatory and other constraints, into which various macroeconomic influences (interest rates, etc.) can be slotted. One of the earliest studies by Greenbaum and Heywood (1973), employed the distinction in microeconomic demand theory between income and substitution effects.[1] Secular increases in real income create a demand for a greater variety of financial claims from individual wealthholders, met by new instruments and financial packages (the income effect). Against this backdrop, cyclical changes in interest rates give rise to substitution effects as people switch into newly developed claims without controlled interest rates.

Silber (1983) focused more directly upon firm-specific responses. Constraints imposed upon a financial firm's ability to optimize its profitability and utility act as a stimulus to innovation at the firm level. The constraints come from regulation, taxation, and the like. A rather similar framework is used by Kane (1984) but the focal point of his analysis is regulation, along with the role of technology in eroding industry (and thus regulatory) boundaries. An 'Hegelian Dialectic' then ensues in which one concept (thesis) inevitably generates its opposite (antithesis). A regulatory action provokes a reaction by firms which then leads to new regulation and in turn to a new adaptive initiative by the firms.[2]

A number of studies have examined product innovation, building on the idea of Lancaster (1966) that products can be viewed as bundles of characteristics (in this case, yield, liquidity, divisibility, price risk, duration, etc). Thus the BIS (1986) analyses the demand and supply of financial characteristics, and changes in demand and supply resulting from monetary policy, technology, regulatory pressures, and competition. Innovation is seen as a mechanism for 'filling in the gaps' and bringing about improvements in the 'characteristics space'.[3]

The basic idea can be illustrated in Figure 12.1. We envisage wealthholders choosing amongst assets according to the two characteristics of expected return and liquidity: essentially a variant of the Tobin–Markowitz expected return–risk analysis in which risk comes from illiquidity. It is assumed initially that two assets are available to hold, A_1 and A_2. Each is represented by a ray through the origin, and the points A_1 and A_2 show, on some objective measure, the expected return and liquidity services which can be obtained from spending a unit of value (pound, dollar) on each

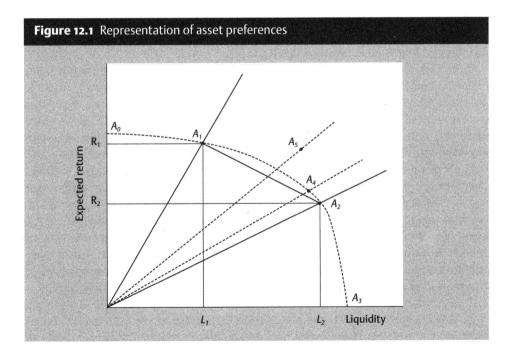

Figure 12.1 Representation of asset preferences

asset. A_1 offers high yield and low liquidity, while A_2 offers low yield and high liquidity. If these are the only assets available, the choices are bounded by the coordinates at A_1 and A_2 (and linear combinations of the two assets).

Over time the number of assets will change, and the nearness of the assets and the gaps between them can be measured by the angle between the rays through the origin. Introduction of the asset A_4 would be a relatively trivial change whereas A_5 would not be because it fills a gap in the product range in an important way. Following Neuman (1935), we can expect market arrangements to provide a more or less continuous spectrum of assets ranging from zero return-full liquidity (A_3) to the highest yield on the asset with complete illiquidity (A_0) as shown by the dashed line. Transactors would then choose assets along this opportunity locus according to their marginal rate of substitution between the two characteristics. Here we have one explanation for financial innovation, in that new claims change the mix of characteristics so as to occupy a previously vacant space. In this way, the proliferation of assets reduces the gaps between claims and completes the market (Lewis, 1990).

Van Horne (1985) treats 'market completeness' more broadly in his analysis of innovation. In a complete market (of Arrow and Debreu type) there is a sufficient number of financial instruments available (e.g. stocks, bonds, futures, options) to hedge every conceivable 'state of the world' that might arise. An incomplete or imperfect financial market is one where there are insufficient instruments available to enable individuals to hedge state-contingent risks if they so wish. Hence financial innovations (new products, instruments) can be viewed as a process of completing the market, i.e. developing (in the limit) a sufficient number of financial instruments to span the whole state space (feasible set of state outcomes). Financial innovations can be seen as a mechanism by which economic entities (individuals, firms, or government) can improve their return/risk trade-offs. Market completeness occurs when no (new) innovation can improve this trade-off.

Miller (1986) and Ross (1989) continue this line of argument. Miller characterizes financial innovations as 'unforecastable improvements' in the array of available financial products and processes. Significant financial innovations are those that endure beyond the expiry of the initial impulses that stimulated them. Unanticipated shocks to the economic environment, such as sharply rising interest rates, provide such impulses. From an examination of financial innovations between 1966 and 1986 he concludes that *regulation* and *taxation* provided the major impetus to financial innovation and that *financial futures* were the most significant innovation over that period. Ross uses agency-theoretic arguments to explain financial innovation. Financial institutions act as intermediaries/marketing agents for individual savers, whose funds they are investing. Institutions have available to them investment opportunities not open to individuals. Securities innovation takes place when financial intermediaries create new securities out of old ones by repackaging them to achieve different risk/return combinations. Examples are STRIPS (separate trading of registered interest and principal of securities) and CMOs (collateralized mortgage obligations). Finnerty (1988: 14) also stresses the importance of what he terms financial engineering ('the design, the development, and the implementation of innovative financial instruments and processes, and the formulation to create solutions to problems in finance') in altering the risk/return characteristics of financial instruments.

Sources of innovation

The preceding studies provide us with a reasonable base for analysing the sources of change. The principal neglect is the international dimension, mainly because the literature is informed by the domestic situation in the USA. As Table 12.1 makes clear, many financial innovations have originated in the Eurocurrency markets in terms of products (rollover credits, medium-term notes), processes (Euroclear), and markets (Euromarkets, IBFs), while many other innovations overlap the domestic and international (currency and interest rate swaps, CHIPS and CHAPS). Some comments on these markets seem warranted.

Despite the importance of Eurocurrency markets in world financing, they are poorly understood. There is in fact no Euromarket as such. Although it is located in terms of book transactions in various Eurocentres, the worldwide market physically consists of networks of telephones, telexes, and computer screens around the world. Nor are there Eurobanks; Euro operations are one compartment of an overall banking balance sheet. This structure was in itself a major innovation.

There is little agreement about the explanations for the rapid growth.[4] One group has emphasized the offshore element, so that the operations in the Eurocurrency markets are seen to be providing substitutes for domestic intermediation. Where the transactions are between banks, Eurocurrency operations act as an international interbank market. Others have concentrated on the currency aspect, looking upon the Eurobanks as adjuncts to the wholesale foreign exchange markets. Yet others have focused upon the cross-border characteristics, seeing the banks' operations as part of a global funds market. There is also the role of some offshore centres as tax havens to be taken into account, for many activities are inter-office transactions, some of which are transfer-pricing undertaken by multinational banks to reduce taxation and evade regulations.

A common thread running through the various explanations is the absence of regulation of various kinds. In the Eurocurrency compartment of their balance sheet, banks are normally free of reserve requirements and deposit insurance premiums, and usually have greater freedom to select the investment portfolio and the range of activities undertaken. A bank is to a large extent an accounting arrangement which can be reorganized and restructured readily, and modern communications facilities enable a divergence between the legal and actual location of banking activities.

Thus the 'escape motive' has been important: banks have sought to avoid regulation by moving business to the offshore markets. In this respect, the markets are a prime example of a regulation product—one description of them borrowing from Friedman's (1969a) analysis is 'duty-free banking' (Lewis and Davis, 1987: 276). The shift of financing to the markets has, in turn, exerted continual pressure on the domestic authorities to alter the regulatory mix and forestall the exit of business.

From the viewpoint of innovation, the importance of the escape motive comes from the ability of the institutions when freed from the regulations to respond rapidly to changing conditions—the hallmark of innovative behaviour. Innovation has been a feature of the offshore markets. The origins of the Eurocurrency markets for both banking and bonds were innovative in that, for the first time on a vast scale, the currency risk of one country was combined with the regulatory environment and political risk of another country—an early illustration of the fungibility of finance. Afterwards, Eurobanking gave banks the freedom to create new instruments and try out new ideas. Thus the recycling crisis of the 1970s was resolved by a new financial instrument—the syndicated credit—enabling long-term financing to be made on the back of short-term deposits of dollars from OPEC countries.[5] When in the 1980s the wealth transfer process internationally reverted to capital market channels and securitized financing came into vogue, while at the same time banks' balance sheet expansion was constrained by capital pressures, new financing facilities were fashioned which combined banking and securities instruments, and provided tailor-made financial structures which blurred long-standing distinctions between banking and securities, and arbitraged different capital markets.[6] Subsequently, when finance for leveraged buy-outs, mergers and acquisitions, and privatizations was needed and had to be raised quickly, the syndicated credit instrument was revived and rejigged and medium-term note facilities introduced.[7] Innovation came simply from allowing markets to do their job.

Table 12.2 Sources of financial innovations

1. **Changing requirements of customers** risk/yield combinations agency costs tax asymmetries scale of financing accounting benefits	4. **Policy changes** regulatory/legislative/supervisory changes
2. **Changed conditions of suppliers** transactions costs capital pressures competition	5. **Technology** technological factors academic research
3. **Environmental changes** interest rates prices, exchange rates	6. **Market completeness (GAPS)** risk-hedging cross-border arbitrage

Putting all of these elements together, Table 12.2 summarizes the factors that provide a stimulus to financial innovation under six headings: (1) changing requirements of customers, including opportunities to reduce or reallocate risk, and arbitrage taxation asymmetries and pricing differences between retail and wholesale markets; (2) changing conditions of suppliers in terms of capital pressures and altered competitive forces; (3) changes in the economic environment from more volatile interest rates, exchange rates, and inflation; (4) changes to the regulatory, supervisory, and legal structure; (5) developments in information technology and academic 'inventions' (e.g. the option pricing model); and (6) factors which close market gaps and lead to more 'complete' markets.

12.2 Consequences for the Demand for Money

THERE is a widespread perception that financial innovation is behind the instability in the demand for money function. This need not necessarily be true. It might be the case that the money supply has become less endogenous/more exogenous, i.e. there has been a regime change. The standard function may have been unable to cope with this change of regime and the different associated dynamic structure. At the same time, if we accept Friedman's (1986) argument that one way by which the financial system responds to a more volatile (e.g. mismanaged) fiat money is by induced financial innovation, then both the money demand instability and the financial innovation could be a consequence of the one thing—money supply variability.

If, on the other hand, we go along with the (seemingly reasonable) idea that financial innovations are responsible for instability in the demand for money function, then we would like to know which of the factors in Table 12.2 are the cause and how long they are likely to last. Only then would we know whether we are dealing with one-off factors or a continuing process. Unfortunately we do not know of any studies that come even remotely close to providing answers to these questions. The answers that we offer are thus necessarily speculative.

Our own assessment of the process of financial innovation highlights three major driving forces. First of all, there is technology. The steep decline in the costs of communication and the widespread introduction of computer technology have had major impacts. The radical reduction in transactions costs implied facilities for the routinization of deals previously regarded as too complex for regular implementation. Hence currency and interest rate swaps, conceptually always feasible, are made computationally practicable, while academic research has made clear that forwards, futures, options, and swaps are all linked and can be priced correctly using constructed portfolios (Black and Scholes, 1973; Smith, Smithson, and Wilford, 1990; Hodges, 1992). Advances in information technology also provide the basis for more efficient monitoring of large volumes of business and provides a ready flow of data for management decisions. At a fundamental level, computerization offers the prospect of instant clearing and in the process can limit the disappearance of money. If alternative earning assets can be liquidated on the spot to finance an act of expenditure, the need to hold money in advance will disappear. The reduction in communication costs also facilitates arbitrage across national boundaries, the integration of the world's capital markets, and the continued growth of currency substitution.

If technology were the only or main factor behind financial innovation, then there would be little reason to expect innovation to slow down. The cost of computer processing power has been falling by an average rate of 30 per cent per year over the past two and a half decades, and shows no sign of bottoming out. We should also note that the previous era of rapid change in money and banking, in the second half of the nineteenth century, was also marked by rapid improvements in communications, coming from the introduction of the penny post, railroads, steamships, and the telegraph.

But technology is not the only influence. Two others widely cited are the experience of the high and variable inflation period of the 1970s, and the cycle of regulation and deregulation. These interact with what almost might be seen as another factor, namely the process of change and innovation emanating from within the industry as a consequence of the ongoing competitive struggle; this in particular seems to be an important element in many of the new instruments and techniques associated with banks' securitized lending.

The 1970s' experience exposed the inefficiency in the more variable climate of the period of the practices inherited from more stable times. In consequence fixed rate loans gave way to variable rate lending. The premium on more flexible ways of doing business, though arising in particular circumstances, nonetheless left a permanent residue as intermediaries invested in the technology and learnt ways of doing business which preserved an efficiency gain even when a more stable environment had been re-established. Involved in a similar way is the regulatory framework. Exposed to new pressures as times change, a given regulatory framework encourages profit-seeking institutions to find ways round the rules. Not all the discoveries become redundant when the regulation is changed or removed or when the pressures calling for innovation around the rules subside.

While regulation itself provokes innovations, deregulation provokes even more. As the regulators discovered that the earlier frameworks were increasingly ill-adapted to accommodate technological change or were of diminishing utility in the light of avoidance-innovation activity, these frameworks were changed. Like the other factors mentioned so far, this reaction appears to have been global, even if the USA and the UK are commonly cited as deregulating most and earliest. Indeed, the deregulation process produces its own dynamic as deregulation in one country shifts the locale of financial activity towards it and puts pressure on legislators in other countries to follow suit. This dynamic dominated the 1980s. The deregulation then changes the rules within which the process of intermediation and the financial markets operate, leading to a new wave of 'innovations' or adaptations. Some of the consequences of deregulation are examined in Chapter 14.

From a longer-term perspective a cycle of regulation, deregulation, and reregula-tion seems plausible without ever arriving at a Hegelian synthesis. Regulation is dis-placed by deregulation as profit-seeking institutions and technical changes cause the regulatory framework to be seen as outmoded and inefficient. Then the performance of the deregulated system results in a crisis, or in persistent strains that invite its reregulation. The new regulations may differ from the old ones, but set in train a rep-etition of the process. Something like this seems to have been played out in the 1990s as deregulation has been followed, first, by new capital controls for credit risks and, later, by extra capital requirements for market risks in the wake of a string of finan-cial scandals, involving derivatives and market trading.

What of the future? Will the process of change and innovation continue? Charles Sandford (1994) argues that by 2020 banks as we know them will have largely disap-peared and many transactions presently passing through banks and other financial intermediaries will be 'disintermediated'. As more financial information is dissemi-nated electronically, individuals will themselves access information before they make decisions about their investments, as they are beginning to do already via the Internet. They will trade globally on electronic markets in which the prices of a vast array of assets are constantly displayed and updated. Advertisements on electronic bulletin boards will match buyers with sellers, borrowers with lenders. Transactions will be instantly verified and settled through a worldwide, real-time payments sys-tem. The long-heralded cashless society may at last arrive.

Whatever the accuracy of this 'crystal-balling', certainly on this interpretation there would seem to be few grounds for expecting financial innovation either to slow down to any great extent or to cease. The next question is: what impact does financial innovation have upon the demand for money? The obvious answer is that it all depends on what sort of innovation takes place. Some innovations have altered both the absolute and relative costs of holding various financial assets as well as reducing the transactions costs associated with exchanging one financial asset for another. This process has occurred both within and across countries, in terms of currency substitution. Second, financial innovation has eroded the dis-tinctions between banks and other financial intermediaries and between interme-diated transactions and market ones. Thirdly, as a consequence, some new financial assets created by innovation are close substitutes for the traditional 'media of exchange' assets included in the definition of money; as a result, the elasticity of substitution for the latter assets should rise, thereby increasing the interest elastic-ity of demand.

On this basis, Thornton and Stone (1992) argue that the effects of financial inno-vation can be represented by supposing that, due to financial innovation, a new money aggregate M^* is appropriate, defined as equal to the old aggregate, M, plus some proportion θ of assets, A, not previously included. Thus,

$$M^* = M + \theta A, \tag{12.1}$$

where the demands for these aggregates in real terms are:

$$(M/p) = y. f(i) \tag{12.2}$$

and

$$A = y.^n g\,(i) \qquad\qquad (12.3)$$

for a given income level, y, and an interest rate i. Thus the demand for M* in real terms equals

$$M^*/p = y.f(i) + \theta(y^n .g(i)\,). \qquad\qquad (12.4)$$

If $\theta = 0$, then obviously financial innovation has no direct effect on the income elasticity of the new aggregate. However, if $\theta \neq 0$, the income elasticity of M^* will change with the level of income if $n \neq 1$, while the interest elasticity of M^* will differ from that of M.

The latter result has some similarity with the earlier analysis of Patinkin (1961). Reviewing the 'innovation' of non-banking financial intermediaries in the 1950s, Patinkin argued that the development could be regarded as providing wealthholders with an asset which is more attractive (more 'liquid') than the bonds previously on offer. This can be represented analytically as equivalent to an increase in the liquidity of bonds in a money–bonds framework. Such an increased liquidity makes bonds a better substitute for money, and thus causes the demand curve for money both to shift leftwards and to become more elastic. This is represented by the shift from D to D' in Figure 12.2. It follows that if the real supply of money remains constant at OC, then the rate of interest must decline from i_1 to i_0.

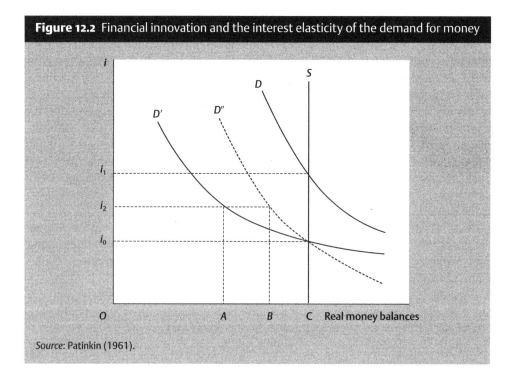

Figure 12.2 Financial innovation and the interest elasticity of the demand for money

Source: Patinkin (1961).

Alternatively, we can see from the diagram that if the monetary authority wishes to raise the interest rate from i_0 to i_2 by open market sales, then it must decrease the real money supply much more in the case of the elastic demand curve D', which characterizes a system with the financial innovations, than in the case of the less elastic curve D'', which characterizes a system without them. But while the innovations may have altered the demand function and imply some constraints on the operation of policy, the central bank can still control interest rates. Financial innovation may compromise stability of the demand for money function, but need not necessarily prevent monetary control.

This framework provides the basis for subsequent discussion. The idea that financial innovation and other structural changes in the financial sector (including deregulation) need not inhibit monetary control is taken up again in Chapters 13 and 14 when considering the transmission of monetary policy. In the meantime, the notion of forming new aggregates, perhaps with different weights, to take account of innovation is explored in the remainder of this chapter.

12.3 Divisia Aggregates

DIVISIA aggregates derive their name from the method of aggregation derived by François Divisia (1925), a French index number theorist. The technique has been applied to the construction of new monetary aggregates where it can usefully be employed to allow for the effects of financial innovation. Instead of adding up the components that make up the monetary aggregates without any assessment of the weights that should be attached to each constituent part, the Divisia approach constructs optimal weights based on index numbers, and ultimately microeconomic consumer theory. Before Divisia approaches were widely known, conventional demand for money functions had been augmented by a set of dummy and other variables to allow for financial innovation (see Taylor, 1987; Hall, Henry, and Wilcox, 1989), but this approach was somewhat *ad hoc*. It simply assumed that all the components within the monetary aggregate have the same weights in the aggregation process, and by implication would all be affected in the same way by financial innovation.

William Barnett (1980) took issue with this and a number of other assumptions in the models of the demand for money based on simple-sum aggregates, on three counts:

1. The conventional approach assumes all assets are perfect substitutes for each other; thus notes and coins are regarded as the same as cheque deposits or building society deposits and are all regarded equally as money, yet at the same time quite different from the excluded items. Evidence on the substitutability between components (Belongia, 1996) indicates elasticities of substitution that are well below the value of infinity required for simple summation.

2. The conventional aggregates ignore shifts between the components, for example, between notes and coins and cheque deposits. When they are added together with equal weights, the volume or quantity of the components within each aggregate such as notes and coin, sight deposits, time deposits, and so on can vary over time without changing the total value of the aggregate. Since the aggregate m is equal to the sum of the components a_i for $i = 1, 2 \ldots, n$, then m could remain unchanged so long as a rise in one component a_i (say) was matched by a fall of equivalent magnitude in another component (a_j). The equal weighting on each component gives each part an equal 'price'.

3. If the assets are not perfect substitutes, contrary to the implicit assumptions, then there is no way of distinguishing between income and substitution effects on monetary asset components. A 'good' aggregate should measure income effects but be unresponsive to price changes representing pure substitution effects, yet a simple-sum aggregate does not allow this. Divisia models internalize price substitution effects by capturing these in relative prices or user costs (which we define below) and changes to the component shares in the total portfolio alter only if substitution *and* wealth effects are present.

The assumptions underlying simple-sum models may have been innocuous when monetary assets had a zero rate of return, since notes and coin (with no explicit yield) should be perfectly substitutable for cheque deposits (which also had a zero yield). Once the process of financial innovation and deregulation began, this undermined the reliability of the assumptions. In the USA, interest-bearing chequable deposits rose from 10 per cent of total cheque deposits in 1980 to nearly 50 per cent at the end of the decade. In the UK, the interest-bearing component of M1 was 15 per cent in 1980 and 59 per cent in 1989 (Podolski, 1992). These own rates of return and differences in liquidity characteristics violated the perfect substitutability assumption.

Barnett's contribution to monetary economics has been to consider a class of aggregates that might overcome these problems and satisfy ideal or 'superlative' properties for the aggregation function. This involves weighting the components in such a way that they reflect the monetary characteristics of each part of the aggregate. Then the shifts between the components due to the effects of substitution and income effects can be identified and the response to financial innovation can be correctly observed.

If we are to construct monetary aggregates based on superlative indices like the Divisia index that avoid Barnett's criticisms, we must begin with consumer theory, index numbers, and aggregation. The first step is to consider issues of *separability, user cost,* and the *Divisia index* itself.

Separability

Separability in the utility function is a simplifying assumption (although it is subjected to empirical testing at a later stage) to allow the applied economist to focus on a subsection of the consumer's general utility function (Swoffard and Whitney, 1988). Underlying the principle of separability is the idea that individuals make decisions in two steps, involving higher-order and lower-order decisions. Higher-order decisions embrace choices over consumption, leisure, and financial asset holding by consumers, and these are assumed to occur first of all. Lower-level decisions, which then follow, consist of the choice over the composition of the financial portfolio given that the size of the portfolio has been determined at the earlier stage. Thus for a utility function

$$u = u(c, L, f(a)),$$
(12.5)

where c is consumption, L is leisure, and $f(a)$ equals total financial wealth, higher-order decisions involve c, L, and $f(a)$ whereas lower-order decisions involve choices over the composition of $f(a)$. In this context, weak separability indicates that changes to utility, arising from alterations to the composition of the portfolio $f(a)$, are unaffected by changes to consumption or leisure, since such lower-order decisions are unaffected by the prior allocation. Formally, this means that the marginal rate of substitution between assets is unaffected by the value of c or L:

$$\frac{(du/da_i)/(du/da_j)}{dc} = \frac{(du/da_i)/(du/da_j)}{dL} = 0.$$
(12.6)

When a subsection of the utility function is separable, it can be isolated from the rest and analysed independently without violating the requirements of consumer theory. Weak separability is a requirement for a group of assets to be aggregated into a block and for each component to be pretested for separability before any kind of aggregation is implemented. Only when separability is assured by parametric or non-parametric tests such as GARP, devised by Varian (1982, 1983), could the separate analysis of $f(a)$ be justified.

The analysis involves the following optimization:

$$\max f(a_i) \text{ subject to } \sum_{i=1}^{n} \pi_i a_i = m,$$
(12.7)

where the sub-utility from the portfolio and the budget constraint are derived independently of c or L. Here m is the total expenditure on monetary services and a_i are the volumes of each asset category held. The only undefined term is π_i, which is the user cost, and we must define this in detail because it is a central concept in the Divisia model.

User cost

The user cost defines the wealth forgone as a result of holding a particular asset a_i. The notion behind this measure is that the components of the monetary aggregate are substitutable to the extent that they offer similar monetary services. If the services differ, then the assets are imperfect substitutes and the extent to which they differ is given by a quantifiable value.

Barnett takes a benchmark asset as the basis of comparison for the user cost, such as a long bond yield or some other high-interest-earning asset. The measure of the liquidity services that an asset provides is reflected in the reduction in the interest earned per period relative to some benchmark rate. Inherent in this concept is Keynes's liquidity preference notion that interest is the reward for the individual to forgo liquidity (services) in the present in exchange for greater purchasing power (command over liquidity) at a later date. The interest forgone is measured as $(R - r_i)$ where r_i is the rate of interest on component a_i, and R is the benchmark yield. The discounted value of this lost interest is

$$\frac{(R - r_i)}{1 + R}$$

and when this is multiplied by the true cost-of-living index to convert the return into a monetary measure the user cost π_i is derived as follows:

$$\pi_i = p^* \cdot \frac{(R - r_i)}{(1 + R)}.$$ (12.8)

Changes in the relative return on asset components will induce shifts in portfolio composition, which the simple-sum aggregates will fail to pick up. Divisia aggregates will register the change through the user cost, π_i, which will alter the entire aggregate. To see how this works we must consider the construction of the Divisia aggregate.

The Divisia index

Taking the user cost of each asset component, a_i, Barnett constructed a new monetary aggregate, known as the *Divisia aggregate*, based on the concepts of separability and user cost. From these foundations he was able to show that the change in the logarithm of the utility function, $f(a_i)$, equals the share weighted change in the logarithm of asset components, a_i. Unlike the simple-sum model, the components are weighted and the weights depend on the user cost. This can be expressed more formally as

$$\text{dlog} f(a_i) = \sum_{i=1}^{n} s_{it} \cdot \text{dlog}(a_{it}),$$ (12.9)

where $s_{it} = \left(\dfrac{\pi_{it} a_{it}}{\sum_{i=1}^{n} \pi_{jt} a_{jt}} \right) = \left(\dfrac{\pi_{it} a_{it}}{m} \right).$

It can be seen from this expression that the index s_{it} depends each period on the proportion of expenditure or asset a_i relative to total expenditure on money services, m.

In practice, the construction of the actual monetary aggregate from this theoretical index-number formulation is given as a discrete approximation to the above:

$$\text{dlog} m_t = \sum_{i=1}^{n} \tilde{s}_{it} \cdot \text{dlog}(a_{it}),$$ (12.10)

where $\widetilde{s}_{it} = 1/2\,(s_{it} - s_{it-1})$ is a weighted average of current and lagged values of s_{it}, the Tornquist–Theil approximation to the Divisia index. Other alternatives are to set $\widetilde{s}_{it}$ as a constant share $\bar{s}_i$ (the transactions-orientated monetary aggregate); or as a weighted average of last period's share and a constant so that $\widetilde{s}_{it} = ((1 - \lambda)s_{it-1} + \lambda\bar{s}_i)$, which is a smoothed Divisia aggregate, based on an empirically determined weight, λ. Each method of forming discrete approximations to the shares gives a different response of the monetary aggregate to changes in the user costs. Both price and quantity adjustments to the aggregate will be translated in different ways into the final Divisia aggregate on the basis of the approximation used. These differences, and the comparison with the simple sum aggregate (where $\widetilde{s}_{it} = 1/n$), yield distinct long-run trend paths and turning points for the monetary aggregate.

Application of Divisia models

When a Divisia approach is used, the demand for money function should be more stable than its simple-sum equivalent and suffer less from the problems that plagued the Goldfeld equation. Through its ability to account for the gradual shift out of certain asset components into others, the Divisia is well placed to deal with financial innovation (see Mullineux, 1996). The variation in the weights is able to deal with changes to the monetary environment and the additional information on the direction of flow of assets out of one component into another is valuable.

While the microeconomic foundations of the approach are sound, limitations arise in the application of the model. The choice of the benchmark is both problematic and crucial to the results. In many cases there is no unique asset which dominates in return over the sample and hence there is no obvious benchmark to use. Models have emerged which allow the switching of the benchmark from one asset to another on the basis of dominant return but the issue remains unsolved. Equally difficult are the problems associated with how to specify correctly the own yields on assets (e.g. quantifying the holding period yields to include returns to non-monetary services), how to specify the monetary aggregate in terms of breadth and construction, and how to deal with quality adjustment and uncertainty in returns.

Nevertheless, despite these difficulties, the evidence for a more stable demand function when Divisia aggregates are used is compelling, suggesting that inappropriate methods were responsible for a lot of the instability in the Goldfeld equation. Chrystal and MacDonald (1994) and Belongia (1996) report results to show that the Divisia model outperformed conventional aggregates in the USA, Australia, Canada, Germany, Switzerland, Japan, and the UK using standard diagnostic tools. The Divisia aggregate is shown to have desirable properties as a leading indicator to predict nominal output and inflation in a test against a St Louis equation for the UK, Australia, Germany, Switzerland, Canada, Japan, and the USA. The superior performance derives from the elimination of distortions due to financial innovations in the late 1970s and early 1980s and the extra information on substitution and income effects, gained by weighting components differently (see Barnett, 1980; Barnett, Offenbacher, and Spindt, 1984; Belongia and Chalfont, 1989).

12.4 Flexible Functional Forms

THE flexible functional form approach to the demand for money has a number of similarities to the Divisia method, and for this reason we wish to consider them conjointly. As before, money enters the utility function, individuals make decisions about the substitutability of assets on the basis of rates of return, and separability becomes a central issue once again. In both models, there is a prior or higher-order decision concerning the level of consumption of goods and leisure relative to the decision to hold financial assets, broadly defined. A second, lower-order decision is then made about the composition of the financial portfolio which is separable from the other decision.

Another similarity between the Divisia and the systems approach to the demand for money comes from the imperfect substitutability of financial assets within the portfolio. These differences derive from the liquidity services that each asset can provide and the relative usefulness of each asset for the purpose of transactions or saving. Obviously, if all assets in the system were perfectly substitutable, there would be little point in modelling them separately as interactive demand functions.

The demand for financial assets has been extensively explored by Ewis and Fisher (1984), Barnett, Offenbacher, and Spindt (1984), Serletis and Robb (1986), and Barr and Cuthbertson (1991, 1992). 'Globally' flexible functional forms are the most general types of these kinds of models, and can cope with any demand system, but they are essentially static and difficult to generalize to dynamic forms. 'Locally' flexible functional forms make some restrictions on the generality of the functional form but remain flexible over a plausible range. They can also be generalized to dynamic forms in which the demand for money is normally estimated. In this section we focus primarily on the class of 'almost ideal demand systems' (AIDS) from the family of 'price-independent generalized logarithmic' (PIGLOG) cost functions.

The AIDS models derive a demand system consistent with microeconomic consumer theory and specify an econometric framework that can determine whether utility-maximizing behaviour is actually observed. They begin by establishing the structure of the equilibrium demands for each asset in the system from the utility function approach. The consumer chooses the desired quantities of each financial asset, $a^*_{1t+1}, a^*_{2t+1}, a^*_{3t+1}, a^*_{4t+1}$ in order to maximize the utility function:

$$u = u(a^*_{1t+1}, a^*_{2t+1}, \ldots a^*_{nt+1}) \tag{12.11}$$

subject to the wealth or budget constraint (w^*_t),

$$\sum_{i=1}^{n} p^*_{it} a^*_{it+1} = w^*_t, \tag{12.12}$$

where p^*_{it} is the expected real price of an asset and a^*_{it+1} denotes desired asset holdings at the start of period $t + 1$.

By maximizing the utility function subject to the wealth constraint, or computing its dual in terms of minimizing the cost of achieving a given level of utility (which turns out to mathematically more tractable), a theoretically consistent solution can be found. Barr and Cuthbertson adopt the PIGLOG family of cost functions and from this general class they choose AIDS functions. The solution yields the set of demand equations giving the quantities demanded as a function of expected prices and total expenditure defined as

$$\ln C(p,u) = (1 - u)\ln a(p^*) + u \ln b(p^*), \tag{12.13}$$

where C is the minimum cost of achieving utility u at price p. The solution produces the share equations:

$$s_i = \alpha_i + \sum_{j=1}^{n} \gamma_{ij} \ln p^*_{jt} + \beta_i \ln\{\frac{w^*_t}{p^*}\}. \tag{12.14}$$

This is a very flexible form that allows each asset demand to be modelled as a share of the total portfolio. The demand system can accommodate luxuries ($\beta_l > 0$) and necessities ($\beta_i < 0$) side by side, and necessities can also be normal or inferior goods. The flexibility of the AIDS model provides a first-order approximation to a wide range of demand functions and this greatly helps in the implementation stage. The model makes considerable demands on the data due to the large number of parameters and cross-equation restrictions that need to be imposed to ensure consistency with the theory.

The demand functions are then examined for their consistency with rational consumer choice theory. They should be homogeneous of degree zero in both prices and wealth and price substitution terms should satisfy Slutsky symmetry

$$\sum_{j=1}^{n} \gamma_{ij} = 0 \tag{12.15}$$

$$\gamma_{ij} = \gamma_{ji}. \tag{12.16}$$

The cost function should also be a concave function of prices, which implies that the substitution effects satisfy a negativity condition:

$$c_{ij} = \gamma_{ij} + \beta_i\beta_j \ln\{\frac{w^*_t}{p^*}\} - s_i\delta_{ij} + s_is_j. \tag{12.17}$$

These three conditions of homogeneity, symmetry, and negativity are necessary and sufficient to ensure a demand system consistent with consumer theory.

At a theoretical level, the system can deal with many of the problems identified by Barnett (1997) for simple-sum money demand equations because the foundations of the models with respect to separability and substitutability are similar. Empirically, the systems-approach equations allow greater flexibility than conventional models. First, asset demands are modelled separately, implying that they are imperfect substitutes (or even complements) and depend on the yield relative to a number of alternatives. Second, the scale or constraint variable in the model is taken from a real budget constraint, and in this respect the equations are not *ad hoc* but are consistent with microeconomic consumer theory. Since the desired long-run demand for any individual asset category depends on a set of expected real prices (yields), and a composite real interest rate, the model is far more like a monetarist portfolio balance approach than the usual Keynesian one derived from motives for holding money, and the allocation of asset shares depends on wealth rather than current income.

Barr and Cuthbertson (1991, 1992) estimate such a model using UK flow of funds data for the personal and corporate sectors. The categories of assets used in the personal sector system are notes and coin, sight deposits, time deposits, building society deposits, and national savings and from these the asset shares (as a proportion of the total portfolio) are calculated. The regression results are reported for the sample 1977(4) to 1986(4). The model satisfies the requirements of consumer theory by exhibiting homogeneity, symmetry, and negativity as described above and the parameter estimates of the model are stable within sample. Results for the corporate sector are similar but include asset categories based on transactions balances (M1), time deposits, public sector debt, and foreign currency deposits. The sample period is the same as before and the model satisfies the requirements of consumer theory.

12.5 Sectoral Disaggregation and Superaggregates

MUCH of the work on Divisia models and AIDS functions of the demand for money has been in parallel with other developments that have taken place to alter the extent or scope of aggregation and disaggregation. Two of them are examined here.

Sectoral disaggregation

Standard monetary aggregates are summations not only over asset types, such as notes and coin, sight deposits, demand deposits, and so on, but also over different subgroups of economic entities. Aggregations such as M0, M1, make an implicit assumption that the underlying theoretical reasons for holding monetary assets are identical across sectors. This assumption can be tested by estimating functions at a disaggregated level and comparing them to the aggregate model.

There are reasons for thinking that the personal sector, company sector, other financial institutions, and overseas sector do not have identical motives for holding liquid assets and do not have equal access to the same set of liquid assets.[8] In the case of the UK, the personal sector holds more liquid cash than either the company sector or the financial institutions sector and holds a significant proportion of total M4 in bank and building society savings accounts. The company sector and financial institutions hold mostly wholesale deposits (not retail deposits) and these are very volatile in comparison with personal sector balances. The corporate sector responds to interest rates on a wide range of alternative assets, many of which are not available to the personal sector. In terms of liabilities (which are usually ignored in demand for money studies), the personal sector has access to two main types of credit (secured mortgage lending and unsecured bank credit card and other short-term loans) whereas firms have access to a wider range of funds, including new equity issues, bond issues, and wholesale markets for commercial paper and bills.

A series of recent papers, many of which originated in the Bank of England, have attempted to build sectoral models using monetary data based on the demand for broad money assets, M4, or the credit counterparts, M4L.[9] The first generation of models, Cuthbertson (1985), Fisher and Vega (1993), and Mizen (1994), estimated individual demand functions for the personal and industrial and commercial company sectors. The personal sector equations looked much like those for the aggregate (which is hardly surprising since the personal sector comprises the bulk of M4 holdings). Industrial and commercial company sector holdings, on the other hand, were far more volatile and difficult to explain—one feature in particular that puzzled empirical researchers was the high income elasticity found in these models.

In a second generation of models, due to Ireland and Wren-Lewis (1992), Mizen (1994), Thomas (1997a,b), Brigden and Mizen (1999), Chrystal and Mizen (1999, 2000), and Chrystal, Janssen, and Nolan (1999), some of this puzzle has been resolved. These papers have taken the demand for money function and modelled the real expenditure decision to which it is related in an interactive way. Thus, the personal sector models involve equations in M4, M4L, and consumption whilst the industrial and commercial companies sector models involve M4, M4L, and investment. For the other financial institutions there is no corresponding real variable, although the sector does include institutional investors, investment trusts, credit corporations, and leasing companies all of which engage in some real activity often via their influence on other sectors' expenditures. The income elasticity and volatility that were questionably large beforehand are much closer to the expected results.

In principle, and so long as the data permit accuracy in estimated relationships, it would seem sensible to examine monetary relationships at the sectoral level or at least to be aware of the important differences with respect to income, interest rates, and other explanatory variables in each sector.[10]

Superaggregates

In Chapter 8 we examined a number of models of currency substitution. This is one area in which financial innovation would seem likely to have been particularly important. The widespread abolition of exchange controls and the introduction of computerized systems make currency substitution possible on a scale not previously feasible. The technology is important because it allows instant quotation of foreign-currency-denominated deposit rates and exchange rates at minimal cost.

Yet early experiments with currency substitution terms in demand for money functions proved to be disappointing. Some of the earlier positive studies (e.g. Brittain (1981) and Miles (1978), were effectively criticized, by Cuddington (1983) for example, and a number of negative findings undermined their conclusions (Bordo and Choudhri, 1982). It was widely expected that currency substitution would be an important factor. Was this anticipation of widespread currency substitution incorrect? And was McKinnon (1984, 1996) mistaken in his belief that the observed instability of national money demand functions (that is, demand for domestically denominated money) could be traced to currency substitution? It seems that as globalization and innovation have continued apace, it was always probable that his contention would prove to be correct ultimately, but simply premature.

A new generation of studies has approached these issues in terms of 'superaggregates' (see Table 12.3). Much of this work was spurred by an interest in the question of the relative stability of European versus national demand for money functions with an eye to the potential advantages of the European Central Bank adopting a Europe-wide monetary policy target prior to full EMU. As a consequence, supranational and national monetary aggregates have been compared for their stability at a European level.[11] If national money demand functions are unstable but EC-wide aggregates formed by adding all the national demands together are not, then the instability at the national level may be due to the behaviour of the holdings of foreign currency deposits by domestic residents. The reasoning is that there are components held abroad by domestic residents that are very volatile, causing the instability observed in national money demand functions. Only in aggregate (at the supranational level) do these effects net out and leave a stable function useful for monetary policy.

A first group of studies typically find that the EC-wide demand for money functions are more stable and adduce that currency substitution, defined as the demand by non-residents for domestic money or *vice versa*, is responsible. The two papers that deserve the greatest attention in this respect are Kremers and Lane (1992) and Lane and Poloz (1992). The first paper investigates the validity of aggregating the demand for money functions at the national level to a supranational function. This amounts to a test of the validity of the assumption that the demand equations have similar functional forms, explanatory variables, and parameter values for all of the (then EMS) countries. Artis *et al.* (1992) show that if Germany or France are excluded from the supra-aggregates the parameter values turn out to be quite different from their values estimated for the full group. The second paper searches for (and finds some) indirect evidence of currency substitution in the (then) nine participating members of the ERM (Germany, France, Italy, UK, Netherlands, Belgium, Denmark, Ireland, and Spain) plus three other G7 countries: USA, Canada, and Japan. Although Filosa (1995) questions whether there is really much currency substitution in Europe after detecting that there is little negative correlation between the residuals of national money demand equations, the aggregated demand for money function of the EC countries participating in the ERM evidences greater stability than the individual national money demand functions.

A later group of studies examined and evaluated the contribution of the first, and has noted that even the superaggregated national aggregates ignore significant

Table 12.3 Principal studies using superaggregates in Europe[*]

Authors	Money concept	Group of countries	Aggregation method[a]	Estimation period	Price level[b]	Real income	Short-term interest rate[c]	Long-term interest rate[c]	Rate of inflation	Currency substitution[d]	Trend[e]	Error-correction parameter	Standard error[f]
(1)	M1	EMS7	er-1979	3/78–4/86	0.42	0.91	—	-1.00	—	1.00	—	—	—
(2)	M1	EMS7	PPP-1985	4/78–4/87	1	1.00	-0.67	—	-1.40	0.08	—	-0.95	0.82
(3)	M1	EMS7	er-1980	2/79–2/90	1	0.99	—	-1.21	—	0.09	—	-0.73	1.17
	M2	EMS7	er-1980	2/79–2/90	1	1.20	—	-0.70	—	0.03	—	-0.38	0.52
(4)	M3	EMS9	er-1987	1/79–4/89	1	1.53	-0.65	—	—	0.02	0.26	-0.34	0.35
	M3	EMS9	er-curr.	1/79–4/89	1	1.33	-0.66	—	—	0 01	0.43	-0.37	0.52
	M3	EMS9	er-curr.	1/77–3/90	1	1.29	-0.72	—	—	0.02	0.46	-0.44	0.50
(5)	M3	EMS6[g]	PPP-curr.	2/79–2/90	1	1.48	—	-0.10[h]	—	—	—	-0.10	0.54
(6)	M1	EMS7	er-curr.	2/79–2/89	1	1.08	-1.16	—	—	-0.13	—	-0.47	0.60
	M3	EMS7	er-curr.	2/79–2/92	1	1.26	-0.68	—	—	-0.09	—	-0.25	0.35
(7)	M3	EC	ec-curr.	1/79–1/92	1	1.25	-0.49	—	—	—	n.a.	-0.53	0.47
(8)	M1	EMS7	er-1990	2/79–4/92	1	1.20	—	-0.14	—	0.07	—	-0.70	0.80

Notes:

[a] er = exchange rate.
[b] Other than in 1, homogeneity is imposed.
[c] Except for (8) where the coefficient is an elasticity, the estimates are semi-elasticities.
[d] In (1) = long-term interest differential US–EMS7; in (2) = $/ECU exchange rate; in (4) = change in $/ECU rate; in (6) = $/ECU deviation from PPP.
[e] In (4) = a segmented trend and in (7) = a segmented and complete trend.
[f] Standard error from EXM × 100.
[g] EMS7 minus Italy.
[h] Long rate minus own rate.

Authors:

(1) Bekx and Tullio (1989)
(2) Kremers and Lane (1990)
(3) Artis et al. (1993)
(4) Monticelli and Strauss-Kahn (1993)
(5) Cassard et al. (1996)
(6) Tullio et al. (1996)
(7) Monticelli (1993)
(8) Artis (1996)

Source: Artis (1996) in Mizen and Pentecost (eds).

components of foreign currency holdings, such as those held by non-residents and those held by residents in banks abroad. Goodhart (1990) and Angeloni *et al.* (1986) make reference to an eight-cell matrix, which we reproduce as Table 12.4, to identify many other possible components, which remain unrecorded in domestic aggregates.

Letting A represent the domestic country and B the foreign country we can categorize the residency, denomination, and location of different money balances. Most of the literature on currency substitution has dealt with the impact of foreign variables on the holdings of domestic currency by domestic residents in domestic banks (cell 1, AAA) or the variation in holdings of foreign currencies by domestic residents in domestic banks (cell 5, ABA). However, this is to consider only two of eight possible component parts of what may be deemed currency substitution even if we restrict ourselves to currency transactions alone. In particular, foreign currency that domestic residents may hold in banks abroad (cell 6, ABB) is neglected along with the possibility of parallel or symmetrical demand for domestic currency by non-residents held in domestic and foreign banks (cells 3, BAA and 4, BAB respectively).

In the European context, there has at least been some attempt to allow for cross-border deposits (CBDs) by adding these to national aggregates to produce super-aggregates (see Artis, 1996 for a survey). How large is the potential misspecification introduced by ignoring CBDs? Studies differ in their answers. Angeloni *et al.* (1986), concluded that the components of CBDs associated with pure substitution and substitution/relocation had not significantly altered for countries such as Germany, the UK, or Spain. In France and Italy, however, there is evidence that they were important, but only for relatively short periods, and in the case of Italy they had been overshadowed by capital relocations since exchange controls were lifted. This led them to conclude that the inclusion of CBDs was not a vitally important issue in Europe. Monticelli and Papi (1995) suggest that some elements of the CBDs are not likely to be substitutable across borders whilst others are. Only the substitutable components are liable to cause instability in national vis-à-vis supranational ones and these seem to be of importance for EC-wide money demand equations.

Perhaps the main issue, noted by Artis (1996), is that, while indirect evidence of the importance of currency substitution might be provided by the relative stability of the

Table 12.4 Definitions of cross-border deposits

	Residents with domestic banks	Residents with foreign banks	Non-residents with domestic banks	Non-residents with foreign banks
In national currency	1 AAA	2 AAB	3 BAA	4 BAB
In foreign currency	5 ABA	6 ABB	7 BBA	8 BBB

Source: Goodhart (1990).

supernational aggregates, the result could also be a statistical artefact. The nature of the aggregation process, in terms of the adding-up procedure and the combination of countries involved, could be responsible for the finding. With the advent of European Monetary Union (EMU) and the removal from circulation of most of the currencies studied, we will probably never find out. A new group of studies will be needed to examine currency substitution at a more global level.

12.6 Conclusions

IN 1962, the Nobel Laureate Lawrence Klein described the ratio of money to income (reciprocal of velocity of circulation) as one of the five 'great ratios of economics' (1962: 183), along with the savings/income ratio (propensity to save), the capital/output ratio (acceleration principle), labour's share of output (income distribution), and the capital/labour ratio (factor proportions). These ratios have all been the basis of empirical examination, but none more so than the ratio of money to income in the form of the demand for money function. (Some studies in fact used the ratio of money to income as the explained variable.) Twenty five years ago, economists thought that they had succeeded in establishing a stable relationship, but the models then fell apart and it has not been possible to reconstruct relatively straightforward functions of the type which featured in early studies.

That failure has acted as a spur for a new wave of theoretical and empirical work. In the previous chapter we examined new theories based around the idea of money as a buffer stock and also econometric advances employing general-to-specific methodology, cointegration and equilibrium correction models. This chapter has explored the role of financial innovation in terms of the processes and source of innovation, its impact on the demand for money, and measurement techniques capable of dealing with innovation. Some of the factors sparking financial innovation such as inflation and high interest rates might be thought of as in the nature of 'one-off' changes resulting from the volatile years of high inflation and energy price shocks. Others such as technology and exchange rate variability show no signs of letting up and appear to have become almost a permanent part of the financial scene. On this basis, there seems no reason to expect financial innovations to cease, placing a premium on estimation methods which can allow for it. A number of techniques have been examined here, including Divisia aggregates, AIDS models, and PIGLOG functions (both unfortunate acronyms), sectoral disaggregation, and supranational aggregates to allow for currency substitution. All have merits and all have resulted in improved estimation, without really convincing that they are 'the' answer.

Perhaps this finding is only to be expected. What comes through from the analyses of financial innovation is that the processes involve a dynamic interaction between information technology, financial engineering, and gap-filling, environmental factors such as interest rates and exchange rates, regulation and deregulation, competition in the financial sector, and the operation of monetary policy. This interactive process is unlikely to proceed smoothly enough to be captured fully by Divisia methods, while the ever-changing cast of characters is difficult to pick up by other methods. The mixture of factors and effects involved becomes clear when we consider deregulation and the consequences that it has for the demand for money, the structure of the financial system, and the operation of monetary policy in following chapters.

Notes

1 An earlier study by Burns (1971) focused on the liquidity and other attributes of claims, and the impact of financial innovation in altering these characteristics.

2 In Hegel's philosophical system, however, the interaction of thesis and antithesis leads to a new concept (synthesis), which then becomes the thesis of the new triad.

3 The idea of analysing needs and characteristics was pioneered for assets by Makower and Marschak (1938) who classified assets in terms of their contribution to the attributes of lucrativity (i.e. profitability) and safety. Lancaster developed his theory for physical products, arguing that consumers make choices not so much between commodities but between alternative bundles of characteristics incorporated in the commodities. For example, people have a need for tooth hygiene and have preferences amongst brands of toothpaste according to what extent they supply the characteristics of prevention of decay and whitening. One difference between goods and financial services is that for physical products the characteristics are immutable for already-produced goods, whereas for financial products the characteristics can be unbundled and traded. This is the basis of derivatives—see Lewis (1990, 1997).

4 Lewis and Davis (1987) provide a detailed account.

5 See Lewis (1986a).

6 Off-the-balance-sheet financing innovations are examined in Lewis (1992b) and references therein.

7 These developments are outlined in Allen (1990).

8 The UK has recently adopted the European System of Regional and National Accounts (1995) (ESA95) and has redefined the sectors into households, private non-financial corporations, other financial corporations. These new definitions are similar to the original sectoral breakdowns and so we use those original terms for ease of exposition even though many of the studies mentioned use the new classifications.

9 The credit counterparts approach is explained in Ch. 14.

10 Of course, if this line of reasoning were to be carried through, there would be no macroeconomics and only individual functions. Irving Fisher argued that although each person's money holding would be 'somewhat rough and dependent on the

accident of the moment' when averaged over 'a large number of people' monetary behaviour 'will be very closely determined' (1911: 149–55).

11 This has been spearheaded by Kremers and Lane (1992); Lane and Poloz (1992); Van Reit (1993); Artis, Bladen-Hovell, and Zhang (1992); Cassard, Lane, and Masson (1996); and Monticelli (1993).

Chapter 13
The Transmission Mechanism

13.1 Money and monetary policy

MONETARY policy is often defined as being synonymous with the quantity of money. For example, in his 1962 survey, 'Monetary Theory and Policy', to which we have already made reference, Harry Johnson defined 'monetary theory as comprising theories concerning the influence of the quantity of money in the economic system, and monetary policy as policy employing the central bank's control of the supply of money as an instrument for achieving the objectives of general economic policy' (1462: 1). More recently, noting the 'consensus among monetary economists that central banks are responsible for inflation', Marvin Goodfriend (1997) went on to add:

The theory of money demand implies that control of the money supply is necessary and sufficient to control the trend rate of inflation . . . money demand may be thought of as the fulcrum by which a central bank controls inflation, and the money supply may be thought of as the lever by which it does so. (1997: 9)

Note the terminology used above to describe the money supply: 'instrument' and 'lever'. The formal theory of economic policy makes a distinction between variables which are under the direct control of the policy-makers, the policy instruments, and variables which can claim some welfare significance and so, although not under the authorities' direct control, are variables the policy-makers wish to influence: these are ultimate target variables or objectives of policy. In between the instruments and the ultimate, or goal, variables, it is possible to distinguish a further category of variables. These intermediate variables are heavily influenced by the authorities' policy instruments without being directly controllable, and they may therefore appear to be good indicators of the combined effect of the use the authorities make of their various policy instruments and may have a temporal lead over the ultimate variables: they may in certain cases be described as forming part of the transmission mechanism through which changes in policy instruments affect the ultimate target variables.

Schematically, the theory suggests that we can think of the sequence

$$I \rightarrow IV \rightarrow UV, \tag{13.1}$$

where I is the set of policy instruments, IV the set of intermediate variables, and UV the set of ultimate variables. The useful properties of intermediate variables may well lead to a case being made out that a particular intermediate or indicator variable should become a target itself.

An example from standard Keynesian fiscal policy analysis clarifies the categorization. In a Keynesian transmission mechanism for fiscal policy, it would be conventional to select as ultimate objectives at least the rate of capacity utilization and the rate of inflation; tax rates of various kinds and rates of government expenditure are the policy instruments which are used to realize desired values for these variables. In view of the multiplicity of instruments, the task of describing or 'indicating' fiscal policy stance would be eased by nominating an intermediate variable. The budget deficit is an obvious candidate; here the policy effects are scaled in net revenue terms, and a thoroughgoing Keynesian analysis would suggest that a demand-weighted version of the deficit would be even better—for not all taxes have the same demand impact.

Further, because the deficit varies not only as a result of variations in the policy instruments but also to an important degree because of non-policy influences, it may be desired to purge the deficit of these influences by normalizing the deficit measurement at full employment. Thus we arrive at the demand-weighted full employment or 'structural' budget surplus measure. This is a coherent example of application of the theory: the nomination of ultimate variables and policy instruments seems relatively unequivocal; at the same time the theory of the transmission mechanism assumed indicates a consistent way of transforming an intermediate variable into an indicator. While this is something of a second-best to using all the information available, say in the form of simulations using a macroeconomic model, it seems likely that there would be communication advantages in using the indicator. Indeed, it would not be difficult to imagine circumstances in which the indicator might be turned into an intermediate target variable.

The true situation is rather more complicated than this example suggests. For a start, views about the transmission mechanism differ. Second, how fine the distinction should be between instrument and intermediate variable in a particular case is a matter of convenience for the purpose in hand, but judgement on this differs from one observer to another and often produces confusion as a result. Third, nominating indicator variables as intermediate targets may give rise to a change in behaviour with the result that the indicator value of the variable becomes compromised. This is the basis of 'Goodhart's Law' (Goodhart, 1984).

When we turn to monetary policy, the position is more complex still. Treasury fiscal actions impinge, albeit through various fiscal and budgetary agencies, directly upon ultimate spending units lying outside the control of the authorities. Monetary policy is implemented through a network of financial intermediaries and markets, none of which is strictly controlled by direct administrative fiat like, say, the rate of the value-added tax (VAT). The 'true' instrument in that sense may be the policy directive given to the Open Market Desk by the central bank's monetary policy committee (e.g. FOMC).

Obviously if for the purpose in hand a particular indicator variable can be taken to be exclusively determined by the policy instruments available, then it will save some unnecessary explanation if that variable is treated in effect as an instrument. This is the classical elision that economists—including Keynes himself—have perpetrated in the case of the money supply. On a strict reading, the money supply—which after all includes the deposit liabilities of commercial banks—is certainly not a policy instrument. It is an intermediate variable. In the *Treatise*, Keynes recognized that 'bank money' as opposed to 'state money' dominates the money stock. Nevertheless, Keynes of the *General Theory* and many other economists elide the distinction between the authorities' control of the interest rate instrument and their influence over the intermediate variable, the money supply, simply treating the money supply as if it were an instrument. Expositions of the standard macroeconomic IS–LM model routinely do this (even though as we saw, Hicks himself did not). This would appear in principle to be perfectly straightforward if we wish to abstract from the control problem in order to focus on other issues. Treating a variable 'as if' it were a policy instrument does not imply that it actually is one. Nevertheless, the practice can create confusion in the minds of those who do not incorporate the 'as if' clause into what they are reading, for the control problem is a major issue in practice. As Lord Kingsdown (Robin Leigh-Pemberton, a former Governor of the Bank of England) once remarked, there is not a switch on the wall in the Governor's office which turns the money supply on and off; it only works the light.

So far we have been considering definitions of the money supply that incorporate the liabilities (deposits) of commercial banks. For a definition of the money supply as the monetary base, the question of what is the instrument—the base itself or the terms (the rate of interest) on which the authorities will decide to meet the excess demand for monetary base—is arguably more a matter of convention. British economists historically have preferred to treat the (money market) rate of interest as the instrument, stressing that the Bank of England has always closely monitored this rate of interest and has often intervened vigorously to enforce a particular value for it. American economists historically have taken the opposite line, stressing that the monetary base is the instrument. This difference reflects alternative ways of examining money supply determination, for in the US tradition the monetary base lies at the heart of the analysis.

13.2 Money Supply Analysis

MONEY supply theories are concerned with the processes governing supply conditions in countries with extensive financial intermediation. Three groups are involved in these processes and the links between the three groups depend upon the institutions, regulations, and financial technology which prevail in individual countries. The monetary authorities issue fiat money and determine the conditions under which the financial intermediaries operate. The public allocates its money holdings between fiat money and the claims of financial intermediaries. Financial intermediaries acquire securities issued by the public and the authorities, and supply their own liabilities in return.

Two major approaches have been developed to analyse the interrelationships. Both are based on identities, yet are shaped by implicit hypotheses about the behaviour of the three participating groups. Those identities used in the USA, although they can be applied in any country with a fractional reserve banking system, revolve around the quantity of base money or total reserves and a 'money multiplier'. Underlying them is the belief, explicitly stated by Brunner (1973), that the money supply process can be decomposed into two parts—one part being the exogenous input of the monetary authorities, the other representing the endogenous reaction of the banks and the public.

In other countries, such as the UK, Australia, France, and Italy, the monetary environment has historically been seen to be less hospitable to such a strict division, because some part of the authorities' behaviour could be rendered endogenous due to a commitment to interest rate or exchange rate targets. For this reason, an alternative mode of analysis has been used, and it has been more useful in these countries to classify the sources of money supply change into 'credit counterparts' by means of the flow of funds without distinguishing the actions of the authorities from others.

Money multiplier approaches

Based on the writings of Friedman and Schwartz (1963) and Cagan (1965), the money multiplier approach builds on the standard analysis in money and banking textbooks, in which bank deposits, D are derived as a multiple $(1/r)$ of banks' holdings of reserves, R. Reserve assets are the monetary liabilities of the central bank, i.e. base or high-powered money, H, divided among the alternative uses as bank reserves and the cash holdings of the non-bank public, C. Thus

$$H = C + R. \tag{13.2}$$

The money supply is defined as

$$M = D + C \tag{13.3}$$

by denoting the ratios C/D and R/D as d and r respectively, one can derive

$$M = \frac{1 + d}{d + r} H = mH, \tag{13.4}$$

which links the money supply to the high-powered money.

The ratio $m = (1 + d)/(d + r)$ is referred to as the *money multiplier*, and under a system of fractional reserve banking (when $r < 1$) must be greater than 1. Part of the bank reserves may be required by law or held by convention, with the remainder held voluntarily by banks in excess of requirements. Accordingly,

$$R = RR + ER, \tag{13.5}$$

where RR is legal reserves and ER is excess reserves, and

$$r = rr + er, \tag{13.6}$$

where rr is the required reserve ratio (RR/D) and e is the excess reserve ratio (E/D), enabling us to rewrite the money multiplier[1] as

$$m = \frac{1 + d}{d + (rr + er)} \; . \tag{13.7}$$

With rr a policy-determined variable, control of the money supply might be achievable by H if the ratios d and e are stable.

The question of the stability of the money supply processes arises because H, d, and e are, in the words of Friedman and Schwartz, 'proximate determinants' in the sense that they are in turn governed by more fundamental factors. The ratios d and e are the outcome of portfolio decisions of the non-bank public and bank sectors, respectively, in response to relative interest rates, summarized by a vector of relevant rates, **i**. If attention is focused on the authorities' actions in supplying base money by means of open market operations altering the central bank's holdings of securities, S, a relationship of the form

$$M = h(S, \mathbf{i}, rr) \tag{13.8}$$

can be substituted for (13.4), along the line of Sims and Takayama (1985). Where open market operations themselves respond to variables such as income or prices by means of a policy reaction function, (13.8) can be decomposed further.[2] The reader may note that many of the variables which would then enter the right-hand side of (13.8) are the same as those which feature in demand-for-money models.

It is fair to say, however, that proponents of the money multiplier identity typically hold to a particular view of the money supply process (Anderson, 1967; Jordan, 1969). This is one in which the monetary authorities provide a particular quantity of base money, from which the banks must meet reserve requirements and obtain their desired holdings of excess reserves and from which the public acquires its currency holdings. Thus the two groups are in competition for a limited amount of base money, with the entire quantity always claimed. Changes in the quantity of the monetary base will create discrepancies between desired and actual reserves of banks, leading to alterations in the banks' acquisition of earning assets and thus their deposits.[3]

This idea is carried though into the *reserves available* approach which focuses upon that part of the monetary base which remains after the public's currency requirements are met. It is a special case of the money base–money multiplier model in which the reserves available to the banking system are treated as exogenous. With total reserves treated as the control variable, we have

$$M = \frac{1 + d}{rr + er} \cdot R. \tag{13.9}$$

The sources of total reserves are member-bank borrowings (BR) from the Reserve Banks and non-borrowed reserves (NBR), the latter arising mainly from system open market operations (along with Federal Reserve float and Treasury currency outstanding). Thus we can rewrite (13.5) as

$$R = NBR + BR$$
$$= RR + ER. \qquad (13.5a)$$

Frequently, reserves required to be held against government demand deposits and time and savings deposits are deducted from the total reserves figure to focus upon the reserves available for private sector demand deposits (and desired excess reserves).

Support for these interpretations of a process running from the quantity of reserves or high-powered money via a money multiplier to the quantity of money is offered from examinations of the relative importance of the public's, banks', and monetary authorities' behaviour in the money supply process for the USA (Brunner, 1987, 1992). Variations in the multiplier are prominent in the short-run, whereas the behaviour of the authorities dominates longer-run movements. When considering short-run movements, it must be remembered that the multiplier models are based on ratios which summarize underlying portfolio equilibrium relationships. Unexpected disturbances create deviations of actual asset ratios from their equilibrium values which are only rectified over time. A decrease in base money, for instance, must instantaneously reduce banks' excess reserve ratios. Variations in asset ratios may then reflect a lag in portfolio adjustment, signalling not the inappropriate nature of the behavioural assumptions, but simply their inapplicability to short-run situations. Of course, finding that H or R is strongly correlated with M does not establish exogeneity, a question taken up later.

Evidence for the UK is different. Figure 13.1 shows a remarkable change in the multiplier; after having fluctuated within a narrow band in the 100 years from 1871 to 1971, it soared in the following years (from around 4 to nearly 10), with a combination of a sharply declining ratio of currency to deposits and a greatly reduced reserve ratio. Much of the latter can be attributed to the ending under Competition and Credit Control in 1971 of the conventional minimum 8 per cent cash ratio which the clearing banks maintained by agreement with the Bank of England. But the years since 1971 have seen a rapid growth of, and British banks' participation in, wholesale markets for liabilities and bought funds.[4] These markets largely obviate the need for a bank to provide for its own cash liquidity needs. Instead, banks can seek out lending opportunities secure in the knowledge that they can buy in reserves to support their loan book—what is known as 'liability management'. By using reserves efficiently, these practices facilitate an economizing in the holding of reserves. Such developments suggest to many the desirability of a money stock formation approach which focuses upon bank lending and its contribution to the quantity of money. The alternative credit counterparts approach does so.

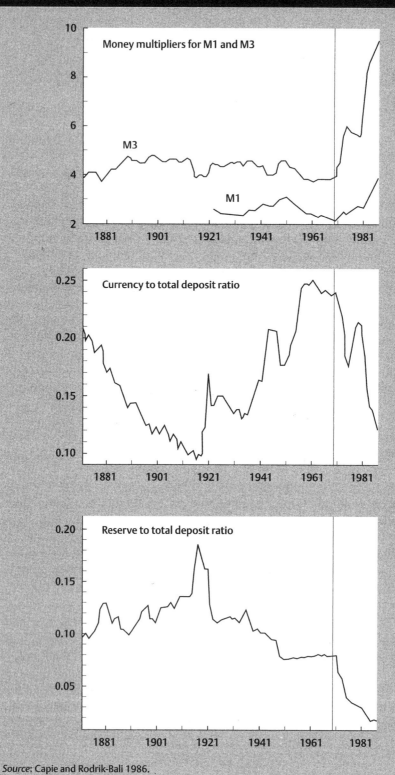

Figure 13.1 Money multipliers, UK, 1871–1985

Source: Capie and Rodrik-Bali 1986.

Credit counterparts approach

This approach, also involving identities, is derived from the flow of funds. Table 13.1 is a simplified four-sector version in which the central bank and the government are aggregated into an official sector, along with the foreign sector, private non-financial sector, and the financial sector (comprising in this case only the banks). Columns (i) and (ii) are the income and expenditure items, showing, for each of the four sectors, how funds have been derived through the earning of revenue and used for expenditures, with any difference constituting the particular sector's net borrowing or net lending (along with unidentified items). The remaining columns (iii)–(viii) show how the net borrowing or lending gives rise to changes in financial assets and liabilities.

The requirement that total income equals total expenditures is simply the familiar national income identity:

$$S + T = (I + G) + (X - Z). \tag{13.10}$$

This can be rearranged to give the parallel financing requirement, for the flow of funds provides the financial counterparts of the income and expenditure items which appear in the national accounts:

$$S - I = (X - Z) + (G - T). \tag{13.11}$$

In this form the identity says that borrowing by the overseas sector to finance an excess of home exports (X) over home imports (Z), together with borrowing by the government sector to finance an excess of its expenditure (G) over its revenue (T), must be matched by net lending by the non-financial private sector of the economy arising from its surplus of savings (S) over capital formation (I). The financial sector is assumed to have no net saving.

Net lending by the non-financial private sector results in its acquiring more financial assets than it issues by incurring liabilities, corresponding to its increase in net financial wealth. The assets may be acquired directly from the overseas and official sectors in the form of capital outflow ($-K$) or additional holdings of official debt issued as cash or bonds ($\triangle C + \triangle GSp$). Alternatively, the acquisition may occur indirectly via the banks (the private financial sector) by savers adding to deposits ($\triangle D$) and net non-deposit liabilities ($\triangle NDL$) in excess of the loans obtained by investors ($\triangle A$). From row 3 we see how the net surplus is allocated across the portfolio, i.e.

$$S - I = \triangle D + \triangle NDL + \triangle C + \triangle GS_p - K - \triangle A. \tag{13.12}$$

By equating (13.12) and (13.11) and rearranging, we obtain

$$\triangle D + \triangle C = (G - T) - \triangle GS_p + (X - Z + K) + \triangle A - \triangle NDL. \tag{13.13}$$

The left-hand side is simply the increase in money supply (M4). The first term on the right-hand side corresponds to the public sector borrowing requirement (or budget deficit). The second is the net sales of government interest-bearing debt to the non-bank private sector. The third term is the net external flows from the balance of

Table 13.1 Simplified flow-of-funds account

	(i) Income	(ii) Expenditure	(iii) Deposits	(iv) Non-deposit liabilities	(v) High-powered money	(vi) Government securities	(viii) Domestic lending	(viii) Foreign lending
1. Official	T	G			$-\Delta H$	$-\Delta GS$		ΔR
2. Foreign	Z	X						$K - \Delta R$
3. Private non-financial	S	I	ΔD	ΔNDL	ΔC	ΔGS_p	$-\Delta A$	$-K$
4. Financial			$-\Delta D$	$-\Delta NDL$	ΔR	ΔGS_B	ΔA	
Total	$S + Z + T$	$I + X + G$	0	0	0	0	0	0

payments identity, as given in row 2 (which includes changes in official reserves along with various short-term bank flows, e.g. non-resident transactions in sterling deposits and assets and the banks' switched position between sterling and foreign currency). The fourth term is bank lending to the private sector, while the last is the increase in net non-deposit liabilities (bank share capital and internal funds less non-financial assets such as bank premises along with any errors and omissions).

Thus we have the credit counterparts by which, in the case of the UK, a change in M4 equals public sector borrowing requirement *less* sales of gilts to non-bank private sector *plus* external influences *plus* increase in bank lending to the private sector *less* increase in net non-deposit liabilities.

Comparing the two approaches

Both approaches are based on identities, and in that sense are equally correct. Why, then, is the money multiplier identity favoured in the USA and the credit counterparts identity preferred in the UK? Our contention is that long-outstanding institutional differences between countries have shaped the approach to the analysis of the money supply.

We first note that the link between the two can be made from row 1 of Table 13.1 where

$$\triangle H + \triangle GS = G - T + \triangle R. \tag{13.14}$$

That is, if the official sector is running a deficit and/or adding to international reserves then it must be issuing high-powered money and interest-bearing government securities. The latter can be acquired by either banks or the non-bank private sector so that

$$\triangle H + \triangle GS_B = G - T - \triangle GSp + \triangle R. \tag{13.15}$$

Substituting the right-hand side of (13.15) into (13.13) gives

$$\triangle M = \triangle H + \triangle GS_B + \triangle A - \triangle NDL. \tag{13.16}$$

The last three items on the right-hand side of (13.16) can be described loosely as the net non-cash assets of the banks and, from the balance sheet of the banking sector in row 4,

$$\triangle GS_B + \triangle A - \triangle NDL = \triangle D - \triangle R. \tag{13.17}$$

Using (13.4) and (13.6) we can rewrite (13.17) as

$$\triangle M = \triangle H + \frac{1 - r}{d + r} \cdot \triangle H = \frac{1 + d}{d + rr + er} \triangle H. \tag{13.18}$$

This derivation immediately suggests one reason why the counterparts framework has been preferred in the UK. As noted previously, an implicit hypothesis underlying Equation (13.18) is that banks' acquisition of non-cash assets is governed by the availability of cash reserves. In short, a supply mechanism determines changes in banks' earning assets. However suitable this assumption is for the United States, it is less applicable for the case of bank lending in the United Kingdom, where the widespread use of the overdraft system means that the usage made of lending limits is largely at the customers' volition. An analysis based on the demand for credit rather than the supply of reserves has been seen to make more sense, and behavioural relationships about the demand for advances can be slotted readily into a framework such as Equation (13.13).

Second, bank lending to the private sector has long been a special focus of monetary policy in the UK, and this is a second reason why the counterparts framework is preferred. To a large degree, economic theory has caught up with this emphasis in terms of what is widely known as the *credit channel*. Early contributions to this literature, such as Jaffee and Russell (1976) and Stiglitz and Weiss (1981), suggested that a rational bank should be cautious about offering credit and should introduce 'quantity rationing' to exclude some 'unsafe' borrowers rather than extending loans to all borrowers who are prepared to pay the going price. This response derives from the inability of the banks to assess perfectly the performance and creditworthiness of the companies to which the loans are extended, giving rise to adverse selection and moral hazard problems. It is likely that banks have a special role in the credit market, particularly with respect to small and medium-sized enterprises unable to access other markets for funds and therefore having a certain dependence on banks for external sources of funds (Bernanke and Gertler, 1995). Factors such as the cash flow, financial wealth, previous loan payments history (see Leland and Pyle, 1977; Diamond, 1984; Fama, 1985) as well as outstanding debt, will be influential in determining the eligibility of a company for access to loans, and these can be monitored by banks under 'relationship banking'. These considerations draw attention to the likely importance of 'quantity variations' resulting from banks' credit decision processes (Stiglitz and Weiss, 1990).

Third, bank lending to the government sector in the UK has in the past frequently been determined more by the fiscal than by the monetary authorities. 'From the point of view of the monetary authorities, the size of the deficit to be financed is an external parameter which they have to accept' (Goodhart, 1975). This was the case before Bank of England independence, and the formal separation of debt management from monetary policy, when the Bank was one cog in a coordinated centralized policy-making machinery. One advantage claimed for the counterparts method is that the components can be identified, respectively, with fiscal policy $(G - T)$, debt management or funding policy $(\triangle GSp)$, exchange rate policy $(X - Z + K)$, and monetary policy $(\triangle A - \triangle NDL)$.

Fourth, the counterparts framework can be readily applied to aggregates which embrace the whole of the banking sector (e.g. M4) and is less readily applicable to the M1 aggregate for a long time preferred in the USA. Finally, the money multiplier has the advantage of isolating the impact of reserve requirements (rr) on the money supply. Since required reserves do not play a role as a policy tool in the Bank of England's monetary policy formulation, this feature is unimportant for the UK system.

Many of these long-standing institutional differences between the USA and the UK have been eroded. M1 is no longer the dominant aggregate in the USA, and the broader aggregates are now accorded greater emphasis. Less lending in the UK is now by means of overdraft than was formerly the case, while more lending in the USA is under loan commitments, both formal and informal. After 1985, the UK government followed the practice of fully funding its deficit by sales of securities. Following Bank of England independence in 1997, the link between monetary and fiscal policy in the UK was formally severed. And in terms of the adoption of base money (termed M0) as one of the monitored monetary aggregates, the UK would seem to have moved closer to US practice. There are further similarities, too, in the operation of monetary policy, examined in the next chapter.

Endogenous money?

When discussing US evidence of a close relationship between H and M, we noted that correlation need not imply causation; H can alter M via a relatively constant money multiplier, but the 'multiplier' may be stable because H is responding to M allowing the nominal money supply to accommodate passively to variations in the demand for money. Endogenous money is one of those concepts for which a fallacy of composition can apply. One individual can augment his/her money holdings by selling assets or reducing expenditures. But it is far from clear that the economy as a whole can do so; one individual's accretion of money may be someone else's loss.

There are some circumstances in which the economy as a whole can adjust its money balances. One is when the central bank stabilizes interest rates and allows the quantity of money to respond to demand. Another is maintenance of a fixed exchange rate which enables money balances to be replenished via overseas transactions. With a fixed rate of exchange and interest rate pegging policies, transactors are afforded some implicit guarantees about their freedom to exchange bonds or foreign securities on demand for money. To this extent (and the account is obviously a highly stylized one) the argument runs that the amount of money actually in existence is determined by *demand*, as excess supplies can be instantaneously liquidated and excess demands satisfied without repercussions for the arguments of the demand function.

However accurate this description is of the 1950s and 1960s, and we have reasons to question it, clearly different institutional arrangements operated in the 1970s. Monetary authorities moved away from interest rate setting to monetary targets, and from fixed to floating exchange rates. Activist monetary policies were followed. All of these are circumstances in which discrepancies between actual and desired money holdings might arise due to monetary shocks, i.e. exogenous money. By the same token, however, monetary policies in the mid- and late 1980s saw some movement back towards previous arrangements, involving interest rate setting, and these policies have continued in the 1990s. In this case, the post-Keynesian 'horizontalists' (Kaldor, 1986; Moore, 1988) contend that the money supply is rendered endogenous. The supply of money function becomes a horizontal line at the administratively-determined nominal interest rate, as opposed to the vertical line in (textbook caricatures of) the quantity theory. If we are to assess this view, we need to examine how monetary policy works, and discussion of endogeneity is deferred to the next chapter.

13.3 Policy Transmission Models

IT is possible to visualize circumstances whereby the precise way in which policy actions feed through the financial and economic system would be of little interest. If open market operations undertaken, say, in the morning had their full effect upon output and prices later that day, then there would be little practical value in the authorities monitoring what happens along the way. Alternatively, if it is not possible either to forecast what is likely to happen or to ascertain what is happening until market operations have fully worked their way through to incomes and prices, the authorities would simply have to sit it out, and stick with whatever policy settings seemed appropriate at the time, even if it takes a long time to find out the appropriateness of the actions taken.

In practice, of course, neither of these extremes holds. Certainly there are lags, but there are factors that can be used to make forecasts and there are also steps along the way that can be observed to form a judgement as to the appropriateness of the forecasts. Monetary policy consists of central banks' actions to affect monetary and financial conditions in pursuit of broader policy objectives. These actions are undertaken in a number of markets and operate via a network of financial institutions. In a complex financial system, the thrust of monetary policy instruments proceeds towards the policy objectives by a transmission process which successively incorporates a number of financial influences as the effects span out from the central bank to the money market, the banking system and other financial intermediaries, and the bond, mortgages and stock markets.

The precise way in which policy actions feed through the financial and economic system is called the *transmission mechanism*, and the various influences represent the *channels* of policy. Actions by the authorities in terms of the instruments, such as discounting, open market operations or repurchase agreements in bills and bonds, and interventions in foreign exchange markets, lack in themselves a common scale upon which they can be aggregated. Variables which are in between the instruments and ultimate goals, i.e. intermediate variables, are intended to solve this index number problem and to indicate how well the financial system is responding to the policy instruments.

Ideas about the transmission mechanism of policy have a fundamental bearing on the choice of indicator or intermediate target variable. So we look first at different views about the transmission mechanism of monetary policy before focusing on the issues involved in choosing an intermediate variable targeting strategy.

The post-war heritage

From the 1950s through to the 1970s the mainstream view of the transmission mechanism of monetary policy stressed that much of what policy did was to exploit credit rationing and imperfections in the markets—either directly, by means of direct controls over the availability and terms of credit, or indirectly via the institutions' sluggish response to interest rate changes stimulated by the authorities' actions. Econometric models adopted an IS–LM-type framework in which monetary policy begins with short-term money market rates and proceeds to longer-term yields and thence, in some cases via the stock market (Tobin's 'q'—see Tobin, 1980e), to expenditures such as fixed investments.

While the model-builders worked assiduously to identify interest rate influences upon expenditures, the rewards were not always commensurate with the effort. In part, this reflected the inadequacy of measures of expected rate of return on new investment and of the real cost of capital. With the latter, difficulties were experienced in measuring the opportunity cost in ways which would take account of inflation expectations and the different impact of inflation and taxation upon various areas of the corporate sector. This problem has not gone away; difficulties still persist in finding a role for the cost of capital in investment equations (see Bernanke and Gertler, 1995).

Monetarists argued that mainstream Keynesian analysis missed the wood while looking for the trees—demonstrations of the monetarist viewpoint favoured heroic single-equation reduced form exercises as contrasted with the structural model approach of the mainstream Keynesian tradition. According to the monetarist approach, the Keynesian tradition underplayed the role of the money supply in the transmission mechanism, sidelining it to a passive role as an inconsequential endogenous output and overlooking the implications of the findings of investigators of the demand for money. Monetarism also faulted the Keynesian prejudice of treating the price level as a parameter or too weakly endogenizing it. Paradoxically—since it does not concern the *monetary* mechanism as such—it was perhaps this last point which was to prove the most telling contribution when inflation took off, and the more so since Keynes himself was a determined opponent of inflation (Meade, 1993).

In fact, up to the point at which the price response is invoked there seems very little to distinguish the monetarist account of the transmission mechanism (see e.g. Friedman and Schwartz, 1963a; Friedman, 1970b) from the Keynesian one as expounded by Tobin and the Yale School (Tobin, 1969, 1978), despite strenuous efforts of both groups to differentiate their products. Surprisingly, much is still made of these differences in elementary textbooks. In both accounts, initial monetary disturbances unbalance portfolios and lead to a rectification process which involves an adjustment of expenditures and asset prices, promoting changes in output and eventually in prices (the Keynesian account placing less emphasis on this) until the aggregate demand for money relationship is again satisfied. Some differences of emphasis arose about the breadth and the relative role of asset price adjustments and possible direct effects of excess money (real balance effects).

Empirical support for the monetarist position seemed to be more persuasive on the US data sample than on the other side of the Atlantic. For example, specific exhibits of the monetarist case in the UK were easily dismissed; money did not appear to be exogenous to output or prices, nor did a stable money multiplier connect prior changes in money to subsequent changes in nominal income on the data set for the 1950s and 1960s (Artis and Nobay, 1969). In retrospect, all this holds together. The strong version of monetarism needed three things: a stable demand for money, a steeply sloped aggregate supply curve and exogenous money. The latter was substantially denied by the fixed-exchange-rate, interest-rate-pegging policies of the time and monetarists were in danger of trying to prove too much in suggesting otherwise.

Conceptions of the dominant features of the transmission mechanism were further developed against the background of a number of significant events. The first of these was the worldwide resort to floating exchange rates after 1973; the second was experience of high and variable inflation and changing expectations of inflation; the third was the actual experience of monetary targeting against a background of financial innovation and deregulation, and the breakdown of the empirical demand for money function.

Floating exchange rates

Friedman's monetarism was essentially a closed economy doctrine—and when applied to an open economy remains an account of what McKinnon calls 'an insular economy'. In such an economy, the exchange rate is just an output variable, with no feedback (see Figure 13.2a). The floating of the exchange rate does have the merit of making an autonomous money supply policy without exchange controls *possible*, but all this does in essence is to make the closed economy results hold fully. The relevant analysis is that of Hume's price–specie flow mechanism and purchasing power parity (see Chapter 8). Price levels in each country are tied to the money stock via the simple quantity theory, $MV = Py$. Prices in each country are brought to conformity with purchasing power parity according to the exchange rate system. Under fixed exchange rates such as implied by an international gold standard, prices in a country are subjected to pressures via the flow of international reserves (specie) calculated to bring them into line with prices ruling elsewhere, while exchange rates remain within the bounds defined by the fixed (e.g. gold) parity. Under floating rates, exchange rates conform to the price levels which result from independent monetary policies.

Friedman enunciated his insular economy view in 1980 in his evidence to the United Kingdom House of Commons Select Committee on the Treasury and Civil Service. When asked whether the exchange rate was not the principal part of the transmission mechanism of monetary policy in the UK, he responded:

I strongly disagree. Monetary policy actions affect asset portfolios in the first instance, spending decisions in the second, which translate into effects on output and then on prices. The changes in exchange rates are in turn mostly a response to these effects of home policy on output and prices and of similar policy abroad. The question is topsy turvy. (1980: 80)

The Keynesian transmission mechanism suggested that floating rates would raise the power of monetary policy by adding devaluation to the effects of a monetary expansion, but received theory was slower to take up the inflationary consequences.

Towards the end of the 1970s much work had been done to integrate the implications of floating rates into the analysis of monetary policy. In the 'financially open economy' (McKinnon's phrase again—see Figure 13.2b), the transmission mechanism has the exchange rate playing an important role from the start, along with the interest rate. The relevant analysis stresses the implications of the exchange rate for pricing decisions and the role of expectations in determining, along with interest rates, what happens to the exchange rate. This is the asset theory of exchange rates which as we saw in Chapter 8 succeeds in integrating elements of both monetarist and Keynesian views.

Among the determinants of the demands for the assets is either the expected behaviour of the exchange rate or the nominal rate of the interest, which in turn is influenced by exchange rate expectations. In order to determine the exchange rate it is necessary to analyse the formation of exchange rate expectations. Tying them to the behaviour of the demands and supplies of money (Dornbusch, 1976) leads to the well-known theoretical result that exchange rates can be expected in the short-run to overshoot their long-run equilibrium. Dornbusch's classic paper on overshooting paved the way for other analyses which capitalize on the overshooting phenomenon (Buiter and Miller, 1981 is a well-known example), and there was considerable interest in the contribution of 'bandwagon', 'bubbles', and similar speculative effects to variations in exchange rates.[5]

If the exchange rate is proximately determined by asset equilibrium, monetary policy may fairly quickly involve exchange rate changes, as the prices of other currencies change in terms of the one whose quantity has altered. Since demands for domestic goods depend on both interest rates and relative prices, policy-induced changes in exchange rates can exert inflationary or deflationary impact on domestic demand via changes in exports and imports (that is, the traded goods sector). There is a transmission mechanism which operates even if the interest rate channel is weak.

Of course, the asset model is one of how exchange rates *might* respond in unmanaged markets, not how exchange rates actually *do* behave. Yet the likelihood of strong and perhaps quite rapid relationships between the exchange rate and major domestic policy objectives means that exchange rate policy cannot be divorced from overall macroeconomic policy, while the links implied in the model between monetary policy, expectations, the exchange rate and domestic prices go some way to providing a theoretical rationale for recent policy emphases which seek to shape market attitudes.

Figure 13.2 Three models of the transmission mechanism

a. Insular economy

Money supply → Interest rate → Output → Prices → Exchange rate

b. Financially open economy

Money supply → Interest rate / Exchange rate → Output → Prices

c. Policy transmission view

Market operations → Interest rate → Exchange rate / Money supply → Output → Prices

Source: McKinnon (1984b), Jonson (1987).

High and variable inflation

The inflation of the 1970s and 1980s was important in influencing views about the transmission mechanism in several ways. It afforded evidence of powerful wealth (extended real balance) effects; it helped to remove any lingering suggestion that it might be appropriate to assume money illusion in transactors' behaviour; it afforded experience of high nominal interest rates via 'Fisher effects' of inflation upon interest rates; it brought home the importance of 'front-end loading'; and it established the importance of forward-looking expectations in economic behaviour.

The worldwide increase in savings in the late 1970s came as a surprise to prevailing economic opinion which held that, if it significantly affected savings behaviour at all, inflation would reduce savings and raise current consumption as consumers sought to anticipate further higher prices by buying more today. As the opposite appeared to happen, economists emphasized the role of wealth effects in the consumption function: as prices rose, consumers would seek to save more as a means of restoring the ratio of wealth (held in nominally denominated assets) to income, an effect anticipated by Mundell (1963a). The experience, simultaneously, of low rates of investment was harder to pin down to specifically monetary causes since the generally uncertain outlook for the resumption of economic growth seemed a powerful reason in itself for this performance. Interest rates, though frequently high were often derisory, even negative, in real terms—i.e. after allowing for inflation. The phenomenon of front-end loading, though, might be held to account for some deterrent effect even when the real interest rate was low. Comparing two projects with the same real return, but different inflation assumptions, it is easy to show that payments of interest and repayments of capital are much larger in proportion to cash flow in the earlier years in a high-inflation scenario than they are in a low-inflation case. Risk-aversion might therefore lead to the rejection of some projects in the high-inflation case which would be pursued at low rates of inflation.

The inflation experience also exposed the irrationality of money illusion and, first in theories of wage determination and then more widely, emphasized the role of expectations. In turn, experience also exposed the limitations of the assumption of adaptive expectations with the fixed lag implied and paved the way for acceptance of forward-looking schemes and the concept of rational expectations.

Monetary targeting and deregulation

Interest in monetary aggregates began in the late 1960s and took hold in the 1970s to some degree under the stimulus of monetarist writings, but also because of the search for intermediate targets in the floating rate, inconvertible currency era. The basic idea was for the central bank to choose a variable—such as the money supply—which theory and evidence suggests is 'midway' between its instruments and the target of inflation, so that this becomes the focus for day-to-day operations.

Monetary targeting relies on three things: a definable quantity of money, a stable demand for the aggregate, and a supply process readily controllable by the authorities. All three have been called into question. The simple quantity equation is based around an amount of money that is used for transactions, but innovations in bank liabilities since deregulation have made the definition of transactions deposits less precise. Liquidity-based definitions of broad money lose meaning as banks come to resemble other financial intermediaries (and vice versa), and even—as in the case of securitization—come to resemble simply a bundle of financial contracts in a disintermediated capital market.

Part of the blurring of the dividing lines has been a reduction of the monopoly over money-transmission services once enjoyed by 'banks', along with the widespread use of credit cards, EFTPOS, ATMs, sweep arrangements, and the like which alter the timing of receipts and payments and the transactions and precautionary demands. Demand for money functions of the simple form used in earlier years have proven difficult to reconstruct.

Finally, monetary control was always going to be more difficult than that of macroeconomic models which treated the quantity of money as a policy variable. Actual performance in the phase of monetary targeting, particularly in the UK in the 1980s, confirmed the non-triviality of the control problem and emphasized the status of money as an intermediate variable; it was not difficult then to consider alternative intermediate target variables and different operating strategies.

In the case of the Bank of England and the Federal Reserve, the market procedures by which interest rate objectives are achieved have remained largely unchanged in

their essentials over a number of decades, and have survived changes to the intermediate variables. Certainly, officials at the Bank of England were never wholly persuaded of the importance which the Thatcher Government attached to money
supply targeting, and did not radically restructure operating strategies in an attempt
to implement them. Since 1844 interest rates have lain at the heart of the Bank's
operations, with the instrument being bank rate (now its dealing rate) and open market operations in bills (now gilt repos). When money supply targets were introduced,
control of interest rates remained; but instead interest rates became a step or *operational target* in achieving the money supply (intermediate) target. In effect, with the
switch to emphasis upon monetary aggregates, the Bank grafted an additional step
into formal operational procedures, thereby retaining continuity with traditional
strategies. Thus the policy sequence became

$$I \rightarrow OV \rightarrow IV \rightarrow UV, \tag{13.19}$$

where OV is the operational variable(s) or target. When interest in monetary targeting waned, the Bank merely broadened the intermediate target set beyond the
money supply to include other things.

A convergence of views

During the 1990s there has probably been a good deal more clarity and agreement
about the nature of the transmission mechanism of monetary policy than there had
been, say, twenty years earlier, and a general view relative to earlier opinions that it
was a good deal more important.

The view of the transmission mechanism in a financially sophisticated open economy as in the McKinnon picture (Figure 13.2b) stresses the active role of the exchange
rate as an asset price like the interest rate and the impact of both on the economy,
with the money supply as an endogenous but not purely passive variable. In the
transmission process, wealth effects and expectational effects add to the impact of
decisions based on variations in interest rates and exchange rates. These effects on
the economy in turn feed back onto the determination of asset prices and the stock
of money.

A schema more in accord with a central banker's view of the world (Jonson, 1987)
starts with market operations and interest rates. In particular, the framework used in
most processes of monetary policy formulation (instruments—operational targets—
intermediate variables—ultimate targets) can be readily superimposed (see Figure
13.2c, which ignores feedbacks). This sequence of market operations, interest rate,
exchange rate, money and credit, output, prices has been augmented by the yield
curve, interest-rate expectations, commodity prices, equity prices, housing activity
and prices, property prices, and the income and capital gearing of households and
business enterprises to give a richer view of the transmission mechanism. These,
along with the new Divisia measures of money in some countries, all serve as information variables.

In this guise, monetary aggregates re-emerge as 'information variables'—variables which provide information about subsequent movements in non-financial economic activity. But even in this role, money supply measures have been joined and increasingly supplanted—by market price data and asset yields. Prior to financial deregulation, monetary policy was seen to affect the macroeconomy through one or more of three possible channels: interest rates; credit rationing (the availability of credit); and the quantity of money. Deregulation immediately removed a number of means of implementing monetary policy—variations in interest rate ceilings, alterations in controlled interest rates, changes in reserve asset ratios, and moral suasion over the supply of credit—without seemingly putting anything in their place. Deregulation was also soon perceived to compromise the money supply policies advocated by monetarists due to financial innovation.

All of this means that the manipulation of money market interest rates now appears to be the principal 'sure thing' in central bank armouries. We turn to this topic in the following chapter.

Notes

1 If rr refers to the reserve requirement which is applicable to demand deposits, then the multiplier (13.7) would be applied to an M1 definition of money. For broader definitions of money, d would need to be widened to include time and savings deposits and the required reserve ratio regarded as a weighted average of the reserve ratio requirements applicable to the various classes of deposits (see Burger, 1971, for a fuller account).

2 Kareken (1967) and Dewald and Lindsey (1972) call expressions such as (13.8), where the money stock is related to exogenous variables, 'pseudo-supply functions'. This is in contrast to the 'true money supply functions' which would reveal the quantity of money that the suppliers would be willing to supply at particular market rates. Such functions require an examination of bank portfolio behaviour, as in Brunner and Meltzer (1987).

3 If, however, banks respond to reserve discrepancies by changing the interest rates paid on deposits and charged for lending, so inducing responses in d and e, the quantitative effects on money may be small. The view thus presupposes that bank interest rates do not respond significantly to changes in bank portfolios (Niehans, 1978).

4 These markets are examined in Lewis and Davis (1987: ch. 4).

5 Investigations of the efficiency of foreign exchange markets do not seem to provide a resoundingly favourable verdict (see e.g. Levich (1989) for a review), and it seems clear that these markets may play host to bubble phenomena (e.g. Blanchard and Watson, 1982). Such bubbles may involve 'rational' investors profiting from the speculative activities of others—see Frankel and Froot (1986).

Chapter 14
Monetary Policy in Practice

14.1 Endogenous/exogenous money

THE previous chapter examined money supply analysis and changing views about how monetary policy impinges on the economy, i.e. views about the transmission mechanism. This chapter examines the *modus operandi*, i.e. how policy actually operated in major countries at the end of the 1990s. At the end of Chapter 13 we noted a convergence of views about the transmission mechanism, and a similar convergence has taken place in policy implementation. While the particular focus is upon the situation in the USA and the UK, broadly similar approaches are being followed elsewhere, including the European Union.

First, however, we go back to the money supply and to the issue of money supply exogeneity/endogeneity. In Friedman's (1969*b*) 'helicopter money' model, the essence of the story revolves around the distinction between nominal and real money balances. Nominal balances come about like 'manna from heaven', and people bid the price level up and down to ensure that, in the long-run equilibrium, real money balances accord with desired levels. In short, the nominal stock of money is determined by supply while the real stock is governed by demand.

When we move outside such simple models, 'supply' need not imply that the nominal money supply is determined by factors which are distinct from demand. One of the merits of the 'money-multiplier' or 'reserves-available' approaches over the 'credit-counterparts' approach is in breaking the money stock into a number of components, reflecting respectively the behaviour of the non-bank public, the actions of banks, and, finally, that of the monetary authorities. Interactions between demand and supply can occur through any of the three groups' resources, but monetarists focus upon the authorities' behaviour and the stability of the money multiplier.

In direct opposition, post-Keynesians such as Kaldor (1970, 1986) have argued that the apparent stability of monetarist empirical relationships comes about because money is a residual in the economy without any causal significance; the authorities have passively supplied money in response to contemporaneous and prior movements in income and thus the demand for money. In reality, neither of the positions we have sketched out of endogenous and exogenous money can be seen as other than caricatures. No central bank has rigidly controlled the stock of money as a policy variable. None has passively ladled out money on demand, other than perhaps in the very short-run.

Not all central banks have been able to exercise control over the amount of high-powered money and some still must residually fund the government deficit and, due to exchange rate commitments, the net balance on private sector foreign exchange transactions. When they do have control, they typically have used it not to force a contraction or expansion of banks' balance sheets via a textbook money multiplier, but to bring about a structure of short-term interest rates consistent with maintenance of exchange rate parity, or economic growth, bank lending, or even the growth rate of the money supply.

But these institutional characteristics do not warrant our going to the other extreme and supposing that interest rate or exchange rate targeting, as it actually operated, implies strict endogeneity of the money stock. Institutional arrangements were never in fact quite so clear-cut as implied. Foreign exchange controls flanked the fixed exchange rate in the UK and many other countries, affording some room for the exercise of domestic monetary policy. Exchange rate expectations undoubtedly alter foreigners' demand for securities and domestic borrowing from overseas, and are associated (under fixed exchange rates unless sterilized) with a variation in the *supply* of money. That they necessarily alter the *demand* for money by an exactly equivalent amount is disputable. Much the same comments apply to an interaction between the demand for credit and the demand for money, as is clear in Brunner and Meltzer's (1976) distinction between credit-market and money-market hypotheses. When interest rates are being stabilized, many short-run increases in the money stock derive from variations in bank lending (as highlighted in the credit counterparts approach). These increases in money may not be demanded, but will always be accepted and willingly held as a store of purchasing power for later spending. Finally, interest rates have never been pegged outright. To enforce a new interest rate peg, the central bank must alter the money supply; in this instance, the money supply is instigating the change, not adapting itself passively to prior events.

Consequently the dichotomy between the view that money is endogenously determined, and that based around a policy-determined, i.e. exogenous, quantity of high-powered money or base money has been drawn too sharply. This becomes apparent when we consider actual policies. Whether central banks could or should operate monetary base control raises a set of different issues, but the question does serve to lead us into subsequent discussion.

Reserves base control

Equation (13.5) in the previous chapter can be interpreted as defining an equilibrium condition for the 'reserves market' in which the supply of reserves, the left-hand side, is equated with the demand for reserves accruing on the right-hand side, from required and desired excess reserves. Given reasonable stability in the latter it follows that variations in the demand for reserves are likely to be dominated by movements in required reserves. With lagged or contemporaneous reserves accounting, these are in turn a reflection of current movements in bank deposits. Central banks argue that they have no alternative but to supply banks with the reserves needed to validate deposit growth if stability of the banking system is to be ensured. All they can do is to influence the cost at which cash is made available to the system, and even here their effective discretionary power is limited. Considering the margin of excess reserves which banks normally hold in modern-day financial systems, the demand for total reserves is highly inelastic with respect to relevant interest rates. Moreover, now that banks practise liability management, they react to any reserve deficiency by bidding more aggressively for deposits and reserves in the wholesale funding markets to support their lending rather than disposing of assets. Any failure of reserves to keep pace with deposit expansion will merely see interest rates spiral upwards seemingly without limit rather than directly impelling banks to contract their lending.

It is possible to visualize events proceeding differently in normal times. Liability management enables banks to 'run but not hide' (Dewald, 1975) from system-wide reserve deficiencies, since with flexible exchange rates and full funding of the government budget, extra issues of deposits by banks cannot pull in more cash to the system as a whole. Banks usually have the alternative of disposing of earning assets to the non-bank private sector, leaving total deposits unchanged. The idea that there is some new breed of banker who will always eschew asset management for liability management is patently false. If interbank rates are bid up high enough, it would pay some banks to sell bills and bonds to the private sector in order to obtain funds for lending out in the interbank market. Liability management is allowed to succeed because the central bank always provides the reserves needed to validate deposit expansion from bank lending. The deposit increase, in turn, provides the non-bank private sector with funds with which to buy the securities sold by the monetary authorities. Indeed, firms may even borrow from the banks in order to buy the bonds—this being one possible hedging strategy should interest rates be expected to fall.

Implications could follow for behaviour 'next time round'. If banks are able to get cash, and at a price not always penal, they are unlikely to rearrange affairs so as to avoid putting themselves into the position of having to seek out cash in the future. Were the consequences of interest rate changes allowed to proceed under alternative arrangements (such as shifting penalty borrowing costs to the banks), behaviour next time around might well be different. After being forced to make up reserve shortages at penalty rates, banks would be likely to exercise much greater care in future when granting overdraft facilities and open credit lines. There would be an incentive for banks individually to refrain from lending and build up reserves when cash shortages are anticipated. Surges in monetary growth may be less likely to occur.

However, this is perhaps to confuse what could be with what is. Goodhart (1992: 728–9) argues that:

Central Banks have historically been at some pains to assure the banking system that the institutional structure is such that the system as a whole can *always* obtain access to whatever cash the system may require in order to meet its needs, though at a price of the Central Bank's choosing; and there has been a further, implicit corollary that the interest rate will not be varied capriciously. The whole structure of the monetary system has evolved on this latter basis, that is, that the untrammelled force of the monetary base multiplier will *never* be unleashed.

One way in which this is achieved in practice is by the presence of various 'safety valves' which allow banks and the financial system generally access to high-powered money. These mechanisms operate via the money market.

14.2 Interest Rates and the Money Market

IN a recent survey of the implementation of monetary policy, Borio (1997: 13–14) observes: 'Currently, virtually all the central banks in the countries considered in this paper [14 major industrial countries] implement monetary policy through market oriented instruments geared to influencing closely short-term interest rates as operating objectives'. The short-term interest rates are money market rates, normally call money rates, and the instruments are those of money market paper.

Call money is the description generally reserved for day-to-day funding and for those loans which, while often of a continuing nature, can be recalled on demand or at short notice (Lewis, 1992*a*). Commercial banks are prominent both as suppliers and demanders of such short-term funds in most money markets, and the interbank market frequently forms the core of money market activity. The USA is the example *par excellence*, although the situation is somewhat similar in France, Germany and Italy.

In the USA, the Federal funds market lies at the centre of the banking system and the money market: it provides a means of distributing reserves held by banks (and other deposit institutions) at the various Federal Reserve Banks (the reserve balances are called Federal funds) throughout the thousands of banks (frequently via brokers); and the rate for overnight transactions is the single most closely watched interest rate. Non-bank entities are excluded from the Federal funds market but they participate in the overnight repurchase market. While non-banks cannot lend Federal funds, repurchase agreements provide banks with immediately available reserve balances when the transaction is cleared, and like Federal funds are exempt from reserve requirements, so that in practice the two markets are closely related.

In the UK no one market is dominant, the money market consists of a number of linked markets, all concentrated in London, including the very large Eurodollar market and the foreign exchange swap market. With the strong growth of new markets which operate alongside the much older markets for eligible bank bills, trade bills, CDs, and Treasury bills, the interbank market and the newer gilt repurchase market (the latter established in January 1996) together constitute well over 50 per cent of the sterling money markets.

Like any financial market, a call money market satisfies holders of financial assets and issuers of debt. To lenders, call money is an outlet for temporarily idle funds which can be employed productively without sacrificing their ready availability. To borrowers, call money allows their indebtedness to be adjusted continuously in line with the daily need for funds. A special need arises from the large banks which straddle the domestic and international payments systems and may experience with little notice withdrawal demands as large customers make payments of all kinds. Access to a call money market enables them to supply considerable amounts to each other and meet unexpected funding needs quickly and cheaply.

The central bank occupies a special position in every national money market. It is primarily through the market for call money that a central bank's operations impinge upon the financial markets as it seeks to control short-term interest rates. The market serves as an automatic regulator when the system as a whole is in balance and as a means of regulating rates when the authorities seek to alter the general level of interest rates. Interbank settlements are the lever. Daily payments made to banks and their customers result (ultimately in the case of net end-of-day settlement, immediately with real-time guaranteed settlement)[1] in transfers of funds between banks, and these are made with 'cash', that is balances which banks hold in operational accounts at the central bank. In the absence of transactions undertaken by the central bank or its clients—especially the government—the settling-up would sum to zero, and through the money market the banks with net inflows of funds could be induced to lend to those with net outflows. When there are transactions involving the central bank—including those on its own account in the markets—the commercial banks can be left with an overall cash deficit or surplus at final settlement. As the source of cash reserves, the central bank is in a strong position to affect financial conditions.

Interest rate determination

Central bank operations in the money market have two dimensions, corresponding to the distinction which Robert Roosa made in 1956 between the 'defensive' and 'dynamic' aspects of policy. One—the 'defensive' dimension—is to facilitate interbank settlements by daily smoothing of the amount of cash. The rationale here is straightforward: since the volatility in cash flows stems from government transactions it is probably more efficient (in the sense that less resources are consumed) for the authorities also to remove the volatility, releasing private sector energies for more productive ends. But the removal of volatility has a cost to market participants in terms of lost trading opportunities, perhaps hindering market growth, and may make it more difficult for the authorities to carry out the other—'dynamic'—aim, which is to engineer imbalances between the demand and supply of reserves and alter credit conditions; many central banks like to 'fine-tune' developments by mixed responses to market pressures.

A cash shortage, for example, can be relieved in several ways. The central bank can buy securities outright—usually involving short-term government paper, although in the UK the Bank of England also deals in commercial bills. In addition, securities can be bought on a sale-and-repurchase basis. Repurchase agreements ('repos') enable the central bank to create a market instrument of the exact maturity that it desires, as well as embodying some automatic stabilization; thus a shortage today and a surplus next week can be smoothed by a one-week sale and repurchase. Swap operations in the foreign exchange market have long been used in Germany, the Netherlands, and Switzerland. Whilst the repurchase is of foreign currency, not domestic securities, the monetary effect is the same. In Canada, the shifting back and forth of government accounts between the Bank of Canada and the chartered banks has the same effect. Finally, cash can be provided through the discount window—the rediscount facility or credit line which authorized institutions (banks, or perhaps money market dealers) have at the central bank. Use of such funds ('borrowed reserves') normally implies some penalty, either monetary (as in the UK) or nonmonetary (as in the USA). Monetary management involves altering the form and the terms on which funds are supplied to the market.

Figure 14.1 depicts the demand and supply of reserves under three regimes: a completely inelastic supply of reserves (S_0); a completely elastic supply (S_1); and where reserves supplied by market operations (R_0) can be supplemented by costly borrowed reserves, giving the supply curve $R_0 A S_2$. This third case corresponds to a situation in which reserves supplied by the central bank are insufficient to meet banks' needs, forcing them into penalty borrowings. The first case is one representation of monetary base control, advocated by monetarists; while the second illustrates a situation where interest rates are rigidly pegged. All three regimes have featured in Federal Reserve and Bank of England policies.

Federal Reserve policies[2]

Briefly, by way of introduction, the Federal Reserve system (the Fed) determines US monetary policy, supervises and regulates member banks, and provides payment services to US government and financial institutions. The Fed consists of the Board of Governors in Washington and twelve Reserve Banks throughout the country. The Federal Open Market Committee (FOMC) consists of the seven Governors plus five of the twelve Federal Reserve Bank presidents voting (one of which is always the New York president). The FOMC decides on a target Federal funds rate and the Federal Reserve Bank of New York operates open market operations in order to achieve this level. The Board of Governors also sets reserve requirements for the banks, while the individual Federal Reserve Banks set the discount rate.

In terms of the key financial markets for implementing monetary policy, the New York Fed intervenes directly in the government securities market: both through repos and outright purchases. It also indirectly affects the Federal funds market by controlling the supply of reserves in the banking system. In this respect, operating procedures focus on achieving a certain degree of tightness or ease in reserve market

Figure 14.1 Interest rate determination in the money market under different reserves regimes

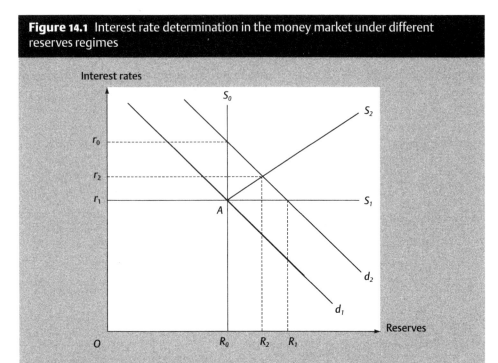

S_0 Monetary base targeting. reserves available to the banking system are fixed once the public's currency requirements are met. In the face of an increasing demand for reserves, reserves are maintained at the level R_0 consistent with the monetary base target, so that the full impact of a shift in demand falls upon interest rates, which rise from r_1 to r_0.
S_1 Interest rate pegging. in response to an increase in the demand for reserves, reserves of amount R_1-R_0 are supplied by market actions to keep interest rates at the level appropriate for overall policy goals.
S_2 Reserves are supplied by a combination of market operations and borrowing facilities. Extra reserves (R_2-R_0) are supplied in response to a shift in demand by allowing institutions to borrow, forcing market rates up to r_2.

conditions, and the FOMC expresses its directives to the New York Fed in terms of a desired degree of reserve pressure. The target is an average level of the Federal funds rate. Earlier the Fed used monetary aggregates as intermediate targets, but these became unreliable as leading indicators.

Our discussion of US monetary policy is based on the reserves-available approach examined earlier. Banks are required to hold a particular proportion of their deposits as reserves (currently 10 per cent of all demand deposits for large banks), RR, and may elect to hold additional reserves, ER. The banks need to meet their reserve requirements over two week 'maintenance periods', based on a lagged reserve requirement: reserves held in the maintenance period relate to deposits held one month previously. Some of these reserves will be obtained by borrowing at the discount window, BR. The job of the New York Fed is to estimate the level of non-borrowed reserves, NBR, needed by the banking system at the target Federal funds rate and compare this to the supply. The difference between the two tells them what quantity of reserves to add to the banking system using open market operations. It does this on a daily basis.

The demand for non-borrowed reserves is given by:

$$NBR = RR + ER - BR. \tag{14.1}$$

Hence, the New York Fed economists need to forecast required reserves, desired excess reserves, and borrowed reserves. They also need to forecast the supply of reserves. Given these forecasts, if the New York Fed feels that an open market operation is necessary on a particular day, it will act at 10.30 a.m. to either add reserves to the banking system or withdraw them from the system. Once the Fed has acted, the Federal funds market continues to operate all day (until 6.30 Eastern time); the Federal funds rate varies depending on the supply of and demand for reserves. If the New York Fed get its sums correct, the Federal funds rate should hover close to the FOMC's target. If it does not, then something has to give.

In the Federal funds market, banks that are below their desired reserve positions borrow from others that are above their desired reserve positions. But, except for borrowing, banks in total cannot augment aggregate reserves in this way—all they can do in the Federal funds market is play 'pass the parcel'. When banks collectively seek more reserves than are available in the market, they succeed only in bidding up the Federal funds rate. As this rate rises, more institutions are induced to borrow at the discount window, which brings reserve supply into line with demand.

Why does it require an increase in the Federal funds rate to elicit greater borrowings? The discount rate is invariably lower than the Federal funds rate, yet banks are extremely wary of using the discount window. This means that the discount rate is not used as a policy instrument but rather the window is used as a safety-valve to relieve short-term liquidity problems in individual banks. Consequently, banks will borrow in the Federal funds market at much higher rates than the discount window because of the bad perception that borrowing at the window creates in the Press and in the markets.[3] Also, excessive use of the window is discouraged by 'moral suasion', i.e. rules which govern the extent and frequency of borrowing, the application of which can be seen as a non-pecuniary cost of borrowing which rises with volume (Goodfriend, 1987). Banks' reluctance to depend upon the good graces of the discount window, when the volume of their borrowing rises, leads them to bid more aggressively for bought funds in the Federal funds market, which puts upward pressure upon rates in that market and the financial system generally. This response defines the upward-sloping segment of the borrowing function shown in Figure 14.2 which provides a representation of the reserves market.

Thus open market operations must balance the banks' needs to meet their reserve requirements against the needs of monetary policy. Upward pressure upon interest rates can be achieved by altering the extent to which banks are forced to borrow in order to satisfy reserve requirements. The Committee is able to do this by varying the supply of non-borrowed reserves. With a demand for reserves of d_1, and a supply of non-borrowed reserves of N_1, borrowings are $(R^* - NBR_1)$ and the Federal funds rate is r_f.

Market operations have been guided by different conceptions of the needs of policy, and most commentators identify three distinct phases. The first, from around 1970 (when targeting of the money stock began) until September 1979, accords most closely to that of endogenous money. At each of the eight meetings each year, the Committee would specify a target rate for the Federal funds rate and a range for the rate until the next scheduled meeting. The trading desk at the Federal Reserve Bank of New York would then supply non-borrowed reserves consistent with that target. In the face of an increase in the demand for reserves from d_1 to d_2, due perhaps to an increase in the quantity of money, interest rates could be allowed to rise to the higher end of the range, but thereafter the increased demand would be accommodated at unchanged interest rates. This is the position illustrated in Figure 14.2, where r_f is the higher end of the target range and additional reserves of (R_2-R^*) are supplied by open market operations which increase non-borrowed reserves from NBR_1 to NBR_2.

However, the situation was never as rigid as that just sketched out. If the expansion of money prompting the increased reserves demanded was judged to be excessive, the interest rate target could be lifted at the next meeting. Or, if deemed desirable, an amendment to the target range could be made in between meetings, by means of a telephone link-up of the Reserve Banks with Washington. Nevertheless, the arrangements clearly had the potential to let through expansions of the money stock in excess of targeted magnitudes.

Accordingly, tactics switched in October 1979 from targeting interest rates to targeting reserves, specifically the amount of non-borrowed reserves. Suppose that NBR_1 is the targeted quantity. An increase in the demand for reserves from d_1 to d_2 no longer elicits an accompanying increase in non-borrowed reserves. There is

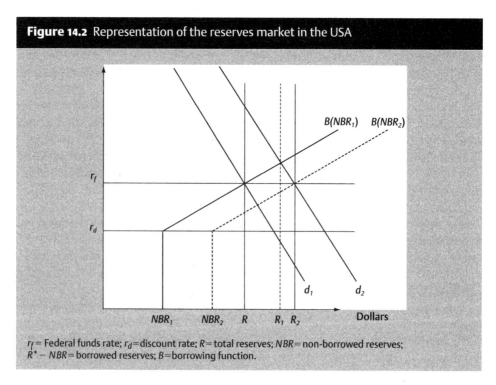

Figure 14.2 Representation of the reserves market in the USA

r_f = Federal funds rate; r_d = discount rate; R = total reserves; NBR = non-borrowed reserves; $R^* - NBR$ = borrowed reserves; B = borrowing function.

nevertheless an increase in total reserves from R^* to R_1, but because the addition is borrowed, the funds rate and other rates are pushed up. This feature was seen (e.g. Wallich, 1984) as a self-regulating mechanism, for the higher rates would tend to push the money supply back over time towards target.

From this description, it is apparent that the new system was not simply one of monetary base control, for the safety-valve of the discount window remained in place. Monetary base control would imply fixing R^*, and in this respect the system was a compromise between one of reserves and interest rate targets. Also, due to the borrowed reserves slippage, and the negligible elasticity of the demand for reserves under lagged reserve accounting, the initial equilibrium between the demand and supply of reserves is again brought about through variations in supply. But unlike in the previous regime, the immediate interest rate consequences of the change in supply would presumably reduce bank lending and the quantity of money and eventually feed back onto the demand for reserves.

Despite this softening of the consequences of a policy of strict reserves control, the interest rate fluctuations experienced were violent enough to be uncomfortable and alongside other considerations, e.g. falling inflation and the advent of the LDC debt crisis in the summer of 1982, led to some retreat from the system in October 1982. Under the new arrangements, borrowed reserves (R^*-NBR_1) were targeted. An increase in the quantity of money, due perhaps to an increase in the demand for money, which raised the demand for reserves from d_1 to d_2, would cause borrowed reserves to rise in excess of the quantity targeted. This created the presumption that non-borrowed reserves should be expanded to NBR_2 so as to keep borrowed reserves unchanged at $R_2-NBR_2(=R^*-NBR_1)$ at the ruling Federal funds rate r_f.

Critics argued that if this was not interest rate targeting, then it was a close relation. In effect, the Federal Reserve controls interest rates by setting a target for the Federal funds rate and using open market operations to keep the funds rate close to the target level. Yet it would seem that the new system was more flexible than the pre-October 1979 regime. The Federal funds rate fluctuated far more on a day-to-day basis, and the Committee operated on a much more judgemental footing. Rather than supply reserves automatically, and correct the position later, an assessment could be taken of the circumstances behind the expansion of the money stock. If the increase is undesired, then non-borrowed reserves could be expanded less than (NBR_2-NBR_1), allowing interest rates to rise above r_f.

While the above framework generally remains in place, like many other central banks, emphasis has moved recently from actions to words—'open-mouth operations'. There is an increased reliance ordinarily upon signalling mechanisms to guide market views on money market rates, which in the USA case takes the form mainly of FOMC announcements of the Federal funds rate target. Since October 1993 the Federal Reserve has announced changes to the funds rate target, and there has been a close relationship between short-term rates and the Fed's target for the funds rate. From October 1993 through to July 1999, for example, the average absolute difference between the Federal funds target and the three-month Treasury bill rate was only 34 basic points (i.e. one-third of 1 per cent). Announcements of the Federal funds rate target are supplemented by public statements of the Chairman and other members of the Board of Governors, which are closely studied as guides to future target rate changes. 'Fed watching' is a long-standing tradition.

Bank of England policies[4]

A similarly eclectic policy is being practised by the Bank of England, also focused around short-term money market rates. While the institutional details are different from the USA, the two systems appear to work along similar lines. Although not formally subject to reserve requirements, all banks in the UK must nevertheless hold 0.5 per cent of their deposits with the Bank of England in non-interest-bearing form. It is a constant sum revised every six months in order to emphasize that this represents a 'tax' to provide funds for the Bank of England and is not intended as a reserve ratio. Separate operational accounts are kept for the clearing of funds through the payments system. Although the government budget deficit is funded fully over the financial year there are substantial day-to-day alterations in the cash position. Banks collectively gain cash when the Exchequer has a deficit, and lose cash when it has a surplus. These daily losses frequently exceed the small operational balances (excess reserves) held by the banks at the Bank. Open market operations undertaken by the Bank of England, mainly in gilt repos and eligible bank-accepted commercial bills, have the aim of providing banks with their cash needs at the end of the day, in the light of their estimates of the budget deficit, flows over the foreign exchanges and gilts markets (which are settled on subsequent days), and shifts in the public's currency holdings (which have large intra-week fluctuations) (see Bank of England, 1988).

Inevitably, these estimates are often incorrect, and there are net drains or additions to the cash position. Yet banks are obliged to keep their operational accounts at the Bank in credit and are unable to borrow reserves through the discount window as in the USA. Instead, two other mechanisms come into play, inherent in the Bank's transactions. Dealing to maintain the desired cash position occurs twice daily (9.45 a.m. and 2.30 p.m.) enabling some intra-day reaction to contrary trends. In addition, there are end-of-day arrangements in the form of an overnight repurchase operation available to the market at 3.30 p.m. and a late overnight repurchase facility to settlement banks at 4.20 p.m., both at penalty rates.

When it seeks to influence market conditions, the Bank of England does not try to alter the supply of reserves, as would be expected from the 'money multiplier' or 'reserves available' formulae. Rather, like the Federal Reserve, it alters the form of and cost at which reserves are supplied, although procedures have altered somewhat over time and depend on whether the authorities wish to send an overt or explicit signal to the markets. In the past, in order to tighten conditions, fewer of the banks' cash needs were met through open market operations and more came from borrowings when the discount houses were forced 'into the Bank'. Unlike banks' borrowing at the discount window of the Federal Reserve, the discount houses almost always had to pay a rate at or above the comparable market rate. Access to the borrowing facility was thus rationed by price (rather than non-pecuniary cost), and usage of it sent a direct signal for bill rates, interbank rates, and bank base (prime) rates to follow. However, the discount houses' special relationship with the Bank ended in March 1997.[5]

Nowadays, interest rate adjustments are brought about via open market operations. These are undertaken with banks, building societies, and securities firms that meet the Bank's eligibility criteria. The counterparties are invited to bid for funds to meet forecast liquidity needs by way of repos of gilts, Treasury bills, eligible local authority and bank bills, marketable UK government foreign currency debt and/or the outright sale of bills, although most operations (54 per cent in April–June 1998 for example) are made using gilt repos (repurchase agreements involving gilt-edged securities, i.e. British government bonds), with an average maturity of around two weeks. Interest rates are responsive to market pressures; the margin between the sterling overnight index average of interbank rates (SONIA) and the Bank's repo rates tends to vary with the size of the money market shortage. But participants in the market are well aware that the Bank can make effective its views by altering the form and cost at which reserves are supplied. Because the market knows that this can happen, there is often no need for it actually to take place and many interest rate changes which could be enforced by market pressures take place 'automatically'.

There is an important historical continuity here. Market operations to make effective an appropriate level of short-term interest rates has lain at the heart of the Bank of England's operations over 150 years: *plus ça change, plus c'est la même chose.*

14.3 The Question of Indicators

OUR examination has revealed that the actual methods of monetary control in the USA and UK bear little resemblance to the money-multiplier approaches which feature in money and banking textbooks. In both countries there now exists a separation of monetary policy from debt management and exchange rate management, which gives the central banks the technical ability to control the quantity of high-powered money quite closely. Neither central bank has used that potential to enforce strict control over the quantity of high-powered money or bank reserves. Both allow the supply of reserves to respond to demand in the short run, partly out of adherence to traditional operating procedures, but mainly to ensure that banks do not run out of cash and thus with an eye to avoiding violent fluctuations in interest rates. Instead, they determine how much of that supply of cash comes from market operations and how much is contributed (actually or potentially) by borrowings or late assistance. This breakdown has implications for the structure of short-term interest rates which feed through the economy.

Markets in other countries offer many variations on these themes but, with deregulation and less reliance upon required reserve ratios and specific controls upon the banking system in the implementation of monetary policy, they seem to be converging on this model. As a result, central banks in all the major industrial countries now guide interest rates via the money market, which in consequence has become more important as a conduit for monetary policy.

Policy targets

Where does this leave money supply and other policy targets? A novelty of the new arrangements is the absence of an intermediate target to perform the role that monetary targets carried before.

From the end of 1973, the Bank of England generally sought to set interest rates with regard to achieving the growth rate of one or more monetary aggregates. Initially the Bank related its daily dealings to a particular level of rates, which tended to be tied rather rigidly to its posted discount rate (the famous bank rate). After August 1981, more market-related techniques were used to achieve a particular level of short rates, again with specific monetary targets in mind, although with the breakdown of demand for money relationships there was no mechanical link between the growth of the aggregates, relative to target, and the setting of interest rates. Table 14.1 sets out the monetary policy targets in operation since 1979. Up to 1997, there were ostensibly three targets: M0, M4 and RPIX (the retail price index excluding mortgage interest payments). However, not too much should be made of this troika. The M0 target was described as a 'guide' and the M4 target as a 'monitoring range' to be assessed in conjunction with a broad range of other indicators including the exchange rate. Only the inflation target has remained in any sense a binding commitment, and from 1997 has become the only target.

A broadly similar evolution has taken place in the USA. Chairman of the Board of Governors, Alan Greenspan describes the changes.

The last 15 years have been a period of consolidating the gains of the early 1980s and extending them to their logical end – the achievement of price stability.

Although the ultimate goals of policy have remained the same over these past 15 years, the techniques used in formulating and implementing policy have changed considerably as a consequence of vast changes in technology and regulation. . . .

Focusing on M1, and following operating procedures that imparted a considerable degree of automaticity to short-term interest rate movements, was extraordinarily useful in the early Volcker years. But after nationwide NOW accounts were introduced, the demand for M1 in the judgment of the Federal Open Market Committee became too interest sensitive for that aggregate to be useful in implementing policy. . . .

As a consequence, by late 1982, M1 was de-emphasized and policy decisions per force become more discretionary. However, in recognition of the long-run relationship of prices and M2, especially its stable long-term velocity, this broader aggregate was accorded more weight, along with a variety of other indicators, in setting our policy stance. . . .

As an indicator, M2 served us well for a number of years. But by the early 1990s, its usefulness was undercut by the increased attractiveness and availability of alternative outlets for saving, such as bond and stock mutual funds, and by mounting financial difficulties for depositories and depositors that led to a restructuring of business and household balance sheets. . . .

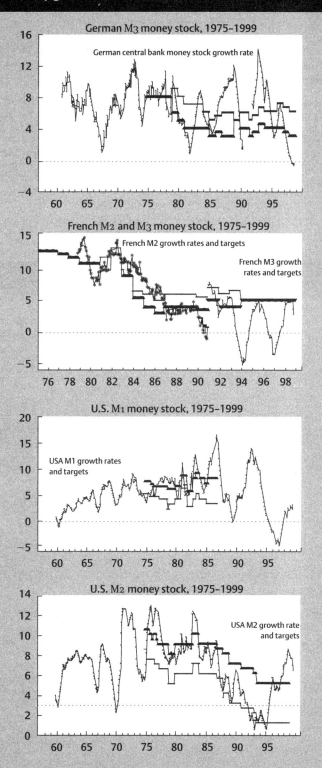

Figure 14.3 Money growth announcements and outcomes

German M3 money stock, 1975–1999

German central bank money stock growth rate

French M2 and M3 money stock, 1975–1999

French M2 growth rates and targets

French M3 growth rates and targets

U.S. M1 money stock, 1975–1999

USA M1 growth rates and targets

U.S. M2 money stock, 1975–1999

USA M2 growth rate and targets

Source: Weber (2000)

Increasingly since 1982 we have been setting the funds rate directly in response to a wide variety of factors and forecasts. We recognize that, in fixing the short-term rate, we lose much of the information on the balance of money supply and demand that changing market rates afford, but for the moment we see no alternative. In the current state of our knowledge, money demand has become too difficult to predict. (Greenspan, 1997: 4–7)

The growth rates of the money supply relative to their targets are shown for Germany, France and the U.S.A. in Figure 14.3. Hence for both (and many other) central banks, the policy is essentially one in which control of short-term interest rates is targeted directly to the economy, and in particular to expected inflation. In all cases, of course, the central bank's influence is over call and other very short-term rates, and not those further along the maturity spectrum. Because of arbitrage operations across the maturity spectrum, operations on short-term rates will spill over into longer rates, to an extent which depends on the market's anticipations of the author-ities' future policies in the money markets; and 'liquidity preference' and 'preferred

Table 14.1 Monetary policy targets in the UK, 1979–2000 (annual % change unless stated otherwise)

Target year[a]	£M3	M4	M0	£ exchange rate (level)	RPIX
1980–1	7–11				
1981–2[b]	6–10				
1982–3[b]	8–12				
1983–4[b]	7–11				
1984–5	6–10		4–8		
1985–6	5–9		3–7		
1986–7	11–15		2–6		
1987–8[c]			2–6		
1988–9			1–5		
1989–90			1–5		
1990–1[d]			1–5	DM2.95[d]	
1991–2[d]		4–8	0–4	DM2.95[f]	
1992–3		3–9	0–4	DM2.95[f]	
1993–4		3–9	0–4		1–4[e]
1994–5		3–9	0–4		1–4
1995–6[g]		3–9	0–4		1–4
1996–7[h]					2½
1997–8[h]					2½
1998–9					2½
1999–2000					2½

[a] As set in the Medium-Term Financial Strategy (MTFS).
[b] Targets were also set for PSL2 and M1 in the 1982 and 1983 MTFS.
[c] 1987–8 MTFS said 'Monetary conditions are assessed in the light of movements in narrow and broad money, and the behaviour of other financial indicators, in particular the exchange rate.' There was no formal target for broad money. Similar references are to be found in the MTFS in 1988–9, 1998–90, and 1990–1.
[d] UK joined the Exchange Rate Mechanism (ERM) of the European Monetary System in October 1990. The 1991–2 MTFS said 'interest rate decisions must now be set consistently with keeping sterling within its announced bands'.
[e] UK left the ERM in September 1992. The new framework was based on an inflation target for RPIX of 1 to 4%, with inflation in lower part of the range by the end of the Parliament. Medium-term monitoring ranges for M4 and M0 were also announced.
[f] Announced in Autumn statement in 1992 after UK left the ERM.
[g] In June 1995 the 1 to 4 range for RPIX was confirmed by the Chancellor and a new target of 2½% or less was announced for beyond the end of this Parliament.
[h] In May 1997 the new Chancellor, Gordon Brown, gave the Bank of England operational independence and set the inflation target at 2½%.

habitat' considerations may make the term structure manipulable to changes in the relative quantities of debt offered at various points in the maturity spectrum. To whatever extent these linkages exist, however, it does not appear that the authorities seek to use them in a conscious way. While the yield curve (ten year less three month nominal interest rates) features prominently in US policy analysis, it is more as an indicator of expected inflation than as an instrument of policy actions. In the UK, the yield curve on index-linked gilts is examined vis-à-vis nominal rates in a similar exercise, and features regularly in the Bank's *Inflation Report*.

In short, market operations constitute the basic policy instrument and the structure of short-term rates is the operational target of policy. Because of constraints upon fiscal policy, it in fact appears that short-term interest rates have to bear the entire burden of short-run adjustment policy. Consequently, the mechanisms by which changes in short-term interest rates impact on the economy, the size of the effects created, and their timing is a key issue in policy formation and the understanding of policy.

Interest rate linkages

A number of factors suggest the linkages to spending and prices as being indirect and complex. For one thing, spending, prices, and other macroeconomic variables respond to a whole range of financial variables, and not just to the interest rate structure. Figure 14.4, based on Akhtar (1997), illustrates some of the mechanisms.[6] Conditions in credit markets generally, including a variety of financial intermediaries, interact with impulses coming from bond, equity and foreign exchange markets, and involve housing and other property markets. Altogether, we can identify five channels by which a change beginning with money market rates will affect aggregate demand in the economy:

1. The effect on real rates of return in the economy.
2. Exchange rate effects, in either nominal or real terms.
3. Money supply or real balance effects, due to the role of money in transactions and as a 'buffer stock'.
4. Wealth effects on spending more generally, operating through the valuation of bonds and equities, and changes in housing and property prices.
5. Credit channel effects, because of the nature of banks as specialist providers of intermediation services and credit.

The supply-side responses to policy changes depend on whether prices and wages are flexible, expectations of wages and prices are sticky, the bargaining/contracting structure of the labour market, and the credibility of the policy change.

All of these have been discussed elsewhere in this volume. Possible supply-side consequences were examined at length in Chapters 9 and 10, as were real balance effects in earlier chapters. Wealth effects are implicit in the valuation of bonds and equities for the demand for money and portfolio balance models. Credit channel

Figure 14.4 Transmission of monetary policy

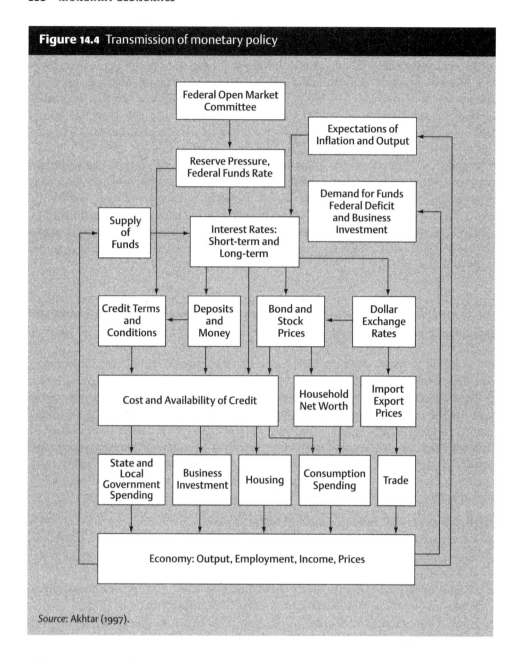

Source: Akhtar (1997).

effects were noted in the previous chapter, and exchange rate effects are covered in the next. This leaves interest rates, discussed at various points throughout this book. We limit ourselves to two observations at this juncture concerning this channel.

First, interest rate setting mechanisms vary widely across markets and countries. At the short end of the market there is a mix of market-clearing, highly flexible, interest rates, and administered, fixed-but-adjustable rates. That is, there are the bill rates, rates on overnight money and other interbank rates of maturities through to three months, rates on certificates of deposit, and so on; on the other, there is the central banks' administered discount rate and those rates for which an element of custom 'market pricing' operates. For interest rates on loans, practices differ from one country to another in terms of fixed, variable, and fixed-but-adjustable rates. Over 80 per cent of company debt in Germany is fixed rate. In the UK, 90 per cent of mortgages in 1992 were variable rate, along with most business loans (Artis and Lewis, 1993). This difference is important when we consider the consequence of more variable interest rates in a deregulated environment later in this chapter.

Second, the authorities' proximate[7] control is over nominal, not real, rates of interest, whereas standard economic analysis emphasizes that it is real, not nominal, rates that are likely to matter most for spending, since those undertaking expenditure plans are assumed not to suffer from money illusion when they make conscious decisions involving interest as an opportunity cost. In the very short run, the distinction is of little consequence; inertia in the movement of prices (and consequently, inertia in expectations of prices) means that a nominal rate change is a real rate change, not simply on impact but over a significant period of time. In the long run, as stressed by Wicksell and by several authors in the new classical macroeconomics tradition, real interest rates are not even proximately controllable by the authorities and attempts to target a real rate may easily yield unstable solutions (unless they feed back to a nominal quantity anchor). Indeed, difficulties of this kind were cited by the authorities in the 1970s as among the reasons for their non-ideological embrace of intermediate targets in the form of money supply targets in a period of high and variable inflation (see Artis and Lewis, 1981: 41–2).

Intermediate target variables

We can distinguish at least two reasons why a target for an intermediate variable might be adopted. The two reasons we have in mind are, first, that the variable in question may be a good contemporaneous indicator of a variable of significance (which itself may be an ultimate variable or just another intermediate variable); second, that it may be a good policy summary and *leading* indicator of a variable or variables of interest.

It is helpful to differentiate the first type of intermediate variable target as an 'indicator'. By assumption an indicator variable has no genuine predictive content, but is useful as a contemporaneous indicator or proxy for a variable of interest, information on which takes some time to collect. For example (we are not concerned with the statistical merits of the argument), in the UK context it is argued that M0 (the monetary base) is a good indicator of current 'money GDP', observations on which do not become available for some time after the event. In this particular case the lead is perhaps not so very long. Still, having regard to the greater inaccuracy of the early GDP guesstimates, the M0 lead would be valuable if the policy objective is to target money GDP and if the relationship between the two is sufficiently robust.

The second type of intermediate variable target is motivated by different considerations. The variable in question is thought of as a reflection in some degree of policy thrust and as having predictive value. In particular, the classic monetary examples are the money supply and the exchange rate. Their particular rationale is that, with a stable demand for money function in the first case and a stable foreign price level in the second, they provide a forecast for inflation—and variations from target imply deviations from the authorities' commitment to control inflation.

Disillusionment with monetary targets grew when it seemed that they met *neither* criterion. Poole's analysis then came into play on the grounds that if a nominal anchor rationale underlies the choice of intermediate target, then the choice should turn on the criterion of robustness. Poole's (1970) classic paper dealt with the choice between the interest rate and the money stock in a context where money income was the ultimate target. Later analysis of the choice between monetary and exchange rate targets has followed the path indicated by the stochastic analysis presented in Poole's paper (see Chapter 15). That is to say, the key test is which of the targets performs best when stochastic shocks are taken into account.

The general result to be derived from such studies is easy to state: interest rate or exchange rate targeting is to be preferred when the instability is from the demand for money function; monetary targeting is generally preferable when the shocks come from domestic spending or from overseas prices; but there are instances too where the results are inconclusive. Formally, the answer will depend on three things: the distribution of shocks assumed, the model, and the content of the objective function. There is no reason to think that these things stay constant over time, but there is little doubt that in the 1980s the perceived distribution of shocks moved against money supply targeting as evidence of instability in money demand functions cumulated.

Some continue to agree with Milton Friedman that a 'monetary total is the best currently available intermediate guide or criterion for monetary policy and I believe that it matters much less which particular total is chosen than that one be chosen' (1969b: 108–9). Broadly speaking, this seemed to be the position of the Bundesbank (Schlesinger, 1994), and it may have been right. Perhaps when financial deregulation has run its course and the system settles down, stability will return to monetary relationships and monetary targets can be resurrected. Yet many of the financial innovations which we identified in Chapter 12 seem likely to produce continuing changes to the demand for money function. In addition, the 'Lucas critique' (Lucas, 1976) and Goodhart's Law (Goodhart, 1984) suggest caution.

Lucas, we recall, argued that it is incorrect to evaluate economic policies by the traditional method of extrapolating econometric equations forward by feeding new values of the explanatory variables into the estimated relationships. This is because changes in policy will themselves induce alterations in the underlying structure of the economy and estimated relationships, i.e. the structure of the economy is not invariant to economic policy. Such feedback is well understood in the physical sciences. In economies, human behaviour may pose special difficulties if well informed and knowledgeable people change their behaviour—and economic relationships—in the face of government policy actions.

Goodhart's Law takes up this point. It states that whenever the authorities do attempt to exploit an observed regularity (e.g. the demand for money), the pattern will change. Insofar as this results from a systematic adaptation of the private sector's behaviour to the perception that the authorities are treating an indicator as a target, we have indeed a Law rather than a coincident observation. A good example is perhaps the reaction of exchange rates to overshoots of monetary targets: instead of depreciating, as would be the expected reaction of the exchange rate to a monetary expansion, an appreciation is the rational (Currie, 1984)—and actually observed (Smith and Goodhart, 1985: 190)—response when the expansion is thought to portend a rise in the interest rate, as under a policy regime in which the authorities are pursuing a target for the money supply.

The argument for a simple monetary rule suggests that sticking to the commitment is of the essence; and that simplicity is warranted because it makes it easy to monitor the authorities' success in maintaining their commitment. The danger is that the authorities will be led to take a ride on a tiger's back, defending the simple rule, for the sake of their reputation, in circumstances in which the rule is hopelessly inappropriate.

The central bank's reputation is an important conditioning variable here. When a central bank is endeavouring to establish credibility for its anti-inflationary policies a simple rule, readily announced and understood, may be needed. Certainly, monetary targets provided a critical nominal anchor in the transition from fixed to floating rates. Once credibility exists, more complex strategies can be followed. In effect, adherence to a simple rule is an instrument for achieving credibility, and when the necessary reputation has been established, it takes the place of the rule.

14.4 Deregulation and the Role of Banks

THE case for monetary targets is eroded further by changing views about the role of banks in the economy. It used to be said that banks perform certain functions which give them a central place in the financial system. Corrigan (1982) in a much cited essay looked to three factors making banks 'special'.[8] One is that banks stand at the centre of the payments system and their liabilities are viewed as money by transactors. Second, banks are the transmission belt of monetary policy. Third, banks are special as producers of information, undertaking credit evaluation and monitoring activities which supplement or substitute for the information available through other sources. In particular, they provide credit or market-enhancing credit guarantees for financial activities which, because of asymmetric information and consequently high evaluation, monitoring, and enforcement costs, cannot easily be funded by securities issues in open markets. The credit channel effects, noted earlier, build on the special lending role of banks, while a related branch of the literature has argued that bank crashes and similar financial disturbances are especially disruptive because the closure of a bank can destroy this private information base and force borrowers onto less well-informed lenders.

A number of writers—notably Tobin (1963), Black (1975), and Fama (1985)—consider this specialness as deriving primarily from the special character of the regulations upon banks. Without these regulations, they argued, banks would look much like other financial intermediaries. Already, with the blurring of the lines between banks and non-banks and between market transactions and intermediated ones, banks have lost much of their distinctiveness. As a result, the monetary system may be seen to be evolving towards a new structure in which central banks are no longer as interested as they were in controlling bank output. Instead, the authorities are aiming at macroeconomic variables, such as the price level, and alterations to the balance sheets of the banks emerge as a by-product of that process rather than a necessary precondition. Banks were the focus of policy when legal restrictions and regulations made them to a large degree quasi-governmental agencies, monopolizing access to cheap credit and enforcing exchange controls and other market constraints. Now banks can no longer be considered part of the 'control core', in Hicks's (1977) terminology, but must instead be grouped with the other endogenously determined parts of the economy.

One area in which banks' responses have become more endogenized is with respect to interest rate variations. Monetary analysis has long assumed that monetary assets bear no interest and with this assumption, 'the' rate of interest represents both the level of market interest rates and the difference between the interest return on money and non-money assets. The analysis begins with an account of how banks create money, and uses balance sheet identities like those in Chapter 13 to show how banks stand relative to the monetary authorities and the general public. With the money supply embracing cash and bank deposits, this means that banks are effectively grouped with the monetary authorities as part of the control core. Bank money is equated with fiat (central bank) money, and both are assumed to bear interest rates set exogenously at zero. In this way the institution of money is inextricably tied to the institution of banking.

This accurately describes many national monetary systems before deregulation, and the structure can itself be traced to a succession of financial innovations in the nineteenth century which transformed banks in Europe from small regional country partnerships into major national and even multinational institutions (European Association for Banking History, 1994). These developments can be seen themselves as the culmination of a process which began in previous centuries with the sovereign or government encouraging the growth of banks as a way of enhancing the State's credit (and reducing the interest cost of state borrowing), and ended with the government sharing its money-creating powers with the banking system (Hicks, 1969). The banks' form of intermediation and their relationship with borrowers made them central to the finance of industrial growth, and government borrowing from the banking system both widened the government's access to credit and enabled it to extend its control over new sources of money creation.[9] As debt money assumed greater significance and more money came to be created as a by-product of the lending activities of banks, interest rates and the availability of bank credit came to be seen as the cornerstone of monetary policy, so that monetary policy became indistinguishable from banking policy.

That is no longer the case as 'marketization' and 'securitization' grows apace. Already well over one-half of home mortgage loans in the USA are securitized in the secondary mortgage market, and it makes more sense to focus on the mortgage market rather than the balance sheet responses of any intermediary grouping when assessing the impact of monetary policy on this sector. Nevertheless, banks continue to dominate some other areas such as small business loans and in the present transitional stage it is still unclear how much of the textbook analysis based around bank intermediation and deposit expansion will survive the wave of innovation. Our analysis retains the standard framework to focus on the response of bank interest rates to monetary policy.

Impact of deregulation

When some part of monetary assets (i.e. bank deposits) bears interest, it is the differential between the interest return on money and non-money assets which must adjust to restore asset market equilibrium following a change in market conditions. If bank interest rates are regulated, relative interest rates between bank deposits and other assets can be readily altered merely by changes in market rates of interest. With deregulation, it becomes a matter of how bank deposit rates are determined.

Payment of interest on bank deposits is possible due to the intermediation activities of banks whereby bank deposits are used to finance holding of other assets. These other assets are themselves substitutes for bank deposits in the portfolios of the non-bank sector. Consider the following representation of the market for bank deposits,

$$D(r_D, r_A, r_K)W = D^S \tag{14.2}$$

in which D^S is the supply of deposits, and in which the demand for deposits, as a proportion of private sector wealth, W, depends on r_D, the banks' deposit rate, r_A, the yield on securities, and r_k, the yield on capital assets. The demand for bank deposits, then, will depend upon the yield on deposits (r_D) and these other assets (r_A, r_K), while competition among banks will ensure that the deposit yield offered will depend upon the yields available on the assets held in the banks' portfolios.

Under regulation, the assets held in banks' portfolios were subject to a number of restrictions. First, there were (and in some cases still are) required cash reserves whereby banks had to hold a certain proportion of deposits as cash or non-interest bearing accounts at the central bank. Second, banks were required to maintain a secondary reserve asset ratio or liquid assets ratio under which a certain proportion of assets was in the form of bills and short-term government securities. Third, new lending of banks was subject to quantitative and qualitative directives which restricted the amount that banks could lend out both in aggregate and to particular sectors. Credit rationing was common. The effect of these asset constraints was to reduce potential earnings, and interest payable, per dollar of deposits. At the same time, interest rate ceilings applied to certain classes of deposits—mainly small retail accounts—and sometimes to certain types of loans, further reducing the level and variability of bank interest rates.[10]

For example, consider the operation of one of these controls, the required reserve ratio (called special deposits in the UK). With the banks subject to a required reserve ratio, s, the deposit rate r_D is given by

$$r_D = (1 - s - er)r_A + s.r_S - c, \tag{14.4}$$

where er represents the excess reserve ratio of the banks, r_S is the interest rate paid on required reserves, r_A is the weighted average yield on banks' asset portfolios, and c is the constant marginal resource cost of deposits. Note the impact of regulation: the imposition of the reserve requirement can be regarded as a form of taxation—a tax on bank intermediation. So long as r_A exceeds r_S, the requirement widens the gap between the cost of funds and the net yield which is sufficient to ensure that the marginal funds can earn profit.

By contrast, if we interpret deregulation as the removal of the reserve requirement (along with the other asset restrictions), then setting $r_S = 0$, we have

$$r_D = (1 - er)r_A - c. \tag{14.5}$$

A process of restrictive monetary policy under deregulation will see banks better able to match the market offerings by raising their own rates. This is because the return on banks' asset portfolios will increase with market rates and, under competitive conditions, the higher return will be passed on to depositors. With r_D responding in this way to variations in r_A, achieving a particular change in relative yields, necessary for portfolio equilibrium, will require a larger change in the absolute level of interest rates.

This argument translates into the familiar IS–LM analysis as an LM schedule which is less elastic with respect to absolute rates of interest, since the fluctuation of bank interest rates with market yields offsets to some extent the tendency of the demand for money to vary with 'the' rate of interest. An increase in the market orientation of banks will have other impacts too, upon the demand for money and the LM curve. In total, four principal effects may be noted:

1. A reintermediation into bank deposit intermediation seems likely to the extent that bank deposit returns were not previously effectively market-determined by the payment of 'implicit' interest in lieu of explicit interest payments. Shifts into now higher-yielding financial instruments which form part of the conventional money supply will increase the demand for money.
2. Transactions balances can be expected to fall, and the interest elasticity of the supply of deposits will increase, as yields become positive in real terms.
3. The interest sensitivity of money demanded, in the longer term, is likely to decrease as bank deposit rates become more responsive to market rates of interest.
4. The income elasticity of the demand for (narrow) money is, however, likely to fall also, as deposits will be held as interest-bearing liquid assets, rather than simply to facilitate transactions.

The first two of these impacts seems likely to produce divergent trends in broad and narrow money and erratic movements of the LM schedule in the transition. The third, as noted, suggests a steepening of the LM curve while the fourth offsets to some degree the change in interest rate elasticity on the LM schedule.

At the same time, conditions in the real sector cannot be expected to remain unchanged in the face of these developments. Deregulation promotes competition and the decline in computation costs makes interest rate variation much cheaper; together, these developments reduce the incidence of credit rationing. In combination with some other developments, the following effects are suggested in terms of the IS curve:

1. The spread of flexi-rate loan contracts and the development of private hedge markets for interest rate futures make it likely that it is the 'permanent' interest rate expected to rule over the life of the loan contract which is relevant for investment decisions. Consequently, the IS curve may exhibit a reduced elasticity with respect to current interest rate movements, insofar as new expenditures are concerned.
2. Under the system of non-price credit rationing, the flow of credit to some sectors was restricted, while others were sheltered from various interest rate or price changes. Interest rate changes since deregulation affect most sectors directly.
3. Under the old system the impact of rationing and interest rate increases fell heavily upon those borrowers seeking new accommodation from the banks. As flexi-rate loan contracts have become commonplace, all borrowers—existing and new—feel the brunt of monetary changes. For existing borrowers, the effect of higher interest rates operates much like a tax in squeezing discretionary income and depressing expenditures.
4. The removal of interest rate ceilings leads to a higher average level of interest rates. Interest costs therefore form a larger proportion of total expenditure, and changes in the rate of interest could have a greater impact on expenditure and budgets.
5. Inflexibilities in other markets could increase interest rate sensitivity. Borrowers are likely to be more sensitive to changes in interest rates if prices in product markets move more slowly.

The last four factors suggest a flattening of the IS curve, while the first suggests some possible offset since what matters when policy changes is the extent to which current short-term rates influence the market's anticipation of the authorities' future policies in the money markets—and thus long-term rates of interest.

14.5 What Do Central Banks Control?

Aᴌᴌ of this undoubtedly puts too fine a gloss on what can often be a relatively blunt instrument. Seymour E. Harris when introducing a symposium 'The Controversy over Monetary Policy' spoke of what he called 'the monetary axe' (1951: 179). About twenty years on from that time, Austen Holmes—then Adviser to the Governor of the Reserve Bank of Australia—was asked by a student in a lecture at Flinders University whether he agreed with the Keynesian or monetarist theories of the transmission mechanism. He responded: 'Well, laddy, it's like this. We take this bloody great axe. We give it a bloody great swing. And we hope that somebody is too stupid to duck.'

That simile seems an appropriate one in the context of the recession of the early 1990s after central banks in a number of countries moved to deflate the asset price boom by raising interest rates. Those unable to duck were the entities which had taken advantage of deregulation, innovation, and greater competition in financial markets during the 1980s to transform their balance sheet positions and increase their financial exposure. In many countries, consumers and business enterprises used the new financial environment greatly to increase their credit to income ratios, and this move towards higher borrowing against assets (real estate and shares) was powerful in stimulating consumption and spending. Interest rate increases may not have been a powerful preventative measure while this adjustment was going on, but at the higher ratios ruling when policy was tightened later in the decade, interest rate variations had considerable influence on those with unhedged positions—a feature also for the Asian crisis in the late 1990s. An unexpected shock to the cost of debt suddenly makes debt-servicing a burden, and asset prices and balance sheets soon look unsustainable. Irving Fisher's 'debt deflation theory' seemed to have become relevant (Fisher, 1933).[11]

Homeowners with floating rate mortgage debt proved to be particularly vulnerable, and the greatly increased financial exposure of the personal sector since deregulation, suggests that for at least some time the transmission mechanism may bear more heavily on the personal sector than the corporate; but this is clearly not the long-run position. The personal sector may reduce its exposure and increasingly take advantage of hedging instruments and swapped contracts—one indication of this is the vast array on offer of part-fixed/part-variable mortgage loans. Nevertheless, the general point remains. When debt ratios are high, the wealth effects of interest rates seem likely to be particularly strong and attention needs to be paid to debt exposures and asset prices in policy formulation.

For the future, one of the consequences of financial change of the kind now in train is that the dividing lines between banks and non-banks and intermediation and markets are becoming progressively more blurred. This development was anticipated and analysed by Fama (1980) and foreshadowed by Tobin (1963) and Gurley and Shaw (1960). A system in which the banking system's responses to monetary policy have become more endogenized has consequences in turn for the use of monetary aggregates as intermediate targets. Benjamin Friedman (1975) and Bean (1983) demonstrated in general terms the inferiority of using an endogenous variable as an intermediate target. The basic idea is that the information contained in the observations of the endogenous variable can be exploited better by transforming it from an intermediate target into an information variable. All that matters when the money supply becomes such an information variable (i.e. indicator) is whether the observed movements provide information which helps to predict future values of the macroeconomic variables such as incomes and prices; the question of whether or not the money supply causes the movements in incomes and prices loses the importance formerly attached to it. Something along these lines seems to have occurred in policy circles with the switch to interest rate controls.

The upshot is that the area of effective policy control is reduced to the central bank's own balance sheet and changes in it brought about by the purchase and sale of securities in the market. There is then the question of the adequacy of monetary control by this means.

Adequacy of market operations

The issue has been posed by Benjamin Friedman (1993: 38):

[I]n a $6 *trillion* economy with more than $25 *trillion* of financial claims outstanding in highly liquid markets where many of those claims change ownership not just easily but frequently, why should it matter whether the Federal Reserve buys $1 *billion* worth of securities or $10 *billion* worth in the course of an entire year? How can such a small difference in Federal Reserve transactions exert a meaningful influence on such matters as how much people choose to work or spend. . . or how much business produces and how they price it?

Dow and Saville (1988) note a similar paradox in the fact that, with so small a quantitative impact in the markets, the Bank of England can exert such widespread effects on interest rates—with many adjustments, e.g. in base rate, happening 'automatically'. They assign a major responsibility for this to the fact that because market rates are indeterminate within a range of their fundamental values, the intervention of the authorities falls on especially receptive ground. The steer given by the authorities accordingly becomes decisive. A closely analogous piece of reasoning may be applied to the intervention by central banks in foreign exchange markets. Here intervention is often trivial in relation to daily turnover but may provide a signal that the market craves.

Still, in the domestic money markets the central bank really is potentially much bigger than it is in the foreign exchange market. What seems to be a pure bootstrap effect may be viewed alternatively as the conclusion of a process of learning in which the driving force is the belief that the central bank could, if it wished, persist in operations which will force the interest rate changes that now take place automatically to take place by arbitrage instead. The key is that the Bank controls the issue of central bank money in the face of demand which is relatively insensitive to interest rates. That is, the reason why the central bank's transactions are so important is that they are conducted with cash or central bank money. This can be produced by the central bank at virtually zero cost and in unlimited amounts for the purpose of market purchases. For market sales, the central bank is limited by the amount of securities it is willing to sell. Accordingly, the authorities' power as a market trans-actor hinges on two factors. One is their monopoly of the manufacture of cash. The second is the continued acceptability of cash in transactions and for settling up imbalances in non-cash payments systems.

Taking this line of argument one step further, there is the question of whether, at an abstract level, market actions are sufficient for monetary stabilization. As we noted in earlier chapters, the workings of a fiat money system have been extensively studied by Patinkin and others. Patinkin (1961) established the minimum precondi-tions which must be set in order to assure the determinancy of the price level. In a general equilibrium framework, some important nominal magnitude needs to be tied down or made in inelastic supply, and since with N assets only $N-1$ rates of return are independent, some rate of return must be exogenously determined. Usu-ally, in monetary theory, the nominal quantity is conceived of as the fiat issue of 'money', used as the means of payment, and the interest rate exogenously set is the zero return on money. As the money supply is cash plus bank deposits, banks are grouped with the central bank as part of the control core in this conception and their deposit rate is assumed to be fixed (at zero).

This is a not unrealistic description of how national monetary systems used to look, but in this chapter we have argued that this grouping is no longer a good description of the way in which the monetary system in many countries is evolving. With the deregulation, banks can no longer be considered part of the core, but must instead be grouped with the other endogenously determined parts of the economy. Thus the area of policy control shrinks, at least at this simplified conceptual level, to the central bank's own balance sheet. The fixed rate of interest then becomes that on central bank money (base money, cash) effectively set at zero. The important nominal quantity which must be fixed is not the quantity of money but the amount of cash, determined by open market operations.

Technology is changing here too. Increasing use of credit cards reduces the demand for money to hold before settlement dates; newer developments promise instant debiting of bank accounts reducing clearing times effectively to zero. These changes affect the demand for money in the traditional transactions sense and seem all too likely to impart instability to the demand for monetary base (Mo) in conse-quence. The extreme of the 'moneyless' society, on the other hand, appears a dis-tinctly unlikely prospect: fortunately, for if monetary policy does not require a stable demand for Mo it does require *some* demand for Mo—otherwise the central bank's ability to influence ('control') the rate of interest would be absent.[12]

Notes

1 With the exception of Canada, most industrial countries have moved to RTGS systems as the main mechanism for settling interbank transactions. Fund transfers are settled at the time of the transfers, which takes place as soon as the sending bank has sufficient funds available in its account at the central bank. The key implication is the need for banks to maintain intra-day settlement balances.

2 This section has benefited from reading Akhtar (1997) and from having discussions with Stephen Millard of the Bank of England.

3 For example, on 16 January 1998 banks were borrowing at a Federal funds rate of 20% rather than at the discount rate of 5%.

4 Recent descriptions are given in the Quarterly Bulletins for May 1997 (p. 204) and August 1998 (p. 202). Earlier accounts are given in Allen (1984), Llewellyn (1990), Shaw (1990), Wilson (1989), and Artis and Lewis (1991).

5 Prior to March 1997, a borrowing facility was held only by the discount houses. Their special role in underwriting the weekly Treasury bill lender and acting as the chosen intermediaries between the Bank and the market was abolished in the reforms of March 1997.

6 Berk (1998) depicts an even more complex process.

7 We may 'proximate' because the Dalton 'cheap money' experiment of 1946–7 convincingly demonstrated that the authorities cannot hold rates at levels well below those which the market regards as appropriate without pumping in liquidity at an inflationary rate. Hugh Dalton, the Labour Chancellor, sought to force long-term rates down from 3 to 2½%, and the authorities found themselves buying more and more securities in the attempt. With the nominal rate which the market expects to rule equal to the real rate plus the expected rate of inflation, the authorities can soon find themselves in the position of chasing after an ever-accelerating target, as their market purchases feed inflation expectations and encourage existing holders of government bonds to take advantage of the unnaturally high price of bonds on offer.

8 The essay and the three others cited at the beginning of the following paragraph are reprinted in Lewis (1995).

9 Much the same process has been evident in terms of close bank-government relations in many rapidly developing countries in Asia.

10 Not all of these controls have applied. Australia was one country where all of these constraints operated under regulation (Davis and Lewis, 1980; Lewis and Wallace, 1997). UK banks prior to 1971 were subject to an 8% conventional cash ratio, a 28% liquid assets ratio, and severe advances directives. Such strict controls were lightened in 1971, reimposed in 1973 and then eliminated in 1981 (Artis and Lewis, 1991). US banks were subject to extensive reserve requirements on all types of deposits and restrictive interest rate ceilings (Friedman, 1970a). The latter were eliminated in 1982 and reserve requirements progressively reduced after that.

11 Irving Fisher argued that a downward economic shock would be magnified by a debt-deflation transmission mechanism involving, *inter alia* debt reduction, falling asset prices and reduced net worth, higher interest rate risk premia, falling confidence, lower profitability and output, contracting money and credit, and reduced velocity (in effect increased money demand). Tobin (1980c: 15) described it as a 'reverse Pigou effect' or 'Fisher effect'.

12 Severe instability in demand for Mo could be problematic in making short-run forecasting of the excess demand for central bank money difficult, but if the operational target is a rate of interest, the authorities can in principle still adjust the scale of their operations in Mo to achieve it.

Chapter 15
Exchange Rates and External Arrangements

15.1 Problems of Paper Money

Iᴛ is in the nature of things for each generation to suppose that it is passing through a unique period of change and tackling unique problems. However, there is one respect in which that view is true of the past three decades, and that is in the transformed nature of the international monetary system. As we emphasized in Chapter 2, the outstanding feature of present monetary arrangements is the determination of the value of money. In the past, the internal currency had intrinsic value or it maintained a fixed (or nearly fixed) relationship to a monetary substance or some other external standard of value. Today no major currency has any commodity link and the value of paper money depends solely on the willingness of others to accept it and ultimately on a faith that its purchasing power will not be depreciated. In short, there is no anchor for the value of money other than that which the central bank establishes.

Milton Friedman's (1986) article is a notable exception, but otherwise the distinctive characteristics of the present monetary order and the implications which they carry for the prosecution of national monetary policies have not received the attention that they deserve. Policy credibility was not an issue when countries were on gold and expected to be so forever—and at the same historic parity. Britain effectively had the same official metallic value from 1717 to 1931, the USA from 1834 to 1934. Central banks' policy objectives were narrowly defined. Monetary policy was subject to the rules of the gold standard which meant that the central banks had to guard their gold reserves and restrict the money supply if these reserves were reduced. Only during times of war or its immediate aftermath was convertibility suspended, and the value of the currency could then vary without causing an ebb or flow of gold abroad. During such periods it was assumed that convertibility would resume (and at the old parity) when the crisis ended; in the meantime a responsible central bank would attempt to find an alternative nominal anchor. Necessarily, in such a system, the central bank had a large measure of independence from the government. The obligation to convert notes into gold at a fixed parity, and to ensure that gold reserves were sufficient to back the currency, protected central banks from political pressures. At the same time the link to gold provided what seems nowadays a remarkable degree of long-term price stability.

All of this has changed. Inflation targeting and the associated tactics, the credibility of policy operations, and the constitution of central banking are now at the heart of monetary policy, and these issues form the basis of the next chapter. This chapter examines external arrangements beginning with the international policy environment, the problems of paper money, and the choices for inflation control. Some theorists argue that a worldwide system of independent paper moneys under floating exchange rates is unworkable. Yet central banks have had to make it work. The policy procedures they have developed—often by trial and error—bear a striking similarity to the 'ideal' agenda for monetary policy laid out by Keynes in 1923 in *A Tract on Monetary Reform*.

The *Tract* was, in many ways, a remarkably forward-looking document. Britain at the time was off gold—temporarily. But the backdrop to policy was the pre-1914 gold standard, to which Britain was expected to return (and did in 1925). There were many who were unhappy that the long-run value of money was determined by unregulated conditions of supply and demand in the gold market. The late nineteenth century fall in the price level was widely attributed to the increased cost of extracting gold from the depleted Californian and Australian mines, as well as to increased gold hoarding in India—a trend that was reversed only by new discoveries on the Klondike in a ten-year boom which began in 1896. Most monetary reformers, however, did not envisage abandoning commodity money. Rather, as in Marshall's tabular standard or Fisher's compensated dollar, the idea was to vary the gold content of the money supply in order to achieve a more stable price level.

Two notable exceptions were Wicksell and Keynes. In *Geldzins and Güterpreise*, published in German in 1898 and translated as *Interest and Prices* (London: Macmillan), Wicksell argued that the gold standard prevented the central bank from adjusting the 'market rate' of interest to the 'natural rate' ('the interest on loans which is neutral in respect of commodity prices, and tends neither to raise nor to lower them' (1936: 102).

They can attain their objective only in so far as they exert an indirect influence on the *money rate of interest*, and bring it into line with the natural rate, or below it, more rapidly than would otherwise be the case ... The question thus arises whether the object in view could not be obtained far more simply, and far more securely through the monetary institutions of the various countries agreeing among themselves to undertake *directly* that alteration in their rates of interest which is necessary and which alone is effective. (1898: 188–9)

Thus his solution was for the establishment of 'an international paper standard', which he called 'an ideal standard of value', giving central banks complete control over the money supply. It would be introduced by the suspension of the free coinage of gold, and he argued

need not ... provide cause for consternation. On the contrary, once it had come into being it would perhaps be the present system which would sound like a fairy tale, with its rather senseless and purposeless sending hither and thither of crates of gold, with its digging up of stores of treasure and burying them again in the recesses of the earth' (1898: 193).

This was the position to which Keynes was heading in *Indian Currency and Finance* (1913).

It is not likely that we shall leave permanently the most intimate adjustments of our economic organism at the mercy of a lucky prospector, a new chemical process, or a change of ideas in Asia . . . A preference for a tangible reserve currency is . . . a relic of a time when governments were less trustworthy in these matters than they are now. (Keynes 1973: 51, 71)

At that time, he looked forward to the day when gold-based currencies would be restricted to one or two countries, the central banks of which would 'manage' what was, in effect, a fiduciary international standard.

That time arrived by 1923 in the *Tract*. Keynes was critical of the policy of returning to gold, both before and after the event (*The Economic Consequences of Mr Churchill*, 1925)[1]. Instead of domestic prices being required to adjust to the exchange rate, he argued in the *Tract* that the exchange rate should be adjusted to a domestic price level consistent with a 'normal' (that is, reasonably full) level of employment. He then went on to sketch an agenda for operating monetary policy under an independent monetary standard. This provides a surprisingly accurate description of how central banking operates in the major countries today.

Keynes outlined 'a method for regulating the supply of currency and credit with a view to maintaining, so far as possible, the stability of the internal price level' (1923: 177). He first asked whether 'stability of prices' or 'stability of exchanges' ought to be the criterion of policy, coming down strongly in favour of prices: 'they should adopt the stability of sterling prices as their *primary* objective—though this would not prevent their aiming at exchange stability as a secondary objective by cooperating with the Federal Reserve Board in a common policy' (ibid. 186). In the absence of this policy coordination, he recommended what was tantamount to a target zone approach in order to 'keep the dollar-sterling exchange steady within corresponding limits, so that the exchange rate would not move with every breath of wind but only when the Bank had come to a considered judgement that a change was required for the sake of that stability of sterling prices' (ibid. 90). Keynes then considered how the objective of stability of prices would be rendered operational 'as regards the criteria, other than the actual trend of prices, which should determine the action of the controlling authority' (ibid. 188), and came up with a 'checklist' of factors not dissimilar to those used nowadays under the 'looking at everything' approach. He also touched on another present-day topic, that of central bank–Treasury relations, by asking whether 'within sufficient wide limits', the Bank of England was 'mistress of the situation' (ibid. 182).

The *Tract* is the source of that famous statement of Keynes ('this *long run* is a misleading guide to current affairs. *In the long run* we are all dead') when rejecting a fixed money-supply rule, based on the long-run quantity theory link between money and prices. Instead, he favoured discretionary monetary policy as a basis for controlling the credit cycle, consistent with his preference for broad, not narrow money. The right policy was to 'watch and to control the creation of credit and to let the creation of currency follow suit' (ibid. 187). This was because the quantity of cash was a backward-looking indicator. It was not the past rise in prices but the future rise which had to be counteracted. (It is interesting that Mo has become an important leading indicator in Britain today precisely because it is a backward-looking indicator of spending, but published faster than GDP.) Finally, in line with current thinking, Keynes considered stable prices could be achieved by monetary policy alone. He did not see wage pressure as a complicating factor.

Yet, there is one important respect in which Keynes's vision differs from modern practice. When Keynes recommended a 'managed currency' in the *Tract* he was doing so for Britain,[2] although he argued that 'the same policy which is wise for Great Britain is wise for the USA, namely to aim at the stability of the commodity-value of the dollar rather than at the stability of the gold-value of the dollar' (ibid. 203). A universal system of managed currencies was beyond his contemplation:

There are probably no countries, other than Great Britain and the United States, which would be justified in attempting to set up an independent standard. Their wisest course would be to base their currencies either on sterling or on dollars by means of an exchange standard, fixing their exchanges in terms of one or the other. (ibid. 205)

A universal system of floating exchange rates was also beyond the conception of Lord Robbins. As late as 1971, Lord Robbins urged:

Rather than let their exchanges fluctuate freely in terms of all other currencies, the authorities of many centres would take steps, as they did in 1931 and again in 1949, to attach themselves at *fixed rates* to one of the larger currencies. The idea of a world in which the exchange rates of every sovereign state are perpetually free to fluctuate in terms of the exchange rates of every other, is purely fanciful. It is perfectly realistic to conceive of floating rates between large *blocs*, the sterling area and the dollar area, for instance. It is not realistic to think of floating rates all round. (Robbins, 1971: 143)

He went on to explain (in the introduction):

The real dispute . . . concerns, not the practicability or the prudence of floating rates here and there or now and then, but rather *whether all rates should be free everywhere and all the time.* (Robbins, 1971: 21)

Yet, however fanciful and unrealistic, floating rates all round is essentially what has transpired. A world system of this form based entirely around independent paper moneys, is unprecedented in monetary history. In the past, major currencies severed the links to a specie base and issued irredeemable paper money, but the departures from a commodity base were temporary expedients in times of war or financial crisis such as the 1930s, were not expected to be permanent and proved not to be so. It is in this respect that modern central bankers have entered uncharted waters.

Economists have long studied the workings of a paper money system, but the models are of a closed economy—Friedman's (1969*b*) 'helicopter money models' and Patinkin's (1965) 'market experiments' are examples. The theory of an international system based around paper currencies is not well developed. Indeed, Kareken and Wallace (1981) and Wallace (1990) contend that a universal system of paper currencies, along with free trade in goods and services, no capital controls, unrestricted portfolio choice, and freely floating exchange rates is 'unworkable'. The equilibrium of such a regime is 'indeterminate' and, without either legal restrictions upon asset holdings or government intervention in the foreign exchange market, equilibrium exchange rates are indeterminate. This indeterminacy results, they argue, because there are no fundamentals governing the demand for items which are intrinsically useless, unbacked, and costless to produce. Without some form of enforcement upon currency holding which prevents one currency from being nearly costlessly substituted for another, the demand for any particular currency is governed, not in part by speculation, but entirely by speculation. The consequence is that the demands for different currencies, exchange rates, price levels, and all nominal values are undefined and the system is, in Kareken and Wallace's words, 'not economically feasible' (1981: 207).

Moreover, the problems of paper money systems at an individual country level have been well documented, the most notable examples coming from the episodes of hyperinflation. Indeed, it is fairly obvious that these kinds of rapid inflations are only technically possible because of the use of paper money. Throughout history, commodity money has been the rule, and it is for this reason, as Forrest Capie (1985: 4) has observed, 'from medieval times to the present day the examples of accelerating and very rapid inflation are few'. Each of those examples is associated with departure from a specie standard made necessary by the need for wartime finance: notably the inflation of the US Revolution, Great Britain during the Napoleonic wars, the US Civil War greenback period, and the much wider and more extensive departures during the First and Second World Wars. In evaluating past experience with such episodes, Irving Fisher wrote in 1911: 'Irredeemable paper money has almost invariably proved a curse to the country employing it' (1911: 131). In terms of an international standard based around fiat currencies, the limited experience in the 1930s with paper moneys and floating exchange rates led policy-makers and men of affairs at the time to contemplate with considerable trepidation a continuing system of free paper currencies.

Despite such warnings, it is easy to understand why those such as Keynes, seeking 'a scientific treatment of currency questions', have been attracted to paper currencies. The appeal of commodity-based money lies in the promise of price and exchange rate stability. A well-managed paper money system can in principle do just as well, perhaps better, in achieving these objectives by avoiding short-run price variability which results from inertia in the adjustment of commodity-based money supply to changes in demand. Indeed, many central banks were originally established in order to provide an 'elastic' supply of money in the context of a commodity monetary standard. This was true of the Federal Reserve System in 1914:

The Federal Reserve was established in the United States with the power to create currency and bank reserves at least somewhat independently of the nation's monetary gold. The Fed was given authority to create currency and reserves by making loans to banks through its discount window or by acquiring securities in the money market. The Fed's mission was to provide an elastic supply of money to smooth short-term interest rates against liquidity disturbances, while preserving the link between money and gold in the long run in order to restrain inflation. (Goodfriend, 1997: 3)

A paper standard can produce these ends at much lower potential social cost by avoiding the inefficiency inherent in tying up of stocks of a valuable commodity for monetary use. If supplied in a proper fashion, paper money can be issued at near-zero social costs—due to its trivial intrinsic content. The worldwide adoption of fiduciary paper money undoubtedly is an acknowledgement, even if unstated, that the benefits of an inconvertible monetary standard are substantial. However, as Milton Friedman (1986) has noted, the true cost of the system is much higher where there is monetary mismanagement. The costs then include the effects upon economic decision-making of unstable exchanges and higher and more variable inflation. Resources will then be diverted into hedging against price level uncertainty via markets for swaps, futures, options and other derivatives.

The essential issue is how to obtain the benefits without these costs. In short, are there grounds for thinking, following Keynes, that governments are more trustworthy than they were? Surprisingly, it is none other than Milton Friedman (1985) who provides an affirmative answer (although it is not governments which are more reliable).

Friedman argues that fiat money has acquired its poor reputation because governments have levied an inflation tax by engaging in inflationary financing. Inflationary money creation has been an attractive source of revenue because it enables governments to impost 'taxation without representation'. These pressures for governments to obtain resources for spending without levying explicit taxes still exist. What has changed is that counter-pressures have developed to limit governments' abuse of power and reduce the political attractiveness of paper money inflation—an application of (although Friedman does not use the term) Galbraith's 'theory of counter-vailing power' (Galbraith, 1952).

One such development is greater sophistication of both the public at large and the financial markets with respect to inflation thanks to the information revolution, which has greatly reduced the cost of acquiring information and which has enabled expectations to respond more promptly and accurately to economic disturbances, including changes in government policy. As a result, for example, nominal interest rates respond more rapidly to expected inflation and any anticipated erosion of the real value of government debt. A second (associated) development is the growth of indexation arrangements for taxation which has reduced the gain from 'bracket creep', when inflation pushes taxpayers into higher marginal tax brackets. A third change is the economizing process which we noted was a feature of the gold standard. Outside money (i.e. high-powered money or the monetary base, Mo) has declined relative to other (sometimes interest-bearing) components of the money stock. This erosion of the tax base reduces the likely revenue from an inflation tax. Friedman estimated that a 10 per cent per year increase in outside money would yield as revenue to the US government, only about seven-tenths of 1 per cent of national income.

Recent inflation performance in the USA, Japan, Europe, and elsewhere perhaps indicates that the preconditions for the successful operation of a paper money system—the exercise of restraint by the issuing authority and/or budget agency—may now exist. Whether this performance can be sustained to allow the irredeemable paper money standard to deliver long-run price stability of the type which marked commodity money systems remains to be seen. The whole point of commodity-based money is that restrictions to inflation are in-built; so long as the monetary structure is tied to a commodity the volume of money is limited by the supply of the commodity. Yet it is only by breaking free of these chains that an independent standard can realize its potential benefits (or its actual costs). Monetary systems can thus be seen as institutional arrangements which, while allowing the monetary authorities to exercise responsibility for money, at the same time usually provide for, or have implicit in them, rules or conventions that constrain or limit the ability of the authorities to pursue inflationary policies. That was precisely the conclusion of the research of the 1980s and 1990s which we reviewed in Chapter 10. In this respect, alternative sets of policies, for example on exchange rates, may serve to govern monetary behaviour.

15.2 Exchange Rate Management

O<small>NE</small> way of thinking about the issues involved is to note that whether its exchange rate is fixed or floating a country is still responsible for its inflation performance. The choice open to a country seeking price stability is whether to do so by means of internal or external stabilization. *Internal stabilization* of the value of money means keeping the purchasing power of national money reasonably stable in terms of goods and services on domestic markets. It may require disconnecting domestic prices from external developments. Flexible exchange rates equilibrate the balance of payments directly, and this freeing of monetary policy makes each country's inflation rate depend essentially on its own national policy (we ignore here complications posed by currency substitution).[3]

External stabilization involves fixing the value of the domestic monetary unit relative to foreign moneys and thus in terms of foreign goods and services. With a fixed exchange rate, the requirement of balance of payments equilibrium without unlimited reserves means that the quantity of (base) money can no longer be used for inflation control. But this 'sacrifice' of monetary autonomy serves to tie the country's inflation rate to that of the fixed exchange rate system.[4]

To this end, exchange rate management involves using the instruments of policy, primarily those of foreign exchange market intervention and interest rate manipulation, in order to influence the course of the exchange rate. In a regime of tight management these instruments are dedicated to targeting a relatively precise value of the exchange rate; in the limiting case, the target may be a fixed exchange rate. The proximate target of exchange rate management is, plainly enough, the exchange rate itself, related to the role of the exchange rate in the transmission mechanism of monetary policy and in particular to the link between monetary policy and inflation. This involves the *nominal* exchange rate, *e*.

Another source of concern stems from the role that the real exchange rate ep/p^* (or its inverse, competitiveness or the cost ratio) plays in the determination of employment and growth. In the short run, with prices sticky, variations in *nominal* exchange rates are highly correlated with variations in *real* exchange rates; but in the medium run the inflation priority, which leads to an emphasis on stabilizing the nominal exchange rate, and the competitiveness priority, which leads to an emphasis on stabilizing the real exchange rate, are more than likely to conflict. Thus a country with a rate of inflation which is already high relative to its competitors faces a dilemma: should it stabilize its nominal exchange rate in order to bear down on inflation, resulting in a decline in the competitiveness of its trading sector, or should it depreciate the currency to maintain competitiveness, thereby stimulating inflation?

Domestic considerations are not alone in giving significance to the exchange rate as a policy target. Exchange rates are of necessity two-sided variables and international responsibilities are likely to entail some degree of commitment to exchange rate stability in the interests of preserving a broader international policy regime, especially when market failure—speculative bubbles and other manifestations of inappropriate exchange market behaviour—seems likely to create problems. The Plaza Agreement and the Louvre Accord in the 1980s to support the US dollar, and support of the yen in the late 1990s are examples.

We first discuss the exchange rate in the transmission mechanism of monetary policy before going on to consider the general case for targeting the exchange rate as an intermediate variable in more detail. We then focus upon experience since 1971.

Open economy monetarism

The combination of the quantity theory and purchasing power parity (PPP) provides a model of the simplest kind which, though far from empirically robust, nonetheless underlies much thinking in this area.[5] If PPP holds, then relative national currency price levels, at least of traded goods, determine the exchange rate; and if the quantity theory holds, national price levels are tied to the corresponding money supplies. Hence relative money supplies determine relative price levels and exchange rates. This simple picture can easily be adjusted to allow for some necessary complications—for example, that while PPP may hold for traded goods prices, domestic price levels also incorporate prices of non-traded goods. With such complications added, the basic proposition is simply that a country's money supply, price level, and exchange rate are determined in a package, given the data for other countries. With output fixed, for example, an x per cent money supply increase will be associated with a rise in prices of x per cent and an x per cent depreciation of the exchange rate. This is the truth behind the phrase that 'the exchange rate is the relative price of two moneys' (see Chapter 8 for a fuller treatment).

This set of relationships may equally well be inverted so as to say that if a country targets its nominal exchange rate, then, subject to any differences in the linkage between non-traded and traded goods prices domestically and overseas, that country's price level will evolve in the same way as prices overseas. This is the essence of a policy of external stabilization of prices. Such an exchange rate targeting policy would of course imply that the money supply would passively adapt to the resultant demand arising from the path of nominal income so brought about. This illustrates the important truth that exchange rate targeting is incompatible with monetary targeting. It also emphasizes that the pursuit of a fixed nominal exchange rate target for inflation control promises control over *relative*, not absolute, inflation: clearly, targeting the Indonesian rupiah would not be intelligent counter-inflation strategy, whereas targeting the US dollar is!

The model as discussed so far has omitted any mention of interest rates. It is interesting to see that if the quantity theory is interpreted as a demand for money relationship and the interest rate is admitted as an additional argument with the usual negative effect, an apparently counter-intuitive result must follow. A rise in interest rates, taking the money supply and real income at home and all foreign variables as given, must result in a *rise* in prices to clear the money market and thence a *fall* (depreciation) in the exchange rate. The rise in interest rates would *reduce* the demand for the (given) stock of money, and since income is given could only occur in equilibrium if prices were to rise.

This conflicts with the conventional prediction that a rise in interest rates—unless it is interpreted as a sign of bad economic management—will lead to a rise (appreciation) of the exchange rate.[6] How is this paradox to be explained? One way of doing so is to view the model involved as a set of long-run equilibrium conditions where in contrast the conventional prediction comes out of a short-run disequilibrium analysis. On this interpretation a rise in interest rates is a sign of bad management in the sense that it implicitly stands in for the expectation of higher inflation and, rationally, in terms of the model, is associated with a rise in current prices, a reduction in the demand for money, and a fall in the exchange rate. (The point is clarified in the Appendix to this chapter.) This interpretation accords with the views expressed by Goodhart (1998) and Sack (1998) that a rise in rates is taken by the financial markets to signal that further rate rises can be expected in the future (see Chapter 10).

An illustration of a version of this approach is given in Figure 15.1. In this version, income is allowed to be flexible in the short run. The model, which is a diagrammatic version of McKinnon (1976), illustrates a world in which fiscal policy is impotent, and in which prices and the exchange rate are determined by the money supply, given supply conditions, and overseas prices; alternatively inverting the model, the money supply, and prices can be determined by the exchange rate, given supply conditions and overseas prices. The economy is taken to be a highly open one, producing and consuming a single composite tradable good which is available from world sources at a price in foreign currency, p^* (in logs). Transport costs are ignored and the Law of One Price applies, so that the pricing line (or aggregate demand curve) is given (in logs) $p = p^* + e$ where e is the exchange rate measured as the domestic currency price of foreign currency. Supply is determined, given fixed nominal wages in the short run, by profit-maximizing entrepreneurs to yield the upward-sloping schedule, *AS*. Then for a given rate of interest (r) and a stock of money, a monetary equilibrium schedule can be drawn as shown (*MM*), its slope dependent on the real income elasticity of money demand. As argued above, a rise in the interest rate, given the money stock, would shift the schedule to the right; we can think of the rate

Figure 15.1 The open economy under global monetarism

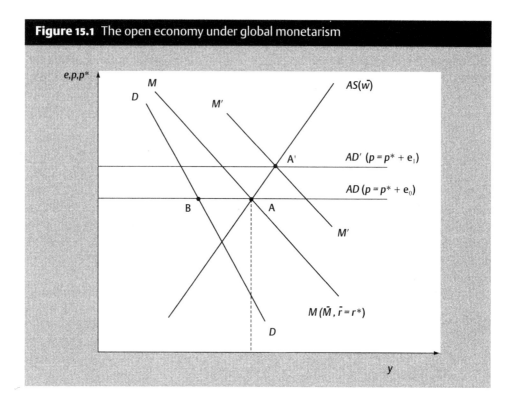

of interest as it would be in a financially open economy in a fully integrated international capital market. The downward-sloping *DD* schedule is a hypothetical *domestic* demand schedule.

Equilibrium, for *po* and *y*, is determined by the intersection of the *AS*, *AD*, and *MM* schedules at A. *DD* is irrelevant except for determining the trade balance (here a surplus) as the distance between domestic absorption B, where *DD* intersects *AD*, and the point A. Fiscal policy (changes in which would shift *DD*) is irrelevant to the determination of output, but obviously is not to the composition of the balance of payments. A monetary expansion will raise prices and output in the short run as the exchange rate falls (from e_0 to e_1, as shown) and real wages drop. In the longer-run (when *AS* is vertical) the monetary expansion can only raise prices and depreciate the exchange rate in proportion. This illustrates the simple, but powerful, model of global monetarism in which the exchange rate's position in the transmission mechanism of monetary policy is critical, unlike closed economy monetarism which treated the exchange rate almost as an addendum (see Chapter 13).

Exchange Rate Targets

Viewed as a part of a causal sequence

$$m \rightarrow e \rightarrow p, y, \tag{15.1}$$

a simple case for treating the exchange rate as an intermediate target variable emerges from two observations: first, that the object of ultimate interest is the variable p or perhaps y (or both); second, that the first link in the chain between m and e may be loose and unreliable. If so, then the desired effects on the ultimate goals of policy may be more reliably achieved by targeting e directly. Evidently, this is just another way of saying that if the demand for money function is unreliable, a policy of accommodating supply to unforeseen shifts while maintaining the exchange rate target is a guarantee of counter-inflationary success. Targeting the money supply itself in these circumstances will not do the trick.

In the framework of the monetary approach, the point can be simply made by reference to Figure 15.2. This uses the same assumptions as the earlier figure. Suppose that the desired price level is p and the overseas price level is p^*. Then the desired result can be achieved, indifferently, by targeting the money supply at M (which underlies the schedule MM) or targeting e at $\bar{e}$, passively supplying the resultant quantity of money demanded. Money and the exchange rate are duals. Suppose, however, that the demand for money is unstable so that the MM schedule corresponding

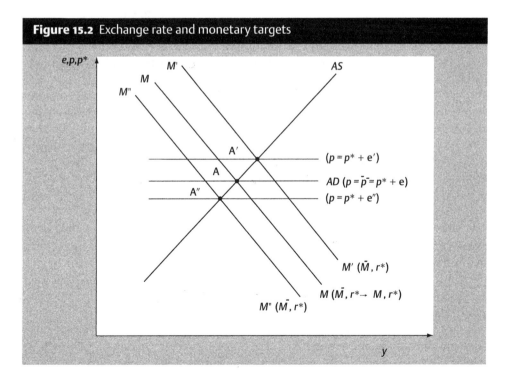

Figure 15.2 Exchange rate and monetary targets

to the supply of money M might shift, as illustrated, between MM' and MM": clearly this would result in corresponding fluctuations in the exchange rate, output, and domestic price level. By contrast, however, the price level may be stabilized by targeting the exchange rate $\bar{e}$: MM then becomes a monetary equilibrium schedule in which the money supply automatically accommodates the demand shocks. There is an exact analogy between the way in which stabilizing the exchange rate endogenizes the money supply to demand and the way in which, in Poole's celebrated closed economy model (Poole, 1970), targeting the interest rate accomplishes the same automatic accommodation (see Chapter 14).

This parallel is exploited in Artis and Currie (1981), Aizenman and Frenkel (1985), and other papers which approach policy choice as a matter of selecting the most robust intermediate variable targets. Specifically, money supply targets and exchange rate targets are compared for their stabilizing properties in the face of various random shocks emanating from domestic expenditures, money demand, foreign prices, and foreign interest rates. In two of the cases—domestic expenditure shocks and foreign interest rate shocks—the results are inconclusive. Instability in money demand functions undermines monetary targeting; as we have seen, maintenance of exchange rates in this case allows the supply of money to respond to demand. Exchange rate targeting is undermined by instability in the foreign price level. Since exchange rate targeting ties the domestic price level to foreign prices, instability in the latter is transferred to the former. Monetary targeting and exchange rate flexibility allow domestic prices to be disconnected from this link.

Thus one important ground for treating the exchange rate as an intermediate target is that the resultant endogenization of, or loss of independent control over, the money supply is actually desirable when there is instability in the demand for money. There are other reasons, too. An important one is the fact that the exchange rate can be observed day-by-day, whereas observations of the money supply only become available with a lag. Thus, even if the demand for money function were reliably stable, greater precision of control on a day-to-day basis could be had from targeting the exchange rate. A further, partly related, point stems from the greater visibility and speed of observation of the exchange rate which makes an exchange rate policy easier for the private sector to monitor than a money supply policy. A monetary authority might therefore gain credibility by committing itself to an exchange rate target (against a low-inflation country), especially if it has followed lax monetary policies in the past (e.g. Hong Kong, Italy, and Britain went down this path in the 1980s).

While these are all arguments for targeting the exchange rate in the context of an overall policy priority on lowering inflation, there is also a set of arguments related to international trade and competitiveness. A trading nation is dependent on buying from abroad goods which have to be paid for in foreign currency, and on selling overseas local production for which payment must often be accepted in foreign currency. Stability of these exchanges of domestic for foreign currency is thus a special convenience. Large changes in real exchange rates appear to produce substantial economic (and social) costs: as the profitability of the trading sector fluctuates, firms will be forced to make costly exit and entry decisions.[7] Perhaps the critical point is that inertia in consumers' purchasing habits implies that a firm which leaves a market faces substantial reinvestment costs if and when it decides to re-enter that market. Price-setting behaviour reflects this. The obvious reason is that exchange rate changes which can produce sharp variations in relative normalized unit labour costs are partly absorbed in variations in suppliers' profit margins.[8]

As we noted earlier, concern of this type about the *real* exchange rate may very well *conflict* with the counter-inflationary purpose of monetary policy and result in an attenuation or attempted limitation of it. Thus Vaubel (1980) has in a graphic phrase noted what he calls the 'implicit emergency clause' of German (and Swiss) monetary policy, in which the ambitions of strict monetary policy have been set aside when the real rate of exchange appreciates too much.[9]

The form that an exchange rate target takes can be varied, depending upon the primary purpose of the policy. A tight counter-inflation policy involving a firm commitment against a low-inflation partner is one possible form for the policy (e.g. Austria). The tighter the commitment, the easier it is to compute the implied inflation rate targets and to monitor the policy. In this instance bands around the central or target rate of exchange should be rather narrow. On the other hand, if the exchange rate target is an acknowledgement of potential possible problems with the demand for money function, a suitable form in which to enter the exchange rate as a target would be as a conditioning variable on the monetary target; that is, the authorities could make the effective width of the band around the monetary target dependent on the level of the exchange rate. If the problem is an apprehension about the extent to which real exchange rates should be allowed to vary, a natural form for the target to take would be that of adjustable limits with a wide band. If other means to manage speculation are not sufficient, such bands should be soft-edged, i.e. should not involve a provocative commitment by the authorities that promotes the damaging 'one-way bet'. All these alternatives have been mirrored in actual or proposed arrangements.

A final comment, but in reality an overriding consideration, concerns the ability of the authorities actually to achieve exchange rate goals. Mrs Thatcher's famous statement 'you can't buck the markets' puts the point clearly enough, and experience offers many illustrations.

15.3 Exchange Rate Arrangements in the 1990s

THE transition from the Bretton Woods era of fixed but adjustable exchange rates to the present international regime of managed floating has involved some sharp changes in perception of the scope and effectiveness of exchange rate policy, none more so than over the last decade.

Table 15.1 shows the position since 1986 for IMF member countries. Altogether

Table 15.1 Exchange rate arrangements of national currencies, 1986–1999

	1986	1989	1991	1993[a]	1995[a]	1997[b]	1999[b]
1. Fixed to							
US dollar	32	32	23	23	23	21	20
French franc	14	14	14	14	14	15	15
Other single currencies	5	5	4	13	8	9	12
SDR	10	7	6	4	3	2	4
Currency basket	30	35	33	27	20	20	13
2. Target zones							
European monetary system	8	9	10	9	10	12	13
Other currency links	5	4	4	4	4	4	4
3. Controlled flexibility	27	26	32	25	38	47	56
4. Independently floating	19	20	29	48	59	51	48
Total[c]	151	152	156	167	179	181	185

[a] 1st quarter.
[b] 2nd quarter.
[c] Classification not always available for some currencies. The method of classifying exchange rate arrangements changed in 1999. Information for 1999 inserted on old basis.

Source: International Monetary Fund Annual Report. Table 11.17 (various issues).

forty-eight countries in 1999 had independently floating currencies, including the USA, Japan, UK, Switzerland, Canada, and Australia (and joined by Indonesia and Korea since 1998 following the Asian currency crisis). If these countries are to achieve price stability, then they do so by means of *internal stabilization*; that is, using monetary policy to keep the purchasing power of a country's money reasonably stable in terms of goods and services on domestic markets.

Matters are different for sixty-four countries which have chosen to peg their currencies to one of the major industrial countries, mostly to the US dollar or French franc, or to a basket of the currencies of the leading countries, so choosing *external stabilization*. External stabilization involves fixing the value of money in terms of foreign moneys (or some other external object); a direct link is thereby created between the macroeconomic behaviour of the domestic economy and that of the country to which it is pegged which precludes the taking of independent, national policies for internal stabilization of prices. By opting for external stabilization, a country forgoes its monetary autonomy and effectively delegates to the major country the responsibility for its inflation performance.

A middle way between these two extremes had been sought by member countries of the European Monetary System (EMS) by adherence to the Exchange Rate Mechanism (ERM), although in practice the system tended to gravitate towards one or other of the two alternatives. The old narrow band ERM sought to combine fixity with flexibility by periodic parity realignments, something like Bretton Woods. Under the wider bands which operated from August 1993 to December 1998, countries had considerable ability—if they wished to do so—to pursue internal stabilization of incomes and prices differently from other members of the system. But, in practice, the countries used internal stabilization to engineer a convergence of policies and macroeconomic outcomes (inflation, interest rates, budgetary policies) in preparation for monetary union—considered in the next section.

The alternative regimes we have discussed are not the only choices on offer. Economic theory offers a continuum of exchange rate systems, ranging from monetary union at one limit through currency boards, multilateral pegs, unilateral pegs, basket pegs, adjustable pegs, crawling pegs, target zones, managed floating to freely floating exchange rates at the other limit. But, now that capital controls and many supports have been lifted, the viability of many of these middle paths between the two limits has been sharply reduced, and this is reflected in actual practice. Table 15.1 shows there has been a marked shift in exchange rate arrangements over the years. In 1999, 25 per cent of countries had independently floating exchange rates (compared with only 8 per cent in 1982). Also, a further 30 per cent of countries had a managed float (although this classification embraces a wide degree of different practices e.g. Singapore's and Thailand's managed floating regimes differ from that of China). Reasons for the declining use of the fixed exchange rate option are not difficult to find.

Fixed parities—how much of a nominal anchor?

The fixing of exchange rates under external stabilization is not in itself sufficient for price stability. It merely fixes relative price relations between the countries which are pegged and allows for only one monetary policy across the linked systems. Obviously that policy could be inflationary, and this would be imported through the fixed peg. However, large inflation rate differentials can arise even when a country anchors itself to a low inflation country, because of significant differences in productivity growth rates. The tendency to absolute (or relative) price equality applies only to tradable goods and services; competition will ensure that there cannot be large and persistent price discrepancies, at least in the longer run, for goods and services of the same quality which are readily transportable. Obvious examples are raw commodities, readily transportable manufacturing goods, and those services carried 'on the wire'. When scaled in terms of a common currency, prices for such internationally traded goods tend to be much the same in all competitive markets. It is this mechanism which produces long-run inflation convergence for countries adhering to a fixed exchange rate peg.

But suppose that one country has a high rate of productivity in its internationally traded goods sector. The country concerned will be able to pay its workers larger wage increases than elsewhere while remaining competitive on world markets. Most likely, wages growth will not be confined to the trade sector and will flow on to wages in the non-traded industries (predominantly services). If productivity in the non-traded services sector is growing more slowly than in other parts of the economy, prices will increase more rapidly for non-traded than for traded goods and services. This is because the wage increases are similar, but productivity growth is different.

In each country the inflation rate is a mixture of inflation in the traded and non-traded sectors. Inflation in traded goods will tend to equality, but the high-productivity country will have more rapid inflation in the non-traded goods sectors and a higher inflation rate overall. The greater is the gap in productivity the greater will be the inflation gap between the countries. Japan had a higher inflation rate than the USA under Bretton Woods. For much the same reasons, inflation in Hong Kong typically has been much higher than in the USA, despite Hong Kong having tied its currency to the US dollar since 1983 using a currency board scheme. While there are special reasons why Hong Kong chose to peg its currency in this manner, the experience is nevertheless instructive for other small countries in showing that a fixed exchange rate can conflict with price stability.

Target zones

Target zones sometimes are advocated as a tool of exchange rate management rather than as a way of providing a nominal anchor for the economy (John Williamson, 1985, 1993). Under such a system, countries—either unilaterally or as part of a regional or multilateral accord—would declare central exchange rate values for their currency, and maintain the actual rate within a specified margin around the central value. At any time, the exchange rate would be allowed to fluctuate only within the band, limiting volatility. The difference from the nominal anchor approach is that the bands themselves would be adjusted from time to time in order to offset changes in inflation rate differentials, preventing misalignments of the real exchange rate like those which opened up the European exchange rate system and the Asian currencies to speculation.

The attraction of target zones comes from the possibility of getting some of the benefits of fixed exchange rates, in terms of reduced volatility, while retaining the advantages of flexibility, in terms of autonomy over domestic monetary outcomes. If a country is to establish a target zone, it must define a central exchange rate in terms of purchasing power parity or equilibrium (sustainable) capital flows, determine the width of the bands, agree upon a mechanism for defending rates, and establish a formula for adjusting the central rate over time. Each of these matters presents considerable conceptual difficulties.

Then there is the problem of maintaining the zones. If the bands are perceived as highly credible in the sense that traders anticipate that the authorities will successfully intervene at the edge of the zone, exchange rates will be nearly fixed. When the exchange rate is near the bottom of its band, the market will expect the rate to revert to central parity; and vice versa, when the rate is near its ceiling. In these ways speculation will be 'helpful' and stabilize the rate within the bands if the band edges are in fact credible and the authorities have the reserves with which to conduct marginal intervention. Krugman (1992) labelled this the 'honeymoon' effect since it gives a stabilizing influence to the exchange rate–fundamental relationship purely from the commitment to intervene at the band edges, resulting in the familiar description of their interaction by an S-shaped curve. This was in fact the experience of some of the European countries, but for many the band edges were not credible and the common pool of foreign exchange reserves held by the central banks with stronger currencies were not forthcoming, leading inevitably to the crises of 1992 and 1993. The lesson, of course, is that once there are doubts as to the viability of the zone, speculation can quickly push the exchange rate over the edge of the band. Very broad bands reduce that possibility, but they may do little to stabilize the exchange rate.

In these circumstances, the objectives must be questioned. A reduction in exchange rate volatility is sought to offer international traders a stable fulcrum against which to set prices, to compare profits, and to plan production and investment decisions across countries. But the merit of target zones in reducing exchange rate uncertainty turns on there being a credible way of keeping exchange rates within the bands. Otherwise, the relevant comparison is not floating versus a fixed (or crawling) peg, but between exchange rates that fluctuate daily and those which, while ostensibly fixed, are adjusted by substantial amounts at longer intervals, often after sustained speculative pressures.

Nevertheless, daily fluctuations of exchange rates under floating are considerable. Whether central banks should or can reduce this volatility remains an open question. As argued in Chapter 8, the central insight of the post-1973 literature on exchange rates is that the exchange rate should be seen as an asset price, responding much like stock prices to investors' asset-holding preferences and a variety of new information. This analogy between the exchange rate and share prices is instructive, as Eichengreen (1993) has noted. The exchange rate reflects the present discounted value of future expected monetary policy outcomes (i.e. fundamentals) in just the same way as the share price indicates the present discounted value of future profits. No one (at least outside of Japan or Hong Kong) argues for stabilizing the price of individual shares or stabilizing the share price index as part of economic policy formulation; however, there is no shortage of those insisting on the desirability of stabilizing the movement of the exchange rate. Granted, the exchange rate can be seen as a rather more important asset price—indeed, the single most important price in the economy (Kenen, 1992). Yet the point remains, and to the extent that exchange rates follow a random walk, many of the factors driving the exchange rate might be seen to be permanent shocks and not temporary fluctuations.

Intervention

Since the volume of net foreign exchange transactions *each day* exceeds the total official reserves of all IMF countries combined, the effect of any central bank's currency transactions upon the overall demand and supply of the national currency must be minimal, although in theory, sterilized intervention can directly alter the exchange rate by changing the relative supplies of domestic and foreign securities. In sterilized intervention policies, foreign exchange transactions are offset in their effects on the domestic monetary base, leaving the quantity of domestic money unchanged. Purchases (sales) of foreign currency securities are matched by sales (purchases) of domestic currency securities, leaving simply a change in the composition of portfolios between domestic and foreign securities. If domestic and foreign securities are relatively close substitutes, so that open market operations in the foreign exchange market differ little in substance from domestic open market operations, the effects on interest or exchange rates may be slight, unless flanked by exchange controls which bring about the needed preconditions.

Even in the absence of a significant portfolio balance effect, sterilized intervention could affect the exchange rate if, by signalling future policy directions, it altered market estimates of the future expected exchange rate. Operators in the foreign exchange market absorb market data on a continuous basis and are highly responsive to information about future events and policy decisions. They may be induced to change their views about the likely future actions of the monetary or fiscal authorities and the impact that these policy actions will have upon the exchange rate.

Sterilized intervention becomes a way to convey this new information to the market. But is intervention the best way of doing so? If the objective is to transmit information for the operators to process, it follows that traders need to know about the action. Why would the authorities convey the information by intervening *unannounced* in the foreign exchange market? And if the authorities by various means make their presence known in the market, why is intervention preferred to simple announcements of the authorities' monetary policy intentions and exchange rate goals? Finally, if actions speak louder than words, why is this particular instrument of policy used?

One answer from Mussa (1981) is that the information is more believable when it is conveyed by means of intervention because the action takes the form of a wager by the central bank on its own information. If the central bank's reputation would be damaged by losses on its intervention account, it has an incentive to follow through with subsequent monetary policy which is consistent with its position-taking in the market. Further, if the market knows this, then it has greater reason to trust the central bank's intervention and view it as a harbinger of later policy actions.

Nevertheless, the capacity to play upon the market's expectations obviously rests on the fulfilment of those expectations; thus for signalling to matter, it must be backed up in the end by the anticipated changes in monetary policy. This requires that policy changes be predictable and consistent, otherwise monetary policy might be seen as trying to serve two masters.

Currency boards

These issues of credibility and consistency are relevant for all countries, but those countries which are in danger of slipping into hyperinflation are, of course, in an altogether different position, and a method of achieving external price stability with credibility is a currency board system. Advocated for Russia by Hanke, Jonung, and Schuler (1993), such a system worked successfully for Yugoslavia (which tied the dinar to the DM) prior to that country's disintegration and currency boards were widely used in the British colonial regimes of Africa, Asia, the Caribbean, and the Middle East, where over seventy once operated. Other than Hong Kong, the most notable current example is that of Argentina, while currency boards operate also in Brunei, Bosnia, Bulgaria, Djibouti, Estonia, and Lithuania. The currency board system gained much publicity in 1998 because of Indonesia's flirtation with a currency board.[10]

Table 15.2 summarizes the features of a typical currency board vis-à-vis a central bank. The principal characteristic is that the board stands ready to exchange domestic *currency* for the foreign reserve currency at a specified and fixed rate. To make this commitment credible, domestic money can be issued only if it is fully backed by foreign reserves. In a classic currency board system there is no central bank, only a monetary authority that issues domestic currency at the fixed rate of exchange for foreign reserve and is required to hold realizable financial assets in the reserve currency. Hence in a currency board system there can be no fiduciary issue. The backing to the currency must be at least 100 per cent. In effect, a currency board is the modern day equivalent of a fully backed gold standard link but with foreign currency assets taking the place of gold reserves.[11]

In principle then, the system is rule-based and transparent; reserve coverage is

---

Table 15.2 A typical currency board versus a typical central bank

Typical currency board	Typical central bank
Usually supplies notes and coins only	Supplies notes, coins, and deposits
Fixed exchange rate with reserve currency	Pegged or floating exchange rate
Foreign reserves of 100%	Variable foreign reserves
Full convertibility	Limited convertibility
Rule-bound monetary policy	Discretionary monetary policy
Not a lender of last resort	Lender of last resort
Does not regulate commercial banks	Often regulates commercial banks
Transparent	Opaque
Protected from political pressure	Politicized
High credibility	Low credibility
Earns seigniorage only from interest	Earns seigniorage from interest and inflation
Cannot create inflation	Can create inflation
Cannot finance spending by domestic government	Can finance spending by domestic government
Requires no 'preconditions' for monetary reform	Requires 'preconditions' for monetary reform
Rapid monetary reform	Slow monetary reform
Small staff	Large staff

Note: The characteristics listed are those of a typical actual currency board or central bank, especially one in a developing country, not those of a theoretically ideal or exceptionally good currency board or central bank.

Source: Hanke, Jonung, and Schuler (1993).

high and clearly defined. The biggest advantage of such a rule-based system is the confidence it creates. It is generally a strong control against inflation since it prevents the monetary authority or central bank from printing money to finance a budget deficit. Similarly, it should protect the currency against speculative attacks since, by law, reserves must at least cover the monetary base. Moreover, the board can earn interest on its foreign assets, thereby pre-empting the seigniorage that foreigners would otherwise reap if foreign currency rather than domestic currency circulated locally (which is the case with 'dollarization').[12]

In practice things are a little more complicated. Like any country on gold, any conversions of domestic currency result in contraction of liquidity and upward pressures on interest rates. Any loss of competitiveness, due for example to the reserve currency appreciating on world markets, can produce a severe deflation of local prices. Hong Kong experienced both of these effects in the late 1990s.

In addition, the total money supply is much bigger than base money, because banks lend a multiple of the reserves they hold. The convertibility and the percentage reserve-currency backing requirements in the currency board system do not extend to bank deposits or any other financial assets. If a person has a bank deposit and wishes to use the currency board to convert it to foreign currency, then the deposit must be first converted into domestic currency and then presented to the currency board. So, if a large number of people want to convert their deposits into foreign currency, the banks would be forced to call in loans, as in a classic banking crisis, unless they are able to borrow reserves from international banks to tide them over. Since an orthodox currency board does not hold reserves against commercial bank deposits and does not engage in open market operations, or provide discount window lending, it is unable to perform a lender of last resort function to help out the banks. Problems with bank liquidity in Argentina in 1995, under a currency board tied to the US dollar, illustrate the vulnerability of this type of system to financial crises (Humpage and McIntire, 1995). Any commodity or 'hard money' standard with a fiduciary component faces the same essential problem.

Speculation and the 'inconsistent quartet'

These problems—competitiveness, interest rates and liquidity and financial crises—have been even more in evidence for other fixed rates systems in the 1990s: the European Monetary System crisis of 1992–3, the Mexican crisis of 1994, and the Asian currency crisis of 1997–8. The European crisis is examined in Artis and Lewis (1993, 1995), the Mexican case in Naím (1995) and Summers (1995), and the Asian crisis in Roubini (1998) and Krugman (1998a).

The trade-off which we noted earlier between inflation control and competitiveness was apparent in all three, although the origins were quite different in Asia as compared with Europe. Reduced competitiveness amongst the Asian economies began with the official devaluation of the Chinese renminbi by 50 per cent in 1994 and was exacerbated after April 1995 when the US dollar (to which their exchange rates were closely tied) began to appreciate. The export slowdown which resulted proved to be a catalyst for the subsequent disaster, for strong growth in the region became increasingly dependent on domestic demand rather than net exports. Countries became focused on rapid development of the infrastructure in terms of public sector projects, real estate developments, and expanding capacity in the industrial sector, fuelled by short-term inflows of foreign capital attracted by the stable exchange rates vis-à-vis the US dollar.

In the European case, the currencies were tied to an appreciating Deutschmark, but otherwise a decline in competitiveness was not accidental but deliberately engineered. This was one of the contradictions of the system. Countries used fixed parities as a means of enforcing convergence of inflation rates and economic performance via declining competitiveness and 'imported credibility'. The system was also used as a vehicle for achieving monetary and political union—under the usual interpretation, the Maastricht Treaty had been seen as requiring a period of 'narrow bands' exchange rate stability as a precondition for entry to EMU. These conditions opened up the ERM to speculation, for even though inflation differentials against Germany were declining for the high-inflation countries, they remained positive and resulted in a cumulative rise in relative national price levels. With fixed nominal exchange rates, this misalignment implied declining competitiveness and a drift in the real exchange rate which the market corrected—in a brutal way.

Both the European and Asian crises illustrate the cumulative nature of currency instability. Once credibility was eroded and traders were presented with the prospect of a one-way bet, speculative crises reminiscent of the final years of Bretton Woods unfolded. Indeed, speculative pressures took on a momentum of their own. As one currency after another fell, the competitiveness of those remaining on the old parities worsened. This raised doubts about the sustainability of interest rate policies and other monetary policy measures used to defend the exchange rate parity.

These monetary policy measures were needed once the abolition of exchange controls effectively removed the possibility that the exchange rate could any longer be treated even as a first approximation as a policy instrument in itself—that is, as being capable of being adjusted without reference to other policy instruments, as with sterilized interventions. Increasingly, exchange rate management and exchange rate policies have come to be seen straightforwardly as the use of monetary policy—unsterilized intervention and interest rate policy—in defence of the exchange rate.

Countries that have committed themselves to an exchange rate peg always run the risk that the interest rates sought on domestic grounds may differ from those required by the maintenance of the peg. In order to preserve an exchange rate parity, it might seem that a country has only to consider whether it will put up with somewhat-higher-than-desired interest rates for a time. But speculation dramatically alters the costs. Since there is a doubt about the exchange rate, interest rates now have to cover the expected rate of realignment, which depends on the probability of a realignment per unit of time and the expected size of a realignment if it occurs—matters about which there may be diverse views. Buying off speculation means interest rates that are a multiple of their previous level.[13] While countries declared in effect that they were prepared to forgo monetary independence, speculators could bet that when it came to the crunch matters might be different and, in so doing, turn an unpleasant, but acceptable, trade-off into an undesirable and possibly politically unacceptable one. So it proved to be the case in all of the crises.

It would seem that a commitment to adhere to a fixed exchange rate and forgo monetary sovereignty is more believable when made by a small country adjoining a large neighbour, such as Holland or Austria, than by nations such as France or the UK. The sustainability of an exchange rate peg is conditioned by the similarity of the productive and financial structures in the economies. If Britain had special problems in these matters in the context of Europe, imagine the difficulties which might emerge if Australia or New Zealand tried to peg their currencies to the yen—or if Indonesia and Thailand tried to peg theirs to the US dollar!

Thus the market made clear to policy-makers seeking to adhere to fixed parities that they would need to find a new solution to the problem of the 'inconsistent quartet': free trade, free capital movements, national policy autonomy, and fixed exchange rates. This policy dilemma, first clearly stated by Henry Wallich (1972), has been restated by Padoa-Schioppa (1998) in the context of European monetary arrangements. The point is well taken: it is not possible to combine all of these four 'desirables' in one system, and successful systems involve some trade-offs. Crisis-affected countries have responded in different ways to this challenge. Mexico, Indonesia, Korea, and Thailand have moved to greater flexibility of rates. Malaysia reimposed exchange controls. The European countries moved to greater fixity, in fact to *irrevocably* fixed exchange rates.

15.4 Monetary Union

ALL of these problems of fixed exchange rates can be removed at a stroke by a move to a monetary union—the ultimate radical solution to the 'inconsistent quartet' problem, in which national policy autonomy is replaced by a sharing of collective monetary sovereignty. Monetary union can be seen as the terminal case of an attempt to coordinate policy between countries. The difference is that in a monetary union there is a firm (indeed irrevocable) commitment from all the countries concerned to adopt a common monetary unit as a unit of account, medium of exchange, and store of value. Policy coordination requires less commitment because the participants retain their currencies and attempt to follow a monetary policy strategy that is jointly beneficial. The justification for coordination is to be found in the spillovers that exist between the participants. On the grounds of the 'prisoner's dilemma' from basic game theory it can be shown that benefits from coordination exist provided all the countries can agree on a common policy and can credibly commit to maintain it. If a country were to renege, the result would be detrimental for all participants as retaliatory policies impinged on each country. The free movement of capital can bring unbearable pressure on monetary authorities until the benefits of opting out outweigh the benefits of maintaining the common policy (Jeanne, 1999). The difficulty of maintaining credibility and avoiding the temptation to bail out has led many to the conclusion that a monetary union is more stable than an attempt to coordinate policy in that currencies which are permanently locked and which ultimately cease to exist cannot fluctuate or be realigned. Sometimes discussed in the context of the ASEAN and the Americas (Mercosur), it has become a reality in Europe—European Monetary Union (EMU).

The EMU process was formulated in the Maastricht Treaty as a series of stages. Stage one began in 1990 when the member states removed any remaining obstacles to the free movement of capital. The second stage began on 1 January 1994, when the European Monetary Institute (EMI) was established with the task of preparing the operations of the future European Central Bank (ECB). The third and final stage involved locking the exchange rates of the member states that fulfilled the conditions for the adoption of a single currency, the euro, whereupon the ECB assumed full responsibility for monetary policy in those countries. That stage began on 1 January 1999 and incorporated eleven countries: Austria, Belgium, Finland, France, Germany, Ireland, Italy, Luxembourg, the Netherlands, Portugal, and Spain (the Euro-11).[14]

How desirable are stable rates?

The old ERM sought to combine fixity of exchange rates (in terms of bands of 2.25 per cent around a central parity rate of exchange) with flexibility (since the central parities could be realigned). When the system broke down under the weight of speculative attacks, with the bands widened to ± 15 per cent and Italy and Britain left floating, there was the question of whether to seek, again, some middle path, to strike out for EMU and complete fixity of rates, or to stay with something like the existing system. At the time, many commentators questioned whether EMU, like the Australian bird of the same name that cannot fly, would ever get off the ground.

To stay with more flexible rates begged the question of why the European Monetary System was established in the first place. Foremost among the reasons was to prevent currency instability. Allowing currencies to fluctuate 15 per cent either side of their central rates might be seen as indistinguishable from a float, although much larger swings than that have occurred outside of Europe. In terms of nominal rates, from February 1985 to January 1988 the dollar prices of the yen and mark both rose by 110 per cent. In the year to August 1993, the yen appreciated 24 per cent against the dollar and 43 per cent against the mark. On seven separate occasions during 1992 the *daily* increase in the US dollar relative to the German mark exceeded 2 per cent. In terms of real rates, Mussa (1986) found that the variance of bilateral real exchange rates (versus the US dollar) for fifteen industrialized countries was on average almost fourteen times higher under floating rates than under the fixed exchange rate regimes. Krugman (1989) argues that such volatility is the result of an interactive process which has taken place over time whereby trade flows and production decisions become desensitized to exchange rate movements, which then permits those rates to become still more volatile because they have so little effect on the real sector.

If such variations in nominal and real exchange rates were to take place within the very different environment in Europe, trading patterns would have to change. Exchange rate stability has been one of the pillars of the unification process, paralleling the increase in trade integration and the single-market programme. Surprisingly, no explicit desired exchange rate regime featured in the Treaty of Rome of 1957 which began the process. It must be recalled that the Treaty was drafted when Bretton Woods operated and fixed exchange rates were the norm. Both the SNAKE and the EMS sought to *restore* some roughly equivalent stability of exchange rates amongst European currencies but failed to do so.

Are floating exchange rates incompatible with the single market? Trade, financial, and monetary integration are discussed in the one breath in the European context, but in principle are separable. Substantial trade can take place under freely floating rates, as now occurs between Canada and the USA, while virtually complete financial integration can exist alongside flexible rates, as shown by the Eurocurrency markets. Yet many would question whether a truly integrated economic market can exist between countries without a common currency, or fixed exchange rates, to facilitate cross-border trade and investment by non-financial enterprises and intensify financial links. It is instructive to note that, on average, trade between a Canadian province and an American state is twenty times smaller than domestic trade between two Canadian provinces, after adjusting for distance and income levels.[15] The Canadian and US markets remain substantially segmented from one another. For other countries this is truer still. As Alan Greenspan (1991) notes: 'since the United States is both a free trade zone and a single currency zone, I cannot dismiss the proposition that a single currency is an important ingredient in a successful free trade zone.'

Fixed parities are regarded as desirable because it is believed that they expand international trade and capital movements and so offer internationally much the same benefits which come in domestic markets from having a uniform national currency. In a national economy, the advantages of having a single currency are obvious—in fact so obvious that they do not receive the attention they deserve—and there seems no reason why they should not apply at a wider level. There are economies of information in having a common medium of quotation. As a unit of account, money is needed for pricing commodities and services, for valuing aggregates, and for making price comparisons. Transactions as well as calculation costs are reduced by having a single medium of exchange. Finally, having a common standard of deferred payments and reducing exchange rate risk facilitates long-term planning and the entering into of long-term contracts.

Consequently, as we move from floating exchange rates to rigidly fixed exchange rates, information costs, transactions costs, and exchange rate uncertainty can be expected to fall but will not be zero if there is a possibility, however remote, of a change in regime in the future. Thus the benefits of fixed exchange rates rest on currencies being *credibly fixed*. In a system in which exchange rates fluctuate in bands around a central parity rate, which itself can be adjusted by discrete realignments, expectations of exchange rate changes consist of two elements: the expected change relative to central parity and the expected realignment. If the bands are perceived as highly credible, exchange rates will be nearly fixed: when the exchange rate is near the bottom of its band, the market will expect the rate to drift back towards central parity; and vice versa, when the rate is near its ceiling. Speculation will be 'helpful' and stabilize the rate. But it is a different story when an expectation of realignment comes into play. So long as there are separate exchange rates they can be realigned, and volatility takes on a different form.

It is a measure of the success of the old ERM that exchange rate volatility in all dimensions was considerably less for ERM currencies than for non-ERM currencies; daily swings in exchange rates were very much smaller, while the occasional large changes in rates—including realignments—were also less (Engel and Hakkio, 1993). This was the experience from 1979 to 1993. Once the system was shown to be vulnerable, the incentives to future speculation were raised. For this reason, stage three of EMU was approached without going through a narrow bands phase,[16] offering no hostages to fortune and presenting no targets to foreign exchange market speculation. In effect, there was the recognition that the basic criterion of convergence was 'sustainable low inflation' and that this should not be threatened by the presence of fiscal overburden. There was no obvious need for an additional qualification of exchange rate stability.

Avoiding the perils of an exchange rate apprenticeship for EMU removed one set of problems, but there was the danger of creating some new ones. The costs of the rapid push to EMU were tied up with whether or not Europe could be said to constitute in the terms of Mundell (1961) an 'optimal currency area'—a question which has been given a thorough airing (Eichengreen, 1992; Smaghi and Vori, 1993). Using the criteria of wage and price flexibility, labour mobility, or even cross-border investment there may be grounds for arguing that Europe is not an optimal currency area. Then again, perhaps the USA and Australia and some other federations are not optimal either, or at least *were* not until unification got under way. The consensus view when European union took place was that the optimal currency area criteria are as much outcomes as prerequisites and therefore the political will to unite was as important as the existence of converged or converging economies.

Monetary autonomy

This leads us to the question of monetary independence. By autonomy over monetary policy we mean that the choice of the money supply and short-term interest rates is left to the monetary authorities of the various nation states, enabling an individual country to influence its exchange rate and rate of inflation. Under a union, with a single currency (the euro) replacing national moneys in general circulation, an independent monetary policy ceases to exist, although each country or at least its central bank has some share in the determination of communal monetary policy.

A monetary union embraces the following conditions:

1. The removal of all capital controls.
2. Permanently fixed exchange rates leading to a single currency.
3. A uniform monetary policy conducted or coordinated centrally.
4. Creation of a new monetary institution, a central bank, to which national issuing banks transfer the task of issuing the standard currency and implementing monetary policy.
5. Enactment of a charter for the central bank which defines its goals, degree of independence, and accountability both to the constituent national central banks and to the respective governments.
6. A common payments and financial system operating under a uniform set of guidelines.
7. A set of parameters for the fiscal budget of the central administration or government.

The basic case against joining any sort of fixed exchange rate regime is that while a country retains all of its existing policy targets, it 'loses' the exchange rate as a shock absorber, through variations in which the objectives may be achieved.[17] Put another way, it would seem that adding the exchange rate to the list of policy objectives 'uses up' a policy instrument. Any such 'counting-rule' argument needs to be treated with care, since the transition from one regime to another seems likely to alter market mechanisms (the Lucas critique) and may enhance the working of other policy measures.

For example, variations in exchange rates can be seen as a means of effecting changes in competitiveness in the face of shifts in relative demand between countries in circumstances where factors of production are relatively immobile and the change in relative prices that would be required may not be easily brought about by market forces in the absence of exchange rate movements (Mundell, 1961). Exchange rate adjustment does not shelter those in declining regions or activities from reductions in real incomes and loss of spending power. Rather it is a device for achieving flexibility of real wages and debts more conveniently when prices and wages geared to the local currency are sticky. Exchange rate changes quickly lower the real wages and incomes of those entities with money illusion and with contracts in terms of the local currency. So runs the standard argument.

In the particular case of European integration, the EU is moving to increase labour and factor mobility, traditionally identified on this standard argument as a key prerequisite for monetary union,[18] since with a common currency and relatively uniform prices and wages ruling across markets, restoration of factor market equilibrium would rely increasingly upon the migration of labour from low to high employment areas. Regional assistance policies are also in place to aid regions.

If it may still be argued (as it clearly can be) that the scope of factor mobility and interregional adjustment assistance is less than that which prevails in the USA, it should be observed that experience with floating rates has weakened the force of the standard argument. And, with more closely integrated markets, 'currency illusion' can be expected to diminish further as transactors become attuned to assessing their position in terms of more than one currency. The result may be that a *nominal* exchange rate change will feed through even more rapidly than at present into home prices, leaving relative prices and the *real* exchange rate unchanged.

Loss of the exchange rate as a shock absorber may possibly matter more for overall macroeconomic policies. Standard neoclassical analysis, however, holds that the equilibrium real exchange rate, like the equilibrium rate of employment and the level of output, is invariant to monetary policy and the nominal exchange rate. Thus the floating rate option carries no consequences for real things, but simply allows a country to choose its own inflation rate. The fixed rate option determines inflation as a consequence of the joint monetary policies of all the countries participating in the exchange rate system or, where the system is operating in asymmetrical fashion, as it was in the EMS, upon the policies of the anchor country (Germany). It is true that later Keynesian analysis, particularly in the elaboration of the 'hysteresis effect' in labour markets, subverts the dichotomy between the real and monetary sides of the economy on which this argument relies, but in doing so it does not reinstate a traditional Phillips curve as a menu for policy choice; in any case, since exchange rate behaviour itself does not appear to preserve real exchange rate equilibrium when nominal rates are floating, it is far from clear that the presence of hysteresis effects in labour markets justifies any predilection for floating rate regimes.

The benefits of union

The gains from monetary union can be briefly summarized as arising from the following: (i) the elimination of exchange (transactions) costs, and (ii) the elimination of exchange rate uncertainty. Gains arising under (i) are formally similar to the gains arising from tariff reduction or removal, but because there are economies of scale in foreign exchange transactions they are difficult to calculate.[19] The larger gains, it is usually assumed, would arise under (ii), i.e. in the eradication of the uncertainty that prevails when rates of exchange are flexible. Of course, only one kind of uncertainty is removed by forming an exchange rate union. The fact of monetary union does not eradicate any of the uncertainties that exist about the relative rates of return from investing in, say, Scotland as opposed to England, for example, though it does remove uncertainty about the exchange rate between the Scottish and English pounds. Because the facilities of the foreign exchange markets allow traders to insure themselves against the risk of exchange rate fluctuation over short horizons, it is the reduction of long-period uncertainty and the beneficial effects of this on production location and investment decisions which are usually most emphasized. That is, an improvement in the functioning of the European capital market is implied which would complement the improvements already set in train by the liberalization programmes begun in 1992 with the single financial market initiative.

However, using the facilities of the forward markets for short-term transactions is not costless. And the costs are not limited to pecuniary ones: time, trouble, and inconvenience are involved as well, so that advantages accruing to intra-union trade from greater stability in exchange rates should not be overlooked. The promotion of trade, in turn, leads to increased competition and greater specialization in areas of comparative advantage, assisting goods market integration. Those who advocated the formation of monetary union often suggested the USA as a model of the positive outcomes of monetary union they had in mind, an example which emphasizes that it is a combination of the large internal market and monetary union to which they were in effect looking. This example also brings out another point which is often overlooked: monetary union is also a political statement designed to promote the feeling of unity and lead on eventually to full political union.

But in general, many of the economic benefits come under the heading of 'the balance of payments'. Loss of the exchange rate instrument makes it easier to finance regional payments imbalances by eliminating or reducing exchange rate risk in financing decisions, since debt in one currency is more nearly a perfect substitute for debt in another member country. In this respect there is a change in regime, as intra-European financing seems likely to prove more efficient than borrowing and lending outside the group. Regime changes may occur in other ways. With firms in uncompetitive regions no longer able to count on exchange rate changes to rescue them from adverse movements in relative prices, prices and wages may have to change directly to bring about the same result. Thus closer economic links within the Community may serve to narrow regional differences in wages and other costs—not least because they become more apparent when stated in one currency unit—so that the discrepancies in competitiveness which give rise to trade imbalances may be less likely to occur and more quickly eliminated if they do. It is to the question of the balance of payments that we now turn.

15.5 The Balance of Payments

IN a regional payments system, which the EU-11 has become, a member economy may indeed sustain current account deficits with other regions more or less indefinitely, since the deficits are always automatically financed by capital inflows from the other partners. It would be regarded as the height of absurdity, for example, for California to worry about its state of payments with the other US states. This is in part because the free movement of goods across state borders keeps regional prices in line with those of other states. Indirectly, this interstate trade in goods and services acts to narrow regional differences in wage and other costs. To some degree also, regional trade imbalances may be offset by government transfer payments if lower tax revenues and higher social security payments result in net transfers from surplus to deficit regions via the central government, although this mechanism operates less effectively in Europe than in the US union.

However, the main reason why regional payments imbalances are ignored—to the extent that we do not even attempt to keep statistics on them—comes from the high substitutability between financial claims issued in the different regions. In response to a payments deficit, members of a region within a country must borrow through the issue of liabilities, or draw down assets or do both, in order to finance the imbalance. If the assets sold, or liabilities issued, were exactly those which members of the surplus regions wanted to buy, prices of the financial claims would remain unchanged, and the current account disequilibrium would be exactly matched by offsetting transactions on the asset account which left the local economies unaffected. In practice, not all assets are readily transferable nationally (for example, many real assets). Nevertheless, relatively minor changes are likely to occur in the prices of those assets which are free to move between regions in order for the facilitating financing mechanism to operate effectively.

This process can continue until national banks and lenders in other regions are unwilling to lend further, or members of the region run out of assets which can be sold off or borrowed against. Most likely, well before these limits are reached, and in response to the growing repayment burden and decline in net assets and wealth, members of the region will revise their economic plans, cut costs and prices, so adjusting expenditures and correcting the imbalance of payments. Notably, this correction is brought about without government intervention. It is prompted by no more than the self-orientated behaviour of individuals and firms looking to their financial positions in response to changes in the physical quantities of the assets in their portfolios. And it may involve little in the way of changes in asset prices so long as members of the deficit regions and financial intermediaries hold large stocks of nationally transferable assets, and portfolio preferences are regionally unbiased.

Something akin to these results obtains for a currency union of sovereign states the currencies of which are pegged unalterably against each other. This is the form taken by EMU in the transition stage to the euro becoming the sole currency (July 2002). A historical analogue of such a system internationally is the gold standard. Then the fixity of exchange rates promoted a high degree of integration of goods markets so that prices for tradable goods moved broadly in step with purchasing power parity relationships. But otherwise the presence of exchange rate uncertainty which exists in other monetary systems introduces a new element into the debt-borrowing equation for it may give rise to costs and externalities that are not explicitly considered in the regional payments model. Or does it?

With the onset of floating exchange rates in 1973, the current account largely replaced the overall balance of payments as an indicator of the need for adjustment in a country's macroeconomic policies (Salop and Spitaller, 1980). For example, the current account is a leading variable among the list of indicators for disciplining international policy coordination (see e.g. Crockett and Goldstein, 1987), and current account developments, actual and prospective, are a prominent component in the IMF's conjectural review and medium-term projections in its *World Economic Outlook*.

However, in an environment of financially integrated markets the long-accepted dichotomy between internal balance and external balance as the appropriate policy framework may no longer be useful. A lack of utility in current account targeting is implicit in the modern intertemporal theory of the balance of payments, as expressed for example by Sachs (1981), Frenkel and Razin (1987) and Razin (1994). The process of global financial integration makes the essential assumptions of that theory more nearly realistic and the policy conclusion succinctly put by Cooper (1981: 269) more relevant: 'In the context of overall savings—investment analysis, countries should not take any particular view of their current account positions at all. Some will draw savings from the rest of the world, others will invest in the rest of the world. Nothing is wrong with this. It is as it should be'.

A convenient starting point is the simplified flow-of-funds account set out in Table 13.1 above. Three equivalent definitions can be provided for a current account deficit (CAD):

$$\text{CAD} = Z - X = K - \Delta R. \tag{15.2}$$

$$= (C + I + G) - Y. \tag{15.3}$$

$$= (I - S) + (G - T). \tag{15.4}$$

The first is obtained from the balance of payments identity and defines the current account deficit as the private capital inflow and borrowings from overseas (K) net of the authorities' addition to international reserves (ΔR). The second expression relates the deficit to the excess of absorption, $A=C+I+G$, over domestic income (Y). In the third equality, the current account deficit is presented as equal to the excess of private sector investment (I) over private sector savings (S) and the government budget deficit ($G-T$).

For any open economy operating in a milieu of floating exchange rates, financial deregulation and high capital mobility, the current account balance can be understood fully only within the framework of a general equilibrium involving the spending and saving decisions of nationals of many countries. The deficits which the USA incurs on the current account of the balance of payments must be matched by surpluses on the part of countries with which it has trading and financial relationships. In the new international financial laissez-faire environment these individual national relationships should be seen as part of an overall pattern of global saving and investment.

If we accept this as a reasonable approximation of reality and if, at the same time, there are national differences in intertemporal time preferences and the marginal efficiency of capital, those areas with low saving propensities and/or high investment propensities will export financial assets and attract an inflow of capital carried, in effect, by an inflow of goods. Interaction of investors in search of the highest rate of return with the behaviour of savers seeking to maximize intertemporal utility determines the efficient worldwide distribution of savings and investment with its counterpart national current account imbalances.

It then follows that if the comparative advantages in present and future goods differ widely across countries (as it has been suggested that they do between Japan and the EU-11 vis-à-vis the USA and the UK), then even large current payments imbalances among countries can persist, contrary to the conventional view that focuses only on the current transactions section of the balance of payments accounts. Viewed in this global setting, the use of macro- and micro-policies *purely* to reduce the size of the current account deficit to some tolerable level does not appear to be desirable. Indeed, it would be positively harmful if American pressure on Tokyo to spend more at home succeeds because the US deficit represents an inflow of foreign capital, financing employment-generating investment expenditure, that America would be denying itself (Higgins and Klitgaard, 1998). The Japanese surplus is the main source of capital for the world system and it ought to be allowed to be put to productive investment. Those who dislike persistent current account deficits are saying that there should never be any systematic trend in net international lending or investment.

From the viewpoint of macroeconomic policy, the implication is that the current account surplus or deficit simply reflect, in the aggregate, individual saving and investment decisions and thus individual lending and borrowing decisions. In the context of international financial laissez-faire, these decisions are made by 'consenting adults' who, we suppose, must know what they are doing. Consequently, if a case for assigning policy priority to the current account is to be made it must rest on identifying externalities in the borrowing process. When global capital markets are undeveloped and imperfect, liquidity constraints provide an example of such externalities and it may be desirable to limit national resort to borrowing from the rest of the world (i.e. to limit the current account deficit). With global capital market integration this becomes a less persuasive argument.[20]

It is in this strict policy sense that the current account 'does not matter', though of course it will matter in other important respects, such as those influencing the overall structure of the economy in the longer term. In the absence of a case for market failure in the savings and investment process, the conclusion is that the authorities should confine themselves to the task of monitoring the internal balance, leaving the current account imbalance and the level of private debt to adjust to their policy setting. But what constitutes internal balance? This is the topic of the next chapter.

Appendix

In the text, the PPP-quantity theory monetary approach to the exchange rate is outlined. With all variables (except for the interest rate and inflation) in logs, the model outlined there can be written as

$$m = p + ay + br \qquad a > 0; b < 0 \tag{A1}$$

and for the 'rest of the world'

$$m^* = P^* + a^* y + b^* r^* \qquad a^* > 0; b^* < 0, \tag{A2}$$

where (A1) and (A2) are demand for money equations in obvious notation.
Eq. (A3) is the PPP equation, with e measured as the exchange rate in units of domestic currency (so a rise is a depreciation)

$$p_T = p_T^* + e, \tag{A3}$$

where the subscript $_T$ refers to traded goods, and equations (A4) and (A5) express a relationship between overall and traded goods prices as

$$p = p_T + k \tag{A4}$$

$$p^* = p_T^* + k^*. \tag{A5}$$

Substitution then gives

$$e=(m-ay-br)-(m^*-a^*y^*-b^*r^*)+(k-k^*). \tag{A6}$$

In stationary equilibrium, with perfect capital mobility, $r=r^*$ and if (for simplicity) the coefficients are the same in both countries and $a=a^*=1$ (income elasticity or money demand is unity), then

$$e=(m-y)-(m^*-y^*)=(m-m^*)-(y-y^*). \tag{A7}$$

To study inflationary equilibrium, assume for additional simplicity that the two countries are of equal size (so the income terms drop out). However, in the domestic country there is inflation; the interest rate incorporates this inflation premium π so $r=r^*+\pi$. Perfect capital mobility requires in equilibrium

$$de=r-r^* \tag{A8}$$

Equation (A7) under these restrictions will read

$$e=(m-m^*)-(b\pi). \tag{A7'}$$

As b is negative, rising prices cause, *ceteris paribus*, a devaluation of the exchange rate.

Since the PPP equation (with $k=k^*=0$) can be inverted to yield the *price* equation

$$p=p^*+e, \tag{A9}$$

it is clear that the price level is higher in the inflationary equilibrium than it is in the stationary equilibrium.

To check this, note that (A1) may also be inverted to give

$$p=m-ay-br \tag{A10}$$

so that the fall in money demand associated with the higher nominal interest rate calls for a higher price level when the money stock and real income are given.

Notes

1 His argument was that returning the pound to its pre-war parity with the dollar— £1=$4.8666—overvalued sterling by 10%, requiring a 10% fall in the money costs of production if the existing volume of British exports was to be maintained. This would meet with intense worker resistance, which could only be overcome by 'intensifying unemployment' without limit.

2 In the *Tract* this was at least clear, whereas in the *General Theory* it was not obvious whether Keynes was directing his message to Britain specifically or worldwide. If the former, the absence of exchange rates from the story is surprising. If Keynes was addressing himself to an 'Atlantic community', then there is no obvious instrument of fiscal policy. Hicks (in private conversation) favoured the second interpretation (Lewis, 1994).

3 Under floating rates, the more the portfolios of transactors are diversified among highly substitute assets denominated in different currencies (i.e. the greater is currency substitution), the more the price level in any country becomes the result of

the joint outcome of the monetary policies of all countries, as under fixed rates (Miles, 1978).

4 Mundell (1969) argued that the 'true' instruments for the respective regimes are the *price* and the *quantity* of money. The exchange rate, according to Mundell, defines the price of one money in terms of others. Under flexible rates, this price adjusts to bring about equilibrium in the balance of payments, while the quantity of money is used as the instrument for achieving the desired rate of inflation. On the other hand, under a fixed rate regime the price of money is used to tie domestic prices to external prices, while the quantity of money must be varied to keep the balance of payments in equilibrium. There is no instrument 'loss' or 'gain' involved in the regime switch.

5 A large volume of empirical work on exchange rate determination is reviewed in MacDonald and Taylor (1989).

6 By contrast, in the standard short-run Keynesian model the interest rate is taken to be the monetary policy instrument and a flow model of international capital movements is added. Then, a rise in the domestic interest rate, relative to foreign rates, causes the exchange rate to appreciate. The increase in the domestic interest rate has deflationary impacts on domestic demand and, to the extent that this bears down on wage inflation and the ability of firms to mark up over costs, reduce prices. The appreciation of the exchange rate adds several further inflation-moderating influences. See Artis and Lewis (1991).

7 Williamson (1985) has been particularly eloquent in pressing these arguments.

8 Another way of putting this would be to say that firms use—as far as they can—a notion of the 'normal' or 'permanent' exchange rate in their pricing decisions. In the literature the extent of the transmission is referred to as the degree of exchange rate 'pass through'.

9 At the analytical level, analyses like those by Dornbusch (1976) and Buiter and Miller (1981) suggest that the real exchange rate will be an immediate casualty of programmes of monetary restraint.

10 Then-President Suharto was considering the system in the face of international and, seemingly, IMF disapproval. A currency board arrangement was also eschewed by the IMF when advising ex-Soviet republics, and Hanke, Jonung, and Schuler (1993) contend that the IMF failed to differentiate between a currency board and a fixed exchange rate operated by a central bank.

11 Once this parallel is drawn it is interesting to note that the equivalent of 'symmetallism' has not arisen in a currency board. This would involve using two (or more) currencies as backing in fixed proportions, and would reduce the tendency for large swings in competitiveness if one reserve currency was subject to wide swings in value relative to other currencies.

12 The term 'dollarization, is applied generically to the use of foreign currency assets and liabilities, although in some cases the dollar is not the main foreign currency of choice of domestic residents. The dollarization literature is quite extensive and has grown rapidly in recent years. Recent surveys can be found in Calvo and Vegh (1997), Giovannini and Turtleboom (1994), Savastano (1992, 1996), and Ize and Levy-Yeyati (1998).

13 Even, in the case of Sweden, money market rates of 500% per annum, and that failed to halt the speculation.

14 Four members of the Union (the EU-15) were excluded: Britain, Sweden, and Denmark (by choice) and Greece. In the case of the other eleven countries, the national currencies were locked in, irrevocably, at the following rates:

1 euro = 1.95583 German mark

= 6.55957 French franc

= 1936.27 Italian lira

= 2.20371 Dutch guilder

= 166.386 Spanish peseta

= 200.482 Portuguese escudo

= 5.94573 Finnish markka

= 0.787564 Irish punt

= 13.7603 Austrian schilling

= 40.399 Belgian franc

= 40.399 Luxembourg franc

Formally, however, from 1 January 1999, the individual national currencies of the EMU members disappeared as separate legal entities. While the national currencies were used in retail transactions in each country between 1999 and 2002, their designation in legal terms is as fixed subdenominations of the euro.

15 Engel and Rogers (1996) and *The Economist*, 18 October 1997, p 100. A recent study (Wall, 1999) confirmed this imbalance. Examining the volume of trade between British Columbia and six Canadian provinces and six comparable US states, he found that the relative volume of province-to-province trade is at least double, and in some cases over ten times higher, than province-to-state trade. This is the position despite the 'relative innocuous border' and the fact that nearly 90 per cent of the Canadian population lives within 100 miles of the US border.

16 The Treaty specified an ERM 'convergence criterion'. This required that the member counties should have participated in the 'normal' bands of the ERM without 'severe tension' and without provoking a devaluation for a period of two years. While the phrase 'normal' was intended to be read as '±2.25%', it was open to the participants simply to declare the ± 15% band to be the 'normal' band, thus satisfying the Maastricht Treaty, and to engage in stage three purely on the basis of convergence and an announcement, ahead of time, of a date and a conversion parity for the introduction of the new single currency for each of the eligible currencies. This is what happened. Interestingly, the term 'normal' was apparently inserted to describe the fluctuation band of ± 2.25% because of an apprehension that the term 'narrow' might be thought to describe only those countries, like Benelux, that might have decided to operate on a still tighter band. How ironical that it proved convenient to let it describe a fluctuation band of ± 15%.

17 Bird (1987) and Chatterji (1989).

18 Mundell (1961), McKinnon (1963), and Laffer (1973).

19 The NEDO has, however, suggested a figure of 1–1.5% of GDP as an upper estimate (Eltis, 1989)—though their calculation overlooks the fact that the overwhelming majority of transactions over the foreign exchanges occur on capital, not trade account, and their figure might for this reason more reasonably be read as a central estimate than as an upper estimate.

20 One of us has argued why, in a small country like Australia, policy-makers might indeed be concerned with such externalities; but the arguments carry less force in the case of the larger economies. See Lewis and Polasek (1990).

Chapter 16
Inflation Control

16.1 The Future of Money

IN the previous chapter and elsewhere in this book, we have highlighted the uniqueness of current monetary arrangements. A system in which essentially every currency in the world is, directly or indirectly, on an irredeemable paper money standard—directly, if the exchange rate of the currency is floating though possibly manipulated, or indirectly, if the exchange rate is effectively fixed in terms of another fiat-based currency—is unparalleled. In Milton Friedman's words, the world has ventured into 'unexplored terrain' (1985: 18).

Fiat money has long existed at an abstract level, in major treatises on money, where what we have called the 'insular economy' model has dominated. Fiat money also corresponds to the 'ideal standard of value' recommended by Wicksell and Keynes (in the *Tract*). Both of these authors favoured a system of managed money, based around irredeemable paper money. Wicksell (1915: 224), in particular, called it 'undoubtedly the ideal which currency systems should endeavour to approach'.

Can this 'ideal' be made to work? Alfred Marshall in 1887 recognized the possibility of using an interest rate policy to stabilize prices—the essence of present-day practice—but held back from actually recommending this policy because he considered it to be practical to implement only on a national basis. Hawtrey (1913) came to much the same conclusion, and we noted earlier the views of Karaken and Wallace as to the unworkability of an international system of paper moneys (Chapter 15). Wicksell, however, had no such qualms in advocating 'an international paper standard'. Keynes's doubts related only to the number of countries participating. For him, the system was fine for the dollar and sterling; other countries would be better off opting for what we have called external stabilization.

The choice between internal and external stabilization as a route to inflation control is another theme which has run through this book. Both Britain and the USA are following through Keynes's suggested approach of 'managed currency', i.e. a commitment to the price level itself enforced by eclectic use of monetary policy to bring about internal stabilization. Britain's inflation target differs little from that which the European Central Bank (ECB) is following for the EU-11. Nevertheless, Britain *still* has the additional option of pursuing external stabilization by entering into EMU, and irrevocably tying its exchange rate to the Union. Inside a fully developed EMU, the problem is simply transferred to the ECB. At this level the external stabilization route to price stability no longer seems plausible unless there is a new Bretton Woods or a return to gold.

In short, the available choices in terms of monetary arrangements seem to all rest on policies to control inflation which are undertaken at the discretion of individual nations or groupings of nations. What remains in dispute are the mechanics—the tactics of inflation targeting—and the constitutional issues—the powers and accountability of the central banks. Before passing on to these, we ask whether there are alternatives which offer a more lasting method to anchor nominal values.

Monetary rules

Endowing a central bank with certain powers and charging it with a duty to stabilize prices is a prescription much in line with the advice that stems from the reputational theory of economic policy and from Rogoff's (1995) model of the optimal 'conservative' central banker. The conception is quite subtle in some ways. It is *not* that the electorate's perception of its own welfare is wrong, only that short-sighted governments will succumb to the temptation to allow inflation to rip for the sake of short-run beneficial impacts on unemployment. Everyone would be better off under a regime which systematically excludes the possibility of 'exploiting' inflation in this way; making the central bank independent or appointing a conservative central banker has the right effect.

Even an independent central bank has discretion, however, and it is the exercise of discretion which can create a problem. A different approach is to adopt a rules-based approach to internal price stability. Monetary authorities like to retain discretion over monetary actions because monetary policy is seen to embrace more than price stability. (This is explicit in the charter of many central banks, e.g. the Federal Reserve—see note 15 below.) There is concern for output fluctuations and a desire to insulate the financial system from financial shocks by varying the money stock in line with changes in money demand. When a central bank has a reputation for anti-inflationary policies it is able to engage in stabilization policies and smooth shocks to the financial sector without exciting the expectation that inflation goals will be sacrificed. A 'reputational monetary policy', perhaps paradoxically, gives a central bank concerned the greatest leverage over the economy. Nonetheless, it is a risky game. Reputation is difficult to win, but easy to lose, and often tackling a number of things is a way of achieving none.

Where such reputation does not exist, it may be necessary in order to earn it for the monetary authorities to deliberately forswear certain activities. Much as Ulysses had himself tied to the mast to resist the lure of the Sirens, it may be necessary for the various monetary authorities to enact or have enacted for them 'self-binding' arrangements with respect to monetary policy. Monetary targets were originally designed with such a purpose in mind, a clear example being the Humphrey-Hawkings legislation of 1978 in the USA which required the Federal Reserve Board to set and achieve pre-specified growth rates of the money supply. This could be taken further, as in the Neal Resolution (H J Res. 409) introduced in 1990, requiring that

The Federal Open Market Committee of the Federal Reserve System shall adopt and pursue monetary policies to reduce inflation gradually in order to eliminate inflation by not later than five years from the date in this enactment of this legislation and shall then adopt and pursue monetary policies to maintain price stability.

Other arrangements are possible. David Friedman (1982), for example, suggested a rule such that money could be printed when the price index gets below some predetermined level and burnt when the price index gets beyond some slightly higher level.

A difficulty with all of these ideas is that there are no rules laid down which cannot be broken. And perhaps they should be broken. Circumstances change, and the old rules may be in need of modification. But then perhaps they should not. There are those who contend that the present international system, whether rule-based or not, or whether money creation is managed by the European Central Bank or the Fed, is incapable of delivering price stability and that the only way to remove inflation policy from the political arena is to undertake a fundamental reform of the monetary system. Reform might come from a return to some form of commodity money, maybe to gold, or from the innovation of private competitive moneys.

Commodity systems

A restoration of the age-old device of ensuring stable prices, namely convertibility into gold, seems unlikely to succeed now that the mystique of gold has been lost—and, once gone, is difficult to reconstruct. There has been a loss of innocence. People have learnt that governments can alter gold parity, tamper with the rules of the game, and change the monetary system. That being so, the faults of a gold standard take on greater significance—these being fluctuations in the relative price of gold, the resource costs, and the potential for instability due to the growth of financial intermediation and debt money (see Chapter 2).

Because its supply is highly inelastic, gold does not bring absolute stability. It does not respond readily to shifts in monetary and non-monetary demand. The secular trend in the price of gold is dependent on mineral discoveries, changes in production techniques, and the depletion policies of the mineral owners. These considerations have led to proposals for other commodity standards, with better price-stabilizing properties. Buchanan (1962) and others suggested a *common brick standard*. Bricks can be made anywhere and if in response to altered liquidity preferences it takes too long to bake new ones, existing houses could always be dismantled. It is thus a commodity with a supply curve which is likely to be stable and highly elastic, allowing it to accommodate shifts in the monetary and non-monetary demands without large changes in the value of the commodity and thus the money stock. A bundle of other commodities could have the same effect, and there have been a number of proposals for monetary systems based on a basket of primary commodities, for example. If the commodities in the basket are non-durables, there would be substantial resource costs from warehousing and spoilage. Durable commodities could share many of the same problems as gold in terms of their supply response.

One way around this issue is to borrow Marshall's (1887) idea of a tabular standard. For example, a proposal which for some time attracted some interest was a standard of four commodities—ammonium nitrate, copper, aluminium, and plywood—chosen because a price index of the four commodities combined tracked the general price index (for the USA) faithfully in the past.[1] The issue of resource costs would not arise since the government would not actually hold the four commodities or issue currency convertible into the commodities. Prices would be defined in terms of a resource unit comprising, say, 50 kg. of nitrate plus 40 kg. of copper plus 35 kg. of aluminium plus 80 sq. m of plywood. This resource unit would be the unit of account—a physical construct paralleling the redefinition of the metre in 1960 in atomic mass. Dowd (1988) made an even simpler proposal for the UK. He suggested the pound sterling simply be redefined as a certain weight of a particular commodity or basket of commodities.

The consequence of such suggestions is to separate the means of payment from the unit of account, and in principle remove 'money' from price determination. Evolution over time of the form of money which was needed under the gold standard to economize on the use of gold and which took place with the growth of the banking system and debt money might be avoided because money as we know it could disappear—an idea borrowed from what is known, perhaps inappropriately, as the *'new monetary economics'*. The argument is that much of the present shape of financial intermediation is a reflection of regulation and outmoded technology. Left to themselves, it is said, financial institutions would evolve into unit trusts or mutual funds linked by electronic fund transfer systems.[2] The whole system could operate like a sweep account, with instant commands via computer terminals to sell and buy securities, and transfer credits to other accounts in settlements of debts. Even hand-to-hand transactions conceivably could be settled by bearer units, with the price in terms of the resource unit of account posted daily in the newspapers in the same way that prices of unit trusts (mutual funds) are advertised now. Financial institutions would offer professional portfolio management, risk pooling, brokerage, and fund transfer facilities[3] but not asset transformation, for 'deposits' in this new world are just claims to primary securities. Since assets of all kinds would be instantly transferable, the vision is of sophisticated barter, made possible by computer technology and negligible transactions costs. With money eliminated from functioning as unit of account, means of payment, and abode of purchasing power, it would no longer matter, in fact no longer exist, and the problems of a monetary economy, i.e. inflation and unemployment would also disappear.

Like the idea of a return to gold, this scenario ignores the lessons of history. A tabular standard is likened to physical definitions of length, weight, volume, time, temperature, and energy, but unlike those other measures there exist opportunities for profit in supplanting or augmenting the official unit of value. Some institutions might be tempted to offer units, especially bearer ones, with a fixed price in terms of the resource unit of account. Those claims would be greatly valued, for savers could then plan future transactions free from concerns about likely conditions in the asset markets, thereby overcoming the uncertainty of barter. There are economies in combining the means of payment and the unit of account. Consequently it might become the practice to state prices in terms of the bearer units, in the same way that contracts written in gold pounds came to be written in paper pounds. The whole process of the erosion of the hoped-for stable standard would be under way again.

The present system of managed money is in some ways the best and the worst of monetary systems. With bad monetary policy, price instability can be much worse than is likely to result from any commodity standard, as history has clearly demonstrated. Properly managed with good monetary policy it can, at least in principle, do just as well as any commodity standard in producing internal and external stability, as history has also shown. Current arrangements have two advantages over the other systems considered here. There is no separation of the unit of account function of money from the transactions function and, if it works properly, it is technically more efficient in that there are fewer resource costs involved. It is also an arrangement attuned to the times. Governments will not willingly return to the discipline of gold convertibility and accept a binding set of international rules. Nor will governments, individually or collectively, readily give up the prestige and seigniorage benefits which come from issuing inconvertible fiat moneys without (as in the European case) some clear commensurate gains.

Here, in some eyes, lies the heart of the matter. Rather than have the monetary system adapt in this haphazard way to 'the times', it may be better to change the system. What one group has in mind is for governments to abandon sovereignty over money and the designation of legal tender, allowing individuals to do business in any money they choose to use and encouraging individuals and firms to offer their own private moneys for use.

Competing currencies

Thus Hayek and others[4] contend that the problem of inflation will only be solved by allowing private institutions to issue money in competition with the public sector. Instead of being 'forced' by legal restrictions to make deposits convertible at full par value in terms of the national currency and having to hold reserves of that currency, private banks could issue notes and/or deposits denominated in terms of different bases, e.g. there could be gold money, oil money, commodity index money. Such issues might be thought to lead to a proliferation of currencies in use, traded against one another at fluctuating prices, so losing the advantages (in terms of a reduction in costs of calculating and transacting) of having a uniform unit of account. Proponents envisage, however, that the provider who chooses the most appropriate base and controls output in such a way that his or her money maintains value over time would capture market share and come to dominate the market. In effect, Gresham's Law will operate in reverse under free competition, and the good money will drive out the bad.

The paramount question raised by competing moneys is that of whether a standardized money is a public good *par excellence*, and hence inappropriate or inefficient for provision by multiple producers or, in the limit, a private monopoly. The basic objection to a badly managed government fiat money system is the resulting instability of prices which renders money less useful in its functions. Yet this alternative has as its central feature the coexistence of several different moneys which would vary in price both within and across countries. Transactions costs and exchange risk would exist in dealing in the various moneys and there would be none of the benefits from having a standard unit of account for the majority of day-to-day transactions. As Kindleberger has argued:

A fixed conversion coefficient between metres and yards permits measurement to take place in either. When the relationship between the yard and the metre fluctuates, however, the public good of a standard of measurement is lost. (1983: 383)

Proponents of competing moneys would retort that this is to confuse standardization with monopoly and that granting the state monopoly rights to issue money may mean the benefits of standardization are outweighed by the tendency of the issuer to indulge in inflationary policies. Standardization could come about spontaneously by the issuers of money homing in on the same commodity or base for denomination. If all banks made their notes and deposits redeemable in gold, then the various claims should trade at par (with a discount indicating doubts about the ability of the issuer to meet withdrawals). In this way, the desire for standardization and the importance of scale economies in information and transactions costs could be put to the market test. If people value uniformity, they would pick and choose among moneys so that a common format emerges, as happened with the competition between video cassette recorder standards, VHS and Beta. But the adoption of the conventional typewriter keyboard offers a cautionary tale.[5] Here externalities have locked society into the use of a less-than-ideal keyboard even though everyone is 'free' to adopt a better model. In any case, for most people, money is rather more important than video recorders (or keyboards) and people elect governments precisely to take decisions which avoid excessive market turmoil and confusion.

It must also be said that there already exists choice in currency. Admittedly there is at present no competition for the national production of monetary units, but under international laissez-faire there is competition internationally.[6] Any citizen can, in the absence of exchange controls, hold purchasing power in US dollars or the euro, and is able to obtain a home mortgage in Swiss francs or Japanese yen. Firms are able to switch from high inflation currencies to low inflation ones.

Of course, such behaviour falls short of subverting the transactions demand for the traditional domestic currency and the discipline it affords over money creation is correspondingly limited. Freedom from exchange control and the potential for currency substitution are very important constraints, but there are costs involved in switching to other moneys and thus they are in themselves not enough to permit neglect of the central problem of designing a system which will assist in obtaining relatively stable prices. This is the topic of the rest of this chapter.

16.2 Inflation Targeting

Price stability

IN one form or another, and by using various means, most of the major countries have adopted what the Australian economist L. G. Melville (later Sir Lesley Melville) described in Adelaide in 1934 during the last era of paper money as a *goods standard*:

So, today, the greater part of the world rejects the gold standard and pledges its adherence to some kind of goods standard. By a goods standard is meant a monetary system under which the quantity of money would be regulated rather with reference to the prices of a selected group of goods than with reference to the quantity of gold.[7]

Current monetary arrangements can be interpreted in this vein. Countries have the objective of using monetary policy to keep the internal value of money reasonably stable in terms of (the underlying value of) a consumer or retail price index.

But what constitutes reasonable stability of prices? Not so long ago Australians seemed prepared to live with around 10 per cent inflation under the socialist government's Wages Accord, while Britons were happy with anything remotely approaching German inflation rates, and the low inflation countries in Europe settled for around 2–3 per cent per annum. But this is no longer the case. Now, as indicated by the recently established European Central Banks' decision to maintain inflation within a corridor of 0–2 per cent per annum, this range has become the international norm. Obviously, credibility in the international low inflation stakes has a lot to do with the changed attitudes. If Japan and the USA can achieve 0–2 per cent inflation, why not others? Competition by competing moneys may not exist domestically, as proposed by free bankers, but as noted, it does internationally and remains a long-run discipline on central banks.

To aim for an annual rise of consumer prices within the range of 0–2 per cent, rather than zero, may be a reflection of the measurement errors inherent in the price indices used to measure inflation. An upward bias in the indices comes in part from improvements in the quality (and price) of existing goods and also from delays in introducing new goods in the 'basket', so that the initial period of declining prices as the commodity moves into mass production is excluded. These, and other factors,[8] may overstate price increases by margins estimated at ⅓ per cent per annum in Australia, ½ per cent per annum in Canada, ½–1 per cent per annum in New Zealand, and as much as 2 per cent per annum in the USA.[9] Yet this does seem a case for having more accurate prices indices, notwithstanding Morgenstern's (1950) strictures on the accuracy of economic statistics.

Alternatively, the specification of a positive target range for inflation may be a recognition that, in present-day labour and product markets, prices are sufficiently inflexible downwards that a gently rising price level overall is needed as a lubricant to ensure that relative price movements occur—what Hahn (1982) called the 'natural rate of inflation'. The argument can be overstated: even with no price inflation, real wage flexibility does not require cuts in nominal wages so long as there is labour productivity growth. Interestingly, in view of the fact that absolute price stability was achieved under the gold standard, there is no overwhelming evidence that wages and prices in Britain or the USA have been less flexible since the Second World War than before the First World War (Allen, 1992). Whatever the reason, the idea of a non-zero inflation target is a very old one. Schumpeter (1954: 713) notes that from Hume through to Wicksell, 'most writers on currency preferred slowly rising to stable prices'.

In other respects, as well, it is not immediately obvious why a permanently rising price level is desirable. A 'creeping' inflation rate of 2 1/2 per cent per annum (like that clocked up under Bretton Woods) implies that the domestic purchasing power of the currency will be halved every generation, i.e. twenty-eight years. The costs which inflation imposes on the holding of money balances for transactions purposes are sometimes encapsulated as the 'shoe-leather' costs of the increased time and cost of making trips to the bank (or ATM) to withdraw currency and replenish cash balances whenever inflation increases, measured in welfare terms as the area of unsatisfied demand beneath a demand for money schedule (such as Figure 7.7 above).[10]

These shoe-leather costs rarely feature in attitudinal surveys. Shiller (1996) posed the question 'Why do people dislike inflation', and the answers of the general public made no mention of time replenishing money balances. However, as noted by Yakir Plessner, Deputy Governor of the Bank of Israel during years when inflation ran at up to 400 per cent per annum, the economizing process occurs in subtle and diverse ways (Plessner, 1994). There is increased activity of the public in the financial markets generally. Employment in the financial services sector expands, and corporations employ accountants and adopt accounting schemes with the aim of managing cash flows and finances more effectively; notably much the same growth in accounting and bookkeeping occurred in German firms during the 1920–3 hyperinflation (Bresciani-Turroni, 1931: 217). Often it is argued that the costs of inflation come about because it is unanticipated and indexation does not exist. Israel carried through the most extensive indexation of any country.

Even greater costs seem likely to emanate from money's role as a unit of account, essentially from the accounting, information, and psychic costs of having a floating standard of value. Household and government budgets are distorted, while the financial structure is weakened as firms substitute debt for equity. People just do not carry log tables around in their heads, and to function properly as a unit of account, money, as the measuring rod, should desirably have a constant value.

Sir John Hicks put these points incisively in his essay *Expected Inflation*:

It is correct, nowadays, to take it that inflation is expected; but it is a mistake to suppose that the expectation is consistent. There is a schizophrenia about inflation. While in part of their behaviour (their investment behaviour, in particular) people show themselves to be inflation-minded, in the rest of it they go on as if they expected prices to be stable. The habits—business habits as well as personal habits—which are based on the assumption of stable prices are too strong to be easily broken. Nor is it just habits (like the division of housekeeping money within the family, one of the most intimate points at which—we have been learning—accelerated inflation hurts); it is also institutions. The accounting system, the tax system, even the general legal system, all are based on the assumption of a stable value of money; if the value of money is seriously changeable, they are twisted out of shape. The accountant's 'profits' cease to be true profits; the taxes that are imposed are different to what was intended; the fines and penalties imposed by the courts, as well as the compensations which they award, lose their proper effect. Now it is of course true that these things can be put right (for a time) by legislation; but only by reopening issues that had been taken to be closed. There is a waste of time in rediscussing them—surely a much more serious waste of time and energy than is involved in holding 'too small' money balances'. (1977: 113–14)

In not allowing for such factors, economic theorists leave a considerable gulf (acknowledged in the *Handbook of Monetary Economics* by Driffill, Mizon, and Ulph, 1990) between the rather meagre costs of inflation formalized rigorously in theoretical models and the 'person-in-the-street' notions of the costs of inflation which would appear to have produced such a groundswell of support for low inflation policies.

Deflation also imposes costs. People will be reluctant to borrow or incur debts if they expect money to increase in value as they will be to lend funds if money is expected to depreciate in value. In this case, moreover, there are grounds for thinking that the ensuing adjustments may not be symmetric. In response to an expected increase/decrease in prices, bondholders will seek to shift out of/into securities vis-à-vis commodities and equities. But whereas bond yields can easily increase to cover the expected deflation of value, the zero interest rate on cash sets a floor for other interest rates. The possibility of a floor to nominal interest rates was discussed earlier in the context of the 'liquidity trap' (see section 5.4 above).

Other objectives

Conventional macroeconomic policy, following Tinbergen's (1956) approach to economic policy, specifies targets derived from the community's and policy-makers' preferences, and instruments such as monetary and fiscal policy which can be adjusted to achieve policy aims. This framework reflects the presumption that the authorities are not exclusively concerned with the inflation rate but have aims relating to unemployment and the balance of payments position. What has happened to these goals?

In the previous chapter, the case was outlined for ignoring the composition of the balance of payments and focusing upon internal balance. On one interpretation, a current account deficit reflects a lack of competitiveness. Or it may be a symptom of macroeconomic demand imbalances, with domestic spending running ahead of production. But the current account deficit is also equal to the excess of private sector investment over private sector savings and the government budget deficit. On this interpretation, the current account deficit is a reflection of savings–investment imbalances, and should be viewed in a global context. For example, if Japan has a high propensity to save and a large current account surplus, it follows that other countries must in aggregate have a current account deficit. In this way the deficit is the result of the natural workings of the international capital market and a myriad of individual decisions about capital formation and savings. There is no more case for interfering with the process internationally than there is domestically.

In practice, things are not so simple. Do markets perceive it the same way? There are enough mercantilists around who see current account surpluses as good and deficits as always bad to pose some concern to policy-makers. If a country running a large current account deficit must be constrained by the worry that a downward shock to the exchange rate might lead to portfolio capital inflows drying up, the balance of payments cannot be ignored and the exchange rate comes back into the picture.

What about employment? The notion that monetary policy should focus primarily, perhaps solely, on controlling inflation implies a large degree of concurrence with monetarist doctrine, the core of which is the 'importance' of money, the natural-rate hypothesis and thus the long-run neutrality of money, striking evidence of which was provided earlier. With this concurrence has come an acceptance that unemployment is best tackled by microeconomic policies, aimed at changing the flexibility of labour markets, rather than macroeconomic policies—this lies at the heart of the supply-sider's argument and Reaganomics.

Whether or not one agrees that inflation is, as Friedman (1987) has put it, 'always and everywhere a monetary phenomenon', it is clear that the process of inflation in real economies involves much more than a costless and automatic marking-up of prices in line with a monetary expansion. The model of inflation as a reverse monetary reform in which successively 'lighter' dollars (pounds may be better in view of the weight analogy) replace the earlier currency, however useful for understanding the steady state implications of monetary shocks, cannot obscure the fact that real-world inflationary processes are marked by sharp changes in relative prices, sharply changing real interest rates, unlegislated real tax changes, and labour market interactions. In the same way a process of disinflation involves disruptive relative price changes and consequential quantity adjustments.

Also, the suggestion of 'hysteresis' in the natural rate of unemployment acts as a reminder that this division of policies into 'micro' and 'macro' may not be quite so straightforward as it seems at first sight. Hysteresis embodies the New Keynesian view that a downward shock to employment can persist for some time. In the extreme case, as in Blanchard and Summer's (1986) insider–outsider model, there is complete hysteresis. The insiders left in employment ignore those now left outside the wage bargaining process. Those long-term unemployed have no influence on labour markets as their workforce skills atrophy. Under partial hysteresis, output and employment are strongly influenced by its own history (Cross, 1988). The conclusion is that adverse demand shocks should be avoided, raising the premium on policy flexibility. But such flexibility has to be exercised against a background of consistency, otherwise it leads simply to short-term politicization of monetary policy.

A policy of stabilizing the trend of prices is compatible with some smoothing of fluctuations in output and employment. A degree of automatic stabilization of aggregate demand is implicit in any policy rule which seeks to prevent prices either falling below, or rising above, the target level. In principle, at least, more discretionary applications of monetary policy need not be excluded. Consider three objectives of monetary policy: price stability, stabilization of output fluctuations, and prevention of liquidity crises. With one instrument and three targets there would seem to be a classic prescription for policy failure. An interesting idea advanced by Niehans (1978) revolves around the observation that these objectives have different time dimensions; one is secular, the second is business-cycle length, and the third is very short-run. This opens up the possibility of conducting monetary-policy operations of different durations for the different objectives. Variations in monetary policy, as reflected in (say) base money, could be imagined as being decomposed into three waves of different frequencies, each assigned to a policy objective with a matching frequency.

In practice, however, this is a difficult game to pull off, the more so the closer the durations of the different cycles. Meeting a liquidity disturbance lasting weeks or months may be unlikely to compromise the long-run trend of prices should policy-makers get it wrong, e.g. supplying liquidity to meet a fluctuation in the demand for money which fails to transpire (although the aftermath of the stock-market crash in 1987 provides a warning). In the case of output fluctuations of several years, the combination of the difficulties of forecasting the economy, data inaccuracies, and revisions, and the lag before the effects of policy take hold makes it likely that policy actions will simply perpetuate the old stop-go cycle.

Often the issues are stated in terms of the long-run versus the short-run Phillips curve. Notably at the Tercentenary of the Bank of England in 1994, Stanley Fischer stated:

There is no favourable long-run trade-off between inflation and growth or inflation and unemployment and therefore low inflation is desirable; but there is a short-run Phillips trade-off . . . denial of the short term trade-off is really very misleading and will get central banks into trouble. The short term trade-off exists.

But this is to address the wrong question. At issue is not the *existence* of a short-run trade-off between inflation and unemployment, but whether it can be *used* for policy purposes. The observed relationship may not be symmetric; an old view—revived in the 1990s with the case of Japan clearly in mind—is that monetary policy can rein in the economy but expansionary policy is like pushing on a string. (Keynes's favourite metaphor was that the mere wearing of larger trousers will not increase one's weight—Hansen, 1949). In small, open economies, the foreign exchanges and international securities markets are important constraints, and these markets' reactions to policy changes may shorten the trade-off or even cause it to disappear.

A central bank's anti-inflationary reputation is important here. A sole objective, readily announced and understood, may be needed when a central bank is endeavouring to establish credibility for its policies. When the necessary reputation has been created, it takes the place of the single objective allowing scope to use monetary policy for short-run stabilization without igniting inflation expectations, prices, and wages. The Federal Reserve's policy in the 1990–3 recession is a case in point; then interest rates were lowered to a new post-Second World War low without seemingly raising expectations of inflation. The exercise was then repeated at the end of the decade. This leads us to the question of tactics.

Tactics

While the case for focusing monetary policy primarily on an inflation objective seems strong, which inflation rate should be targeted and how should it be measured? Should a conventional index be used or a truncated index or a reweighted index? Should inflation rates be smoothed or a core component extracted from the raw data? When an inflation target is specified, how far ahead should the target realistically be set? How long do current changes to monetary policy take to pass through via the transmission channels to prices? If the target is set consistent with the transmission lag, the intermediate variable for monetary policy becomes an inflation *forecast* target (Artis, Mizen, and Kontolemis, 1998). How is inflation then forecast? These are some of the tactical issues posed by inflation targeting.

An obvious starting point is the nature of the target for prices. Ever since 1958, Milton Friedman has argued the case for an intermediate target in the form of a growth rate in the money supply (then 3–5 per cent per annum) required for price stability. The Bundesbank has ostensibly followed this kind of monetary targeting strategy, although recent studies of Bundesbank policy (e.g. Bernanke and Mihov, 1997) give reasons for thinking that the Bundesbank has been inflation targeting all along since overshoots of monetary targets have always been justified with an appeal to a reliable record on inflation. In this respect, there has been a preference amongst central banks to define a target in terms of a monetary policy *outcome* rather than an *instrument* or *intermediate variable*. A target could be defined in terms of inflation (as in the UK and the EU-11), or nominal income, or reference made to a general index of monetary conditions (as in Canada and the USA).

New Zealand was the first country to shift from an intermediate target to an inflation target, adopting a 0–2 per cent target in March 1990. Since then inflation targets have been declared (in time sequence) by Canada, Israel, UK, Sweden, Finland, Australia, Spain, and the European Central Bank. An inflation target has the advantage that the central bank has a single objective for monetary policy. Both a nominal income target and a monetary conditions target, in contrast, allow for deviations in more than one economic variable (Bean, 1983, 1998; Goodhart, 1994; Meade, 1994). Allowing for deviations from 'equilibrium' output by using a nominal income target has the advantage that policy-makers will not be inclined to make matters worse by engineering a disinflation in the face of adverse supply shocks as they might do with an unqualified inflation target. The disadvantage is that lags in the receipt of data on which the target is based and revisions would typically mean that policy-makers could only react to new information about the target variable on a quarterly basis rather than the typical monthly basis for price data. In any case, in practice the choice may not be so stark since an inflation-targeting regime will normally carry provision for adjustment of the target (although how this is done matters for the credibility of the regime).

Using a target stated in terms of a general index of monetary conditions would ensure that the external consequences of a tight monetary policy through the exchange rate were taken into account more explicitly. An index of conditions help-fully takes into account the legitimate point that external factors matter and avoids excessive exchange rate appreciation as a result of an unchecked zeal to eradicate inflation. It also addresses the question of who should take care of the exchange rate in a world of delegated responsibility for monetary policy, which features less directly when the objective is focused on a domestic target. This may be of impor-tance to a central bank in a small open economy.

The issue of whether the target should be in the price level or the inflation rate has not surfaced in practice. Most observers have concluded that a target in the price level is a vastly more difficult objective than a target in inflation. With price-level tar-geting, overshoots must be corrected for in subsequent periods by deflation whilst with inflation targets an overshoot can be overlooked by allowing for 'base drift', since it is the change in the price series year-on-year that matters, not the level of the price index.[11] Conversely, of course, with an explicit price level target any under-shoots would be corrected by future increases in prices, in order to prevent 'negative' base drift. It is this latter feature which makes price level targeting attractive to those concerned by the possibility of hitting the zero lower bound (ZLB) of inflation targets, implying deflationary policies in terms of 'true' inflation (i.e. once upward measure-ment biases in price indices are taken into account). This leads to the next question: 'inflation in what index?'

There is general recognition that the prices series targeted should be accurate, timely, and readily understood by the general public (Bernanke and Mishkin, 1997). All of the countries with inflation targets have so far chosen some version of the con-sumer price index, acknowledging that a central purpose of inflation control is to improve the decision-making environment for consumers in the countries con-cerned (Ball and Mankiw, 1994). Internationally, however, perhaps in order to pro-mote stability of exchange rates, it might be considered desirable that the variation across nations in the inflation rate of that index should not exceed some relatively small magnitude (say, 3 percentage points); if so, it might be sensible to adopt tar-geting of wholesale prices indices, on the grounds that these consist largely of trad-able goods prices for which the Law of One Price can be expected to hold. In a related, though not identical context, McKinnon (1988) advocated such a choice of index to be targeted. A clear disadvantage in such a choice, however, is that volatil-ity in wholesale price index inflation is clearly greater than that in consumer price index inflation.

More generally, there are competing criteria that make a target more or less desir-able. The price index should (probably) be 'of interest to consumers' in that it should not exclude components that are likely to form a large share of the typical con-sumer's expenditure basket. In that sense, the index should be as inclusive as possi-ble to represent accurately the general rise in prices of a representative basket of goods for an average consumer. Nor should the index respond perversely to changes in the stabilization instrument. In Australia and the UK, for example, where a large proportion of the housing stock is owner-occupied, variable-rate mortgage interest payments form a large part of the typical consumer's expenditure basket, and the targeted series omit mortgage interest payments. Ideally, also, the index should not be too 'lumpy' or volatile since this is likely to induce volatility in the instrument of monetary policy and create greater uncertainty in financial markets.

One procedure is to surround the central target rate by triggers; for example, in Bank of England practice these are set at ±1 per cent around the target rate. The bands permit some volatility in the recorded rate of inflation and insulate the monetary instrument from excessive variation. But the bands cannot be too wide, or the discipline of the target is lost. There are other ways of dealing with these problems.

Another possibility is to delete components of the index that are particularly volatile. This might imply that the target should exclude items such as food, which have strong seasonal effects, and energy prices, which have jumps corresponding to supply shocks, or interest costs, which cause perverse movements in inflation when there are changes to the monetary policy instrument. These items simply add noise. It is possible to go too far in 'smoothing by eliminating', however, since there is a danger of excluding those items in which the consumer is most interested.

Rather than arbitrarily choosing some items to be excluded it is possible to use adjusted measures of central tendency, such as trimmed means and medians, which are preferred (more efficient) measures of central tendency when the cross-sectional price distributions are highly leptokurtic.[12] These measures for underlying inflation avoid arbitrary omissions by excluding components that are at the tails of the distribution on the basis of information regarding the distribution of relative price movements. Another statistical technique is to trim the extreme tails of the distribution. By how much to do so, depends on the kurtosis of the sample—trimming should increase with the sample kurtosis (see Bryan, Cecchetti, and Wiggins, 1998, for example). An alternative is the weighted median. The weighted median puts half of the distribution on each side of its value and is not adversely affected by extreme values of the distribution as the mean will still be affected by asymmetry of probability mass.

However useful these measures are for internal consumption within the central bank and policy circles, they may all be too 'clever' in the sense of failing the test of being readily understood by the general public. On this score, a more understandable result may come from using a core measure of inflation, which is based on the common trend of the individual price indices. For example, the model of Bryan and Cecchetti (1993) extracts core inflation by using a weighting scheme that removes the noise from the true inflation signal in the observed time series of individual price series. The key assumption is that core inflation is uncorrelated at all leads and lags with the noise component, which is comprised of relative price disturbances. Given this property it is possible to extract the core component by using a Kalman filter algorithm.

Figure 16.1 illustrates the different approaches for the UK against the level of retail price inflation excluding mortgage interest payments (RPIX). Price data for sixty-four categories of goods from 1974 to 1996 are used to construct alternative measures of inflation. In the upper panel the calculations of inflation for RPIX, a weighted median, and the 25 per cent trimmed mean shows that, in general, the headline RPIX is higher than the other measures. In the lower panel the Stock-Watson dynamic filter provides a core extraction of inflation that reflects the path of RPIX. Unlike the other measures of central tendency the extracted core is not always below the RPIX

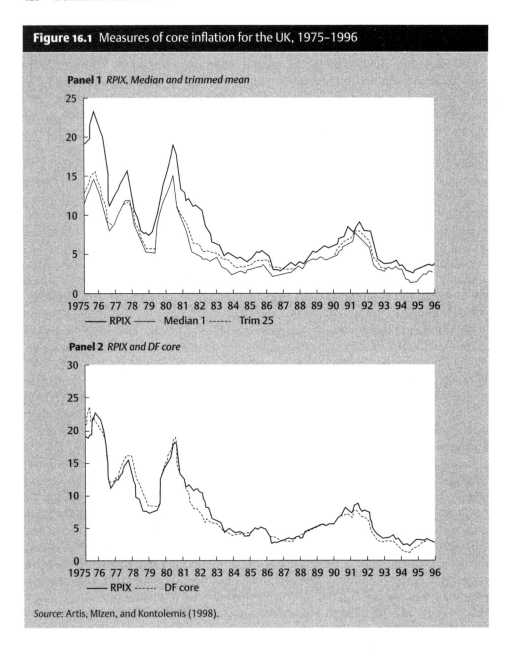

Figure 16.1 Measures of core inflation for the UK, 1975–1996

Panel 1 *RPIX, Median and trimmed mean*

—— RPIX —— Median 1 ------ Trim 25

Panel 2 *RPIX and DF core*

—— RPIX ------ DF core

Source: Artis, MIzen, and Kontolemis (1998).

figure but exceeds the headline rate for a large part of the 1970s and early 1980s. Although it uses a different method to remove the erratic components from the inflation series, the core tracks RPIX in which the target is specified quite well. However, in recent years when inflation targeting has operated, there is very little to separate the three measures, and the contrast between this period and the earlier years of high and volatile inflation is shown most strikingly in the figure.

Nevertheless, some authors still question whether a central bank should consider a single measure at all. The view put forward by Britton, Fisher, and Whitley (1998) is that no summary measure is adequate. Haldane (1998) argues that the best results will be obtained from a mixture of measures from many models which include 'off-model' information for inflationary risks and potential regime shifts such as those which obviously have occurred since 1975. This leads us to the question of indicators. But, again, we note that suspicion of measuring inflation by an index of prices is an old one in economics. The Austrian School, in particular, was dismissive towards those who placed 'an uncritical trust in index figures' (Schumpeter, 1954: 1094).

The question of indicators

Obviously a novelty of present arrangements in a number of countries is the absence of an intermediate target to perform the role that exchange rates (under Bretton Woods) and then monetary targets carried before. The classical theory of economic policy provides a framework for understanding one of the key features of inflation targeting—that it is inherently non-transparent in terms of the transmission methods while being fully transparent (albeit with a lag) in terms of outcomes. It also makes clear Svensson's (1997a) argument that the intermediate variable in inflation targeting is the inflation *forecast*. In the classical theory, firm distinctions are drawn between policy instruments, intermediate variables, and the ultimate variables of policy interest. A causal structure is presumed so that changes in instruments lead reliably to changes in the intermediate variable which plays a role in the transmission mechanism that ultimately conveys an effect on the goal variables of interest. Monetary targeting can be thought of this way: the central bank's instruments produce changes in the intermediate variable, the money supply, which lead—with a lag—to changes in the price level. Given that the links in the sequence are reliable, a price-stability oriented central bank can be monitored for the quality of its policy simply by keeping track of the current movement of money supply. Svensson pointed out that, under inflation targeting, the role of intermediate variable, at least from the monitoring point of view, is taken by the inflation forecast. If the forecast does not fall within the announced target bands for good reasons, the central bank is not doing its job. The analogy falters at this point, to the extent that the forecast of inflation does not play the same role in the transmission mechanism of monetary policy as the money supply did in the traditional schema.

The monitoring issue of course arises because the monetary policy transmission mechanism takes time, so that the effectiveness of policy actions to control inflation can be discerned only after a long delay, a problem which is exacerbated by the inherent publication lag with prices data. Keynes in the *Tract* was well aware of the consequences: 'If we wait until a price movement is actually afoot before applying remedial measures, we may be too late. "It is not the *past* rise in prices but the *future* rise that has to be counter-acted"' (1923: 187).[13]

Friedman (see Chapter 7) four decades ago estimated the lags from money to prices as being eighteen to twenty-four months, and this estimate of the time interval has stood up remarkably well, despite the impact that rational expectations was meant to have had upon speeding up policy transmission when monetary changes are anticipated. Thus Lane and Van Den Heuvel (1998) reproduce the Bank of England's assessment that eighteen months to two years is the lag from implementation to full effect of monetary policy. For shorter horizons, the issue of Friedman's 'long and variable lags' in monetary policy transmission arises: the lags imply that not all of the policy measures will have worked themselves through. Longer horizons, on the other hand, involve greater uncertainty and even less precision over the effects of risks on inflation.

Given the lags in the monetary transmission process, inflation targeting is really inflation-*forecast* targeting in practice. The monetary authorities alter the monetary instrument, i, to ensure that a specific target in inflation is hit m-quarters hence. Alternatively they may form an optimal sequence for the policy instrument, i, derived from a forward-looking policy rule based on a forecast horizon, n, for expected inflation, $E_t\pi_{t+n}$:

$$i = \lambda(E\pi_{t+n} - \pi^*), \tag{16.1}$$

where the target is specified as π^*, and the feedback parameter is λ. The choice of the pair (λ, π) can be determined by optimizing methods using a loss function representing the cost of disinflation, as in Batini and Haldane (1998). Whichever means is used to choose the optimal value for the monetary policy instrument, given the transmission lags, a central bank will need to form a forecast of its value n-quarters ahead to adjust policy today (Bernanke and Woodford, 1997).

In practice, neither the choice of the best horizon nor the forecasting of inflation can be done with any precision. There is a very prominent place for judgement in these matters, and apparent agreement that 'a wide variety of factors and forecasts' should be taken into account (Greenspan, 1997). Attaching particular significance to a single indicator would imply either that the response function from monetary indicators to outcomes is fixed and invariant or would involve discarding information that is relevant to a changing feedback rule. At the same time, the often conflicting signals of the indicators have to be interpreted and this requires a model, either formalized econometrically or in policy-makers' heads. Econometric models are inevitably vulnerable to rapid changes in structural relationships and conditioned by underlying assumptions about interest rates and data variables. Use is consequently made of survey material, private sector forecasts, and a range of financial market data.[14]

'Looking at everything', while technically efficient in the sense that it uses all available information, may result in policy confusion and create a bias towards inaction (not necessarily a bad thing). It may also reduce accountability since there is no way to judge the appropriateness of policy for some years—and then it is too late. How much freedom of action should the central bank have and in what ways can it be held accountable for its actions?

16.3 **Constitutional Issues**

THE strength of inflation targeting is its transparency in terms of outcomes and the inability of the monetary authority to deny the upshot of policy in the inflation figures, as opposed to the 'mumbo-jumbo' of monetary conditions and expressions such as 'ease' or 'tightness' of monetary policy. But who is responsible—the government or the central bank? Should a central bank have goal or instrument independence or both, and what other things should it do?

Independence

Independence or autonomy can imply a number of different things: independence of thought and opinion; independent advice; independence over day-to-day operations; independence to formulate policy; or independence to set objectives. Obviously a certain degree of independence is necessary if a central bank is to provide an 'outside' input on government policy questions. Some separation from normal political processes is desirable for the execution of policies which affect market participants. But independence is rarely meant literally in the sense of a central bank having the right to conduct policy free of any constitutional safeguards and political and institutional constraints. Only the European Central Bank with both goal and instrument independence, limited accountability, and confidentiality of the meetings of its governing council can be said to be in this position, and it qualifies easily for the title of the most independent central bank in the world.[15] Independent national central banks, by contrast, typically have instrument independence but not goal independence and invariably are subject to strict accountability.

Economists have constructed a number of measures of central bank independence by quantifying various aspects of central banks' institutional and political structures. Table 16.1 compares the rankings of seven different studies. Germany, Switzerland, and the USA in that order turn out as the most independent on these grounds. In one respect this is not surprising. A traditional motive for central bank independence derives from notions of the separation of power and checks and balances in democratic processes. These ideas surface most strongly in federal systems where constitutions have been drafted with an eye to curb central government financial powers. This idea provides a link between the formal independence of central banks in the USA, Germany, and Switzerland and the federal structure of their political systems. In the same way that an independent judiciary enables the power to make laws to be separated from the power to judge on the basis of them, the idea of an independent central bank is to separate the power to spend money (vested in government) from the power to create it (the central bank). Clearly the same factors were at work in the federal European Union, with the additional twist

Table 16.1 Ranking of central banks' independence in various studies

Country	1	2	3	4	5	6	7	Mean
Australia	0.50	0.25	0.25	0.33	0.69	0.45	0.20	0.38
Austria	—	—	—	0.66	0.69	0.86	—	0.73
Belgium	0.50	0.50	0.50	0.33	0.53	0.29	0.60	0.46
Canada	0.50	0.50	0.83	0.33	0.84	0.70	0.20	0.55
Denmark	—	—	0.50	—	0.61	0.68	—	0.59
Finland	—	—	0.50	—	0.69	0.58	—	0.59
France	0.50	0.50	0.50	0.33	0.53	0.42	0.40	0.45
Germany	1.00	1.00	1.00	1.00	1.00	1.00	1.00	1.00
Greece	—	—	—	—	0.30	0.79	—	0.54
Ireland	—	—	—	—	0.53	0.68	—	0.60
Italy	0.50	0.50	0.37	0.33	0.38	0.38	0.40	0.40
Japan	0.50	0.75	0.83	0.33	0.46	0.27	0.60	0.53
Netherlands	0.50	0.50	0.83	0.33	0.76	0.64	0.80	0.62
New Zealand	—	—	0.25	0.33	0.23	0.41	—	0.30
Portugal	—	—	—	—	0.23	—	—	0.23
Spain	—	—	0.25	—	0.38	0.32	—	0.31
Sweden	0.50	0.50	0.50	0.33	0.42	0.39	0.40	0.43
Switzerland	1.00	1.00	1.00	1.00	0.92	0.97	1.00	0.98
UK	0.50	0.50	0.50	0.33	0.46	0.53	0.40	0.46
USA	1.00	0.75	0.75	0.50	0.92	0.77	0.60	0.75

Notes: 1. Bananian, Laney, and Willett (1983); 2. Bade and Parkin (1985); 3. Alesina and Summers (1993); 4. Burdekin and Willett (1990); 5. Grilli, Masciandaro, and Tabellini (1991); 6. Cukierman (1992); 7. Eijfinger and Schaling (1992).

Source: Masciandaro and Spinelli (1994).

that the ECB had to be at least as independent as the Bundesbank if the Germans were to join and give up the mark.

Focusing on the laws and statutes governing the relationship between the central bank and the government of the day takes us only so far. That independence in itself is not sufficient for sound money is vividly demonstrated by the German hyperinflation of 1922–3. The inflation started *after* the Reichsbank had been given a high degree of independence by the 'Autonomy Law' of 1922 (Caesar, 1994). Also, during the First World War, both the Bank of England and the Federal Reserve were in conflict with the governments of the day over war financing, and in both cases the banks were subordinated to government, despite retaining formal independence. In the case of the USA, Congress passed the *Overman Act* and used the threat of takeover to circumscribe the Fed's independence.

Autonomy is consequently better defined *de facto* rather than *de jure*, and informal influence may be more effective than formal independence. For example, the Bank of Japan was never intended to be independent of government, and one of the legislated responsibilities of the Ministry of Finance is to supervise the Bank of Japan. The Bank of Japan thus does poorly in the formal 'rankings'. Nevertheless it is widely perceived as being highly independent (Cargill, 1989), and has considerable anti-inflationary credibility in the markets. Much then depends on the personalities of the officials involved and the unwritten conventions which evolve. The high watermark of powerful central banks, in the 1920s, was also a period in which strong personalities were governors—Montague Norman of the Bank of England, Benjamin Strong of the Federal Reserve Bank of New York, Hjalmar Schacht of the Reichsbank, and Emile Moreau of the Banque de France. Alan Greenspan, Chairman of the Board of Governors of the Federal Reserve provides a contemporary example.

Accountability

Accountability is another important consideration. This is not the same thing as independence. For an institution to be held to be accountable for its actions implies that it has some autonomy when undertaking them. In principle, a central bank could have independence and not have to account for its policies, except in the market place. Yet persistent actions by a central bank to thwart government policies would be likely to see the removal of the bank's independence, unless its actions coincided with public opinion. On this view, the essential factor which underpinned the independence of the Deutsche Bundesbank—and low inflation in Germany—was the public support for the policies of the Bundesbank[16] stemming from a strongly held fear of inflation in Germany, which can be traced back to the hyperinflation of the 1920s.

The point is if public bodies are to earn the respect and approval of the people, then they must be seen to be exercising policies which are in the public's long-run interests. Indeed, their legitimacy as public institutions rests on such a process of open scrutiny. This monitoring process is, in turn, aided if there are clear (and sensible) goals—such as price stability—which the central bank has a mandate to achieve and can be held responsible for if they are not attained, and this is the basis of inflation targets. However, the assessment of whether the target has been hit or missed can only be made after the two-year Friedman lag has elapsed, since the full effects of present policy cannot be determined until all of its effects have been transmitted to prices. Current monetary policy decisions have to be based on a forecast of inflation several years ahead and any justification of policy depends on the reliability of the forecast information. Thus the construction of forecasts is crucial and publication of the basis for the forecasts is central to accountability. Experience shows that the inherent lack of transparency in terms of policy transmission produces laudable efforts to make up for it using inflation reports, press statements, minutes of policy review meetings, and cross-examination by parliamentary and congressional committees.

Yet, accountability can be overdone; continuous supervision erodes independence. Congressional oversight of the Federal Reserve—the Chairman and other officials appeared forty-six times before Congress in 1990—means that it is difficult, if not impossible, for the Federal Reserve to sustain a generally unpopular monetary policy course in the absence of substantial support from the President and Congress (Akhtar and Howe, 1991).

The case against independence

There are two arguments against a separation of powers in the case of monetary policy. One is Milton Friedman's view that money is too important for it to be left to central bankers and unelected officials. The elected government must ultimately be responsible and the institutions engaged in the formulation and execution of monetary policy should not be operating on the basis of a fundamentally different principle than that applied to other government bodies. Otherwise, there is the likelihood of creating 'a system of rule by men and not by law' (1963: 235), with the danger that an unrepresentative meritocracy would exercise control. Friedman considers that 'the case against a fully independent central bank is strong indeed' (ibid. 239).

Historically, central banks were rarely entrusted with the responsibility for determining the level of prices. Long-run price stability was provided by the gold standard, and the decision as to whether the country was on gold or suspended convertibility usually required legislative action or government statute. Indeed, central banks were there to water down the gold standard; they were expected to ease the constraints of the 'cross of gold' and provide an 'elastic currency' to alleviate periodic financial crises. This expectation gave the central bank some leeway in the short run, but ultimately there was the necessity to respond to the balance of payments and maintain gold convertibility.

Nevertheless, like statutory authorities, governmental control over monetary policy need not preclude taking the *technical responsibility* for achieving the objectives of policy out of the hands of elected politicians, while leaving the setting of the objectives themselves to the government (or parliament). The New Zealand model which got inflation targeting under way is one way of combining these elements in which a legislated 'sunshine clause' gives the Reserve Bank full responsibility over monetary policy for a specified period to bring about the 0–2 per cent inflation goal. This can be overridden only in exceptional circumstances, and then only by Act of Parliament. The result is that the objectives of monetary policy are open to public debate, while the detailed methods by which these ends are to be achieved are devolved to 'technicians', in much the same way as occurs with other statutory instrumentalities. These technicians can be called to account for their actions on a periodic basis by politicians, but otherwise policy is distanced from political influence.

The second argument against central bank autonomy is based on the concern that in solving one problem, others may be created. A particular issue is the need for economic policies to be coordinated. Many forces impact upon inflation and economic performance, and an independent monetary policy increases the difficulty of achieving coordination between monetary and other government policies. Some of the most difficult dilemmas for monetary policy arise from a failure to coordinate the stances of fiscal and monetary policies. Two of the major macroeconomic policy blunders of recent times, at least in terms of their external impacts—the Reagonomics experiment in the early 1980s and German unification—are good illustrations. Both of these episodes demonstrate that monetary policy cannot offset the effects of an inappropriate fiscal policy; rather, it will accentuate the costs by raising interest rates domestically and externally by more than otherwise would be the case. Moreover, when there are large fiscal budgets there is always the risk that a variety of subtle political pressures brought to bear upon the central bank will result in some monetization of the debt in order to reduce pressures upon interest rates. It follows that some coordination of fiscal and monetary policy could actually enhance a central bank's counter-inflationary credibility: independence *within* government may be valuable since it gives the central bank leverage over other policy settings.

The difficulty is that governments, not central banks, are the ones inclined to cheat on inflation, and a precommitment of some kind not to interfere (excessively or at all) in monetary policy is needed. Granting independence may be a solution to this problem but independence carries with it a moral obligation to account for the actions taken, as Blinder (1998) has argued. In this respect precommitment has some value; independence may be sufficient but the desire for democratic accountability usually makes a publicly declared target necessary. The lesson to be learned from the recent experience of central bank independence and inflation targeting is 'do what you say and say what you do' (Artis, Mizen, and Kontolemis 1998). This would certainly explain why inflation reports, press statements, minutes of policy review meetings, and other forms of demonstrating consistency between what the central bank is 'saying' and 'doing' have proliferated among newly independent central banks.

Other functions

The now burgeoning literature on central bank independence, exploring many of these issues, has focused almost entirely on the implications of independence for macroeconomic performance. But a central bank is more than a national monetary agency. It carries out a range of other functions which include *inter alia* custodian of the banking system, oversight of the payments system, agent for public debt issues, manager of foreign reserves, etc.

Prudential supervision is an area of responsibility which has expanded significantly in recent years. Some central banks (e.g. the Fed) continue to combine monetary policy and bank supervision, but in the vast majority i.e. twenty of the twenty-four countries in Table 16.2 the functions are separated, with supervision vested in a separate authority. Ought an independent central bank to carry out functions such as prudential supervision? Do these other functions deflect the central bank from its principal job of conducting monetary policy? Does the provision of emergency credit to the financial system compromise the settings of monetary policy instruments?

Considering the last of these, we imagine by analogy with Richard Musgrave's (1959) stabilization, allocation, and distribution branches of a fiscal agency, that the

Table 16.2 Monetary policy and bank supervisory agencies in various countries

Country	Monetary policy agency	Bank supervisory agency	Status
Australia	Reserve Bank of Australia	Australia Prudential Regulation Authority	Separated
Austria	ESCB (National Bank of Austria)	Ministry of Finance	Separated
Belgium	ESCB (National Bank of Belgium)	Banking and Finance Commission	Separated
Canada	Bank of Canada	Office of the Superintendent of Finance Institutions	Separated
Denmark	Danmarks Nationalbank	Finance Inspectorate	Separated
Finland	ESCB (Bank of Finland)	Bank Inspectorate, Bank of Finland	Separated
France	ESCB (Banque de France)	Banque de France, Commission Bancaire	Separated
Germany	ESCB (Deutsche Bundesbank)	Federal Banking Supervisory Office	Separated
Greece	Bank of Greece	Bank of Greece	Combined
Hong Kong	Hong Kong Monetary Authority	Hong Kong Monetary Authority	Combined
Ireland	ESCB (Central Bank of Ireland)	Central Bank of Ireland	Separated
Italy	ESCB (Banca d'Italia)	Banca d'Italia	Separated
Japan	Bank of Japan	Ministry of Finance, Bank of Japan	Separated
Luxembourg	ESCB (Luxembourg Monetary Institute)	Luxembourg Monetary Institute	Separated
Mexico	Banco de Mexico	National Banking and Securities Commission	Separated
Netherlands	ESCB (De Nederlandsche Bank)	De Nederlandsche Bank	Separated
New Zealand	Reserve Bank of New Zealand	Reserve Bank of New Zealand	Combined
Norway	Norges Bank	Banking, Insurance and Securities Commission	Separated
Portugal	ESCB (Banco de Portugal)	Banco de Portugal	Separated
Spain	ESCB (Banco de España)	Banco de España	Separated
Sweden	Sveiges Riksbank	Swedish Financial Supervisory Authority	Separated
Switzerland	Swiss National Bank	Federal Banking Commission	Separated
UK	Bank of England	Financial Services Authority	Separated
USA	Federal Reserve System	Federal Reserve System, OCC. FDIC, State government agencies	Combined

Source: Updated from Haubrich (1996) and Goodhart and Schoenmaker (1996).

central bank has a policy branch, a financial assistance branch, and payments branch. The policy 'branch' supplies base money consistent with the stance of monetary policy. In the financial assistance 'branch', emergency credit is supplied to institutions that are temporarily illiquid. This involves the 'branch' lending to individual banks, with finance coming from the sale of government securities. Since loans replace securities in the portfolio, there is no expansion of the monetary base, and no alteration to monetary conditions, from its actions. Activities in the payments 'branch' depend on the type of settlement system which operates. If we focus, for simplicity, upon a gross settlements system, the job of the 'branch' is to prevent 'gridlock' from developing in the system when payments cannot proceed because certain institutions have insufficient funds in their accounts at the central bank. Liquidity would be provided to these institutions on a secured basis within a day or overnight by means of repurchase agreements. In this way, the injection of liquidity would be automatically reversed later in the day or next day. Again there need be no conflict with monetary policy objectives.

There may be conflicts of interest in other ways. A regulator may be concerned about the effects that tight monetary policy has upon the profitability, bad debts, and capital positions of the banks that it supervises. When the regulator is also the central bank, it may be tempted to pull its punches and moderate the counter-inflationary stance of policy. Another possible conflict may come about if there are some failures of banks which reflect poorly on the regulatory competence of the central bank; its acumen in conducting monetary policy may then be called into question. There were some examples of this in the wake of the Asian financial crisis in the late 1990s. Finally, there may be a conflict between the breadth of responsibilities and independence. Independence carries a lot of political power, and that needs accountability. The wider are the powers that a central bank has, the more it will be called to account, while multiplicity of functions may make it harder for the public to judge the central bank's overall performance. Separation of functions may be the price to be paid for greater independence and focus over monetary policy. This proved to be the case in the UK and Australia, and this trend accelerated when the European System of Central Banks (ESCB) adopted a Bundesbank-style separation as the norm for monetary union.

16.4 Conclusions

THIS book has examined the workings of a number of different monetary systems—commodity money in a variety of forms, paper money with fixed and floating exchange rates, and various tabular standards. In our view history teaches that no monetary system can offer a cast-iron guarantee of price stability. Any arrangement will have some potential for inflation and offer some opportunities for inflation control. That is as true of the current system of irredeemable paper money, floating exchange rates, and international financial laissez-faire, as it is of the gold standard. If governments are able to resist inflation under a commodity standard, they are surely capable of resisting inflation under a system of managed money. What is needed is for people to decide upon the basic principles that are to define the workings of the monetary system and then agree to abide by them.

One such set of principles was outlined by Keynes in *A Tract on Monetary Reform*. In the *Tract*, Keynes proposed 'a scientific treatment of currency questions', at the centre of which was a system of 'managed currency':

The governors of the system would be bank-rate and Treasury Bill policy, the objects of government would be stability of trade, prices, and employment, and the volume of paper money would be a consequence of the first ... and an instrument of the second, the precise arithmetical level of which could not and need not be predicted. (1923: 196)

As regards the criteria, other than the actual trends of prices, which should determine the action of the controlling authority ... Actual price-movements must of course provide the most important datum; but the state of employment, the volume of production, the effective demand for credit as felt by the banks, the rate of interest on investments of various types, the volume of new issues, the flow of cash into circulation, the statistics of foreign trade and the level of the exchanges must all be taken into account. The main point is that the *objective* of the authorities, pursued with such means as are at their command, should be the stability of prices. (ibid. 188–9)

At that time, Keynes noted: 'It will be observed that in practice we have already gone a long way towards the ideal of directing bank rate and credit policy by reference to the internal price level and other symptoms of under- or over-expansion of internal credit' (ibid. 185).

Present-day central bankers have gone much further down the route to Keynes's ideal and his prescription of seventy-seven years ago is a remarkably accurate picture of how monetary policy operates in a large number of countries today. Keynes's emphasis upon the primacy of interest rates, the endogeneity of the money supply, and the need to 'look at everything' finds ready echoes in current strategies adopted by many modern central banks.[17]

However, today's central bankers are operating managed currencies under conditions quite different from those which Keynes envisaged. He thought there might be, at most, two managed currencies globally. A worldwide system of free paper currencies was beyond his contemplation. The difficulty of this arrangement is that paper money can produce 'the best of times and the worst of times'. It is the best system because it is possible by following an appropriately calibrated monetary path for a paper money system to do just as well as any commodity money in producing price and exchange rate stability, yet at a much lower social cost. It is the worst of systems because the monopoly over production and the freedom from the rigour of convertibility makes it possible for a government to expand the money supply virtually without limit. This wide range of possible outcomes has led some leading theorists to argue that a world system of paper money would leave exchange rates 'indeterminate' and is therefore 'not economically feasible' (Kareken and Wallace, 1981).

The practical reality they ignored is that while a central bank's leverage over domestic markets rests on its monopoly position over the supply of base money, no central bank monopolizes the world supply. Each national currency must compete for a place in the portfolios of international transactors, and the potential for currency substitution under 'competing currencies' acts as a powerful constraint upon monetary policies. In order to placate expectations about future policies, and protect the value of money, governments of all persuasions have felt the need to establish the credibility of policies.

Keynes wrote the *Tract* in an era when central banks had a large degree of independence from government, and one of the ways of promoting policy credibility today has been to turn back the clock and give central banks the autonomy which was removed in much post-Second World War legislation. Inflation targeting has been another, frequently concurrent change. These reforms to central banks in many cases have occurred simultaneously with reforms to fiscal policy and labour markets. Perhaps these changes have simply coincided with a period of low inflation in the developed world, and thus it is too early to say for sure that inflation targeting has produced a lasting regime change. But there is certainly the prospect of one.

Notes

1 Known as the ANCAP standard, the idea is discussed in Fama (1983), Greenfield and Yeager (1983), and Hall (1982). The following comments are based on Lewis (1985).

2 Giddy (1986), Karaken (1986), McCulloch (1986), and Goodhart (1988) developed the ideas.

3 A recent conception of how financial intermediaries might evolve is given in Sandford (1994).

4 Vaubel (1979), Salin (1984), and Dowd (1988).

5 The argument is that, once adopted, the standard QWERTY keyboard is very difficult to displace, even though more efficient designs are available. The problem is that training schools and operatives are accustomed to the QWERTY keyboard so that individual employers find it uneconomic to introduce more efficient keyboards—even though starting from scratch a collective decision would favour an alternative configuration. An interesting account of how the QWERTY layout came to be adopted can be found in David (1985), although not everyone agrees with the 'market-failure' interpretation (see *The Economist*, 3 Apr. 1999, p. 72). The situation for currencies is not dissimilar in that currency use is dependent on the range of facilities and services offered for that currency, upon customary accountability, and, of course, legal tender laws.

6 International currency competition, we note, kept the great currencies from being debased in the Middle Ages. Coins could always be debased by reissuing them in a base form (with more alloy) to make them go further. But in this case the sovereign ran the risk of losing the mint trade of professional traders and dealers who could always turn to the services of overseas mints. By virtue of the competition in money, the great currencies—the Venetian ducat, the Dutch guilder, and the pound sterling—maintained their value for centuries (Cipolla, 1956).

7 Cited in Mason (1963).

8 In addition, infrequent revisions to weights may exaggerate the increase in the cost of living, when consumers shift from goods which have become relatively expensive to cheaper alternatives.

9 In the USA, 'virtual price stability' has been interpreted to be about 2% inflation (Feldstein, 1992).

10 The first study was by Martin Bailey (1956). For a recent analysis see Chadha, Haldane, and Janssen (1998).

11 Base drift also arose in the context of money supply growth targets, in particular whether overshoots should be corrected in the next target range set. Invariably they were not.

12 In these circumstances, it is more likely that a draw may be obtained of one observation in one tail of the distribution that is not balanced by an equally extreme observation in the opposite tail.

13 The quotation referred to by Keynes is from Hawtrey (1923).

14 The yield curve is one such source of information. It is possible to extract the expected sequence of future short rates from the spot rate yield curve. The sequence of future rates can then be treated as a corresponding forward rate curve. Under the assumption of negligible liquidity premia, the forward curve reveals the market's expectation of future short-term interest rates. Add to this Irving Fisher's decomposition of nominal interest rates into expected real returns and inflation premia and, with assumptions about the behaviour of real rates, there emerges an indicator of expected inflation which can be compared with estimates from other sources (including, for example, the interest rate futures market).

15 The primary objective of the ECB is to maintain price stability. It has to support the general economic policies of the Community but 'without prejudice to the objective of price stability' and is not allowed to take instructions from Community institutions or bodies, any government or from any other body. This precedence on price stability is similar to the Bundesbank, and can be contrasted with the US Federal Reserve which is charged 'to promote effectively the goals of maximum employment, stable prices, and moderate long-term interest rates'.

16 Jacques Delors once remarked that not all Germans believe in God, but all Germans believe in the Bundesbank.

17 It is also interesting to observe that Keynes's views, written in a very different era, still have a great deal of influence on present-day central bankers. Mervyn King, the Deputy Governor of the Bank of England responsible for monetary policy, recently admitted Keynes's *Tract* has had an influential effect on his own thinking and this is corroborated by the numerous citations it receives in his speeches.

Bibliography

Adam, C. S. 1991. Financial innovation and the demand for sterling M3 in the UK 1975-86. *Oxford Bulletin of Economics and Statistics*, 53: 401-24.

Aizenman, J., and Frenkel, J. A. 1985. Optimal wage indexation, foreign exchange intervention and monetary policy. *American Economic Review*, 75: 402-23.

Akerlof, G. A. 1973. The demand for money: a general equilibrium inventory-theoretic approach. *Review of Economic Studies*, 40: 115-30.

—— 1979. Irving Fisher on his head: the consequences of constant target-threshold monitoring of money holdings. *Quarterly Journal of Economics*, 93: 169-87.

—— and Milbourne, R. 1980. The short-run demand for money. *Economic Journal*, 90: 885-900.

Akhtar, M. A. 1997. *Understanding Open Market Operations*. New York: Public Information Dept., Federal Reserve Bank of New York.

—— and Howe, H. 1991. The political and institutional independence of US monetary policy. *Banca Nazionale del Lavoro Quarterly Review*, 178 (Sept.): 343-89.

Alesina, A., and Summers, L. 1993. Central bank independence and macroeconomic performance: some comparative evidence. *Journal of Money, Credit and Banking*, 25: 151-62.

Alexander, S. S. 1952. Effects of a devaluation on the trade balance. *International Monetary Fund Staff Papers*, 2: 263-78.

Allen, S. 1992. Changes in the cyclical sensitivity of wages in the United States, 1891-1987. *American Economic Review*, 82: 122-40.

Allen T. J. 1990. Developments in the international syndicated loan market in the 1980s. *Bank of England Quarterly Bulletin* 30(1): 71-7; repr. in *The Globalization of Financial Services*, ed. M.K. Lewis, Cheltenham: Edward Elgar, 1999.

Allen, W. A. 1984. Recent developments in monetary control in the United Kingdom in *Improving Money Stock Control*, ed. L. H. Meyer, Boston: Kluwer-Nyhoff.

Andersen, P. S. 1985. The stability of money demand functions: an alternative approach. *BIS Economic Papers* 14, April.

Anderson, L. C. 1967. Three approaches to money stock determination. *Federal Reserve Bank of St Louis Review*, Oct.: 6-13.

Angeloni, I. C., Cortarelli, C., and Levy, A. 1986. Cross-border deposits and monetary aggregates in the transition to EMU. *Journal of Policy Modelling*, 16: 29-54.

Aoki, M. 1977. *Optimization of Stochastic Systems*. New York: Academic Press.

Archibald, G. C., and Lipsey, R. G. 1958. Monetary and value theory: A critique of Lange and Patinkin. *Review of Economic Studies*, 26: 1-22.

Arrow, K. J. 1964. The role of securities in the optimal allocaton of risk-bearing. *Review of Economic Studies*, 31: 91-96.

—— 1974. General economic equilibrium: purpose, analytic techniques, collective choice. *American Economic Review*, 64(3): 253-72.

—— and Debreu, G. 1954. Existence of an equilibrium for a competitive economy. *Econometrica*, 22: 265-90.

—— and Hahn, F. H. 1971. *General Competitive Analysis*. San Francisco: Holden-Day and Edinburgh: Oliver & Boyd.

Artis, M. J. 1996. Currency substitution in European financial markets, in *The Macroeconomics of International Currencies: Theory, Policy and Evidence*, ed. P. D. Mizen and E. J. Pentecost. Cheltenham: Edward Elgar.

Artis, M. J., Bladen-Hovell, R., and Zhang, W. 1993. A European money demand function, in *Policy Issues in the Operation of Currency Unions*, ed. P. R. Masson and M. P. Taylor. Cambridge: Cambridge University Press.

Artis, M. J. and Currie, D. A. 1981. Monetary and exchange rate targets: a case for conditionalizing. *Oxford Economic Papers*, Suppl. 33: 176-200.

Artis, M. J., and Lewis, M. K. 1974. The demand for money: stable or unstable? *The Banker*, 124: 239–47.

—— —— 1976. The demand for money in the UK: 1963–73. *Manchester School*, 44: 147–81.

—— —— 1981. *Monetary Control in the United Kingdom*. Oxford: Philip Allan.

—— —— 1984. How unstable is the demand for money in the UK? *Eco-nomica*, 51: 473–6.

—— —— 1991. *Money in Britain: Monetary Policy, Innovation and Europe*. Oxford: Philip Allan.

—— —— 1993. Après le déluge: monetary and exchange-rate policy in Britain and Europe. *Oxford Review of Economic Policy*, 9(3): 36–61; repr. in *Readings in Macroeconomics*, ed. J. Jenkinson, Oxford: Oxford University Press, 1996.

—— —— 1995. Has the EMS a future?, in *EMU After Maastricht: Transition or Revaluation*, ed. D. Currie and J. D. Whitley. London: Lothian Foundation Press.

—— Mizen, P. D., and Kontolemis, Z. 1998. Inflation targeting: what can the ECB learn from the recent experience of the Bank of England? *Economic Journal*, 108: 1810–25.

—— and Nobay A. R. 1969. Two aspects of the monetary debate. *National Institute Economic Review*, 49: 33–51.

Aschheim, J. 1961. *Techniques of Monetary Control*. Baltimore: Johns Hopkins University Press.

Baba, Y., Hendry, D. F., and Starr, R. M. 1992. The demand for M1 in the USA 1960–88. *Review of Economic Studies*, 59: 25–61.

Backhouse R. E. 1991. The debate over Milton Friedman's theoretical framework: an economist's view, Dept. of Economics Discussion Paper 91-22, University of Birmingham.

Backus, D. K., and Driffill, J. 1985. Inflation and reputation. *American Economic Review*, 75(3): 530–8.

Bade, R., and Parkin M. 1985. *Central Bank Laws and Monetary Policy*. Depratment of Economics, University of Western Ontario, mimeo.

Bailey, M. J. 1956. The welfare costs of inflationary finance. *Journal of Political Economy*, 64(2): 93–110.

—— 1971. *National Income and the Price Level* 2nd Edn. New York: McGraw-Hill.

Ball, L. 1997. Efficient Rules for Monetary Policy, *NBER Working Paper*, 5952, March.

—— 1998. Policy Rules for Open Economies, Research Discussion Paper (RDP9806). Sydney, Reserve Bank of Australia.

Bananian, K., Laney, L. O., and Willett, T. D. 1983. Central bank independence: an international comparison. *Economic Review*. Federal Reserve Bank of Dallas, March, 1–22.

Bank for International Settlements. 1986. *Recent Innovations in International Banking*. Basle: Bank for International Settlements.

Bank of England. 1988. *Bank of England Operations in the Sterling Money Market.* London: Bank of England.

Barnett, W. A. 1980. Economic monetary aggregates: an application of index number and aggregation theory. *Journal of Econometrics*, 14(1): 11–48.

—— 1982. The optimal level of monetary aggregation. *Journal of Money, Credit and Banking*, 14: 687–710.

—— 1997. Which road leads to stable money demand? *Economic Journal*, 107: 1171–85.

—— Barr, D. G., and Cuthbertson, K. 1990. Modelling the flow of funds with an application to the demand for liquid assets by the UK personal sector, in *Economic Modelling at the Bank of England*. London: Chapman & Hall.

—— Fisher, D., and Serletis, A. 1992. Consumer theory and the demand for money. *Journal of Economic Literature*, 30(4): 2086–119.

—— Offenbacher, E. K., and Spindt, P. A. 1981. New concepts of aggregated money, *Journal of Finance*, 36(2): 497–505.

—— —— —— 1984. The new divisia monetary aggregates. *Journal of Political Economy*, 92(6): 1049–85.

Barr, D. G., and Cuthbertson, K. 1991. Neoclassical consumer demand theory and the demand for money. *Economic Journal*, 101: 855–76.

—— —— 1992. An interdependent error feedback model of UK company sector asset demands. *Journal of Money, Credit and Banking*, 24(1): 83–95.

Barro, R. J. 1976. Rational expectations and the role of monetary policy. *Journal of Monetary Economics*, 2, (Jan): 1–32.

—— 1977. Unanticipated monetary growth and unemployment in the United States. *American Economic Review*, 67: 101–15.

Barro, R. J. 1978. Unanticipated money, output and the price level in the United States. *Journal of Political Economy*, 86: 549–80.

Barro, R. J. 1981. *Money, Expectations and Business Cycles: Essays in Macroeconomics*. New York: Academic Press.

—— and Gordon, D. B. 1983*a*. A positive theory of monetary policy in a natural-rate model. *Journal of Political Economy*, 91(4): 589–610.

—— —— 1983*b*. Rules, discretion and reputation in a model of monetary policy. *Journal of Monetary Economics*, 12(1): 101–21.

—— and Santomero, A. M. 1972. Household money holdings and the demand deposit rate. *Journal of Money, Credit and Banking*, 4: 397–413.

Batini, N., and Haldane, A. G. 1998. Forward-looking rules for monetary policy. *NBER Conference on Monetary Policy Rules*, Islamorada, Florida, Jan.

Batts, J., and Dowling, M. J. 1984. The stability of the demand-for-money function in the United Kingdom: 1880–1975, *Quarterly Review of Economics and Business*, 24: 37–48.

Baumol, W. J. 1952. The transactions demand for cash: an inventory theoretic approach. *Quarterly Journal of Economics*, 66: 545–56.

Bean, C. 1983. Targeting nominal income: an appraisal. *Economic Journal*, 93: 806–19.

—— 1998. The new UK monetary arrangement: a view from the literature. *Economic Journal*, 108: 1795–809.

Bekx, P., and Tullio, G. 1989. A note on the European Monetary System, and the determination of the DM-dollar exchange rate. *Cahiers Economiques de Bruxelles*, 123, 3ème trimestre, 329–43.

Belongia, M. T. 1996. Measurement matters: some recent results in monetary economics re-examined. *Journal of Political Economy*, 104(5): 1065–83.

—— and Chalfant, J. A. 1989. The changing empirical definition of money: some estimates from a model of the demand for money substitutes. *Journal of Political Economy*, 97(2): 387–97.

—— and Chrystal, K. A. 1991. An admissible monetary aggregate for the United Kingdom. *Review of Economics and Statistics*, 73(3): 491–502.

Bergstrand, J. H., and Bundt, T. P. 1990. Currency substitution and monetary autonomy: the foreign demand for US demand deposits. *Journal of International Money and Finance*, 9: 325–34.

Berk, J. M. 1998. Money transmission: what do we know and how can we use it? *Banca Nazionale del Lavoro Quarterly Review*, 205 (June): 145–70.

Bernanke, B., and Gertler, M. 1995. Inside the black box: the credit channel of monetary policy transmission. *Journal of Economic Perspectives*, 9: 27–48.

—— and Mihov, I. 1997. What does the Bundesbank target? *European Economic Review*, 41: 1025–53.

—— and Mishkin, F. S. 1997. Inflation targeting: a new framework for monetary policy. *Journal of Economic Perspectives*, 11(2): 97–116.

—— and Woodford, M. 1997. Inflation forecasts and monetary policy. *Journal of Money, Credit and Banking*, 29: 653–84.

Bilson, J. F. O. 1978. The monetary approach to the exchange rate: some empirical evidence. *International Monetary Fund Staff Papers*, 25: 48–75.

Bird, G. 1987. *International Macroeconomics*. London: Macmillan.

Black, F. 1970. Banking and interest rates in a world without money. *Journal of Bank Research*, 1: 9–20.

—— 1975. Bank funds management in an efficient market. *Journal of Financial Economics*, 2: 323–39; repr. in *Financial Intermediaries: The International Library of Critical Writings in Economics*, 43, ed. M. K. Lewis, Cheltenham: Edward Elgar, 1995.

—— and Scholes, M. 1973. The pricing of options and corporate liabilities. *Journal of Political Economy*, 81: 637–55.

Black, S. W. 1977. *Floating Exchange Rates and National Economic Policy*. New Haven, Conn.: Yale University Press.

Blanchard, O., and Summers, L. 1986. Hysteresis and the European unemployment problem. *National Bureau of Economic Research Macroeconomics Annual*, 2: 263–303. Cambridge, Mass.

Blanchard, O., and Watson, M. W. 1982. Bubbles, rational expectations and financial markets, in *Crisis in Economic and Financial Structure*, ed. E. Watchel. Lexington, Mass.: Lexington Books.

Blaug, M. 1968. *Economic Theory in Retrospect*, 2nd ed. London: Heinemann Educational Books.

—— Eltis, W., O'Brien, D., Patinkin, D., Skidelsky, R., and Wood, G. E. 1995. *The Quantity Theory of Money: From Locke to Keynes and Friedman*. Aldershot: Elgar.

Bleaney, M. F. 1993. The formal analysis of risk-loving behaviour in financial markets. *Revista Internazionale di Scienza Economiche a Commerciali*, 40: 909–13.

Blinder, A. 1998. *Central Banking in Theory and Practice*. Cambridge, Mass.: MIT Press.

—— and Maccini, L. 1991. Taking stock: a critical assessment of recent research in inventories. *Journal of Economic Perspectives*, 5: 73–96.

Bloomfield, A. I. 1959. *Monetary Policy under the International Gold Standard: 1880–1914*. New York: Federal Reserve Bank of New York.

Bordo, M. D., and Choudhri, E. U. 1982. Currency substitution and the demand for money: some evidence for Canada. *Journal of Money, Credit and Banking*, 14: 48–57.

Borio, C. E. V. 1997. The implementation of monetary policy in industrial countries: a survey. *BIS Economic Papers*, 47 (July).

Boughton, J. M. 1979. Demand for money in major OECD countries, *OECD Economic Outlook*, Occasional Studies, Jan.

—— 1991. Long-run money demand in large industrial countries. *International Monetary Fund Staff Papers*, 38: 1–32.

—— and Tavlas, G. S. 1990. Modelling money demand in large industrial countries: buffer stock and error-correction approaches. *Journal of Policy Modelling*, 12: 433–61.

Brainard, W. C. 1967. Uncertainty and the effectiveness of monetary policy. *American Economic Review, Papers and Proceedings*: 57(2): 411–25.

—— 1976. Comments and discussion on

Goldfield, 1976, in *Brookings Papers on Economic Activity*, 3: 732–6.

Branson, W. H. 1977. Asset markets and relative prices in exchange rate determination. *Sozialwissenschaftliche Annalen*, 1: 69–89.

—— and Henderson, D. W. 1985. The specification and influence of asset markets, in *Handbook of International Economics*, Vol. ii, ed. R. W. Jones and P. B. Kenen. Amsterdam: North-Holland.

Bresciani-Turroni, C. 1931. *The Economics of Inflation: A Study of Currency Depreciation in Post-War Germany 1914–1923*; trans. London: Allen & Unwin, 1937.

Brigden, A., and Mizen, P. D. 1999. Money, credit and investment in the UK industrial and commercial companies sector. *Bank of England Working Paper* 100.

Brittain, B. 1981. International currency substitution and the apparent instability of velocity in some western European economies and the US. *Journal of Money, Credit and Banking*, 13: 135–55.

Brittan, S. 1981. How to end the monetarist controversy. *Hobart Paper* 90. London: Institute of Economic Affairs.

Britton, E., Fisher, P., and Whitley, J. 1998. The inflation report projections: understanding the fan chart. *Bank of England Quarterly Bulletin*, 38 (Feb.): 30–7.

Brock, W. A. 1974. Money and growth: the case of long-run perfect foresight. *International Economic Review*, 15: 570–7.

—— 1990. Overlapping generations models with money and transactions costs, in *Handbook of Monetary Economics*, vol. i, ed. B. M. Friedman and F. H. Hahn, 2nd reprint, Amsterdam: North-Holland, 1996.

—— and Holmes, C. H. 1997. A rational route to randomness. *Econometrica*, 65(5): 1059–95.

Bronfenbrenner, M., and Mayer, T. 1960. Liquidity functions in the American economy. *Econometrica*, 28: 810–34.

Brown, A. J. 1939. Interest, prices and the demand for idle money. *Oxford Economic Papers*, 2 (May): 46–69.

Bruce N., and Purvis D. D. 1985. The specification and influence of goods and factor markets in open-economy macro-economic models, in *Handbook of*

International Economics, ii, ed. R. W. Jones and P. B. Kenan. Amsterdam : Elsevier.

Brunner, K. 1968. The role of money and monetary policy. *Federal Reserve Bank of St Louis Review* (July): 8–24.

—— 1973. A diagrammatic exposition of the money supply process. *Schweizerischen Zeitschrift für Volkswirtschaft und Statistik,* 4 Dec.: 481–533.

—— 1987. Money supply, in *New Palgrave Dictionary of Economics,* ed. P. Newman, M. Milgate, and J. Eatwell. London: Macmillan.

—— 1992. Money supply, in *New Palgrave Dictionary of Money and Finance, ii,* ed. P. Newman, M. Milgate, and J. Eatwell. London: Macmillan.

—— and Meltzer, A. H. 1976. An aggregative theory for a closed economy, in *Monetarism,* ed. J. L. Stein, Amsterdam: North-Holland.

—— —— 1987. Money supply. *Working Paper* GPB87-14, University of Rochester.

Bryan, M. F., and Cecchetti, S. G. 1993. The consumer price index as a measure of inflation. *Economic Review of the Federal Reserve Bank of Cleveland,* 29: 15–24.

—— —— and Wiggins, R. L. 1998. Efficient inflation estimation. *NBER Working Paper,* 6183.

Buchanan, J. M. 1962. Predictability: the criterion of monetary constitutions, in *In Search of a Monetary Constitution,* ed. L. B. Yeager. Cambridge, Mass.: Harvard University Press.

—— Burton, J., and Wagner, R. E. 1978. *The Consequences of Mr Keynes.* Hobart Paper 78. London: Institute of Economic Affairs.

Buckley, A. 1986. *Multinational Finance.* Oxford: Philip Allan.

Budd, A., and Holly, S. 1986. Economic viewpoint: does broad money matter? *London Business School Economic Outlook 1985–89,* 10: 16–22.

Buiter, W. H., and Miller, M. H. 1981. Monetary policy and international competitiveness: the problems of adjustment. *Oxford Economic Papers,* Suppl. 33: 143–75.

Burdekin, R. C., and Willett, T. D. 1990. Central bank reform: the federal reserve in international perspective, mimeo.

Burger, A. E. 1971. *The Money Supply Process.* Belmont, Calif.: Wadsworth.

Burns, J. M. 1971. On the effects of financial innovations. *Quarterly Review of Economics and Business,* 11(2): 83–95.

Burstein M. L. 1963. *Money* Cambridge, Mass.: Schenkman.

Caesar, R. 1994. Central banks and governments: issues, traditions, lessons. Discussion paper 94/1994, University of Hohenheim.

Cagan, P. 1956. The monetary dynamics of hyperinflation, in *Studies in the Quantity Theory of Money,* ed. M. Friedman. Chicago: University of Chicago Press.

—— 1958. Why do we use money in open market operations? *Journal of Political Economy,* 66: 34–46.

—— 1965. *Determination and Effects of Changes in the Stock of Money 1865–1960.* New York: National Bureau of Economic Research.

Calvo, G. A., and Rodriguez, C. A. 1977. A model of exchange rate determination under currency substitution and rational expectations. *Journal of Political Economy,* 85: 617–24.

—— and Vegh, C. A. 1992. Currency substitution in developing countries: an introduction. *Revista de Análisis Económico,* 7: 3–28.

—— —— 1997. From currency substitution to dollarization and beyond: analytical and policy issues, in *Essays on Money, Inflation and Output,* ed. G. A. Calvo. Cambridge, Mass.: MIT Press.

Cantillon, R. 1734. *Essai sur la nature du commerce en général,* ed. with English trans. H. Higgs. London: Macmillan, 1931.

Canzoneri, M. 1985. Monetary policy games and the role of private information. *American Economic Review,* 75(4): 1056–70.

Capie, F. 1985. Conditions in which hyperinflation has appeared. *Carnegie-Rochester Conference Series on Public Policy,* Apr.

Cargill, T. F. 1989. *Central Bank Independence and Regulatory Responsibilities: The Bank of Japan and the Federal Reserve,* Monograph Series in Finance and Economics, 21. New York: Salomon Brothers Center.

Carr, J., and Darby, M. R. 1981. The role of money supply shocks in the short-run demand for money. *Journal of Monetary Economics*, 8: 183–99.

Carr, J., Darby, M. R. and Thornton, D. L. 1985. Monetary anticipations and the demand for money: reply. *Journal of Monetary Economics*, 16: 251–7.

Cassard, M., Lane, T. D., and Masson, P. R. 1997. Core-ERM money demand and effects on inflation. *Manchester School* 65, 1–24.

Cassel, G. 1922. *Money and Foreign Exchange after 1914*. London: Macmillan.

Chadha, J. S., Haldane, A.G., and Janssen, N. G. J. 1998. Shoe-leather costs reconsidered, *Bank of England Working Paper* 86.

Chambers, S. P. (1934), 'Fluctuations in capital and the demand for money', *Review of Economic Studies*, 2: 38–50.

Chatterjee, S. 1999. Real business cycles: a legacy of countercyclical policies? *Business Review*, Jan./Feb. Philadelphia: Federal Reserve Bank of Philadelphia.

Chatterji, M. 1989. Themes in public policy. Inaugural lecture, University of Dundee, 8 Nov.

Chick, V. 1986. The evolution of the banking system and the theory of saving, investment and interest. *Economies et Sociétés*, 20: 111–26.

Chow, G. 1966. On the long-run and short-run demand for money. *Journal of Political Economy*, 74: 111–31.

—— 1977. *Analysis and Control of Dynamic Economic Systems*. New York: Wiley.

Chrystal, K. A., and MacDonald, R. 1994. Exchange rates and financial innovation: the sterling dollar rate 1972–90. *Federal Reserve Bank of St Louis Review*, 76(2): 73–109.

—— and Mizen, P. D. 2000a. A dynamic model of consumption, money and lending for the household sector, *Bank of England Working Paper*, forthcoming.

—— —— 2000b. Other financial corporations: Cinderella or ugly sister of empirical monetary economics, *Bank of England Working Paper*, forthcoming.

Cipolla, C. M. 1956. *Money, Price and Civilization in the Mediterranean World: Fifth to Seventeenth Century*. Princeton: Princeton University Press.

Clower, R. W. 1965. The Keynesian counterrevolution: a theoretical appraisal, in *The Theory of Interest Rates*, ed. F. H. Hahn and F. Brechling. London: Macmillan.

—— 1967. A reconsideration of the microfoundations of monetary theory. *Western Economic Journal*, 6: 1–9.

—— (ed.) 1969. *Monetary Theory*. Harmondsworth, Middx: Penguin

Coghlan, R. T. 1978. A transactions demand for money. *Bank of England Quarterly Bulletin*, 18: 48–60.

Cooper, R. N. 1981. Comment on Sachs. *Brookings Papers on Economic Activity*, 1: 269–82.

—— 1982. The gold standard: historical facts and future prospects. *Brookings Papers on Economic Activity*, 1: 1–45.

Cordon, W. M. 1983. The logic of the international monetary non-system, in *Reflections in a Troubled World Economy*, ed. F. Machlup, G. Fels, and H. Miller-Groeling. London: Macmillan.

Corrigan, E. G. 1982. Are banks special? *Federal Reserve Bank of Minneapolis Annual Report*, 2–18; repr. in *Financial Intermediaries: The International Library of Critical Writings in Economics*, 43, ed. M. K. Lewis. Cheltenham: Edward Elgar, 1995.

Courakis, A. S. 1978. Serial correlation and a Bank of England study of the demand for money: an exercise in measurement without theory. *Economic Journal*, 88: 537–48.

Covick O. E. 1974. The quantity theory of drink — a restatement. *Australian Economic Papers*, Dec.: 171–7

Cowen, T., and Kroszner, R. 1987. The development of the new monetary economics. *Journal of Political Economy*, 95: 576–90.

Cramp, A. B. 1962. Financial intermediaries and monetary control. *Economica*, 29: 143–51.

Crockett A., and Goldstein M. 1987. *Strengthening the International Monetary System: Exchange Rates, Surveillance and Objective Indicators*. Washington, DC: International Monetary Fund.

Cross, R. (ed.) 1988. *Unemployment Hysteresis and the Natural Rate Hypothesis*. Oxford: Blackwell.

Croushoure, D. 1990. Money in the utility function: an adequate microfoundation of money? Federal Reserve Bank of Philadelphia, mimeo.

Cuddington, J. T. 1983. Currency substitution, capital mobility and money demand. *Journal of International Money and Finance*, 2: 111–33.

—— 1989. Review of *Currency Substitutability: Theory and Evidence for Latin America* by V.A. Canto, and G. Nickelsberg (Boston: Kluwer). *Journal of Money, Credit and Banking*, 21(1): 267–71.

Cukierman, A. 1992. *Central Bank Strategy, Credibility and Independence*. Cambridge, Massachusetts: MIT Press.

Cukierman, A., and Liviatan, N. 1991. Optimal accommodation by strong policymakers under incomplete information. *Journal of Monetary Economics*, 27(1): 99–127.

Culbertson J. M. 1958. Intermediaries and monetary theory: a criticism of the Gurley-Shaw theory. *American Economic Review*, 48 : 119–31.

Currie, D. A. 1984. Monetary overshooting and the exchange rate. *Manchester School of Economic and Social Studies*, 52: 28–48.

Cuthbertson, K. 1985. Sterling bank lending to UK industrial and commercial companies. *Oxford Bulletin of Economics and Statistics*, 47: 91–118.

—— 1988. The demand for M1: a forward-looking buffer stock model. *Oxford Economic Papers*, 40: 110–31.

—— 1991. The encompassing implications of feedforward versus feedback mechanisms: a reply to Hendry. *Oxford Economic Papers*, 43: 344–50.

—— and Taylor, M. P. 1986. Monetary anticipation and the demand for money in the UK: testing rationality in the shock-absorber hypothesis. *Journal of Applied Econometrics*, 1: 355–65.

—— —— 1987a. Buffer stock money: an appraisal, in *The Operation and Regulation of Financial Markets*, ed. D. A. Currie, C. A. E. Goodhart, and D. T. Llewellyn. London: Macmillan.

—— —— 1987b. The demand for money: a dynamic rational expectations model. *Economic Journal*, (Suppl.), 97: 65–76.

—— —— 1987c. Monetary anticipations and the demand for money: some evidence for the UK. *Weltwirtschaftliches Archiv*, 123: 509–20.

—— —— 1992. A comparison of the rational expectations and general-to-specific approaches to modelling the demand for M1. *Manchester School*, 60: 1–22.

David, P. 1985. CLIO and the economics of QWERTY. *American Economic Review, Papers and Proceedings*, 75: 332–7.

Davidson, J., Hendry, D. F., Srba, F., and Yeo, S. 1978. Econometric modelling of the aggregate time-series relationships bet-ween consumers' expenditure and income in the UK. *Economic Journal*, 88: 661–92.

Davidson, P. 1978a. Why money matters: lessons from a half-century of monetary theory. *Journal of Post-Keynesian Economics*, 1(1): 46–70.

—— 1978b. *Money and the Real World*, 2nd edn. London: Macmillan.

Davis, K. T., and Lewis, M. K. 1980. *Monetary Policy in Australia*. Melbourne: Longman Cheshire.

Debreu, G. 1959. *Theory of Value: An Axiomatic Analysis of Economic Equilibrium*, Cowles Foundation for Research in Economics, Monograph 17. New York: Wiley.

Dewald, W. G. 1975. Banking and the economy. College of Administrative Science, University of Ohio, mimeo.

—— and Lindsey, D. E. 1972. A critique of standard money supply models, Report 7216. Division for Economic Research, Dept. of Economics, Ohio State University.

Diamond, D. W. 1984. Financial intermedia-tion and delegated monitoring. *Review of Economic Studies*, 51: 393–414, repr. in *Financial Intermediaries, International Library of Critical Writings in Economics*, 43, ed. M. K. Lewis. Cheltenham: Edward Elgar, 1995.

Dillard, D. 1955. The theory of a monetary economy, in *Post-Keynesian Economics*, ed. K. K. Kurihara. London: Allen & Unwin.

Divisia, F. 1925. L'indice Monetaire et la Theorie de la Monnaie. *Revue d'Economie Politique*, 39: 980–1008.

Dornbusch, R. 1976. Expectations and exchange rate dynamics. *Journal of Political Economy*, 84(6): 1161–76.

Dow, J. C. R. 1958. The economic effect of monetary policy 1945-57. *Committee on the Working of the Monetary System, Principal*

Memoranda of Evidence, 3, HMSO 1966: 76–105.

Dow, J. C. R., and Saville, I. D. 1988. *A Critique of Monetary Policy*. Oxford: Oxford University Press.

Dowd, K. 1988. Private money: the path to monetary stability. *Hobart Paper* 112. London: Institute of Economic Affairs.

—— 1996. *Competition and Finance: a Reinterpretation of Financial and Monetary Economics*. London: Macmillan.

—— and Lewis, M.K. (eds) 1992. *Current Issues in Financial and Monetary Economics*, London: Macmillan.

Drake, L. M. 1992. The substitutability of financial assets in the UK: the implications for monetary aggregation. *Manchester School*, 60(3): 221–48.

—— and Chrystal, K. A. 1994. Company-sector money demand: new evidence on the existence of a stable long-run relationship for the United Kingdom. *Journal of Money, Credit and Banking*, 26(3): 479–94.

—— —— 1997. Personal sector money demand in the UK. *Oxford Economic Papers*, 49(1): 188–206.

Driffill, J. 1988. Macroeconomic policy games with incomplete information: a survey. *European Economic Review*, 32(2–3): 513–41.

—— Mizon, G., and Ulph, A. 1990. The costs of inflation, in *Handbook of Monetary Economics*, ed. F. H. Hahn and B. M. Friedman. Amsterdam: North-Holland.

Durand, D. 1942. *Basic Yields of Corporate Bonds 1900–1942*. Technical Paper 3, New York: National Bureau of Economic Research.

Edgeworth, F. Y. 1895. Thoughts on monetary reform. *Economic Journal* 5: 434–51.

Eichengreen, B. (ed.) 1985. *The Gold Standard in Theory and History*. New York: Methuen.

—— 1992. Is Europe an optimum currency area? CEPR Discussion Paper 478, in *The European Community After 1992: The View from Outside*. London: Macmillan.

—— 1993. International monetary arrangements for the 21st century, *Working paper* cg3-021, Center for International and Development Economics Research. Berkeley and Los Angeles: University of California Press.

Eijffinger, S., and Schaling, E. 1992. Central Bank Independence: Searching for the Philosophers' Stone. Suerf Colloquium, Berlin, mimeo.

—— —— 1993. Central bank independence in twelve industrial countries. *Banca Nazionale del Lavoro Quarterly Review*, 184 (Mar.): 49–89.

—— and De Haan, J. The political economy of central bank independence. *Special Papers in International Economics*. 19. Princeton: Princeton University.

Eika, K. H., Ericsson, N. R., and Nymoen, R. 1996. Hazards in implementing a monetary conditions index. *Oxford Bulletin of Economics and Statistics*, 54(4): 765–90.

Eltis, W. A. 1989. The obstacles to European Monetary Union, NEDO, mimeo.

Engel, C., and Hakkio, C. S. 1993. Exchange rate regimes and volatility. *Federal Reserve Bank of Kansas City Economic Review*, 3rd quarter, 43–58.

—— and Rogers, J. H. 1996. How wide is the border? *American Economic Review*, 86: 1112–25.

Engle, R. F., and Granger, C. W. J. 1987. Cointegration and error correction: representation, estimation and testing. *Econometrica*, 55: 251–76.

Eshag, E. 1963. *From Marshall to Keynes: An Essay on the Monetary Theory of the Cambridge School*. Oxford: Blackwell.

Estrella, A., and Mishkin, F. 1998. Rethinking the role of the NAIRU in monetary policy: implications of model formulation and uncertainty, NBER, mimeo.

European Association for Banking History e.V. 1994. *Handbook on the History of European Banks*. Aldershot, Hants: Edward Elgar.

Ewis, N. A., and Fisher, D. 1984. The translog utility function and the demand for money in the United States. *Journal of Money, Credit and Banking*, 16(1): 34–52.

Fama, E. F. 1980. Banking in the theory of finance. *Journal of Monetary Economics*, 6: 39–57.

—— 1983. Financial intermediation and price level control. *Journal of Monetary Economics*, 12: 7–28.

—— 1985. What's different about banks? *Journal of Monetary Economics*, 15: 29–39; repr.

in *Financial Intermediaries*, International Library of Critical Writings in Economics, 43, ed. M. K. Lewis. Cheltenham: Edward Elgar, 1995.

Feenstra, R. C. 1986. Functional equivalence between utility costs and the utility of money. *Journal of Monetary Economics*, 17: 271–91.

—— 1992. Money in the utility function, in *New Palgrave Dictionary of Money and Finance, ii*, ed. P. Newman, M. Milgate, and J. Eatwell. London: Macmillan.

Feige, E. L. 1967. Expectations and adjustments in the monetary sector. *American Economic Review Papers and Proceedings*, 57: 462–73.

Feldman, G. D. 1993. *The Great Disorder: Politics, Economics and Society in the German Inflation 1914–1924*. New York and Oxford: Oxford University Press.

Feldstein, M. 1992. The recent failure of US monetary policy. *NBER Working Paper* 4236. New York: National Bureau of Economic Research.

Fellner, W., and Somers, H. 1941. Alternative approaches to interest theory. *Review of Economics and Statistics*, 23: 43–8.

—— —— 1949. Notes on 'stocks' and 'flows' in monetary interest theory. *Review of Economics and Statistics*, 31: 145–6.

Filosa, R. 1995. Money demand stability and currency substitution in six European countries. BIS Working Paper 30. Basle: Bank for International Settlements.

Finnerty, J. D. 1988. Financial engineering in corporate finance: an overview. *Financial Management*, 17(4): 14–33.

Fischer, S. 1974. Money and the production function. *Economic Inquiry*, 12: 518–33.

—— 1977. Long-term contracts, rational expectations and the optimum money supply rule. *Journal of Political Economy*, 85: 191–205.

—— 1979. Capital accumulation on the transition path in a monetary optimizing model. *Econometrica*, 47: 1433–9.

—— 1994. *Modern Central Banking*. Tercentenary of the Bank of England, Central Banking Symposium, June.

—— and Cooper, J. P. 1973. Stabilisation policy and lags. *Journal of Political Economy*, 81: (4): 847–77.

Fisher, I. 1911a. *Elementary Principles of Economics*. New York: Macmillan.

—— 1911b. *The Purchasing Power of Money*, (revised edn., 1913). New York: Macmillan.

—— 1920 *Stabilizing the Dollar* New York: Macmillan

—— 1923. The business cycle – largely a 'Dance of the Dollar'. *Journal of the American Statistical Association*, 18: 1024–8.

—— 1925. Our unstable dollar and the so-called business cycle. *Journal of the Am-erican Statistical Association*, 20: 179–202.

—— 1930. *The Theory of Interest*. New York: Macmillan

—— 1933. The debt-deflation theory of great depression. *Econometrica*, 1: 337–57.

—— 1934. *Stable Money: A History of the Movement*. New York: Adelphi.

Fisher, P., and Vega, J. L. 1993. An empirical analysis of M4 in the United Kingdom. *Bank of England Working Paper* 21.

Frankel, J. A. 1979. On the mark: a theory of floating exchange rates based on real interest rate differentials. *American Economic Review*, 69: 610–22.

—— 1983. Monetary and portfolio balance models of exchange rate determination, in *Economic Interdependence and Flexible Exchange Rates*, ed. J. S. Bhandari and B. H. Putnam. Cambridge, Mass.: MIT Press.

—— and Froot, K. 1986. A tale of fundamen-talists and chartists, *NBER Working Report 1854*. New York: National Bureau of Economic Research.

Frenkel, J. A. 1976. A monetary approach to the exchange rate: doctrinal aspects and empirical evidence. *Scandinavian Journal of Economics*, 78: 169–91.

—— 1977. The forward exchange rate, expectations and the demand for money: the German hyperinflation. *American Economic Review*, 67, (Sept.): 653–70.

—— and Razin, A. 1987. *Fiscal Policies and the World Economy*. Cambridge, Mass.: MIT Press.

Friedman, B. M. 1975. Targets, instruments and indicators of monetary policy. *Journal of Monetary Economics*, 1 (Oct.): 443–73.

—— 1993. The role of judgement and discretion in the conduct of monetary policy: consequences of changing financial markets, *Working Paper 4599*. New York: National Bureau of Economic Research.

Friedman, B. M., and Hahn, F. H. (eds.) 1990. *Handbook of Monetary Economics*, ii, 2nd reprint. Amsterdam: North-Holland, 1996.

Friedman, D. 1982. Gold, paper or . . . .: is there a better money? *CATO Institute of Policy Analysis*, Sept., 23.

Friedman M. 1948. A monetary and fiscal framework for economic stability. *American Economic Review*, 38: 245–64.

—— 1953a. The methodology of positive economics, in *Essays in Positive Economics*. Chicago: University of Chicago Press.

—— 1953b. The case for flexible exchange rates, in *Essays in Positive Economics*. Chicago: University of Chicago Press.

—— 1956. The quantity theory of money: a restatement, in *Studies in the Quantity Theory of Money*, ed. M. Friedman. Chicago: University of Chicago.

—— 1958. The relationship of prices to economic stability and growth. *85th Congress, second session, Joint Economic Committee Print*. Washington, DC: US Government Printing Office.

—— 1959. *A Program for Monetary Stability*. New York: Fordham University.

—— 1961. The lag in effect of monetary policy. *Journal of Political Economy*, 69(5); in *The Optimum Quantity of Money and Other Essays*. London: Macmillan, 1969.

—— 1962. *Price Theory: a Provisional Text*. Chicago: Aldine.

—— 1963. Should there be an independent monetary authority?, in *In Search of a Monetary Constitution*, ed. L. Yeager. Cambridge, Mass.: Harvard University Press.

—— 1964. The monetary studies of the National Bureau; The National Bureau enters its 45th year, 44th Annual Report, National Bureau of Economic Research, Repr. in *The Optimum Quantity of Money and Other Essays*. London: Macmillan.

—— 1966. Interest rates and the demand for money. *Journal of Law and Economics*, 9: 71–85.

—— 1968a. The role of monetary policy. *American Economic Review*, 58(1): 1–17.

—— 1968b. Money: the quantity theory. *International Encyclopedia of the Social Sciences*, 10. London: Macmillan.

—— 1969a. The Euro-dollar market: some first principles. *Morgan Guaranty Survey*; (Oct.): 4–14. Repr. in *The Globalization of Financial Services*, ed. M. K. Lewis. Cheltenham: Edward Elgar, 1999.

—— 1969b. *The Optimum Quantity of Money and Other Essays*. Chicago: Aldine.

—— 1970a. Controls on interest rates paid by banks. *Journal of Money, Credit and Banking*, 2: 16–32.

—— 1970b. A theoretical framework for monetary analysis. *Journal of Political Economy*, 78: 193–238.

—— 1970c. *The Counter-Revolution in Monetary Theory*, Occasional Paper 33. London: Institute of Economic Affairs.

—— 1971. *A Theoretical Framework for Monetary Analysis*, NBER Occasional Paper 112. New York: National Bureau of Economic Research.

—— 1973. *Money and Economic Development*, Horowitz Lectures of 1972. New York: Praeger.

—— 1976. Comment on Tobin and Buiter, in *Monetarism*, ed. J. L. Stein. Amsterdam: North-Holland.

Friedman M. 1980. Memorandum on monetary policy in Treasury and Civil Service Committee, *Memoranda on Monetary Policy*, Series 1979–80. London: HMSO.

—— 1985. Monetary policy in a fiat world. *Bank of Japan Monetary and Economic Studies*, 3(2): 11–18.

—— 1986. The resource costs of irredeemable paper money. *Journal of Political Economy*, 94: 642–7.

—— 1987. Quantity theory of money, in *The New Palgrave Dictionary of Economics*, ed. J. Eatwell, M. Milgate, and P. Newman. London: Macmillan.

—— and Meiselman, D. 1963. The relative stability of monetary velocity and the investment multiplier in the United States, 1897–1958, in *Stabilization Policies, Papers prepared for the Commission on Money and Credit*. Englewood Cliffs: Prentice-Hall.

—— and Schwartz, A. J. 1963a. Money and business cycles. *Review of Economics and Statistics*, 45: 32–64.

Friedman M., and Schwartz, A. J. 1963b. *A Monetary History of the United States 1867–1960*. Princeton: National Bureau of Economic Research.

—— —— 1970. *Monetary Statistics of the United States*. Princeton: National Bureau of Economic Research.

—— —— 1982. *Monetary Trends in the United States and the United Kingdom: Their Relation to Income, Prices and Interest Rates 1867–1975*. Chicago: University of Chicago.

Frisch, R. 1933. Propagation problems and impulse problems in dynamic economics, in *Economic Essays in Honour of Gustav Cassel*: 171–205. London: Allen & Unwin.

Froot, K. A., and Frankel, J. A. 1989. Forward Discount Bias: Is it an Exchange Rate Premium? *Quarterly Journal of Economics*, 104: 139–161.

Galbraith, J. K. 1952. *American Capitalism: The Concept of Countervailing Power*. Boston: Houghton Mifflin.

Gallarotti, G. M. 1989. The classical gold standard as a spontaneous order. *CATO Institute Seventh Annual Monetary Conference*, Feb., Washington.

Gandolfi, A. E., and Lothian, J. R. 1976. The demand for money from the Great Depression to the present. *American Economic Review*, 66 (May): 46–51.

Garber, P. M., and Grilli, V. U. 1986. The Belmont-Morgan syndicate as an optimal investment banking contract. *European Economic Review*, 30: 649–77.

Garcia, G., and Pak, S. 1979. Some clues in the case of the missing money. *American Economic Review*, 69: 330–4.

Ghatak, S. 1983. *Monetary Economics in Developing Countries*. London: Macmillan.

Giddy, I. 1986. Assetless banking, in *Strategic Planning in International Banking,* ed. P. Savona and G. Sutija. London: Macmillan.

Giovannini, A. 1992. Bretton Woods and its precursors: rules versus discretion in the history of international monetary regimes. Discussion Paper 661, London: Centre for Economic Policy Research.

—— and Turtelboom, B. 1994. Currency substitution, in *Handbook of International Macroeconomics*, ed. F. van der Ploeg. Oxford: Blackwell.

Girton, L., and Roper, D. 1981. Theory and implications of currency substitution. *Journal of Money, Credit and Banking*, 13(1): 12–30.

Goldfeld, S. M. 1973. The demand for money revisited. *Brookings Papers on Economic Activity*, 3: 577–638.

—— 1976. The case of the missing money. *Brookings Papers on Economic Activity*, 3: 683–739.

—— and Sichel, D. E. 1987. Money demand: the effects of inflation and alternative adjustment mechanisms. *Review of Economics and Statistics*, 69: 511–15.

—— —— 1990. The demand for money, in *Handbook of Monetary Economics*, i, ed. B. M. Friedman and F. H. Hahn. Amsterdam: North-Holland.

Goldsmith, R. W. 1969. *Financial Structure and Economic Development*. New Haven, Conn.: Yale University Press.

Goodfriend, M. 1987. *Monetary Policy in Practice*. Richmond: Federal Reserve Bank of Richmond.

—— 1997. Monetary policy comes of age: a 20th century odyssey. *Federal Reserve Bank of Richmond Economic Survey*, 83(1): 1–22.

Goodhart, C. A. E. 1975. *Money, Information and Uncertainty*. London: Macmillan.

—— 1978. Monetary policy, in *Demand Management*, ed. M. Posner. London: Heinemann.

—— 1984. *Monetary Theory and Practice: The UK Experience*. London: Macmillan.

Goodhart, C. A. E. 1988. *The Evolution of Central Banks*. Cambridge, Mass.: MIT Press.

—— 1990. International financial linkages, LSE Financial Markets Group Special Paper, 21.

—— 1992. Monetary base, in *New Palgrave Dictionary of Economics*, ed. P. Newman, M. Milgate, and J. Eatwell. London: Macmillan.

—— 1994. What should central banks do? What should be their macroeconomic objectives and operations? *Economic Journal*, 104: 1424–36.

Goodhart, C. A. E. 1998. *1998 Keynes Lecture in Economics*, British Academy, London, 29 Oct.

—— and Crockett, A. D. 1970. The importance of money. *Bank of England Quarterly Bulletin*, 10: 159–98.

—— and Shoenmaker, D. 1996. Should the functions of monetary policy and banking supervision be separated? *Oxford Economic Papers*, 47(4): 539-60.

Gordon, R. J. 1984. The short-run demand for money: A reconsideration. *Journal of Money, Credit and Banking* 16(4): 403–34.

Granger, C. W. J., and Newbold, P. 1974. Spurious regressions in econometrics. *Journal of Econometrics*, 2: 111–20.

Graves, P. E. 1980. The velocity of money: evidence for the UK, 1911–1966. *Economic Inquiry* XVIII: 631–9.

Greenbaum, S. I., and Heywood, C.V. 1973. Secular change in financial services industry. *Journal of Money, Credit and Banking*, 5: 571–603.

Greenfield, R. L., and Yeager, L. B. 1983. A laissez-faire approach to monetary stability. *Journal of Money, Credit and Banking*, (Aug.): 302–15.

Greenspan, A. 1991. Opening remarks. *Policy Implications of Trade and Currency Zones.* Kansas City: Federal Reserve Bank of Kansas City.

—— 1997. Speech at Center for Economic Policy Research, Stanford University, 6 Sept.

Gregory, T. E. 1933. Money, in *Encyclopedia of the Social Sciences*, 10: 601–13. New York: Macmillan.

Grice, J., and Bennett, A. 1984. Wealth and the demand for £M3 in the UK 1963–78. *Manchester School*, 52: 239–71.

Griliches, Z. 1967. Distributed lags: a survey. *Econometrica*, 35: 16–49.

Grilli, V., Masciandaro, D., and Tabellini, G. 1991. Public financial policies in industrialized countries. *Economic Policy*, 13: 342–92.

Gurley, J. G., and Shaw, E. S. 1960. *Money in a Theory of Finance*. Washington, DC: Brookings Institution.

Guttentag, J. M., and Lindsay, R. 1968. The uniqueness of commercial banks. *Journal of Political Economy*, 76(5): 991–1014.

Haberler, G. 1961. A survey of international trade theory. *Special Papers in International Economics*, 1. Princeton: Princeton University Press.

Hacche, G. 1974. The demand for money in the UK: experience since 1971. *Bank of England Quarterly Bulletin*, 14: 284–305.

Hahn, F. H. 1965. On some problems of proving the existence of equilibrium in a monetary economy, in *The Theory of Interest Rates*, ed. F. H. Hahn and F. P. R. Brechling. London: Macmillan.

Hahn, F.H. 1973. *On the Notion of Equilibrium in Economics*. Cambridge: Cambridge University Press.

—— 1977. Keynesian economics and general equilibrium theory, in *Microeconomic Foundations of Macroeconomics*, ed. G. C. Harcourt. London: Macmillan.

—— 1982. *Money and Inflation*. Oxford: Blackwell.

Haldane, A. G. 1998. On inflation targeting in the UK. *Scottish Journal of Political Economy*, 45: 1–32.

Hall, R. E. 1982. *Inflation: Causes and Effects*. Chicago: University of Chicago Press for the National Bureau of Economic Research.

—— and Mankiw, N. G. 1994. Nominal income targeting, in *Monetary Policy*, ed. N. G. Mankiw. Chicago: University of Chicago Press.

Hall, S., Salmon, C., Yates, T., and Batini, N. 1998. Uncertainty and simple monetary policy rules: an illustration for the UK. *Bank of England Working Paper*, 96.

Hall, S. G., Henry, G. G. B., and Wilcox, J. 1989. The long-run determinants of UK monetary aggregates, *Bank of England Discussion Paper*, 41.

Hamburger, M. J. 1977. The demand for money in an open economy: Germany and the UK. *Journal of Monetary Economics*, 3: 25–40.

Hanke, S. H., and Schuler, K. 1991. Ruble reform: a lesson from Keynes. *Cato Journal*, 10: 655–66.

—— Jonung, L., and Schuler, K. 1993. *Russian Currency and Finance*. London: Routledge.

Hansen, A. H. 1949. *Monetary Theory and Fiscal Policy*. New York: McGraw-Hill.

—— 1953. *A Guide to Keynes.* New York: McGraw-Hill.

Harper I. R., and Coleman A. 1992. New monetary economics, in *New Palgrave Dictionary of Money and Finance,* iii ed. Newman, P. Milgate, M., and Eatwell, J. London: Macmillan.

Harris, L. 1985. *Monetary Theory.* Singapore: McGraw-Hill.

Harris, S. E. and others. 1951. The controversy over monetary policy. *Review of Economics and Statistics*, 33 (Aug.): 179–200.

Harrison, R. 1998. Monetary conditions indices: theory and evidence. Bank of England, mimeo.

Harrod, R. 1965. *Reforming the World's Money.* London: Macmillan.

—— 1969. *Money.* London: Macmillan.

Haubrich, J. G. 1996. Combining bank supervision and monetary policy. *Economic Commentary*, Federal Reserve Bank of Cleveland, (Nov.): 1–5.

Hawtrey, R. 1913. *Good and Bad Trade.* London: Constable.

—— 1923. *Monetary Reconstruction.* London: Longmans Green.

Hayek, F. 1976*a*. *The Denationalisation of Money,* Hobart Paper 70. London: Institute for Economic Affairs.

—— 1976*b*. Choice in currency—a way to stop inflation? Occasional Paper 48. London: Institute of Economic Affairs.

Heller, H. R. 1965. The demand for money: the evidence from the short-run data. *Quarterly Journal of Economics*, May, 79: 291–303.

Hendry, D. F. 1979. Predictive failure and econometric modelling in macroeconomics: the transactions demand for money, in *Economic Modelling*, ed. P. Ormerod. London: Heinemann.

—— 1985. Monetary economic myth and econometric reality. *Oxford Review of Economic Policy*, 1: 72–84.

—— and Ericsson, N. R. 1983. Assertion without empirical basis: an econometric appraisal of 'Monetary trends in . . . the United Kingdom' by M. Friedman and A. Schwartz. Bank of England Panel of Academic Consultants, Paper 22: 45–101.

—— —— 1991. An econometric analysis of UK money demand, in *Monetary Trends in the United States and the United Kingdom*, M. Friedman and A. J. Schwartz. *American Economic Review*, 81: 8–37.

—— and Mizon, G. 1978. Serial correlation as a convenient simplification, not a nuisance: a comment on a study of the demand for money by the Bank of England. *Economic Journal*, 88: 549–63.

Hicks, J. R. 1933. The application of mathematical methods to the theory of risk, presented at the Meeting of the Econometric Society in Leyden, Sept.–Oct. 1933.

—— 1935. A suggestion for simplifying the theory of money, *Econometrica*, (new series), 2: 1–19.

—— 1937. Mr Keynes and the 'Classics': A suggested interpretation. *Econometrica*, 5: 147–59.

—— 1939. *Value and Capital.* Oxford: Clarendon Press.

—— 1946. *Value and Capital*, 2nd edn. Oxford: Clarendon Press.

—— 1955. Economic foundations of wage policy. *Economic Journal*, 65: 389–404.

—— 1967. Monetary theory and history—an attempt at perspective, in *Critical Essays in Monetary Theory*. Oxford: Clarendon Press.

—— 1969. *A Theory of Economic History.* Oxford: Clarendon Press.

—— 1973. Equilibrium and the trade cycle. *Economic Inquiry*, 18: 523–34.

—— 1974. *The Crisis in Keynesian Economics.* Oxford: Blackwell.

—— 1977. *Economic Perspectives.* Oxford: Oxford University Press.

—— 1982. The credit economy, in *Money, Interest and Wages: Collected Essays in Economic Theory*, ii, Oxford: Blackwell.

—— 1986. Managing without money. Discussion Paper 65, Dept. of Economics, University of Hong Kong.

—— 1989. *A Market Theory of Money.* Oxford: Oxford University Press.

—— and Allen, R.G.D. 1934. A reconsideration of the theory of value. *Economica*, 1: 52–76.

Higgins, M., and Klitgaard, T. 1998. Viewing the current account deficit as a capital inflow. *Current Issues in Economics and Finance,*

4(13). New York: Federal Reserve Bank of New York.

Hirshleifer, J. 1965. Investment decision under uncertainty: choice-theoretic approaches. *Quarterly Journal of Economics*, 79: 509–36.

—— 1966. Investment decision under uncertainty: applications of the state-preference approach. *Quarterly Journal of Economics*, 80: 252–77.

Hodges, S. D. 1992. Financial engineering: new approaches to managing risk exposure, in *New Issues in Financial Services*, ed. R. Kinsella. Oxford: Blackwell.

Hoover, K. D. 1988. Two types of monetarism. *Journal of Economic Literature*, 22: 58–76.

Houthakker, H. S. 1977. The breakdown of Bretton Woods. Discussion Paper 543, Harvard Institute of Economic Research.

Hume, D. 1752. Of money, of the balance of trade, and of interest, in *Essays Moral, Political and Literary*. London: Oxford University Press (repr. 1963); repr. in *International Finance*, ed. R. N. Cooper. London: Penguin, 1969.

Humpage, O. F., and McIntire, J. M. 1995. An introduction to currency boards. *Federal Reserve Bank of Cleveland Economic Review*, 31(2): 2–11.

International Monetary Fund. 1988. Japan's liquidity trap. *World Economic Outlook*, Box 4.1, Sept.

Ireland, J., and Wren-Lewis, S. 1992. Buffer stock money and the company sector. *Oxford Economic Papers*, 42: 209–31.

Ize, A., and Levy-Yeyati, E. 1998. Dollarization of financial intermediation: causes and policy implications. Working Paper WP/98/28. Washington: International Monetary Fund.

Jacobs, J. 1998. *Econometric Business Cycle Research*. Dordrecht: Kluwer Academic Press.

Jaffee, D., and Russell, T. 1976. Imperfect information, uncertainty and credit rationing. *Quarterly Journal of Economics*, 90: 651–66.

Jeanne, O. 1999. Currency crises: A perspective on recent theoretical developments. *CEPR Discussion Paper* 2170, June.

Johansen, S., and Juselius, K. 1990. Maximum likelihood estimation and inference on cointegration — with

applications to the demand for money. *Oxford Bulletin of Economics and Statistics*, 52: 169–210.

Johnson, H. G. 1958. The balance of payments. *Pakistan Economic Journal*, June; repr. H. G. Johnson, *Money, Trade and Economic Growth*. London: Unwin University Books, 1962.

—— 1962. Monetary theory and policy. *American Economic Review*, 52: 335–84.

—— 1963. A survey of theories of inflation. *Indian Economic Review*, 6(4); repr. in *Essays in Monetary Economics*. London: Allen & Unwin, 1967.

—— 1969. The case for flexible exchange rates. *Federal Reserve of St Louis Review*, 51(6): 12–24.

—— 1971. The Keynesian revolution and the monetarist counter-revolution. *American Economic Review*, 61: 1–14.

—— 1972. Inflation: a monetarist view, in *Further Essays in Monetary Economics*. London: Allen &.Unwin.

—— 1976. Money and the balance of payments. *Banca Nazionale del Lavoro Quarterly Review*, 116: 3–18.

Joines, D. H. 1985. International currency substitution and the income velocity of money. *Journal of International Money and Finance*, 4: 303–16.

Jones, R. A. 1976. The origin and development of media of exchange. *Journal of Political Economy*, 84: 757–75.

Jones, R. W., and Kenen, P. B. 1985. *Handbook of International Economics*, vol. ii. Amsterdam: North-Holland.

Jonson, P. D. 1976. Money and economic activity in the open economy: the UK 1880–1970. *Journal of Political Economy*, 84: 979–1012.

—— 1987. Monetary indicators and the economy. *Reserve Bank of Australia Bulletin*, Dec. 5–15.

Jordan, J. L. 1969. Elements of money stock determination. *Federal Reserve Bank of St Louis Review*, 51 (Oct.): 10–19.

Kaldor, N. 1939. Speculation and economic stability. *Review of Economic Studies*, 7: 1–27.

—— 1970. The new monetarism. *Lloyd's Bank Review*, July: 1–18.

—— 1986. *The Scourge of Monetarism*, 2nd edn. Oxford: Oxford University Press.

Kane, E. J. 1984. Technological and regulatory forces in the developing fusion of financial services competition. *Journal of Finance*, July: 759–73.

Kanniainen, V., and Tarkha, J. 1986. On the shock-absorption view of money: international evidence from the 1960s and 1970s. *Applied Economics*, 18: 1085–101.

Kareken, J. 1967. Commercial banks and the supply of money: a market determined rate. *Federal Reserve Bulletin*, 53: 1699–712.

—— 1986. Federal bank regulatory policy: a description and some observations. *Journal of Business*, 59: 3–48.

—— and Wallace, N. (eds.) 1980. *Models of Monetary Economies*. Minneapolis: Federal Reserve Bank of Minneapolis.

—— —— 1981. On the indeterminacy of equilibrium exchange rates. *Quarterly Journal of Economics*, May: 207–22.

Kavanagh, N. J., and Walters, A. A. 1966. The demand for money in the United Kingdom 1877–1961: preliminary findings. *Bulletin of the Oxford Institute of Economics and Statistics*, 28: 93–116.

Kenen P. B. 1992. *EMU after Maastricht*. New York: Group of Thirty.

Kent, R. J. 1985. The demand for the services of money. *Applied Economics*, 17: 817–26.

Kessel, R. E. 1965. *The Cyclical Behavior of the Term Structure of Interest Rates*, Occasional Paper 91. New York: National Bureau of Economic Research.

Keynes, J. M. 1913. *Indian Currency and Finance*. London: Macmillan.

—— 1920. *The Economic Consequences of the Peace*. New York: Harcourt Brace & Howe.

—— 1923. *A Tract on Monetary Reform*. London: Macmillan.

—— 1925. *The Economic Consequences of Mr Churchill*, repr. in part, in *Essays in Persuasion*. London: Macmillan 1931

—— 1930. *A Treatise on Money*. London: Macmillan.

—— 1933. The theory of a monetary economy, in *Der Stand und die nächste Zukunft der Konjunkturforschung, Festschrift für Arthur Spiehoff*. Munich: Duncker & Humblot.

—— 1936. *The General Theory of Employment, Interest and Money*. London: Macmillan.

—— 1937a. The General Theory of Employment. *Quarterly Journal of Economics*, Feb.; repr. in *The New Economics*, ed. S. E. Harris. London: Dobson, 1947.

—— 1937b. The theory of the rate of interest, in *The Lessons of Monetary Experience: Essays in Homer of Irving Fisher*, repr. in *Readings in the Theory of Income Distribution*, ed. W. Fellner and B. F. Haley, for the American Economic Association.: London, Allen & Unwin, 1950.

—— 1973. *The Collected Writings of John Maynard Keynes: The General Theory and After*, xiii: P. I, Preparation; xiv: P. II, Defence and Development, ed. D. Moggridge for the Royal Econometric Society. London: Macmillan.

Khan, M. S. 1974. The stability of the demand-for-money function in the United States, 1901–1965. *Journal of Political Economy*, Nov.-Dec., 82: 1205–19.

Kindleberger, C. P. 1983. Standards as public, collective and private goods. Institute for International Economic Studies, University of Stockholm, repr. series, 217.

—— 1984. Financial institutions and economic development: a comparison of Great Britain and France in the eighteenth and nineteenth centuries. *Explorations in Economic History*, 21: 103–24.

King, R. G. 1982. Monetary policy and the information content of prices. *Journal of Political Economy*, 90: 247–79.

—— 1983. On the economics of private money. *Journal of Monetary Economics*, 12: 127–58.

Kiyotaki, N., and Wright, R. 1989a. On money as a medium of exchange. *Journal of Political Economy*, 97: 927–54.

—— 1989b. A contribution to the pure theory of money. Federal Reserve Bank of Minneapolis, Research Dept. Staff Report 123, Aug.

Klein, B. 1974. Competitive interest payments on bank deposits and the long-run demand for money. *American Economic Review*, 64: 931–49.

Klein, L. R. 1950. Stock and flow analysis in economics. *Econometrica*, 18 (July): 236–52.

—— 1962. *An Introduction to Econometrics.* Englewood Cliffs, NJ.: Prentice-Hall.

Knetter, M. M. 1989. Price discrimination by US and German exporters. *American Economic Review*, 79: 198–210.

—— 1993 International comparisons of pricing to market. *American Economic Review*, 83: 473–486.

Knight, F. 1921. *Risk, Uncertainty and Profit.* Boston: Houghton Mifflin.

Kouri, P. J. K. 1976. The exchange rate and balance of payments in the short run and the long run: a monetary approach. *Scandinavian Journal of Economics*, 78: 280–304.

Kouri, P. J. K., and Porter, M. G. 1974. International capital flows and portfolio equilibrium. *Journal of Political Economy*, 82(3): 443–67.

Koyck, L. M. 1954. *Distributed Lags and Investment Analysis.* Amsterdam: North Holland.

Kreinin, M. E., and Officer, L. H. 1978. The monetary approach to the balance of payments: a survey. *Princeton Studies in International Finance*, 43. Princeton University.

Kremers, J. J. M., and Lane, T. D. 1990. Economic and monetary integration and the aggregate demand for money in the EMS. *International Monetary Fund Staff Papers*, 37 (4): 777–805.

—— —— 1992. The implications of cross-border monetary aggregation. *International Monetary Fund Working Paper*, 92/71. Washington, DC: IMF.

Krueger, A. O. 1983. *Exchange Rate Determination.* Cambridge: Cambridge University Press.

Krugman, P. R. 1988. Target zones and exchange rate dynamics, *NBER Working Paper 2481*. New York: National Bureau of Economic Research.

—— 1989. *Exchange-Rate Instability.* Cambridge, Mass.: MIT Press.

—— 1992. *Currencies and Crises.* Cambridge, Mass.: MIT Press.

—— 1998a. Japan's trap. http://web.mit.edu/krugman/www/Japtrap.html.

—— 1998b. What happened to Asia? http://web.mit.edu/krugman/www/disinter.html.January.

Kydland, F. E., and Prescott, E. C. 1977. Rules rather than discretion: the inconsistency of optimal plans. *Journal of Political Economy*, 85(3): 473–91.

—— —— 1982. Time to build and aggregate fluctuations. *Econometrica*, 50: 1345–70.

—— —— 1991. Hours and employment variation in business cycle theory. *Economic Theory*, 1: 63–81.

Lacey, R., and Danziger, D. 1999. *The Year 1000.* London: Little, Brown and Company.

Laffer, A. 1973. Two arguments for fixed rates, in *The Economics of Common Currencies*, ed. H. G. Johnson and A. K. Swoboda. London: Allen & Unwin.

Laidler, D. E. W. 1966a. Some evidence on the demand for money. *Journal of Political Economy*, 74: 55–68.

—— 1966b. The rate of interest and the demand for money — some empirical evidence. *Journal of Political Economy*, 74: 543–55.

—— 1971. The influence of money on economic activity: a survey of some current problems, in *Monetary Theory and Monetary Policy in the 1970s*, ed. G. Clayton, J. C. Gilbert, and R. Sedgwick. London: Oxford University Press.

—— 1980. The demand for money in the US — yet again, in *On the State of Macroeconomics*, ed. K. Brunner, and A. H. Meltzer. Amsterdam: North-Holland.

—— 1982. *Monetarist Perspectives.* Oxford: Philip Allan.

—— 1984. The buffer stock notion in economics. *Economic Journal*, 94, Suppl.: 17–34.

—— 1993a. *The Demand for Money: Theories, Evidence, and Problems*, 4th edn. New York: Harper & Row.

—— 1993b. *The Golden Age of the Quantity Theory.* Hemel Hempstead: Harvester-Wheatsheaf.

—— and Parkin, J. M. 1970. The demand for money in the UK 1956–67: some preliminary estimates. *Manchester School*, 38: 187–208.

—— —— 1975. Inflation: a survey. *Economic Journal*, 85: 741–809.

Lancaster, K. J. 1966. Change and innovation in the technology of consumption. *American Economic Review*, 56(2): 14–23.

Lane, T., and Van Den Heuvel, S. 1998. The United Kingdom's experience with inflation targeting, Working Paper 98/87. International Monetary Fund.

—— and Poloz, S. S. 1992. Currency substitution and cross-border monetary aggregation: evidence from the G-7, *IMF Working Paper 92/81*.

Lange, O. 1942. Say's Law: a restatement and criticism, in *Studies in Mathematical Eco-nomics and Econometrics*: 49–68, ed. O. T. Lange *et al*. Chicago: University of Chicago Press.

Latané, H. A. 1954. Cash balances and the interest rate—a pragmatic approach. *Review of Economics and Statistics*, 36: 456–60.

Laumas, G. S., and Mehra, Y. P. 1977. The stability of the demand for money function. *Journal of Finance*, 23, (3), 911–16.

Leijonhufvud, A. 1987. Constitutional constraints on the monetary powers of government, in *The Search for Stable Money*, ed. J. A. Dorn and A. J. Schwartz. Chicago: University of Chicago.

Leland, H., and Pyle, D. 1977. Information asymmetries, financial structures and financial intermediaries. *Journal of Finance*, 32: 371–87, repr. in *Financial Intermediaries, International Library of Critical Writings in Economics*, 43, ed. M. K. Lewis. Cheltenham: Edward Elgar, 1995.

Lerner, A. P. 1938. Alternative formulations on the rate of interest. *Economic Journal*, 48 (June): 211–30.

—— 1944. *Economics of Control*. New York: Macmillan.

Levich, R. M. 1989. Is the foreign exchange market efficient? *Oxford Review of Economic Policy*, 5: 40–60.

Lewis, M. K. 1978. Interest rates and monetary velocity in Australia and the United States. *Economic Record*, 54 (Apr.): 111–126.

—— 1980. Are banks controlled because they are different, or different because they are controlled? *Economic Papers* 63: 25–40.

—— 1985. Money and the control of inflation in the UK. *Midland Bank Review*, Summer: 17–23.

—— 1986a. The future of banking, in *Transactions of the Manchester Statistical Society*, 18 Feb.: 1–18; repr. in *The Globalization of Financial Services*, ed. M. K. Lewis. Cheltenham: Edward Elgar, 1999.

—— 1986b. Financial services in the United States, in *Personal Financial Markets*, ed. R. L. Carter, B. Chiplin, and M. K. Lewis. Oxford: Phillip Allan.

—— 1990. Liquidity, in *Foundations of Economic Thought*, ed. J. Creedy. Oxford: Blackwell.

—— 1992a. Call money market, in *New Palgrave Dictionary of Money and Finance*, i, ed. P. Newman, M. Milgate, and J. Eatwell. London: Macmillan.

—— 1992b. Off-the-balance-sheet activities, in *New Palgrave Dictionary of Money and Finance*, iii, ed. P. Newman, M. Milgate, and J. Eatwell. London: Macmillan.

—— 1993. International financial deregula-tion, trade and exchange rates. *Cato Journal*, 13(2): 243–72.

—— 1994. Monetary policy: do we need a new agenda? *Economic Record*, 70(211): 434–55.

—— 1995. *Financial Intermediaries: The International Library of Critical Writings in Economics*, 43. Cheltenham: Edward Elgar.

—— 1997. Derivative markets, in *The Australian Financial System: Evolution, Policy and Practice*, ed. M. K. Lewis and R. H. Wallace. Melbourne: Addison-Wesley Longman.

—— and Davis, K. T. 1987. *Domestic and International Banking*. Oxford: Philip Allan.

—— and Polasek, M. 1990. Whither the balance of payments? *Australian Economic Review*, 3rd quarter: 5–16.

—— and Wallace, R. H. 1997. *The Australian Financial System: Evolution, Policy and Practice*. Melbourne: Addison-Wesley Longman.

Lewis, W. A. 1949. *Economic Survey, 1919–1939*. London: Allen & Unwin.

Liviatan, N. 1965. On the long-run theory of consumption and real balances. *Oxford Economic Papers* (new series), 17: 205–18.

Llewellyn, D. T. 1990. Money market opera-tions of the Bank of England and the determination of interest rates, in *Current Issues in Monetary Economics*, ed. T. Bandyopadhyay and S. Ghatak. London: Harvester Wheatsheaf.

Lloyd, C. L. 1962. The real balance effect: *Sine Qua* what? *Oxford Economic Papers* (new series), 14: 267–74.

Lohmann, S. 1992. Optimal commitment in monetary policy: credibility versus flexibility. *American Economic Review*, 82(1): 273–86.

Long, J. B., and Plosser, C. I. 1983. Real business cycles. *Journal of Political Economy*. 91, (Feb.): 39–69.

Longbottom, A., and Holly, S. 1985. Econometric methodology and monetarism: Professor Friedman and Professor Hendry on the demand for money. *Discussion Paper*, 131, London Business School.

Lowe, P., and Ellis, L. 1997. The smoothing of official interest rates, paper presented to Reserve Bank of Australia Conference on Monetary Policy and Inflation Targeting, July.

Lucas, R. E. Jnr. 1972. Expectations and the neutrality of money. *Journal of Economic Journal*, 4: 103–24.

—— 1973. Some international evidence on output-inflation trade-offs. *American Economic Review*, 63: 326–34.

—— 1976. Econometric policy evaluation: a critique. in *The Phillips Curve and Labor Markets*, ed. K. Brunner and A. H. Meltzer, *Carnegie-Rochester Series on Public Policy*, 1: 9–46. Amsterdam: North-Holland.

—— 1980. Equilibrium in a pure currency economy. *Economic Inquiry*, 18: 203–30.

—— 1987. Money demand in the United States: a quantitative review, paper given at Carnegie-Rochester Conference, Nov.

—— 1994. Review of Milton Friedman and Anna J. Schwartz's 'A monetary history of the United States, 1876–1960'. *Journal of Monetary Economics*, 34: 5–16.

—— and Prescott, E. C. 1971. Investment under uncertainty. *Econometrica*, 39(5): 659–81.

—— and Rapping, L. A. 1969. Real wages, employment and inflation. *Journal of Political Economy*, 77: 721–54.

—— and Stokey, N. L. 1987. Money and interest in a cash in advance economy. *Econometrica*, 55: 491–513.

Lusher, D. W. 1942. The structure of interest rates and the Keynesian Theory of interest. *Journal of Political Economy*, 50 (Apr.): 274.

Lutz. F. A. 1940. The structure of interest rates. *Quarterly Journal of Economics*, 55: 36–63; repr. in *Readings in the Theory of Income Distribution*, ed. W. Fellner and B. Haley. Philadelphia: American Economic Association, 1946.

MacDonald, R., and Milbourne, R. 1990. Recent developments in monetary theory. *Dundee Discussion Papers in Economics*, 9, Apr. University of Dundee.

—— and Taylor, M. P. 1989. Exchange rate economics: an expository survey. In *Exchange Rates and Open Economy Macroeconomics*, ed. R. MacDonald and M. P. Taylor. Oxford: Blackwell.

MacKinnon, J. G., and Milbourne, R. 1988. Are price equations really money demand equations on their heads? *Journal of Applied Econometrics*, 3: 295–305.

McCallum, B. T. 1976. Rational expectations and the estimation of econometric models: an alternative procedure. *International Economic Review*, 17: 484–90.

—— 1983. The role of overlapping generations models in monetary economics. *Carnegie-Rochester Conference Series on Public Policy*, 18: 9–44.

—— 1993. Macroeconomics after two decades of rational expectations, *NBER Working Paper* 4367. National Bureau of Economic Research.

—— 1995. Two fallacies concerning central bank independence. *American Economic Review*, 85(2): 207–11.

—— and Whittaker, J. K. 1979. The effectiveness of fiscal feedback rules and automatic stabilisers under rational expectations. *Journal of Monetary Economics*, 5: 171–86.

McCandless, G.T. Jnr., and Weber, W.E. 1995 Some monetary facts. *Federal Reserve Bank of Minneapolis Quarterly Review*, Summer: 2–11.

McCulloch, J. H. 1986. Bank regulation and deposit insurance. *Journal of Business*, 599: 79–85.

McKenzie, R. B., and Tullock, G. 1978. *Modern Political Economy*. New York: McGraw-Hill.

McKinnon, R. I. 1963. Optimum currency areas. *American Economic Review*, 53: 717–25.

—— 1976. The limited role of fiscal policy in an open economy. *Banca Nazionale del Lavoro Quarterly Review*, June: 95–119.

—— 1982. Currency substitution and instability in the world dollar standard. *American Economic Review*, 72: 320–33.

—— 1984*a*. Why floating exchange rates fail. *Discussion Paper 72*. Rome: Banca d'Italia.

—— 1984*b*. An international standard for monetary stabilization. *Policy Analyses in International Economics,* 8. Washington, DC: Institute for International Economics.

McKinnon, R. I. 1985. Two concepts of international currency substitution, in *The Economics of the Caribbean Basin*, ed. M. Connolly and J. McDermott. New York: Praeger.

—— 1988. Monetary and exchange-rate policies for international financial stability: a proposal. *Journal of Economic Perspectives*, 2(1): 83–103.

—— 1993. The rules of the game: international money in historical perspective. *Journal of Economic Literature*, 31: 1–44.

—— 1996. *The Rules of the Game: International Money and Exchange Rates*. Cambridge, Mass: MIT Press.

—— and Oates, W. 1966. *The Implications of International Economic Integration for Monetary, Fiscal and Exchange Rate Policy,* Princeton: Princeton Studies in International Finance, 16.

Makinen, C. E., and Woodward, G. 1986. Some anecdotal evidence relating to the legal restrictions theory of money. *Journal of Political Economy*, 94: 260–5.

Makower, H., and Marschak, J. 1938. Assets, prices and monetary theory. *Economica*, 5: 261–88.

Malkiel, B. G. 1992. Term structure of interest rates, in *New Palgrave Dictionary of Money and Finance,* iii, ed. P. Newman, M. Milgate, and J. Eatwell. London: Macmillan.

Mankiw, N. G., and Summers, L. H. 1986. Money demand and the effects of fiscal policies. *Journal of Money, Credit and Banking,* 18: 415–29.

Marini, G. 1985. Intertemporal substitution and the role of monetary policy. *Economic Journal*, 95: 87–100.

—— 1986. Employment fluctuations and demand management. *Economica*, 53: 209–18.

Markowitz, H. 1952. Portfolio selection. *Journal of Finance*, 7: 77–91.

—— 1959. *Portfolio Selection: Efficient Diversification of Investment*. New Haven Conn.: Yale University Press.

Marschak, J. 1934. The meeting of the Econometric Society in Leyden, Sept.-Oct. 1933. *Econometrica*, 2: 187–203.

Marshall, A. 1887. Remedies for fluctuations of general prices; repr. in *Memorials of Alfred Marshall*, ed. A. C. Pigou. London: Macmillan, 1925.

—— 1890. *Principles of Economics.* New York: Macmillan.

—— 1923. *Money, Credit and Commerce*. London: Macmillan.

—— 1926. *Official Papers,* ed. by J. M. Keynes. London: Macmillan.

Masciandara, D., and Spinelli, F. 1994. Central Banks' Independence. *Scottish Journal of Political Economy*, 41(4): 434–443.

Mason, W. E. 1963. *Clarification of the Monetary Standard*. Philadelphia: Pennsylvania State University Press.

Mayer T. 1975. The structure of monetarism, pt. 1. *Kredit and Kapital*, 8(2): 191–218.

Meade, J. E. 1975. The Keynesian revolution, in M. Keynes (ed.), *Essays on John Maynard Keynes*. Cambridge: Cambridge University Press.

—— 1978. The meaning of internal balance. *Economic Journal*, 88: 423–35.

—— 1993. The meaning of internal balance. *American Economic Review*, 83(6): 3–9.

—— 1994. *Full Employment without Inflation*. London: Social Market Foundation.

Meiselman, D. 1962. *The Term Structure of Interest Rates*. Englewood Cliffs, NJ: Prentice-Hall.

Meltzer, A. P. 1963. Yet another look at the low level liquidity trap. *Econometrica*, 31(3): 545–9.

Metzler L. A. 1951. Wealth, saving, and the rate of interest, *Journal of Political Economy*, 59(2): 93–116.

Menger, C. 1892. On the origin of money. *Economic Journal*, 2: 239–55.

Merton, R. C. 1971. Optimum consumption and portfolio rules in a continuous time model. *Journal of Economic Theory*, 3(4): 373–413.

Milbourne, R. 1987. Re-examining the buffer stock model of money. *Economic Journal*. Suppl., 97: 130–42.

—— 1988. Disequilibrium buffer stock models: a survey. *Journal of Economic Surveys*, 2: 187–207.

Miles, M. A. 1978. Currency substitution, flexible exchange rates and monetary independence. *American Economic Review*, 68: 428–36.

Mill, J.S. 1821. *Elements of Political Economy*. London: Baldwin, Cradock & Joy.

Mill, J.S. 1848. *Principles of Political Economy*. London: J. W. Parker.

—— 1871. *The Principles of Political Economy with Some of Their Applications to Social Philosophy*, 7th edn. London; repr. 1965, ed. J. M. Robson. Toronto: University of Toronto Press.

Miller, M. H. 1986. Financial innovation: the last twenty years and the next. *Journal of Quantitative Analysis*, 21: 459–71.

—— and Orr, D. 1966. A model of the demand for money by firms. *Quarterly Journal of Economics*, 80: 413–35.

Milner, C., Mizen, P. D., and Pentecost, E. J., 1996. The impact of intra-European trade on sterling currency substitution. *Weltwirtschaftliches Archiv*, 132 (1): 160–71.

Minford, P. 1986. Rational expectations and monetary policy. *Scottish Journal of Political Economy*, 33: 317–33.

—— 1992. *Rational Expectations Macroeconomics: An Introductory Handbook*. Oxford: Blackwell.

Minsky, H. P. 1977. A theory of systemic fragility, in *Financial Crises: Institutions and Markets in a Fragile Environment*, ed. E. J. Altman and A. W. Sametz. New York: Wiley.

—— 1978. The financial instability hypothesis: a restatement. *Thames Papers on Political Economy*, Autumn.

—— 1986. *Stabilizing an Unstable Economy*. New Haven, Conn.: Yale University Press.

Mizen, P. D. 1992. Should buffer stock theorists be broad or narrow-minded? Some answers from aggregate UK data 1966–89. *Manchester School*, 60(4): 403–18.

—— 1994. *Buffer Stock Models of the Demand for Money in the UK*. Basingstoke: Macmillan.

—— 1997. Microfoundations for a stable money demand function. *Economic Journal*, 107: 1202–12.

—— Moggridge, D., and Presley, J.R. 1997. The papers of Dennis Robertson: the discovery of unexpected riches. *History of Political Economy*, 29(4): 573–91.

—— and Pentecost, E. J. 1994. Evaluating the empirical evidence for currency substitution: a case study of the demand for sterling in Europe. *Economic Journal*, 104: 1057–69.

—— and Presley, J. R. 1995. Persistent negative reactions in Cambridge to Keynes' General Theory—some new evidence. *Scottish Journal of Political Economy*, 42(4): 639–51.

—— —— 1996. The real balance effect and stability analysis in classical monetary theory. *Scottish Journal of Political Economy*, 43(1): 32–47.

—— and Tew, B. 1996. Proposals to ensure a smooth transition to European Monetary Union by 1999. *World Economy*, 19(4): 407–23.

Monticelli, C. 1993. All the money in Europe? An investigation of the economic properties of EC-wide extended monetary aggregates, mimeo.

—— and Papi, L. 1994. EU-wide monetary aggregates: an assessment of competing approaches. Conference paper EEA Congress, Maastricht, 1994.

—— and Strauss-Kahn, M. O. 1993. European integration and the demand for broad money. *Manchester School*, 61: 345–66.

Moore, B. J. 1988. *Horizontalists and Verticalists: The Macroeconomics of Credit Money*. Cambridge: Cambridge University Press.

Morgenstern, O. 1950. *On the Accuracy of Economic Observations*. Princeton: Princeton University Press.

Morton, W. A. 1950. Trade, unionism, full employment and inflation. *American Economic Review*, 40: 13–39; repr. in *Inflation*, ed. R. J. Ball and P. Doyle, Penguin, 1969.

Mullineux, A. 1996. *Financial Innovation, Banking and Monetary Aggregates*. Cheltenham: Edward Elgar.

Mundell, R. A. 1961. A theory of optimum currency areas. *American Economic Review*, 51(4): 657–65.

—— 1962. Appropriate use of monetary and

fiscal policy for internal and external stability. *International Monetary Fund Staff Papers*, 9 (Mar.): 70–79.

—— 1963*a*. Inflation and real interest. *Journal of Political Economy*, 71: 280–83.

—— 1963*b*. Capital mobility and stabilization policy under fixed and flexible exchange rates. *Canadian Journal of Economics and Political Science*, 2 (Nov.): 475–85.

—— 1969. Toward a better international monetary system. *Journal of Money, Credit and Banking*, 13: 625–48.

—— 1973. A plan for a European currency, in *The Economics of Common Currencies: Proceedings of the Madrid Conference on Optimum Currency Areas*, ed. H. G. Johnson and A. K. Swoboda. London: Allen & Unwin.

Muscatelli, V. A. 1989. A comparison of the rational expectations and general to specific approaches to modelling the demand for M1. *Oxford Bulletin of Economics and Statistics*, 51: 353–75.

Musgrave, R. A. 1959. *The Theory of Public Finance*. New York: McGraw-Hill.

Mussa, M. 1976. The exchange rate, the balance of payments and monetary and fiscal policy under a regime of controlled floating. *Scandanavian Journal of Economics*, 78: 229–48.

—— 1981. *The Role of Official Intervention*. New York: Group of Thirty.

Mussa, M. 1986. Nominal exchange rate regimes and the behavior of real exchange rates: evidence and implications. *Carnegie-Rochester Conference Series on Public Policy*, 25: 117–214.

Muth, J. F. 1960. Optimal properties of exponentially weighted forecasts. *Journal of the American Statistical Association*, 55(290): 299–306.

—— 1961. Rational expectations and the theory of price movements. *Econometrica* 29(3): 315–35.

Naím, M. 1995. Latin America the morning after. *Foreign Affairs*, 74(4): 45–61.

Nelson, E. 2000. UK Monetary Policy. A guide using Taylor rules. Bank of England mimeo.

Nerlove, M. 1958. *Distributed Lags and Demand Analysis for Agricultural and Other Commodities*, US Dept. of Agriculture, Handbook 141.

Washington, DC: Government Printing Office.

—— 1967. Distributed lags and unobserved components in economic time series, in W. Fellner *et al.*, *Ten Economic Studies in the Tradition of Irving Fisher*, New York: Wiley.

Neuman, A. M. 1935. The doctrine of liquidity. *Review of Economic Studies*, 3(1): 81–99.

Newberry, D. M. G., and Stiglitz, J. E. 1981. *The Theory of Commodity Price Stabilisation: A Study in the Economics of Risk*. Oxford: Clarendon Press.

Niehans, J. 1977. Exchange rate dynamics with stock/flow interaction. *Journal of Political Economy*, 856: 1245–57.

—— 1978. *The Theory of Money*. Baltimore.: Johns Hopkins University Press.

Obstfeld, M. 1984. Multiple stable equilibria in an optimising perfect-foresight model. *Econometrica*, 52: 223–8.

Officer, L. H. 1984. *Purchasing Power Parity and Exchange Rates*. Greenwich, Conn.: JAI Press.

Ohlin, B. G. 1937. Alternative theories of the rate of interest. *Economic Journal*, 47: 423–7.

Okun, A. M. 1981. *Prices and Quantities: A Macroeconomic Analysis*. Oxford: Blackwell.

Ostroy, J. M. 1973. The informational efficiency of monetary exchange. *American Economic Review*, 64(3): 597–610.

—— and Starr. R. M. 1974. Money and the decentralisation of exchange. *Econometrica*, 42(6): 1093–111.

Padoa-Schioppa, T. 1988. The European monetary system: a long-term view, in *The European Monetary System*, ed. S. F Giavazzi, S. Micossi, and M. Miller, Cambridge: Cambridge University Press.

Paish, F. W. 1958. The future of British monetary policy. Committee on the Working of the Monetary System, *Principal Memoranda of Evidence*, 3, HMSO 1966: 182–88.

—— 1959. Gilt edged and the money supply. *The Banker*, 109: 17–25.

Pakko, M. R., and Pollard, P. S. 1996. Purchasing power parity and the Big Mac. *Federal Reserve Bank of St Louis Review*, 71(1): 3–21.

Patinkin, D. 1948. Relative prices, Say's Law and the demand for money. *Econometrica*, 16: 135–54.

Patinkin, D. 1949. The indeterminacy of absolute prices in classical monetary theory. *Econometrica*, 17: 1–27.

—— 1951. The invalidity of classical monetary theory. *Econometrica*, 19: 135–51.

—— 1961. Financial intermediaries and the logical structure of a monetary economy. *American Economic Review*, 51: 95–116.

—— 1965. *Money, Interest and Prices.* 2nd edn. New York: Harper & Row.

—— 1969. The Chicago tradition, the quantity theory and Friedman. *Journal of Money, Credit and Banking*, 1(1) 46–70.

—— 1972. *Studies in Monetary Economics.* Harper International edition, New York: Harper Row.

—— 1976. *Keynes' Monetary Thought*, Durham, NC: Duke University Press.

—— 1987. Walras' Law. *Wider Working Papers* WP13, June. Hebrew University of Jerusalem and World Institute for Development Economics Research.

—— 1993. Irving Fisher and his compensated dollar plan. *Federal Reserve Bank of Richmond Economic Quarterly*, 79(3): 1–33.

Patterson, K. D. 1987. The specification and stability of the demand for money in the UK. *Economica*, 54 (213): 41–55.

Persson, T., and Tabellini, G. 1993. Designing institutions for monetary stability. *Carnegie-Rochester Conference Series on Public Policy*, 39, Dec.

Phelps, E. S. 1968. Money wage dynamics and labour market equilibrium. *Journal of Political Economy*, 76: 678–711.

Phelps, E.S. *et al.* (eds) 1970. *Microeconomic Foundations of Employment and Inflation Theory.* New York: Norton.

—— 1988. Seven schools of macroeconomics. *Arne Ryde Memorial Lecture.*

—— and Taylor, J. B. 1977. The stabilising powers of monetary policy under rational expectations. *Journal of Political Economy*, 85: 163–90.

Phillips, A. W. 1958. The relation between unemployment and the rate of change of money wage rates in the United Kingdom, 1861–1957. *Economica*, 25: 283–99.

Pigou, A. C. 1917. The value of money. *Quarterly Journal of Economics*, 32: 38–65.

—— 1941. *The Veil of Money.* London: Macmillan.

—— 1945. *Lapses from Full Employment.* London: Macmillan.

Plessner, Y. 1994. On the costs of inflation: Israel's example. *Journal of Economic Perspectives*, 8(2): 204–7.

Podolski, T. 1992. Financial innovation and the money supply, in *New Palgrave Dictionary of Money and Finance*, 2, ed. P. Newman, M. Milgate, and J. Eatwell. London: Macmillan.

Poole, W. M. 1970. Optimal choice of monetary policy instrument in a simple stochastic macro model. *Quarterly Journal of Economics*, 84(2): 197–216.

—— 1980. Comment on paper by Tobin. *Brookings Papers on Economics Activity*, 1: 79–85.

Porter, M. G. 1974. The interdependence of monetary policy and capital flows in Australia. *Economic Record*, 50(1): 1–20.

Prais, Z. 1975. Real money balances as a variable in the production function. *Journal of Money, Credit and Banking*, 6 (Nov.): 535–43.

Prescott, E. 1986. Theory ahead of business-cycle measurement. *Federal Reserve Bank of Minneapolis Quarterly Review*, Fall: 9–22; repr. in *Real Business Cycles, Real Exchange Rates and Actual Policies*, ed. K. Brunner and A.H. Meltzer, Carnegie-Rochester Series on Public Policy 25. Amsterdam: North-Holland.

Price, L. D. D. 1972. The demand for money in the UK: A further investigation. *Bank of England Quarterly Bulletin* 12(1): 43–55.

Purvis D. D. 1980. Monetarism — a review. *Canadian Journal of Economics,* 13(1): 96–121.

Radcliffe Report, 1959. *Committee on the Working of the Monetary System Report*, Cmnd. 827. London: HMSO.

Ramsey, F. P. 1928. A mathematical theory of saving. *Economic Journal*, 38: 47–61.

Ratti, R. A., and Jeong, B. W. 1994. Variation in real exchange rate as a source of currency substitution. *Journal of International Money and Finance*, 13(5): 537–50.

Razin A. 1994. The dynamic optimising

approach to the current account: theory and evidence, in *Understanding Interdependence: The Macroeconomics of the Open Economy.* Princeton: Princeton University Press.

Robertson, D.H. 1922. *Money;* (revised edn. 1928.) Cambridge: Nisbet & Co.

—— 1937. Alternative theories in the rate of interest. *Economic Journal,* 47: 423–43.

Robbins, L. 1971. *Money, Trade and International Relations.* London: Macmillan.

Robinson, J. 1938. A review of the economics of inflation by Bresciani-Turroni. *Economic Journal,* Sept.; repr. with additions in *Collected Economic Papers,* i., Oxford: Blackwell, 1960.

Robinson, J. 1951. The Rate of Interest. *Economica,* 19: 92–111; repr. in *Collected Economic Papers,* ii, Oxford: Blackwell.

—— 1970. Quantity theories old and new. *Journal of Money, Credit and Banking,* 2 (Nov.): 504–12.

Rogers, C. 1989. *Money, Interest and Capital: A Study in the Foundations of Monetary Theory.* Cambridge: Cambridge University Press.

Rogoff, K. 1985. The optimal commitment to an intermediate monetary target. *Quarterly Journal of Economics,* 100(4): 1169–89.

—— 1987. Reputational constraints on monetary policy. *Carnegie-Rochester Conference Series on Public Policy,* 26: 141–82.

—— 1995. The purchasing power parity puzzle. *Journal of Economic Literature,* 34(2): 647–68.

Roosa, R. V. 1956. *Federal Reserve Operations in the Money and Government Securities Markets.* New York: Federal Reserve Bank of New York.

Ross, S. A. 1989. Institutional markets, financial marketing, and financial innovation. *Journal of Finance,* 44: 541–56.

Roubini, N. 1998. The asian currency crisis of 1997 URL:http//www.stern.nyu.edu/_roubini/NOTES.

Sachs, J. 1981. The current account and macroeconomic adjustment in the 1970s. *Brookings Papers in Economic Activity,* 1: 201–68.

Sack, B. 1998. Does the Fed act gradually? A VAR analysis. Working Paper 17, Federal Reserve Board of Governors FEDS.

Salin, P. (ed.) 1984. *Currency Competition and Monetary Union.* The Hague: Martine Nijhoff.

Salop J., and Spitaller E. 1980. Why does the current account matter? *International Monetary Fund Staff Papers,* Mar.: 101–34.

Samuelson, P. A. 1938. A note on the pure theory of consumer behavior. *Econometrica,* 4: 61–71.

—— 1947. *Foundations of Economic Analysis.* Cambridge, Mass.: Harvard University Press.

—— 1958. An exact consumption-loan model of interest with or without the social contrivance of money. *Journal of Political Economy,* 66: 467–82.

—— 1970. The fundamental approximation theorem of portfolio analysis in terms of means, variances, and higher moments. *Review of Economic Studies,* 37(4): 537–42.

—— 1971. Maximum principles in analytical economics. *Les Prix Nobel en 1970.* Stockholm: 273–88.

Sandford, C. S. jun. 1994. Financial markets in 2020. *Federal Reserve Bank of Kansas City Economic Review,* 79(1): 19–28; repr. in *The Globalization of Financial Services,* ed. M. K. Lewis. Cheltenham: Edward Elgar, 1999.

Santomero, A. M., and Seater, J. J. 1981. Partial adjustment in the demand for money: theory and empirics. *American Economic Review,* 71: 566–78.

Sargent, T. J. 1977. The demand for money during hyperinflation under rational expectations, I. *International Economic Review,* 18 (Feb.): 59–82.

—— 1979. *Macroeconomic Theory.* New York: Academic Press.

—— 1999, Comment on 'Policy rules for open economies' by Lawrence Ball in J. B. Taylor, *Monetary Policy Rules,* Chicago: Chicago University Press.

—— and Wallace, N. 1973. Rational expectations and the dynamics of hyperinflation. *International Economic Review,* 14 (June): 328–50.

—— —— 1975. Rational expectations, the optimal monetary instrument, and the optimal money supply rule. *Journal of Political Economy,* 83: 241–57.

—— 1981. Some unpleasant monetarist arithmetic. *Federal Reserve Bank of Minneapolis Quarterly Review,* 5(3): 1–17.

Savastano, M. A. 1992. The pattern of currency substitution in Latin America: an overview. *Revista de Análisis Económico*, 7: 29–72.

—— 1996. Dollarization in Latin America: recent evidence and some policy issues, in *The Macroeconomics of International Currencies: Theory, Policy and Evidence*, P. D. Mizen, and E. J. Pentecost. ed. Aldershot: Edward Elgar.

Say, J. B. 1821. *A Treatise on Political Economy*, translated by C. R. Prinsep from the 4th French edn. London: Longmans. 1st edn., Paris, 1803.

Schlesinger, K. 1994. On the way to a new monetary union: The European Monetary Union. *Federal Reserve Bank of St Louis Review*, 76(3), May/June, 3–10.

Schumpeter, J. A. 1954. *History of Economic Analysis*, repr. London: Routledge.

Schwartz, A. J. 1992. Banking school, currency school, free banking. In *New Palgrave Dictionary of Money and Finance*, Vol. i, ed. P. Newman, M. Milgate, and J. Eatwell. London: Macmillan.

—— 1998. Schwartz on Friedman. *The Region*, 12(3): 5–8.

Scitovsky, T. 1969. *Money and the Balance of Payments*. Chicago: Rand McNally

Serletis, A., and Robb, A. L. 1986. Divisia aggregation and substitutability among monetary assets. *Journal of Money, Credit and Banking*, 18(3): 430–46.

Shaw, R. 1990. Recent developments in the money markets, in *The Future of Financial Systems and Services: Essays in Honour of Jack Revell*, ed. E. P. M. Gardener. London: Macmillan.

Shiller, R. 1996. Why do people dislike inflation? National Bureau of Economic Research, New York (mimeo), cited in J. S. Chadha, A. G. Haldane, and N. G. J. Janssen (1998).

—— 1978. Rational expectations and the dynamic structure of rational expectations models: a critical review. *Journal of Monetary Economics*, 4: 1–44.

Shuetrim, G., and Thompson, C. 1998. The implications of uncertainty for monetary policy. Sydney: Reserve Bank of Australia, mimeo.

Sidrauski, M. 1967. Rational choice and patterns of growth in a monetary economy. *American Economic Review*. 57(2): 534–44.

Silber, W. L. 1983. The process of financial innovation. *American Economic Review*, 73(1): 89–95.

Sims, G. E., and Takayama, A. 1985. On the demand for and supply of money: an empirical study. *Keio Economic Studies*, 22: 1–26.

Sinclair, P. J. N. 1991. The scope and nature of monetary economics. *University of Oxford Applied Economics Discussion Paper Series*, 113, July. Oxford: Institute of Economics and Statistics.

Skidelsky, R. 1996. *Keynes*. Oxford: Oxford University Press.

Slutsky, E. E. 1937. The summation of random causes as the source of cyclic processes. *Econometrica*, 5: 105–46. (Original Russian version: 1927.)

Smaghi, L. B., and Vori, S. 1993. *Rating the EC as an Optimal Currency Area*, Temi di discussione, 187. Rome: Banca D'Italia.

Smith, C. W. jun., Smithson, C. W., and Wilford, D. S. 1990. *Managing Financial Risk*. New York: Harper & Row.

Smith, R. G., and Goodhart, C. A. E. 1985. The relationship between exchange rate movements and monetary surprises: results for the United Kingdom and the United States compared and contrasted. *Manchester School*, 53: 2–22.

Solow, R. M. 1956. A contribution to the theory of economic growth. *Quarterly Journal of Economics*, 70: 65–94.

Spencer, D. E. 1985. Money demand and the price level. *Review of Economics and Statistics*, 67: 490–6.

Starleaf, D. R. 1970. The specification of money demand-supply models which involve the use of distributed lags. *Journal of Finance*, 25(4): 743–60.

Stiglitz, J. E., and Weiss, A. 1981. Credit rationing in markets with imperfect information. *American Economic Review*, 71: 393–410.

—— —— 1990. Banks as social accountants and screening devices for the allocation of credit. *Greek Economic Review*, 12: 85–118; repr. in *Financial Intermediaries, International*

Library of Critical Writings in Economics, 43, ed. M. K. Lewis. Cheltenham: Edward Elgar, 1995.

Stock, J. 1998. Monetary policy in a changing economy: indicators, rules and the shift towards intangible output, paper presented to IMES conference, Japan, 18–19 June.

Summers, L. 1995. Ten lessons to learn. *Economist*, 23 December, http: //www.economist. com/archive.

Svensson, L. 1996. Inflation forecast targeting: Implementing and monitoring inflation targets. *Bank of England Working Paper* 56.

—— 1997a. Inflation targeting, some extensions, Institute for International Economic Studies, mimeo.

—— 1997b. Optimal inflation contracts, 'conservative' Central Banks and linear inflation contracts. *American Economic Review*, 87(1): 98–114.

—— 1998. Inflation targeting as a monetary policy rule. Institute for International Economic Studies, mimeo.

Swan, T. W. 1955. Longer-run problems of the balance of payments, repr. in *The Australian Economy*, ed. H. W. Arndt and W. M. Corden. Melbourne: Cheshire, 1963.

—— 1960. Economic control in a dependent economy. *Economic Record*, 36 (Mar.): 51–66.

Swoffard, J. L., and Whitney, G.A. 1988. Comparison of nonparametric tests of weak separability for annual and quarterly data on consumption, leisure and money, *Journal of Business and Economic Statistics*, 6(2): 241–6.

Taylor, J. B. 1979. Staggered wage setting in a macroeconomic model. *American Economic Review, Papers and Proceedings*, 69: 108–13.

—— 1980. Aggregate dynamics and staggered contracts. *Journal of Political Economy*, 88: 1–23.

Taylor, M. P. 1987. Financial innovation, inflation and the stability of the demand for broad money in the UK. *Bulletin of Economic Research*, 39: 225–33.

Theil, H. 1958. *Economic Forecasts and Policy*. Amsterdam: North-Holland.

—— 1964. *Optimal Decision Rules for Government and Industry*. Amsterdam: North-Holland.

Thomas, R. S. J. 1997a. The demand for M4: A sectoral analysis, p. 1 - The personal sector. *Bank of England Working Paper Series* 61.

—— 1997b. The demand for M4: A sectoral analysis, P. 2 — The company sector. *Bank of England Working Paper Series* 62.

Thornton, D. L., and Stone, C. C. 1992. Financial innovation: causes and consequences, in *Current Issues in Financial and Monetary Economics*, 81–109, ed. K. Dowd and M. K. Lewis. London: Macmillan.

Thornton, H. 1802. *An Enquiry into the Nature and Effects of the Paper Credit of Great Britain*; repr. with an Introduction by F. A. von Hayek. London: Allen & Unwin, 1939.

Tinbergen, J. 1952. *On the Theory of Economic Policy*. Amsterdam: North-Holland.

—— 1956. *Economic Policy: Principles and Design*. Amsterdam: North-Holland.

Tobin, J. 1947. Liquidity preference and monetary policy. *Review of Economics and Statistics*, 29: 124–31.

—— 1956. The interest elasticity of transactions demand for cash. *Review of Economics and Statistics*, 38(3): 241–7.

—— 1958. Liquidity preference as behaviour towards risk. *Review of Economic Studies*, 25(1): 65–86.

—— 1963. Commercial banks as creators of money, in *Banking and Monetary Studies*, ed. D. Carson, Homewood, Illinois: R. D. Irwin; repr. in *Financial Intermediaries: The International Library of Critical Writings in Economics*, 43, ed. M. K. Lewis. Cheltenham: Edward Elgar, 1995.

—— 1965a. Money and economic growth. *Econometrica*, 33: 671–84.

—— 1965b. The theory of portfolio selection, in *The Theory of Interest Rates*, ed. F. Hahn and F. P. R. Brechling. London: Macmillan.

—— 1969. A general equilibrium approach to monetary theory. *Journal of Money, Credit and Banking*, 1(1): 15–29.

—— 1972. Friedman's theoretical framework. *Journal of Political Economy*, 80 (5) 852–63.

—— 1978. Monetary policies and the economy: the transmission mechanism. *Southern Economic Journal*, 44: 421–31.

—— 1980a. Stabilization policy ten years

after. *Brooking Papers on Economic Activity*, 1: 19–72.

Tobin, J. 1980b. Discussion, in *Models of Monetary Economics*, ed. J. Kareken and N. Wallace. Minneapolis: Federal Reserve Bank of Minneapolis: 83–90.

—— 1980c. *Asset Accumulation and Economic Activity*. Oxford: Blackwell.

—— 1992. Money, in *New Palgrave Dictionary of Money and Finance Vol ii*, ed. P. Newman, M. Milgate, and J. Eatwell, London: Macmillan.

—— and Brainard, W. C. 1963. Financial intermediaries and the effectiveness of monetary controls. *American Economic Review*, 53(2): 383–400.

—— —— 1968. Pitfalls in financial model building. *American Economic Review May; Papers and Proceedings* repr. in J. Tobin *Essays in Economics*, i, Chicago: Markham, 1971.

—— and Buiter, W. 1976. Long-run effects of fiscal and monetary policy on aggregate demand, in *Monetarism*, ed. J. L. Stein. Amsterdam: North-Holland.

Townsend, R. M. 1980. Models of money with spatially separated agents, in *Models of Monetary Economies*, ed. J. Kareken and N. Wallace. Minneapolis: Federal Reserve Bank of Minneapolis.

Toynbee, A. J. 1954. *A Study of History*, vii. London: Oxford University Press.

Trautwein, H-M. 1993. A fundamental controversy about money: Post-Keynesian and new monetary economics, in *Macroeconomic Theory: Diversity and Convergence*, ed. G. Mongiovi and C. Ruhl. Aldershot: Edward Elgar.

Tucker, D. 1966. Dynamic income adjustment to money supply changes. *American Economic Review*, 56: 433–49.

Tullio, G. E. de Souza, and Guicca, P. 1996. The demand for money functions in Europe and in Germany before and after the fall of the Berlin Wall, in *The Control of Inflation in the Transition to EMU*, ed. P. de Grauwe, S. Micossi, and G. Tullio. Oxford: Oxford University Press.

Turnovsky, S. J. 1980. The choice of monetary instruments under alternative forms of price expectations. *Manchester School*, 48: 39–63.

Ulph, A., and Ulph, D. 1975. Transactions costs in general equilibrium theory. *Economica*, 42(168): 355–72.

Van Horne, J. C. 1985. Of financial innovations and excesses. *Journal of Finance*, 40: 621–31.

Van Reit, A. G. 1993. Studies of EC money demand: survey and assessment. *De Nederlandsche Bank Quarterly Bulletin*, 63–75.

Varian, H. R. 1982. The non-parametric approach to demand analysis. *Econometrica*, 50(4): 945–73.

—— 1983. Non-parametric tests of consumer behaviour. *Review of Economic Studies*, 50: 99–110.

Vaubel, R. 1979. Free currency competition. *Weltwirtschaftliches Archiv*, 113: 435–459.

—— 1980. International shifts in the demand for money, their effects on exchange rates and price levels and their implications for the pre-announcement of monetary expansion. *Weltwirtschaftliches Archiv*, 116: 1–44.

Vickers, J. 1986. Signalling in a model of monetary policy with incomplete information. *Oxford Economic Papers*, 38(3): 443–55.

Viner, J. 1937. *Studies in the Theory of International Trade*. London: Allen & Unwin.

Voss, C. A. 1984. Technology push and need pull. *R & D Management*, 14(3): 147–51.

Wall, H. J. 1999. How important is the U.S. — Canada border? *International Economic Trends*, Federal Reserve Bank of St Louis, Aug.

Wallace, N. 1983. A legal restrictions theory of the demand for money and the role of monetary policy. *Federal Reserve Bank of Minneapolis Quarterly Review*, Winter: 1–7.

—— 1990. Why markets in foreign exchange are different from other markets. *Federal Reserve Bank of Minneapolis Quarterly Review*, Winter: 12–18.

Wallich, H. C. 1972. *The Monetary Crisis of 1971 — The Lessons to be Learned*. Per Jacobsson Lectures. Bank for International Settlements.

—— 1984. Recent techniques of monetary policy. *Federal Reserve Bank of Kansas City Economic Review*, May: 21–30.

Walras, L. 1954. *Elements of Pure Economics*, trans. and ed. W. Jaffé. Homewood, Ill.: Irwin; 1st edn., Lausanne, Switzerland: 1874–7; definitive edn., Paris: Pichon, 1926.

Walsh, C. E. 1995a. Optimal contracts for central bankers. *American Economic Review*, 85(1): 150–67.

—— 1995b. Is New Zealand's Reserve Bank Act of 1989 an optimal Central Bank contract? *Journal of Money, Credit and Banking*, 27(4), pt. 1: 1179–91.

—— 1998. *Monetary Theory and Policy*. Cambridge, Mass: MIT Press.

Walters, A. A. 1965. Professor Friedman on the demand for money. *Journal of Political Economy*, 73: 545–51.

—— 1967. The demand for money — the dynamic properties of the multiplier. *Journal of Political Economy*, 75: 293–8.

Weber, A. 2000. Monetary policy rules and EMU, conference paper, EMU: A First Birthday Party, South Bank University, 10, March 2000.

Weiss, L. 1980a. The role for active monetary policy in a rational expectations model. *Journal of Political Economy*, 88: 221–33.

Weiss, L. 1980b. The effects of money supply on economic welfare in the steady state. *Econometrica*, 48: 565–78.

Wenninger, J. 1988. Money demand — some long-run properties. *Federal Reserve Bank of New York Quarterly Review*, 13 (1): 23–40.

Westaway, P., and Walton, D. 1991. Endogenous financial innovation and the demand for M0'. In *Money and Financial Markets*, ed. M. P. Taylor. Oxford: Blackwell.

White, L. H. 1987. Accounting for non-interest-bearing currency: a critique of the legal restrictions theory of money. *Journal of Money Credit and Banking*, 19: 448–56.

Whittle, P. 1963. *Prediction and Regulation by Linear Least-Square Methods;* 2nd edn. revised. Minneapolis: University of Minnesota Press, 1983.

Wicksell, K. 1898. *Interest and Prices*, 1st edn., Jena: Germany; trans. London: Macmillan, 1936; repr. 1962, New York: Augustus Kelley.

—— 1906. *Lectures in Political Economy*, ii. 1915 edn. trans., London: Routledge & Kegan Paul, 1935.

Wieland, V. 1996. Monetary policy, parameter uncertainty and optimal learning. Board of Governors of the Federal Reserve System, May, mimeo.

—— 1998. Monetary policy and uncertainty about the natural unemployment rate. Board of Governors of the Federal Reserve System, Apr., mimeo.

Williamson, J. 1976. The benefits and costs of an international monetary non-system, in *Reflections on Jamaica*, M. Bernstein *et al.*, Essays in International Finance, 15, International Finance Section, Princeton: Princeton University.

Williamson, J. 1983. *The Exchange Rate System*, Washington DC Institute for International Economics, rev. edn. 1985.

—— 1985. *The Exchange Rate System*. Washington, DC: Institute for International Economics.

—— 1993. Exchange rate management. *Economic Journal*, 103: 188–97.

Wilson, J. S. G. 1989. *The London Money Markets*. SUERF Papers on Monetary Policy and Financial Systems, 6, 2nd edn. Tilburg: SUERF.

Woodford, M. 1998. Optimal monetary policy inertia, Paper presented at the Money, Macro and Finance Research Group Conference, London, Sept. 1998.

Wren-Lewis, S. 1984. Omitted variables in equations relating to prices and money. *Applied Economics*, 16: 483–96.

Yaari, M. 1969. Some remarks on measures of risk aversion and on their uses. *Journal of Economic Theory*, 1: 315–29.

Yates, A., and Bhundia, A. 1998. Interest rate stepping: some stylised facts and tentative explanation. *Bank of England*, mimeo.

Yeager, L. B. 1968. The essential properties of the medium of exchange. *Kyklos*, Fasc. 21(1): 45–68.

—— 1992. Monetary constitutions, in *New Palgrave Dictionary of Money and Finance*, ii, ed. P. Newman, M. Milgate, and J. Eatwell, London: Macmillan.

Yellen, J. L. 1996. Monetary policy: goals and strategy. Remarks at the National Association of Business Economists, Washington, DC, Mar. 1996.

Yule, G. U. 1927. On a method of investigating periodicities in disturbed series, with special reference to Wolfer's sunspot numbers. *Philosophical Transactions of the Royal Society Series A*, 226: 267–98.

Zervoyianni, A. 1988. Exchange rate overshooting, currency substitution and monetary policy. *Manchester School*, 56: 247–67.

—— 1992. International macroeconomic interdependence, currency substitution and price stickiness. *Journal of Macroeconomics*, 14: 59–86.

Author Index

Subject Index